LIBERTY'S NEMESIS

LIBERTY'S NEMESIS

THE UNCHECKED EXPANSION OF THE STATE

Edited by Dean Reuter and John Yoo

Encounter Books New York • London

First American edition published in 2016 by Encounter Books, an activity of Encounter for Culture and Education, Inc., a nonprofit, tax exempt corporation.
Encounter Books website address: www.encounterbooks.com

Manufactured in the United States and printed on acid-free paper. The paper used in this publication meets the minimum requirements of ANSI/NISO Z39.48–1992 (R 1997) (*Permanence of Paper*).

FIRST AMERICAN EDITION

LIBRARY OF CONGRESS CATALOGING-IN-PUBLICATION DATA
Names: Reuter, Dean, 1960– editor. | Yoo, John, editor.
Title: Liberty's nemesis: The unchecked expansion of the state/edited by Dean Reuter and John Yoo.
Description: New York: Encounter Books, 2016. | Includes bibliographical references and index.
Identifiers: LCCN 2015037272| ISBN 9781594038372 (hardcover: alk. paper) | ISBN 9781594038389 (ebook)
Subjects: LCSH: Abuse of administrative power—United States. | United States—Politics and government—2009– | Obama, Barack.
Classification: LCC E907 .L53 2016 | DDC 973.932092—dc23
LC record available at http://lccn.loc.gov/2015037272

CONTENTS

Introduction 1
Dean Reuter

1. The Ad Hoc Implementation and Enforcement of Health Care Reform 13
Jonathan H. Adler

2. A Multifaceted Assault on the Second Amendment 27
Bob Barr

3. Religious Liberty 41
Gerard V. Bradley and Robert P. George

4. Is *Chevron's* Game Worth the Candle? Burning Interpretation at Both Ends 57
Ronald A. Cass

5. Immigration: Executive versus Congressional Action 71
Linda Chavez

6. Operation Choke Point and the Bureaucratic Abuses of Unaccountable Power 81
Charles J. Cooper

7. Cheating Marriage 91
John C. Eastman

8. The Fannie/Freddie Fiasco: Executive Overreach in the Regulation of Financial Markets 105
Richard A. Epstein

9. Executive Interference with a Supposedly Independent Agency: The Federal Communications Commission 117
Harold Furchtgott-Roth

10. Promoting Small Business Capital Formation: The Promise of Venture Exchanges 137
Daniel M. Gallagher and Troy A. Paredes

11. Executive Overreach: Dodd-Frank 151
C. Boyden Gray and John Shu

12. Threats to Due Process and Free Speech on Campus 169
Samantha Harris and Greg Lukianoff

13. Congress in an Era of Executive Overreach 181
Senator Orrin G. Hatch

14. A Stylized Model of Agency Structure for Mitigating Executive Branch Overreach 191
F. Scott Kieff

15. The Radicalization of the National Labor Relations Board 209
William J. Kilberg and Thomas M. Johnson, Jr.

16. Disparate Impact: The Way of the New World 221
Peter N. Kirsanow

17. Muddied Waters: How the EPA and Corps of Engineers Redefined Their Authority over State Waters 229
Adam P. Laxalt and Lawrence VanDyke

18. The Separation of Powers in an Administrative State 239
David McIntosh and William J. Haun

19. Scandal at the IRS 255
Cleta Mitchell

20. Federal Overreach in Environmental Regulation: "A Severe Blow to the Constitution's Separation of Powers" 271
Patrick Morrisey and Elbert Lin

21. Criminal Law and the Administrative State: How the Proliferation of Regulatory Offenses Undermines the Moral Authority of Our Criminal Laws 283
Michael B. Mukasey and John G. Malcolm

22. FTC Overreach on Advertising Enforcement Threatens the Free Flow of Valuable Information 299
Maureen K. Ohlhausen

23. Preemption without Representation 311
E. Scott Pruitt

24. Unilateral Actions of President Obama in Voting and Elections 319
Hans A. von Spakovsky

25. The Designation of Systemically Important Financial Institutions by the Financial Stability Oversight Council and the Financial Stability Board 331
Peter J. Wallison

26. The FTC, Unfair Methods of Competition, and Abuse of Prosecutorial Discretion 351
Joshua D. Wright

Conclusion 363
John Yoo

Author Biographies 371

Acknowledgments 387

Notes 389

Index 545

INTRODUCTION

Dean Reuter

This book is an examination and critique of the expanding power of the federal government. The volume is unique in several ways. First, it is not a rant. It is a careful study and documentation of problems created by agencies given too much authority and sometimes overreaching—exceeding even their generous grants of authority to act. Second, our contributors are particularly qualified to write on these topics, and the list of contributors is long. Most have themselves toiled in the halls of the federal government, while others have worked at the state level, sometimes fending off incursions by the federal government. Many contributors are current or former heads of administrative agencies that assert unprecedented powers; all have special insight into the functions and dysfunctions of the federal government, its penchant for overreach, the administrative state, and what it all means for our liberty. This is particularly poignant since the battle for liberty was presumably won by our founders, who loathed the idea of unfettered government and so created the Constitution we cherish today. Third, whereas some chapters focus on particular agencies or discrete areas of law and policy, others examine the incentives and structures operating throughout the federal government that create the readiness to delegate power to the regulators and then allow them to exercise that power, and more, unilaterally. Finally, our writers propose solutions to both the discrete and the thematic problems they identify, outlining the path back to a government that works to foster success and freedom—to promote the greater good, not to punish.

Our contributors do all this in the shadow of the significant fact that, according to two respected economists, federal regulations have cost the United States economy approximately $38.8 trillion.[1] Indeed, federal regulations have decreased economic growth by about 2 percent annually between 1949 and 2005.[2] *Reason Magazine* drives the astonishing point home: "the average American household receives about $277,000 less annually than it would have gotten in the absence of six decades of accumulated regulations—a median household income of $330,000 instead of the $53,000 we get now."[3]

Our writers, while not exactly alone in this critique, are working actively against the trend of administrative law scholarship. Most administrative law scholars are vocal and committed defenders of the regulatory state.[4] The more cynically minded would say that this might be so because it adds to the mush and the muddle that is prime material from which to churn out scholarship. The canonical text, our Constitution, stands athwart these modern-day insights and necessities, these scholars insist. Thus, this obsolete and imperfect Constitution[5] should be read to accommodate the bureaucracy, not the other way around. Accordingly, it now seems appropriate to state the names of, and to note the contributions made to our enterprise by, various public servants, attorneys, scholars, and activists. Professor Jonathan H. Adler will discuss the arbitrary and capricious implementation and enforcement of Obamacare; former Congressman Bob Barr will address the many-headed threats facing the Second Amendment; Professors Gerard V. Bradley and Robert P. George will address the crisis of religious freedom in America today; Chair of the Center for Equal Opportunity Linda Chavez will explicate the realities of the immigration issue's presidential versus congressional action dimensions; law school dean emeritus and former commissioner of the U.S. International Trade Commission (ITC) Ronald A. Cass will discuss the courts' relationship to the administrative state and its overreach; stellar Supreme Court advocate Charles "Chuck" J. Cooper will discuss how America's civil service and bureaucracy abuse their unaccountable power; Professor Richard A. Epstein will focus on presidential overreach in regulating the financial markets; Professor John Eastman will address the same-sex marriage controversy; Harold Furchtgott-Roth, a former commissioner of the Federal Communications Commission (FCC) and currently a senior fellow at the Hudson Institute, will speak to the Obama White House's interference in the FCC's "network neutrality" rulemaking; Daniel M. Gallagher and Troy A. Paredes, former commissioners at the U.S. Securities and Exchange Commission (SEC), will explicate the potential of venture exchanges for small businesses; former White House Counsel C. Boyden Gray and securities litigator John Shu will describe the overreach embedded within the Dodd-Frank statute; Samantha Harris, Director of Policy Research at the Foundation for Individual Rights in Education, and the Foundation's CEO, Greg Lukianoff, will discuss how campus speech is imperiled every day; Senator Orrin Hatch will explain the role of Congress at a time when the President is incessantly overreaching; F. Scott Kieff, a commissioner of the ITC, will analyze a model for decreasing the probability of Executive Branch overreach; Gibson, Dunn & Crutcher attorneys William J. Kilberg and Thomas M. Johnson will point out the radicalization of the National Labor Relations Board; labor attorney Peter N. Kirsanow will address the new realities of disparate impact jurisprudence and what it means for civil liberties; Nevada's Attorney General Adam Laxalt and that state's Solicitor General Lawrence VanDyke will catalogue the history behind and the implications of the Environmental Protection Agency (EPA) asserting power over state waters; former Congressman David McIntosh and attorney William Haun will discuss the imperiled separation of powers in the modern administrative state; attorney and activist Cleta Mitchell will recount the story of the scandal-driven Internal Revenue Service (IRS); West Virginia Attorney General Patrick Morrisey and that state's Solicitor General Elbert Lin will explain how the federal government has overreached in formulating and applying its environmental regulations; former U.S. Attorney General Michael Mukasey and John Malcolm, former Deputy Assistant Attorney General in the Criminal Division at the U.S. Department of Justice, will explain how the proliferation of regulatory offenses undercuts the moral force of criminal legislation; Maureen Ohlhausen, a commissioner of the Federal Trade Commission (FTC), will address how the FTC's advertising enforcement policies threaten the free flow of valuable information; Oklahoma Attorney General E. Scott

Pruitt will explain how the Obama administration is harming the states by preempting state policies on undocumented immigrants; former Federal Election Commission commissioner Hans A. von Spakovsky will examine voting and elections; former White House Counsel Peter J. Wallison will expound on how many of the key financial institutions were designated by the Financial Stability Oversight Council and the Financial Stability Board; and finally, Joshua D. Wright, a commissioner of the Federal Trade Commission, will address the FTC's Unfair Methods of Competition jurisprudence and relatedly its abuse of prosecutorial discretion.

It is axiomatic that as the federal government expands, individual liberty contracts.[6] Although the federal government is capable of enlarging our liberties and charged with defending our country, it most often acts domestically by limiting our options for action or taking our money to fund a project that might reflect the interests of only a temporary majority. As our contributors describe, a most intense concentration of power is happening within the federal agencies.[7] And it is happening not just because of actors, including the President, within the Executive Branch, but with the cooperation of Congress, the courts, and even some of the states.

How, exactly, did we come to this point? Isn't such an accumulation of power impossible under our Constitution? After all, the genius of the American Constitution lies in its structure and its design to prevent the concentration of great powers.[8] Every tyrannical or despotic governing ruler in history survived only because he hoarded and exercised unilateral power. Recognizing this, our founding fathers drafted a Constitution that carefully divided power in a manner that would prevent any one person, any cadre or cabal, or even any single branch of government, from accumulating outsized power. Though the structure of the Constitution still holds today, its carefully prescribed balance of power is dangerously near a tipping point. The founders rightly perceived that human nature would lead those in power to seek still more power. However, by dividing power at the outset, they reasoned that everyone seeking greater power would be confronted and checked by others asserting and jealously guarding their own power. With everyone in government pushing with equal force against everyone else, the delicate balance of power would be preserved.[9] Maintaining this balance of power requires a certain faithfulness by all. Thomas Jefferson, describing the limits under which the federal government ought to operate, wrote, "I had rather ask an enlargement of power, from the nation, where it is found necessary, than to assume it by a construction which would make our powers boundless. Our peculiar security is in possession of a written Constitution. Let us not make it a blank paper by construction."[10] Jefferson, like his founding brothers, was arguing in favor of a limited federal government, backed by a written constitution that must not be read out of existence by the very people charged with enforcing its limits. Our contributors, though, show that significant actors in government have allowed the administrative state to gain new powers and to exceed or overreach even those powers granted to it by others.

Power is divided in two fundamental ways by our Constitution—horizontally and vertically. At the federal level, the horizontal division of power is between the three branches of government. Under the Vesting Clauses of the Constitution each branch is assigned particular powers.[11] Article I gives Congress the legislative authority.[12] Article II gives the responsibility to execute the laws to the Executive Branch, headed by the President.[13] The judicial power, the power to say what the law is by deciding cases and controversies, is given to the courts, established by Article III.[14] In addition to these structural safeguards assigning particular and limited power to specific branches of government, there are features of the Constitution that limit power. For example, although Congress has the power to legislate, its authority is limited to enumerated, or listed, powers.[15] And Congress is itself divided into two houses, each of which must pass identically worded bills before they can become law, making it difficult to act.[16] Even then, the President has the power to veto a bill passed by Congress and, then again, by a supermajority vote, Congress can override the President's veto.[17] Likewise, although the judiciary has a distinct role, Article III states that judges become judges only when they are appointed by the President, and they must be confirmed by the Senate.[18] Judges can rule an act of Congress, duly signed by the President, as unconstitutional on its face because it exceeds the enumerated powers of the federal government, or rule that it is being implemented in an unconstitutional manner by the Executive Branch. And although they enjoy lifetime tenure (provided they observe "good behavior"), judges can be impeached by Congress.[19] The President's powers in executing the laws can be severely limited by Congress through its "power of the purse": its ability to appropriate with conditions or limitations, or withhold altogether, funds for use by the Executive Branch.[20] Likewise, the President can be impeached and removed from office by Congress, but only during a trial over which the Chief Justice of the United States presides.[21] The horizontal separation of powers at the federal level and these other features were put in place to make it difficult, if not impossible, for any one branch of government to use or even accumulate tyrannical amounts of power.

The vertical separation of powers divides power between the states and the federal government, and it is a further hindrance on the accretion of power at the federal level. Because our federal government is a government of limited, enumerated powers, those powers not specifically granted to it by the Constitution are reserved for the states or the people.[22] The states each retain their sovereign, independent authority under our constitutional design.[23] The federal government, properly understood, was born out of an agreement between the states, who decided as precisely as possible what powers the federal government should and should not have. Power was derived from the people as sovereigns and ceded in some measure to the states in order to organize society. Some limited parts of this power were, under the agreement memorialized by the Constitution, given to the federal government as our country was organized. Even though the predecessor organizing document of our country, the Articles of Confederation, had an insufficiently strong central government, the founders remained wary of investing the federal government with too much power.[24]

The vertical separation of powers has been under attack for generations, with power gradually and sometimes precipitously shifting from the states to the federal level. This has at times happened in the face of opposition from one or more states trying to guard its own powers, though it also has happened, somewhat unpredictably, with the active participation of the states. So as time has passed, power has moved "vertically," away from the people and the states and to the federal government. This is problem enough but, most unfortunately, it is compounded by the erosion of the separation of powers at the federal level and the resultant rise of the administrative state.

Some of the accumulation of power at the federal level is consistent with the Constitution, as it has been amended. When Congress was given the power to lay and collect income taxes, the federal government was able to collect more money from the citizens of the states.[25] Money in the coffers of the federal Treasury, and under the control of the federal government, meant more power at the federal level. Every dime of transportation money a state accepts today comes with myriad restrictions and requirements—a laundry list of that which the state must not do and must do (some having very little to do with transportation). Of course, with few exceptions, the money the federal government spends comes from within one or another state. Likewise, the Seventeenth Amendment changed the manner in which U.S. senators are elected.[26] Arguably, the new (and current) system of direct election by the people of the states makes senators less accountable to the state legislatures, which results in more power at the federal level.

Too much power at the federal level is never a good thing, but we have seen that concerns could be lessened if power, even great power, were adequately divided at the federal level. But over the past several decades, all branches of the federal government, and all levels of government, have been complicit in the accumulation of power at the federal level within the administrative state, allowing the administration to reach beyond the constitutional limits of its power.[27] After power rose to the federal level, how, then, did that power slide to the administrative agencies? Why weren't the other branches of the federal government jealously guarding their power in a way that would prevent the slide?

A century or so ago President Woodrow Wilson determined that the federal government must engage "experts" to make the rules under which we all must live.[28] Wilson's prolific academic career, which spanned several decades, championed the separation of politics (by which he understood partisan politics) and administration. Regrettably, doing so also erodes accountability. Nonetheless, doe-eyed, Wilson approvingly wrote, "Government does now whatever experience permits or the times demand."[29] Wilson unashamedly, and successfully, argued that Congress was too busy and lacked the expertise to pass sensible laws on the many diverse matters of need for the quickly growing nation, and that it was so riven with politics that its direct exercise of power on these matters of specificity was not to be trusted. The solution was to delegate its powers to experts housed in federal agencies.[30] Congress would legislate in broad strokes, giving general direction, and the experts would fill in the details and make the policy decisions to which their expertise, devoid of political considerations, led them. This formulation had an intuitive appeal one hundred years ago when the federal government was an infant, but even then it was unconstitutional if those agency experts, when filling in the details of the laws passed by Congress, either legislated or exceeded the authority granted to them by law.

Because all legislative power is vested, by the Constitution, in the legislature, agencies (part of the Executive Branch) have no legislative power whatsoever. Furthermore, Congress cannot delegate its legislative power to agencies—the constitutional infirmity arises when unelected and unaccountable agencies exercise the authority to legislate, to make law. Even if Congress delegates non-legislative power to agencies, legal problems arise when those agencies exercise more power than has been properly granted. Holding true to the founders' fears, experience has shown that once agencies have power, they use it—agencies are very adept at identifying wrongs and wrongdoers and adopting all manner of rules and regulations to control conduct.[31] When they legislate or exceed properly delegated powers, agencies overreach, exceeding the legal limits of their authority. As the following chapters show, this happens all too often.

Congress, of course, itself errs by delegating legislative power to the agencies[32] in what is best described as a win-win-lose situation. Congress and the agencies win, but we lose. Congress happily claims credit when it passes sweeping "reform" laws, and the unaccountable agencies just as happily accept the power. Congress then avoids blame when the agencies, who can't be held accountable by the people, fill in the unpopular details with their regulations. We are left with a new regime of onerous restrictions and no one to blame but "the system."

Congress compounds the problem when it fails to provide meaningful oversight of agencies.[33] It has several powers it could use to constrain agencies, but it fails. For example, it uses no regular reauthorization process during which it could revisit statutory limitations on agencies. It has no consistent budgetary process during which it could threaten an errant agency's funding level or freedom of action. Stunningly, Congress sometimes has no input at all on agency budgets for powerful newer entities, like the recently created Consumer Financial Protection Bureau and other fee-generating agencies that use their power to extract their own funding from those they regulate. We easily recognize the impropriety of letting a small-town judge take a cut of all the traffic fines he upholds, even if that money goes into the general courthouse funds instead of directly into his own pocket. Why does Congress enact a scheme that allows an agency budget to be increased with the many fees and fines the agency extracts? Partly because, for every dime the agencies collect from the regulated community, Congress has to collect one less dime in taxes.

At least, we can say, Congress purports to limit agency authority by prescribing the agencies' means of regulating. The Administrative Procedure Act (APA), passed in 1946, mandates particular steps that most agencies must follow when promulgating regulations, including requiring greater deliberation by giving public notice of proposed rules and the opportunity for public comments.[34] Unfortunately, agencies now routinely avoid these requirements by several creative and illicit work-arounds, while Congress and even the courts too often stand mute, failing to require compliance by the agencies.[35] So even this means of limiting agency action is being eroded.

Congress could do much more. Members of Congress occasionally deign to fight overregulation by proposing corrective legislation. Two such bills recently in Congress, the Regulatory Improvement Act of 2014 and the Searching for and Cutting Regulations that Are Unnecessarily Burdensome (SCRUB) Act of 2014, seek to launch a commission to identify and eradicate antiquated and burdensome regulations. This commission would be a creature of Congress's will. It would list regulations for statutory repeal—the same general way that Congress exercises its power over trade, military bases, and, subject to a time limit, D.C. legislation. Although some journalists seem to think that "the cure is dubious and the disease exaggerated,"[36] the bills would be a step in the right direction. First, although President Obama has already asked the agencies to get rid of outdated regulations, they have little incentive to rock the boat—unless Congress hangs the specter of rocking it for them, leading Congress (the regulator of the regulators, almost an intonation of *Qui custodiet ipsos custodes?* or Who guards the guards?) to scrutinize what the agency has been up to in other matters as well. Second, while it is true that regulated parties generally do have the right to add their input to agency rulemaking during the notice and comment phase, such is not always the case. At any rate, the regulators do not have to accommodate those concerns; they need only consider them. Third, even if retrospective review by Congress causes gridlock, it is necessary.

The courts, too, are complicit in the growth of regulatory power by allowing the delegation of legislative power in the first place, permitting it whenever there is an "intelligible principle" provided by Congress to guide agency action as it expounds upon the grant of power, a very low hurdle.[37] The judiciary has compounded its head-in-the-sand approach with a host of cases since then—*Chevron*,[38] *Auer*,[39] and *City of Arlington*,[40] all discussed in the chapters that follow—that keep judges' "hands off" when presented with a challenge to agency rules.

The courts go even farther by deferring to final agency action, including when a beleaguered member of the regulated community dares to contest an agency enforcement action. Agencies have become judge, jury, and executioner. Given deliberately vague statutes passed by Congress, agencies make the rules by filling in the gaps, often without consulting anyone beyond the agency walls. The courts defer to the agency interpretations of their statutes. Then the agencies conduct fact-finding missions and enforcement actions, building a case. Agency attorneys then bring the case before an administrative law judge (ALJ), who is typically an employee of the same agency. The "accused" does not enjoy the due process and protections of the rules of evidence found in an independent Article III court.[41] The ALJ makes his ruling, typically finding on behalf of the agency, and only then can the private party appeal to the Article III court; even then, the Article III tribunal will begin its consideration with a heavy presumption in favor of the agency's finding.[42] So in addition to long and expensive delays, the unfortunate regulated citizen's day in a real court begins with a heavy thumb on the scales in favor of the agency.[43]

In defense of the courts, deference to agency action is seated in a belief that agency results reflect some coherent policy view espoused by Congress and advanced by agency officials who are at least indirectly accountable to the President, Congress, and the people.[44] In contrast, the reasoning continues, judges are life-tenured—and thus once appointed are even less accountable—so they should be extremely constrained when questioning the delegation of power by Congress or overturning an agency action.[45] But as we have seen, in practice, agency officials are themselves accountable to virtually no one. They use congressional indifference and judicial deference to their actions as license to employ and even exceed even the generous powers Congress has delegated. Allowing congressional delegation to agencies and deferring to agency decisions might have seemed sensible—although wisdom is a different thing altogether from constitutionality—when they were few, small, and without much power. A new world is upon us now, however. Despite this, the courts seem to be living in a 1950s world, where federal agencies had not yet accumulated the massive powers, thoroughgoing political insulation, and emboldened brashness they now possess.[46]

The President, too, is a wink-and-a-nod conspirator in the modern-era arrangement that has given us the administrative state and its overreach. Presidents influence and sometimes directly guide policy decisions at the agency level, yet they conveniently avoid responsibility for complications that might arise. President Obama famously claimed he had no sway over the IRS, part of a cabinet-level agency, when it became embroiled in a scandal over delaying applications for tax-exempt status by conservative-leaning not-for-profit organizations.[47] Yet, in another matter, President Obama strongly voiced his preference that net neutrality be adopted (and it has been described as "an unusual, secretive effort" of the Obama White House),[48] which was followed to the letter by the FCC,[49] an independent agency. Such a change should be made, under the APA, only after a public notice and comment period. Those members of the public who oppose the President's policy choice on net neutrality might be correct in thinking that their comments during an ensuing comment period would not be fairly considered.

Within the pages that follow, our contributors give dozens of examples of Congress delegating too much authority to agencies, and agencies thanking them by regulating well beyond even these generous delegations of power. Agencies have gone beyond exercising powers they should not but do possess, to exercising powers they do not even have. But to be clear, although the Obama administration and its agencies have perfected the art of exercising domestic power and overreaching their granted authority, this President is not the first to overreach, and he is doing so on a playing field that has been decades in the making. His administration did not create this problem, though it is certainly exacerbating it. It is a problem that must be solved; thankfully, it is a problem that can be solved.

1.

THE AD HOC IMPLEMENTATION AND ENFORCEMENT OF HEALTH CARE REFORM

Jonathan H. Adler

On March 23, 2010, President Barack Obama signed the Patient Protection and Affordable Care Act (PPACA) into law. One week later, he signed a set of amendments to the PPACA, the Health Care and Education Reconciliation Act (HCERA). These steps completed the enactment of President Obama's signature domestic policy achievement: a fundamental reworking of America's health care system and health insurance markets. Often referred to as the "Affordable Care Act," "ACA," or simply "Obamacare," the PPACA contains a series of mandates, regulatory proscriptions, taxes, and subsidies designed to expand health insurance coverage and make health insurance more affordable, particularly for those with preexisting conditions.

Signing health care reform into law was not the end of the story. The PPACA had still to be implemented. Given the size, scope, and complexity of the law, this has been no easy task. The Obama administration has not contented itself with implementing health care reform as written, however. Since 2010, the administration has repeatedly departed from the text of the law, altering and ignoring provisions it did not like, did not wish to implement, or otherwise found objectionable. These changes have alleviated or delayed the law's burdens on some constituencies, while increasing the burdens borne by others. Whether or not such decisions made good policy sense, they were not authorized by Congress. Millions of Americans are subject to the PPACA's penalties and mandates as a consequence of administrative action, instead of legislation enacted by the people's elected representatives. The PPACA, as it has been implemented, is quite different from the PPACA that Congress enacted and the President signed into law.

DELAYING THE EMPLOYER MANDATE

The PPACA imposes a "shared responsibility" requirement obligating employers with more than fifty employees to provide qualifying health insurance to their employees.[1] Employers who fail to comply with this "employer mandate" are required to pay a penalty or "tax" that can reach $2,000 per employee beyond the thirtieth employee.[2] This provision exposes larger employers to substantial penalties if they fail to offer qualifying health insurance. Unsurprisingly, some employers reduced their number of full-time employees—either by laying off workers or reducing their hours—to reduce their financial exposure.[3]

Section 1513 of the PPACA provides that the employer mandate "shall apply to months beginning after December 31, 2013."[4] In other words, this provision of the law was due to take effect at the start of 2014. In July 2013, however, the Obama administration announced in a blog post that it would delay the employer mandate by a year.[5] The stated reason for this delay was "the complexity of the requirements" imposed on employers and "the need for more time to implement them effectively."[6] Later that month the IRS published a guidance detailing the "transition relief" to be afforded employers from the employer mandate and its associated information-reporting requirements.[7]

Seven months later, in February 2014, the Treasury Department announced further delays of and modifications to the employer mandate.[8] Treasury declared that the mandate would be delayed until 2016 for firms with fewer than one hundred employees. In addition, Treasury announced that firms with over one hundred employees would only need to provide qualifying insurance to 70 percent of their full-time employees in 2015, and 95 percent of employees thereafter, to avoid the statutory penalties. The administration not only waived the effective date for the employer mandate, it also invented a new set of staggered requirements for employers.

In announcing the second delay, administration officials said it was intended to help employers adjust to the law's requirements. Some observers saw more political motivations. "By offering an unexpected grace period to businesses with between 50 and 99 employees, administration officials are hoping to defuse another potential controversy involving the 2010 health-care law," reported Juliet Eilperin and Amy Goldstein of the *Washington Post*.[9] "Not coincidentally, the delays punt[ed] implementation beyond congressional elections in November," added the *National Journal*'s Ron Fournier.[10]

In justifying these delays, the Treasury Department claimed that it has broad authority to offer "transition relief" in implementing a complex law like the PPACA. That may be true in other cases but not here. When Congress provides that a given legal requirement takes effect on a date certain, that is when the legal requirement takes effect. If, as the administration has claimed, the employer mandate penalty is a tax, that tax liability for noncomplying employers began to accrue at the start of 2014. As Congress did not delegate the Executive Branch authority to waive or delay this requirement, no such authority exists.

Agencies often fail to meet statutorily prescribed deadlines—and courts often give agencies time to catch up with their obligations—but that is not what is at issue here. The PPACA does not instruct the IRS to impose the mandate by a certain date. Rather, the PPACA provides that employers become liable for noncompliance as of a certain date. Further, the IRS did not seek to meet a statutory deadline and fail. Instead it purported to offer prospective relief from a liability imposed by statute.

Nothing in the PPACA authorizes the Executive Branch to waive the application of the employer mandate penalties. The text of the PPACA is quite clear. It provides that the employer mandate provisions "shall apply" after a date certain. Were this not enough, other provisions of the PPACA reinforce the statutory requirement. For example, the PPACA details the amount of the employer penalty to be assessed in 2014 and then provides for the penalties to be adjusted for inflation in subsequent years.[11]

That Congress expected the employer mandate to take effect in 2014 is reaffirmed by the fact that implementation of this requirement is essential for the proper implementation of other parts of the law. For instance, the employer mandate reporting provisions are essential to determining eligibility for tax credits and cost-sharing subsidies in state health insurance exchanges. These tax credits were to be available beginning January 1, 2014, and serve as the trigger for assessing the penalty.[12] The tax credits and employer penalties were supposed to take effect together, and the administration never suggested delaying the credits (though it did waive verification of eligibility).[13] Further, as Ezra Klein reported in 2009, the employer mandate was essential for passage of the PPACA given the way the Congressional Budget Office scored health care reform proposals.[14]

The Treasury Department claimed that delaying the effective date of the employer mandate was an ordinary exercise of its "longstanding authority to grant transition relief when implementing new legislation."[15] Despite this claim, the Treasury Department failed to identify an applicable precedent that would justify waiving a tax liability prospectively as the administration did. Treasury cited cases in which the IRS waived potentially applicable penalties or allowed deferred payment of tax liabilities, but not cases in which a pending tax liability was waived prospectively. It is one thing for the IRS to defer a payment deadline or decline to seek penalties for noncompliance; either could be justified as an exercise of enforcement discretion for which precedent exists. It is quite another to waive an accrued tax liability—repeatedly and selectively—without legislative authorization. Such an action is unlawful.

Even legal commentators who have been generally supportive of this administration's implementation of the ACA have acknowledged that the Treasury Department lacked the legal authority to delay the employer mandate. University of Michigan law professor Nicholas Bagley, for instance, wrote in the *New England Journal of Medicine* that these delays "appear to exceed the scope of the executive's traditional enforcement discretion" and cannot be justified as an exercise of Executive Branch authority to prioritize limited agency resources.[16] As Bagley explained, the employer mandate delays cannot be justified as the sort "discretionary judgment[s] concerning the allocation of enforcement resources" approved by the Supreme Court in *Heckler v. Chaney*.[17] In his view, the purported precedents relied upon by Treasury provided "slim support for a sweeping objection that will relieve thousands of employers from a substantial tax for as long as 2 years."[18] Precisely.

The assertion of unilateral authority to delay the employer mandate—if ratified and accepted as a precedent for agency action in the future—could mark a dramatic shift in the separation of powers. As Bagley explained,

> the Obama Administration's claim of enforcement discretion, if accepted, would limit Congress's ability to specify when and under what circumstances its laws should take effect. That circumscription of legislative authority would mark a major shift of constitutional power away from Congress, which makes the laws, and toward the President, who is supposed to enforce them.[19]

Given the weakness of the legal justifications offered by the Treasury Department, it is fair to wonder whether Treasury attorneys even considered whether the IRS had authority to defer the employer mandate before the action was taken. When Mark Mazur, Assistant Secretary of the Treasury for Tax Policy, was questioned by the House Oversight and Government Reform Committee, he admitted to not knowing whether any such analysis had been conducted.[20] Specifically, he said he did not "recall" any inquiries within Treasury as to its authority to delay the mandate. In other words, by all accounts it appears the administration made its decision to delay the employer mandate and only then sought to determine whether it had legal authority to do so. Regrettably, this is not the only example of the unlawful execution of the PPACA.

"IF YOU LIKE IT, YOU CAN KEEP IT"

One of the most prominent political obstacles to the enactment of comprehensive health care reform was the fact that a large portion of Americans were satisfied with their existing health insurance. For this reason, President Obama and most congressional supporters of the PPACA repeatedly promised that the health care reform law would not result in anyone losing their existing health insurance. "If you like your health insurance plan, you can keep it," the President promised again and again.[21] This commitment became something of a mantra, only it was not true.

The PPACA imposes a suite of minimum coverage and other requirements on all private health insurance plans. This was a key part of the law. Existing insurance plans that do not meet all of these requirements are noncompliant and are illegal under the PPACA. The law contained a "grandfather" provision allowing the continuation of some such plans for a limited time, but this provision was relatively narrow and interpreted by the Department of Health and Human Services in an even narrower way.[22] As written, the PPACA would ensure that many who liked their preexisting health insurance plans would not be allowed to keep them.

In 2013, many Americans were distressed to learn that their existing health insurance plans would be canceled for failing to meet the PPACA's minimum coverage requirements. Modest year-to-year changes in preexisting plans even resulted in the loss of "grandfather" status. This was an anticipated effect of the law.[23] As the *Wall Street Journal* reported, the White House always knew that not everyone who liked their health insurance would be able to keep it, even if some officials believed most affected consumers would be happy to be forced to obtain "better" plans.[24]

On November 14, 2013, President Obama announced a purported fix to this problem. According to the President's announcement, made in a press conference, insurance companies would be allowed to renew policies that were in force as of October 1, 2013, for one additional year, even if they failed to meet relevant PPACA requirements.[25] The Department of Health and Human Services subsequently released guidance documents detailing the policy.[26] As with the delays of the employer mandate, there was no clear legal authority for this change. Indeed, no citation of legal authority accompanied the President's announcement or the subsequent letter from the administration to state insurance commissioners encouraging them to allow the renewal of noncompliant plans.

The PPACA's prohibition on the issuance of noncompliant health insurance plans is clear. This requirement cannot be waived by administrative fiat. Even if the federal government promised not to take any enforcement actions against insurance providers for issuing such plans, the legal requirement remained on the books, so the relevant health insurance plans remain illegal under federal law. Health insurance companies are only allowed to offer insurance plans that provide the prescribed list of "essential benefits."[27] Further, only insurance plans that provide such benefits satisfy the minimum coverage requirement (the individual mandate).[28] Although the PPACA authorizes the administration to waive the individual mandate penalty due to "hardship"—in this case, a loss of coverage and an increase in health insurance prices caused by the PPACA itself—insurers' obligations to offer compliant health plans cannot be waived by administrative fiat. A presidential announcement cannot overcome the legal jeopardy health insurers could face should they agree to renew such plans and seek to enforce any terms that have been declared illegal under the PPACA and its implementing regulations.

The only legal justification the administration offered for this move was "enforcement discretion." Specifically, the administration claimed it was not changing the law so much as it was merely announcing that it would not enforce relevant requirements for a given time period. This legal justification does not work, however.[29] The President was not merely announcing a new enforcement policy. He was actively encouraging private insurance companies and state insurance commissions to violate the law.

While the Executive Branch maintains the discretion over how the laws are to be enforced, such discretion does not entitle administrative agencies to disregard statutory provisions that are deemed unwise or inconvenient, let alone the authority to waive legal obligations that are written into federal law. The constable's authority to decide not to arrest every lawbreaker is not the authority to waive the law's obligations. An agency's authority to allocate resources in accord with the Executive Branch's policy choices does not allow it to disregard unwanted statutory mandates. Such authority exists only to the extent that it is delegated by Congress.

Although the administration claimed it was relying on "enforcement discretion," the announced policy did more than pull back enforcement of the law's requirements. It also sought to impose new obligations on private insurers. Specifically, the new administration policy conditioned the exercise of enforcement discretion on private insurers agreeing to a series of disclosures to those who might wish to renew their policies for an additional year. As detailed in a guidance letter explaining the change, insurers wishing to renew their policies would be required to provide their customers with a notice explaining that the relevant policies fail to comply with the PPACA's requirements, that other more comprehensive policies are available, and how such policies can be obtained. Whether or not requiring such disclosure is a good idea, nothing in the PPACA authorized the administration to take this step.

The President's announcement could not bind state insurance commissioners. As Professor Bagley notes, primary enforcement of the various insurance regulations remains with state insurance commissions, who are under no obligation to follow the administration's lead.[30] The President's decision could not change relevant state laws either.

Apart from the legality of the move, state insurance commissioners raised concerns about its practical effects too. Health insurance policies must be approved by each state's insurance commission before they may be sold. This approval process typically requires submitting rates and plan specifications and can take quite some time. By the time of the President's announcement, most insurance companies had already approved their offerings for 2014, and many state insurance commissions showed little interest in revisiting these determinations.

Had the administration sought to allow for the renewal of noncompliant plans, it had other options. The grandfather provision of the PPACA, as written, does not indicate when, and under what circumstances, year-to-year plan revisions cause an insurance plan to lose its grandfathered status.[31] The Department of Health and Human Services filled that gap through regulations—regulations that interpreted the scope of the clause quite narrowly, forcing insurers to cancel a large number of plans.[32] If the administration had second thoughts about the way it chose to implement the PPACA in this regard, it could have either sought legislative reform or revised the implementing regulations through a supplemental rulemaking. Instead, it simply announced a "change" in the law.

TAX CREDITS IN FEDERAL EXCHANGES

Another central feature of the PPACA is the authorization of state-based health insurance "exchanges," government-managed marketplaces for the purchase of health insurance. Congress intended these marketplaces to empower consumers to compare competing health plans by providing standardized comparative information. Exchanges were also designed to facilitate government regulation of insurance markets and provide a conduit for the provision of tax credits and subsidies for the purchase of qualifying health insurance plans. Here again, the administration implemented the PPACA in an illegal fashion.[33]

Section 1311 of the act directs each state to create an "American Health Benefit Exchange."[34] Despite the obligatory language of Section 1311, the PPACA gives each state a choice of whether to take responsibility for (and bear the cost of) operating its own exchange. States that agreed to set up their own exchange were eligible for start-up funds from the federal government. Moreover, the PPACA provides for tax credits and cost-sharing subsidies for low-income individuals who purchase qualifying health insurance on state-established exchanges. Should a state refuse to create its own exchange, another provision requires the federal government to create an exchange for that state.[35]

As written, the PPACA only provides tax credits and cost-sharing subsidies for the purchase of qualifying health insurance plans in exchanges that are "established by the State" under Section 1311. Specifically, the PPACA authorizes tax credits for each month in a given year in which a taxpayer has obtained qualifying health insurance. As defined by the law, a "coverage month" is any month in which the taxpayer is "covered by a qualified health plan . . . that was enrolled in through an Exchange established by the State under section 1311."[36] The amount of the tax credit is also calculated with reference to a qualifying health insurance plan "enrolled in through an Exchange established by the State under [Section] 1311."

If a state refuses to establish its own exchange, the federal government is required to "establish and operate" an exchange for that state.[37] While a federal exchange may operate like a state exchange, nothing in the PPACA authorizes the provision of tax credits or cost-sharing subsidies to individuals who purchase health insurance in federal exchanges. To the contrary, the relevant provisions of Section 1401 only provide for tax credits for the purchase of health insurance in state-established exchanges.

When the PPACA was enacted, it was generally assumed that most if not all states would willingly create exchanges.[38] As President Obama explained shortly after signing the legislation into law, "by 2014, each state will set up what we're calling a health insurance exchange."[39] Few expected that many states would refuse. But despite the administration's best efforts to encourage state cooperation, some three dozen states refused to create their own exchanges.

Faced with the prospect that widespread state refusal to establish exchanges under the PPACA would make tax credits and cost-sharing subsidies unavailable in much of the country, the Internal Revenue Service sought a fix. Specifically, the IRS promulgated regulations in May 2012 providing that tax credits would be available for the purchase of qualifying health insurance plans in states established under either Section 1311 or 1321, without regard for whether the exchange was established by a state or established by the federal government.[40] To justify its decision, the IRS explained,

> The statutory language of section 36B and other provisions of the Affordable Care Act support the interpretation that credits are available to taxpayers who obtain coverage through a State Exchange, regional Exchange, subsidiary Exchange, and the Federally-facilitated Exchange. Moreover, the relevant legislative history does not demonstrate that Congress intended to limit the premium tax credit to State Exchanges. Accordingly, the final regulations maintain the rule in the proposed regulations because it is consistent with the language, purpose, and structure of section 36B and the Affordable Care Act as a whole.[41]

Although commentators argued that the express language of the PPACA precluded the IRS interpretation, this paragraph—lacking any citation to relevant statutory provisions, legislative history, or other legal authority—was the entirety of the IRS's justification for the rule when promulgated.[42]

Months later, under pressure from members of Congress to offer a more complete explanation, the Department of the Treasury began to identify potential authority for its rule. Specifically, the Treasury Department suggested that the language of Section 1321 could be interpreted to make a federally established exchange "the equivalent of a state exchange in all functional respects," including an exchange for purposes of determining eligibility for tax credits.[43]

According to Treasury's new reasoning, an exchange established by the federal government under Section 1321 may be treated as an exchange established by the state under Section 1311 because the Department of Health and Human Services (HHS) is required to "establish and operate *such Exchange* within the State."[44] "Such exchange," according to Treasury, is a Section 1311 exchange and should be treated as such for the purposes of authorizing tax credits and cost-sharing subsidies. Concluding otherwise, Treasury maintained, would undermine the PPACA's stated purpose of expanding health insurance coverage.

Treasury's interpretation would be a plausible interpretation of the relevant statutory text were it not for repeated references to the states' role in establishing those exchanges through which tax credits may be offered. As noted before, Section 1311 expressly requires that an authorized exchange must be "established by a State." Section 1304(d) also clearly defines "state" as "each of the 50 States and the District of Columbia."[45] Yet even if one were to set this language aside, as the Treasury Department suggests, and conclude that a Section 1321 exchange is the equivalent of a Section 1311 exchange, this is not enough to establish that tax credits are available to offset the costs of qualifying health insurance plans in either type of exchange.

The eligibility requirements for the tax credits are not found in either Section 1311 or Section 1321 but in Section 1401, which creates Section 36B of the Internal Revenue Code. This section repeatedly defines qualifying health insurance plans eligible for tax credits as those purchased "through an Exchange *established by the State*" under Section 1311. So even if one reads Section 1321 to provide that an exchange established by the federal government is, for all intents and purposes, a Section 1311 exchange, a federal exchange is still not an exchange "established by the State" as required by Section 1401.

The repeated reference to the states' role in creating the relevant exchanges is significant. Not all references to exchanges in the PPACA reference this role as Section 1401 does. Section 1421, for example, provides tax credits to small businesses that make nonelective contributions to employee plans offered through an exchange. Yet, whereas Section 1401 repeatedly references exchanges "established by a State," Section 1421 only references "Exchanges." Under the Treasury Department's interpretation, the additional language in Section 1401 is reduced to surplusage.

The Treasury Department claimed that its interpretation merely reaffirmed well-established congressional intent. Yet neither the federal government—nor anyone else—has ever identified a single contemporaneous statement indicating that tax credits would be available for the purchase of health insurance in federal exchanges under the PPACA. The lack of any such statement is more than a bit conspicuous, especially since numerous health care reform proposals considered prior to the enactment of the PPACA conditioned subsidies on state cooperation.[46]

Because the availability of tax credits for the purchase of health insurance in exchanges triggers imposition of the employer mandate penalty and increases the number of people subject to the individual mandate penalty, the IRS rule became quite controversial. Four separate lawsuits against the rule were filed by states, employers, and individuals affected by the IRS rule. One, *King v. Burwell*, reached the Supreme Court.

On June 25, 2015, a divided Supreme Court held the IRS rule reflected a "fair construction" of the PPACA.[47] Writing for a six-justice majority, Chief Justice John Roberts explained that allowing for the provision of tax credits in federal exchanges would fulfill the PPACA's broad purpose "to improve health insurance markets, not destroy them."[48] The Chief Justice conceded that "State and Federal Exchanges are established by different sovereigns" and that the statute's definition of "State" did not encompass the federal government; he concluded that it was nonetheless "ambiguous" whether an exchange "established" by HHS could qualify as an exchange "established by the State."[49] While the conclusion that tax credits are limited to state-created exchanges reflects "the most natural reading of the pertinent statutory phrase," such a reading would not be consistent with what the Court's majority saw as "Congress's plan."[50] On this basis, and over a strong textualist dissent by Justice Antonin Scalia, the Court upheld the IRS rule.

CONCLUSION

These examples are but the most conspicuous instances of unlawful administrative action implementing the PPACA. There are others.[51] At the time of this writing several lawsuits remain pending that challenge the administration's failure to abide by the PPACA's text. These include suits challenging the employer mandate delay, the expenditure of funds for health insurance subsidies never appropriated by Congress, and the administration's attempt to impose taxes on state and local government health insurance plans.[52] Legal concerns have also been raised about the Obama administration's handling of risk corridors, its decision to stop enrollment in transitional high-risk pools prior to the legislative deadline, and its willingness to authorize subsidies for insurance plans purchased outside of health insurance exchanges.[53]

Not all of these controversies will be resolved in court, however. Jurisdictional obstacles may prevent lawsuits challenging some of the administration's unilateral revisions to the PPACA. For examples, no individuals might satisfy the requirements of Article III standing where the effect of an administrative action was to postpone a deadline or extend a statutory benefit beyond the scope of the statute. That does not make the actions any more lawful. It only means that they cannot be challenged in court.

On March 9, 2010, as the PPACA neared final passage, House Speaker Nancy Pelosi famously remarked that "we have to pass the bill so that you can find out what is in it—away from the fog of the controversy."[54] In her view, the law's many features would be revealed by experience. Speaker Pelosi was correct that many would not understand what the PPACA would mean until after it was enacted, but she should have also added that to know what the law would mean for Americans, the PPACA would actually have to be implemented—and implemented without much regard for the actual statutory text.

2.

A MULTIFACETED ASSAULT ON THE SECOND AMENDMENT

Bob Barr

Bill Clinton was not a subtle president. The manner in which his administration handled firearms issues, especially during his first two years in office, was no exception. Crime, or more particularly, fighting the perception that he was "soft on crime," was a major theme in Clinton's victory over incumbent President George H.W. Bush in 1992. Clinton realized early on that a primary vehicle with which to convey this "tough-on-crime" image was placing gun control front and center as a legislative initiative in 1993 and 1994.

The Brady Bill was signed into law by Clinton on November 30, 1993.[1] This was followed less than a year later with passage of the so-called Clinton Gun Ban, which placed severe restrictions that lasted for a decade on a wide variety of firearms.[2] However, the blowback from the 1994 gun ban—a major factor in the Republicans regaining control of the U.S. House of Representatives that year for the first time in four decades—cramped the ability of the Clinton administration to enact further gun control legislation during the remainder of his time in office.

He never really gave up trying, but even after being weakened following his impeachment by the House of Representatives in December 1998, Clinton's efforts to implement his gun control agenda were rarely disguised; instead, he generally openly attempted to employ such measures for political gain as much as for the substance of gun control.

Thus, the agreement reached between the Clinton administration and Smith & Wesson in 2000, designed to implement an industry standard for gun locks and other "safety" technology,[3] was largely a public relations ploy and predictably fell apart shortly after the following election.[4] But it illustrated the manner in which Clinton operated in the firearms arena following the electoral damage he sustained as a result of the 1994 mid-term election: with a decidedly anti-Second Amendment set of beliefs, he was ultimately more concerned with the public relations and political benefits of pressing that agenda rather than the ultimate legal implementation of the measures.

That approach changed significantly after Barack Obama's election in 2008. The team of President Obama, Vice President Joe Biden, Attorney General Eric Holder, and now, Holder's successor, Loretta Lynch, is at its core more firearms-averse than its Democratic predecessor; but it is far more subtle and nuanced about how it implements its policy. The Obama administration is more concerned with Second Amendment substance than Bill Clinton ever was. To a degree, this approach to gun control is the result of political reality. The renewed strength of the National Rifle Association (NRA) and other grassroots, Second Amendment–focused organizations, coupled with the strong majorities that pro-gun members enjoy in both houses of Congress, has forced the Obama administration to turn to non-legislative means to implement its anti-gun agenda—tactics willingly employed by this President in other areas as well.

President Obama himself has been relatively transparent about his desire to push the limits of unilateral, executive power in order to implement anti-firearms measures that Congress clearly would not support. In this, he is adopting former Clinton advisor Paul Begala's characterization of executive power—"Stroke of the pen . . . Law of the land. Kind of cool."[5]

Although the Obama administration has met with only partial success in its drive to implement gun control measures through executive action, the damage to the processes of government, and to the fundamental, individual right to keep and bear arms as codified in the Second Amendment[6] and upheld in case law by the U.S. Supreme Court in 2008 and 2010,[7] has been anything but insignificant. This chapter explores a few of the many non-legislative measures and procedures employed by the Obama administration to implement its anti-Second Amendment agenda.[8]

In the mixed bag that is the Obama administration's executive action on gun control, we do see some actions that are little more than public relations ploys or measures to burnish the President's credentials with the more liberal wing of his Democratic Party. For example, on January 16, 2013, at least partially in response to the horrible mass murder spree by deranged killer Adam Lanza at Sandy Hook Elementary School in Newtown, Connecticut, the month before,[9] Obama announced twenty-three executive gun control measures.[10] The list included such non-substantive directives as launching a "national dialogue" by the Secretaries of Health and Human Services and Education on "mental health" issues and a national "safe and responsible gun ownership campaign."[11]

Other actions included in the January 2013 executive actions list are more substantive and problematic. And, while some of the announced actions may not be problematic, many Americans remain deeply concerned with the manner in which this administration has sought to circumvent Congress and the public debate that is an essential component of the federal legislative process.

Other executive measures affecting the Second Amendment and firearms issues discussed in this chapter relate to

- the Arms Trade Treaty (ATT) adopted by the United Nations General Assembly in April 2013 and signed by U.S. Secretary of State John Kerry on September 25, 2013;
- Operation Choke Point;
- Operation Fast and Furious;
- efforts to circumvent the long-standing congressional prohibition on the Centers for Disease Control and Prevention (CDC) pressing a gun control agenda;
- regulatory overreach by the Bureau of Alcohol, Tobacco, Firearms, and Explosives (ATF);
- regulatory overreach by the State Department; and

- regulatory overreach by the Department of Health and Human Services.

ARMS TRADE TREATY

On April 2, 2013, following more than a decade of debate throughout most of which the United States vigorously opposed the effort, the U.N. General Assembly adopted an Arms Trade Treaty (ATT).[12] It was signed by U.S. Secretary of State John Kerry on September 25, 2013.[13] To date, 130 nations have signed the treaty, with 69 having ratified it.[14] It entered into force and effect on December 24, 2014.[15]

Even though it is certain the U.S. Senate will not ratify the ATT—absent a massive shift in party control and philosophy—the fact that the United States is a signatory to it means, by its terms and pursuant to the Vienna Convention on the Law of Treaties, that our country is "obliged" not to engage in actions that would "defeat [its] object and purpose."[16] This means not engaging in actions, such as *opposing* gun control efforts, that are contained in the terms of the treaty itself and, more problematic, which might be contrary to any companion, foundational documents that reflect its "object and purpose" and on which it is based.[17]

This means that President Obama could, if he so desires, use the fact that his administration has *signed* the ATT as justification for taking executive action to quietly implement anti-firearms measures. If he does this and if such actions become known, it would then be up to the courts to undo such acts (unlikely) or Congress to do so by appropriations riders or specific prohibitory or limiting legislation (both of which are subject to presidential veto). These remedial steps are never certain and, even if successful, take time, time during which rights are abridged and during which it becomes increasingly difficult to dismantle the effects of those problematic actions.

Arguably, even if a President signs a treaty, another President can "unsign" it.[18] There is no clear consensus among international law experts as to the effect of such a move.[9] However, at a minimum, "unsigning" a treaty would appear to remove any legal obligation on the part of that country to comply with the terms or objects of the treaty.[20]

In Congress, once a treaty has been signed by an administration, it remains "on the shelf" indefinitely, and along with it, the possibility of a president citing it as justification to do or not to do something relating thereto. There remains a risk also that a treaty thus sent to the Senate, even if it languishes there for years (as the U.N. Convention on the Law of the Sea),[21] could be quickly slipped off the shelf, dusted off, and approved by a Senate suddenly favorable to its adoption.

Meanwhile, the myriad provisions of the ATT (which are now in effect for the nations that have signed or ratified it) present and will continue to pose increasingly burdensome issues for the U.S. government and for American companies and individuals engaged in international transactions subject to the extremely broad terms of references in the ATT and its underlying instruments (e.g., transfers of military armaments in certain circumstances, civilian arms sales, brokering and commercial sales of firearms and ammunition, transport of hunting firearms and related equipment, etc.).

Unless clear and decisive action is taken to revoke or at least mitigate the effect of the Obama administration's signing of the ATT (which the U.S. Senate could undertake by expressly voting down the ATT), and absent firm measures by the United States to mitigate the effects of the treaty's provisions affecting international trade and commerce involving firearms, the ATT will pose more problems for the U.S. government, for American companies that import and export firearms and related goods, and for individual citizens seeking to travel internationally to participate in legitimate hunting or other lawful activities involving firearms.

OPERATION CHOKE POINT

In what can be described only as a classic "end around" maneuver, the Obama administration in 2013 directed two federal agencies—the Department of Justice and the Federal Deposit Insurance Corporation (FDIC)—to pressure banks and other financial institutions regulated by the federal government to sever their business relationships with what were described as lawful but "high-risk" businesses.[22] This was a thinly veiled move to cut off the ability of firearms and firearms-related businesses to secure financing necessary for their operations.

The scenario thus presented by Operation Choke Point was deceptively if devastatingly simple. Firearms retailers, as any businesses selling merchandise to the public, must as a practical matter be able to maintain bank accounts in order to accept checks and credit cards and to maintain a line of credit (reflecting the fact that firearms sales vary greatly from season to season if not month to month). If, under the regulatory scheme overseen by the FDIC, such a retailer suddenly receives a letter from their bank that—because they are engaged in a "high-risk" business or industry—the bank is shutting down their account(s), that retailer is presented with immediate and potentially devastating options. They may simply be forced to closer their doors, since no such business can operate on a "cash only" basis (which would itself trigger government scrutiny). Such a notice would force the business to suddenly search for a bank that will accept their business (a move made difficult because they have already being tagged as "high risk") or cause them to dramatically shift their business operation into less "high-risk" retailing.

Operation Choke Point led to a firestorm of criticism, especially from the firearms industry and from members of Congress.[23] The controversy figured in the Senate confirmation hearings for Loretta Lynch, who was sworn into office as Eric Holder's successor as Attorney General on April 27, 2015. Although Lynch promised to look into the controversy as Attorney General, and despite ongoing congressional scrutiny, the effort by the Obama administration to improperly strangle businesses engaged in the lawful commerce of firearms and ammunition has not yet been killed.

A report on Operation Choke Point issued in May 2014 by the House Oversight and Government Reform Committee, chaired at the time by Rep. Darrell Issa (R-CA), concluded that the inception and implementation of the program was unlawful.[24] For example, the committee found that the program was designed not only to cut off truly "high-risk" and questionable business operations but also to prevent lawful firearms and firearms-related businesses from being able to finance perfectly *legal* transactions.[25] In addition, the committee concluded that the Department of Justice lacked legal authority for the manner in which it was carrying out the operation, which ultimately was designed to use the implicit threat of regulatory investigations and prosecutions to pressure financial institutions into cutting off firearms and firearms-related businesses from financial resources essential for their survival.[26]

Subsequent to the House Oversight and Government Reform Committee report, the offices of the Inspectors General for both the Department of Justice and the FDIC initiated investigations of Operation Choke Point.[27] The pressure against this clear abuse of regulatory and prosecutorial power by the Obama administration has continued in the 114th Congress that convened in January 2015, and it appears the congressional actions have borne fruit. In a January 28, 2015, letter, the FDIC clarified its position and directed that banks should *not* assess "risk" based on industry- or business-wide criteria but rather assess each customer's operations and history.[28] The FDIC also mandated that before a business could be choked off from financing, such action must be put in writing by the examiner.[29]

Whether this congressional and public scrutiny will truly stop the clear abuses of power perpetrated by Operation Choke Point remains to be seen; but the operation stands as a stark reminder of the many tools and agencies with which the federal government can target legitimate firearms and firearms-related businesses.

OPERATION FAST AND FURIOUS

In one operation (for which even the Obama administration felt embarrassment), Operation Fast and Furious revealed serious flaws in law enforcement techniques employed by the Department of Justice and the ATF. In its zeal to apprehend, prosecute, and publicize illegal trafficking in firearms, the ATF permitted approximately 2,000 firearms to be sold or transferred to criminal elements, including known high-level Mexican drug cartel figures.[30] Several of the firearms permitted to be sold or transferred to criminal elements during Operation Fast and Furious were subsequently recovered on the Arizona side of the Mexican border (as recently as July 2013 in a gang-style shooting in Phoenix[31]) and at the scene where U.S. Border Patrol Agent Brian Terry was killed in December 2010.[32]

The political fallout from the Fast and Furious scandal has been significant. A U.S. Attorney was forced to resign,[33] and Attorney General Holder was held in contempt of Congress on June 28, 2012—the first time a sitting member of a president's cabinet has been held in criminal contempt of Congress.[34] The citation was the result of the Obama administration's adamant refusal to turn over to the Congress documents relating to Fast and Furious,[35] despite public statements by Obama promising "transparency."

The use of "sting operations" in federal law enforcement investigations is nothing new, whether in undercover drug cases or investigations involving illicit trafficking in firearms. However, the irresponsible, almost cavalier, manner in which Fast and Furious was carried out by the Obama administration's Department of Justice and its component agency, the ATF, reveals a clear predisposition to "go after" firearms cases without due regard for the consequences.

THE CENTERS FOR DISEASE CONTROL AND PREVENTION

The CDC, a formal agency within the Department of Health and Human Services that is headquartered just outside of Atlanta, Georgia, has existed for nearly seven decades (though it has undergone several name changes).[36] The agency was formally established in 1946 to control malaria, at the time a serious and highly communicable disease, particularly in the Deep South.[37]

Typical of the mission creep that infects virtually all federal bureaucracies, however, the CDC has constantly grown in size, budget, and jurisdiction. It now claims jurisdiction over, and spends taxpayer monies on, such non-disease matters as disabilities, injury control, workplace hazards, terrorism, domestic violence, suicide, sexual violence, and many others.[38]

Gun control advocates have for years attempted to shoehorn "gun violence" into the mission and work of the CDC—claiming it should be dealt with as a "public health issue" rather than a law enforcement matter. This effort moved into high gear during the Clinton presidency but drew on "research" linking gun violence to "public health" dating to the late 1970s.[39] In response to Clinton's attempt to employ the CDC in moving his anti-gun agenda forward, in 1996 the Republican-controlled Congress made it clear that funds would not be appropriated for the CDC to engage in such a political foray.[40]

Obama, however, always watchful for opportunities to advance his gun control agenda without engaging in a frontal assault, has attempted to nudge funds to the CDC for such purposes. The heartbreaking Sandy Hook school shooting in December 2012 provided him such an opening. As part of his January 16, 2013, announcement, Obama issued a Presidential Memorandum, entitled "Engaging in Public Health Research on the Causes and Prevention of Gun Violence."[41]

The Presidential Memorandum, directed to the Secretary of HHS, repeats the gun control mantra that "gun violence is also a serious public health issue."[42] This language is used routinely by gun control advocates to justify expanding the resources and powers of the federal government far beyond law enforcement to implement their agenda. The memorandum then makes the leap to the powers enjoyed by Obama to direct HHS and CDC to "conduct or sponsor research into the causes of gun violence and the ways to prevent it."[43]

There is no power inherent in the presidency, implied by the Constitution or directed by federal law, that provides a legitimate basis for the effort "directed" by the Obama memorandum. As with many actions undertaken by contemporary American presidents, however, saying it is so can make it so if neither the Congress nor the courts step in and tell him "no." Thankfully, in this particular instance, and much to the chagrin of gun control advocates, the presidential effort to employ federal resources to "study" gun violence as a "public health issue" has thus far fallen flat, because Congress has refused to reinstate funding for such an effort (as it first did in 1996).[44]

Obama persists though. The public relations effort to shift the gun debate from one of law enforcement and related problems to "public health" continues undeterred by congressional appropriations limits. Ways around such "technicalities" are many. For example, a report titled *Priorities for Research to Reduce the Threat of Firearms-Related Violence* was recently produced for the CDC by the National Academy of Science with outside monies from several private and quasi-private entities and even one "anonymous donor."[45] The CDC Foundation itself is a donor for this project.[46]

Clearly, this effort to make gun control a public health issue follows the manner in which the anti-tobacco lobby shifted the public debate from one of individual choice to public health over the course of five decades, to the point now where the Food and Drug Administration

(FDA) enjoys legal authority to regulate virtually all tobacco products. Indeed, Dr. Mark Rosenberg, former head of the CDC, has proudly and publicly proclaimed just such a goal, at one point telling the *Washington Post*, "We need to revolutionize the way we look at guns, like we did with cigarettes . . . dirty, deadly and banned."[47] Zealots like Rosenberg—armed with the significant resources of non-government, anti-gun benefactors Michael Bloomberg, George Soros, and innumerable foundations and private funding sources—will continue to provide tools outside the regular order of our constitutionally based government, with which policy makers like Clinton and Obama will be able to press their agenda even in the face of clear, contrary congressional directives.

ATF REGULATORY EFFORTS

As the primary federal agency with regulatory jurisdiction over firearms, the potential is great for the ATF to be abused by presidents as a means of undercutting or circumventing Congress or simply taking actions of which Congress would not approve.[48]

In the summer of 2011, for example, the ATF sent letters to more than 8,000 federal firearms licensees (FFLs—businesses and individuals engaged in the regular sale or purchase of firearms) in the four states bordering Mexico (Arizona, California, New Mexico, and Texas).[49] The letters required the FFLs to report to the bureau any and all sales to anyone not also an FFL in any five-day period "of two or more semi-automatic rifles capable of accepting a detachable magazine and with a caliber greater than .22."[50] There was no particular basis in law or other regulations for this "multiple sales reporting requirement," and it was disingenuously published by the ATF as an emergency rule change. With the support of the NRA,[51] several plaintiffs quickly challenged the ATF's actions as contrary to existing, statutory reporting requirements[52] and an unnecessary, costly, and unfair burden on lawful firearms retailers. Although the government's position thus far has been sustained by the courts,[53] a regulatory move to expand the reporting requirement beyond these border states was withdrawn by the ATF in the face of public opposition by the firearms industry and Second Amendment groups.[54]

Another arena in which the ATF has pressed the regulatory envelope involves expansion of the category of persons prohibited under federal law from acquiring or possessing firearms,[55] a matter clearly within the jurisdiction of Congress. In January 2014, the ATF published a proposal that would have greatly expanded the categories of persons prohibited from possessing firearms based on having been "adjudicated as a mental defective" or "committed to a mental institution."[56] As noted in comments filed in opposition to the proposal, such broadening language not only conflicted with court decisions interpreting the statutory language, but also raised serious due process concerns.[57] This initiative by the ATF appears to be among those included in President Obama's list of twenty-three "Executive Actions" announced in January 2013.[58]

While a "review" of the categories of persons prohibited from possessing firearms may not present substantive or jurisdictional concerns, attempting to change federal law by rule change without congressional approval, as the administration is attempting, is another matter entirely.

On February 13, 2015 (a Friday), the ATF published a proposal to ban an entire category of popular rifle ammunition—M855/SS109 5.56x45 mm rounds—used by millions of civilian shooters in the immensely popular AR-15 rifle.[59] The move by the ATF would have eliminated the ammunition's three-decades-old "sporting purposes" exemption from being considered "armor piercing."[60] But it was quickly denounced by industry and sporting associations alike as arbitrary and not fact-based.[61] The degree of widespread opposition caused the ATF less than one month later to back away (for the time being at least) from the proposed ban.[62]

However, the attempt by the ATF to push through reversal of a thirty-year policy, based on a sudden decision that an entire category of popular rifle ammunition is now considered by the ATF to be "armor piercing" and therefore unlawful for civilian use, stands as a clear reminder of how quickly and arbitrarily the ATF can adjust its regulatory sights. The ATF's actions also illustrate how it can attempt to use the regulatory power over ammunition to effectively ban an entire class of firearm (in this case, the popular AR-15 rifle).

Other, recent regulatory moves by the ATF that conflict with congressional action or policies include bans on importation of certain categories of ammunition;[63] reversal of policy on use of "stabilizing braces" on AR-15-style pistols often used by amputees;[64] arbitrary limitations on

National Firearms Act Trusts, thus making it more difficult for lawful trusts and corporations to acquire and keep firearms governed by the National Firearms Act;[65] and regular, if not frequent, additional administrative and reporting requirements for FFLs.[66]

REGULATORY OVERREACH BY THE DEPARTMENT OF STATE

Insofar as the Department of State has jurisdiction over certain transactions involving the transfer or transportation of firearms between the United States and other countries (including for hunters, brokers, and importers and exporters of firearms and ammunition), this federal department, too, has been enlisted by the Obama administration as an enabler of extra-congressional executive action against firearms.

The primary statutory vehicle by which the State Department engages in this exercise regarding exporting rifles, handguns, and ammunition is ITAR—International Traffic in Arms Regulations.[67] (The Commerce Department is responsible for monitoring and regulating shotguns and shotgun shells.)[68] There are well-established rules under which U.S. citizens have for many years temporarily exported up to three non-automatic firearms and up to 1,000 rounds of ammunition, with a relative minimum of paperwork required (so long as properly declared to Customs Service).[69] No longer. In its continuing anti-firearm effort, in early 2015 the Obama administration had the State Department enforce a three-year-old set of additional and highly burdensome paperwork requirements for temporary exports of firearms and ammunition under ITAR.[70]

In 2010 and 2013, in other arbitrary anti-firearm moves, the State Department disapproved the re-importation into the United States of collectible military rifles[71] and some 800,000 military-surplus M-1 Garand rifles and carbines from our ally South Korea.[72] These moves reversed long-standing policy by the federal government that such rifles, no longer used by the military but prized by sportsmen and collectors, posed no law enforcement danger and therefore could be re-imported and sold to civilians in the United States. The State Department claimed in its policy reversal that the rifles might be used for "illicit purposes" (as if any firearm could not be so misused by the wrong person) and therefore for public safety reasons could no longer be imported.[73]

One does not have to be involved in high-level diplomatic activities to run afoul of the State Department's anti-firearms agenda. This is the same department that reversed itself in October 2009 when then Secretary of State Hillary Clinton declared that U.S. opposition to the drafting of the ATT would cease and that the United States would no longer oppose the effort, culminating in her successor—John Kerry—formally signing the treaty on behalf of the United States in 2013.[74]

REGULATORY OVERREACH BY THE DEPARTMENT OF HEALTH AND HUMAN SERVICES

Not to be left behind in the Obama administration's executive-action-based gun control agenda, even the Department of Health and Human Services has climbed on the bandwagon. In December 2014, for example, HHS issued proposed "Guidelines" for early childcare providers that recommends—this is no joke—a ban on all "objects manufactured for play as toy guns on the premises [of child care providers] at any time."[75] The proposal also included firearms storage requirements of the sort expressly invalidated in the 2008 *Heller* opinion.[76] Compliance with the "voluntary" guidelines would be accomplished through *inspections*, including random, unannounced inspections of childcare homes and facilities.[77]

While the guidelines are ostensibly "voluntary," they must be taken seriously. Such guidelines frequently come to be attached to federal funding sources used to entice state and local regulatory bodies to adopt them and they often morph over time into mandatory requirements. Many state and local government regulatory bodies frequently adopt such proposed federal guidelines as their own. Concerned parties that filed comments in opposition to the proposed HHS guidelines were wise to do so.

CONCLUSION

Our discussion scratches the surface of the many ways in which the Obama administration has attempted to implement its anti-firearms agenda through executive actions. It should serve at the same time as a clear warning of just how many ways are available to *any* president to circumvent the regular constitutional process, by using regulatory and rulemaking powers ceded to the Executive by modern Congresses.

These dangers are only enhanced in the absence of a proactive and aware Congress mindful of its crucial responsibility to ensure presidents operate within, and consistent with, the letter and the intent of the law and the policies of the underlying legislation.

3.

RELIGIOUS LIBERTY

Gerard V. Bradley and Robert P. George

In a series of actions beginning on August 1, 2011, the Obama administration has sought to redraw America's map of religion and society. The boundary lines on the envisioned chart divide human activity into two basic realms. The first is "public" life, defined expansively to include not only law and political affairs but commercial and social intercourse too. This space is to be governed by positive norms promulgated by public authority, which have, assertedly, the peculiar value of originating (to adapt a phrase derived from *Planned Parenthood v. Casey*) not in anyone's or any group's moral code or religious doctrine but in the requirements of liberty for all.[1] Non-conforming religious norms of conduct have no sway.

The second realm, the province of religion, is limited to "private" space. Religion is there subsumed within an encompassing project of individual self-definition (that is: assimilated to the "conscience" or "dignity" or "identity" of the acting person). This area is the realm of subjectivity. The foundation of value here is neither moral truth nor one's obligations to a greater-than-human source of meaning and value. The metric of worth is instead authenticity—one's subjective sense of one's own deepest, and thus true, self. In perhaps the most startling relevant position adopted by the administration (in the *Hosanna-Tabor* litigation), the Equal Employment Opportunity Commission (EEOC) argued that *churches* should be understood as aggregations of persons, all expressing themselves in a similar way.[2]

The administration's efforts would finally solve the religio-political problem—the "church-state" question—at the heart of modern liberalism. It would do so with a touch of magic: religion would simply vanish from the radar screen of public authority. It would not count in public, and in private it would register, and be regulated, under non-religious descriptions (as the way some persons self-identify, or choose to express themselves within a like-minded cohort). The administration has deployed the full array of Executive Branch weapons in its campaign: administrative rulemaking; executive orders; law enforcement discretion; contracting and procurement policy; legislative proposals; arguments of policy as well as of statutory and constitutional interpretation in judicial proceedings; and even the presidential "bully pulpit." We will supply examples of each.

This breathtakingly audacious campaign has so far been only partly successful. One reason is that the Supreme Court has stymied the initiative at a few critical points, most notably in the *Hosanna-Tabor* and *Hobby Lobby*[3] decisions. Another reason is that the campaign is, well, breathtakingly audacious. The administration has not, however, been decisively defeated. On the contrary: its vision is intact, and it operates on the strategic offensive, choosing favorable grounds upon which to press its case against religion.

The prospects for the administration's success are better than average. Congress has been supine, even where by a simple majority action it could block the administration, or at least seize the political initiative on select issues by forcing the President to veto corrective legislation. Meanwhile, the Executive's bold program synthesizes, and is propelled by, strong cultural tailwinds. Among these winds is the waxing of same-sex "marriage" as the *sine qua non* of charity and even of justice toward some people who have in the past been poorly treated. The diminishing cultural and moral authority of America's churches and religious leaders promotes the administration's agenda. The American believer seems, moreover, to be increasingly a syncretist, someone who assembles an *ad hoc* religious identity, so that the proposal to understand one's religion as one's own spiritual brand resonates with many persons' experiences and desires.

The administration has, to be sure, taken broadly conventional positions in some Supreme Court religion cases (involving legislative prayer, prisoners' beards, and secondary rules implementing religious nondiscrimination in the workplace).[4] And most of what it does is unrelated to the boundary revisions we take up here. But the administration also has regularly exploited a cluster of sexual-equality and sexual-identity issues, especially effective access of women to reproductive services and of non-heterosexuals to marriage, with the conscious aim of redrawing this country's map of religion and society.

I.

A. "Contraception" Mandate

In the beginning was the HHS "contraception" mandate. The Affordable Care Act, which was enacted on March 23, 2010, requires group health plans and health insurance issuers to cover without cost-sharing certain "preventive care and screenings" for women.[5] On August 1, 2011, the Department of Health and Human Services announced that among these covered services would be all FDA-approved contraceptives, including those (IUDs and "emergency contraceptives") that act sometimes as abortifacients.[6] Because the ACA also requires employers of fifty or more workers to offer health insurance,[7] the administration's rulemaking effectively compelled employers—including religious institutions—to subsidize contraception and early abortion for their female workers and covered dependents.

On August 3, 2011, the Obama administration promulgated an exception to the "contraception" mandate for some religious employers who conscientiously objected to it.[8] This "exemption" was limited to those non-profits that employed and served "primarily" its own adherents and whose "purpose" was "inculcation of religious values."[9] Ever since, the administration has invariably said that its goal is to exempt only churches and other houses of worship. So it has; no religious hospital or charity could qualify for the exemption. Nor could any college or university.

Even this limited concession did not reflect a positive evaluation of religious liberty. The administration has invariably maintained in litigation over a related "accommodation" for other religious non-profits that the sense of the exemption lay not in some special concern for churches but in simple efficiency: female employees of churches which condemn "contraception" would not use the free "preventive services" anyway.

Perhaps the most controversial offensive in the administration's campaign has been that waged against religious non-profit employers who object to the "contraception" mandate. Critics blasted the initial August 3, 2011, "exemption" as so narrow that it would not have extended to Jesus and the apostles (who primarily served as evangelists to persons outside their own religious community).[10] The administration has since promulgated several versions of a wider "accommodation" for religious non-profit employers (such as the University of Notre Dame).[11] This "accommodation" (*not* an exemption!) has gone through five iterations.[12] It currently permits an objecting, qualifying employer to inform *either* its insurance administrator *or* the government of its conscientious religious objection, and then—according to the Obama administration—it is relieved of all meaningful participation.[13] (This either/or rule stems from Supreme Court compulsion, in cases involving *Wheaton College*[14] and the *Little Sisters of the Poor.*[15]) According to the scores of religious employers litigating the matter, though, the "accommodation" still imposes a "substantial burden" upon their religious exercise in violation of the Religious Freedom Restoration Act.[16]

The Supreme Court has taken up and will resolve the non-profits' challenges to the "contraception" mandate during the 2015–2016 term. We venture no prediction about the Court's likely decision. We are certain, however, that the administration will continue to defend the remarkable position it has taken in lower court "accommodation" cases, namely, that there is such a "compelling state interest" in women's reproductive health services that what it calls the "seamless" free delivery of those services to every woman of reproductive age overrides all considerations of religious freedom.[17] The administration is willing to "accommodate" religious employers' objections *only* to the extent that doing so has no adverse impact upon "seamless" delivery. In other words, the administration asserts, and argues vigorously, that there is a "compelling interest" in making no exceptions. Religious employers who do not conform face ruinous penalties and thus extinction.

The government's position regarding religious employers in the profit-seeking sector of the economy has been even more startling. HHS asserted in *Burwell v. Hobby Lobby Stores* that neither the named corporate party nor its individual owners "can even be heard under" the Religious Freedom Restoration Act.[18] The Supreme Court recognized that this claim would have "dramatic consequences."[19] Indeed it would.

The administration asserted in *Hobby Lobby* that *corporations* simply "cannot exercise religion."[20] Perhaps because it was engaged at the time in dozens of "mandate" lawsuits with corporate employers (albeit non-profits), HHS simultaneously asserted that a profit-motive was somehow incompatible with exercising religion.[21] Partly because several religious liberty claimants in Supreme Court cases have been profit-seeking businesses, a Court majority easily refuted the administration's claim,[22] which required essentially that the government extend a facsimile of the non-profits' "accommodation" to Hobby Lobby.[23]

B. Government Contractors

All too often, very young children manage to illegally enter the United States (many through Mexico) without an accompanying adult caregiver.[24] For many years the United States contracted with the humanitarian arms of various churches to provide needed supervision and care.[25] These organizations—almost all of them Catholic or evangelical Protestant—have long done the job well and cost-effectively. They have done so because they can recruit especially motivated workers and because so many of these children are accustomed to trusting churches in a way that is based upon their experience at home—they would never trust government.

On Christmas Eve 2014, the Obama administration published an interim final rule that disrupted this long-standing arrangement and that might terminate it altogether. On the chance that a female child-migrant might have been impregnated by sexual abuse, *every* contractor must provide "timely, unimpeded access to . . . emergency contraception."[26] If a pregnancy is confirmed, *every* contractor "must ensure that the victim receives timely and comprehensive information about all lawful pregnancy-related medical services and timely access to" reproductive services, including abortion.[27] The rules contain *no* exceptions for religious or moral objections to these new requirements, notwithstanding the administration's acknowledgment (in the preamble) that some grantees and contractors have such objections.[28]

C. Sexual Orientation and Gender Identity

On July 21, 2014, President Obama issued Executive Order 13672,[29] which was implemented by a Department of Labor rule published on December 9, 2014, and became effective on April 8, 2015.[30] The 2014 order and implementing rule were an unwarranted interpretation of Title VII's ban on "sex discrimination." It added "sexual orientation and gender identity" to the prohibited bases of discrimination. Executive Order 13672 looks like a down payment upon the stalled Employment Non-Discrimination Act (ENDA),[31] which the President seeks to deliver without Congress's assent.

American presidents since World War II have generally specified the non-discrimination requirements when it comes to federal *contractors*. Congress has, however, generally superintended the strings attached to federal *grants*. And so reports that the administration has decided or is likely to decide that grantees too must abide by SOGI (sexual orientation/gender identity) non-discrimination rules[32] represent a significant overreach. If these reports are true, the President would make a huge balloon payment on ENDA.

Both contractors and grantees retain a right under the federal rules to hire staff on religious bases.[33] But it is unclear if these rules extend to a refusal to hire or retain a staffer who professes the religion of the contractor or grantee but who engages in immoral sexual conduct (which would be the case, for example, even if a staffer was civilly married to a member of the same sex). The Obama administration would likely deny that immoral conduct by a co-religionist qualifies for the exception. Or would it insist that the "equal dignity" of staffers of a different SOGI constitutes a compelling government interest that all those who do business with the federal government must honor? Or both?

D. Defense of Marriage Act

On February 23, 2011, Attorney General Eric Holder announced that the President had instructed the Justice Department to cease defending the constitutionality of the federal Defense of Marriage Act (DOMA) in judicial proceedings.[34] President Obama judged that there was no reasonable basis for defending DOMA. Refusing to defend a statute was itself a highly unusual (though not quite unique) executive action.

The Supreme Court thus took up in *United States v. Windsor* the question of DOMA's constitutionality (more exactly, that of the Section 3 definition of "marriage" as the union of a man and a woman),[35] without benefit of an executive argument in its favor.[36] Decided on June 26, 2013, *Windsor* effectively held that federal marriage laws must conform to state laws, so that a couple legally married and living in New York, for example, would be legally married there for both state and federal purposes.[37]

Since *Windsor* was decided, the Obama administration has aggressively moved to establish a "place of celebration" rule for federal marital status. The government has established by rule or practice almost all across the federal corpus (save for a few arenas governed unequivocally by statute, such as VA benefits, copyright, and some Social Security matters) that no matter where a couple *resides* (whether or not same-sex couples could legally marry in that state), they are "married" for federal legal purposes so long as they *celebrated* a civil marriage somewhere. All federal personnel are therefore expected to treat as spouses the parties to a civil same-sex marriage, even where the domicile state would not do so and even where the federal actor holds sincere religious scruples against doing so. The administration has implemented this policy without making any provision for religious objections.

For example, the Family and Medical Leave Act (FMLA) defines its beneficiaries to include "a husband or a wife, as the case may be."[38] In 1995 the Department of Labor promulgated a rule making the law of the state where an employee *resides* in control for FMLA purposes.[39] In a proposed rule published on June 27, 2014, the department reversed course.[40] The new rule, which became final on February 25, 2015, establishes that a marriage could be composed of two "husbands" or two "wives."[41] It also specifies that FMLA eligibility is to be determined according to the laws of the state where a couple's marriage was celebrated.[42]

Of course any employer could complain that being made to treat two persons in an immoral sexual relationship as "spouses" violates the Religious Freedom Restoration Act (RFRA).[43] So, too, could federal contractors, grantees, and others who are "substantially burdened" (the triggering RFRA term) by application of any of the government's remapping initiatives.[44] That is precisely what Hobby Lobby and so many religious non-profits have done to fend off the "contraception" mandate. But the administration is certain to deny that eligibility provisions that are unappealing to some religious institutions impose a "substantial burden" (because, the government will argue, no one has a right to be a grantee or contractor, and these institutions' religious scruples are not in any way being compromised). Any possibility for judicial relief is diminished each time the administration ascribes overriding value to the notion of an equal "dignity" for everyone's sexual self-determination or reproductive freedom. Indeed, the administration's position is unmistakably that there is a "compelling state interest" in making no exceptions when it comes to same-sex "married" couples.

In any event, RFRA applies to *all* federal government actions, including all of those so far described here.[45] RFRA's requirements therefore constitute, in the first instance and principally, a duty upon all federal lawmakers and law enforcers to treat the "exercise of religion" as that statute directs.[46] And so, assuming that the President would not serially violate his own understanding of his constitutional duty to "take Care" that RFRA (among other laws) "be faithfully executed,"[47] the administration must hold that the actions so far catalogued *comply* with RFRA. Its conscientious judgment must presumably be that, notwithstanding RFRA's high valuation of religious liberty, it is making things go as they ought to go.

* * *

The most apt account of the Obama administration vision for religion in public life that we have seen is in a New Mexico Supreme Court opinion from the *Elane Photography* case.[48] That court in 2013 ruled in favor of a lesbian couple who asserted that, under the state law outlawing discrimination on grounds of sexual orientation in all "public accommodations," a wedding photographer was bound to photograph their "commitment ceremony."[49] Concurring in that result, Justice Bosson recognized that the photographers—the Huguenins—acted out of a sincere Christian belief that the ceremony celebrated an immoral sexual relationship and that memorializing it in pictures made them complicit in the immorality.[50]

Justice Bosson wrote, tellingly, that the Huguenins are "free to think, to say, to believe, as they wish; they may pray to the God of their choice and follow these commandments in *their personal lives*."[51] In the world of "the marketplace, of commerce, of public accommodation," they must "compromise."[52] They "must channel their conduct, not their beliefs, so as to leave space for other Americans who believe something different."[53] They must adhere to the "glue that holds us together as a nation, the tolerance that lubricates the varied moving parts of us as a people."[54] This is "the price of citizenship."[55]

II.

On many occasions during the course of its *Kulturkampf*, the Obama administration—and the President himself—has made clear that the core of religious liberty is "freedom of worship."[56] We have already seen that beyond "freedom of worship" lies treacherous territory for believers who would negotiate public life according to their religious norms. We have seen, more exactly, the administration maintain that religious exercise is either impossible (perhaps a better phrase is to be ignored) or heavily outweighed by the asserted requirements of sexual and reproductive freedom.

It is worth noting that "worship" is, in settled First Amendment law, a (if not *the*) irreducible religious activity. It is an undertaking that has no secular analogue.[57] One consequence of this designation is to put "worship" in an unenviable First Amendment position. Under prevailing judicial norms of interpretation, "worship" is speech "subject matter" and not "viewpoint." Public authorities may therefore discriminate against "worship" where it could not do so against a religious "viewpoint."[58] For example, New York authorities (as in *Bronx Household of Faith*) may constitutionally deny school meeting space for "worship," whereas they could not do so for a secular group engaged in its signature activity, or for a church that sponsored a lecture defending, say, the Christian viewpoint on a secular subject matter.[59] And perhaps authorities must do so, because to promote "worship" is, perforce, to promote religion, which presumptively violates the asserted Establishment Clause norm of "neutrality" between "religion" and "non-religion."[60]

"Worship" is in any event inseparable from the concept of a "minister" (used here generically to denote anyone who conducts or orchestrates "worship") and from "church," used broadly to indicate any worshiping community. If "freedom of worship" is the core of religious liberty, one would expect that the Obama administration would take a very generous view of these two corollary terms.

So it was predictable that counsel for the EEOC would begin her argument in the 2012 Supreme Court "ministerial exception" case by saying that "[t]he freedom of religious communities to come together to express and share religious belief is a fundamental constitutional right."[61] Not so predictable (perhaps) was her next assertion: "But it's a right that must also accommodate important governmental interests in securing the public welfare."[62] Then the government drew back even further from the defense one might possibly have expected. After listening to government counsel's argument, the Chief Justice asked her, "Is there anything special about the fact that the people involved in this case are part of a religious organization? . . . Is [this freedom] . . . any different from any other group of people who get together for an expressive right?"[63]

Counsel for the EEOC answered: no.[64]

As the Court in *Hosanna-Tabor Evangelical Lutheran Church and School v. EEOC* recounted this scene from oral argument, EEOC "thus see[s] no need—and no basis—for a special rule for ministers grounded in the Religion Clauses themselves."[65] It follows under the EEOC's view, then, "that the First Amendment analysis should be the same, whether the association in question is the Lutheran Church, a labor union, or a social club."[66] Indeed, EEOC argued in its brief that "it would violate the First Amendment" if employment discrimination laws were used "to compel the ordination of women by the Catholic Church or by an Orthodox Jewish Seminary."[67] These churches could successfully fend off such an intrusion, EEOC asserted, by invoking not the religion clauses but the "implicit" First Amendment right to "freedom of association."[68]

"We find this position untenable," wrote the Chief Justice for the Court.[69] He explained that the First Amendment itself "gives special solicitude to the rights of religious organizations."[70] The justices repudiated the administration's remarkable view, which would erase the distinctively religious character of churches and assimilate them to the broader category of "expressive associations."

The High Court's decisive rejection does not mean that the administration's transposition of religion into speech, and church into an aggregation of expressive individuals, was stillborn on January 11, 2012. On the contrary, the administration's secularized view of religion suffuses the re-mapping campaign examined here. And it can operate without judicial molestation, so long as (for the most part) no plaintiff suffering from a "substantial burden" upon religious exercise can persuade a court that his (or her or its) case depends precisely upon the transposition rejected in *Hosanna-Tabor*.

The administration's audacious campaign has more far-reaching aspirations. It seeks to pierce the veil protecting religious belief as such from public obloquy. *Orthopraxy* in public and commercial life doubtlessly tends in our society to engender an *orthodoxy*. Even if at first it is instigated by the need to conform to legal rules, what people do habitually establishes social expectations and thus customary norms of behavior. Before long the legal norms are part of the cultural furniture. It is then not long before a "consensus" about what is truly owed to other persons "evolves." Then a mainstream belief about what justice entails is born, and those who would do otherwise are not only legally restrained but the subjects of social censure and stigma. They would behave badly.

This dynamic movement from doing to believing is promoted especially when legal norms are introduced, justified, and enforced with heavy moral ballast. The legal norms considered here have been defended as imperatives of "gender equality," "women's health," "sexual self-determination," and "equal dignity" for "equal love." The "contraceptive" mandate and satellite issues of "reproductive freedom" are all promoted as defenses in a "war on women." The government surely seeks to stigmatize any negative moral judgment of homosexual relations not only as irrational but as so mistaken and hurtful as to be tantamount to racism. So Solicitor General Donald Verrilli could not deny, during oral argument of the Sixth Circuit same-sex "marriage" cases, that the *Bob Jones University* impact—exemption negated—might be down the road for religious institutions that hold to the view of marriage that the President says he held until just four years ago.[71]

Perhaps the most probative evidence of the President's intention to stigmatize resistance to whatever achieves (somehow) the status of being on the "LGBT agenda" was his April 8, 2015, announcement (through the statement of close advisor Valerie Jarrett) that he was throwing the full support of his administration behind legal prohibitions on reparative therapies for minors (with their parents' consent).[72] These therapies, which are currently unlawful in California, New Jersey, Oregon, and the District of Columbia,[73] treat some instances of same-sex attraction as psycho-sexual developmental problems or as the effects of sexual abuse. Accordingly, some therapists seek to restore (in those instances) a person's authentic heterosexual identity through counseling.

The President's statement did not say that he would call for a federal ban on reparative therapy (the constitutional basis of which would be dubious).[74] Instead, it indicated that the administration would be supportive of further efforts to ban these therapies at the state level.[75] It is difficult to understand why, save that President Obama has been captured by an unscientific, and even irrational, ideology. Evidence for the propositions that "sexual orientation" is to a significant degree "plastic"—that is, subject to experiential and social influences[76]—and that sexual abuse frequently causes aberrational "acting out" is plentiful. These two propositions are nearly unchallenged in the relevant scientific communities.

In fact, the President's position is very nearly absurd. As Johns Hopkins psychiatrist Paul McHugh recently wrote of laws banning reparative therapies, "A doctor who would look into the psychological history of a transgendered boy or girl in search of a resolvable conflict could lose his or her license to practice medicine. By contrast, such a physician would not be penalized if he or she started such patient on hormones that would block puberty and might stunt growth."[77]

More prosaically, these laws—and now the President of the United States—would say this to an anxious teenage boy who has, perhaps, had a homosexual encounter: any professional who would help you to *like* a girl is a criminal. But any professional who will help you to *be* a girl is a hero.

III.

The Obama administration's re-mapping of religion and society is unprecedented in at least four important ways, *besides* its breathtaking aim to make religion disappear from view.

One. The specific allowance for both individual and institutional exemptions from onerous, but ostensibly neutral, general laws, is significantly below the accustomed federal norm, dating from around 1965 until the end of the George W. Bush presidency.

Two. Never before has the federal Executive been rebuffed by the Court for taking positions that—to use a plain term—were too *secularized*. In general, since World War II the federal Executive has often been at odds with the Court. But in most instances it has been because the government defended positions more religion-friendly (again, speaking plainly) than the Court was prepared to accept. This has been almost uniformly the pattern in cases of public aid to religious schools and where public authority sponsors or conducts a religious observance. These two categories account for the vast bulk of Supreme Court Establishment Clause cases. And the pattern was nearly without exception, pre-Obama: a secularized Court rejected the pro-religion submissions of the Executive.

The cases that come closest to being counter-examples involved the Selective Service law's conscientious objector provisions during the Vietnam era. In *Seeger* and *Welsh* the Court read those provisions expansively to include avowedly non-religious conscientious objections.[78] In these cases the Solicitor General (Archibald Cox and Erwin Griswold, respectively) argued that the law as written simply did not permit such a reading.[79] Without suggesting that a statute that made explicit provision for non-religious conscientious objection would be either unconstitutional or unjust, we think it rather clear that the solicitors general were right. And we do not concede that, by making the statutory phrase "religious training and belief" include "non-religious training and belief,"[80] the justices acted as friends to religion.

Three. From the founding right up until yesterday, America's federal government and the states entered into and sustained a mutual partnership with religious institutions to serve the common good. In this tradition, "public" works comprised some that were governmental and, often, more that were religious. These joint ventures have included government assistance to religious schools, hospitals, charities, and even straightforward missionary works (among Native Americans and in foreign locales strategically interesting to the United States). By and through its actions described herein, the Obama administration has shown a muscular resolve to dispense with, in principle entirely, these institutional helping ministries. The administration has used both carrot and stick, the one to induce these ministries to secularize and the other to drive them from the field.

There have been over the last two centuries or more some short-term episodes of similar animus against these helping institutions, including occasional federal legislative and executive drives against parochial education. But these drives were aimed at specifically Roman Catholic schools and petered out by World War II. Since World War II the courts have often taken aim at Catholic schools, and the Supreme Court appeared by the mid-1970s to be utterly indifferent to their survival. The federal Executive invariably opposed this judicial impulse. But the present administration's animus is more ecumenical and global (for it includes *any* religious employer).

Four. From the founding until perhaps the day before yesterday, Americans and their presidents believed that our country's security and prosperity depended in some *essential* way upon the virtue of the people. Because our country's commitment to liberty meant that government could do little directly to inculcate virtue in citizens, the essential precondition of security and prosperity depended heavily upon the exertions of religious institutions. The Obama administration seems to be indifferent (judging from our third point), and even hostile, to that religious contribution to national success. More startlingly, the administration seems—by its demarcation of the world into realms of law and subjectivity—to have rejected altogether the connection between private character and public well-being.

The Obama's administration's campaign against religion is both deeply ideological and merely political. It is political in that the administration's most extravagant aggressions—including those described here—inflict collateral damage upon religious belief, conduct, and institutions. In these cases the administration's goal is not exactly anti-religious, even though the damage inflicted is enormous and disproportionate (think of the administration's unwillingness to concede anything to religion on the "contraceptive" mandate, or its seemingly gratuitous exclusion of religious providers of services to unaccompanied child migrants). In these cases religious people and institutions happen to stand in the way of achieving ostensibly secular goals, such as "gender equality," full "dignity" for "sexual minorities," universal access to the means of "reproductive health," and so on.

When imperatives of this urgency are not in play, as they are not in matters like prisoners' diets and grooming, the Obama administration has taken more or less conventional religious liberty positions.[81] And we would grant that, when administration officials from the President on down praise religion in speeches and profess their respect for believers, they could pass a lie detector test while doing so. But when matters of what these officials deem to be great urgency are in play, the administration has plainly been politically ruthless. No price extracted from religion for the sake of, for example, "marriage equality," is too great.

The administration's campaign is thus deeply ideological: it cannot be explained—or even grasped—save by reference to its fanatical commitment to a set of disputed ideas about sexuality and gender, which are denied by many if not most Americans and which are surely belied by our political and cultural traditions. We say "fanatical" advisedly; by it we mean simply that the administration's pursuit of its ideological goals is relentless, single-minded, and fails to take account of important relevant goods and interests that its actions adversely affect. And the administration's campaign cannot be understood save by reference to its peculiar conception of the nature and value of religion in its individual and social manifestations, as well as in its civil and political effects. Here too the administration has adopted views at odds with most Americans and surely contrary to the positions of the founders and of the entire constitutional and political tradition until very recently. In all the administration has, it surely seems, placed itself in the vanguard of a revolution in our political and legal culture.

4.

IS *CHEVRON'S* GAME WORTH THE CANDLE?
Burning Interpretation at Both Ends

Ronald A. Cass

STARTING WITH *CHEVRON*

Keeping executive officials from running amok, as they tend to do when given too much uncontrolled discretion—expanding the reach of official power and threatening liberty (the subject of this volume)—is a central concern of constitutional government.[1] So, too, is keeping judges from expanding their reach to cover decisions committed to the political branches, going beyond the decision of concrete cases to become general overseers of government.[2] The trick is doing both at the same time, especially without giving added freedom to the legislature, the branch our founding generation feared most.[3]

The *Chevron* doctrine—as elaborated following the Supreme Court's decision in *Chevron U.S.A. v. Natural Resources Defense Council, Inc.*[4]—was an effort to accomplish this trick: giving legislative directives their due but keeping both administrative and judicial discretion in check. It was intended to provide a simple, uniform rule for judicial review of agency decisions. Courts would ensure that agencies follow legally binding statutory commands and do not exceed their legal authority. That part of *Chevron* follows directly from courts' constitutional role under Article III and from Section 706 of the Administrative Procedure Act (APA).[5]

Chevron also clarified a rule of statutory construction largely (though not always explicitly) implemented in the APA and in pre-APA precedent: when agencies are charged with implementing unclear statutory language, courts would presume that the law gives the relevant agency discretion to take any action that fits a reasonable construction of that language.[6] For example, the Communications Act of 1934 directed the Federal Communications Commission to allocate radio licenses as "the public convenience, interest, and necessity" require.[7] Congress did not need to add, "the FCC has discretion to decide how it will implement this command." The agency's discretion was clear from the broad, vague terms chosen to frame its charge.[8]

Chevron extended that approach to settings where the space potentially covered by the law's command (and, necessarily, the scope of the discretion being granted) was more limited. As the Court framed the general point respecting administrative discretion encapsulated in *Chevron*, "We accord deference to agencies under *Chevron* . . . because of a presumption that Congress, when it left ambiguity in a statute meant for implementation by an agency, understood that the ambiguity would be resolved, first and foremost, by the agency, and desired the agency (rather than the courts) to possess whatever degree of discretion the ambiguity allows."[9] That approach did not permit the agency to dictate the law's meaning; the agency's application of the law based on a reasonable reading of what the law allowed it to do would not bind future agency determinations, much less courts, to accept this as the only reasonable reading of what the law says the agency *must* do.[10]

Understood this way, *Chevron* was not a rule of judicial *deference* to agency interpretations of law; instead, it was a canon of statutory construction regarding the scope of discretionary agency authority bounded by law.[11] While *Chevron*'s merits and demerits can be, and have been, debated, its basic structure should have been common ground.

CHEVRON SLIPPING: TOO MUCH DEFERENCE AND TOO LITTLE

A funny thing happened, however, on the way to the judicial forum. As courts went about filling up *Chevron* in peculiar ways, *Chevron*-as-interpretive-canon frequently gave way to other visions.

One is *Chevron* as direction for courts to cede responsibility for "saying what the law is."[12] The language of "deference" associated with the doctrine led some judges to back away from serious inquiry into laws' meaning, leaving agencies to do work previously reserved for courts. In *Babbitt v. Sweet Home Chapters of Communities for a Great Oregon*,[13] for example, the Supreme Court deferred to the Secretary of the Interior on the scope of his authority to protect endangered species, essentially allowing the Secretary to make a determination on the substance of a legal term rather than on a policy issue permitted within a statutory mandate as interpreted by a court. The Court decided that the law permitted the Secretary to interpret the statutory prohibition on letting anyone "take" endangered animals (a complement to the prohibition on killing or maiming endangered species) to include indirectly and unintentionally causing harm to endangered species—a radical departure from the well-understood meaning of the term "to take" in a wide array of rules respecting wildlife.[14] In this instance, there was no ambiguity respecting the meaning of a charge to the administrator except in the sense that one could contest any legal term; deferring to the Secretary was tantamount to allowing him to resolve the sort of question that is quintessentially given to Article III courts.

Other times, courts have done exactly the opposite, torturing statutory language to produce results that eliminate agency discretion. Even where a law clearly speaks in language redolent of a design to grant discretion to the administrator implementing the law, judges have elevated inferences about greater statutory purposes over sound construction of the law. *Massachusetts v. Environmental Protection Agency*[15] may be the clearest example. The provision at issue in *Massachusetts* was § 202(a)(1) of the Clean Air Act, stating that the Administrator of the Environmental Protection Agency (EPA) shall "prescribe . . . standards applicable to the emission of any air pollutant from any class or classes of new motor vehicles or new motor vehicle engines, which *in his judgment* cause, or contribute to, air pollution which may reasonably be anticipated to endanger public health or welfare."[16] The administrator of the EPA demonstrably had *not* made a judgment that the substances at issue in the case (greenhouse gases) "cause, or contribute to, air pollution which may reasonably be anticipated to endanger public health or welfare." However, overriding the administrator's view of the scope of his discretion and the judgments he did make respecting how best to exercise that discretion, the Supreme Court determined that the substances were covered under the law's definition of "pollutant" and that the administrator was required to decide whether they contribute to air pollution that endangers public health or welfare—in an opinion strongly suggesting that there can be only one possible outcome to this exercise of administrative discretion.[17]

Massachusetts plainly (though not expressly) discards *Chevron* as a guide for decision. It not only rejects the administrator's reading of the statute; it rejects as well the administrator's decision respecting a matter that the law plainly commits to the administrator's discretion. If this case stands for something more than a rule of special solicitude for environmental causes (a more than plausible reading of the decision), the lesson is that judges at times will rebel against *Chevron*'s apparent choice between expansive discretion (when there is ambiguity, silence, or evident commitment of an issue to an administrator) or no discretion (when the question is what the law says).[18] Administrative decisions on matters the law plainly entrusts to administrative judgment, if they grate too much against judicial sensibilities, still may be found to be at odds with the law.

EXTRAORDINARY CASES VERSUS TRADITIONAL TOOLS

Another set of cases in which *Chevron* sometimes is set aside are those described by the courts as "extraordinary." Two cases that illustrate the possibilities in this genre are *Food & Drug Administration v. Brown & Williamson Tobacco Co.*[19] and *King v. Burwell.*[20] Brown & Williamson challenged an FDA decision to define the term "drug" in its governing statute to include nicotine and to define the term "drug delivery device" to include cigarettes. The majority of the Supreme Court agreed, finding the meaning of these terms clear from the law's structure, the context (including other legislation respecting tobacco regulation), and history (including contemporaneous rejection of the notion that the law covered nicotine as a drug and tobacco as a drug delivery device, along with decades of consistent adherence to that view by the agency). Justice O'Connor's opinion for the Court, thus, appears consistent with a typical "traditional tools" approach to *Chevron*'s Step One: an interpretation of the statute by the Court using the traditional tools of statutory construction, here concluding that there was no ambiguity respecting the issue before the Court and no intention to grant the agency discretion to regulate a substance and product outside its authority.[21]

Having said that, however, O'Connor's opinion went on to say,

> Deference under Chevron to an agency's construction of a statute that it administers is premised on the theory that a statute's ambiguity constitutes an implicit delegation from Congress to the agency to fill in the statutory gaps. See Chevron, 467 U.S., at 844. In extraordinary cases, however, there may be reason to hesitate before concluding that Congress has intended such an implicit delegation.[22]

Justice O'Connor added, "This is hardly an ordinary case."[23] The inference drawn by a number of observers was that the Court had signaled its disinclination to apply *Chevron* in extraordinary cases if that might lead to a result out of keeping with justices' instincts on broader policy considerations (whether that meant justices' own policy instincts or their instincts respecting policy considerations embedded in a broader set of legal commands).

While *Brown & Williamson* did not need a different rule than standard *Chevron* to reach the majority's result, the Court has found other cases sufficiently important—because of the scope of the policy issues they raise or the politically or publicly sensitive nature of the matters implicated—to invoke the "extraordinary cases" language. One case that did this in notable fashion is *King v. Burwell*, a challenge to an Internal Revenue Service (IRS) interpretation of a provision in the Patient Protection and Affordable Care Act (ACA), colloquially known as "Obamacare."[24]

The ACA set up a mechanism for states to create health care exchanges under Section 1311 (codified at 42 U.S.C. § 18031)—essentially, government-run marketplaces for purchasing health insurance policies. The act also provided for creation of federally run exchanges, established and operated by the Secretary of Health and Human Services (HHS), under ACA Section 1321 (now 42 U.S.C. § 18041), in cases where states declined to create state exchanges. The federal exchanges then would allow residents of the states without exchanges to have access to broadly similar sorts of insurance policies as are available on state exchanges (but not necessarily identical insurance options). The ACA provided for subsidies available through tax credits for policies purchased though "an Exchange established by the State under Section 1311 [42 U.S.C. §18031]."[25] IRS issued a rule interpreting that term to mean *both* exchanges established by the state under Section 1311 and exchanges established by the Secretary of HHS under Section 1321.

Most of the attention to the challenge to that rule in *King* (in Court and out) focused, naturally enough, on debate over whether "an Exchange established by the State" under one section of the law could and should be interpreted to mean "an Exchange established" by a different, federal official—the Secretary of HHS—under a completely different provision of the law.[26] The decision for the Court, however, also went out of its way to say that *Chevron* did not apply.

The court of appeals below had found that the provision in the law was ambiguous and that *Chevron*, therefore, demanded deference to the administrator.[27] The Supreme Court did not disagree with the conclusion that the statutory provision was ambiguous. It could have, in light of its ultimate disposition of the case based on the majority's own reading of the law—although it would be more than a little difficult to credit the Court's statutory construction as resting on an unambiguously clear reading of the law.[28] Instead, the majority quoted *Brown & Williamson*'s statement regarding extraordinary cases and then said,

> This is one of those cases. The tax credits are among the Act's key reforms, involving billions of dollars in spending each year and affecting the price of health insurance for millions of people. Whether those credits are available on Federal Exchanges is thus a question of deep "economic and political significance" that is central to this statutory scheme; had Congress wished to assign that question to an agency, it surely would have done so expressly. . . . It is especially unlikely that

> Congress would have delegated this decision to the IRS, which has no expertise in crafting health insurance policy of this sort.[29]

In other cases, the Court had noted that a law should not be presumed to confer authority on administrators to decide major questions of policy without saying so expressly, and certainly not to decide such questions in ways that are at odds with established practice. The Court framed the point pithily in *Whitman v. American Trucking Associations, Inc.*: "Congress, we have held, does not alter the fundamental details of a regulatory scheme in vague terms or ancillary provisions—it does not, one might say, hide elephants in mouseholes."[30]

That observation, sometimes referred to as a special "major questions" rule for *Chevron*, actually was but another standard canon of statutory construction, another application of "traditional tools." The sense of this canon is that it is reasonable to read statutes as consistent with prior rules unless they plainly contradict them. For the same reasons, it is reasonable to read statutes as not giving administrators authority to make U-turns on major policy questions unless the law clearly grants that power. This understanding was the basis for the decision in *Whitman* that the EPA administrator had overstepped her bounds, making her decision on the scope of her authority under the Clean Air Act unreasonable.[31]

DAMN THE CANONS—FULL SPEED AHEAD: INTERPRETATION FIT FOR A *KING*

King took a different, though partially related, tack. It reasonably said, in the same spirit as *Whitman*, that the law should not be presumed to grant administrators discretion over major policy issues without saying so—either saying so expressly or with a commitment of authority in terms that plainly imply such discretion, as the Communications Act did in its broadly phrased grant of radio spectrum licensing authority to the FCC. Rather than use that observation to assert that the contested provision of the ACA had to be applied in line with its plain meaning, however, the *King* majority said that it would *not* defer to the administrator, then adopted the same construction of the law as the IRS without finding anything in prior law—or anything substantial other than a general appreciation of the law's *broadest* purposes—to support that interpretation.[32] The majority rejected established canons of statutory construction, such as the canon against interpretations that make statutory language unnecessary, citing as its reason the law's "inartful drafting," which the *King* majority attributed to the ACA's congressional sponsors' choosing to replace ordinary legislative procedures with special rules that reduced both transparency and participation in the legislative process.[33] In the majority's words, "As a result, the Act does not reflect the type of care and deliberation that one might expect of such significant legislation."[34]

Instead of *requiring clarity* to change prior law (through judicial construction or judicial acceptance of administrative constructions) as *Whitman* did, the Court in *King* declared a provision that was clear on its face to be ambiguous because the majority deemed the law's drafting deficient—in more colloquial language, you just can't expect laws to mean what they say when the drafting is secret and sloppy. In these justices' view, the provision as drafted was out of keeping with what the law's drafters wanted to do. The assertion that the matter at issue in *King* was too important for the ambiguity to support a presumption of administrative discretion under *Chevron* was a free-standing observation, not tied to an established interpretive rule. It at once ousted future administrators of authority to exercise discretion at odds with the Court's interpretation of the ACA and created a potential new category of *Chevron*-ineligible cases.

The problem with *King* is not the majority's observation that important policy questions should not automatically be presumed to have been committed to agency discretion. Instead, it is the fact that the Court tossed off this observation without any guidance as to how judges should determine which questions are so important as to fall outside of *Chevron*'s scope. Limiting the point to situations like *Whitman* where the discretion asserted encompassed making major changes to established legal rules—or tying the point to any other similarly cabined setting—would supply the missing constraint on judicial discretion to apply or disregard *Chevron*.

Perhaps the best reading of *King* is that it did not mean to carve out a new category of cases. Just as trying to draft a law with marginal political support under extreme time pressure (before the political balance would have tipped against the law's passage) brings out the worst legislative instincts, highly visible litigation seems to bring out judges' worst instincts respecting basic predicates of laws' interpretation. As Justice Holmes famously put it, "Great cases, like hard cases, make bad law." If the *King* dictum respecting *Chevron* is limited to the peculiar, and peculiarly politicized, arguments in that case, little damage will have been done to broad legal precepts. If it is taken seriously in the future, *Chevron*'s clarity (at least a degree of its remaining clarity) will be but one victim of courts' tendency in "great cases" to head a bit off the rails.

FROM *RULE* TO *FEEL*: DEFERENCE BY DEGREES

Beyond carving out exceptions to *Chevron* or twisting its application, judges also have attempted to avoid the seemingly bipolar choice between wholly non-deferential judicial interpretation of statutory terms and broad deference to agency interpretations by creating tests that allow courts a broader panoply of options under formulae more flexible than (original) *Chevron*. The clearest case is *United States v. Mead Corp.*[35] *Mead* presented the question whether a U.S. Customs Service decision on the proper tariff classification for certain "day planners" deserved deference under *Chevron*.

Viewed in the context of *discretion* rather than *deference*—that is, understanding that *Chevron* deference is merely a description of the way courts should identify the range of choices left to administrators—the answer should have been clear. The relevant law, the Harmonized Tariff System of the United States (HTSUS), combines U.S. tariff undertakings with an international coding system. It is a voluminous and complex document; the HTSUS has more than 17,000 classification categories and subcategories, covers thousands of pages, and has a 60-page index and over 850 pages of general notes.[36] Just reciting these facts belies the notion that this document was designed for judicial scrutiny rather than administrative implementation. The primary sort of judgment called for in implementing the law is practical, assessing what classification best fits particular products, what similarities or differences suggest which category is the best match among the potential alternatives. Although this design does not confer discretion on administrators to classify "day planners" as steel beams or lingerie, it would seem undeniably to confer discretion to choose between the closest available categories (in this case, subcategories of a single tariff classification).[37]

The *Mead* majority, however, focusing on deference's domain, crafted a different rule, one that turns on a multiplicity of factors to guide judicial choice among a larger set of deference levels. The opinion for the Court first declares, "The fair measure of deference to an agency administering its own statute has been understood to vary with circumstances, and courts have looked to the degree of the agency's care, its consistency, formality, and relative expertness, and to the persuasiveness of the agency's position."[38] The Court made clear that it was not going to make its list of circumstances fit a clear test of any sort, settling for an "it depends" standard.

So, for example, the level of formality of the administrative process that produced the decision was deemed to be important; the majority observed that most of the cases that had extended *Chevron* deference were instances of notice and comment rulemaking, which it described as "a relatively formal administrative procedure tending to foster the fairness and deliberation that should underlie a pronouncement" that has the force of law.[39] But the Court also declared that this sort of formal decision-making was neither necessary nor sufficient for *Chevron* deference.[40]

Mead further muddied the water by declaring that administrative decisions that did not merit *Chevron* deference still could qualify for *Skidmore* deference. Apart from its questionable reach back to pre-APA precedent, "*Skidmore* deference" is an oxymoron. The point of the Court's decision in *Skidmore v. Swift & Co.*[41] was that when administrative decisions lack "controlling authority" within some sphere—when the law has not given the administrator discretion respecting those decisions—while courts still may find those decisions provide useful information, the administrative decisions are *not* entitled to deference. Instead, courts may choose to give an administrative judgment some weight in its determination respecting the application of statutory language to a given setting, and "[t]he weight of such a judgment in a particular case will depend upon the thoroughness evident in its consideration, the validity of its reasoning, its consistency with earlier and later pronouncements, and all those factors which give it power to persuade, if lacking power to control."[42]

Skidmore's description of how courts might treat this category of administrative decisions is the *opposite* of deference; it is merely an input to independent judgment. It is a way of saying, "I'll listen to what you have to say, but then I'll decide for myself what to do." That explains why the difference between *Chevron* and *Skidmore* was described this way:

> *Chevron* deference is what I give to my wife. I know we're going to wind up doing what she says, so we start out with the presumption that that's what we're going to do. *Skidmore* deference is what she gives to me. . . . [W]e do what I say when she's persuaded that she wants to do it anyway. And that's why the notion of *Skidmore* deference is a wonderful concept for courts.[43]

While *Mead*'s approach is a more straightforward means of avoiding the limited set of choices associated with *Chevron*, it is even more problematic than most of the *Chevron*-stretching decisions. *Mead* significantly reduces certainty about the test judges will use to assess law's meaning respecting agency discretion in a much wider class of cases than the "extraordinary cases" exception carved out in *Brown & Williamson* and *King*, for instance. It also divorces the concept of "deference" from that of "discretion," blurring the line between the roles assigned to courts and agencies. In the end, *Mead* substitutes *feel* for *rule*.

RETURN TO RULES AND LAW

As a matter of *policy*, arguments can be advanced for a variety of different rules regarding the scope for administrative discretion and the weight to be given to agency determinations regarding their authority.[44] As a matter of *law*, it should be clear that more definite, more predictable, less malleable rules are preferable and that federal courts must play the central role in saying what boundaries Congress has placed around official discretion.[45] The Supreme Court made exactly this point as recently as 2013, in a case where both the majority and the dissent were concerned with drawing lines around uncabined administrative discretion. As the majority put it,

> [So far as the role of the courts is concerned, risks associated with excessive administrative power are] to be avoided not by establishing an arbitrary and undefinable category of agency decisionmaking that is accorded no deference, but by taking seriously, and applying rigorously, in all cases, statutory limits on agencies' authority. Where Congress

> has established a clear line, the agency cannot go beyond it; and where Congress has established an ambiguous line, the agency can go no further than the ambiguity will fairly allow. But . . . [i]f "the agency's answer is based on a permissible construction of the statute," that is the end of the matter.[46]

That, in a nutshell, is the instinct that at times was, and in all cases should have been, the basis for the rule in *Chevron.*

Yet the occasional clear statement of *Chevron*'s rule is not by any means a predictable norm for the Supreme Court or for other courts, and its application is even less predictable.[47] Differences among the various applications of *Chevron,* in fact, have left observers wondering whether the test now has two steps, as generally assumed, or one or three.[48] Taken together with the exceptions made for "extraordinary cases" (a category defined thus far by assertion more than by application of well-honed analytical tools) and the muddled rule of *Mead* along with its revival of *Skidmore*—less charitable commentators might liken this to a horror movie with a population of "undead" who cannot be killed—*Chevron* is not the rule it could and should have been.

The question now is whether the game is worth the candle. The goal of keeping *administrative* discretion within legal bounds without expanding *judicial* discretion beyond the pale of law interpretation reserved for Article III courts—without giving courts discretion to alter the application of laws in ways less responsive to checking by the political branches than are administrative exercises of discretion—is met only episodically under the current, nominally *Chevron*-esque, regime. Courts now, in keeping with some precedent, can intervene to direct results at odds with administrative exercises of discretion that are consistent with legislative directives (more so than the judicial ruling) or defer to administrative interpretations of core statutory terms, even when those conflict with the law's evident meaning.

Worse still, the current regime gives additional cover to Congress when it steps outside (or sidesteps) the role of law making assigned by the Constitution. There are reasons to wonder whether a reinvigorated nondelegation doctrine can stop Congress from assigning unstructured authority to administrators in ways that expand both potential executive power and legislative power.[49] Without that check, however, Congress is free to write flabby, unclear laws that pass important questions of public policy—and of laws' meaning—down the line to administrators and judges, allowing legislators to claim credit for tackling big issues while escaping responsibility for difficult judgments and unpopular consequences.[50]

Perhaps the best course at this point is to scrap the *Chevron* framework and return to the terms laid out in the APA's Section 706. Rightly understood, that section directs courts to interpret the law, to say what the law commands, and to assess the reasonableness of administrative actions. That is in essence the original *Chevron* test. Courts are to prevent administrators from stepping over lines laid down by statute and to allow reasonable exercises of discretion that do not cross those lines. Possibly—just possibly—starting over will encourage courts to get this right. Then again, as Boswell's report of Samuel Johnson's aphorism on multiple marriages says, this may simply be the triumph of hope over experience. But when experience has been this bad, what's left but hope?

5.

IMMIGRATION
Executive versus Congressional Action

Linda Chavez

Of all President Obama's executive actions, the one that has generated the most controversy was his decision on November 20, 2014, to defer deportation for up to five million persons illegally present in the United States. Currently, an estimated eleven million persons reside illegally in the United States.[1] Most entered the United States without official authorization—the largest number crossing our southern border with Mexico. However, an estimated 40 percent of illegal immigrants came to the United States with valid visas but overstayed or violated the terms of those visas. For more than a decade, Congress has attempted to pass laws that would deal with the status of this latter population but has failed repeatedly, most recently in 2013 when the Senate passed a comprehensive immigration reform bill but the House of Representatives failed to take it up. In his statement announcing his actions, President Obama said, "I continue to believe that the best way to solve this problem is by working together to pass that kind of common sense law. But until that happens, there are actions I have the legal authority to take as President—the same kinds of actions taken by Democratic and Republican presidents before me—that will help make our immigration system more fair and more just."[2]

But were President Obama's actions in line with what previous presidents had done? And under what authority was he acting? After all, he had on numerous occasions declared that he couldn't simply act without congressional authority. "With respect to the notion that I can just suspend deportations through executive order, that's just not the case,"[3] he said in 2011 and repeated more than twenty times[4] before suspending deportations for nearly half of the current illegal population. As of this writing, the administration's executive action is on hold while suits challenging it wend their way through federal courts, but there is little question that the President pushed the limits of his executive power.

While it is true that previous presidents have issued executive orders (a route President Obama chose not to take) to allow groups of people to enter or remain in the United States in conflict with immigration laws in place at the time, President Obama's actions were far broader in scope, applying to more than a third of the illegal population present. A fact sheet on previous major executive actions on immigration by the Pew Research Center notes that most were targeted narrowly at groups like Ethiopians fleeing Ethiopia's Marxist dictatorship in the 1970s, whereas those that affected more people "were eventually formalized or superseded by legislation, though sometimes—as often happens with complicated subjects such as immigration—the new laws led to new issues."[5] President Obama's actions were not intended to deal with a pressing concern that could not be dealt with legislatively. His clear intent was to rebuke Congress for failing to act.

Before discussing the legal implications of the President's actions, it is important to understand exactly what he did and did not do. First, contrary to popular criticism, the President did not issue a presidential executive order suspending deportations, much less give amnesty to anyone. Instead, he directed the Secretary of Homeland Security to prioritize deportations of persons unlawfully present in the United States and to expand the Deferred Action for Childhood Arrivals (DACA) program[6] to include new categories of eligible participants.

On the same day the President announced his plan to defer deportation of certain classes of illegal immigrants, Secretary of Homeland

Security Jeh Johnson issued a memorandum that outlined the department's enforcement and removal policies "to prioritize threats to national security, public safety, and border security,"[7] citing the well-recognized principle of prosecutorial discretion in law enforcement in the face of limited resources. A recent study by the American Action Forum, a center-right public policy group headed by economist and former Congressional Budget Office director Douglas Holtz-Eakin, estimated that the federal government would have to spend $400–600 billion to address removal of the current illegal population and prevent future illegal immigration.[8] Given budget constraints (the total annual DHS appropriations for fiscal year 2015 was $39.7 billion[9]), it is hard to argue that the department can apprehend, detain, and ultimately deport the eleven million persons unlawfully present in the United States. Nor is there much evidence of the political will to do so even among the most ardent opponents of illegal immigration. Had the administration's actions gone no further than to recognize formally what had been the de facto policy of all recent administrations with respect to illegal immigrants living in the United States—namely, to concentrate resources on removing those illegal immigrants who have broken other laws—they might not have aroused much furor. But the President's goal was much more ambitious, and the DHS Secretary issued additional memoranda that went far beyond outlining deportation priorities.

In all, Secretary Johnson issued a dozen memoranda instituting new immigration policies that day. Some were uncontroversial, or nearly so, including strengthening security along the U.S.-Mexico border, improving pay for immigration officers engaged in removal operations, and enabling businesses to hire and retain highly skilled foreign-born workers. By far the most contentious of the memoranda was one entitled "Exercising Prosecutorial Discretion with Respect to Individuals Who Came to the United States as Children and with Respect to Certain Individuals Who Are Parents of U.S. Citizens or Permanent Residents,"[10] resulting in a program often referred to as Deferred Action for Parents of Americans (DAPA). The original DACA program was instituted through executive action as well, in a legal memorandum issued on June 15, 2012, by then Secretary of Homeland Security Janet Napolitano.[11] The idea for a program to provide legal status to immigrants who came to the United

States illegally as children dates back to a bipartisan bill known as the DREAM Act (Development Relief and Education for Alien Minors Act) first introduced in 2001 by Senators Dick Durbin (D-IL) and Orrin Hatch (R-UT).[12] However, that bill never became law.

Although versions of the DREAM Act were either introduced as standalone legislation or incorporated into other bills in every subsequent Congress, none made it through final passage, largely because of widespread Republican opposition.[13] However, the Obama administration's 2012 actions granting temporary legal status to certain illegal immigrants who had arrived before they reached age sixteen, provided they met certain criteria, did not meet broad public opposition. Opinion polls showed that a majority of Americans favored adjusting the legal status of childhood arrivals; polling after the 2012 presidential elections by the Democratic polling firm Lake Research Partners and the Republican firm the Tarrance Group found that 57 percent of voters favored the action, while only 26 percent opposed.[14] Two years after the program was initiated, 643,000 childhood arrivals had received a temporary legal status, though no path to U.S. citizenship, and of those, 428,000 received two-year work permits. The criteria required applicants to be less than thirty-one years old; to have arrived prior to their sixteenth birthday and remained continuously since before June 16, 2007; to have obtained or be in the process of obtaining a high school degree or its equivalent or to have been an honorably discharged veteran of the U.S. Armed Forces or Coast Guard; and to have no convictions for any felony (or significant or multiple misdemeanor offenses) or to otherwise pose no national security or public safety threat.[15] Since many of these individuals had simply accompanied their parents (sometimes as babies in arms), spent most of their lives in the United States, spoke English, graduated from American schools, and were well integrated into their communities, they were the most sympathetic category of illegal immigrants.

Nonetheless, a group of Immigration and Customs Enforcement (ICE) officers, joined by the State of Mississippi, filed suit in the district court for the Northern District of Texas seeking a preliminary injunction to prevent the DHS from implementing DACA. The district court dismissed the ICE officers' claims "without prejudice for lack of subject-matter jurisdiction" and Mississippi's claim for lack of standing.[16] On appeal, a unanimous, three-judge panel of the Fifth Circuit upheld the lower court's "dismissal of Plaintiff's claims for lack of subject matter jurisdiction," holding that "[n]either Mississippi nor the Agents have alleged a sufficiently concrete and particularized injury that would give Plaintiffs standing to challenge DACA."[17] The issues of standing would come up again in legal challenges to President Obama's DAPA program.

In his primetime address to the nation announcing DAPA, President Obama issued a challenge to Congress: "To those members of Congress who question my authority to make our immigration system work better, or question the wisdom of me acting where Congress has failed, I have one answer: Pass a bill."[18] His actions, however, virtually guaranteed that efforts under way at the time to reach a compromise on immigration legislation in the House of Representatives would grind to a halt. Coming just days after a congressional election in which Republicans gained eight senators and thirteen House members, the President's defiant tone infuriated GOP lawmakers. Even some Democrats objected, with Senator Joe Donnelly (D-IN) issuing a statement before the President's speech that "[t]he president shouldn't make such significant policy changes on his own."[19] Similarly, Senator Joe Manchin III (D-WV) told White House aides that he disagreed with the President's actions: "To put it through now is the wrong thing to do. . . . I told them I wasn't comfortable."[20] As the *New York Times* noted in its coverage of the President's speech, the President "chose confrontation over conciliation . . . as he asserted the powers of the Oval Office to reshape the nation's immigration system and all but dared members of next year's Republican-controlled Congress to reverse his actions on behalf of millions of immigrants."[21] And Republican members soon attempted to overturn it using Congress's power of the purse over DHS funding.

In December 2014, Congress passed an omnibus spending bill that included funding for all government agencies except DHS, which Congress funded only through February 2015 by a continuing resolution. The action came after threats of an entire government shutdown over the president's immigration order orchestrated by Senators Ted Cruz (R-TX) and Mike Lee (R-UT) and other conservatives in the House and Senate. The hope was that with Republicans gaining control of the Senate and gaining additional, more conservative members in the GOP-controlled

House, they could derail the President's executive action when the new Congress convened in January. Senator Cruz's efforts ultimately failed when even fellow Republicans deserted him, and the continuing resolution funding DHS contained no provisions blocking the President's immigration effort.[22] In late February, conservative members of Congress again tried to use the funding bill to reverse the President's actions. But while the House passed a DHS funding bill that eliminated funding for both the original DACA program and DAPA, the Senate refused to pass the measure, insisting on a clean appropriations bill without amendments restricting DACA and DAPA. After weeks of resisting, Speaker of the House John Boehner finally brought the Senate bill to a vote in the House on March 3, 2015, bucking his most conservative fellow House Republicans. The bill passed 257–167 with only 75 Republicans voting in favor.[23] Meanwhile, what Republicans in Congress failed to do a federal district court judge in Texas accomplished: putting at least a temporary halt to the President's plans.

On December 3, 2014, Texas Attorney General and Governor-elect Greg Abbott filed suit challenging the Obama administration's executive actions on behalf of the state; he was joined by sixteen other states. Nine other states would eventually join the effort, which sought a declaratory judgment against DAPA, the expansion of DACA, and the DHS's newly defined priorities on apprehension, detention, and deportation of illegal immigrants. The suit claimed that the directives violated the duty set forth in Article II, Section 3 of the Constitution that the President "take Care that the Laws be faithfully executed" and that the actions also violated the Administrative Procedure Act.[24] The suit, filed in the District Court for the Southern District of Texas, was assigned to Judge Andrew S. Hanen. On February 16, 2015, Judge Hanen issued a memorandum of opinion and ordered a preliminary injunction to halt implementation of the DAPA program, which was set to begin accepting applications May 19, 2015, and stop three provisions that expanded DACA, which would have eliminated the age cap, extended work authorizations from two to three years, and adjusted the entry date requirement to January 1, 2010.

It is important to understand what Judge Hanen's opinion said and what it did not say. The opinion dealt with only three issues: whether the plaintiffs—twenty-six states, including Texas—had standing to sue;

whether the DHS has the authority to defer deportation and grant other relief for parents of Americans and lawful permanent residents (the so-called DAPA directive); and whether the DAPA was legally adopted. The order did not affect the existing DACA program, a point the judge made clear at the onset.

The judge's opinion dealt definitively with two of these issues. First, as in the earlier suit against DACA, the initial issue for the court to decide was whether the plaintiffs had standing to sue and could show that the parties had suffered or would suffer actual damages if DAPA and the other measures were allowed to take effect. Judge Hanen determined that at least one of the states, Texas, had standing to sue because DAPA imposed a financial burden on the state to provide certain benefits—namely, drivers' licenses, which Texas claimed would cost nearly $200 per eligible immigrant.

Second, Judge Hanen determined that in promulgating DAPA, DHS did not follow the proper procedural requirements under the Administrative Procedure Act. He reached no conclusion on whether the administration's actions were constitutional. In doing so, he followed the canon of judicial restraint that if there is a non-constitutional ground for deciding a case, the court prudently avoids making a judgment on its constitutionality. By relying on the APA, Judge Hanen did not need to address the plaintiffs' constitutional claims.

On the issue of prosecutorial discretion, Judge Hanen's memorandum was mixed. He noted "the law is relatively clear on enforcement discretion and, thus, the Court will not address it at length."[25] The judge added, "[T]his Court finds that Secretary Johnson's decisions as to how to marshal DHS resources, how best to utilize DHS manpower, and where to concentrate its activities are discretionary decisions solely with the purview of the Executive Branch, to the extent that they do not violate any statute or the Constitution."[26] However, Judge Hanen went on to say that the DAPA program seemed to go beyond mere prosecutorial discretion. "The DHS does have discretion in the manner in which it chooses to fulfill the expressed will of Congress. It cannot, however, enact a program whereby it not only ignores the dictates of Congress, but actively acts to thwart them." While the judge's memorandum and order of injunctive relief are not the final word—he will rule on the merits of the plaintiffs' claims after hearings in July 2015—his pronouncement that "DAPA does not represent mere inadequacy; it is complete abdication"[27] leaves little room for doubt which way he is likely to rule.

The administration appealed the order for injunctive relief to the Fifth Circuit, which upheld Judge Hanen's injunction in a 2–1 ruling on May 26, 2015.[28] Further appeals will follow, with the Solicitor General likely to file a petition for certiorari with the U.S. Supreme Court in the fall of 2015.

Ultimately, the courts will decide the legal issues, but as Keith E. Whittington writes in his book *Constitutional Interpretation: Textual Meaning, Original Intent, and Judicial Review*, "Whereas the unelected denizens of the federal judiciary are primarily responsible for what the text requires—the legal constitution—other members of the federal government are perhaps more concerned with what the text suggests—the political constitution."[29] President Obama's decision to usurp Congress's role in settling the contentious issue of what to do about the eleven million illegal immigrants living in the United States has deeply muddied the immigration debate on the merits. His motivation was nakedly partisan; and the timing was geared to deflect attention from the stunning defeat Democrats suffered in congressional elections just two and a half weeks earlier. But it also derailed efforts under way among House Republicans to seek some way forward on immigration reform. As the *Wall Street Journal* reported immediately after the election, Speaker of the House John Boehner and President Obama had held secret talks on immigration reform for more than a year. Moreover, House and Senate Republicans were discussing moving individual immigration bills to increase visas for high-tech workers, according to press reports.[30]

By acting unilaterally, President Obama made it difficult or impossible for Republican lawmakers to move such measures forward. And, unfortunately, that seems to have been part of President Obama's aim. Had President Obama really wanted to fix our broken immigration system—including to provide a path to citizenship for the millions of illegal immigrants living here—he could have acted within the first two years of his administration, when Democrats controlled both houses of Congress. But immigration reform was not on the President's agenda, and it only became so when he saw it providing an electoral advantage to Democrats.

Few astute political analysts doubt that Republicans have been badly hampered in their quest to regain the White House by the party's growing unpopularity among Hispanics, driven largely by the immigration issue. Although immigration reform is not Hispanic voters' top issue (the economy and education outrank it),[31] 66 percent of them say passing new immigration legislation is extremely or very important, according to a 2014 poll by Pew Research.[32] In 2012, Mitt Romney won only 27 percent of Hispanics' votes and 26 percent of Asian voters[33] after advocating that illegal immigrants "self-deport." But it is not just Hispanic or Asian voters who may be turned off by some Republicans' harsh rhetoric. Romney's former deputy campaign manager, Katie Packer Gage, writing in *Politico* says, "taking a hard-line position on immigration loses . . . more votes in the general election than it wins . . . in the GOP primaries."[34] Gage's opinion research firm, Burning Glass Consulting, "survey[ed] likely Republican voters in Iowa, New Hampshire, and South Carolina and likely general election voters in [ten] swing states" and found that "GOP nominees chasing the relatively small group of anti-immigration primary voters—and giving opponents ammunition to portray them as anti-immigration—risk alienating [24] percent more voters in a general election than they attract."[35]

President Obama's actions goaded Republicans, who, for the most part, resisted making illegal immigrants the focus of their criticism and directed their ire at the President. Nonetheless, the President set himself up to be the liberator of millions of illegal immigrants who hide in the shadows of American life, no doubt hoping to solidify Democratic Party support among Hispanic voters. Whether he succeeds will depend in part on whether the courts ultimately vindicate his policies. But even in the highly unlikely event that his executive actions survive, they will not solve the problem.

One of the arguments against providing legal status to those who have broken our laws is that doing so merely encourages more people to come illegally. Opponents of legalization have noted that President Ronald Reagan's amnesty, which gave legal status to three million illegal immigrants in 1986, led to the current situation, with a threefold increase in illegal immigrants in the past thirty years. When some 47,000 unaccompanied minors crossed our borders in the summer of 2014,[36] many critics accused DACA for encouraging the surge, even though it occurred two years after DHS instituted DACA and the newly arrived minors were ineligible to benefit from it because the policy stipulated only those who arrived before 2007 could apply. Indeed, the number of unaccompanied minors has fallen dramatically in the wake of detentions and efforts in Central America to discourage minors from leaving, as well as stepped-up efforts by Mexico to deport Central Americans transiting Mexico on their way north.[37] So, too, have the overall numbers of illegal immigrants. At its peak in 2007, the illegal population was some 12.2 million persons.[38] More than a million illegal immigrants have left since the recession began in 2009, and fewer persons are caught crossing the border illegally now than at any point since 1972.[39]

Despite the appeal of the argument that amnesty simply encourages future waves of illegal immigration, the real driver of illegal immigration is current immigration law. Our outdated laws ignore U.S. labor needs, center on family reunification rather than skills, and are hopelessly unenforceable. The Immigration Reform and Control Act of 1986 (IRCA)[40] created a bureaucratic nightmare of government overreach in the hopes of stemming future flows of illegal immigration. Instead of adopting sensible, market-based measures to increase the number of persons admitted to the United States to create legal avenues for needed workers to migrate here, the law penalized employers for hiring undocumented workers. This did nothing to slow illegal immigration and only created federal interference in the employment process for businesses. Worse, it made all employers—including individuals who hire someone on a full-time, or even part-time, basis to clean their homes, babysit their children, or cut their grass—into quasi-enforcement agents who must verify legal statuses by inspecting (and maintaining for years copies of) birth certificates, drivers' licenses, Social Security cards, and other documents.[41] Ordinary Americans and many small businesses routinely flout the law. It should be replaced with a flexible, market-driven system that gives priority to immigrants whose skills would benefit our economy, the kind of policy that most Republicans would under other circumstances embrace. But President Obama's actions have made the prospects for passing any meaningful comprehensive reform far less likely—and that will hurt not just future immigrants but all of us.

6.

OPERATION CHOKE POINT AND THE BUREAUCRATIC ABUSES OF UNACCOUNTABLE POWER

Charles J. Cooper[1]

> *The greatest evil is not done now in those sordid "dens of crime" that Dickens loved to paint. It is not even done in concentration camps and labor camps. In those we see its final result. But it is conceived and ordered (moved, seconded, carried and minuted) in clear, carpeted, warmed, and well-lighted offices, by quiet men with white collars and cut fingernails and smooth-shaven cheeks who do not need to raise their voice.*
>
> —*C.S. Lewis*

In late 2012, the federal bank regulators began to pressure the banks to close the accounts of certain merchant customers. Banks were warned that those that refused to terminate the targeted customers would be subjected to repeated examinations, heightened regulatory scrutiny, and possibly even criminal prosecution. In the understated words of the head of the American Bankers Association, "this put [the banks] in a difficult business position."[2]

It has actually put their merchant customers in an *impossible* business position. For the past three years, banks have been terminating the accounts of responsible, law-abiding businesses.[3] Without warning and without recourse, these customers have been left by many banks unable to cash their checks, pay their bills, and deposit their receipts. Their businesses were not illegal. The government did not press charges or even have grounds to suspect that the law had broken. These law-abiding Americans—who pay their taxes and play by the rules, have devoted their lives to starting and growing small businesses, and have worked hard to make their American dreams a reality—have simply fallen victim to their own government's abuse of power. They have fallen victim to Operation Choke Point.

WHAT IS OPERATION CHOKE POINT?

Operation Choke Point is a government regulatory campaign to coerce banks to deny service to law-abiding members of perfectly legal industries by threatening those banks with regulatory retaliation. It is being carried out by the Federal Deposit Insurance Corporation (FDIC), the Office of the Comptroller of the Currency, and the Federal Reserve, acting under the leadership and with the cooperation of the Department of Justice. These agencies are using their authority to regulate the banking system to coerce banks to cut off legal businesses from the financial system. The banks are the "choke point" that the regulators use to deprive those disfavored businesses of the financial oxygen necessary to commercial success—indeed, to survival.

Bank regulators have selected the targets of Operation Choke Point. It seems clear that these businesses are being targeted solely because of the political biases and animus of the Obama administration. Congressional investigations have revealed that Operation Choke Point targeted payday lenders, for example, because some agency officials consider payday lending "unsavory" and "a particularly ugly practice."[4] One senior FDIC official openly explained that he "literally can not stand pay day lending" and that he "sincerely" and "passionate[ly]" believes that payday lenders "do not deserve to be in any way associated with banking."[5] No friend to the Second Amendment, the current administration has also used Operation Choke Point to target gun and ammunition businesses.

These regulators have no authority to conduct Operation Choke Point. The Federal Deposit Insurance Act provides them with authority to supervise the banks only by prescribing internal bank controls and systems, as well as specific standards for credit underwriting, interest rate exposure, and asset growth.[6] No law authorizes them to deny banking services to lawful businesses they consider "unsavory." No statute confers on them the authority to act as the moral gatekeepers of the financial system, picking and choosing bank customers upon whom to bestow a government seal of approval.

Because they do not possess the statutory authority over merchant customers to carry out Operation Choke Point, the regulators chose instead to abuse their authority over banks and to turn those banks against their customers. Banks refusing to close the accounts of customers out of favor with the administration soon learned that their regulators had discovered a reason to question their "safety and soundness." Those that stood by their customers were subjected to intense scrutiny, more frequent and harsher examinations, and regulatory harassment. Under the guise of supervising bank safety and soundness, the regulatory agencies and the Justice Department weaponized the banks in their political wars.

To acquire leverage over the banks, the regulators needed a fulcrum. Traditional safety and soundness criteria were objective standards, crafted to protect banks from genuine threats to their financial soundness and to ensure that the banks complied with the law. Such standards would not have permitted regulators to single out businesses that, although unpopular with the powers that be in Washington, were nevertheless perfectly lawful and financially sound commercial enterprises. To carry out Operation Choke Point, a more subjective standard was needed, one that would permit regulators to give free rein to their beliefs and biases.

"Reputation risk" provided this standard. As originally conceived and defined by the regulators, reputation risk was the risk that a bank might acquire a bad reputation either by providing poor service to its customers or by contracting with third parties who provided poor service to bank customers in the name of the bank.[7] In 2008, however, the FDIC expanded the concept to include bad publicity about third parties used by the bank to provide customer service in the name of the bank "whether or not the publicity is related to the institution's use of the third party."[8] With Operation Choke Point, reputation risk was expanded further still, this time to embrace the risk posed to a bank even by negative publicity associated with one of its customers. With this evolved standard in hand, Operation Choke Point could demand that banks not only protect their own reputations but also pass judgment on the reputations of their customers.

Because this new notion of reputation risk is vague and inherently subjective, it leaves the banks with no concrete standards to apply when passing these judgments and, more significantly, with no standards to which they might reliably turn when defending their decisions before their federal regulators. It is a standard, therefore, that "can all too easily become a pretext for the advancement of political objectives, which can potentially subvert both safety and soundness and the rule of law."[9]

Operation Choke Point has subverted the banks and the rule of law. Federal regulators have expanded their authority to supervise bank safety and soundness into a power they should not and genuinely do not possess: to advance their own political agendas by controlling access to essential banking services. Although their guidance documents to the banks do little to establish what constitutes a reputation risk, the regulators themselves have left no doubt in their informal backroom dealings with the banks about the judgments they expect those banks to make regarding which customers deserve to have a bank account and which customers have a "bad reputation" and thus must be expelled from the financial system.

Indeed, the regulators have even taken matters into their own hands and sought to give certain industries a bad reputation. FDIC personnel ensured that the chair's talking points and correspondence with Congress always mentioned pornography dealers alongside payday lenders, in an effort to convey a "good picture regarding the unsavory nature of the businesses at issue."[10] One FDIC official explained in an internal e-mail message (produced to Congress) that he felt "strongly that including payday lenders in the same circle as pornographers and on-line gambling businesses will ultimately help with the messaging on this issue."[11]

Lest there be any doubt as to its "messaging on this issue," the FDIC then published a list of "high-risk" industries in which such "disreputable merchants" are to be found:[12]

Ammunition Sales	Life-Time Memberships
Cable Box De-scramblers	Lottery Sales

- Coin Dealers
- Credit Card Schemes
- Credit Repair Services
- Dating Services
- Debt Consolidation Scams
- Drug Paraphernalia
- Escort Services
- Firearms Sales
- Fireworks Sales
- Get Rich Products
- Government Grants
- Home-Based Charities
- Life-Time Guarantees
- Mailing Lists/Personal Info
- Money Transfer Networks
- Online Gambling
- PayDay Loans
- Pharmaceutical Sales
- Ponzi Schemes
- Pornography
- Pyramid-Type Sales
- Racist Materials
- Surveillance Equipment
- Telemarketing
- Tobacco Sales
- Travel Clubs

This list made it abundantly clear that the vague and malleable concept of reputation risk provides the regulators with ample leeway to compel banks to close the accounts of businesses they deem "unsavory," to deny those businesses access to the banking system, and, ultimately, to purge those merchants and business models from American commerce.

With their new tool in hand, the bank examiners began to go bank to bank and to demand that the accounts of specific types of customers be closed. In the back rooms of banks around the country, these examiners explained that banks continuing to serve "reputationally risky" customers will suffer consequences. As one examiner reportedly told a banker who hesitated to succumb to this pressure, "I don't like this product and I don't believe it has any place in our financial system. . . . Your decision to move forward will result in an immediate, unplanned, audit of your entire bank."[13] The message to bankers could not be more clear: If the bank refuses to turn against the customers targeted by the regulators and exile them from the banking system, the regulators will turn on and punish the bank itself.

The experience of one bank that refused to knuckle under confirms that these threats were not idle. In the early days of Operation Choke Point, the FDIC became aware that a bank was doing business with a single payday lender.[14] Because this bank served a merchant in one of the thirty industries targeted by Operation Choke Point, the FDIC undertook with the State of Ohio a joint compliance and risk management visit of the bank. When the bank again concluded that it had no valid reason for closing the payday lender's account, an FDIC field supervisor and two supervisory examiners, along with three Ohio state officials, including the Chief Examiner of the state, held a conference call with the bank to discuss their concerns about payday lending.

When this failed to produce the desired result, the FDIC regional director for the Midwest, M. Anthony Lowe, personally wrote to the bank to express the FDIC's definitive position that "activities related to payday lending are unacceptable for an insured depository institution." In the event that the recalcitrant bank—after an impromptu compliance examination, a follow-up conference call with state and federal regulators, and an official letter from the FDIC regional director responsible for the oversight of the bank—had failed to get the message, Lowe also promised that "[m]embers of our Region's Senior Management will contact you in the near term to schedule a meeting to further discuss our concerns relative to the aforementioned relationship."

For over two years, the nation's gun dealers, pawn shops, tobacco vendors, and payday lenders have watched as one bank after another has chosen to yield to the backroom threats of regulators and closed their accounts. In most cases, the banks were provided no explanations. These businesses had no opportunity to defend themselves. They had no way even of knowing that their own government was responsible for their treatment by their banks. Operation Choke Point has cost some Americans their businesses, their jobs, and their livelihoods, all to satisfy the political biases of federal regulators. They have been powerless to defend themselves against this lawless agency action. And yet even as these regulators were coercing banks to deny financial services to these law-abiding businesses in lawful industries, other agencies in the administration were seeking to facilitate and encourage financial services for felons openly engaged in criminal enterprises. In early 2014 the Department of the Treasury's Financial Crimes Enforcement Network issued guidance "to enhance the availability of financial services" for marijuana growers and dealers, whose activities are federal crimes.[15]

OPERATION CHOKE POINT IS UNLAWFUL AND UNCONSTITUTIONAL

Operation Choke Point is both illegal and unconstitutional. Federal bank regulators have imposed binding rules of conduct without following the procedures prescribed by the Administrative Procedure Act. They have exceeded their statutory authority and have exercised powers that Congress did not confer upon them. And they have violated the United States Constitution by depriving citizens of their good names and their property without due process of law.

The agencies responsible for Operation Choke Point have violated the APA.[16] The APA requires that federal agencies first provide the public with notice that they plan to impose a binding standard on regulated industries and then permit the public to comment on the agency's proposed regulation.[17] This "notice and comment" rulemaking requirement promotes open and informed government, allowing the interested parties to know what the agencies are doing and allowing the agencies themselves to benefit from the input of those who are going to be regulated, and who might be harmed, by the proposed rule.[18] Operation Choke Point never opened its subjective and manipulable standard of reputation risk to this process.

Refusal to follow notice and comment rulemaking has produced the very result that the authors of the APA sought to avoid: arbitrary and abusive agency action.[19] The absence of any clear definition of reputation risk and of any concrete standards that both the agencies and the banks can use to assess reputational risks creates ample room for regulatory judgments that are purely subjective, enabling regulators to reach whatever decision satisfies their needs or biases. This is the very definition of arbitrary and capricious agency action.

These agencies have exceeded their statutory authority under the federal banking statutes.[20] Bank regulators are charged with ensuring that law-abiding Americans have access to banks that are "safe and sound."[21] They are not charged with regulating the American economy, policing public morals, or giving force of law to their personal political prejudices. They have no more authority to pressure a bank to close the accounts of law-abiding businesses that they find "unsavory" than the IRS has to deny tax-exempt status to charitable organizations that the administration views as political adversaries, as discussed by Cleta Mitchell in another chapter. In short, there is simply no law that authorizes these agencies to do what they are doing.

But Operation Choke Point has a more fundamental problem: it violates the Constitution. It deprives American citizens of their liberty and their property without the due process of law required by the Fifth Amendment to the United States Constitution. Americans may not be deprived of their reputations or of their right to carry on their chosen lawful trade and hold a bank account without being afforded due process of law.[22] Operation Choke Point brands responsible, law-abiding Americans, who are pursuing lawful callings, as "fraudsters," "high-risk businesses," and "reputation risks." It has succeeded in stripping many of them of their bank accounts, which in turn destroyed their businesses, without offering them any explanation or opportunity to defend themselves. The Constitution forbids such lawless attacks on the liberty and property of American citizens.

OPERATION CHOKE POINT AND THE RULE OF LAW

To say only that the banking agencies have acted in excess of their statutory and constitutional authority, however, is ultimately to miss the point of, and to understate the case against, Operation Choke Point. These are lesser-included offenses in Operation Choke Point's assault on the rule of law. Operation Choke Point fails to follow proper procedure in much the same way that a military coup d'état fails to respect the chain of command. These agencies have broken the law, to be sure, but what is even more insidious is that they are operating *outside* the law.

These agencies have left the paths by which power may be exercised constitutionally. They have engaged in what Professor Philip Hamburger has aptly described as administrative off-roading:

> The Constitution generally establishes three avenues of power. It authorizes the government to issue binding edicts through legislative and judicial acts and to exercise force through executive acts. Nonetheless, like many who enjoy the strength of their vehicles, the government

> frequently prefers to drive off-road, pursuing binding power down paths of its own choosing.[23]

Federal agencies—almost all of them—have been driving off-road for decades. Few have careened so recklessly off course, however, as have the agencies responsible for Operation Choke Point. It is their conscious and strategic disregard for the paths established by the Constitution and by the law that raises special alarm. Operation Choke Point is not so much illegal as it is anti-legal.

When the bank regulators devised their subjective and manipulable standard of reputation risk, they arrogated to themselves a power to make law that belongs to the legislature. But when they ceased to rely on even that standard and abandoned even the pretext of promoting bank safety and soundness, when they began to abuse their regulatory power by threatening any bank that refused to close the accounts of customers whom these regulators personally disfavor, they were not exercising legislative, judicial, or executive power. They were exercising a kind of coercive power that the Constitution denies to all branches of the federal government. Operation Choke Point relies on the very sort of unbridled power against which our Constitution was designed to protect.

President Obama has set the example for his lawless administrative state. The power he claims—to rule by executive order with the stroke of his pen—is a power that suited the emperors and pontiffs, the kings and queens, and the dictators and despots of Europe. It is a power, however, that is radically alien to the American Constitution. President Obama has rejected both the separation of powers and the fundamental principle of Anglo-American law that no man, not even the President, is above the law. He has asserted the sort of absolute prerogative power that has always been anathema to the American political tradition.

In conceiving and ordering Operation Choke Point, President Obama's subordinates have only followed their leader in abandoning obedience to the Constitution and to the rule of law. In place of due process and principles of open government, they have substituted arbitrary commands and backroom threats. In place of the will of the people as given force through the enactments of the legislature, they have substituted their own personal political biases. In place of legitimate regulatory authority, they have substituted raw power.

CONCLUSION

C.S. Lewis depicted Hell as a bureaucracy. President Reagan, too, warned of the dangers posed to liberty by the quiet men who administered the edicts of the Soviet Union's absolutist masters in the Kremlin. The Soviet Union has departed the world stage, but the threat that unaccountable power poses to liberty remains. We must now decide "whether we believe in our capacity for self-government or whether we abandon the American revolution and confess that a little intellectual elite in a far-distant capitol can plan our lives for us better than we can plan them ourselves."[24] To acquiesce in the assumption of such power by the quiet men of the administrative state in Washington is to submit to the rule of an elite, albeit one neither small nor intellectual, and to become complicit in "the betrayal of our past, the squandering of our freedom."[25]

7.

CHEATING MARRIAGE

John C. Eastman[1]

> *The Court has cheated both sides, robbing the winners of an honest victory, and the losers of the peace that comes from a fair defeat. We owed both of them better. I dissent.*
>
> —*Associate Justice Antonin Scalia*[2]

At the conclusion of his opinion dissenting from the Court's holding in *United States v. Windsor* that Section 3 of the federal Defense of Marriage Act was unconstitutional, Justice Antonin Scalia accused the Court's majority of cheating. The fight being waged from one end of the country to the other is, according to Justice Scalia, a political and policy dispute, not a legal dispute, and its resolution therefore belongs in the political process and not in the courts. The Court could have covered itself "with honor," he noted, "by promising all sides of the debate that it was theirs to settle and that [the Court] would respect their resolution." "We might have let the people decide," Justice Scalia added, but the Court did not, and thereby cheated both sides of the case, depriving the former of an honest victory and the latter of a fair defeat.

The cheating of which Justice Scalia accused his colleagues is that of interfering with the political process. It is the kind of cheating that lies at the heart of a debate about the appropriate role of the courts in our form of government; a debate that dates back at least a half century to the 1960s-era "activism" of the Warren Court and to the counter "originalism" movement of the 1980s. While the adherents to the Warren Court's model, those in the majority in *Windsor*, might in candid moments acknowledge that their view of the judiciary's role is not that of our nation's founders, they would not accept Justice Scalia's description of their enterprise as cheating. They would prefer instead to regard their work as an advanced stage of the delivery of justice, a prime example of the evolved role for a judiciary giving voice to a living constitution.[3]

But another kind of cheating occurred in the case, cheating of the more traditional sort, which, in the end, might be even more pernicious than the cheating Justice Scalia cited. The case was, in significant measure, a collusive suit, with critical litigation strategies implemented by parties nominally on opposite sides of the case but who were, in truth, collaborating to achieve the same outcome. This cheating involved federal executive officials at the highest levels of government who manipulated not the judicial process, for the courts involved seemed to have become willing participants, but the law itself. The purpose of this chapter is to document what transpired and to raise a red flag about the threat posed to the rule of law by the advance-the-agenda-at-any-cost tactics employed by actors in the Executive Branch.

PROLOGUE

In 1993, the Hawaii Supreme Court held that Hawaii's marriage law, which like every other marriage law in the country at the time defined marriage as between one man and one woman, was a classification based on sex and therefore subject to strict scrutiny under the Equal Protection Clause of the Hawaii Constitution.[4] Although the court remanded to the trial court for further consideration rather than ordering that a marriage license be issued to the same-sex plaintiffs, most observers believed that the ruling would prove fatal to Hawaii's marriage law.[5]

Concerns about whether same-sex "marriages" performed in Hawaii would have to be recognized elsewhere because of the U.S. Constitution's

Full Faith and Credit Clause arose across the country and in Congress.[6] The U.S. Supreme Court has long recognized a public policy exception to the Full Faith and Credit Clause that likely would have allowed other states to *not* recognize same-sex "marriages" performed in Hawaii in contravention of those states' contrary marriage policy. That public policy exception was bolstered by an act of Congress in 1996 and by state statutes or constitutional amendments in roughly three dozen states over the course of the next decade.[7]

Congress passed the Defense of Marriage Act (DOMA) in 1996, explicitly noting that the law was adopted in the wake of the Hawaii Supreme Court decision "to protect the right of the States to formulate their own public policy regarding the legal recognition of same-sex unions, free from any federal constitutional implications that might attend the recognition by one State of the right for homosexual couples to acquire marriage licenses."[8] Parroting language in the Full Faith and Credit Clause itself, Section 2 of DOMA provided that no state had to give "effect" to such marriages performed in other states.[9] Section 3 of DOMA defined marriage for purposes of federal law as it had traditionally been understood—a union of one man and one woman.[10] The law was passed by overwhelming majorities in Congress—342–67 in the House of Representatives; 85–14 in the Senate—and signed into law by President Clinton.

On January 26, 2009, less than a week after taking office as President, Barack Obama nominated Harvard Law School Dean Elena Kagan to the position of Solicitor General of the United States. In her opening remarks during her confirmation hearing, Kagan emphasized the "critical responsibilities" that the Solicitor General owes to Congress, "most notably the vigorous defense of the statutes of this country against constitutional attack." In her response to follow-up written questions, Kagan stated that her role as Solicitor General would be to "advance . . . the interests of the United States, as principally expressed in legislative enactments and executive policy." "I am fully convinced," she added, "that I could represent all of these interests with vigor, even when they conflict with my own opinions. I believe deeply that specific roles carry with them specific responsibilities and that the ethical performance of a role demands carrying out these responsibilities as well and completely as possible."[11] She even asserted that the obligation to defend acts of Congress also applied in situations where the policy of the new administration with respect to the law differed from that of a previous administration: "The cases in which a change between Administrations is least justified are those in which the Solicitor General is defending a federal statute. Here interests in continuity and stability combine with the usual strong presumption in favor of defending statutes to produce a situation in which a change should almost never be made."[12]

Kagan was confirmed on March 19, 2009.

That same month, a lawsuit challenging DOMA was filed in Massachusetts, while another case involving DOMA was already pending in California.[13] The Solicitor General's office normally does not get involved in federal district court litigation; its primary task is to handle representation of the United States before the Supreme Court. But the office does occasionally take an active role at the district court level in high-profile litigation in order to articulate the position of the United States and to shape the litigation. That happened with the DOMA cases, and what transpired is telling.[14]

The initial pleadings filed in the cases defended the law in strong terms, as is customary, and also raised jurisdictional objections to the court's authority even to hear the case.[15] The Department of Justice (DOJ) even argued that states had a right, under the long-recognized public policy exception to the Constitution's Full Faith and Credit Clause, not to recognize marriages performed elsewhere that were not consistent with the state's own public policy, comparing the same-sex marriage case to a prior case involving adult incest, a comparison that reportedly caused the President to "hit the roof."[16] But shortly after Elena Kagan was confirmed as Solicitor General, the Department of Justice pleadings changed rather dramatically, both in substance and in tone. In the *Smelt* case, for example, even while continuing to argue that the district court lacked jurisdiction to consider the case, the Department of Justice expressly disavowed DOMA in the reply brief it filed on August 17, 2009: "With respect to the merits, this Administration does not support DOMA as a matter of policy, believes that it is discriminatory, and supports its repeal."[17] The department also made clear in that brief that it would continue to defend the law despite its policy disagreement only "as long as reasonable arguments can be made in support of their constitutionality."[18] But as we subsequently learned, the department was already laying the groundwork for a future case in which it would refuse to defend DOMA in circuits that had not yet rejected heightened scrutiny analysis. As acting Assistant Attorney General Tony West noted, it didn't "take a rocket scientist to know that one of these days someone is going to file a challenge to DOMA in a circuit that has yet to decide whether gays and lesbians should be considered a suspect class," a determination that would subject DOMA to heightened scrutiny.[19] The DOJ then repudiated the various rationales for DOMA that had been explicitly relied upon by Congress, offering up instead a rationale that had not been mentioned by Congress—permissible under rational basis review (a point the department highlighted in its briefing in the *Gill* case) but a guaranteed path to defeat under heightened scrutiny.[20]

On September 18, 2009, the Department of Justice filed its reply brief in the *Gill* case pending before Judge Joseph L. Tauro, U.S. District Court for the District of Massachusetts, in Boston. In it, the department repeated the language from the *Smelt* reply brief that the Obama "[a]dministration does not support DOMA as a matter of policy, believes that it is discriminatory, and supports its repeal." Remarkably, it also explicitly repudiated all of the rationales that Congress advanced in support of DOMA in 1996, thereby setting the stage for the refusal to defend DOMA once it was challenged in the Second Circuit (which at the time had not yet ruled on the level of scrutiny to be applied).

Less than a year later, on July 8, 2010—shortly after the Senate Judiciary Committee had concluded its hearings on the nomination of Elena Kagan to the position of Associate Justice—the district court in Massachusetts rejected the Department of Justice's feeble defense of DOMA and ruled that Section 3 of DOMA violated the equal protection component of the Fifth Amendment's Due Process Clause.[21] Then, on August 24, 2009, the federal district court in California dismissed the *Smelt* case for lack of jurisdiction, as the Department of Justice had requested.[22]

Elena Kagan was confirmed as Associate Justice of the Supreme Court on August 5, 2010. The next day, President Barack Obama "marked her ascension with a jubilant televised celebration in the East Room of the White House."[23]

On November 9, 2010, Edith Windsor filed a lawsuit against the United States, alleging that Section 3 of the Defense of Marriage Act denied her a spousal exemption from the federal estate tax solely because her deceased spouse, Thea Spyer, was another woman. According to the allegations in the complaint, because of DOMA the federal government did not recognize the marriage of Windsor and Spyer, which had been performed in Canada in May 2007.[24] On December 3, 2010, after a pre-trial conference, Magistrate Judge James Francis issued an order setting February 9, 2011, as the deadline for the United States, defendant in the case, to file its motion to dismiss.[25] That deadline was subsequently extended to March 11, 2011, pursuant to a revised scheduling order entered by Magistrate Judge Francis on January 28, 2011, apparently the result of a plea for an extension that Assistant Attorney General Tony West had made in a telephone call to Roberta Kaplan, Edie Windsor's attorney, at the explicit behest of Attorney General Eric Holder.[26]

On February 23, 2011, Attorney General Eric Holder announced that the Obama administration would no longer defend the Defense of Marriage Act. In his statement, he noted that the administration had defended DOMA in jurisdictions "in which binding circuit court precedents hold that laws singling out people based on sexual orientation, as DOMA does, are constitutional if there is a rational basis for their enactment."[27] But he added that there were now two cases pending in the Second Circuit, "which has no established or binding standard for how laws concerning sexual orientation should be treated."[28] As a result, he and the President had determined that "classifications based on sexual orientation should be subject to a more heightened standard of scrutiny" and that Section 3 of DOMA "fails to meet that standard and is therefore unconstitutional."[29] "Given that conclusion," Holder stated, "the President has instructed the Department not to defend the statute in such cases," a determination with which Holder "fully concur[red]."[30]

General Holder also announced that he had "informed Members of Congress of this decision, so Members who wish to defend the statute may pursue that option," and that he would "instruct Department attorneys to advise courts in other pending DOMA litigation of the President's and my conclusions that a heightened standard should apply, that Section

3 is unconstitutional under that standard and that the Department will cease defense of Section 3."[31]

It is exceedingly rare for the government to decline to defend a statute, in part because of the President's constitutional obligation to "take care that the laws be faithfully executed." To be sure, the Constitution also imposes on the President, by oath, the duty to "preserve, protect and defend the Constitution of the United States," but the almost universal practice of the Department of Justice to reconcile these at-times conflicting duties has been to defend the laws despite any constitutional concerns by the Executive. The only exceptions recognized by the DOJ have been extremely narrow: laws that intrude on the executive powers of the President, and laws that are "clearly unconstitutional" under existing Supreme Court precedent.[32] Neither of those exemptions applied in the *Windsor* case.

The near-universal practice of the Department of Justice to defend all laws in cases that did not fit within either of those two narrow exemptions developed after a controversy during the late 1970s, in which the Carter administration had argued that it could decline to present in court any defense of an arguably constitutional federal statute that the department had determined for itself (independently of Congress and the judiciary) to be unconstitutional.[33] After the department notified Congress of its decision not to defend a federal statute that prohibited public broadcast licensees from using their licenses to endorse or oppose candidates for public office, the Office of Senate Legal Counsel warned the Senate that if the statute were struck without a defense, the precedent would be established that the Executive Branch could nullify laws with which it disagrees by a default in court.[34] The district court dismissed the action for lack of an adversarial party (the Senate had intervened as an amicus curiae rather than a party), but while the appeal was pending, the DOJ under a new Attorney General at the outset of the Reagan administration advised the court of appeals that it would renew its defense of the statute.[35]

The concerns that arose out of that controversy led to the adoption of 28 U.S.C. § 530D, which requires the Attorney General to notify Congress any time he decides not to defend any act of Congress on the ground that he believes the act is unconstitutional. That law presumes that Congress would take up the defense when the Executive refused to do so. The contrary view would effectively give to the President a post-enactment veto power that the Supreme Court has expressly held to be unconstitutional.[36] It would sanction a "suspension" power that the Take Care Clause was specifically designed to prevent.[37]

One of the charges leveled against King George III in the Declaration of Independence was that he suspended laws adopted by the colonies until his assent to them should be obtained and then, once suspended, utterly neglected to attend to them.[38] The concern was that the king was reasserting a power that had provoked serious tension between Parliament and the Stuart kings during the seventeenth century, where laws properly enacted through the political process were "dispensed with," or suspended, at the whim of the monarch.[39] Early state constitutions also refused to countenance the view that the Executive had the power to suspend laws.[40]

The ratification debates reveal that the Take Care Clause was adopted to prevent the President in the new constitutional system from being able to exercise a power to suspend duly enacted laws with which he disagreed.[41] But as the Senate Legal Counsel recognized in response to the department's actions in *League of Women Voters*, the ability to suspend or even "nullify" a law can be as effectively accomplished indirectly by non-defense and default in response to a constitutional challenge as it can be directly accomplished by refusal to enforce the law.

The DOJ's claim that the President can decline to defend any statute that he believes to be unconstitutional, even when perfectly reasonable arguments in support of its constitutionality exist, creates a serious risk that the judicial system might be manipulated to give the President a de facto post-enactment veto or suspension power. That risk manifested itself in the *Windsor* case, for the department did more than simply decline to defend the Defense of Marriage Act; it actively joined in the plaintiffs' attack on the constitutionality of DOMA and even sought to undermine the defense being provided by the U.S. House of Representatives by defaulting on the rationales Congress had for its overwhelming approval of the law and then using those defaults to attack the law.

The legislative history of DOMA contains several rationales that Congress asserted were both important and furthered by the Defense of Marriage Act, including the development of relationships that are optimal for procreation and encouraging the creation of stable relationships that facilitate the rearing of children by both of their biological parents.[42] In several prior court decisions, those rationales were held to be more than sufficient to uphold the law's constitutionality.[43] Yet in the *Gill* case and elsewhere, the department "disavowed" all of the rationales that had been identified by Congress and had been successfully relied on to defend DOMA, choosing instead to rely on a hypothesized interest in maintaining the status quo.[44]

Then, in *Windsor*, the DOJ mischaracterized the rationales actually advanced by Congress, contending instead that "the legislative history demonstrates that the statute was motivated in significant part by animus towards gays and lesbians."[45] Indeed, the department made concession after concession in the district court that no lawyer, complying with the ethical obligation to zealously advocate for his client, would have made.[46] It contended that opposite-sex and same-sex couples are "similarly situated," for example, a threshold inquiry under equal protection analysis that was clearly untrue.[47] It unnecessarily equated the view that homosexual conduct is immoral with animus toward gays and lesbians; it accused Congress of having the "bare desire to harm a politically unpopular group"; and it contended that "Congress's interest in 'promoting responsible procreation and childrearing'" is "not materially advanced by" Section 3 of DOMA.[48] The department even urged the court to apply heightened scrutiny after acknowledging that numerous other courts, including the Supreme Court, had applied rational basis review to sexual-orientation classifications.[49] And then, having "disavowed" or mischaracterized the rationales actually relied upon by Congress, the department argued that Section 3 must be held unconstitutional because, under heightened scrutiny, "a statute must be defended by reference to the 'actual [governmental] purpose behind it, not a different 'rationalization'" (such as the one the department itself had offered in the *Gill* case).[50]

The Department of Justice's conduct in the district court was thus a far cry from the long-standing policy that the department "has a duty to defend the constitutionality of an Act of Congress whenever a *reasonable argument* can be made in its support, even if the attorney general concludes that the argument may ultimately be unsuccessful in the courts."[51] It did not come close to "zealous advocacy" for the client—the United States itself, the policies of which are reflected in the laws, not the personal views of the President or the Attorney General—that the standards of ethical conduct require. It instead amounted to a manipulation of the judiciary in order to have a duly enacted act of Congress declared unconstitutional: much more than just the declining to defend to which it had alerted the court back in February, this was an overt about-face, joining forces with the plaintiff to attack the constitutionality of the statute that was its duty to defend, "switching sides to advocate that the statute be ruled unconstitutional," as the court of appeals would later put it.

Worse, the DOJ's conduct was designed not just to lose the particular case, but to obtain a decision from a higher court that would operate as binding authority throughout the nation. That led it to take some truly bizarre actions in the district court. For example, in order to preserve the district court's jurisdiction to issue a substantive ruling rather than merely a default judgment, the department filed a motion to dismiss to provide a merely technical adversarial-ness that was necessary for the Court's jurisdiction, in light of the department's position that Congress itself did not have legal standing to intervene on behalf of the United States. The department then filed a brief *opposing its own motion to dismiss and supporting the plaintiff's motion for summary judgment.*[52] In doing so, it even accused the Congress that enacted DOMA of doing so out of "animus."[53] Not surprisingly, particularly in light of the department's outcome-determinative concessions and advocacy in favor of the plaintiff, the district court ruled on June 6, 2012, *without benefit of oral argument*, that Section 3 of DOMA was unconstitutional.

True to form and to its interest in securing a binding precedent from a higher court, the Department of Justice then proceeded a week later to *appeal* the judgment against DOMA that it had just *won* from the district court and then to argue *against* its own appeal. The appeal was expedited because of the plaintiff's motion that was granted without opposition from the United States but over the opposition of the Bipartisan Legal Advisory Group of the U.S. House of Representatives (BLAG), which alone had been defending DOMA in the trial court. Opening briefs were due in a little over a month in early August, and oral argument was scheduled for the month after that—lightning speed for a case in the court of appeals.

But not satisfied with even that expedited consideration, the plaintiff and the U.S. Department of Justice both filed petitions for certiorari before judgment. Windsor's petition was filed on July 16, 2012, supported by a brief filed by the Department of Justice on August 31, 2012, urging the Court to take the case (if it did not take one of the other cases addressing the constitutionality of Section 3 of DOMA already pending before it). The Department of Justice argued, as it had in its own petition before judgment in a case from the Ninth Circuit, that "the question of Section 3's constitutionality is a matter of 'such imperative public importance as to justify the deviation from normal appellate practice and to require immediate determination in this Court'" before judgment by the court of appeals.[54] And even though the district court had applied a rational basis standard of review, the department continued to press for heightened scrutiny by using the language of intermediate review rather than rational basis review in its brief supporting Windsor's petition for certiorari: "Section 3 of DOMA denies to same-sex couples legally married under state law significant federal benefits that are otherwise available to persons lawfully married under state law," the DOJ argued. "Because such differential treatment bears no *substantial relationship* to any *important governmental objective*, Section 3 violates the guarantee of equal protection secured by the Fifth Amendment."[55]

The department then filed its own petition for writ of certiorari before judgment on September 11, 2012, and filed a supplemental brief the day after the Second Circuit's ruling, urging the Court to grant its petition for certiorari in the *Windsor* case rather than its earlier petition in the parallel case in Massachusetts.[56] Although the department's lawyers explained that the reason for its changed position was that the Second Circuit's decision was "not constrained by prior precedent" requiring the application of mere rational basis review (as was the First Circuit in the Massachusetts case)—and they desperately wanted the Supreme Court itself to adopt heightened scrutiny—it undoubtedly had not escaped their attention that Justice Kagan would have to recuse herself from the Massachusetts case.[57]

Oral argument was held in the court of appeals on September 27, 2012, before Chief Judge Jacobs and Judges Straub and Droney, and the case was decided just three weeks later on October 18, 2012. Again, lightning speed, apparently in an attempt to leapfrog the Massachusetts case from which Justice Kagan would be recused and provide the Supreme Court with an alternate vehicle with which to consider the constitutionality of DOMA.

As it had done in the district court below, the Department of Justice did not just *decline to defend* Section 3 of DOMA; it affirmatively attacked its constitutionality. And even though the district court had applied rational basis review in its decision, the department continued to advocate for the application of heightened scrutiny, devoting more than twenty-five pages of its forty-five-page brief to that part of the argument.[58] "[D]iscrimination based on sexual orientation merits heightened scrutiny," it contended (even while acknowledging that other courts had held that only rational basis review applies and that the Supreme Court itself had never applied heightened scrutiny to sexual-orientation classifications), and "[u]nder that standard of review, Section 3 of DOMA is unconstitutional."[59] Most significantly, the DOJ continued to advance the "disavowal" strategy that appears to have been launched the summer before in the *Smelt* and *Gill* cases. "[U]nder any form of heightened scrutiny," it argued, "a statute must be defended by reference to the 'actual [governmental] purposes' behind it, not different 'rationalizations.'"[60]

The department also repeated a number of key, outcome-determinative concessions, such as the claim that same-sex couples are "similarly situated" to "opposite-sex couples"; that the "legislative history demonstrates that the statute was motivated in significant part by disapproval of gay and lesbian people and their intimate and family relationships"; that another of Congress's rationales ("defending and nurturing the institution of traditional, heterosexual marriage") "does not support Section 3" of DOMA; and that Congress's asserted interest in "encouraging responsible procreation and child-rearing" was "not materially advanced by Section 3 of DOMA."[61]

With advocacy like that from the United States Department of Justice, which was supposed to be *defending* the law, it is little wonder that the court of appeals not only affirmed the district court's judgment but adopted the department's extensive request to apply heightened scrutiny.

The Department of Justice repeated its abdication in the Supreme Court. As it had in the court of appeals, the Department of Justice sought review of a ruling that had just gone in favor of the position for which it was advocating. It challenged the legal standing of the Bipartisan Legal Advisory Group of the U.S. House of Representatives to defend the statute on behalf of the United States, claiming that "no counsel will be heard" to present the position of the United States contrary to the Attorney General. It argued that BLAG's members were only individual legislators who had no Article III standing, rather than (as the House resolution confirmed) a body acting on behalf of the House as an institution. It again pressed hard for the Court to adopt heightened scrutiny, and it made a slew of unnecessary concessions that undermined the defense of DOMA that BLAG was trying to provide.

In his opinion for the Court, Justice Kennedy picked up many of the themes advanced by the Department of Justice, including several aspects of the false narrative that had been spun. Most significantly, Justice Kennedy asserted DOMA was passed only out of animus toward gays and lesbians, based on arguments to that effect made by the Department of Justice. Had the lawsuit been the result of a truly adversarial process, those false claims would not have been conceded by the party responsible for defending the law.

The Supreme Court itself strongly warned in *Windsor* that such conduct would put "the integrity of the political process . . . at risk" should it become "a common practice in ordinary cases." The refusal-to-defend trend is unfortunately becoming a "common practice" and poses a serious threat to the rule of law itself. It "jeopardize[s] the equilibrium established within our constitutional system" that is necessary for a proper adjudication of important constitutional issues.

This threat to the rule of law may well be a consequence of these cases every bit as tragic as the "breathtakingly subversive idea" of treating same-sex relationships as "marriage" and the "deinstitutionalization" of that profoundly important societal institution that will predictably result.[62] As Abraham Lincoln warned 177 years ago, in a speech before the Young Men's Lyceum of Springfield, Illinois, with "the perpetrators of [lawless] acts going unpunished, the lawless in spirit, are encouraged to become lawless in practice; and having been used to no restraint, but dread of punishment, they thus become, absolutely unrestrained. . . . [I]f the laws be continually despised and disregarded, . . . the alienation of [the people's] affections from the Government is the natural consequence; and to that, sooner or later, it must come."[63]

The perpetrators of lawlessness about which Lincoln warned were simply mobs taking the law into their own hands. What we are witnessing now, with the "cheating" described in this chapter and the aftermath of cheating it has spawned, is lawlessness by those at the very highest echelons of political power, by elected officials whose sworn duty is to defend the laws, not undermine them. The alienation of the people from their government is therefore a much greater risk than it was in Lincoln's day, for then the government merely sat by and watched the lawlessness unfold.

8.

THE FANNIE/FREDDIE FIASCO
Executive Overreach in the Regulation of Financial Markets

Richard A. Epstein[1]

FANNIE AND FREDDIE: THE STATUTORY SCHEME

The residential home market is one of the largest and most complex financial markets in the United States. These loans are typically originated by private banks to their customers. In earlier times, these loans were private transactions in which the United States played no significant role. But in line with the ever-expanding role of government, the United States established the Federal National Mortgage Association, or Fannie Mae, in 1938, which in turn became a public traded company—a so-called government sponsored enterprise (GSE) in 1968. Its companion organization, the Federal Home Loan Mortgage Corporation, or Freddie Mac, was created as a GSE in 1970. The function of both these organizations is to supply a "secondary" market that allows the originators of mortgages to sell them off to other parties and use the proceeds of sale to initiate another cycle of lending, all in a conscious effort to increase the level of home ownership in the United States. To do their job Fannie Mae and Freddie Mac have the power both to purchase home mortgages and to guarantee their payments to private parties who purchase these issues, often in complex pools of mortgage-backed securities. Between them they invested in over $5 trillion in mortgage-backed securities.

The operation of these companies was by the original plan subject to their own independent boards of directors, but the policies that they enacted were heavily influenced by their dual status as hybrid federal and private institutions. That federal involvement had powerful influences on the lending policies adopted by Fannie and Freddie, and the federal oversight carried with it important consequences. Most notably, the Housing and Community Development Act of 1992 imposed on Fannie and Freddie "an affirmative obligation to facilitate the financing of affordable housing for low- and moderate-income families" while maintaining "a strong financial condition and a reasonable economic return," two clearly inconsistent obligations.[2] At the same time it was widely understood that there was an implicit federal government guarantee against the losses generated by the lending activities undertaken under the aegis of Fannie and Freddie. As is common in these cases, there was no explicit accounting for the cost of either the affordable lending program or its implicit guarantee.

Programs of this sort look attractive during good times. But they generate serious complications when matters start to go bad, as happened at the end of the housing boom in 2007 and 2008. At this point the hard question becomes how best to administer these programs, a matter that normally puts strains on the delicate balance between the legislative and executive branches of government. It falls to Congress to pass general legislation on matters within its enumerated powers, so long as these laws respect the substantive protections the Constitution provides to all individuals. It then falls to the President of the United States "to take care that the Laws be faithfully executed."[3] The word "be" in that sentence is no grammatical anomaly. It signals that the President must also oversee actions done by his authorized agents. These include members of his cabinet, including of course the Secretary of the Treasury. Still, the executive power today is not fully lodged in the President but parceled out among independent agencies set up by Congress, virtually all of which are given extensive powers to adopt rules and regulations in order to achieve basic statutory objectives.

This approach has special urgency in connection with the contentious government bailout of the Federal National Mortgage Association and its somewhat smaller companion, the Federal Home Loan Mortgage Corporation. That bailout took place on September 6, 2008, at the height of the financial crisis.[4] During this time, the administration similarly treated American International Group, but Lehman Brothers was left to dangle in the wind. With Fannie and Freddie, the United States Treasury, under the assertive leadership of then Secretary of the Treasury Henry Paulson, prevailed upon the Federal Housing Finance Agency (FHFA), an independent agency, to subject both Fannie Mae and Freddie Mac to conservatorships. Those conservatorships were to be operated by the FHFA's then director, James Lockhart, who was shortly thereafter replaced by a former high-level Treasury employee, Edward DeMarco.[5] The FHFA had been set up on July 8, 2008, under the Housing and Economic Recovery Act (HERA) to deal with what was thought, rightly, at the time to be an impending financial crisis.[6] As everyone agrees, the risk of bank runs is serious enough that there is a legitimate role for the government to play as a banker of last resort that can, with its open credit lines, intervene in order to stabilize markets. I will not debate here whether the negative collateral consequences of government bailouts are worse than the negative collateral consequences of non-bailouts, a topic on which there is massive disagreement. Instead, here the key question goes to the propriety of the regulatory actions of the FHFA and Treasury pursuant to their statutory powers.

To put this issue into relief, it is critical to set out briefly the statutory framework. Congress well understood that any bailout of major private institutions is fraught with potential abuse. As with the exercise of all government powers, the dangers run in opposing directions. The government can act so harshly toward the private party that it confiscates wealth under the guise of debt relief. Or the government can act so cooperatively that it gratuitously bestows public funds on private parties. These two opposing risks are at stake any time the government exercises its eminent domain or general power of rate regulation. Indeed, it operates any time the government decides to make a transfer of government property to private entities.[7] In both these settings, a sound institutional framework establishes safeguards against both risks. One example among many involves the rate regulation of natural monopolies, which was perhaps the single most important issue before the Supreme Court from the end of the Civil War to the beginning of the Second World War.[8] Make the rates too low, and the company cannot recover its invested capital. Make them too high, and the firm continues to reap the monopoly profits that the system of rate regulation is intended to control. The upshot is an elaborate set of procedural and substantive protections to guard the common carrier—the government agency can take care of itself in how it sets the rates and other terms and conditions of service.

The same problem arises in connection with the 2008 bailouts. Bailouts are by definition individual events that cannot follow the regulatory principles which govern rate of return for firms (e.g., electric companies or other public utilities) that operate in stable industries. Any bailout transaction necessarily requires some individualized negotiation over the structure of a deal. HERA's initial assumption was that the Treasury would enter into arm's-length negotiations with the financial institution that was slated to receive the bailout, with the Treasury representing the United States and the trustees representing the financial institution. If the parties struck a deal that met their mutual satisfaction, it would help to allay the charges that the shareholders of the firm were being exploited without their consent.

That optimistic conclusion does not answer the related question of whether the deal given by the government was too sweet to the private party. In order to deal with this problem, Section 1117 of HERA provided for the "[t]emporary authority of Treasury to purchase obligations and securities," which was subject to the huge caveat that "[n]othing in this subsection requires the corporation to issue obligations or securities to the Secretary without mutual agreement between the Secretary and the corporation."[9] The Treasury's power was further hemmed in by the requirement that the Secretary first determine that an "emergency" requires the use of this power, which can then only be exercised subject to conditions needed to "protect the taxpayers." That list of conditions covers the full range of preferences, priorities, amounts, and maturities of the obligations or securities to be purchased, coupled with the creation of a plan that, critically, will allow for "the orderly resumption of private market funding or capital market access," taking into account the "probability" that Fannie and Freddie can discharge their repayment obligations.[10] Keeping each entity as "a private shareholder-owned company" was also on the list of relevant considerations, as were restrictions on the ability of the corporation to pay "dividends and executive compensation" during the period that these obligations remained in effect. Section 1117 did not contemplate the power of the Treasury to strip the board of its ability to represent the corporation.

The full picture emerges, however, only by looking at the FHFA, which has the power to throw any corporation that is in financial distress into either a receivership or a conservatorship under its control.[11] At this point, the FHFA then steps into the shoes of the displaced director and thus owes the same fiduciary duties toward the shareholders. To be sure, there are complex questions concerning the direction in which the FHFA should take the management of Fannie and Freddie once the takeover is complete. But neither conservatorship nor receivership allows it simply to claim the assets for itself or to hand them over in full to the Treasury, even under some kind of agreement.

The basic choices are two. First, the FHFA can throw the company into receivership, which means that the FHFA "shall place the regulated entity in[to] liquidation."[12] In the alternative, it can place the regulated entity into a conservatorship where the statutory duties run as follows:

> The Agency may, as conservator, take such action as may be—
> (i) necessary to put the regulated entity in a sound and solvent condition; and
> (ii) appropriate to carry on the business of the regulated entity and preserve and conserve the assets and property of the regulated entity.[13]

A conservator's goal is to continue the operations of a regulated entity, rehabilitate it, and return it to a safe, sound, and solvent condition.[14]

Under HERA, the FHFA also has the power to take over the operation of any corporation and either to throw it into receivership, at which point it would be liquidated, or to keep it alive in conservatorship, at which point it would continue operations in standard form.

PAULSON AND THE 2008 BAILOUT

In principle, the FHFA should have operated as an independent entity, but from the outset that was not the case. The driving force in these negotiations was Hank Paulson, who essentially prevailed on the FHFA to force out the directors and then to do the deal with the government. Paulson made it clear that, regarding the deterioration of Fannie and Freddie, "FHFA, the Federal Reserve and the Treasury have moved to address this difficult issue" and "conservatorship was the only form in which [Paulson] would commit taxpayer money to the GSEs."[15] The statement was an open arrogation of powers that Paulson did not have, for he did not have the right to speak for the FHFA or for the Federal Reserve. Nor would it make the slightest difference in this case that the FHFA agreed to have Paulson speak on its behalf, for that very abdication of authority is itself a breach of the FHFA's statutory duties as conservator.

With Paulson's action, the entire HERA framework buckles because Treasury is running both sides of the deal. This point has serious consequences for the deal that was essentially struck: the Senior Preferred Stockholder Agreement (SPSA), under which the Treasury agreed to advance up to $200 billion (later raised to $400 billion) to Fannie and Freddie in exchange for a commitment fee of $1 billion and a senior preferred stock that carried with it a 10 percent dividend, which would increase to 12 percent if the two companies chose unilaterally to defer payments to some future time.[16] In addition, the FHFA gave the Treasury a warrant to purchase at a nominal price up to 79.9 percent of the common stock—a number chosen because it was just below the 80 percent figure that would have required the Treasury to consolidate Fannie and Freddie into the federal budget.

In one sense this deal followed the form that was entered into between the Federal Reserve Bank of New York and AIG for a bailout figure of $85 billion. There the dividend rate was 14 percent, with the same nominal warrant for 79.9 percent of the stock. But there was a crucial difference between the two cases. Since Fannie and Freddie were GSEs (government sponsored enterprises), it was easier for Paulson to force out their respective boards. But the AIG Board remained in place and approved the deal, which it thought was better than any alternative. That bailout worked in the sense that the retained 20 percent of common stock had substantial value. Nonetheless, Starr International, led by the former head of AIG, Hank Greenberg, sued to challenge that takeover. All these claims were rebuffed in an able opinion in *Starr International Co. v. Federal Reserve Bank of New York*.[17]

Because AIG retained its board while Fannie and Freddie did not retain theirs, the analogous principles of corporate law should take away from the FHFA and Treasury the normal protection of the business judgment rule because of the evident self-dealing in the case.[18] Under the fair value rule, the government should have the burden of proving that this deal was fair to all shareholders—a contentious issue outside the scope of this chapter.

THE THIRD AMENDMENT OF 2012

The closely contested nature of the 2008 SPSA stands in stark contrast to the Third Amendment, which on August 17, 2012, was signed by Edward DeMarco, now the head of the FHFA and a former high-level Treasury official, and Timothy Geithner, the Secretary of the Treasury during the first term of the Obama administration. Here again the self-dealing reverses any presumption in favor of the deal. The terms were so lopsided that there can be no dispute that all the gain goes to the Treasury and none to the shareholders of Fannie and Freddie. The deal provided that, with a small exception, all of the future earnings of Fannie and Freddie would be subject to a dividend sweep, meaning that they would be paid over to the Treasury in full, without reducing the amount of preferred stock in Treasury's hand, which at that time amounted to about $187 billion. It was clear that this decision was made in secret, without any independent fairness opinion for the shareholders. It was also made at a time when the underlying businesses of both Fannie and Freddie had returned to fiscal health, so that they were now in a position to pay off the 10 percent dividend on the full $187 billion without compromising the financial health of either entity. The action thus amounted to an outright expropriation of all the future profits of these two corporations. As of this writing, in June 2015, if all the excess dividends had been treated as a return of capital, the outstanding preferred issues of the two companies would be somewhere between $30 and $40 billion, reducing the future dividend payments accordingly.[19]

The Treasury tried to justify this action by saying that the two companies benefited because they would no longer have to strain to come up with the 10 percent dividend on an annual basis. But the point has no merit given that there *never* was an obligation to pay the 10 percent dividend; under the SPSPA both Fannie and Freddie had the option to accrue payments indefinitely, which a solvent company would not do because of the extra cost. Normally, fair value determinations require sophisticated financial analysis. But in this case, the enormity of the breach is evident on the face of the agreement. It is a classic case of Executive Branch overreach that involves both the FHFA and Treasury.

THE JUDICIAL RESPONSE: *PERRY V. LEW*

The question then arises as to the nature of the judicial response to the problem. Lawsuits were, of course, not long in coming, and they followed two different paths. The first theory treated the case as a breach of fiduciary duty, for which the proper remedy is to undo the transactions to negate the self-dealing. The easiest way to accomplish this is to credit all excess dividend payments as a return of capital that reduces the amount of outstanding preferred shares. This cash remedy does not raise the further question of whether the FHFA should take steps, as it is authorized to do under the quoted statutory passages, to return both companies to the private market now that the financial crisis has passed. There is no strict requirement under HERA as to when this ought to be done. But there is a strong argument that a court should require the transition now that it is clear the FHFA has acted in consistent violation of its statutory duties. Though the issue has not yet been pressed in litigation, FHFA should not be trusted with doing anything that involves other people's money.

The second approach argues that stripping both companies of all their assets, after taking control over all functions, amounts to a taking—except in name—of all firm value. The only way that the Takings Clause can have any effect is if it ensures that stratagems like this do not yield handsome rewards to the parties that impose them, as has long been recognized in other cases.[20] On this theory, the argument is that even if the taking is for a public use, the decline in the value of the shares, attributable to the legal effect of the regulations, sets the amount of the award, to which statutory interest has to be added as of August

17, 2012. To be sure, the shares traded at a positive value after August 17, 2012, but that market response was only a reflection of the general view that the Third Amendment would be found to be either a breach of fiduciary duty, a taking, or both, so the shares would continue to have residual value. The clear implication is that if the government wins its litigation on the Third Amendment, the share value will in fact drop to zero, because what value are shares that have neither dividend, liquidation, or voting rights?

Ultimately, the government might yet win. The litigation in question came to a head on September 30, 2014, in *Perry Capital LLC v. Lew*.[21] Without any discovery, the court gave the government a full victory on the case, whose downward pressure on the private shares in Fannie and Freddie continues unabated today. In effect, District Court Judge Royce Lamberth showed the usual, if undeserved, judicial deference to government on a variety of procedural and substantive grounds. The initial parry was procedural, as the government placed extensive reliance on the claim that the FHFA shall "as conservator or receiver, and by operation of law, immediately succeed to—(i) all rights, titles, powers, and privileges of the regulated entity, and of any stockholder, officer, or director of such regulated entity with respect to the regulated entity and the assets of the regulated entity."[22] The implication of the claim that the FHFA inherits all shareholder rights is that the shareholder has no power whatsoever to sue the FHFA for breach of fiduciary duty. This reading means that all the duties of conservatorship cannot be enforced by their beneficiaries, which in turn means that this procedural section is part of the outright plan of confiscation. It is highly unlikely that this section should be read this way; a more sensible meaning is that no shareholder should be able to bring a derivative suit against the FHFA when it brings or settles cases with third parties.

Those agreements with third parties in many cases could result in payments to Fannie and Freddie or in a release of claims owing to them. What the legislation does is give FHFA virtually unlimited power to make those deals. But it does not allow any funds that are paid into Fannie and Freddie to be distributed by FHFA as it sees fit. To allow it to disregard any and all shareholder obligations is to allow these extreme standing claims to swallow the entire case. It is a sad commentary that the Executive Branch would put this extravagant reading on the provision, and sad as well that Judge Lamberth should accept this procedural bar against all recovery. Certainly no one could argue that standing is missing in the traditional sense that requires a party to have a direct financial stake in the outcome of the case.

This procedural argument was then followed by a substantive argument that is equally incredible. As the argument goes, since the conservatorship gave the FHFA complete control over the matter, "the plaintiffs' property interests—whatever they may have been prior to the Third Amendment—were extinguished."[23] Again, this conclusion is reached without any explicit discussion of the conservator's duty under the statute, whose key provisions set out earlier were not even cited. Accordingly, the district court concluded that in this instance the shareholders in question also failed under the pliable test for regulatory takings under *Penn Central Transportation Co. v. City of New York*,[24] because the shareholders did not have sufficient "investment-backed expectations" that their shares would retain value. But for what reason would they invest in shares other than for the financial return and control rights?

EXECUTIVE OVERREACH AND JUDICIAL ACQUIESCENCE

It should be clear that if this decision were generalized, the government could confiscate the wealth of any corporation by the following two-step approach: first, use the conservatorship to bring any corporate assets under its control, and second, enter into a sweetheart agreement to transfer all the asset value into the government's coffers. The statutory scheme does not authorize anything like that, at least if all of its provisions are read as part of a whole of what was in general a well-conceived statute. The moral of the story, then, is that Executive Branch overreach may be used to transform sensible legislation into a regulatory monster, even when the legislation could have achieved its proper goals if it had been read in the correct fashion. In certain cases of Executive Branch overreach there is some judicial pushback, which there seems to be in the immigration area. But property rights in the eyes of many courts are not human rights, so an exceedingly low threshold applies to government takings. The matter has not yet found its way to the Supreme Court, and indeed may not get there if the lower courts all affirm the government's aggressive stance. But the Court will surely take the case if the government loses, as it well ought to in this case. Either way, the key point is that Executive misrule remains the order of the day. In some cases, Congress, which now sees massive dollar inflows into federal coffers, will be reluctant to correct the administrative perversion of its statutory scheme. So it lies with the courts to intervene if Executive abuse is to be countered at all. It is too early for a final judgment on these matters, but the early returns are far from encouraging.

9.

EXECUTIVE INTERFERENCE WITH A SUPPOSEDLY INDEPENDENT AGENCY

The Federal Communications Commission

Harold Furchtgott-Roth

Generations of Americans have read the *Federalist Papers*,[1] essays written by Alexander Hamilton, John Jay, and James Madison to encourage ratification of the Constitution. Many of the *Federalist Papers* emphasize the importance of the separation of powers, often with reference to Montesquieu. Partly in reaction to the absence of separation of powers under the British monarchy and under the Articles of Confederation, Madison even paraphrases Montesquieu: "The accumulation of all powers, legislative, executive, and judiciary, in the same hands, whether of one, a few, or many, and whether hereditary, self-appointed, or elective, may justly be pronounced the very definition of tyranny."[2]

Given such a warning, one might reasonably assume that the federal government would permanently eschew concentrating powers in one agency. But even in the early years of the Republic, separation of powers was not uniformly followed.[3] Perhaps worse, when powers were separated, Madison's tyranny was sometimes present.[4] The greatest early deviation from Madison's view, almost a century after his writing, was the establishment of the Interstate Commerce Commission (ICC).[5] As an "independent agency," the ICC combined "all powers, legislative, executive, and judiciary, in the same hands."[6] Although an independent agency left to its own devices can become a Madisonian tyranny,[7] an independent agency willing to accept outside domination can also be at the mercy and whim of an interfering executive.

The Federal Communications Commission, like the Securities Exchange Commission and the Federal Trade Commission, is an independent agency, *not* (like the Department of Transportation or Department of Energy) a creature of the Executive Branch.[8] To be sure, the President has lawful ways to influence the FCC's actions: He appoints commissioners of both parties when vacancies arise (once a year, more or less); he names the chair from among the sitting commissioners; and Executive Branch agencies such as the Commerce Department and Justice Department occasionally convey their views in comments reviewable by the public.[9] But there are critical checks on presidential power in this area. By statute, the five-member FCC must include two members not from the President's party, and all commissioners are subject to Senate confirmation.[10] Commissioners do not serve at the pleasure of the President and are both entitled and expected to exercise their best judgment even when that judgment departs from the President's.

As such, the organization of the FCC follows a pattern from the ICC that is designed to shield independent commissions from direct presidential influence and thereby dilute the effect of transitory political events on agency policy-making.[11] As early as 1935, Supreme Court Justice George Sutherland described independent commissions as follows:

> The commission is to be non-partisan; and it must, from the very nature of its duties, act with entire impartiality. It is charged with the enforcement of no policy except the policy of the law. Its duties are neither political nor executive, but predominantly quasijudicial and quasilegislative. . . . [I]ts members are called upon to exercise the trained judgment of a body of experts appointed by law and informed by experience.
>
> . . .

> [It is] a body of experts who shall gain experience by length of service; a body which shall be independent of executive authority, *except in its selection*, and free to exercise its judgment without the leave or hindrance of any other official or any department of the government.[12]

There are sound reasons for maintaining FCC independence from undue Executive Branch influence. First, the FCC undoubtedly exercises the power to adjudicate individual cases.[13] The Supreme Court has long acknowledged the importance of protecting the independence of those who engage in adjudicatory functions, even if they do so only occasionally.[14] Indeed, since the founding of our nation, it has been acknowledged that an executive officer "'should not hold his office at the pleasure of the Executive Branch' if one of his 'principal dut[ies]' 'partakes strongly of the judicial character.'"[15]

Second, in addition to its adjudicatory functions, the FCC serves as an expert administrator with technical expertise in the industries over which it holds regulatory sway. "'The work of this commission [is] of a most exacting and difficult character, demanding persons who have experience in the problems to be met—that is, a proper knowledge of both the public requirements and the practical affairs of industry.'"[16] The need to rely on the technical expertise of commissioners provided additional support for the need to insulate the individual commissioners from political influence and was embodied in the creation of the Federal Trade Commission[17] and all subsequent independent agencies. Independence from Executive Branch influence is necessary to safeguard the commissions from partisan politics and enable the commissioners to make expert decisions based on empirical data.[18]

Third, the FCC has substantial rulemaking authority not vested in the Executive Branch. Congress could have written, and the President could have signed, the Communications Act to empower the Executive to promulgate regulations over the communications industry.[19] But the Communications Act did not. Similarly, the FCC has substantial enforcement authority under the Communications Act not vested in the Executive Branch. Congress could have written and the President could have signed a law assigning enforcement authority to the Executive Branch, but they did not.

In its ordinary proceedings, the FCC of course takes into consideration the views of the administration, as well as the views of those who participate in the commission's public proceedings. The views of the administration, in ordinary proceedings, are given more or less weight depending on the views of a particular commissioner, but never have the administration's views been preclusive of other views in a public proceeding. Until now.

Over the past year, something has gone awry. In several cases of extremely high importance, President Barack Obama has exercised outsized, overt influence on the FCC's decision-making, acting not simply as one advocate among many but as the most powerful voice, often to the exclusion of others, in policy debates. Indeed, in several cases the President has effectively countermanded his own FCC chair, directing results inconsistent with those the agency had previously proposed. In each of these cases, the FCC has acceded to his wishes, effectuating precisely the policy result he has requested at the cost of basic principles of separation of powers and its own independence. In this chapter we discuss three recent cases of presidential overreach in the communications policy space: (1) network neutrality, (2) government-operated broadband networks, and (3) government subsidies for broadband connectivity to schools and libraries.

NET NEUTRALITY: REGULATING THE INTERNET AS A PUBLIC UTILITY

On February 26, 2015, the FCC supplanted a fifteen-year-old bipartisan policy framework governing the regulation of broadband Internet access service with a new, highly contested, and likely unlawful regime that subjects broadband service to the system of rules developed many decades ago to regulate monopoly railroad and telephone services.[20] While the popular press has focused on the agency's adoption of "net neutrality" (or "open Internet" rules), the FCC's decision went well beyond that specific issue. Its new framework imposes on broadband Internet service providers (ISPs) a broad swath of regulations having nothing to do with Internet openness—regulations never intended to apply to broadband service. The FCC's action reflected a sudden about-face from the approach the agency had proposed in mid-2014. The change in course, which shifted from a light-touch approach that would have protected Internet openness, was driven first and foremost by aggressive intervention on the part of President Obama and, according to press reports, his top aides.[21]

Background

Debates over the regulatory treatment of broadband Internet access have focused on two separate but intertwined issues: the appropriate legal classification of broadband service and the proper role, if any, of "net neutrality" requirements (i.e., disclosure mandates and limitations on an ISP's ability to block, speed up, or slow down Internet traffic). The classification issue extends back to the 1980s, when the FCC differentiated between services involving the mere transmission of information (which it called "basic" offerings) and those that involved both transmission and processing of information (which it called "enhanced" offerings). In the Telecommunications Act of 1996 (hereafter referred to as the 1996 Act),[22] Congress codified slightly different concepts, using the term "telecommunications service" to refer to basic transmission services that were sold to the public,[23] which has generally been interpreted by the commission and the courts as meaning on a common carrier basis (i.e., sold to a wide class of users on a non-discriminatory basis). The 1996 Act defined the term "information service" to describe a "capability for generating, acquiring, storing, transforming, processing, retrieving, utilizing, or making available information via telecommunications."[24]

In a 1998 report to Congress, the commission (led by Bill Kennard, the second chair appointed by President Clinton) explained that ISPs "conjoin the data transport with data processing, information provision, and other computer-mediated offerings, thereby creating an information service."[25] In 2002, the agency formally adopted this view, determining that cable modem service was an integrated information service and not the bundled provision of distinct transmission (telecommunications service) and processing (information service) components.[26] In 2005, the Supreme Court upheld this approach in its landmark *Brand X* decision,[27] prompting the FCC to extend the "integrated information service" classification to wireline, wireless, and powerline-provided broadband service.[28] Although the agency briefly considered reclassifying broadband Internet access as the bundled provision of telecommunications service and information service in 2010, it quickly backed away.[29]

The related debate over "net neutrality" dates to an address by FCC Chair Michael Powell, who in 2004 articulated four "Internet Freedoms." Consumers, Powell argued, should (1) have access to their choice of legal content, (2) be able to run applications of their choice, (3) be permitted to attach any devices they choose to their home connections, and (4) receive meaningful information regarding their service plans.[30] The following year, the FCC adopted a non-binding "Policy Statement" largely tracking these freedoms.[31] In 2008, the agency issued a decision purporting to enforce the Policy Statement against an ISP that had (the FCC argued) violated its precepts, but the U.S. Court of Appeals for the D.C. Circuit struck down that decision in 2010, finding that the FCC had failed to establish any appropriate legal basis on which it could justify its action.[32]

In December 2010, the FCC issued its first *Open Internet Order*.[33] That decision subjected wireline, cable, and fixed wireless ISPs to a no-blocking rule, a no-unreasonable-discrimination requirement, and a host of transparency mandates requiring disclosure of their network practices to consumers and Internet content providers. Mobile wireless providers were subject to a more limited no-blocking requirement and to the disclosure mandates, but not to the non-discrimination rule. These rules were not based on specific mandates within the Communications Act (though the agency did cite a collection of provisions meant to regulate voice and video services). Instead, the FCC focused on Section 706 of the 1996 Act, which directed the FCC to take actions removing "barriers to the deployment of infrastructure investment."[34] While the agency had previously viewed this provision as merely telling it what to do with its other statutory powers, it now interpreted it to afford the FCC independent regulatory authority, not found in other provisions and unrelated to removing barriers to deployment of infrastructure investment.

After broadband provider Verizon appealed the ruling (along with other providers that dropped out as the litigation progressed), the D.C. Circuit overturned the no-blocking and non-discrimination rules. In *Verizon v. FCC*, the court rejected Verizon's arguments that Section 706 did not provide any independent authority and that the net neutrality rules would not promote broadband deployment.[35] The court then considered whether the no-blocking and non-discrimination rules were nevertheless unlawful because they treated ISPs as common carriers, in direct violation of Communications Act language to the contrary.[36] The court distinguished the network neutrality rules at issue from the FCC rules governing data roaming, which allows one mobile wireless carrier to use another's network to serve its customers.[37] The data roaming rules had not barred all unreasonable discrimination but had simply required that carriers interact with others on "commercially reasonable" terms; in a previous decision, the D.C. Circuit had found that those rules did not impose common carrier requirements.[38] The net neutrality rules, on the other hand, gave ISPs far less latitude. They therefore were common carrier requirements and unlawful.[39] The court left the transparency rule, which did not impose common carrier requirements, in place.[40]

Following the court's *Verizon* decision, Chair Tom Wheeler stated that the court had provided a "roadmap" for the adoption of sustainable open Internet rules—one grounded in retaining broadband Internet access's classification as an information service.[41] The Notice of Proposed Rulemaking (NPRM) that the FCC adopted in May 2014 followed this path, proposing retention of the information service designation and reliance on Section 706.[42] The NPRM tentatively concluded that mobile broadband services should continue to be subject to a distinct set of open Internet rules reflecting the unique technical and market characteristics of such service and that the arrangements by which ISPs and other networks interconnected should not be addressed in any new open Internet decision.[43]

The President's Role

While parties drafted and filed comments on the FCC's proposal following the May 2014 NPRM, "an unusual, secretive effort" commenced "inside the White House," aimed at defeating the FCC's Section 706 proposal and attempting to impose instead a regime that reclassified broadband service and treated it as a public utility.[44] Senior White House aides, "[a]cting like a parallel version of the FCC itself," developed an alternative approach, in consultation with activists and representatives from Internet companies. White House staffers were told "not to discuss the process openly."[45]

On November 10, 2014, in a YouTube video and a press statement issued while he was in China, a country noted for an Internet lacking basic freedoms, the President publicly proposed the plan that his staff had developed during its parallel process. Repudiating both Chair Wheeler's May proposal and another approach that Wheeler had reportedly favored less than a week before, the President announced, "I believe the FCC should reclassify consumer broadband service under Title II of the Telecommunications Act—while at the same time forbearing from rate regulation and other provisions less relevant to broadband services."[46] (The Communications Act allows the FCC to "forbear" from enforcing certain statutory provisions or rules when it finds, based on statutorily prescribed requirements, that the mandates are no longer necessary.[47])

Although he acknowledged that the FCC "is an independent agency," he asked that the FCC "implement the strongest possible rules to protect net neutrality." These "bright-line rules" included (1) a new no-blocking rule; (2) a "no throttling" rule prohibiting ISPs from intentionally slowing down or speeding up content; (3) increased transparency requirements; and (4) an explicit ban on "paid prioritization"—a hypothetical practice in which an ISP would charge a content provider to prioritize that provider's content over other providers' content.[48] Whereas the FCC had proposed to continue subjecting mobile ISPs to different requirements than fixed ISPs, the President argued that "the FCC should make [its net neutrality] rules fully applicable to mobile broadband."[49] And while the agency had proposed to exclude interconnection between ISPs and other networks from the scope of its order, President Obama asked the FCC to "to apply net neutrality rules to points of interconnection between the ISP and the rest of the Internet . . . if necessary."[50]

According to the *Wall Street Journal*, the White House effort had "boxed in Mr. Wheeler," who was forced to "[line] up behind Mr. Obama."[51] The same day as President Obama's announcement, Wheeler issued a statement thanking the President for his input and explaining that the agency would be unable to issue a final order in December, as had been expected. "The more deeply we examined the issues around the various legal options," he explained, "the more it has become plain that there is more work to do."[52] Reclassification, he noted, "raise[s] substantive legal questions," as well as "policy issues that run the gamut from privacy to universal service to the ability of federal agencies to protect consumers."[53] It was clear that Chair Wheeler's proposal to retain the "information services" classification would not prevail.

The Result

On February 26, the FCC adopted its 2015 *Open Internet Order*, which largely tracked the President's proposal (and, accordingly, departed dramatically from the framework on which the FCC had sought comment).[54] Consistent with the President's request, the FCC reclassified broadband Internet access as a telecommunications service subject to common carrier regulation. The FCC also used its forbearance authority to peel away certain requirements (though it left in place a great many mandates).[55] Just as the President had requested, the agency adopted a new no-blocking rule, a "no throttling" rule, increased transparency requirements, and an explicit ban on "paid prioritization."[56] As the President had requested, the agency opted to subject mobile providers to the same set of requirements as fixed providers. And as the President had asked, the FCC changed course and opted to regulate Internet interconnection.[57] Rationalizing the commission's abdication to the President, network neutrality advocate and former Special Assistant to President Obama Susan Crawford stated, "[T]he FCC, although an independent agency, can read the President's speeches like everyone else, sense the change in the wind, and act accordingly."[58] The agency, in her words, appears to be one that makes decisions not based on law, existing regulations, its expertise, court decisions, or a public record compiled through its public notice; rather, the FCC could and even should make decisions based on the "change in the wind" coming from the White House.[59] That is hardly the description of an independent agency.

* * *

President Obama's intervention in the *Open Internet* matter played a central role in dramatically shifting the FCC's course—from a light-touch regime consistent with well over a decade worth of bipartisan consensus to a new, untested, and aggressive regime treating the Internet as a public utility. In every relevant respect, the FCC shifted course to align with the President's views—views developed in a secretive, parallel process bearing no relationship to the notice and comment process required by law. Moreover, the FCC's changed approach led to multiple appeals, filed by a broad array of industry groups and broadband providers—appeals that likely would have been avoided had the commission pursued the path laid out in the NPRM. These appeals, which could well find their way to the Supreme Court, are likely to require still further proceedings before the FCC as it works to cure the order's defects, further extending uncertainty in the broadband marketplace and harming consumer interests.

The President was able to intervene in the details of an independent agency's proceedings only because the chair and some of his fellow commissioners permitted him to do so. Although the President does not have the power to remove commissioners from office,[60] he does have the power to designate a different chair if one does not follow his suggestions.[61] The President also has the power to favor accommodating commissioners with the possibility of appointments to higher office and the power to withhold such appointments from the uncooperative.[62] In short, the President can exercise substantial influence over an independent agency whose commissioners are willing to be influenced.

MUNICIPAL BROADBAND: PREEMPTION OF STATE LAWS

On the same day it adopted its network neutrality rules and reclassified broadband Internet access, the FCC usurped state sovereignty over what powers they must give to towns and municipalities. Specifically, the FCC preempted state laws that imposed conditions on the deployment and operation of municipally owned broadband networks. Here, as in the other cases discussed in this chapter, the FCC's action was driven not primarily by the legal and policy arguments put forth during the public comment period, but rather by the President's expression of his views on this critical issue of state and federal power.

Background

In recent years, there has been increasing enthusiasm among some parties in the communications sector about the potential for government-owned and -operated broadband networks to compete with privately owned companies. Advocates of such "municipal broadband" networks assert that broadband service in the United States is lagging in terms of speeds, prices, and availability. Evidence, however, is to the contrary.[63] Advocates also argue that municipalities should be primary providers of a service that, in their view, is properly considered a public utility. Opponents of municipal broadband networks, on the other hand, point out that a number of these projects have not lived up to expectations, unnecessarily put taxpayer dollars at risk, undercut incentives for private-sector providers to invest in broadband infrastructure, and distract local governments from their core functions by diverting investments away from basic infrastructure such as schools or roads.

Fearing the potential harms associated with government broadband networks, various states (twenty-one as of June 1, 2014) have enacted laws restricting their localities' ability to build or operate such systems.[64] Some states require local officials to seek citizen approval of a municipal broadband project through a referendum. Other states have enacted "level playing field" requirements to ensure that municipal networks do not enjoy an unfair competitive advantage over private-sector providers.[65] Finally, some states have barred such networks altogether or have imposed population-based or other restrictions on the type of municipal entity that can provide broadband service.

Although the effect of these restrictions has been the subject of considerable debate, the D.C. Circuit's *Verizon* decision shifted the course of the discussion by suggesting to some that the FCC might have authority to invalidate these state laws. As detailed earlier, the *Verizon* Court held that Section 706 of the 1996 Act gave the FCC authority to regulate for the purpose of removing barriers to broadband infrastructure investment.[66] Writing in a separate opinion, Judge Laurence Silberman expressed his view that "[a]n example of a paradigmatic barrier to infrastructure investment would be state laws that prohibit municipalities from creating their own broadband infrastructure to compete against private companies."[67]

Judge Silberman's opinion was pure *dicta* and overlooked two important legal barriers to the use of Section 706 to preempt state laws regarding government broadband networks. First, Section 706 is an instruction equally to *both* the FCC *and* state commissions, not just to the FCC. If the purpose of Section 706 were related to preemption—as opposed to the statutory language of removing barriers to infrastructure investment with specific examples given—it would only instruct the FCC. Second, preemption is nowhere mentioned in the text of Section 706. An attempt by the FCC to preempt state-imposed municipal broadband restrictions pursuant to Section 706 could violate the "clear statement" rule articulated by the Supreme Court in *Gregory v. Ashcroft* (1991).[68] An aspect of this principle requires courts to "start with the assumption that the historic police powers of the States were not to be superseded by the Federal Act unless that was the clear and manifest purpose of Congress."[69] Third, in its 2004 decision in *Nixon v. Missouri Municipal League*,[70] the Supreme Court concluded that Section 253 of the act did not empower the FCC to preempt a Missouri law prohibiting municipal telecommunications service. Although the *Nixon* decision addressed the FCC's preemption authority under Section 253 and not Section 706,[71] its core reasoning highlights the problem inherent in *any* regime permitting federal preemption of state municipal broadband legislation: federal preemption cannot *create* local authority where none had previously existed.[72] The FCC cannot *require* a state to give particular powers to localities, which are wholly creatures of state law.

Notwithstanding these legal barriers, municipal broadband advocates took Judge Silberman's offhand remark as the hook they were looking for. Chair Wheeler and President Obama proved to be willing partners. Several months after the D.C. Circuit's decision, in June 2014, Chair Wheeler choreographed the shift in federal policy after a visit to Chattanooga, Tennessee.[73] Municipal broadband advocates regard Chattanooga's municipal broadband system—operated by the city's municipal electric utility, the Electric Power Board of Chattanooga (EPB), and subsidized by local ratepayers and by both federal and state taxpayers and untaxed entities—as the "poster child" for municipally owned networks. Today, customers within EPB's electric service territory have the option of subscribing to gigabit-per-second Internet service. However, EPB has not been able to offer its broadband and video services to residents in surrounding areas because of a territorial restriction under Tennessee law.[74] Following his trip to Chattanooga, Chair Wheeler telegraphed that he was amenable to an approach in which the FCC preempted state limitations on government broadband networks and indicated his willingness to use an FCC response to a petition as the vehicle to address the issue. In a blog published on the FCC's website, Wheeler wrote, "I believe that it is in the best interests of consumers and competition that the FCC exercises its power to preempt state laws that ban or restrict competition from community broadband. Given the opportunity, we will do so."[75] Six weeks later, EPB responded to Chair Wheeler's invitation by filing a petition asking the FCC to strike down the Tennessee law.[76] In an apparently coordinated move, the City of Wilson, North Carolina, filed a separate petition with the FCC the same day seeking preemption of restrictions in that state.[77]

The President's Role

While the EPB and City of Wilson petitions were still pending before the FCC, the administration weighed in on the preemption issue. On January 13, 2015, shortly before the President's State of the Union address, the White House issued a report entitled "Community-Based Broadband Solutions"[78] and a related "fact sheet."[79] In its report, the administration asserted that many consumers in the United States either lack access to or do not have a meaningful choice among high-speed broadband connections.[80] To increase consumer choice, the White House called for a policy response that encourages municipal broadband deployments.[81]

The following day, at the headquarters of Cedar Falls Utilities (a municipal broadband provider in Iowa), President Obama formally announced his support for the EPB and City of Wilson petitions. The President stated,

> I believe that a community has the right to make its own choice and to provide its own broadband if it wants to. . . . And if there are state laws in place that prohibit or restrict these community-based efforts, all of us—including the FCC, which is responsible for regulating this area—should do everything we can to push back on those old laws.

The administration also submitted a letter to the FCC urging the commission "to utilize its authority to address barriers inhibiting local communities from responding to the broadband needs of their citizens."[82]

There is no economic evidence that government-provided services, such as those in the communications sector, can be delivered at a lower cost or higher quality than privately provided services. Most economic theory, and the empirical evidence of approximately a century of failed socialist experience around the world, yields the exact opposite conclusion. The United States under President Clinton led an international effort to explain the benefits of private enterprise over government-owned enterprises under failed postal-telegraph government bureaucracies. President Obama still sought to have America revert to government ownership of communications services where every other country in the world had utterly failed.

The Result

On February 26, 2015, the FCC voted along party lines to effectuate President Obama's directive, relying on Section 706 to grant EPB's petition in its entirety and largely granting the City of Wilson's petition. In so doing, the FCC sought to distinguish *Gregory* and *Nixon* through a bizarre analytical construct. The FCC's core finding was that, whereas the commission may preempt state laws that *regulate* municipal broadband service, it may not preempt state laws that flatly *prohibit* municipal broadband service.[83] In dissent, Commissioner Ajit Pai pointed out that this distinction "does not make any sense" and "leads to an exceptionally strange result," in that "once the people's elected representatives allow municipalities to offer any Internet service at all, the camel's nose owns the tent."[84] As of this writing, Tennessee's Attorney General has appealed the FCC's order to the United States Court of Appeals for the Sixth Circuit, and the National Association of Regulatory Utility Commissioners (which represents state public service commissions) has intervened in support of Tennessee's appeal.[85]

E-RATE: A MASSIVE EXPANSION OF A CONSUMER-FUNDED SUBSIDY

In December 2014, the FCC voted to increase the size of its "E-Rate" subsidy mechanism, under which fees paid by telecommunications users are used to provide improved communications services to schools and libraries, by a whopping 62 percent, from a maximum of $2.4 billion per year to $3.9 billion per year.[86] The commission sought to transition the E-Rate program from the dial-up era to better support broadband-enabled digital learning. There are, however, serious questions about whether such a massive spending increase, funded by increases in consumers' monthly phone bills, was necessary to achieve that goal. Moreover, as economists have often observed, the fee structure to pay for the E-Rate program is inefficient and punishes consumers.[87] And, as in the other cases discussed in this chapter, the FCC's move to expand the E-Rate program was undertaken at the direction of the White House.

Background

The Telecommunications Act of 1996 charged the FCC with adopting policies to ensure that consumers in all regions of the nation have access to advanced telecommunications services. Among other things, Congress required the FCC to ensure that all schools and libraries had access to such services "for educational purposes at rates less than the amounts charged for similar services to other parties."[88]

Implementing this congressional directive, the FCC created the E-Rate program in 1997, establishing multiple categories of services that schools and libraries could purchase at a discounted rate subsidized by the program, which was funded by telecommunications consumers. The FCC capped annual E-Rate expenditures at $2.25 billion until 2010, when it voted to index the cap to inflation.[89] Before its most recent expansion, the E-Rate program was capped at just over $2.4 billion.[90]

The President's Role

Early in his second term, President Obama realized that the FCC was a convenient tool available to advance his educational platform. Soon thereafter, the FCC began to move in lockstep with the President. On June 6, 2013, President Obama launched the ConnectED Initiative, an effort to "connect 99 percent of America's students to the Internet through high-speed broadband and high-speed wireless within 5 years."[91] Of course, even by the FCC's own 2008 estimates, the vast majority of American households had access to two or more competitive broadband providers.[92] No doubt, most schools and libraries had broadband access as well. The press release announcing the plan noted that the President was "calling on the FCC to modernize and leverage its existing E-Rate program to meet that goal."[93]

In addition, the fact sheet accompanying the President's announcement stated that he was "further directing the federal government

[FCC] to make better use of existing funds to get this technology into classrooms."[94] During the press conference in which he announced that he was "directing the . . . FCC to begin a process" to reform the E-Rate program, the President added, "[and] for those of you who follow politics in Washington, here's the best news—none of this requires an act of Congress."[95] In response to a question, then White House spokesman Josh Earnest denied that this was an end run around Congress but told reporters that "the President has advocated and administrated the unilateral action to get this done. We're not going to wait for Congress to act."[96]

Just over a month later, the FCC issued a 175-page proposal to reform the E-Rate mechanism. Although the FCC's proposal was months in the making, and largely had been developed well before the President announced his ConnectED Initiative, the agency's acting chair at the time, Mignon Clyburn, tied it closely to the President's wishes: "[President Obama] announced his ConnectED initiative and called on the FCC to bring high-speed Internet to 99% of U.S. students within five years. Answering the President's call will require modernizing E-Rate."[97]

After the Senate approved President Obama's second-term FCC chair nominee, Tom Wheeler, he too began to emphasize his alignment with the administration on E-Rate reform.[98] Using the same language as the President, Chair Wheeler stated in a January 2014 blog post, "I am firmly committed to meeting the goal of connecting 99 percent of America's students to high-speed broadband within five years."[99] Only four days later, in his 2014 State of the Union address, the President said, "Last year, I also pledged to connect 99 percent of our students to high-speed broadband over the next four years. Tonight, I can announce that with the support of the FCC . . . we've got a down payment to start connecting more than 15,000 schools and twenty million students over the next two years."[100] Chair Wheeler issued a statement in response: "The Federal Communications Commission shares the President's commitment to seizing the opportunities of digital learning, which is why we've already launched an effort to modernize our successful E-Rate program—the nation's largest education technology program."[101] Four days later, the FCC issued a press release indicating that it would "invest an additional $2 billion over the next two years to support broadband networks in our nation's schools and libraries," "represent[ing] a doubling of investment in broadband."[102] These figures represent 40 percent of public school children and a large percentage of all school children.[103] The administration makes no representation that the 20 million students in 15,000 schools had no access to broadband services. Using the White House talking points, Chair Wheeler said, "[t]his investment is a down-payment on the goal of 99 percent of America's students having high-speed Internet connections within five years."[104] The *New York Times* described the announcement as "an effort to meet President Obama's promise to provide broadband service" for schools.[105] Indeed it was.

The choreographed rollout was completed two days later in a speech in which Chair Wheeler stated that "E-Rate modernization is at the top of my agenda and why I support President Obama's goal of connecting 99 percent of all students to high-speed broadband capacity in five years—or faster. . . . The President has set the goal of, within five years, connecting 99 percent of America's students to digital learning opportunities through high-speed broadband in their schools and libraries. I subscribe to that goal."[106]

The Result

Over the next ten months, the FCC adopted two orders that together implemented President Obama's vision, including a massive increase in spending paid for by taxes on consumers. In July 2014, just months before mid-term congressional elections, the FCC approved an order adopting goals and rule changes designed to ensure affordable access to high-speed broadband, maximize the cost-effectiveness of spending for E-Rate-supported purchases, and improve the overall administration of the program.[107] Notably, the agency elected not to raise the spending cap at that time. For that step, it waited until just *after* the elections: In December 2014, the commission adopted a second order, setting out major new policy changes and increasing the annual spending cap from $2.4 billion to $3.9 billion.[108] Both orders were adopted in partisan 3–2 votes.

Republican Commissioner Pai took Democratic Chair Wheeler to task for the blatantly political nature of the process:

> [W]e're discussing whether to spend an additional $1.5 billion each year to pay for the promises made last summer. That's a $7.5 billion

> payoff over five years for the entrenched interests that thrive under the bureaucratic yoke of today's E-Rate program. That's a 17.2% telephone tax increase for American families that are still struggling to make ends meet in this lackluster economy. . . . It's no accident that a spending increase was promised *before* the election and the tax increase to pay for it is coming *after* the election.[109]

There is, to be sure, room for debate about the policy choices that were made throughout the E-Rate modernization process, including whether or not such a sizable increase in the spending cap was warranted. What cannot be ignored, however, is the consistent presence of the Obama administration looming over the FCC and directing it at every step of the process. The E-Rate program is by far the largest federal program providing support for school broadband connectivity. It is also a program administered by a purportedly independent agency not under the control of the White House. Yet it is clear that the E-Rate modernization effort and its 17.2 percent tax increase on consumers reflected yet another instance of FCC decision-making designed to fulfill the policy preferences of the Obama administration, and undertaken in close coordination with the President's staff. Here again, we see an FCC that is acting less as an independent agency and more as an Executive Branch entity.

* * *

Montesquieu, Madison, and other advocates of the separation of powers might not have approved of the nineteenth- and twentieth-century development of independent agencies such as the FCC in the American government. Combining the powers of the three principal branches of government, independent agencies have suffered the shortcomings political philosophers have long predicted.

Independent agencies such as the FCC have political tendencies. As the discussion in this chapter indicates, the current FCC too often has departed from the intended role of an independent agency and acted instead as an arm of the Executive Branch, seeking first and foremost to implement the President's demands. Even absent corrections in the courts, which are sure to come with regard to at least some of these matters, the political allegiance to the Executive Branch undermines the commission's credibility as an independent, expert institution.[110] To restore this credibility, the FCC must return to the vision articulated by Justice Sutherland, under which an independent agency is "non-partisan," acts "with entire impartiality," and eschews "political [and] executive" activities, instead choosing to "exercise the trained judgment of a body of experts appointed by law and informed by experience."[111] Justice Sutherland's prescription would not remedy all of the maladies from the FCC's combination of the powers of government, but it would go far toward restoring its patina of independence.

10.

PROMOTING SMALL BUSINESS CAPITAL FORMATION
The Promise of Venture Exchanges

Daniel M. Gallagher and Troy A. Paredes[1]

I. WHY SMALL BUSINESS MATTERS

Small business is the lifeblood of our economy. Even today's largest companies—household names like Ford, GE, Microsoft, and Google—can trace their origins to entrepreneurs and innovators who turned their nascent ideas into thriving enterprises. The success of every business depends on the hard work, imagination, and determination of individuals. But that's not all. The success of a business also depends on its ability to raise capital.

We believe that the U.S. Securities and Exchange Commission (SEC), as the federal agency charged with facilitating capital formation, needs a "growth agenda" to ease overreaching regulatory burdens and dictates that hold back small business. The SEC has a three-part mission: to protect investors; to maintain fair, orderly, and efficient markets; and to facilitate capital formation. Too often, the goal of capital formation is downplayed, if not outright overlooked, as the SEC imposes intrusive and burdensome regulations on businesses in the name of "investor protection." Indeed, a "more-regulation-is-better-than-less" perspective seems to prevail at times, as if regulation, even when well intentioned, does not regularly disadvantage investors. Regrettably, this leads to the kind of regulatory overreach that stifles capital formation—particularly for small business, which is less able to bear the fixed costs of regulatory burdens—and cuts off investment options for investors. Pursuit of a growth agenda for small business would recognize the value of capital formation for issuers and investors alike. The regulatory change we advance in this essay would help bring the SEC back into alignment with its capital formation mission, eliminating at least one of the impediments to growth that results when regulation goes too far.

Small business, whether it remains small or turns into a Fortune 500 company, benefits society. Small business provides opportunities to entrepreneurs and business owners by allowing them to achieve their dreams, to employees by creating jobs, to consumers by innovating new products, to suppliers by giving them new buyers, and to investors by allowing them to support businesses they believe in. The following amplifies our perspective.

First, behind each small business is an entrepreneur—an individual with an idea that he or she hopes to turn into a reality. Often, entrepreneurs create something entirely new. Other times, they take another's idea and make it more effective, less complicated, or more efficient. These days, entrepreneurs are taking age-old goods and services and overlaying new technology to revolutionize them. The phone in your pocket, for example, allows you to do so much more than talk to a friend or even take a photo.

This entrepreneurial spirit and drive reinforces the virtues of innovation, tenacity, self-reliance, and self-discipline that move an economy—indeed, a society—forward. Especially appealing is the fact that entrepreneurism is democratic rather than aristocratic. It gives all of us the opportunity to pursue our dreams and to chart a path for ourselves based on the merits of our ideas and the effort we invest in pursuing them—provided, of course, that entrepreneurs have access to capital at critical points to develop the business.

Second, small business creates jobs. New, growing businesses require more employees. It is no surprise, then, that they create a disproportionate number of jobs in the United States.[2] Employees not only benefit from having a steady paycheck, but they may also share in the upside of the company's growth through stock or other incentive awards. Increased employment, in turn, drives increased demand for goods and services across the economy.

Third, small business innovation creates new goods and services that increase our standard of living. New and emerging companies might spot a targeted market opportunity—a niche that is not occupied, or that is underserved, by existing companies—and be nimble enough to exploit it. Other start-ups aim to be disruptors—turning an existing market on its head. Sometimes the change is even more pronounced as consumers come to depend on a new good or service as part of their daily lives in a way that they never could have imagined. Such innovations do not just disrupt a market; they *create* one.

Even when the benefits are merely incremental, they are beneficial. For example, an entrepreneur may open a new dry cleaner or bakery, which makes life a little easier or tastier for people in the neighborhood. At the other end of the spectrum, the benefits from small business can be revolutionary, such as when a biotech start-up discovers a new drug to cure a disease or when a few friends in a dorm room come up with a new way for us to access information and communicate with each other. Whether the benefits simply make life a little more convenient or enjoyable day-to-day or more fundamentally transform how we live, society is better off.

Fourth, as small businesses grow, they challenge incumbent businesses to run themselves more efficiently and to invest more in research and development. To stay ahead of innovative competitors, larger companies must continue to come up with and commercialize new ideas. Small business, in other words, spurs big business to be more creative and entrepreneurial. Incumbent businesses that do not meet the challenge risk being displaced: the creative destruction of capitalism in action.[3] The benefits of such competition are well known: better products, lower prices, and an overall more dynamic economy that can anticipate and respond to consumers' interests and society's needs.

Fifth, and perhaps most importantly to the SEC, small business is good for investors.[4] New and emerging enterprises provide investors with a wider range of investment options and the chance to earn substantial returns by backing small companies with a lot of growth potential.

Put in terms of the SEC's mission, giving investors the opportunity to invest in small business is not just consistent with investor protection—it *is* investor protection. Investor protection is not just about protecting investors from fraud, manipulation, and other abuses. It is about enabling investors to succeed. Even as it is essential for investors to be appropriately safeguarded from wrongdoing, it is also essential to recognize that investors are better off when they are offered more investment choices.

Yes, investing in small companies and other new businesses has its risks, but there is no reward without taking some risk. Provided that misconduct is properly policed, risk alone is not grounds for the SEC or any other government agency to stop investors from investing in businesses they believe in. "Merit review"—the process of the government picking winners and losers by passing judgment on the merits of a company and its offering—was rejected long ago, and for good reason, when the federal securities laws were initially crafted.

Capital formation is the basic mechanism by which we achieve all of these benefits—that is to say, by which we live better lives and, we would add, by which the U.S. maintains its competitive edge. Without the ability to efficiently raise the capital they need to get off the ground and prosper, new and emerging companies cannot produce their goods and services, invest in research, expand their facilities, hire employees, compete aggressively, and generate wealth for American investors. Indeed, in the U.S., the vast majority of business financing comes through capital markets, rather than through banks, making well-functioning capital markets critical to the success of small business.

With all the good that small business does, it is imperative that the SEC have a sharp focus on promoting capital formation for small business. The SEC has made some progress in recent years, but not enough. Much more can and must be done, and the commission must be willing to think outside the box. Accordingly, we recommend the promotion of "venture exchanges" as one promising component—not to the exclusion of other good ideas—of an SEC growth agenda comprising steps that make it easier for entrepreneurs and other small businesses to raise the capital they need to succeed.[5]

For venture exchanges to take root, the SEC will need to recalibrate its regulatory scheme to allow the marketplace flexibility to fashion a trading venue that focuses on the unique needs of smaller companies and their investors. Ensuring that regulation does not unnecessarily hinder economic growth is at the core of redressing regulatory overreach in economic matters, and that is what we strive for with our following recommendation.

II. CAPITAL FORMATION AND THE CURRENT REGULATORY STATE OF AFFAIRS (IN BRIEF)

The SEC's rules and regulations already contain many accommodations to ease the burden on small business. These accommodations have been adopted over the years, sometimes of the agency's own volition and sometimes only through Congress's compulsion. For example, SEC reporting requirements under the Securities Exchange Act of 1934 (the '34 Act) are scaled so that "smaller reporting companies" (generally, companies with under $75 million in float[6]) are exempt from particular financial statement reporting requirements[7] and other disclosure obligations[8] that larger companies must satisfy. Smaller companies also are given more time to prepare their quarterly and annual federal securities law filings[9] and are exempt from some especially burdensome requirements, like the requirement to have auditors attest to the effectiveness of internal controls under Section 404(b) of the Sarbanes-Oxley Act.[10]

Small business also can raise limited amounts of capital in offerings that are exempt from the regulatory demands of Section 5 of the Securities Act of 1933 (the '33 Act).[11] Rules 504 and 505 of Regulation D under the '33 Act permit private (i.e., unregistered) offerings of up to $1 million and $5 million, respectively.[12] Rule 506 of Regulation D permits private offerings of unlimited amounts to "accredited investors"[13] and is widely used by new and growing companies.[14] Regulation A has long permitted quasi-public offerings if certain tailored disclosure requirements are met.[15] The Jumpstart Our Business Startups (JOBS) Act of 2012 has made it easier for companies to avail themselves of Regulation D and Regulation A when seeking new capital.[16]

The JOBS Act ushered in two other significant reforms to promote small business capital formation. First, the legislation creates a new class of post-IPO company—emerging growth companies, or EGCs.[17] EGCs benefit from an "on-ramp" to the public markets that reduces disclosure and related burdens for these companies.[18] This IPO on-ramp reflects a congressional response to the concern that regulatory overreach under the federal securities laws has discouraged companies from going public—the specific concern being that too many companies have chosen to stay private to avoid the regulatory costs of being public, especially in the aftermath of the Sarbanes-Oxley Act. Notably, the commission could have (and should have) taken the lead in building an on-ramp to the IPO market without Congress having to force its hand, but it did not, despite its mission to facilitate capital formation. Congress had to step in. Second, the JOBS Act creates a framework for "crowdfunding": a mechanism for very small companies to fund themselves by tapping into a broad base of retail investors, each of which would make a small equity investment in the company. One can think of crowdfunding as leveraging the "wisdom of the crowd" to evaluate the merits of an investment.[19]

Despite these substantial efforts, more can and should be done by the SEC to promote small business. Making it easier for new and smaller companies—the drivers of so much prosperity in the U.S.—to access the capital they need to start up and to thrive should be a top SEC goal, but this has not been the case often enough.

To this end, the commission needs to embrace a holistic approach to small business capital formation. This holistic approach would be motivated by the principle that a small business, whatever its exact stage of development, should be able to access the capital it needs to innovate and grow.[20] The SEC, in turn, should scale back undue regulatory burdens and dictates that stifle entrepreneurs and emerging companies from raising the funds they need. Entrepreneurism should be open to everybody, including those who are not wealthy or well-connected and thus cannot fund their own dreams or tap into their professional or social networks for backing. And entrepreneurs and small business should not have to rely on borrowing from banks, which are not always willing to lend on terms that smaller companies and their founders can accept.

When it comes to fostering small business in particular, the SEC should have a flexible, innovative regulatory mindset attuned to the specific needs and wherewithal of new and emerging companies.

III. VENTURE EXCHANGES

While our discussion so far has focused on the initial issuance of securities (i.e., the sale of securities by a company to investors), secondary liquidity (i.e., aftermarket trading) in those securities is also important. Without question, the SEC needs to support the primary issuance of securities by making the capital-raising process itself less burdensome, costly, and time-consuming. But the commission cannot ignore subsequent trading of the securities that a company sells to raise capital. Investors may need or want to exit their investment for any number of reasons (e.g., education, retirement, illness, other investment opportunities) and may be reluctant to invest their money in the first place if they are not confident that they will be able to sell their holdings quickly and at a fair price. If investors are very concerned about the liquidity of their assets, they will demand an illiquidity discount in the value of the shares they do buy to compensate for the risk that they will not be able to sell easily. Promoting liquidity thus not only protects investors by ensuring that they can exit their positions efficiently; it also boosts the valuation of initial issuances, resulting in more capital being made available to companies in the first place. Put differently, secondary liquidity promotes capital formation.[21]

Regarding smaller companies, concerns about the lack of secondary liquidity have increased recently, ironically as a result of some of the reforms to facilitate primary issuances. For example, the JOBS Act raises the shareholder threshold at which a company that has not publicly issued securities must still register with the SEC and become subject to '34 Act mandatory reporting requirements.[22] While we support increasing the threshold so that companies can raise more capital privately without becoming subject to the costs and burdens of the '34 Act, it is axiomatic that the change in the threshold could result in companies staying private longer, with more and more shareholders holding restricted securities that they cannot readily resell. The problem is especially acute for start-ups and other growing enterprises because so many employees are granted stock, as compensation, that they may want to sell. A solution that we support, although it is not the subject of this essay, is to ease regulatory restrictions to encourage secondary liquidity for privately issued securities.[23]

A more pressing concern to some is that the revisions to Regulation A could result in a company issuing up to $50 million annually in shares using a scaled disclosure regime. While we support the Regulation A reforms, to the extent that revised Regulation A proves to be a success as a vehicle companies use to raise capital, the question is raised as to where those shares will trade. Shares issued in a Regulation A offering are freely tradable (i.e., they are not "restricted" like shares issued in a private placement) and can be held by non-accredited investors. The expectation is that the shares will likely trade in the over-the-counter (OTC) market. Furthermore, at least some of the smaller companies that use the JOBS Act IPO on-ramp to go public may have difficulty reaching the quantitative thresholds necessary to list shares on one of today's existing exchanges. These EGCs, too, may only have the option to trade OTC.

In theory, small and emerging companies that have issued shares publicly, including under Regulation A, could achieve an exchange listing.[24] Both of the current primary listing venues for corporate equities in the United States—NYSE and NASDAQ—have scaled requirements for listing small cap companies.[25] But the regulatory requirements and listing standards when going public and trading on one of these small cap markets are still costly and burdensome for small companies to meet and maintain.[26] Indeed, the regulatory costs and burdens of being a public company can stifle the IPO market by discouraging a company from going public in the first place, although the IPO on-ramp has been very helpful. Moreover, these small cap stock markets are characterized by the same basic market structure on which the entire U.S. equities market is based; and, as we explain further on, we are concerned that the structure of today's equity markets may not be particularly conducive to smaller companies. The bottom line is that for a small company, the costs and burdens of issuing shares to the public and listing on one of the current exchanges may not be worth it.

As a result, today's secondary markets are largely binary: a company that goes public can seek to be listed on an exchange—a status which, despite its benefits, results in the imposition of substantial regulatory burdens—or it can trade OTC. Small and emerging companies need another option.[27] What might that option be? Especially promising are so-called venture exchanges, where listing is less costly and burdensome and where the market structure can be tailored to promote the creation and martialing of liquidity for small companies. Venture exchanges would be a middle ground between today's exchanges and the OTC market. In fashioning the scaled regulatory regime that would allow venture exchanges to take shape, one would need to scrub current exchange listing standards and SEC regulations to search for requirements that do not make sense for small companies. These are not hard to find. Despite the Administrative Procedure Act, the Paperwork Reduction Act, the Regulatory Flexibility Act, and other procedural protections that should constrain the commission from overreaching, regulations are often blanketed on all companies equally, notwithstanding the disproportionately costly impact for small business.[28] Even regulations that seem justified when adopted may become outmoded as circumstances change, or they may not be warranted in hindsight as benefits fail to materialize or costs come in higher than expected. A retrospective review that focuses on how key rules have affected small business would be instrumental in deciding how to reform the regulatory regime. This should include not just a rule-by-rule assessment but an evaluation of the cumulative burden of regulatory mandates.[29] By eliminating or tailoring listing standards and SEC regulations that do not stand up to a thorough cost-benefit analysis, we can allow small companies to list on a venture exchange.

So what would this regulatory construct look like? To begin, a venture exchange would be a national securities exchange: a new exchange registered with the SEC or a tier of an existing registered exchange. It would, among other things, have scaled listing standards, market surveillance obligations, SEC oversight, and price transparency. Like existing exchanges, it would be a place where any investor could transact—it would not be limited to institutions or wealthy individuals.[30]

In this short essay, we are unable to take up all of the operational, technological, and other features of a venture exchange that would need to be addressed; nor can we tackle every regulatory change that would be needed. Rather, we offer three of what may be several guiding features for shaping the needed regulatory reform to give venture exchanges a shot at making a real difference for small business capital formation.

First, the SEC must re-examine its long-standing view of equity market structure to make it work for venture exchanges. The current U.S. market structure is focused, if only implicitly, on trading in larger public companies. SEC rules, particularly the "national market system" regulatory regime adopted in 2005—or "Reg. NMS"—has resulted in computerized, highly interconnected trading venues that promote fast execution at the best price.[31] The data tell us that, when it comes to the performance of the U.S. equity markets, investors on the whole seem to be better off today than in the past, as it has never been easier or cheaper to transact and there is abundant competition among trading venues.[32]

What is not clear is whether things have translated into a marketplace that functions well enough for the listing and trading of small cap stocks.[33] When it comes to market structure, the most acute concern for small cap stocks is a lack of liquidity.[34]

The basics of market structure are fundamental to the discussion, and we believe that the absence of small cap liquidity is likely caused, at least in part, by the SEC's market structure rules being a poor fit for small and emerging companies. The fix, then, is for the rules to change so that venture exchanges have the flexibility to create a marketplace that focuses on enhancing liquidity in small cap shares.

Specifically, a venture exchange would be permitted to fashion its trading environment to aggregate and deepen liquidity for the smaller companies that trade there.[35] Today's market structure regulatory regime tends to disperse liquidity among different marketplaces.[36] For example, statutory "unlisted trading privileges" mean that the exchange that lists the security cannot keep all the trading in that security to itself; other exchanges are allowed to trade the security as well.[37] Reg. NMS, in turn, requires that orders be routed to the exchange with the best price available for execution. Venture exchanges would instead be permitted to elect to be exempt from these rules to concentrate trading in a small cap security on the exchange where the company lists. Similarly, venture exchanges could be allowed to require broker-dealers participating in the exchange to transact customer orders for stocks listed on the exchange on the exchange itself, rather than internalizing (i.e., trading against the broker's own inventory) or taking the order to an alternative trading system (an ATS or so-called dark pool).[38]

In addition, a venture exchange would be permitted to determine the characteristics of trading that occurs on the exchange. For example, rather than engaging in continuous trading, orders could be allowed to batch, with periodic auctions held to match outstanding buy and sell orders at specific points throughout the day.[39] And a venture exchange might be permitted to choose its own "tick size," or the increments in which shares trade, if the exchange determines that larger spreads would incentivize market making and thus increase liquidity.[40] Allowing venture exchanges or issuers, or both, the flexibility to compensate market makers and other liquidity providers is also worth considering.

These alternative market structure choices hold out the promise of creating a virtuous circle. Broker-dealers could be incentivized to make markets in a security, thus adding still more liquidity, if they know they can come to a single venue, display their bid, and ask, and that counterparties will execute against their position. This dynamic is especially important for enticing liquidity in otherwise low-liquidity names, which may stand in sharp contrast to the optimal market structure when it comes to higher-liquidity names, where the ability to trade in competing venues can give rise to important investor benefits without compromising liquidity to any appreciable degree. The broker-dealers quoting in the stock of small and emerging companies trading on a venture exchange, as well as those underwriting new issuances, may also be interested in writing research on the stocks they trade or underwrite, which would directly benefit the investing public, particularly retail investors who are more likely to read research than dense, turgid corporate filings.[41]

Second, a venture exchange would be a national securities exchange, and thus state law registration and qualification requirements for the purchase and sales of securities would be preempted for listed shares.[42] To date, preemption of state "blue sky" regulation has been limited to offerings on the NYSE, AMEX, or NASDAQ's national market, or on national securities exchanges with "substantially similar" listing standards. This latter point has historically been interpreted quite strictly, with the commission requiring listing standards very similar to the main exchanges.[43] The SEC can do it differently: even though a venture exchange's listing standards might depart from those of one or more of the named exchanges, the venture exchange's listing standards should nonetheless be found to meet the requirements for blue sky preemption if they are scaled appropriately for smaller companies.[44] Similarly, listing shares on a national exchange currently triggers the same periodic reporting requirements for all companies, regardless of size, subject to only a handful of exceptions.[45] This is also unnecessary: the SEC has the authority to subject venture-exchange-listed companies to a more tailored reporting regime, such as the semiannual, scaled periodic disclosure requirements required of issuers under recently adopted Tier 2 of Regulation A.[46] This accommodation for Regulation A issuers may serve as a useful model for a tailored reporting regime for other small companies seeking to do an IPO. Whether the Regulation A model or another model is pursued, we would welcome further scaling of the registration requirements of the '33 Act and the ongoing disclosure requirements of the '34 Act for smaller public companies—continuing the important work that began with the IPO on-ramp of the JOBS Act.[47] Undue regulation should not be the reason a viable company chooses to remain private and forgo the capital-raising and liquidity benefits of trading publicly.

As for a venture exchange's listing standards, they would be scaled as well. This would include lifting certain corporate governance mandates that companies trading on the NYSE and NASDAQ must meet, many of which are rooted in the Sarbanes-Oxley Act. The goal of easing such listing standards, as well as certain quantitative standards relating to items such as share price and market value, is to address the concern that listing standards themselves may deter a smaller company from going public.[48] To be clear, venture exchanges would still have listing requirements, but we would expect them to strike a better cost-benefit fit for smaller companies by avoiding overly burdensome and prescriptive requirements that unjustifiably impede capital formation.[49] More to the point, there is no reason to adhere to the current listing standards as if they were etched in stone and inviolable.

Third, investor education is essential. Investors need to be aware that purchasing a venture-exchange-listed stock is very different from purchasing a stock listed on other exchanges, with different attendant risks as well as potential rewards. The SEC, the exchanges themselves, and others could help educate investors about what it means to invest in a venture-exchange-listed company. This could include informing investors of the nature of small cap companies, the SEC requirements the companies are subject to, the scaled listing standards on a venture exchange, and the effects of the market structure for small caps. Many investors still recall a time when the NYSE was where blue chips were listed and NASDAQ was home to upstart (at least by comparison to blue chip names) technology companies. As venture exchanges seek to build their brands, bring in high-quality companies for listing, and attract investors, we are optimistic that investors will become informed about what distinguishes venture exchanges from other trading venues. The SEC's Office of Investor Education and Advocacy could help by preparing alerts and other materials that highlight for retail investors the pros and cons of investing in a smaller company that trades on a venture exchange.[50] Specialized ticker symbols might also be worth considering as a way to indicate to investors that they should evaluate what is different about investing in a small cap company listed on a venture exchange.[51]

Some complain that venture exchanges are markets for lemons. Companies may list on venture exchanges because they are not seasoned enough to make it in the "big leagues," the critique goes. A disproportionate number of these companies go on to fail, and those that succeed will depart for one of the established exchanges as soon as they are able. These dynamics have been cited as contributing at least in part to the demise of one early attempt at creating a venture-type exchange, the American Stock Exchange's Emerging Company Marketplace.[52]

In one sense, this is exactly what one would expect from venture exchanges. Younger companies are more likely to fail, but with higher potential risk comes higher potential reward. And we should expect—and perhaps even *want*—companies to move up from a venture exchange tier when they are ready. One might even measure the success of a venture exchange by the number of companies that "graduate."[53] Venture exchanges might very well end up looking like a pipeline, with small companies taking the opportunity to grow and attract the capital that the venture exchange affords before making the jump to the main exchange.

So how do you solve (or at least substantially mitigate) the lemons perception? By ensuring that companies that fail do so based on the merits of the business, not because of fraud or deceit. Even as smaller companies may be burdened by fewer regulatory mandates when trading on a venture exchange, they should be subject to sound regulation and vigorous anti-fraud enforcement and sophisticated surveillance programs at the exchanges to monitor for signs of misbehavior. There should be no easing up on Rule 10b-5 or other anti-fraud provisions under the federal securities laws because a company trades on a venture exchange.

By striking the regulatory balances we call for in this essay, we believe that it is possible for venture exchanges to be seen as credible and legitimate venues where "good" companies want to list.

* * *

Small business is a critical part of the economic fabric of our country, and we have an obligation to make sure that these enterprises have access to the capital they need to innovate and grow. This requires the SEC to apply a small-business-focused mindset to ensure that its rules work for small business, rather than leaving them to struggle with unreasonably strict or inflexible rules that can snuff out the benefits of small business. Venture exchanges have the potential to overcome the challenges of the past and significantly improve trading in the securities of small and emerging companies. We are not saying that they are without risk; nor are we guaranteeing an outcome. We are saying that the SEC should pull back the overreach of current regulatory burdens and restrictions that stifle the innovation of venture exchanges as a listing and trading venue for smaller companies looking to raise capital. Simply put, the marketplace, not the government, should decide the ultimate viability of venture exchanges.

11.

EXECUTIVE OVERREACH
Dodd-Frank

C. Boyden Gray and John Shu[1]

I. WHAT IS DODD-FRANK?

The Dodd-Frank Wall Street Reform and Consumer Protection Act of 2010 and the entities it created provide examples of executive overreach in the financial regulatory arena.[2] The Democrats controlled both houses of the 111th Congress, which pushed Dodd-Frank into law, ostensibly in response to the financial crises of 2008 and 2009.[3] President Obama signed Dodd-Frank into law on July 21, 2010.[4] Many believe that Dodd-Frank is the most significant and complex legislation targeting the financial industry since the Securities Exchange Act of 1934.[5] Dodd-Frank's intent, according to its title page, is "[t]o promote the financial stability of the United States by improving accountability and transparency in the financial system, to end 'too big to fail,' to protect the American taxpayer by ending bailouts, to protect consumers from abusive financial services practices, and for other purposes."[6]

There are legitimate questions about whether the Dodd-Frank agencies are constitutionally organized,[7] whether the act delegates unlimited power to agencies, and whether the act grants litigants sufficient due process, as we discussed originally in a 2010 white paper.[8] We focus here on Executive Branch overreach under Dodd-Frank's aegis, because (1) the act grants its agencies broad rulemaking, interpretative, and discretionary authority beyond effective oversight of either Congress or the judiciary, (2) those agencies have improperly exceeded even those unprecedentedly expansive statutory limits, and (3) those agencies have ignored and/or not followed the law.

II. DODD-FRANK ENABLED IMPROPER EXECUTIVE BRANCH OVERREACH

Executive Branch overreach, or Executive overreach, is generally defined as when the President of the United States or an Executive Branch administrative agency acts or attempts to act in such a way that it exceeds its statutory powers or constitutional powers, or encroaches on the powers belonging to Congress, the judiciary, or the several states.[9] For example, on January 4, 2012, President Obama recess-nominated Richard Cordray as director of the Bureau of Consumer Financial Protection and three members to the National Labor Relations Board, even though the U.S. Senate was still in *pro forma* sessions.[10] Two years later, the U.S. Supreme Court ruled 9–0 that President Obama exceeded his authority; the President may not make recess appointments when the U.S. Senate is in *pro forma* sessions because the Senate alone determines whether it is in recess.[11] Senator Orrin Hatch (R-UT) commented when the Court released its opinion, "[t]oday, the Supreme Court emphatically rejected President Obama's brazen efforts to circumvent the Constitution, bypass the people's elected representatives, and govern above the law. . . . The Court has reaffirmed the Senate's vital advice-and-consent role as a check on executive abuses."[12]

National Labor Relations Board v. Noel Canning did not directly affect Director Cordray's recess appointment, because the Senate confirmed Director Cordray on July 16, 2013, and the Consumer Financial Protection Bureau (CFPB) subsequently purported to "ratify" all the actions which he took prior to his confirmation.[13] But because the CFPB refuses to rescind and re-promulgate the actions that the CFPB took during Cordray's unlawful appointment, those actions remain under a cloud of uncertainty.

Executive Branch agencies have existed since the beginning of the Republic. The Departments of War, State, Treasury, and Navy were America's first agencies. The Interstate Commerce Act of 1887, which President Grover Cleveland signed into law, created the Interstate Commerce Commission, America's first independent regulatory commission.[14]

President Franklin Delano Roosevelt, with his "New Deal," vastly expanded the federal government's programs, reach, and administrative agencies. In 1935 and 1936, the U.S. Supreme Court found much of the New Deal unconstitutional.[15] The Court changed direction in 1937, however, opening the floodgates for the modern administrative state.[16]

The CFPB, since it became active in July 2011, is the main example of agency overreach as a result of Dodd-Frank. The CFPB, by intentional design, (1) is massive and complex, (2) is insulated from meaningful review or oversight, and (3) has broad and pervasive authority. The CFPB, by statute and by its own volition, is now enmeshed in common aspects of everyday life, such as residential mortgages, student loans, and automobile financing. Perhaps the CFPB's most shocking examples of agency overreach, however, are its regulating issues, which Dodd-Frank specifically exempted from the CFPB's jurisdiction, and the CFPB's alleged racism, sexism, and ageism toward its own employees, which is symbolic of its structural unaccountability.

What Is the CFPB?

The CFPB is an administrative agency whose mandate is to "regulate the offering and provision of consumer financial products or services under the Federal consumer financial laws."[17] This means that it has the authority—or at least it asserts authority—to implement and enforce all consumer-related laws involving finance and credit, and thus the power to dictate credit allocation in the U.S. economy.[18] The CFPB has the power to administer, enforce, and implement federal consumer financial law with exclusive rulemaking authority, which means that it defines what products and conduct fall within its jurisdiction and enforces its own regulations.[19] The CFPB may exempt any entity, product, or service from its jurisdiction if the CFPB determines that the exemption is "necessary *or* appropriate."[20] Dodd-Frank requires the courts to give the CFPB extra deference regarding the meaning or interpretation of any provision of federal consumer financial law.[21] The act permits its own Financial Stability Oversight Council (FSOC) to set aside only a CFPB final regulation, if and only if the FSOC decides upon a two-thirds vote that the regulation in question endangers the U.S. banking or financial system.[22] The FSOC cannot overturn the CFPB's supervisory and enforcement actions or unofficial "guidance." Because the CFPB is one of the FSOC's ten voting members, this veto provision actually requires a seven-ninths supermajority of non-CFPB members, rendering this provision toothless.

CFPB's Structure

The CFPB is able to behave as if it were beyond effective oversight because, in part, Dodd-Frank made it so. The act intentionally housed the CFPB within the Federal Reserve, placing one protected entity (the CFPB) within another (the Fed), which essentially means that the CFPB is neither an executive agency nor an independent agency.[23] This structure was a political compromise, which Senator Bob Corker (R-TN) and Congressman Frank (D-MA), who originally envisioned a free-standing cabinet agency, managed.[24] In fact, Dodd-Frank shields the CFPB from Executive Branch management or oversight.[25]

Congress does not have the power of the purse over the CFPB because the CFPB director determines his own budget, which the Federal Reserve Board "shall transfer to the [CFPB] from the combined earnings of the Federal Reserve System."[26] Dodd-Frank specifically states that the CFPB's funds from the Federal Reserve System "shall not be subject to review by the Committees on Appropriations of the House of Representatives and the Senate."[27] Dodd-Frank further states that all monies "obtained by or transferred to the Bureau Fund [the Consumer Financial Protection Fund] shall not be construed to be Government funds or appropriated monies" and "shall not be subject to apportionment."[28] Those monies are solely "under the control of the [CFPB's] Director."[29]

The CFPB's current base budget amount is up to 12 percent of the Federal Reserve System's 2009 operating expenses.[30] From fiscal years 2010–2014, if the CFPB director, at his own discretion, felt that amount insufficient, Dodd-Frank authorized Congress to appropriate $200 million each year to the CFPB, totaling $1 billion.[31] Presumably Congress had oversight authority over that $200 million per year appropriation, although the act is unclear on that issue and pre-authorized the money.[32]

The CFPB reported that its fiscal year (FY) 2014 actual budget was more than $497.9 million, its FY2015 estimated budget is $582.0 million, and its FY2016 estimated budget is $605.5 million.[33] The CFPB, however, is entitled to receive up to $618.7 million for FY2015 and $631.7 million for FY2016.[34] Additionally, the CFPB director has wide discretion over the management, use, and disbursement of other monies, such as those in the Consumer Financial Civil Penalty Fund, which totaled $159.0 million at the end of FY2014 and is estimated to be $180.1 million at the end of FY2015.[35] For these reasons, the CFPB has boasted that it enjoys "full independence" from Congress.[36] In comparison, the FY2014 budget for the FTC's Bureau of Consumer Protection was $188 million, or less than two-fifths of the CFPB's budget.[37]

Most of the CFPB's budget is from the Fed, which also has no oversight or appropriations power over the CFPB.[38] For example, the Federal Reserve Board may not (1) intervene in *any* CFPB matter or proceeding, (2) appoint, direct, or remove any CFPB officer or employee, nor (3) merge or consolidate the CFPB or its functions and/or responsibilities with any part of the Federal Reserve Board or the Federal Reserve banks.[39] Furthermore, the Federal Reserve Board may not delay, prevent, or review any CFPB rule or order.[40] Dodd-Frank, in fact, states that the Fed may *delegate* to the CFPB the power to examine entities subject to the Federal Reserve Board's jurisdiction for compliance with the federal consumer financial laws.[41]

One example of the CFPB's poor monetary stewardship is its controversial renovation of headquarters, which it rents from the Office of the Comptroller of the Currency (OCC).[42] The renovation project's estimated cost jumped from $55 million in 2010 to $215.8 million in 2014, which calculates to nearly $600 per square foot.[43] CFPB management did not obtain CFPB Investment Review Board (IRB) approval, as CFPB guidelines require, before going ahead with the project.[44] In fact, CFPB management ignored IRB guidance.[45] CFPB officials repeatedly refused to answer basic questions before the U.S. House Financial Services Committee, such as identifying the person or persons who authorized the renovation project, because "the CFPB was unable to locate any documentation of the decision to fully renovate the building."[46] When Congresswoman Ann Wagner (R-MO) directly asked Director Cordray at a March 3, 2014, hearing, "Who signed off? Who gave the authorization?" with respect to the renovation project, he shot back, "Why does that matter to you?!"[47]

That is the way the head of an overreaching, unaccountable agency answers Congress, under oath.

CFPB's Wide-Ranging, "Abusive" Authority

One of the CFPB's stated objectives is to protect consumers "from unfair, deceptive, or abusive acts and practices and from discrimination."[48] The CFPB may halt a company or service provider from "committing or engaging in an unfair, deceptive, or abusive act or practice" with respect to offering or transacting in a consumer financial product or service.[49] In fact, Dodd-Frank makes it unlawful for consumer financial product companies or service providers to "engage in any unfair, deceptive, or abusive act or practice."[50] The act extends this liability to any entity that "knowingly or recklessly provide[d] substantial assistance" to the offender.[51]

Dodd-Frank does not define what constitutes an "abusive" act or practice, except to say that the CFPB cannot define something as "abusive" unless (1) it "materially interferes with the ability of a consumer to understand a term or condition of a consumer financial product or service," or (2) it takes "unreasonable advantage" of a consumer's "lack of understanding" of the "material risks, costs, or conditions of the product or service" or a consumer's "inability" to protect his own interests "in selecting or using a consumer financial product or service."[52] Dodd-Frank vests the CFPB with the sole discretion to interpret these terms, along with when and how they are applied to consumer financial products and services and the consumer financial industry as a whole.[53]

"Abusive," as used in the act, is not in any previous federal or state consumer protection statute. The term "abusive" also does not seem to include the concepts of deception or fraud, which would mean that the CFPB could declare illegal even products and services whose terms, conditions, risks, costs, and competitive alternatives are fully disclosed, so long as the CFPB labels them "abusive," even *after* the customer transaction is completed. Thus, one might say the act's legal standard is essentially "the CFPB will know it when it sees it," because each and every consumer has different abilities to understand a term, condition, material risk, and cost; and each and every consumer has varying levels of ability or desire to protect his or her own interests.

The CFPB, before issuing rules regarding unfair, deceptive, or abusive practices and acts, must "consult with the Federal banking agencies, or other Federal agencies, as appropriate, concerning the consistency of the proposed rule with prudential, market, or systemic objectives administered by such agencies."[54] The CFPB must perform cost-benefit analyses prior to issuing rules.[55] The CFPB must also follow the requirements of the Administrative Procedure Act when issuing rules.[56] These statutory requirements do not apply to the CFPB's "guidance" or enforcement actions.

Thus, on March 23, 2012, CFPB Director Cordray stated that he does not intend to make rules to define or set standards for what is "abusive" but instead will use enforcement actions to do so, which means that consumers and lenders will not know what the CFPB believes is "abusive" until the CFPB goes after the lender.[57]

The CFPB may also choose "favorites," given that it has the power to exempt entire classes of covered persons, service providers, consumer financial products, and consumer financial services from any of its rules.[58] It is not clear whether the CFPB must engage in cost-benefit analyses or consult with any other regulator or agency when issuing exemptions. Thus, the CFPB's charter, rulemaking authority, and enforcement power are so vast that the CFPB essentially has the power to self-determine which entities it affects and rewrite the consumer financial protection laws as it sees fit, instead of leaving that authority to only Congress.[59]

The CFPB, through enforcement actions, may "seek all appropriate legal and equitable relief including a permanent or temporary injunction as permitted by law."[60] It has its choice of weapons, including restitution, contract rescission or reformation, returning money or real property, compensation for unjust enrichment, paying damages, seeking monetary civil penalties, and enjoining a business from doing business.[61] The CFPB also has its choice of arenas: it may choose to sue in any federal district court or "any court of competent jurisdiction of a state in a district in which the defendant is located or resides or is doing business," or it may conduct an adjudication before its own administrative law judge, which gives the CFPB a home-turf advantage.[62]

CFPB Disregards Dodd-Frank's Motor Vehicle Dealer Exemption

Dodd-Frank § 1029 specifically exempts auto and other motor vehicle dealers from CFPB's jurisdiction.[63] The act maintains the Fed's and the FTC's respective preexisting responsibilities.[64]

The CFPB, however, (1) still wanted to regulate auto dealers;[65] (2) realized it could do so because all automobile leases and a significant percentage of automobile purchases involve a finance or insurance product; and (3) automobile dealers sell finance or insurance products that go even beyond purchase loans or leases, such as paint chip or tire wear and tear insurance, thus placing themselves under the CFPB's jurisdiction in the agency's eyes.[66]

Dodd-Frank's imprecise language again enables the CFPB to overreach. For example, the language of § 1029(b), "Certain Functions Excepted," which covers exceptions to the auto dealer exception, is unclear as to whether a dealer for a particular automobile manufacturer is considered to provide "retail credit or retail leases . . . directly to consumers" if they are done through the manufacturer's finance arm.[67] The language is also unclear as to whether an automobile manufacturer's finance arm is considered an "unaffiliated third party finance or leasing source" when their dealers naturally "routinely assign" retail credit and/or retail leases to the manufacturer's finance arm, especially because that finance arm often provides better interest rates and other conditions than other entities.[68]

On March 21, 2013, the CFPB issued a "bulletin" providing "guidance about compliance with the fair lending requirements of the Equal Credit Opportunity Act (ECOA) and its implementing regulation, Regulation B, for . . . all indirect auto lenders within the jurisdiction of the Consumer Financial Protection Bureau (CFPB)."[69] It revealed the CFPB's new interpretations of the ECOA, Regulation B, "indirect" lenders, and creditors.[70] Because a "bulletin" is not a "rule," the CFPB purports to avoid Dodd-Frank's and the APA's statutory rulemaking requirements; the bureau maintained secrecy about its plans, did not permit any outside input or comment, and did not provide lenders/creditors an implementation period to conform to the CFPB's new "standard," even though the bulletin essentially operated as a rule, which in and of itself is problematic.[71]

The bulletin also stated that it would not apply to "small" lenders, even though all lenders of all sizes are subject to the ECOA and Regulation B.[72] The CFPB's guidance bulletin essentially concluded that a lender may be held liable for a motor vehicle dealer's discriminatory practices *even if the lender had no actual knowledge of those practices*.[73] The CFPB used a theory of "disparate impact" and its own policy preferences to reach this conclusion, even though (1) neither the ECOA nor Regulation B has this standard, (2) the disparate impact theory never has been approved specifically in the ECOA context, and (3) the CFPB's March 2013 bulletin did not explain the required statistical data or methodologies the CFPB must use to identify such disparities.[74] Moreover, the CFPB announced its plan to use "disparate impact" *in a different bulletin*, once again not an actual rule.[75]

Generally speaking, a plaintiff may establish liability in a disparate impact claim without proof of intentional discrimination, so long as an identified business practice has a disproportionately adverse effect on certain protected classes of individuals and are unjustified by a legitimate rationale or not in sound business considerations.[76] Plaintiffs may not rely on statistical disparity alone; they must show that the defendant's policy or policies caused that statistical disparity.[77] For example, racial imbalance alone does not establish a *prima facie* disparate impact case.[78]

The CFPB's bulletin stated that, in its view, a potential ECOA violation occurs when a motor vehicle dealer's interest rates disparately impact a protected class of consumers based on race, color, religion, national origin, sex, marital status, age, receipt of public assistance income, or exercise of rights under the Consumer Credit Protection Act.[79] To get around the Dodd-Frank § 1029 exception, the CFPB essentially redefined "creditor" to include indirect lenders, thus bringing credit decisions within the CFPB's authority, such as (1) when a creditor evaluates an applicant's information, establishes a buy-rate, and then communicates that buy-rate to the dealer, indicating that it will purchase the obligation at the designated buy-rate if the transaction is consummated; or (2) when a creditor provides rate sheets to a dealer establishing buy-rates and allows the dealer to mark up those rates.

The CFPB's bulletin even helpfully "suggested," as Mario Puzo's Don Vito Corleone would have done,[80] ways for lenders and auto dealers to avoid liability, such as (1) monitoring and addressing the effects of markup policies as part of a "robust fair lending compliance program"; (2) imposing controls or otherwise revising dealer markup or "reserve" policies; (3) eliminating dealer discretion to mark up buy-rates; and (4) compensating dealers using a different mechanism, such as a flat fee per transaction.[81] The CFPB essentially instructed auto dealers and their lenders how the CFPB wanted them to conduct their businesses in order to minimize, but not eliminate, the chances of CFPB prosecution. The CFPB, in part because of its ability to shut down their businesses and inflict massive fines, made the auto dealers and their lenders an offer they could not refuse: comply with the CFPB's "suggestions" and "guidance," or die.[82] The CFPB's behavior is administrative agency overreach at its worst.[83] Even Senator Elizabeth Warren (D-MA), the CFPB's godmother, realized the weaknesses inherent in the CFPB's guidance bulletin: she called for Congress to give the CFPB specific authority to regulate automobile dealers and their lenders, which she would not have done if the CFPB's actions were on solid footing.[84]

The CFPB's overreaching behavior raised enough concerns that both Democrat and Republican House Representatives, in late May and late June 2013 respectively, demanded explanations from the CFPB; the CFPB sent a short response letter without providing substantial details.[85] Former CFPB assistant director Rick Hackett publicly questioned whether the CFPB had the legal authority to regulate automobile dealers and their lenders.[86]

After the CFPB extended its *enforcement* power, it needed a formal rule extending its *supervisory* authority over nonbank finance companies, such as automobile manufacturers' finance arms, as "larger participants" so that the CFPB could examine them, go through their accounting books and the like, including their advertising and marketing, payment processing, and other critical daily operations. Accordingly, in June 2015 the CFPB issued an actual rule doing just that.[87] The CFPB stated that it considered automobile manufacturers' finance arms to be "captive" nonbanks which "generally," but not always, do indirect lending.[88] The CFPB, on its own, declared as "larger participants," and thus within its supervisory and enforcement jurisdiction, "any nonbank auto finance company that makes, acquires, or refinances 10,000 or more loans or leases in a year," which essentially meant all of them.[89] In 2014 alone, auto manufacturers sold more than 16,500,000 new vehicles in the United States alone, which calculates to more than 1,375,000 new vehicles per month, and does not include the financed purchases of used or certified pre-owned vehicles.[90] The CFPB's June 2015 rule also redefined certain automobile leases in order to include them in those under the CFPB's expanded jurisdiction and authority.[91]

The CFPB's power grab, if allowed to continue, could have immense impacts. The automobile dealers and their lenders greatly fear the CFPB. Dodd-Frank permits the CFPB, through enforcement actions, to "seek all appropriate legal and equitable relief including a permanent or temporary injunction as permitted by law."[92] This includes recovery of its "costs," which the act does not limit only to legal costs—encompassing the aforementioned "choice of weapons."[93] As noted before, the CFPB has its choice of venues as well, from federal district courts to state district courts to the home-turf advantage of its own ALJ.[94] For example, a respondent must answer a CFPB complaint within fourteen days, and the CFPB's rules require only the Office of Enforcement, and no other, to disclose documents.[95] Discovery is very limited.[96] Only the hearing officer has the power to issue subpoenas, and he or she has full discretion.[97] CFPB administrative enforcement appeals are even more weighted in the CFPB's favor; the CFPB director is the sole appellate decision-maker, and he has unfettered discretion in managing the process and reaching his decision.[98] The CFPB's administrative hearing rules provide no applicable standard of review that the director must apply when reviewing the administrative law judge's decision.[99] The director, at any time prior to issuing the final decision, may raise and determine any other matters outside the scope of the issues specified in the notice(s) of appeal as long as the director deems the issues to be "material."[100]

On June 4, 2015, CFPB Director Cordray issued his first administrative enforcement appellate decision, in the matter of PHH Corporation.[101] It is indicative of how he, and perhaps future directors, will wield their practically limitless power.[102] He upheld in part and reversed in part ALJ Cameron Elliot's November 2014 recommended decision, which found that PHH Corporation, a mortgage lender, violated the Real Estate Settlement Procedures Act (RESPA), 12 U.S.C. §§ 2601–2617, when it accepted illegal reinsurance premium kickbacks for mortgage loans that closed on or after July 21, 2008.[103] In terms of dollar amount, Director Cordray increased ALJ Elliot's $6,442,339 penalty to $109,188,618, *a seventeen-fold increase.*[104] Director Cordray reached that dollar amount because he interpreted RESPA's liability attachment points and disgorgement requirements, and the accompanying case law, very differently than ALJ Elliot did.[105] He further imposed heavy injunctions on PHH, some lasting up to fifteen years.[106] He also issued an "unredacted version" of his decision "for the parties, and a redacted version for the public."[107] Director Cordray stated that he used a "preponderance of the evidence standard" and that his "review as to both facts and law is *de novo*," meaning that he gave the ALJ no deference at all.[108]

This decision is important because it establishes CFPB precedent for interpreting RESPA, handling future administrative proceedings and settlement demands, the breadth of disgorgement calculations (especially when consumer restitution is unavailable), and the applicability of existing case law and interpretative rules to the CFPB director's decision-making. As of the time of this writing, PHH has appealed to the D.C. Circuit.[109]

CFPB Allegedly Discriminated and Retaliated Against Minority, Women, "LGBTQ*," and Older Employees

As the *Washington Post* reported,[110] and as the House Financial Services Committee further detailed, the CFPB allegedly illegally discriminated and retaliated against its minority, women, "LGBTQ*," and older employees, even though it is supposed to protect these groups against predatory or discriminatory practices and acts.[111] The evidence shows that the CFPB's alleged discrimination and retaliation goes back to at least May 2012, if not earlier, less than a year after the CFPB went live in July 2011.[112] The CFPB's alleged discrimination and retaliation are terrible examples of an administrative agency ignoring the law, particularly the "authoritarian, untouchable, unaccountable, and unanswerable" managers at a structurally protected agency that sees itself as beyond oversight.[113]

CFPB employees allege that the CFPB continually violated the law, even after the employees and the U.S. Congress put the CFPB and its leadership on notice.[114] The U.S. House of Representatives Committee on Financial Services, Subcommittee on Oversight and Investigations held its most recent public hearing on the CFPB's alleged discrimination and retaliation on June 25, 2015.[115] At that hearing, Oversight and Investigations Subcommittee Chair Sean Duffy (R-WI) stated that (1) CFPB management discriminated and retaliated against employees based on "race, age, gender, and sexual orientation"; (2) the CFPB had "the worst track record" of all the federal financial regulatory agencies when it came to protecting its employees against discrimination; (3) the CFPB's *per capita* number of Equal Employment Opportunity (EEO) complaints is far higher than at other federal agencies; (4) the CFPB's Office of Equal Opportunity & Fairness, Office of Civil Rights, and Office of Minority & Women Inclusion are at "the heart of the problem"; and (5) "CFPB leadership refuses to take meaningful action to prevent this behavior and protect its employees," despite ample and repeated notice and warning.[116] In the first half of FY2015, compared to the FDIC, the OCC, and the Federal Reserve, the CFPB had the most EEO complaints, even though it has the fewest actual number of full-time (or equivalent) employees.[117]

The CFPB's minority, women, "LGBTQ*," and older employees accused the CFPB of favoring white males and creating a hostile work environment.[118] CFPB employees alleged that CFPB management systemically engaged in "bullying" and retaliated against employees who filed complaints, such as lowering performance ratings and thus preventing raises or promotions.[119] CFPB employees also claimed that CFPB human resources failed for months to respond to their formal complaints.[120] The CFPB hired an outside investigator, Misty Raucci of the Defense Investigators Group, to investigate claimants like Angela Martin.[121] Raucci stated that she received so many pleas for help regarding discrimination and retaliation claims that it turned what was supposed to be taking "only two to five statements" into a six-month process.[122] She testified that she found the complainants credible, and she found that the CFPB's general environment "is one of exclusion, retaliation, discrimination, nepotism, demoralization, devaluation, and other offensive working conditions which constitute a toxic workplace for many of its employees. . . . The corrosive environment of the CFPB workplace was engendered by the bureau's perpetual failure to uphold its own EEO policies."[123] Raucci also testified that CFPB managers used their internal EEO policies against complaining employees.[124]

CFPB employees further testified that many CFPB managers were "racist" and made inappropriate remarks.[125] For example, CFPB employees testified that they internally referred to the CFPB's Office of Consumer Response as "The Plantation" because practically all of the employees were African Americans assigned to menial tasks such as data entry, and the CFPB managers gave them fried chicken lunches.[126] Racism at the CFPB was so prevalent that CFPB managers apparently felt comfortable allegedly discriminating and retaliating against a senior equal employment specialist who worked in the CFPB's own Office of Civil Rights and had more than twenty years of previous EEO experience at different agencies.[127] CFPB managers did not spare immigrants from their racism; they allegedly openly referred to a naturalized U.S. citizen CFPB employee, Ali Naraghi, who had previously worked at the Fed with top marks for over fourteen years, as "a f****** foreigner."[128]

It is, perhaps, no surprise that the CFPB's managers showed markedly different patterns when rating employees of different races and ages, according to its own data.[129] CFPB managers ranked white employees better than minority employees in performance reviews, which affect pay raises and bonuses.[130] Overall, in 2013 white CFPB employees were twice as likely to receive the agency's top grade of "5 stars" compared to the CFPB's minority employees; 74.6 percent of whites received ratings of either 4 or 5 stars, compared to 65.5 percent of Asians, 65.2 percent of Hispanics, and 57.6 percent of African Americans, according to a CFPB internal report.[131] Minority employees disproportionately received 3-star ratings, the lowest grade given out in large numbers: 42.4 percent of African Americans, 34.5 percent of Asians, 34.8 percent of Hispanics, and 24.4 percent of Caucasians.[132] In these reviews, 20.7 percent of white employees received a 5-star rating, compared to 10.5 percent of African American employees.[133] Employees less than forty years old received an average rating of 3.94 stars, while older employees received an average rating of 3.78 stars.[134] The CFPB also significantly discriminated against employees based on their union status: non-unionized employees received an average rating of 4.04 stars, while unionized employees received an average rating of 3.79 stars.[135] With respect to both race and gender, among similarly experienced and educated CFPB employees, the pay disparity went as high as $60,000 per year for some positions.[136] In 2012 and 2013, CFPB management repeatedly dismissed or ignored the pleas for help from the CFPB's employee union, the National Treasury Employees Union (NTEU), which detailed the CFPB's discrimination and retaliation.[137]

The CFPB views itself as combating Wall Street's and mortgage companies' alleged racial discrimination and "predatory lending," which purportedly contributed to the 2008 financial collapse.[138] The CFPB, however, appears to be untouchable when it comes to its own alleged discrimination, retaliation, and civil rights violations against its minority, female, "LGBTQ*," and older employees. Robert Cauldwell, president of NTEU Chapter 335, which represents CFPB employees, described the CFPB as an agency of "[h]ubris, persecution, retaliation, discrimination."[139] He is seeking a civil suit against the CFPB for discriminating against him due to his sexual orientation.[140] Cauldwell stated, "I don't think the CFPB is scared of Congress."[141]

III. CONGRESS HOLDS THE SOLUTIONS TO EXECUTIVE OVERREACH

The courts can do much to prevent the CFPB's overreaches, either in judicial review of the CFPB's actions or judicial review of the constitutionality of the agency itself. But the courts are not the only branch of government that can—and should—act to prevent the CFPB from violating its constitutional and statutory limits.

Congress and the President can fix the problem of agency overreach resulting from Dodd-Frank—if they want to. This may not be possible until at least January 21, 2017. For even if Congress drafted a series of perfectly structured, perfectly worded bills preventing the CFPB and other Dodd-Frank agencies from overreaching or abusing their powers, the President has to sign them, or Congress must override his vetoes. The President has firmly and repeatedly stated that he considers Dodd-Frank one of his signature achievements and that he will actively oppose any attempt to modify or repeal the act.[142] Moreover, the 114th Congress does not have enough votes in either house to override a presidential veto, especially when powerful minority-party senators and representatives aggressively defend the Dodd-Frank agencies, to the point where they accused majority-party committee members of being racist because they held hearings on serious allegations of racism, sexism, and other discrimination and retaliation at a Dodd-Frank agency.[143]

Still, various senators and representatives have introduced many bills designed to modify Dodd-Frank and its agencies.[144] Some even managed to pass their respective congressional house. Some examples include the following: in June 2015, Senator Richard Shelby (R-AL) placed S. 1484, the Financial Regulatory Improvement Act of 2015, on the Senate's legislative calendar.[145] On May 19, 2015, Senator David Perdue (R-GA) introduced S. 1383, the Consumer Financial Protection Bureau Accountability Act of 2015, which would amend Dodd-Frank to change the CFPB's funding from the Fed to the annual congressional appropriations process.[146] On April 13, 2015, Representatives Frank Guinta (R-NH) and Ed Perlmutter (D-CO) introduced H.R. 1737, the Reforming CFPB Indirect Auto Financing Guidance Act of 2015, which would declare the CFPB's March 21, 2013, bulletin without force or effect and would affect future CFPB "guidance."[147] The bill has bipartisan support in the form of 112 co-sponsors.[148] On March 4, 2015, Congressman Sean Duffy (R-WI) introduced H.R. 1265, the Bureau Advisory Commission Transparency Act of 2015.[149] The bill would require each of the CFPB's advisory committees and subcommittees to be subject to the Federal Advisory Committee Act, which would effectively make their proceedings public.[150] In April 2015, the bill passed the House, 401–2, and is now in the Senate Committee on Banking, Housing, and Urban Affairs.[151] On April 22, 2015, the House passed Congressman Robert Pittenger's (R-NC) H.R. 1195, the Bureau of Consumer Financial Protection Advisory Boards Act; the vote was 235–183.[152] The bill would make permanent the CFPB's advisory boards that focus on smaller institutions and credit unions, and add another permanent advisory board focusing on small businesses.[153]

IV. CONCLUSION

Dodd-Frank agency overreach issues will continue to be important. For example, every month the CFPB's twelve data-mining programs collect and monitor information on approximately 600 million personal credit card accounts, and the CFPB plans to monitor 95 percent of all credit card transactions by 2016.[154] The CFPB already gathers data on millions of mortgages, bank accounts with overdraft fees, automobile sales, credit scores, and payday loans, and student loans.[155] The CFPB is currently reviewing the entire student loan servicing industry and it plans to establish rules governing the $1.2 trillion student debt market.[156] This will place the CFPB in direct conflict with the U.S. Department of Education, which owns or guarantees approximately $1.1 trillion in federal student loans, issues and enforces rules governing loan servicers, and structures their federal contracts.[157]

The CFPB will also likely try to regulate out of business the industries it does not like. For example, the CFPB's plans to regulate the payday loan and vehicle title loan industries might reduce the number of these loans by 70–82 percent and kill off monoline payday loan stores.[158] The CFPB knows that its proposed rules "would likely make the small stores that offer payday loans unprofitable on average" and that most of these small stores are in minority communities.[159]

The Dodd-Frank agencies' controlling regulatory philosophy appears to be "We know better than anyone what is best for you." Perhaps Justice Owen Roberts regretted his vote in *Parrish* when he wrote, "[I]t is plain that this Act creates personal government by a petty tyrant instead of government by law. . . . all these matters are buried in the bosom of the Administrator and nowhere else."[160]

12.

THREATS TO DUE PROCESS AND FREE SPEECH ON CAMPUS

Samantha Harris and Greg Lukianoff[1]

In February 2015, Laura Kipnis, a prominent feminist professor at Northwestern University, published an essay in the *Chronicle of Higher Education* decrying the climate of "sexual panic" on campus in what she called the "post-Title IX landscape."[2] Her essay criticized the university's restrictions on faculty/student relationships—even among those from different departments—and briefly mentioned a case in which a Northwestern student filed a Title IX lawsuit against the university over alleged sexual advances by a professor. Kipnis's essay was a pointed criticism of the current campus climate—one she believes is marked by an "obsession with helpless victims and powerful predators"—and it struck a nerve.

Soon after the article's publication, a group of offended students petitioned the university administration for a "swift, official condemnation" of Kipnis's article, claiming that the university's silence in the face of her criticism was hurtful to victims of sexual misconduct.[3] The administration said it would "absolutely" consider the petition.[4]

Kipnis was soon notified that two students had filed Title IX complaints against her, based on the essay and a subsequent tweet about the essay sent from her personal account.[5] According to Kipnis, the Title IX investigation that followed was nothing short of Kafkaesque. She was told she would not learn of the details of the complaints against her until her first meeting with the investigators. She was told she could not have an attorney present—only a "support person" who would not be allowed to speak. She was asked to keep the charges against her confidential. As she described it, "I'd plummeted into an underground world of secret tribunals and capricious, medieval rules, and I wasn't supposed to tell anyone about it."[6] The university even disregarded its promise to issue findings within sixty days, leaving Kipnis's future uncertain until well after the sixty-day deadline.

Then Kipnis took a risk: she published a second, scathing essay in the *Chronicle of Higher Education*, detailing what she called her "Title IX inquisition" by a "kangaroo court."[7] That same night, Kipnis received a letter from Northwestern's outside law firm, which informed her that the "preponderance of evidence does not support the complaint allegations."[8] This affirms what our organization, the Foundation for Individual Rights in Education (FIRE), has found: universities cannot defend in public what they try to get away with in private. But if Kipnis had decided to keep quiet about her ordeal—as school policies often directly order many students and professors—there is no telling what would have happened to her.

How did we arrive at a point where a law intended to protect women from discrimination in education is being used, as one writer put it, "as a means by which professors are put on trial for their tweets"?[9] The answer is the federal government.

The Executive Branch, particularly the Office for Civil Rights (OCR) of the Department of Education, has dramatically expanded its power over the years. It has shifted from a focus on overt sexual and racial discrimination to the adoption and enforcement of a "hostile environment" theory that has led to significant restrictions on free speech on campus.

Although this expansion began in the 1990s, OCR's overreach has dramatically accelerated under the Obama administration, most notably since 2010. Over the past five years, OCR has ignored the Administrative

Procedure Act (APA), investigated scores of colleges, given itself new and imagined powers, and has made it essentially impossible for universities to comply with its new decrees. Throughout all of these initiatives, OCR has encouraged the policing of speech and a reduction in due process for accused students.

We have seen an uptick in "politically correct" censorship and outrageous due process violations on campus in recent years. Though campus "P.C. Never Died" (as one coauthor wrote in 2010) after its supposed heyday in the 1990s, in the last few years P.C. speech policing and moral panics seem to be dominating campuses once again.[10] It is easy to attribute this to the real problem of biases among students and administrators and the problem of groupthink. But what we have learned at FIRE is that the secret engine behind universities' massive overreaction to offended students is the fear of an investigation by the increasingly aggressive Department of Education.[11]

A BRIEF HISTORY OF TITLE IX, 1972–2010

The key text of Title IX of the Education Amendments of 1972 is brief: "No person in the United States shall, on the basis of sex, be excluded from participation in, be denied the benefits of, or be subjected to discrimination under any education program or activity receiving Federal financial assistance."[12]

In the landmark 1977 case *Alexander v. Yale*, a federal court ruled that schools could be liable under Title IX not just for overt discrimination but also for not responding to allegations of sexual harassment by professors.[13] This was a significant development, but further expansion of Title IX was slow and measured over the following decade. When the Department of Education was created in 1980, its newly formed Office for Civil Rights took over the enforcement of Title IX from the now-defunct Department of Health, Education, and Welfare. In the early 1980s, courts grappled with whether Title IX extends to employment discrimination at educational institutions receiving federal funds[14] and the extent to which Title IX covers private institutions that receive federal funding indirectly.[15]

Colleges and universities, meanwhile, began to enact speech codes—prohibitions on expression that was protected under the First Amendment but that could offend others based on their race, religion, or sex. Broadening language borrowed from the employment setting, universities adopted sexual and discriminatory harassment policies that were ostensibly aimed at preventing the campus from being a hostile environment for women and minority students. In reality, they prohibited constitutionally protected speech.[16]

In the mid-1990s, the phenomenon of campus speech codes converged with the expansion of Title IX by both the federal judiciary and OCR. In 1994, OCR investigated Santa Rosa Junior College after two women complained about comments made about them on an online college bulletin board that included "anatomically explicit and sexually derogatory terms."[17] In a letter to the college, OCR concluded that the offensive speech had created a "hostile educational environment" for the complainants and directed the college to adopt a policy banning, among other things, online speech that "has the purpose or effect of creating a hostile, intimidating or offensive educational environment."[18] Soon thereafter, when the University of Massachusetts faced criticism over a proposed, broad harassment policy in 1995, "[t]he chancellor at the Amherst campus, David K. Scott, responded to criticism by suggesting that a code was required by Federal Department of Education regulations."[19]

Meanwhile, courts began to rule that Title IX indeed required schools to respond effectively not just to *quid pro quo* harassment by faculty but also to allegations of student-on-student sexual harassment resulting in a hostile environment.[20] In 1997, OCR released its *Sexual Harassment Guidance*, which affirmed that schools must respond to student-on-student harassment that creates a "hostile environment" because a failure to do so "permits an atmosphere of sexual discrimination to permeate the educational program and results in discrimination prohibited by Title IX." OCR's 1997 guidance also presented peer sexual assault as an example of harassment (and, by extension, discrimination) under Title IX.[21]

By 1999, the Supreme Court had addressed the issue of institutional liability for peer "hostile environment" harassment, ruling in *Davis v. Monroe County Board of Education* that an educational institution could be liable for peer harassment under Title IX, but only when the conduct in question was "so severe, pervasive, and objectively offensive that it can be said to deprive the victims of access to the educational opportunities or benefits provided by the school."[22]

Although OCR's 2001 *Revised Sexual Harassment Guidance* cited the speech-protective *Davis* standard approvingly,[23] universities continued to adopt overly broad speech codes, citing federal anti-discrimination law as the rationale. Concerned that universities were misinterpreting these laws to require the prohibition of constitutionally protected speech, OCR's then assistant secretary wrote in a July 28, 2003, "Dear Colleague" letter, "I want to assure you in the clearest possible terms that OCR's regulations are not intended to restrict the exercise of any expressive activities protected under the U.S. Constitution."[24]

OCR's concern for free speech proved to be short-lived. Within five years, OCR guidance had moved away from the *Davis* standard. In a September 2008 pamphlet titled "Sexual Harassment: It's Not Academic," OCR defined sexual harassment simply as conduct that "is sexual in nature," "is unwelcome," and "denies or limits a student's ability to participate in or benefit from a school's education program."[25] The pamphlet also lists examples of sexual harassment, including "making sexual propositions" and "telling sexual or dirty jokes," which are unambiguously protected under the First Amendment.

AGGRESSIVE ENFORCEMENT UNDER THE OBAMA ADMINISTRATION: 2010–PRESENT

After many years of gradual expansion, things began to change dramatically in the fall of 2010. Under the leadership of then Assistant Secretary for Civil Rights Russlynn Ali, OCR began taking a much more aggressive stance toward the enforcement of federal anti-discrimination laws, including Title VI of the Civil Rights Act of 1964 and, in particular, Title IX.

On October 26, 2010, OCR issued a Dear Colleague letter on the subject of bullying and discriminatory harassment.[26] The main purpose of that letter was to remind educational institutions that some of what they might regulate as "bullying" would also constitute discriminatory harassment, thus triggering responsibilities under Title VI, which prohibits discriminatory harassment at schools receiving federal funding. However, there were several troubling aspects to the letter.[27] Most notably, it failed to replicate the speech-protective understanding of student-on-student (or peer) hostile environment harassment contained in previous OCR guidance, omitting any reference to an objective component—a "reasonable person" standard—in the assessment of harassment claims.

THE APRIL 2011 DEAR COLLEAGUE LETTER

Then, on April 4, 2011, OCR issued an unprecedented Dear Colleague letter on the subject of schools' obligation, under Title IX, to respond to claims of sexual harassment and sexual violence.[28] In that letter, OCR mandated that institutions "must use a preponderance of the evidence" (more likely than not) standard in their grievance procedures for claims of sexual violence and harassment. The 2011 letter also mandated that "[i]f a school provides for appeal of the findings or remedy, it must do so for both parties," a provision that is eerily similar to constitutionally impermissible double jeopardy.[29]

Universities—some of which had been using more rigorous evidentiary standards—scrambled to comply with this new requirement, with Stanford University even lowering its evidentiary standard from "beyond a reasonable doubt" to "a preponderance of the evidence" in the middle of a student's proceedings.[30] One anonymous administrator, writing in the higher education publication *Inside Higher Ed*, called the April 2011 Dear Colleague letter "a 19-page document that at best complicates my work, at worst undermines my judgment and my ability to make good decisions for my institution and my students," and noted, "I do not appreciate having my hands tied by the presumption of guilt the Dear Colleague Letter portrays."[31]

The April 2011 Dear Colleague letter likely violated the APA by creating new substantive rules without providing for notice and comment as required by the act.[32] OCR argues that the letter does not create new legal requirements and thus is not subject to notice and comment under the APA, but court decisions and even guidance from the Executive Branch's own Office of Management and Budget belie that argument.[33]

THE FEDERAL "BLUEPRINT"

OCR's unprecedented intrusion into campus life intensified yet further in May 2013, when OCR, together with the Department of Justice, entered into a resolution agreement with the University of Montana that OCR referred to as "a blueprint for colleges and universities throughout the country."[34] The agreement stemmed from a May 2012 OCR/DOJ joint investigation into the university's handling of sexual assault claims.

In this "blueprint," OCR mandated a breathtakingly broad definition of sexual harassment, one that, if taken literally, prohibits large amounts of constitutionally protected expression. According to the blueprint, "sexual harassment should be more broadly defined as 'any unwelcome conduct of a sexual nature.'"[35] The blueprint also explicitly states that expression need not be "objectively offensive" to constitute sexual harassment, meaning that if a listener takes offense to sex- or gender-related speech for any reason, no matter how irrationally or unreasonably, the speaker has engaged in sexual harassment.[36]

This is an unconstitutional standard that conflicts with decades of legal precedent regarding the permissible scope, under the First Amendment, of campus harassment policies.[37] The blueprint, therefore, leaves universities in an impossible situation: violate the First Amendment or risk an OCR investigation and possible loss of federal funding.

Because of the threat to free speech, a large number of civil liberties organizations—including FIRE, the American Council of Trustees and Alumni, the Goldwater Institute, the Electronic Frontier Foundation, and the Student Press Law Center—pushed back against the blueprint. In a coalition letter sent to OCR in July 2013, FIRE and other groups argued that the blueprint posed a substantial threat to student and faculty speech and called for its retraction.[38] U.S. Senator John McCain, in a scathing letter to the Department of Justice, wrote, "Without congressional authorization or even any formal agency rulemaking, Assistant Attorney General Thomas Perez and a group of lawyers in the DOJ's Civil Rights Division have single-handedly redefined the meaning of sexual harassment at all universities and colleges across the country that receive public funding."[39]

The blueprint also sent shock waves through colleges and universities, which were still working to comply with the mandates of the 2011 Dear Colleague letter. At a June 2013 meeting of the National Association of College and University Attorneys, OCR attorney John DiPaolo faced pushback from university attorneys who felt that OCR had gone too far in its regulation of colleges and universities.[40]

In addition to the free speech issues, the blueprint also imposed a massive administrative burden on the University of Montana, providing other universities with an illustration of what was to come should they be deemed out of compliance with the ever-expanding requirements of Title IX.[41] The resolution agreement identified more than forty distinct actions that the University of Montana had to take to comply with Title IX. Many of these provisions required detailed reporting to the federal government, including an annual assessment of its anti-harassment efforts, as well as all of its sexual assault training materials and policy revisions.[42]

One provision, which drew particular ire from UM faculty, required the university to turn over to the federal government the names of faculty who did not attend mandatory sexual assault training sessions.[43] After negotiation, the government agreed to allow UM to report employee training compliance "by sector, such as the College of Arts and Sciences, or other schools within the larger university."[44]

The final UM policy, reviewed and approved by OCR and DOJ, prohibits discrimination and harassment on the basis of seventeen different categories, including "political ideas"—far more than required by federal anti-discrimination law.[45] Because the terms of the resolution agreement require UM's anti-harassment efforts to be monitored closely by OCR and DOJ, the agencies now oversee the application of harassment law to conduct and expression well beyond the purview of their mandates under Titles VI and IX.

NATIONAL EFFECTS OF OCR OVERREACH

In a November 2013 letter to coauthor Lukianoff, OCR backed away from its statement that the Montana agreement was a national blueprint. It wrote that "the agreement in the Montana case represents the resolution of that particular case and not OCR or DOJ policy."[46] Unlike in 2003, however—when OCR used a Dear Colleague letter to clarify that its policies did not require the prohibition of constitutionally protected speech—OCR never communicated this important shift to universities themselves.[47]

As a result, the blueprint continues to have a substantial impact on universities' efforts to revise their sexual harassment policies to comply with Title IX. Over the past several years, many universities, including

Penn State, the University of Connecticut, Clemson University, Colorado College, and Georgia Southern University, have revised their sexual misconduct policies to include the blueprint's broad definition of sexual harassment.[48] The number of institutions defining sexual harassment as any "unwelcome conduct of a sexual nature" will increase until OCR explains that such a definition is not required.

During this time, the number of sexual violence complaints filed under Title IX—and thus, the number of universities under OCR investigation—has been growing tremendously. *Inside Higher Ed* reports that the number of sexual violence complaints filed under Title IX went from just 9 in 2009 to 102 in 2014 and to 51 by April 2015.[49] This increase stems both from a coordinated effort by student activists and from the federal government's increased focus on the issue.[50]

To handle all of these investigations, OCR will need yet more resources. In February, the Obama administration requested "a 31 percent increase in the budget of its Office for Civil Rights, to deal, in part, with more federal investigations of colleges accused of mishandling sexual assault cases."[51]

The number of accused students who have filed lawsuits against their universities alleging unfair treatment in campus sexual misconduct proceedings has also grown dramatically. More than forty-five such lawsuits have been filed since OCR issued the April 4, 2011, Dear Colleague letter.

This increased risk of investigation and litigation, coupled with the complex and shifting regulations related to Title IX, has left universities in an impossible position. As a result, an entire cottage industry has sprung up around higher education risk management, with organizations that offer—for a hefty price tag—to supply universities with all of the information, training materials, and advice that they need to be Title IX compliant.

Even the federal government itself has taken note of OCR's heavy-handed tactics. A 2015 report of the Senate's bipartisan Task Force on Federal Regulation of Higher Education specifically criticized the Department of Education's tendency to "make significant changes in policy without following the APA's notice and comment procedures," citing OCR and, in particular, OCR's April 2011 Dear Colleague letter, as an example.[52]

WHITE HOUSE TASK FORCE TO PROTECT STUDENTS FROM SEXUAL ASSAULT

The federal government's increased focus on Title IX has not been limited to OCR. In January 2014, President Obama established the White House Task Force to Protect Students from Sexual Assault, which was given a "mandate to strengthen federal enforcement efforts and provide schools with additional tools to help combat sexual assault on their campuses."[53] In April 2014, the Task Force issued its first report, "Not Alone," which prescribed increased federal governmental involvement in virtually every aspect of campuses' handling of sexual assault claims.[54]

Among other things, the report promised that the Departments of Justice and Education would develop "trauma-informed" sexual assault training programs for universities, would evaluate and test various models for adjudicating claims of campus sexual assault, and would solicit participants for a "sex offender treatment program targeting college perpetrators." The report also said OCR would be "strengthening its enforcement procedures in various ways." The Task Force further recommended that universities conduct campus climate surveys to assess the extent of sexual assault on campus and announced that it would "explore legislative or administrative options to require schools to conduct a survey in 2016."[55]

The Task Force's website, notalone.gov, also makes it easier than ever for students to file a federal complaint against a university. The home page contains a prominent link for students on "how to file a complaint"; students who navigate to that page are then told, "if your school does not respond appropriately [when you report sexual misconduct], file a complaint with the Office for Civil Rights (OCR)."[56]

LEGISLATIVE EFFORTS

Even the Legislative Branch has joined the effort to expand OCR oversight. In July 2014, a bipartisan group of senators introduced the Campus Accountability and Safety Act (CASA), aimed at improving universities' response to allegations of sexual misconduct on campus. One shocking provision empowered OCR to impose fines of up to 1 percent of an institution's operating budget per Title IX violation, with no cap—and to keep that money for itself. While 1 percent might not seem like much, it is a staggering figure in light of recent OCR findings letters—including that at the University of Montana—that have found more than forty Title IX violations at a given institution.[57] Fortunately, when a new version of CASA was introduced this year, the bill was revised so that the funds collected would go not to OCR but rather to grant programs for institutions to develop trauma-informed trainings, bystander intervention programs, and other prevention and response efforts.[58] The federal government, however, could still collect money in excess of the actual amount of the institution's federal funding when Title IX violations are found.

This federal overreach into campus affairs is not limited to Title IX enforcement. According to the report of the bipartisan Task Force on Federal Regulation of Higher Education, "the Department of Education issues official guidance to amend or clarify its rules *at a rate of more than one document per work day*," on issues ranging from student eligibility for financial aid, to accreditation, to distance learning programs (emphasis in original). As a result, the report finds,

> [C]olleges and universities find themselves enmeshed in a jungle of red tape, facing rules that are often confusing and difficult to comply with. They must allocate resources to compliance that would be better applied to student education, safety, and innovation in instructional delivery. Clearly, a better approach is needed.[59]

CONCLUSION

The consequences of this federal overreach have been disastrous. Student and faculty expression is governed by campus harassment policies fashioned in response to OCR directives that impose vague, subjective restrictions on speech protected by the First Amendment. Faculty face a chilling effect on their own expression both inside and outside of the classroom and fear a formal complaint filed by offended, hypersensitive students. According to Professor Kipnis, many professors "now live in fear of some classroom incident spiraling into professional disaster" and "routinely avoid discussing subjects in classes that might raise hackles."[60] Harvard Law School Professor Jeannie Suk has written that many criminal law professors are now afraid to teach rape law, because "it's not worth the risk of complaints of discomfort by students."[61]

Meanwhile, sexual assault victims are funneled into campus judicial systems overseen by administrators whose primary loyalty lies with their employer, not justice. In campus judicial systems, accused students are routinely subjected to unfair proceedings that afford them few, if any, due process protections. And because colleges, at most, can expel students, rapists—who are often serial predators—are free to continue their behavior off-campus.

Claiming ever-expanding, extralegal powers out of thin air, OCR is forcing universities to perform an impossible task, stripping college students of core civil liberties, and failing to properly address campus sexual misconduct. Fortunately, OCR is not above the law. Lawmakers should investigate the agency's claims to authority and its recent activity in congressional hearings. Litigation under the First Amendment and the Administrative Procedure Act can and should correct the agency's overreach.

Students, faculty, administrators, and the general public should also demand that colleges adopt a clear, constitutional definition of harassment following the Supreme Court's *Davis* standard. Only this definition appropriately balances the twin necessities of protecting freedom of expression while prohibiting truly harassing conduct.

Finally, law enforcement must be the primary institution for addressing sexual assault on campus. Instead of doubling down on a broken campus judicial system, lawmakers should empower and fund local police departments to properly respond to campus rape. The criminal justice system alone has the resources, expertise, and authority to investigate allegations, retrieve evidence, and arrest and try alleged perpetrators. Only the criminal justice system provides those accused of such serious criminal activity the necessary procedural protections to ensure a fair verdict in which all parties may trust.

13.

CONGRESS IN AN ERA OF EXECUTIVE OVERREACH

Senator Orrin G. Hatch

The central means by which our Constitution ensures limited federal government is the separation of powers. Our nation's founders knew, in the sage words of Sir William Blackstone, that "in all tyrannical governments . . . the right both of making and of enforcing the laws is vested in one and the same man, or . . . body of men; and wherever these two powers are united together, there can be no public liberty."[1]

To safeguard our liberties, the Constitution vests legislative power in Congress, executive power in the President, and judicial power in the courts. This prevents any one branch from becoming too powerful, as each branch must work with the others to accomplish its designs. The separation of legislative and executive powers is particularly important, because a body with power both to make and to carry out laws is a body with power to do almost anything it wants.

Throughout his time in office, President Obama has consistently undermined the separation of powers and sought to aggrandize the power of the presidency at the expense of Congress. He has brazenly announced that he "won't take no for an answer"[2] when Congress refuses to go along with his far-left agenda and instead declared, "[W]hen Congress won't act, I will."[3] These are not just words. In far too many cases, the President has backed up his threats of unilateralism with action.

The Obama administration's abuses of the executive power are legion—so legion that a short essay such as this can barely scratch the surface. Three broad themes, however, capture much of the administration's objectionable disregard of the laws. First, the administration has repeatedly ignored or rewritten laws passed by Congress. Second, the administration has used congressional inaction as an excuse to assume legislative authority. Third, the administration and its allies have undermined the confirmation process by weakening Senate rules and claiming authority to bypass the Senate altogether.

These abuses all share a common trait: they have expanded presidential power at the expense of Congress and the rule of law. The damage that President Obama has inflicted on the separation of powers has been considerable, though, as I shall explain, not irredeemable.

DEFYING AND REWRITING EXISTING LAWS

The first way that the Obama administration has undermined the separation of powers is through defying or rewriting duly enacted statutes. The Constitution vests in Congress the power to write laws. The President can veto Congress's product but has no authority to revise laws that he does not like. President Obama, however, has not been satisfied with his constitutionally defined authority. When faced with laws he does not like, or thinks could be improved, rather than seek statutory fixes from Congress he has decided to rewrite the laws himself—or else ignore them.

The most egregious rewrites have involved Obamacare. Barely had the law passed before the President was rewriting it for political convenience. First came a series of "delays" of statutory mandates. The administration began by delaying the deadline for states to decide whether to set up a health care exchange. Then it delayed the employer mandate. Then it delayed the open enrollment deadline. Then it delayed the closing date for special high-risk pools for individuals with preexisting conditions. Again the administration delayed the employer mandate. Again it delayed the high-risk pool closing date. Again it delayed the open enrollment deadline.[4] All of these delays came in defiance of express statutory deadlines written into the law by Congress and signed by this President.

Next followed a series of revisions to the law to make it more politically palatable. These were not revisions through the traditional, constitutionally mandated procedure of bicameralism and presentment, whereby Congress amends a statute and the President signs the changes into law. Rather, these were unilateral rewrites through executive fiat, premised on inapplicable or entirely absent statutory authority.

First, the administration rewrote Obamacare's minimum coverage requirements, claiming as authority an Internal Revenue Service practice that permits the agency to adjust how a new tax is phased into operation. But the IRS's occasional use of temporary transitional relief does not empower a different agency—the Department of Health and Human Services—to alter or decline to enforce statutory requirements for years on end. Next, the administration enlarged the law's hardship exemption to allow just about anyone who wishes to avoid the individual mandate to do so. The actual text of the statute specifies that a health plan is unaffordable when it exceeds 8 percent of household income.[5] But the administration's rewrite allows anyone whose plan is canceled to receive an exemption by attesting that they consider other available plans to be "unaffordable," regardless of the plans' cost.[6] This has the benefit of saving individuals from paying a penalty for not carrying health insurance—a politically popular result, to be sure—but the statute nowhere permits the administration's change. Political convenience is no excuse for ignoring clear statutory text.

Two more rewrites merit mention. First, the administration twisted a minor provision in the Medicare statute beyond recognition in order to prevent major, Obamacare-mandated cuts to the Medicare Advantage program. This minor provision authorizes the administration to make bonus payments to so-called "demonstration projects" designed to improve the delivery of health services.[7] It was never intended to make up for a multibillion-dollar shortfall in Medicare funds.

Second, and most notoriously, the administration claimed authority to provide subsidies for *federally* established exchanges based on a provision in Obamacare authorizing subsidies for *state*-established exchanges.[8] The administration took this tack to defray the costs of the law for residents of states without state-sponsored exchanges. But a desire to save people money, or to make a legislative monstrosity workable, does not justify ignoring or rewriting statutory text. The Constitution binds the President to the text of the laws that Congress passes. By usurping legislative authority from Congress, President Obama has undermined the separation of powers.

The Obama administration's defiance of statutory mandates has not been limited to Obamacare. In the context of environmental regulation, the administration claimed vast authority under the Clean Air Act to regulate power plants solely on the basis of carbon emissions, notwithstanding a complete lack of any statutory provision empowering it do so. The administration also claimed not to be bound by the act's numerical thresholds. The Supreme Court rightly rejected these extreme positions.[9] Other instances of open defiance include releasing the "Taliban Five" from Guantanamo Bay without first notifying Congress, as required by the National Defense Authorization Act, and refusing to turn over documents subpoenaed by Congress, an act of defiance so brazen that it led the House of Representatives to hold the Attorney General in contempt.[10]

USURPING CONGRESS'S ROLE

In addition to defying or rewriting existing laws, President Obama has also used Congress's decisions *not to act* as grounds for assuming legislative power. There is, of course, no Congress-did-not-act-so-the-President-can clause in the Constitution. The President is not some sort of stopgap against congressional gridlock. Rather, Congress and the President are two independent branches with separate, constitutionally defined powers. Failure by one to act does not give the other leave to usurp authority.

But that is precisely what President Obama has claimed. Employing his so-called "pen and phone" strategy, he has repeatedly exercised legislative-like power to implement his own, preferred policies when Congress has refused to bow to his wishes. For example, after Congress declined to raise the minimum wage, President Obama decided he was going to act on his own and issued an executive order requiring federal contractors to raise the minimum wage paid to their employees. He ignored the fact that a federal statute already governs the minimum wage for federal contractors and that this statute requires the wage to match prevailing rates in the surrounding region. But as in other areas, existing law was no impediment to President Obama.[11] Congress had failed to act, so he overrode Congress and implemented the policy he preferred. Never mind the separation of powers.

Education is another field that has proved fertile for President Obama's usurpation of legislative power. For several years now, it has been clear that No Child Left Behind is unworkable. Although the idea of setting rigorous nationwide education standards is laudable, the bill's one-size-fits-all approach has proved too rigid for the many divergent challenges schools face. States have struggled mightily to meet the law's strict benchmarks, with the threat of diminished funding hanging constantly overhead.

Rather than work with Congress to fix No Child Left Behind and set realistic goals going forward, President Obama has opted to use waivers to force states to adopt his own preferred set of education policies. The administration grants waivers to states that relieve them from No Child Left Behind's requirements but attaches conditions to the waivers that obligate states to meet new requirements made up by the administration. Some of these new requirements are commendable—they include improving teacher quality, expanding high-performing schools, and building better data systems—but they bear little resemblance to the provisions of the law itself.[12] In using waivers to rewrite No Child Left Behind rather than working with Congress to fix it, the Obama administration has usurped legislative authority.

Finally, there is immigration. For years the President has decried Congress's resistance to comprehensive immigration reform that provides a pathway to citizenship. Over this period he has also decreed increasingly expansive enforcement carve-outs for various classes of illegal immigrants. First he exempted illegal immigrants brought here as children. Then veterans. Then, last year, he exempted parents of U.S. citizens and lawful permanent residents. In each of these moves, the President said he was acting because Congress had refused to. But Congress's decision not to pass comprehensive reform does not give the President *carte blanche* to implement whatever policies he thinks best. Indeed, the failure of Congress to act highlights the absence of a national consensus on immigration reform. The decision to grant lawful status to broad categories of immigrants is a legislative, not an executive, function, and by his unilateral action the President inhibits the development of a national consensus. Through the exercise of prosecutorial discretion the President may decline to enforce laws against certain individuals, but such discretion requires individualized assessments of particular cases.[13] Sweeping changes that affect millions of people is not discretion; it is legislation.

UNDERMINING THE CONFIRMATION PROCESS

The final category of executive overreach under President Obama centers on the confirmation process. A core component of the constitutional system of checks and balances is the Senate's role in confirming nominees. The advice and consent requirement safeguards against the danger of incompetent, corrupt, or ideologically extreme executive appointees.

Lately, however, the Obama administration and its allies have worked to weaken Senate rules to ease confirmation of controversial nominees, and in some cases even sought to cut the Senate out of the process entirely. With regard to Senate rules, in 2013–2014 Senate Democrats—at the White House's urging—invoked the so-called nuclear option to lower the threshold for cloture on all nominations except Supreme Court nominations from sixty to fifty votes.[14] In so doing, Democrats seriously damaged one of the Senate's key institutional hallmarks and sharply curtailed the ability of dissenting senators to challenge ill-advised nominations.

For over two centuries, the Senate has been a vital forum for deliberation and debate. Early in the nation's history, visitors flocked to the Senate gallery to hear legends like Daniel Webster, Henry Clay, and John C. Calhoun address the nation's most pressing issues. Debates on nominees have been an important part of this history. Most have been confirmed. Some have not. But throughout the years a key feature of the Senate has been members' right to fully air their views on matters of importance. By lowering the threshold for ending debate on nominees, Democrats undermined a defining Senate feature. Time will tell how far the damage extends.

At the same time that Senate Democrats were weakening the consideration of nominees, the White House was attempting to cut the Senate out of the appointment process entirely. After several of his nominees to the National Labor Relations Board ran into opposition, President Obama decided the solution was to bypass the Senate altogether through recess appointments. Article II of the Constitution gives the President "power to fill up all vacancies that may happen during the recess of the Senate."[15] This means the President can appoint officials without Senate confirmation when the Senate is in recess. So President Obama made the appointments.

But there was a problem. *The Senate was not in recess.* Although the Senate did not convene in regular session, it held a series of *pro forma* sessions during the period President Obama made the appointments. Unbowed, President Obama claimed that the *pro forma* sessions did not count, that the Senate was not really in session during this period, and that therefore he had power under the Recess Appointments Clause to make the appointments unilaterally.

The President's claims were breathtaking. He claimed that he—not the Senate—determines when the Senate is in session for purposes of the Recess Appointments Clause and that therefore he—not the Senate—sets the bounds of the recess appointment power. This argument turns the system of checks and balances on its head. No more is the Senate a check on the President's appointment power, with a narrow exception for when the Senate is unable to transact business. Rather, the President himself gets to determine when his appointees need Senate confirmation and when they do not.

And even this description is too charitable, for the Senate *was* able to transact business during the *pro forma* sessions that the President did not count. In fact, the Senate passed a bill during one of them. What the President asserted, then, was the power to appoint officials without Senate confirmation *during periods when the Senate is in session and passing legislation.* It is hard to see this as anything other than a frontal assault on the Senate's role in the confirmation process and an attempt to expand presidential power beyond reasonable bounds. The Supreme Court rejected the President's claims unanimously.[16]

THE CONGRESSIONAL RESPONSE

If the separation of powers and the liberty it protects are to survive, then a serious response to these usurpations is required. Congress must act to ensure that all three branches of government check the abuses of a President determined to trample all obstacles to his far-left agenda.

First, Congress should use the tools within its power to alter the behavior of the Executive Branch. Foremost among these is the confirmation power, or rather, the power to withhold confirmation of presidential nominees. The federal government today is a sprawling leviathan, with programs and offices too numerous to count. Even the most effective and strong-willed President cannot exert any degree of detailed control over the bureaucracy from the Oval Office. Instead, all presidents must rely on appointees to put their agenda into effect.

The Constitution's requirement that the Senate consent to the President's nominees for senior posts is an enormous check on the President's power. Unfortunately, the Senate's effective exercise of this power reached a low point in the 113th Congress, when the President's allies used the newly lowered cloture threshold to rush through as many nominations as the Senate's calendar allowed. Happily, however, the new Republican Senate majority in the 114th Congress offers the prospect of greater scrutiny of the President's nominees and the opportunity to ensure that those willing to warp the law to implement the President's agenda never receive confirmation. Vigorous and effective oversight after confirmation can also help ensure that Executive Branch officials remain true to their commitment to the rule of law even in the face of the President's ideologically extreme agenda.

Congress should also reform the administrative process. The Administrative Procedure Act is nearly seventy years old. It embodied the New Deal's optimism about the federal government's ability to cure all of society's ills. But the APA is structured to facilitate heavy-handed command-and-control regulation, which in turn leads to outdated and ineffective schemes. Many years of experience have also taught agencies and outside groups how to manipulate numerous loopholes in the regulatory process. These abuses have become so commonplace that they now often pass without notice. Congress should act to fix these problems by restoring regulatory transparency, requiring evidence-based rulemaking, and ensuring that agencies comply with their basic duty to conduct cost-benefit analysis for any new regulations.

Second, Congress should ensure that the President is held accountable for his actions through meaningful judicial review. The role of the federal judiciary in the administrative process has thus far escaped significant legislative attention. This is unfortunate. Given the broad authority that Congress has ceded to the President, the courts often stand as the only true independent check on his power. Recent abuses by the political branches, however, have created serious obstacles to effective and appropriate judicial review of the regulatory process.

To begin with, Congress has routinely passed vague laws that grant agencies extraordinarily flexible powers that are both unwise and constitutionally troublesome. Judicial deference to agency interpretations of these laws has magnified this problem to an extreme degree. Although originally intended as a means of curtailing judicial activism, *Chevron*[17] and associated doctrines have resulted in a gross misallocation of lawmaking authority. Such doctrines have turned courts into rubber stamps rather than effective checks on administrative overreach. The threat of toothless judicial oversight became even more real when the President's allies in the Senate allowed him to pack the D.C. Circuit with compliant judges disinclined to engage in meaningful review of the administration's questionable activities.

Next, Congress's creation of broadly available private rights of action to challenge administrative decisions and regulatory actions has opened yet another avenue for abuse of the courts. While these provisions provide important opportunities for regulated parties to defend their liberties, too often they have allowed groups with no concrete stake in the process to use the courts as a means to drive their own ideological agendas. Worse yet, the administration has taken to colluding with these sorts of ideological litigants, using settlement agreements to skirt the rulemaking process's procedural safeguards. Inconsistent efforts by the judiciary to define the constitutional limits on standing have also inadvertently created a perverse environment where businesses with real skin in the game are shut out of court while special interest groups with no meaningful injury in fact are allowed to litigate.[18]

Restoring the constitutionally proper judicial role is vital to returning accountability to the regulatory process. When reviewing agency action, courts should hear only real cases and controversies where litigants have concrete interests at stake. But when courts do rule, they should say firmly what the law is and not simply ratify what regulatory agencies want the law to be. Legislation to ensure meaningful reform on these fronts—and to thereby bring the administrative state more in line with the Constitution—must be one of Congress's top priorities.

Third, Congress must stop enabling executive overreach through irresponsible legislation. The unfortunate truth is that many of President Obama's abuses are rooted in Congress's irresponsible, unwise, shortsighted, or counterproductive drafting. Sometimes Congress has enabled executive overreach by shielding agencies from accountability. Consider, for example, how Congress acceded to the Obama administration's demands in crafting the Dodd-Frank banking "reform" law. At the President's urging, Congress created a new agency called the Consumer Financial Protection Bureau with complete freedom from congressional oversight, absolute authority to set its own budget, and near immunity from judicial review.[19] By agreeing to these changes, Congress eliminated its ability to check this new agency in any meaningful way.

At other times, Congress has granted massive amounts of vague authority to the Executive Branch, thereby inviting administrative abuse. Consider, for example, the EPA's costly new rules regulating carbon dioxide. Although Congress plainly did not intend to authorize the EPA to regulate carbon dioxide emissions, the Clean Air Act's operative language is so vague as to facilitate motivated misinterpretation. Overbroad delegation thus enabled a vast overreach by the President that Congress never meant to authorize.

Congress has also invited abuse by failing to act. Consider, for example, the Department of Education's waiver conditions to implement its own agenda—one completely divorced from the purposes of the statute. The administration has succeeded only because Congress enacted broad waiver authority in the original law and then failed to reauthorize the law after it expired in 2007.[20] Congress's inaction has invited, without authorizing, the administration's unilateralism.

Responsibly legislating is not an easy task. It requires difficult compromises, political risks, and much hard work. Nevertheless, the consequences of inaction—namely, overreach by the Executive Branch—create an imperative for Congress to act. In this short chapter, I offer ideas on how Congress can reclaim its rightful role as the primary lawmaking body in our constitutional system and once again serve as a crucial check against executive encroachment.

President Obama has done significant damage to the separation of powers. It will take consistent, focused effort to right his wrongs.

14.

A STYLIZED MODEL OF AGENCY STRUCTURE FOR MITIGATING EXECUTIVE BRANCH OVERREACH

F. Scott Kieff[1]

With so many reasons to be grateful to the framers and our other intellectual forebears for implementing the many constructive approaches in U.S. institutions and organizations of government, we should not be surprised to find within our system an existing model of agency structure that goes a long way toward mitigating Executive Branch overreach and other excessive political influence.[2] This chapter explores one such model that already exists but is often overlooked: a largely independent commission adjudicating commercial law, with a structure similar to that of the U.S. International Trade Commission (ITC).

Several crucial caveats are due at the outset. The first is that like most other agencies, the ITC is itself imperfect, a work in progress, and ever a candidate for improvement. The second is that the bulk of the credit for the salutary attributes of the agency model explored in this chapter lies with a few key internal structural elements of the ITC. The focus here is therefore on the rules of the game rather than any particular players or team. The third is that one size rarely fits all and that mitigation of undue political influence from the Executive Branch or elsewhere is just one goal to be weighed against many when conducting an overall assessment of any agency structure.[3] Nor is such undue political influence a problem uniquely facing any one administration over others or any one side of the political spectrum over the other. Finally, this chapter builds on and presumes familiarity with the broad and deep legal literature on the theory and practice of administrative agencies.[4] With all of these caveats in mind, the agency model explored here in merely stylized or summary fashion is offered to positively engage in constructive dialogue with readers across the political spectrum about one type of tool for mitigating effects that are widely recognized to be pernicious.

Rising from the shadow of the Civil War's violent political divisions, when the country was funded almost entirely by import tariffs rather than the modern income tax, the essential structure of the agency model explored here traces its intellectual roots to the famous Harvard economics professor Frank W. Taussig, who was appointed the first chair of the ITC's predecessor (the Tariff Commission).[5] After having long advocated for a very independent commission so as to de-politicize the import component of U.S. international trade, Taussig oversaw the creation of an agency structured to do only fact-finding, analysis, adjudication, and technical advising, leaving policy-making to the political branches of government.

The ITC is somewhat like the many other independent administrative agencies, such as the Federal Trade Commission (FTC) and Securities and Exchange Commission (SEC). Each of these commissions is often seen as less subject to political pressure than typical Executive Branch agencies, such as the Department of Justice (DOJ) Antitrust Division and the Department of Commerce Patent and Trademark Office (PTO), because each is not within any Executive Branch department.[6]

But unlike almost all of the other independent commissions, there are several essential statutory features of the ITC's structure that enable significantly greater independence, most of which date back to the statute creating the original Tariff Commission:[7]

- six members, appointed by the President and confirmed by the Senate, with no more than three from any one political party;[8]
- nine-year staggered terms for each member;[9]
- the position of chair rotates among the members every two years, switching party every time;[10]
- each member has the same vote on substantive matters;[11]
- any four members can overrule the chair on administrative matters;[12] and
- analytical studies assigned by and technical assistance provided to both political branches, including both houses of Congress.[13]

As a result of these structural features, the commission staff generally work closely with all six of the commissioners' offices, recognizing that every two years the chair will rotate and that many of the commissioners have a good chance of serving as chair. This incentivizes close coordination among the members and the commission staff, which has long helped the ITC operate by consensus on internal administrative matters as well as on substantive decisions. Such coordination and support from the staff help ensure the best factual record is assembled and enable resulting published work products, including those for the majority as well as minority dissents and concurrences, to be written with moderation, careful explanation, and citation to the law and record. This, in turn, strengthens external confidence in the agency's expertise and independence among reviewing courts and the elected branches of government, including both houses of Congress, across the political spectrum.

In contrast, the FTC is generally understood to act in a way that more closely reflects the views of its chair because it has an internal structure more common among independent agencies. It has five members and they serve for slightly shorter terms of seven years. But for a number of reasons, including the fact that the chair of the FTC can serve for the individual commissioner's entire term, the chair can direct the agency staff in a way that other FTC commissioners cannot.[14] This allows the FTC chair to have much more influence than the chair's control over the agenda would itself afford or than the chair's single vote on matters before the commission would imply. Furthermore, because of the Sunshine

Act, it is generally not appropriate for more than two commissioners to directly interact outside an open meeting, which can have the effect of further empowering the chair.

Because each of these distinctions can be seen as mere matters of degree, a comparative example across several agencies that handle the same subject matter can illustrate the relative benefits of this model structure. To that end, the following discussion briefly outlines the major agencies that operate in the U.S. patent system, including the ITC. As sketched in the following figure, these range from the group on the left, which comprises ordinary Executive Branch agencies including the PTO and DOJ, to the group in the middle of independent commissions including the FTC and ITC, and the group on the right of courts comprising the many district courts, the U.S. Court of Appeals for the D.C. Circuit (CADC), the U.S. Court of Appeals for the Federal Circuit (CAFC), and the Supreme Court.[15] Also shown in the figure are the basic topical components in a patent dispute that are actually decided by each agency. For the PTO, this includes only the basic requirements for a valid patent, often collectively called validity. For the DOJ and the FTC, this includes only antitrust issues.[16] For the FTC and the courts, this includes all aspects of patent disputes from validity to infringement and remedies, as well as antitrust. In addition, the figure points out that moving from left to right there is an increasing mix of substantive topic areas being considered at one time in each matter before an agency, along with an increasing recognition of political independence.

The differences sketched in this figure have practical impact that might inform the past decade of debates surrounding the U.S. patent system, which emphasize concerns about the extensive costs, delays, and inaccuracies resulting from decisions reached by lay judges and juries charged with adjudicating patent cases in U.S. district courts but who generally lack expertise in deciding patent issues.[17] This chapter highlights a contrasting view. Exploring various approaches to resolving disputes in patent cases, the chapter highlights a set of underappreciated benefits of patent jury trials that, in turn, highlight underappreciated benefits of the stylized model for an agency structure exemplified by the ITC.[18] More particularly, the chapter explores how both jury trials and a very independent agency such as the ITC increase predictability and

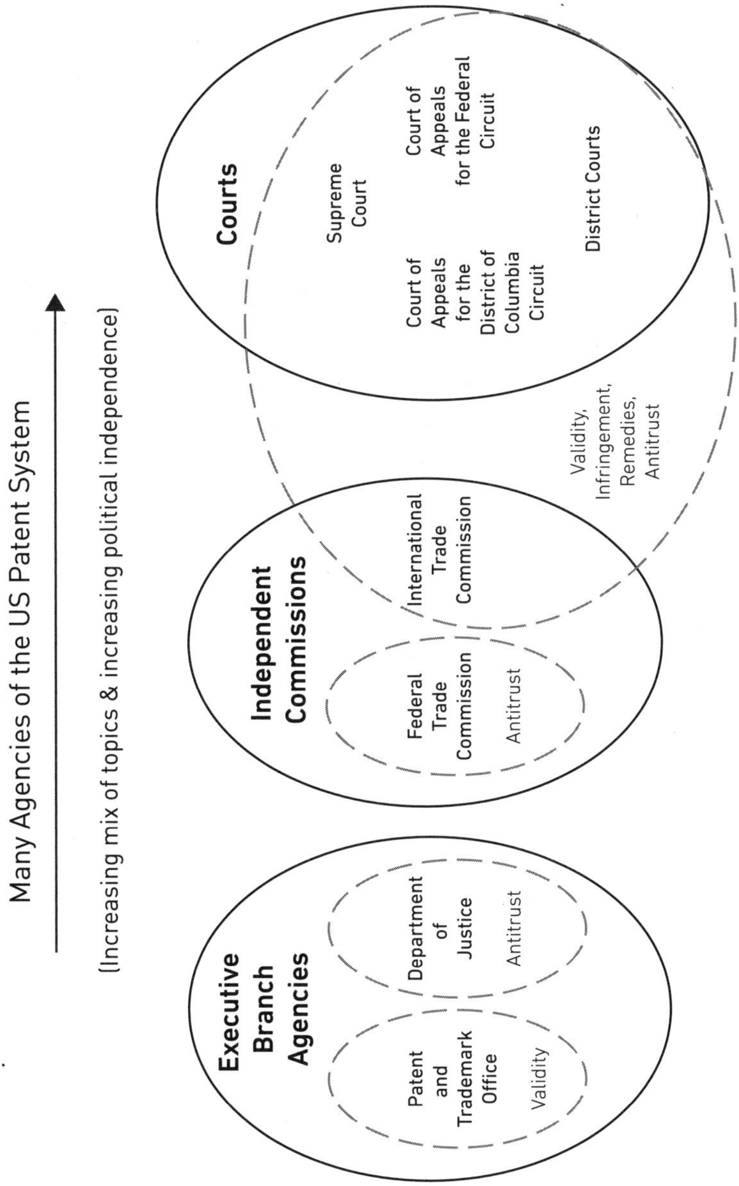

Source: Commissioner Kieff, United States International Trade Commission

level the playing field by decreasing the role that fashion and politics can play in disputes.

To be sure, from matters of demographic characteristics to the general reputation of a given party in the geographic region of the courthouse and its jury pool, a host of factors relating to fashion and politics have long been recognized to play too great of a role in ordinary civil trials, including those involving patents.[19] Many of the more invidious aspects of this effect have been targeted by helpful reforms, but still more progress should always be considered.[20] Civil litigation in the U.S. is generally considered to primarily rely on a decision-making process under which the judge neutrally applies the procedural rules and resolves legal questions, and either the judge or the jury neutrally decides the open factual questions, all while generally deferring to policy judgments made by the other branches of government out of court.[21] In contrast, our society has often recognized that certain decisions ultimately involve a sufficiently large amount of normative and political content of the type that would be well suited to delegation to various government officials who operate within structures designed to be more responsive to politics and fashion.[22] While not typically considered the topic of mainstream political debates because they are too far down in the weeds of the arcane field of patent law, popular sentiment about many aspects of the patent system—which we may call fashion—has often been a prominent component of actual policy debates. And those most able to influence this popular sentiment can meaningfully increase the relative role that it plays, instead of detailed factual analysis of particular cases, in driving policy outcomes within those agency decisions designed to respond to such input.

Although many commentators and policy makers see patents as tools that societies use to encourage inventors to invent, significant and politically diverse voices among those studying and implementing the U.S. patent system have instead focused on the role of strong, predictable rules for patent procurement and enforcement in facilitating competition and the commercialization of inventions.[23] One key difference between these views about the core goal of a patent system lies in who is the target: inventors in particular or a diverse set of market actors in general. Another key difference is in the mechanism contemplated to stimulate the behavior of the particular target.

The process of getting an invention commercialized requires coordination among a large number of complementary users of an invention, including venture capitalists, managers, marketers, laborers, and often the owners of other inventions. Such coordination can be greatly facilitated by allowing inventions to be patented and then using dispute resolution procedures to enforce those patents that have relatively low administrative costs and less reliance on flexible discretion over subjective factors. When an inventor has a patent backed by credible enforcement in court, then that patent can act like a beacon in a dark room to draw to itself all of those interested in that technology and start conversations among them.[24] As long as the patent is predictably enforced, this beacon effect is followed by a bargain effect: those parties know that only those who strike deals with each other involving the patent can avoid being excluded by the patent in court.[25] Through the enforcement of that patent right and those contract rights, the government is able to help patentees and their contracting parties appropriate the returns to any of their rival inputs to developing and commercializing innovation—labor, lab space, capital, etc.—without the government itself having to trace the relative contributions of each participant and with less risk that political influence will affect outcomes.[26] This decentralized, ad hoc coordination occurs spontaneously, without the government having to amass any of the specified information it would need to directly target each of the parties.[27] Instead, each party brings its own expertise and other assets to the negotiating table and knows—without necessarily having to reveal it to other parties or the government—enough about its own level of interest and capability to decide whether to strike a deal or not.

Economic history has taught that a defining feature of the early U.S. patent system, central to its economic success, was the way in which it used a property rights approach to facilitate private ordering in the process of getting inventions put to use.[28] Giles S. Rich, one of the two principal drafters of the statute that implemented the patent system operating in the United States from 1952 through the end of the twentieth century, was explicit in focusing on the role of patents in facilitating coordination among many diverse market participants in order to commercialize innovation, rather than on getting inventions made.[29] Not only was Rich a principal drafter of the statute, but he also went on to be the longest-sitting federal judge in the U.S., serving on the court that heard most of the appeals in the U.S. patent system. By the time of his death, Judge Rich was widely regarded as the world's most famous patent scholar and jurist and as the father of the modern U.S. patent system.[30]

This view of patents has a broad and deep tradition in the U.S. It is evident in Abraham Lincoln's description of the patent system as having "added the fuel of interest to the fire of genius, in the discovery *and production* of new and useful things."[31] It has been embraced by leading jurists of commercial law from diverse political perspectives, such as Learned Hand and Jerome Frank, who immediately recognized the power of the U.S. Patent Act of 1952 in strengthening patents and who championed strong patents as tools for helping smaller market entrants compete against larger, established firms.[32] Both major political parties in the U.S. have similarly embraced this approach when in control of the Executive Branch. A very diverse pair of U.S. Presidents decided to adopt an approach to patents like that in the '52 Act.[33] President Carter, a Democrat, decided after a careful study to put forth a statute designed to strengthen the patent system by creating the Federal Circuit; and President Reagan, a Republican, signed the bill to much fanfare after Congress passed it.[34]

While targeting inventors to stimulate them to make inventions has much appeal, the difference between the goals of inventing and commercializing reveals some key institutional features of the patent system. Consider that the goal of getting inventions made may be accomplished by the use of targeted incentives that are alternatives to patents, such as tax credits, prizes, grants, rewards, and the like.[35] Providing these targeted incentives requires an immense amount of information about who exactly should be targeted and how large the incentive should be, and those operating under the regime have stronger incentives to seek their own rewards than to discipline the giver to be more frugal in giving rewards to others.[36] Not only is amassing all of that information difficult for the government, but large, established market actors will often be better able than smaller market entrants to wield the political influence needed to get the government to act on that information to their benefit.

One feature that patents have in contrast with other such rewards is that the patent applicants themselves bring to the government much of the information needed to grant and enforce the patent. Patent applicants do this through the process of submitting and prosecuting their patent applications. Likewise, the patent system leaves the competitors of the patentee and of the patentee's business associates in a position where these competitors are putative infringers of the patent. As a result, these competitors have strong incentives to invalidate the patent by bringing to the government's attention the rest of the relevant information needed to evaluate the validity of the patent, either when the patent is asserted against these competitors in court or during patent office reexamination.[37]

Importantly, a focus on incentives to commercialize is mindful of incentives to invent: both indirect from patents and direct from other inducements such as invention's famous mother, necessity, as well as innate curiosity, the direct funding of basic research by governments and private actors, first mover advantage, and the like. But focus on commercializing should prevail over focus on invention because it is likely to accomplish both goals without most of the collateral costs of a system primarily focused on making inventions and with a range of mechanisms for minimizing and mitigating the collateral costs of enforcing property rights in patents.

For example, the commercialization view takes seriously the risk of hold-up, which requires both asset specificity and opportunism.[38] As a result, this view of patents sees the patent law doctrines relating to the prior art as designed to ensure that valid patent claims do not cover technology in which, or even toward which, potential patent hold-up victims are likely to have significantly invested.[39] Similarly, it views patent law's doctrines relating to the disclosure that must be provided in a patent as designed to help third parties avoid making reasonable investment-backed expectations in the territory that could be targeted for threat of patent hold-up by valid patent claims.[40] This view allows for remedies in particular cases of patent infringement to be meaningfully decreased or even eliminated based on specific factual evidence of asset specificity and opportunism, including evaluating the interaction between them.[41]

While court litigation is more expensive and time-consuming than many of the administrative proceedings, this time and money is a fair price to pay for their important benefits.[42] Decisions in patent jury trials are closely tethered to the underlying factual record, which helps them avoid error, helps appellate courts correct errors that do arise, and meaningfully attenuates the influence of politics and fashion.[43] Such a detailed factual record requires significant time and money to assemble and thoroughly vet. But it is highly effective at proving historical and technological facts, such as whether a particular document of alleged prior art was in the public domain on a particular date and what technological content it communicated to people of ordinary skill in the art. In contrast, the massive savings in time and money associated with various administrative proceedings before the PTO to retest a patent's validity come precisely through reliance on the expertise of their decision-makers, which is the gravamen of the enhanced deference accorded such decisions by reviewing courts under principles of administrative law.

Fears about political influence driving outcomes at the PTO are not without foundation in recent history, under both Democratic and Republican administrations. The elimination of effective patent protection for computer software through the Supreme Court's 1972 *Benson* decision was generally recognized to have been the direct result of intensive influence wielded by IBM general counsel Nicholas Katzenbach over the U.S. Department of Justice, which he headed as Attorney General during the Kennedy/Johnson administration. A similar influence was applied, albeit ultimately unsuccessfully, during the first Bush administration, in the lead up to the 1994 appellate court *Alappat* decision, after the PTO commissioner had made the decision to reconstitute the office's internal Board of Appeals to hold a rehearing before a specially packed board decided to reject the patent on a type of software.[44]

None of this should suggest ill motive, illegality, or immorality on the part of any of the private or government actors or organizations in these cases. Private parties have appropriate interests in petitioning their government officials, and government officials have appropriate interest in receiving such input. And when particular courts have significant room to maneuver within a given policy space, similar opportunities for influence become focal points for influencing decision-making by those courts as well as by agencies.[45] Yet these well-recognized opportunities for influence of politics and fashion in the patent system can be avoided when the main path across the playing field is through the more fact-based decision-making of a patent jury trial.

An additional important benefit of patent jury trials over most administrative proceedings is that they tether issues of patent validity and infringement together before a single decision-making body. This provides important self-disciplining effects on both patentees and alleged infringers. And this self-disciplining, in turn, helps rein in the arguments presented by both sides from more distracting extremes that might introduce errors into the underlying judgment. For example, an alleged infringer may argue that the patent is invalid for being so expansive as to encompass a putative piece of prior art (e.g., a journal article or example of public use). But the alleged infringer will typically be self-disciplined by the realization that such a broad interpretation of the patent is more likely to support a finding of patent infringement if it turns out that piece of putative prior art fails to knock out the patent.[46] Of course, the patentee faces the same self-discipline in reverse.

Similar self-disciplining occurs when arguments over the remedies for patent infringement must be made before the same body that hears arguments over various defenses to infringement.[47] The adjudicated infringer arguing for lower damages (decreased value) would be constrained in making arguments about putative anticompetitive effect that might result from a patent's essential nature (extremely high value) or about a patent's failure to meet the statutory subject-matter criteria because it would preempt an entire field (also extremely high value).

On top of these self-disciplining effects, patent jury trials have a demonstrated record of mitigating the serious risks imposed on the entire system by bad faith arguments.[48] A direct way to mitigate that problem is to allow courts to award attorneys' fees and other actual damages against a party, on either side, who presses an argument in bad faith.[49] These damages could even be trebled in egregious cases.[50] Alleged infringers rightfully worry about the *in terrorem* impact of the high cost of baseless litigation, which can allow plaintiffs with bogus patents to shake down large companies for large numbers of expensive settlements. And small inventors rightfully worry that baseless arguments about invalidity could bleed patentees dry through years of litigation. Such a system of bad-loser-pays is used with some success in several other areas of U.S. law and in many areas of law in the U.K.[51] It would be especially useful in proceedings that include the self-disciplining effects just explored, such as administrative agencies like the ITC. It should not be expected to significantly decrease the frequency of litigation; but it should reasonably be expected to decrease its overall length and cost, because when both sides know their evidence can be tested in court (or by an agency like the ITC), they know that evidence will have to comply with the rules of evidence and procedure. This gives parties incentives to exchange evidence of the factual basis for viewing their opponent's case as truly infirm, which puts them on notice that continuing on the same path brings with it real risk.

Nevertheless, responding to popular concerns about patent jury trials, the 2011 America Invents Act significantly increased the depth and breadth of available internal PTO procedures to more closely scrutinize patent examination in the first instance and increased opportunity for patent revocation through reexamination or review after patents have issued. With a large budget of $2.5–3 billion (over twice the budget of the main agency charged with regulating the entire U.S. securities markets, the SEC), the PTO has been rapidly increasing its pool of internal administrative patent judges—these are the officers who review the final determination of the patent examiners—from a historical high of about eighty in 2009 to roughly double that number in 2012 and plans to double the number again in the coming year or two.[52]

This vast increase came on top of a decade of enhanced scrutiny of the putative antitrust implications of the substantive and procedural rules relating to remedies for patent infringement. This marked increase in antitrust scrutiny of patents occurred in both the DOJ, with a budget of approximately $160 million, and the FTC, with a budget of approximately $300 million, beginning with joint hearings in 2001 and including the 300-page FTC report more recently issued in 2011.[53]

While these PTO, DOJ, and FTC budget numbers are not offered as precise accountings for detailed comparison, they generally inform the broad discussion in at least two key ways. First, they give a reasonable sense of relative magnitude. For example, while the PTO handles trademarks as well as patents, the trademark side is a much smaller part of the PTO's overall operation. And while the DOJ and the FTC also handle a much broader set of antitrust matters not involving intellectual property (IP), and the FTC has a large consumer protection docket, both the DOJ and the FTC have been highlighting their IP-focused work in their annual budget justifications for years and both have been devoting resources toward their significant actions relating to IP over the past decade.[54] Second, all three of these agencies have deployed various enhanced procedures of a type that lead to the non-enforcement of a patent rather than to its enforcement. Put differently, they all have the direct effect of working against patents, never for them. When the relevant agency (such as the PTO or FTC) only has power to focus on one of the core substantive areas of a patent dispute, such as validity of the patent or the proper remedy for patent infringement, the proceeding often does not include the important self-disciplining tensions that usually cabin the arguments made by parties on both sides of a district court patent litigation, which typically involves all substantive areas of a patent case.[55]

In contrast to the other administrative agencies discussed here, the ITC uses only a portion of its more modest total budget of $80 million to deploy several significant sets of professional staff with extensive experience in all three main aspects of IP, mainly patent, cases: (1) validity and enforceability, (2) infringement, and (3) remedy.[56] It does so in a time frame widely regarded as significantly faster for the parties than district court litigation, while being at least somewhat less expensive for the parties.[57] These groups of ITC staff include the following:

- a large department of expert patent litigators (the Office of Unfair Import Investigations) who operate independently of the commission under formal conflict of interest rules in furtherance of their legal duty to represent the public's interest in each case in which they elect to participate, which is most of them;
- a large department of expert IP (mostly patent) lawyers who represent the commission's interests in following applicable statutes and precedents for adjudicating patent cases (the Office of General Counsel's IP team), most of whom have extensive patent experience and many of whom served as law clerks at the CAFC;
- a group of five to six administrative law judges and their staff of permanent law clerks, who collectively spend all of their time adjudicating IP disputes, mostly involving patents; and

- the six commissioners, each of whom has as least one full-time senior counsel with extensive IP experience devoted to IP matters, mostly involving patents.

The numbers tell a compelling story. Section 337 investigations at the ITC are fast, with a median time to adjudication of fourteen months.[58] They are also inexpensive for the government to run, with an estimated marginal cost to the ITC per investigation of about $57,000.[59] This makes an ITC investigation faster than the PTO's Inter Partes Review (IPR) and at a very manageable cost to the government.

The relative independence, speed, and expertise of ITC patent proceedings were highlighted when the ITC was recently faced with its most high-profile patent case in a generation, which involved the so-called smartphone wars between Apple and Samsung.[60] This ITC case happened to result in the enforcement of a patent rather than elimination of a patent or significant restriction on patent enforcement. The almost unanimous reaction from the major media that had long been calling for faster, more expert adjudication of patent cases was very critical of the outcome, without in most instances even addressing the particular facts or reasoning of the published record or decision.[61]

In that case, after the ordinary full trial proceedings before the administrative law judge, with active involvement of the expert patent litigation attorneys from the ITC's Office of Unfair Import Investigations representing the public's interest, the ITC made special, supplemental solicitations for public input on the public interest. These solicitations addressed, among other things, concerns about anticompetitive effects of patent enforcement in the context of technological standard-setting organizations and putative commitments to issue licenses on so-called RAND or FRAND (fair, reasonable, and non-discriminatory) terms. The PTO, the DOJ, and the FTC all provided formal submissions, as has occurred in prior ITC proceedings raising similar issues. They largely reflected the FTC's decade of actions expressing significant skepticism about patent enforcement but focused largely on only the broad, general policy concerns of the FTC about antitrust implications of patents, rather than on the particulars of the case at hand.

The result was an extensive record developed through a thorough factual investigation and detailed legal and economic analysis into the core underlying economics of patent hold-up, including detailed evidence about whether particular parties were surprised, were opportunistic, or made asset-specific investments; what particular patents were related to which particular standards; whether they were essential to those particular standards; what specific terms were involved in any relevant licensing commitments that were made; how each of the particular parties acted in relation to those commitments, etc. Based on this record, the ITC issued a detailed decision spanning roughly 150 pages, including approximately 35 pages devoted to the analysis of this evidence, and an accompanying thoughtful dissenting opinion of approximately 10 pages setting forth detailed reasoning closely tied to the factual record, which focuses largely on a different reading of the facts relating to the specific actions of the parties regarding their particular negotiating behaviors.[62]

Simply put, the ITC processes and opinions involved highly experienced government staff, with a dramatically faster time frame and significantly lower cost than district court litigation, relying on government officials having extensive expertise in the relevant technology, economics, industrial dynamics, and law, focused on the facts with extensive and very detailed published opinions that tie the application of the law to the facts of the case. And while the basic remedy often used in ITC proceedings is one that can easily appear to be blunt at first blush—an exclusion order—the ITC also issues cease and desist orders that are *in personam*, against only those parties involved in the proceeding, and it has a demonstrated track record of very carefully tailoring orders of either type to mitigate hold-up problems in particular cases.[63] This all gave significant guidance to future government decision-makers and private parties about how the law would be applied to facts of future cases, which would increase certainty and predictability that can help parties organize their affairs and conduct their governmental and commercial activities based on the facts relevant to particular cases.

Yet, when the Executive Branch intervened in the case afterwards to set aside the ITC's remedy, the only public information it provided was contained in a single three-page letter, containing only a few lines of text explaining how it was based on the facts of this case.[64] This provided little information to academics, government officials, and businesses, in the U.S. or around the world, about what facts or reasons triggered this different outcome.

The combination of the response by the public media and the response from the Executive Branch provides little guidance for future decision-makers around the world about how particular types of evidence about what specific types of economic issues will have what particular types of legal significance in future cases. Instead, whether correct or not, some might read both as suggesting that significant traction can be gotten using the less legally formal tools of popular sentiment or political influence. The field of political economy demonstrates that the efficacy of these sorts of strategies and tactics tend to favor large, established businesses, which sometimes can come at the expense of competition and innovation.[65] Significant concerns have already been raised that political considerations could feature more prominently in IP enforcement in the future.[66]

This chapter takes seriously the concerns raised by critics of patent jury trials as an important benchmark against which to measure patent litigation proceedings before the ITC. In so doing, it shows how ITC proceedings go a long way in directly satisfying the concerns raised by critics of patent jury trials without triggering the costs raised by the particular administrative procedures involving the PTO, DOJ, and FTC, which are often advocated by those critics. More specifically, the chapter explores the ways in which proceedings like those conducted at the ITC are significantly less long, are less expensive, and involve much more (and much more diverse) patent law expertise than the typical patent jury trial. ITC proceedings also are structured to turn on facts rather than political influence. As a result, they have a long track record of reaching outcomes favoring both sides, patentees and alleged infringers, depending on the facts of the particular case.

Given the significant complexity and thoroughness of each of the organizations and procedures mentioned in this chapter, its discussion of them is far from exhaustive. Rather, the chapter highlights some of the ways that the concerns of the critics of patent jury trials can be meaningfully addressed without triggering what appear to be various deleterious side effects of the reform mechanisms they seek to implement. To the extent that these negative side effects are appropriately considered to be unintended consequences, the chapter outlines important reasons alternative reforms should be considered—for example, increased reliance on patent jury trials and increased reliance on proceedings before the ITC or an ITC analog.[67]

The chapter explores the ITC as a model agency structure that goes a long way in mitigating the pernicious effects of Executive Branch overreach. The basics are simple: (1) internal structure designed to incentivize the heaven of collaboration and reasoned moderation through the threat of the hell of deadlock and long-standing internal disputes; and (2) a set of substantive law topics that are commercial in nature (thereby giving strong incentives for private parties to bring to the agency the relevant facts on the various sides of each issue) and simultaneously in dispute (thereby providing each side with self-discipline against hyperbole).

15.

THE RADICALIZATION OF THE NATIONAL LABOR RELATIONS BOARD

William J. Kilberg and Thomas M. Johnson, Jr.[1]

For many years, there was a shared understanding between Republicans and Democrats about the federal government's role in labor relations that was, if not quite a consensus, at least a negotiated truce. President Roosevelt and the New Deal Democrats had passed the Wagner Act, also known as the National Labor Relations Act (NLRA), which protected the rights of employees to join labor unions, bargain collectively with their employers over the terms and conditions of employment, and strike if necessary.[2] A generation later, Republicans could take credit for the Taft-Hartley Act (passed over President Truman's veto), which eliminated certain types of strikes and boycotts, authorized states to enact "right-to-work" laws to ensure that employees could opt out of unions, and protected free speech during union campaigns.[3]

Presidents of both parties nominated qualified candidates to serve as members of the National Labor Relations Board, the federal agency that acts as an arbiter in disputes between management and labor and polices the legal boundaries between the Wagner and Taft-Hartley Acts.

The NLRB was respected for its expertise—so much so that its attorneys, rather than the appellate specialists in the Office of the Solicitor General, argued the board's cases in the U.S. Supreme Court. Meanwhile, politicians on both sides of the aisle assumed that unions would always be an indelible fixture of American political life. As late as the Nixon administration, Republican Secretary of Labor George Shultz could golf with the head of the AFL-CIO George Meany without raising any eyebrows.[4]

This détente between Republicans and Democrats no longer exists, principally because union strength no longer appears as inevitable as it once was. Union participation as a percentage of the total workforce has declined from a high of 28.3 percent in 1954 to 11.1 percent in 2014.[5] In the private sector, 24.2 percent of the workforce was unionized in 1973; that number now stands at a mere 6.6 percent.[6] Republicans recognize that federal intrusions into the workplace that once were taken for granted in the name of promoting "industrial peace" now must be reconsidered in light of an increasingly competitive, globalized, and non-unionized workforce. Democrats, on the other hand, feel increasing pressure from unions to preserve existing pro-labor rules and promote new ones in the hope that the government can reverse the steady decline of union influence by fiat.

As a result, the National Labor Relations Board has become a much more political and politicized institution. That trend did not start with President Obama, but, more than any other, his administration has placed its thumb on the regulatory scales in favor of unions—ignoring constitutional and statutory limits in the process.

When the Senate refused to confirm his controversial nominations to the board, the President made the appointments unilaterally during a brief "intra-session" recess of the Senate—an action that the Supreme Court later held unconstitutional under Article II's Advice and Consent Clause.[7] As a Senator and presidential nominee, Obama championed legislation that would effectively replace secret-ballot elections with signature drives run by union supporters that are prone to coercion and abuse.[8] When Congress refused to enact this so-called Employee Free Choice Act, the NLRB proceeded to engineer much the same result through a rule that dramatically reduces the time to conduct elections in order to prevent union opponents from mobilizing.[9] The President has also repeatedly bypassed Congress to issue pro-union executive orders: For example, one requires government contractors to post pro-union notices in the workplace, while another prohibits the same contractors from seeking reimbursement from the federal government for any costs incurred in opposing union campaigns.[10]

What explains this administration's zeal in expanding executive power to promote union interests at the expense of the rule of law? And does the President's strategy even offer hope to those who wish to restore collective bargaining as the preferred means by which management and employees interact on issues such as wages, benefits, and job protection?

The President's pro-union agenda has its roots in an established liberal narrative about the correlation between strong unions and a strong economy. According to this narrative, unions are necessary to preserve the middle class and grow the economy because unions ensure "fair" wages. Thus, this theory posits, to promote a strong middle class, the government must promote strong unions. Liberals credit unions in substantial part for the growth of the economy in the decades following World War II. And they claim that the country lost its way when President Reagan ordered air traffic controllers back to work during the 1981 PATCO strike and fired those who refused. Emboldened by Reagan's victory against PATCO, they argue, employers ever since have pushed a pro-management, deregulatory agenda that has weakened unions and contributed to a shrinking middle class.

The remedy, from the liberal perspective, is clear: Economic necessity, married to principles of distributive justice, requires expansive administrative action to provide unions with the political power necessary to regain the influence they have lost since Reagan declared war on organized labor. Liberal policy prescriptions include, among other things, that government contractors and other employers must pay "fair" wages sought by unions, rather than competitive wages set by the market; employers must not be allowed to speak or act against unions during organizing campaigns; and employers must not be able to enforce neutral workplace rules that could have an incidental effect on union organizing.

The problem with the liberal narrative is that it misdiagnoses the problem and thus is incapable of prescribing the proper solution. The evidence does not support the conclusion that organized labor's declining fortunes have contributed to a shrinking middle class. Union participation in the workforce has been in decline since 1954, but income stagnation is a more recent phenomenon.[11] Furthermore, from the mid-1970s until at least the turn of the century, middle-class contraction resulted most often from more people climbing the economic ladder into higher income brackets.[12] This data refutes the idea that unions, already in decline for decades, were responsible for ensuring that most Americans enjoyed a certain standard of living.

It is also untrue that Republican policies precipitated the decline in union fortunes. Rather, the decline in union density is principally the result of increased competition and technology in the post–World War II period.[13] The Wagner Act's inflexible contract-based system was designed for an industrial age, in which the supply of low- and moderately skilled labor in places like assembly plants and rail yards was vital to economic success. As companies became more automated, however, employees were viewed less as interchangeable cogs in a machine and more as individuals with unique talents and skill sets. The employee on the line became less valuable than the employee who could operate the computerized system that runs the line.

But collective bargaining agreements are almost always seniority-based, restrict workers to narrow job classifications, and apply strict work rules, thus making it difficult or impossible for employers to leverage the particular skill sets of individual employees and reward employees according to merit. Instead, under the union model, employees are paid the same negotiated wage "premium" regardless of the price that the market would bear for their services. While this wage "premium" has remained steady since the 1970s, studies show no increase in productivity or other offsetting benefits associated with unionization.[14]

To the contrary, the union model has introduced distortions into the marketplace. By lifting wages above competitive rates, unions increase the costs of production, which are passed on to consumers in the form of higher prices.[15] As a result, unionized companies lose business to non-union competitors, reducing total employment in a unionized workplace below market levels.[16] For example, since the late 1970s, unionized American companies have faced steep competition from foreign manufacturers, whose lower costs have often produced cheaper goods.

The lower prices benefited consumers, which increased overall demand. This led to the proliferation of non-union foreign-owned plants within the United States and thus more American jobs.[17]

President Reagan's showdown with PATCO must be understood against the backdrop of these powerful historical and economic trends. To be sure, Reagan's actions raised public awareness and showed that it was possible to successfully counteract the deleterious effects that unions could impose on the economy. But the innovation and entrepreneurship of the American people in the preceding decades had set the stage for that moment. Outside America, the results were the same: Margaret Thatcher had her "PATCO moment" in Great Britain around the same time when she cut off government subsidies to the coal industry during a 1984 union strike. And like America, nearly every European country has experienced a drop in union participation over the past thirty years.[18]

While the world economy has moved on, the union lobby in the United States has not. Unions remain a strong political presence within the Democratic Party, contributing hundreds of millions of dollars in political contributions and expenditures as well as in-kind contributions.[19] Not coincidentally, the one place where unions have *not* declined is the public sector, which is relatively immune from the competitive pressures of the market. In fact, union membership in the public sector has increased from 32.8 percent in 1977 to 35.7 percent according to recent statistics[20] In 2010, for the first time, there were more unionized workers in the public sector (7.9 million) than in the private sector (7.4 million).[21] The vitality of public-sector unions and the absence of competition have resulted in wages and benefits that are unrelated to productivity and out of line with the private workforce.[22] Compensation and pension costs have driven many state governments today into financial distress, and Republicans and Democrats at the state level are waging pitched battles over public pension and health care reform.

The clash between competing liberal and conservative views of unions and the desperation of the labor lobby has resulted in a National Labor Relations Board that is increasingly marginalized and radicalized. But it is also a board that continues to play an outsized role in American labor relations relative to the political branches. Having failed for years to repeal or amend Taft-Hartley, Democrats now seek to circumvent it through administrative action. Democrats thereby hope that they can "retrofit" the old union model onto a modern economy that cannot sustain it.

Through his policies, President Obama has encouraged and accelerated this shift in decision-making from Congress to the board. Of the many examples of this tendency, there are three categories of policy initiatives that merit sustained discussion: undermining state "right-to-work" laws, which have been enacted now in half the states; minimizing the speech rights of management and employees who want a non-unionized workforce; and interfering with neutral policies that could have an incidental chilling effect on union organizing.

First, the board has looked for opportunities to counteract state "right-to-work" laws, which make it illegal for an employer to run a "closed shop" in which union membership is made a condition of employment. These laws reflect the prerogatives of the states that adopt them, and federal efforts to invalidate or circumvent them undermine constitutional federalism, as specifically recognized in the Taft-Hartley Act amendments and by the Supreme Court.[23] Such laws are also increasingly popular because they provide employees with a measure of freedom over whether or not to join a union. But because the laws introduce competition and threaten a union's political grip on a workplace, they are unpopular with labor.

In its most brazen attack on these laws, the NLRB in 2011 attempted to stop the Boeing Corporation from opening a new plant, for new work, in a right-to-work state.[24] Specifically, the board claimed that Boeing violated the NLRA by placing a new assembly line in South Carolina (a right-to-work state) instead of expanding its existing unionized facility in Everett, Washington. Boeing's planned expansion did not cost any unionized employees their jobs; to the contrary, Boeing had openly discussed plans that would continue the growth of employment at its Everett facility. But the government claimed that Boeing was attempting to circumvent the union, and acting out of anti-union animus, by placing new work outside of Washington in a less union-friendly jurisdiction. The upshot of this unprecedented theory is that management could never use as economic leverage the threat to place new work in a new, non-union facility—despite the fact that unions have comparable economic tools at their disposal in the form of strikes. While the union ultimately withdrew its charge, the board's complaint, if successful, would have nullified a $2 billion investment in South Carolina and dislocated thousands of employees who had already been hired in connection with the new project.[25]

More recently, the board has expressed willingness to re-examine a long-standing rule that exempts employees in right-to-work states from having to pay dues for unions to process grievances on their behalf.[26] Under federal law, even if an employee opts out of union membership in a right-to-work state, the union still acts as the exclusive representative for all employees in the covered unit (even the opt-outs).[27] Because all employees must utilize the exclusive union grievance process to resolve their employment issues, the board historically has held that non-member employees do not need to pay for the costs of such grievances in right-to-work states for their protection.[28] If the board reconsiders this rule, and permits unions to charge non-members for administrative costs, it would effectively impose a tax on employees who choose to exercise their statutory right to opt out of union membership.

Second, under Obama, the board has repeatedly attempted to curtail the speech rights of management and the speech and voting rights of dissenting employees in order to enhance the political power of unions during election campaigns.

The most prominent example of this is the new NLRB rule that amended the procedures for determining whether a majority of employees wish to be represented by a labor organization for purposes of collective bargaining.[29] Among other things, this rule allows "ambush" elections by shortening an election campaign period to as few as ten days, thereby making it more difficult for management or dissenting employees to oppose the union in any concerted fashion.

This rule is a solution in search of a problem, as most election petitions are already processed quickly. The median time for an organizing election in 2010, for example, was only thirty-eight days, and the general counsel has described the board as having done an "outstanding" job in meeting target timeframes.[30] While Congress passed a resolution disapproving the "ambush" election rule under the Congressional Review Act, the President vetoed the resolution, and the rule took effect in mid-April 2015.[31] In the month afterward, there was a 32 percent increase in the number of election petitions filed with the NLRB.[32]

Besides limiting the time that employers have to campaign in advance of a union election, President Obama's board has also made it easier for unions to gerrymander workplaces to help ensure favorable election results. In its 2011 *Specialty Healthcare* decision, the board for the first time placed a heightened burden of proof on employers to make it more difficult for management to challenge the scope of the "bargaining unit" proposed by the union, that is, the group of employees eligible to vote on whether or not to be represented.[33] The net effect of this change is that it will now be easier for unions to organize very small groups of employees within a workplace, creating "micro-units" for bargaining purposes.

Under prior law, presumptions in certain industries favored a "wall-to-wall" bargaining unit of all employees at a particular salary or experience level within a facility. But under the new *Specialty Healthcare* test, unions will be able to single out and certify as a bargaining unit the most pro-union part of a workplace, wherever it exists—for example, the men's shoes section at a large department store.[34] The result will be more balkanized and adversarial work environments, in which groups of employees performing similar job duties could receive different wages, benefits, or job protections. This test is currently being challenged in several federal courts of appeals as inconsistent with the NLRA and NLRB precedent.[35]

The President has even extended his attack on free speech in the workplace by requiring employers to deliver the administration's pro-union messages. One of the President's first acts was to issue an executive order that requires nearly all government contractors to post a notice of employees' rights in "conspicuous places" in its plants and offices.[36] That notice, as developed by the Department of Labor, requires the employer to affirm the right of employees to form, join, and support a union, to bargain collectively with their employer, to strike or picket, and even to wear "union hats, buttons, t-shirts, and pins in the workplace."[37]

In 2011, the NLRB sought to expand the scope of the notice-posting requirements from government contractors to all employers covered by the NLRA.[38] Under the final rule, failure to post the required notice could serve as evidence of an unfair labor practice and could toll the statute of limitations on any unfair labor practice charge brought against an employer.[39] The D.C. Circuit ultimately invalidated the rule, reasoning that provisions of the Taft-Hartley Act prohibited the board from punishing employers for speaking (or refusing to speak) on matters relating to collective bargaining.[40] The court reasoned that the applicable provisions of Taft-Hartley, which have roots in the First Amendment, prevent the government from requiring an employer to post a one-sided notice that effectively encourages employees to unionize.[41]

Third, the board has expanded its mandate to shape company policies on employee discipline, confidentiality, and non-disparagement, among other things. The board's cudgel in this arena is Section 7 of the NLRA, which protects the right of employees to discuss the terms and conditions of employment and to otherwise engage in "concerted activity" with other employees.[42] The board's jurisdiction in this area extends to practically *all* workplaces, not simply ones where unions already exist or are likely to be present.

The board's most prominent and controversial use of Section 7 has been in policing corporate social media policies, which aim to prevent employees from posting an employer's confidential information online or using social media to harass other employees or disparage the work environment. In a series of memoranda, the board has sought to sharply limit company policies that restrict employee comments on sites like Twitter or Facebook.[43]

To be sure, employee speech is valuable and discussion with management about employment terms and conditions ought to be permitted and encouraged. But the board has gone beyond encouraging productive discourse and has restricted employers' ability to enforce neutral civility rules that are a baseline expectation for workplace behavior. For example, in one case, the board invalidated a car dealership's policy that read that "[n]o one should be disrespectful or use profane language which injures the image or reputation of the Dealership."[44] The dealership had used this rule to justify its termination of an employee who had posted disrespectful and disparaging comments about the dealership on Facebook. A divided NLRB held that employees would reasonably construe the rule as prohibiting communications protected by Section 7 of the act.[45] In another decision, the board invalidated Costco's rule that employees not post electronically any statements that "damage the Company, defame any individual or damage any person's reputation."[46] The board even invalidated Costco's rules that prohibited employees from electronically sharing "confidential" information, such as employees' names and contact information, payroll data, and unauthorized postings of company property.[47] In a third decision, a divided board held that merely asking employees to keep internal human resources or legal investigations confidential could violate the NLRA.[48]

The board has also taken aim at "at will" employment policies, which typically provide that an employee has no expectation of future employment for any set period of time. These policies merely state the default rule of most employment relationships in the United States. But the board has taken the position that such policies violate the NLRA if they are written in a way that could suggest that the rule cannot be changed through union organizing or collective bargaining.[49]

Further, the board has attempted to use Section 7 to limit employers' freedom with regard to the types of contractual provisions they can enter into with their employees. In 2012, the NLRB held in *D.R. Horton, Inc.* that an employer had violated Section 7 by mandating that its employees sign an arbitration agreement restricting them to single employee complaints and prohibiting the filing of joint or collective actions against the employer. The board reasoned that the agreement "unlawfully restrict[ed] employees' Section 7 right to engage in concerted action for mutual aid or protection."[50] The Fifth Circuit subsequently overturned this decision and held that arbitration agreements containing class waivers were permissible, notwithstanding Section 7's protections of collective action.[51] Despite the circuit court's disapproval, the board later reaffirmed its original *D.R. Horton* decision.[52]

These measures, taken together, represent President Obama's federal labor legacy: invalid recess appointments, intrusions on federalism, aggressive curtailment of employee and management speech, and officious intermeddling in workplace policies. The board claims that these policies will help restore the middle class. But the middle class has moved on and no longer looks to the board as its protector. While powerful unions may have coincided with the strong middle class of the mid-century, the President has yet to learn that correlation is not causation.

The President cannot stop the economic tides, which will continue to determine the future of unions in the American workplace. But his administration can thrash about in the waves, introducing distortions that hurt the economy and ordinary workers. Congressional reforms could help ensure that the NLRB acts in the future as a neutral umpire attuned to the realities of today's economy, rather than as an advocate for labor. Senate Republicans, for example, have introduced an NLRB Reform Act that would increase the number of board members from five to six and ensure equal representation of Republicans and Democrats.[53] The proposed act would also hold the NLRB more accountable by providing parties with easier access to the courts and encouraging the board to process cases in a more timely fashion. Congress could also consider reintroducing the TEAM Act, which was passed by a Republican Congress in the mid-1990s and vetoed by President Clinton.[54] Under current law, it is illegal for employees to form any type of voluntary association to present their concerns to management, thus providing costly trade unions with a federally enforced monopoly over group communication. The TEAM Act could free employees and management to develop and pursue more efficient, less costly avenues for employee input into the terms and conditions of employment.

With reforms like these, it may be possible to reach a new political consensus on the role the government should play as intermediary between management and labor. That consensus would recognize that some industries may still benefit from the union model of rigid job classifications, extensive work rules, and lockstep wage and benefit increases. But any such consensus would also need to be attuned to the reality that the country no longer has a significant unionized workforce. The policies pursued by President Obama—in which trade union influence is artificially inflated at the expense of constitutional limits, individual liberties, and economic growth—do not represent that future.

16.

DISPARATE IMPACT
The Way of the New World

Peter N. Kirsanow

No sooner does a government attempt to go beyond its political sphere and enter upon this new track than it exercises, even unintentionally, an unsupportable tyranny; for a government can only dictate strict rules, the opinions for which it favors are rigidly enforced, and it is never easy to discriminate between its advice and its commands.

—Alexis de Tocqueville[1]

Various Executive Branch agencies within the Obama administration have been churning out both advice and commands pertaining to race and ethnicity that would make Tocqueville blanch. There are few areas in the public sphere immune from Executive Branch dictates regarding race and the manner in which everyone—from employers to educators to financial institutions—must comport themselves to avoid sanctions by various federal agencies, primarily for failing to take sufficient steps to avoid the disparate impact of certain policies or practices on racial minorities.

The administration's insistence on micromanaging the "correct" racial percentages often has deleterious consequences for the purported beneficiaries of such racial bean counting. For example, the EEOC's attempt to discourage the use of criminal background checks because of the ostensible negative effect on minority applicants for employment actually results in significantly fewer minorities being hired.[2] And the mismatch effect created by racial preferences in college admissions supported by the administration results in more minority students dropping out of, and otherwise doing poorly in, schools for which they are ill-prepared.[3]

The concept of disparate impact achieved traction first in the employment context in *Griggs v. Duke Power*.[4] There, the Supreme Court found that a facially neutral employment policy (such as requiring a high school diploma for certain jobs) had a disparate impact on black applicants. The Court held that any such policy, even if adopted and enforced neutrally, must be job-related and consistent with business necessity. Otherwise, the policy would violate the prohibition against race discrimination in employment under Title VII of the Civil Rights Act of 1964.

The concept of disparate impact in employment often is in tension with Title VII's statutory prescription against disparate *treatment*. Some employers, in order to get the "right" number of minority employees and applicants to avoid a disparate impact claim, engage in disparate treatment—i.e., racial discrimination against majority employees or applicants. This, absurdly, places employers between the proverbial rock and a hard place: be sued for racial discrimination for trying to avoid a disparate impact lawsuit, or be sued for disparate impact for trying to avoid a discriminatory treatment lawsuit. The Supreme Court allows that an employer may avoid liability for the former if it has a "strong basis in evidence" that it may be liable for the latter.[5]

Despite its Red Queen quality, at least the use of disparate impact in the employment context has been blessed by the Supreme Court . . . for now. But as Justice Scalia notes in his concurring opinion in *Ricci v. DeStefano*, "[R]esolution of this dispute merely postpones that evil day in which the Court will have to question whether, or to what extent, are the disparate impact provisions of Title VII of the Civil Rights Act of 1964 consistent with the Constitution's guaranty of equal protection?"[6] The Obama administration, however, has extended the concept well beyond the employment context into areas for which its use has dubious legal or policy support. A few examples follow.

AFFIRMATIVELY FURTHERING FAIR HOUSING

The Obama administration's Department of Housing and Urban Development (HUD) has promulgated a rule,[7] colloquially known as Affirmatively Furthering Fair Housing (AFFH), which incorporates disparate impact theory and its conceptual cousin, affirmative action, into housing policy. Through the AFFH, HUD seeks to engage in both racial and social engineering by requiring public housing authorities (PHAs) to take "proactive steps beyond simply combatting discrimination to foster inclusive communities and access to community assets for all persons protected under the Fair Housing Act. More specifically, it means taking steps proactively to address significant disparities in access to community assets."[8]

There are several infirmities with the AFFH rule. First, disparate impact claims are not cognizable under a plain statutory reading of the Fair Housing Act of 1968.[9] There is absolutely no evidence that when Congress passed the act, it adopted disparate impact liability. Indeed, HUD did not even attempt to claim in the AFFH that there is any support whatsoever for disparate impact in the text of the act. Instead, HUD merely noted that "[HUD] has long interpreted the Act" to include a disparate impact component. Thus, by simply stating that it has the power to apply disparate impact theory to housing, HUD has arrogated that power to itself.[10] A neat tautological trick, but nonetheless suspect, even under *Chevron* deference.[11]

Notably, the AFFH provisions regarding the classification of citizens by race violate the plain meaning of the Equal Protection Clause of the Constitution. AFFH Section 5.154(c) provides in pertinent part:

> *Fair housing data provided by HUD*. HUD will provide program participants with nationally uniform local and regional data on patterns of integration and segregation; racially and ethnically concentrated areas of poverty; access to assets and education, employment, low-poverty, transportation, and environmental health, among others; disproportionate housing needs; data on individuals with disabilities and families with children; and data on discrimination. HUD will

> also provide PHA site locational data . . . the distribution of housing choice vouchers, and occupancy data.

Quite simply, there is only one way to provide data on "integration and segregation" and "racially and ethnically concentrated areas of poverty": by violating the Equal Protection Clause. Government classification of individuals on the basis of race is inherently suspect and subject to strict judicial scrutiny. The classification must serve a compelling state interest and be narrowly tailored to serve that interest in order to pass constitutional muster.[12] This is particularly true where the government—in this case HUD—purports to grant *benefits* on the basis of race. HUD does so by providing "access to assets in education, employment, low-poverty, transportation, and environmental health." Furthermore, the rule compels PHAs to engage in constitutionally prohibited racial balancing by requiring PHAs to reduce "racial and national origin concentrations."[13] The only plausible means to discharge this mandate is to engage in racial discrimination, however well intended or benign.

Furthermore, the rule steals a disparate impact base. HUD maintains people often live in areas primarily populated by their own racial or ethnic groups. HUD describes this phenomenon as "segregation," despite the fact that legal segregation has been dead for more than sixty years. HUD then magically transforms middle- or lower-income populations into a protected class based simply on disparate impact: "disproportionate housing needs [*sic*] when the percentage of extremely low-income, low-income, moderate-income and middle-income families in a category of housing need are members of a protected class is at least 10% higher than in the category as a whole."[14] HUD's focus on disparate impact, and the almost complete absence of a discussion by the department of disparate treatment, suggests disparate impact in this regard is based less on race than on income.

Finally, HUD evinces executive racial presumptiveness on an impressive scale. *De jure* racial segregation no longer exists. Thus, "racially concentrated neighborhoods" are largely a function of income and voluntary residential choices. Among such choices—at least for some members of racial and ethnic minorities—is that they prefer to live near friends, relatives, and members of their own racial and ethnic groups. HUD, however, presumes to know better what is in minorities' best residential interests, assuming the role of national racial chef and pronouncing that neighborhoods with, say, a 25 percent black, 20 percent Hispanic, 10 percent Asian, and 45 percent white mix is where Americans prefer—or should prefer—to live. This is surely the type of overreach against which Tocqueville warned.

EEOC GUIDANCE ON CRIMINAL BACKGROUND CHECKS

In April 2012, the EEOC issued a new policy guidance regarding hiring people with criminal records.[15] Although the EEOC presents this guidance as a mere refinement of a previous guidance, the EEOC's triumphalism accompanying it suggests that it is intended to broadly discourage the use of criminal background checks in hiring.

The EEOC's claim of authority to regulate the use of criminal background checks is based on a strained interpretation of disparate impact. "Convicted criminals" is not a protected class under Title VII. Black and Hispanic men are, however, more likely to have criminal records than are white and Asian men, or black, Hispanic, white, or Asian women. Therefore, the use of criminal history in hiring has a disproportionate impact on black and Hispanic men. This disparate impact, according to the EEOC, constitutes discrimination on the basis of race.

This is totem pole disparate impact. As debatable as the Court's decision interpreting Title VII in *Griggs* may have been, at least the Court had some evidence on which to base its finding that the education and testing requirements in that case were not job-related. No such evidence undergirds the EEOC guidance on criminal history in employment.[16] The EEOC completely ignored this aspect of *Griggs*. The EEOC adduced no evidence regarding whether applicants with criminal records are better, comparable, or worse employees than people without criminal records.[17] Without such data, the EEOC cannot determine whether a criminal history is in fact immaterial in predicting an applicant's job performance. EEOC failed to consider that even if an ex-offender does not exhibit so-called counterproductive work behaviors, if he commits a crime, it will cost the company money and manpower. The likelihood that a particular employee will be arrested and therefore unable to come to work is a legitimate business concern, and one that social science can predict with some accuracy.[18] This undercuts the EEOC's use of disparate impact theory as applied to criminal records. If a criminal history is a meaningful prediction of an applicant's job performance, then employer use of criminal history is job-related and consistent with business necessity. Whether or not its use has a disparate impact on minorities is legally irrelevant.

Aside from the guidance's questionable legal foundation, it presents practical problems for employers, similar to that in *Ricci*. The guidance insists that employers conduct an "individualized assessment." The individualized assessment is conducted after the employer has considered the seriousness of the applicant's offense, the length of time that has elapsed since the offense, and whether the offense is related to the job sought. The guidance strongly recommends that an employer then give the applicant a chance to explain his criminal record. This introduces an element of subjectivity into the hiring process, leaving an employer exposed, once again, to disparate *treatment* claims. Such disparate treatment claims could arise in two ways. First, minority applicants could claim that they were treated differently for a consciously innocent reason—i.e., the employer developed a better rapport with one candidate than the other. So the mere fact that the process was not uniform exposes the company to a disparate treatment suit. Second, in an attempt to avoid a disparate impact suit, an employer could preferentially hire minority applicants instead of white applicants, thus creating an opportunity to be sued by white applicants. Rocks and hard places abound when Executive Branch agencies issue dictates on the basis of race.

LENDING ON THE BASIS OF RACE

The Department of Justice and the Consumer Financial Protection Bureau aggressively use disparate impact to accuse banks of discrimination in lending. In 2011, the DOJ obtained a $335 million settlement from Countrywide on the grounds that black and Hispanic borrowers were charged higher fees and rates than white borrowers and that 10,000 minority borrowers also received subprime mortgages when similar white borrowers received more favorable terms.[19] Bear in mind that the essence of disparate impact or "statistical discrimination" is that the government usually is not able to prove disparate *treatment*. For example, in the Countrywide case, there was no evidence that Countrywide had a policy of intentionally discriminating against blacks and Hispanics. Neither did the complaint provide any evidence that individual mortgage brokers were consciously discriminating against blacks and Hispanics. Indeed, if individual brokers were deliberately discriminating against blacks and Hispanics, it must have been a conspiracy on a massive scale, given that during the four years in question Countrywide originated nearly 200,000 loans to Hispanics and 90,000 loans to blacks.[20] The DOJ alleged only that Countrywide gave brokers discretion in setting loan rates and fees, did not require brokers to document why they varied loan offers, did not track and remedy racial disparities in loans, and had a compensation structure that rewarded employees for putting borrowers in higher-priced loans.[21] These practices, the DOJ said, resulted in African Americans and Hispanics, as groups, receiving less favorable loans than whites; and this, purportedly, constitutes discrimination. (Interestingly, the DOJ did not address the loan terms received by Asian Americans. Did they receive more favorable loan terms than whites, or did they receive loan terms more akin to those received by African Americans and Hispanics?)

As in the housing field, the problem with this approach is that it is difficult to prove anyone engaged in actual racial discrimination. Hundreds of thousands of loans and millions of individual decisions are involved in this case. How can the DOJ demonstrate that thousands of Countrywide employees were individually deciding to discriminate against African American and Hispanic loan applicants? How can the DOJ disentangle all the individual motivations and decisions that led to the loans in these cases? The DOJ compared borrowers who had similar, but not identical, credit profiles. Given that mortgage brokers had the authority to both lower and raise the standard rate, some bargaining was probably involved in this process. The mortgage broker whose livelihood is implicated in his decisions is naturally inclined to look much more closely at each individual profile than are the DOJ attorneys who are simply running the numbers. Furthermore, the broker will try to make as much money as possible off each loan. It is simply impossible to prove that thousands of people were engaging in invidious discrimination based solely on these numbers, and numbers are all the DOJ had.

But the details of the accusation were irrelevant. All that mattered was that the accusation of racial discrimination had been made and expensive, lengthy litigation had started. Those two things are enough to send banks scrambling to settle. The DOJ repeatedly deployed this tactic against banks large and small—from Countrywide (now part of Bank of America) to the Fort Davis State Bank.[22]

The DOJ extracts huge settlements from its victims based on mere allegations of disparate impact. Countrywide disgorged $335 million,[23] PNC paid $35 million for the alleged sins of National City Bank,[24] and tiny Fort Davis State Bank (total assets: $78.5 million; equity capital: $6.68 million) looked under the couch cushions and offered up $159,000.[25]

These settlements were earmarked first to compensate the alleged victims of the banks' malfeasance.[26] But what happens to any money that is left over after the supposed victims have been compensated? Does the money go back to the bank? Does it go into the United States Treasury? No. It is given to organizations that "provide services . . . targeted at African-American and Hispanic potential and former homeowners."[27] The DOJ has refused to provide a complete list of organizations that are eligible to receive these funds but did state that the National Urban League and Operation Hope were among the organizations.[28] Thus, the DOJ uses tendentious lawsuits to enrich these organizations and others like them (all supporters of disparate impact, of course).[29] The entire process is perhaps best described as a shakedown, with the ancillary effect of promoting the sort of racial engineering favored by bureaucrats.

The foregoing are but a few examples of departments and agencies within the Obama administration relying on suspect legal rationales and, arguably, exceeding their statutory authority in furtherance of a vision best described as a form of racial egalitarianism. The various rules, guidances, and policies, contrary to Martin Luther King, Jr.'s vision, are fixated on the color of Americans' skin.

Unsurprisingly, this overreach has done little to improve the racial environment in America and has arguably worsened it. Several polls taken during the Obama administration show that Americans believe race relations have deteriorated markedly over the last few years. State-sponsored racial discrimination, history shows, nearly always has that affect. Sadly, the Obama administration's racialist legacy promises to be part of that history.

17.

MUDDIED WATERS
How the EPA and Corps of Engineers Redefined Their Authority over State Waters

Adam P. Laxalt and Lawrence VanDyke[1]

> *The powers reserved to the several States will extend to all the objects which, in the ordinary course of affairs, concern the lives, liberties, and properties of the people, and the internal order, improvement, and prosperity of the State.*
>
> —*Publius (James Madison), Federalist No. 45*

Water is precious and clean water is invaluable. Few states understand this more than Nevada, where bustling cities are canvassed by desert landscapes. Sagebrush is Nevada's state flower for a reason: things struggle to grow here. But thanks to the Humboldt, Carson, Walker, and Truckee rivers in northern Nevada, agriculture thrives in the Great Basin. There, Nevadans grow crops, including alfalfa and garlic, and raise livestock from cattle to bees. This delicate desert ecosystem is regulated and maintained at the state and local levels, where citizens directly consult their elected representatives and express their needs.

A new federal regulation threatens this balance. The Environmental Protection Agency (EPA) and the U.S. Army Corps of Engineers (Corps of Engineers) (hereafter referred to as the agencies) have published a rule expanding the scope of waters covered by the Clean Water Act (CWA). Rather than preserve the state's role as the primary regulator of intrastate waters, the new definition expands the jurisdiction of the CWA to cover agricultural waterways and rain-filled ditches. This land grab contradicts Supreme Court precedent and goes well beyond the agencies' constitutionally delegated authority.

This expansion of power also imposes financial and regulatory burdens on states in violation of the Tenth Amendment. By introducing a costly case-specific analysis of whether a variety of other waters—or, occasionally, even roadside ditches—fall within the CWA's ambit, the new rule leaves nothing but specifically excluded waters outside its jurisdiction. Thus, the rule wrests control and stewardship from local authorities and threatens to impose unpredictable, arbitrary costs on the states. In fact, Nevada's agricultural ditches and canals are implicated, even though many of these channels remain dry for most of the year. This unconstitutional overreach of power has left states with no option but to legally challenge the agencies' new rule.

I. JUDICIAL HISTORY OF "WATERS OF THE UNITED STATES"

Since 1975, the EPA and the Corps of Engineers have attempted to push the definition of "waters of the United States" beyond any reasonable limit.[2] The term "navigable waters" originally retained its plain meaning and constrained the text of the CWA, encompassing waters that were "'navigable in fact' or readily susceptible of being rendered so."[3] In *United States v. Riverside Bayview Homes*, the Court determined that the congressional recasting of "navigable waters" as "waters of the United States" relaxed this strict reading and allowed the Corps of Engineers to assert jurisdiction over a wetland physically adjacent to navigable waters.[4] Since *Riverside Bayview Homes*, the Court has twice rejected agency attempts to stretch the definition of "waters of the United States" to cover isolated wetlands and other spuriously connected waters.[5]

These two denials of agency jurisdiction form a clear precedent: "waters of the United States" does not cover disconnected, ephemeral waters. This limitation was first outlined in *Solid Waste Agency of Northern Cook County v. United States Army Corps of Engineers* (*SWANCC*) when the Court invalidated a Corps of Engineers rule that asserted jurisdiction over an isolated, intrastate pond.[6] The Court held that the rule exceeded the Corps of Engineers' authority under the CWA.[7] In reaching this conclusion, the Court limited its holding in *Riverside Bayview Homes* to confer jurisdiction only over those wetlands that "actually abut[] on" traditional navigable waters, not "nonnavigable, isolated, intrastate waters."[8] Five years later, in *Rapanos v. United States*, the Court affirmed the *SWANCC* holding, clarifying that it applied to wetlands as well as ponds.[9]

Due to a split majority, two tests emerged from *Rapanos*. The plurality opinion, authored by Justice Scalia, defined "waters of the United States" as those that include "relatively permanent, standing or continuously flowing bodies of water" and secondary waters that have a "continuous surface connection" to those waters.[10] Justice Kennedy's solo concurrence, on the other hand, created a "significant nexus" requirement.[11] He proposed determining jurisdiction based on whether wetlands "significantly affect the chemical, physical, and biological integrity of other covered waters."[12]

II. CONFLICT WITH THE SUPREME COURT

The agencies' new rule violates the Supreme Court's precedents. While the EPA and the Corps of Engineers purport to strike a course between the Scylla and Charybdis of the two plurality tests, it ultimately founders on both. The latest definition of "waters of the United States" runs afoul of both *Rapanos* tests by expansively defining tributaries, extending per se coverage to nebulously adjacent waters, and creating a case-specific category to capture any waters that may fall through the jurisdictional cracks.

In past rules, the agencies' jurisdiction was limited to primary waters that implicated "interstate or foreign commerce."[13] But the agencies' new rule would establish per se jurisdiction over practically all tributaries that flow into primary waters. Defining a tributary as "a water that contributes flow, either directly or through another water" to a traditional navigable water, the agencies sweep into their jurisdiction ephemeral streams that fill with rainwater and ditches that are usually dry.[14]

In a feat of gymnastics, the agencies attempted to square their definition of tributaries with the "continuous surface connection" and "significant nexus" tests from *Rapanos*. It cannot be done. Many tributaries, by their ephemeral nature, fail to maintain a "continuous surface connection" to primary waters as required by the *Rapanos* plurality.[15] Even Justice Kennedy's looser "significant nexus" test cannot stretch so far as to include such inconsequential "tributaries."[16] Moreover, the agencies' inclusion of tributaries that contribute flow through *non-jurisdictional waters* suggests that only explicitly exempted waters will be non-jurisdictional.[17] Even a generous reading of the final rule reveals the agencies' blatant power play: should the new rule survive the Supreme Court, the EPA might better be characterized as the Environmental *Micromanagement* Agency.

The agencies also sidestepped the Court's clear exclusion of isolated wetlands by exerting per se jurisdiction over all "adjacent" waters. These waters include all waters "bordering, contiguous, or neighboring" traditional navigable waters even if "separated by constructed dikes or barriers . . . and the like."[18] Nesting its definitions, the agencies expansively described "neighboring" as "located within 100 feet of the ordinary high water mark" or "located within the 100-year floodplain."[19] By definition, these waters lack a *continuous* surface connection;[20] they need only share a minimal connection with a navigable water once every decade or century.[21] Nevertheless, the agencies argue that adjacent waters affect the "chemical, physical, *or* biological" properties of jurisdictional waters.[22] But they twist Justice Kennedy's words. He required that the connection be "chemical, physical, *and* biological."[23] The nexus between two "adjacent" waters is less than tenuous; it is imagined.

Lest any waters fall through the regulatory cracks, the final rule allows the agencies to assert jurisdiction over "similarly situated" waters that pass their version of the "significant nexus" test on a *case-by-case* basis.[24] This discretionary nightmare conflicts with all but Justice Kennedy's solo concurrence in *Rapanos*, where both the plurality and the dissent found a case-specific approach unsupported by precedent.[25] Furthermore, those eight justices recognized the infeasibility of such time-consuming and costly determinations.[26] Despite these legal hurdles and practical warnings, the agencies created this "vague catch-all category" that will leave states and citizens clueless as to where and when the agencies will claim jurisdiction.[27]

In short, the agencies' new rule fails to adhere to even the most lenient limits set by the Court. The agencies have again claimed for themselves "the discretion of an enlightened despot," which is not "befitting a local zoning board," much less a federal agency.[28]

III. CONSTITUTIONAL CONFLICTS

After losing in *SWANCC*, the EPA and the Corps of Engineers were supposed to define the limits of their jurisdiction in conformity with the Constitution. In 2006, a frustrated Supreme Court observed that the new rule failed this mission.[29] As Chief Justice Roberts observed, "Rather than refining its view of its authority in light of our decision in *SWANCC*, . . . the Corps of Engineers chose to adhere to its essentially boundless view of the scope of its power. The upshot today is another defeat for the agency."[30] Undaunted by that defeat, the agencies created a new rule that conflicts not only with the Court's precedent but with the Constitution's Commerce Clause and the Tenth Amendment as well.

By pushing the new rule to the outer limits of Congress's commerce power, the agencies exceeded their interpretive capacity. In cases of constitutional overreach, the Court will "construe the statute to avoid such problems."[31] In both *SWANCC* and *Rapanos*, that is precisely what the Court did. Rejecting the Corps of Engineers' interpretation, the Court cautioned the agency against creating "an administrative interpretation of a statute invok[ing] the outer limits of Congress' power" without "a clear indication that Congress intended that result."[32]

Yet the new rule does just that. Invoking "jurisdiction . . . to the maximum extent permissible under the Commerce Clause,"[33] the agencies' definitions—such as their definition of "adjacent," which exceeds literal adjacency[34]—reach further beyond the Constitution than they did in *SWANCC* and *Rapanos*. The new rule should therefore receive the same negative treatment from the Court.

The new rule also impermissibly redefines the role of states in regulating water by requiring them to play second fiddle to federal agencies. Typically, the Court hesitates to defer to an agency's interpretation that infringes on traditional state authority.[35] That is certainly the case here.

The Supreme Court,[36] Congress,[37] and the text of the CWA[38] all recognize water rights as an area of traditional state power. Though it acknowledges this foundation, the rule proceeds to cast the states in a supporting role, requiring them to be "authorized by the EPA to administer the permitting programs."[39] This reorganization of roles in regulating water abuses the generous deference typically given to agencies.

IV. INTERNAL STATUTORY AND REGULATORY CONFLICTS

In addition to constitutional concerns, the agencies' definitions are unreasonable because they go beyond the plain language of the CWA.[40] Such capricious interpretations deserve no deference. Instead, the agencies must offer definitions that predictably emerge from the text of the statute. Whatever a roadside ditch in dry season may be, it is definitely not "water." As the Court noted in *Rapanos*, the term "waters of the United States" must include "at bare minimum, the ordinary presence of water."[41] This understanding adheres to the purpose of the CWA, which was established to cover the "Nation's *waters*."[42] If the definition is recast to include judicially excluded wetlands and ephemeral streams, the change must come from Congress, not the agencies. As it is written now, the plain language of the act bars the broad definitions offered in the new rule.

The agencies protect their boundless definitions as nothing but a marginal increase in their jurisdictional waters. Noted UC Berkeley economist David Sunding disagrees.[43] After criticizing the EPA's methodology, he concluded, "The errors, omissions, and lack of transparency in EPA's study are so severe as to render it virtually meaningless. The agency should withdraw the economic analysis and prepare an adequate study of this major change in the implementation of the CWA."[44] The majority of these flaws arise from underestimating the increase in jurisdictional waters because of a mistaken methodology.[45] As the Nevada Association of Counties noted, "[t]he economic analysis does not acknowledge or recognize that, under the proposal, additional waters, currently not jurisdictional . . . will become jurisdictional."[46] Because the agencies' cost-benefit analysis relied on this faulty calculus, it suffers the same shortcomings. By not responding to these criticisms, the agencies have proceeded with an ill-advised rule that will incur unpredictable costs on states and their citizens.

In what amounts to a regulatory sleight of hand, the final rule repeatedly invokes its "expansion" of the exempted categories as evidence of its limited jurisdictional grab. However, these "exemptions" are not really new.[47] The categories now excluded from the rule are mostly waters that have *always* been excluded in practice.[48] A brief glance at the list—which includes "small ornamental waters" and "puddles"[49]—makes this abundantly clear. The fact that the agencies felt the need to clarify that these waters are exempt testifies to the breadth of its definitions.

V. STATE, LOCAL, AND PRACTICAL CONFLICTS

Supposing the final rule was facially constitutional and consistent with current statutes, it would still amount to an atrocious policy for practical reasons. Many of the negative results can be traced to a common source: the rule is riddled with ambiguities. As a result, public and private parties will incur severe litigation costs as they attempt to divine the precise definitions of the new rule. The agencies will also see a spike in their paperwork, and states will shoulder new costs as they attempt to comply with the vague definitions. But even if the rule were clear, opposition would persist because the agencies disingenuously trample underfoot the rights of states and localities over their land.

The supreme irony of the final rule is that it purports to provide clarity while actually creating ambiguity. The new rule supposedly "reflects the agencies' goal of providing simpler, clearer, and more consistent approaches for identifying the geographic scope of the CWA,"[50] but it provides none of these things. Instead, the agencies "eliminated the definitions of floodplain and riparian area,"[51] preferring rather to "interpret specific aspects of the significant nexus standard in light of the science, the law, and the agencies' technical expertise."[52] As another example, the term "contribute flow" is not defined, leaving groundwater flow and evapotranspiration (the evaporation of moisture) up for grabs.[53] Moreover, the EPA's Science Advisory Board deemed it "appropriate to define 'other waters' as waters of the United States on a case-by-case basis," dispelling any hope of clarity or certainty.[54] In other words, the agencies will know it—and let us know—when they see it.

Apart from the new rule failing to achieve its mission, its ambiguities may create economic problems. For example, litigation costs would likely increase for private parties seeking exemptions. However, the usual cost of litigation pales in comparison to the penalties the EPA could impose if a private party received an unsympathetic ruling. Private parties may be forced to pay for the permits rather than run the risk of unaffordable penalties, such as fines up to $37,500 per violation each day.[55]

The final rule would also burden intermediary agencies and citizens by sweeping more waters into the Section 404 Permit Program.[56] As the Nevada Association of Counties observed, "the Corps, which oversees the 404 permit program, is already severely backlogged in evaluating and processing permits."[57] The predicted increase of jurisdictional waters could only aggravate these delays.[58] The process already requires, on average, more than two years and hundreds of thousands of dollars for an individual permit or more than three-quarters of a year and tens of thousands of dollars for a nationwide permit.[59] And citizens cannot ignore these requirements without running the risk of *criminal* liability.[60]

States will also incur severe administrative costs as a result of the final rule. For every new water encompassed within the "waters of the United States," each state must enact water quality standards (WQS) or allow the EPA to impose its own.[61] If newly designated "waters of the United States" fail to meet these standards, states must issue pollution restrictions known as total maximum daily load (TMDL) standards.[62] States with their own National Pollutant Discharge Elimination Systems (NPDES), found in compliance with the CWA, will need to increase their investment in these programs to accommodate for the newly jurisdictional waters.[63] The number of permits required to keep up with this federal overreach will burden the agencies and overwhelm state and local intermediaries that administer these permits.

These regulations achieve a common end: undermining state and local governments. According to the new rule, "States [will] administer approved CWA section 404 programs for 'waters of the United States' within the state, except those waters remaining under Corps jurisdiction . . . as identified in a memorandum of Agreement between the state and the Corps."[64] The forthcoming memoranda will include "[a] description of waters of the United States within the State over which the Secretary retains jurisdiction, as identified by the Secretary."[65] Put simply, the agencies expect the states to do all the heavy lifting in implementing the new rule, except when the agencies want control over a given water.

Nevada, like any other state, cannot afford the unnecessary costs of a sloppy redefinition of "waters of the United States." With a tight biannual state budget,[66] Nevada's economy should not be the plaything of the EPA or the Corps of Engineers. The money wasted on satisfying the agencies would have to be redirected from vital expenditures such as education, police, and firefighting.

VI. CONCLUSION

The founding fathers defined the scope of the national government to let states do what they do best: tend to their needs and the needs of their citizens. The EPA and the Corps of Engineers would recast this federalist vision as a regulatory nightmare. Subscribing to the delusions of King Midas, the agencies would chill federalism in the belief that they can perfect any water they touch.[67]

More could be said, but the problems with the final rule highlighted in this chapter sufficiently demonstrate the agencies' disregard for the Constitution, the Supreme Court, the states, local governments, and the people. For that reason, Nevada has joined numerous states in opposing the final waters of the United States rule to keep power in the hands of those most responsive and most capable of serving and protecting their citizens.[68]

18.

THE SEPARATION OF POWERS IN AN ADMINISTRATIVE STATE

David McIntosh and William J. Haun

When Americans are asked about the "most important" part of our Constitution—the truly indispensable guarantee within it—they usually cite the provisions within the Bill of Rights. That answer, however, is not the founders'. As James Madison noted in *Federalist* No. 47, "[n]o political truth is certainly of greater intrinsic value, or is stamped with the authority of more enlightened patrons of liberty," than the need for separated governmental power.[1] While, as Justice Scalia frequently puts it, "[e]very banana republic has a bill of rights,"[2] the separation of executive, legislative, and judicial authority into coordinate branches prohibits any one government actor from exercising total power—what the *Federalist* characterized as "the very definition of tyranny."[3]

With such high stakes, the threat modern regulatory agencies pose to the separation of powers cannot be ignored. Modern regulatory agencies effectively exercise the entire range of governmental power—legislative, executive, and judicial.[4] Their function is as threatening as their scope: many agencies write law through rulemaking, enforce it—increasingly with armed police—and then adjudicate it with an administrative law judge (ALJ) who works for the agency.

The modern administrative state was founded on premises that supplant the separation of powers. These premises—that agencies staffed with "experts" will face "modern" problems better than elected officials and that administration is more "efficient" than legislating—still undergird agency operations today. The three constitutional branches have engaged in a gradual surrender of power to the administrative state. This essay strives to outline this problem and propose solutions that can both (1) restore current administrative power to the appropriate constitutional branch and (2) impose separation-of-powers principles on agency actions and procedures. As Justice Scalia noted in his seminal dissent in *Morrison v. Olson*, "just as the mere words of the Bill of Rights are not self-effectuating, the Framers recognized '[t]he insufficiency of a mere parchment delineation of the boundaries' to achieve the separation of powers."[5] We argue that the power agencies exercise is often the "legislative" or "judicial" power that the Constitution confines to other branches of government. We believe that those vested with genuine constitutional authority have a responsibility to reclaim the power that is rightfully theirs.

I. THE ADMINISTRATIVE STATE, FUELED BY EXPANSIVE DELEGATION, ERODES THE SEPARATION OF POWERS

Article II of the U.S. Constitution vests the nation's entire "executive power" with the President and requires that he "take care that the laws be faithfully executed."[6] As Justice Scalia thoroughly explained in his *Morrison* dissent, this ensured that a single branch of government would possess administrative capability with political accountability.[7] By linking administrative power to that of the President's, the Constitution limited the nature of administrative power (as the President's is limited to executive power) and rendered it politically accountable—preserving the founders' guarantee of a "wholly popular" government as articulated in *Federalist* No. 14.

The modern administrative state finds its roots in the Progressive Era and not the founding. Rather than extoll the virtue of limited, separated power, modern administrative agencies uphold President Woodrow Wilson's charge: "The period of constitution-making is passed now. We have reached a new territory in which we need new guides, the vast territory of *administration*."[8] Well before his presidency—even before President Wilson was Professor Wilson—Wilson began articulating a view of government administration echoed today among both Democrats and Republicans, the need to run government "like a business."[9] Separation of powers, with its demands of compromise, debate, minority protections, fixed procedures, and slow movement, was inefficient, Wilson argued, and stood in the way of "progress."

In contrast, Wilson wanted to "free us from the idea that checks and balances are to be carried down through all stages of organization."[10] Wilson carved a distinction between the separation of executive, legislative, and judicial power in the Constitution with the "actual division of powers" that include "legislative and judicial acts of the administration."[11] This allowed Wilson to embrace a role for administrative power that—as the New Deal would reveal—would be untethered not only from the Executive Branch but also from the Constitution's structural constraints. Madison in the *Federalist* counted on executive, legislative, and judicial branches to jealously guard their respective power. But the Progressive combination of political expediency and ideology corroded the incentives to guard one's power. First, the Congress abdicated its powers by delegating to agencies. Then, the courts—succumbing to political pressure to uphold these delegations of legislative power—followed.

The Constitution contains vesting clauses that expressly place a certain power within a certain branch: the legislature possesses all the legislative power "herein granted," the executive is granted the entire executive power of the United States, and the U.S. Supreme Court, along with other inferior courts that Congress creates, receives the judicial power. The fact that the Constitution does not expressly prohibit one branch from delegating some of its power does not mean that the Constitution is "no more than a generalized prescription that the functions of the Branches should not be commingled too much."[12] Applying the maxim *expressio unius est exclusio alterius*—the mention of one or more elements of a class excludes others—to the vesting clauses produces the conclusion that no branch may appropriate another branch's powers.[13] As evidence, many state constitutions barred such delegations at the founding,[14] and the vesting clauses themselves state the nature of power that accords with a particular branch. The Constitution notwithstanding, as Professor Gary Lawson has explained, "[t]he Supreme Court has not invalidated a statute on nondelegation grounds since 1935."[15]

Delegation defenders may respond, credibly, that "a certain degree of discretion, and thus of lawmaking, *inheres* in most executive and judicial action, and it is up to Congress, by the relative specificity or generality of its statutory commands, to determine—up to a point—how small or how large that degree shall be."[16] But there has been almost no interest in either the Congress or the courts in actually specifying the characteristics and limits of acceptable delegation. As Justice Thomas explained while concurring in the judgment in *Department of Transportation v. Association of American Railroads*, even where a judicial "reluctance to second-guess Congress on the degree of policy judgment is understandable," it is an abdication of judicial duty to assume "that any degree of policy judgment is permissible when it comes to generally applicable rules regarding private conduct."[17] Some power is inherently legislative and cannot be delegated. But neither the Congress nor the courts have defined the limits, so legislative power has been lumped in with Executive Branch agencies. With the refusal to define the line between executive discretion and legislative power, the separation itself has eroded.[18]

The Court seems disinterested in determining the limits of acceptable delegation, resting simply on the general premises of modern administrative power: "in our increasingly complex society, replete with ever changing and more technical problems, Congress simply cannot do its job absent an ability to delegate power under broad general directives."[19] In addition to this belying the structure of our Constitution, it also belies the reality of administrative regulation that often stifles innovation and is slow to respond to technological changes. For example, the Food and Drug Administration's broad definition of "medical device," applying to "any instrument" affecting bodily structure, is over forty years old and even applies to mobile applications. But the FDA has yet to provide any regulatory guidance as to mobile health applications, leaving innovators confused as to what technology they may acceptably develop.[20]

Broad delegation has the effect of surrendering consequential, long-term policy choices to administrative agencies, even when it was unintended by the delegating Congress.[21] The Telecommunications

Act of 1996 delegated authority to the Federal Communications Commission to regulate telecommunications differently than information services.[22] While modern technology makes this distinction irrelevant, the FCC continues to regulate even where it is unclear that it possesses statutory authority to do so—such as in establishing "net neutrality" rules. Perhaps the most threatening example of agency delegation being mismatched to modern innovation is in the environmental context. The Environmental Protection Agency asserts, with the support of the U.S. Supreme Court, that the Clean Air Act of 1970 (CAA) allows it to regulate greenhouse gas emissions despite the fact that "[f]or the first three and a half decades of the Act's existence," it never applied to greenhouse gas emissions.[23]

The Progressives' presumption of agency expertise cloaks the real purpose of avoiding democratic accountability for policy decisions. Just as the Left exhorts the courts to apply "evolving" interpretations of the Constitution to arrive at desired policy outcomes, it uses the regulatory state to promote policies that are not supported by majorities in the legislative process. The founders understood that political actors would seek to gain power by favoring factions and at the same time deflect responsibility while aggrandizing their ambitions.[24] To constrain these human impulses, the founders developed the structure of separate and countervailing powers together with electoral accountability. By delegating legislative authority to administrative agencies, the modern Congress slips around these safeguards. Political actors can take credit for good policies (e.g., "I voted for clean air.") while avoiding any accountability for how that program is implemented (e.g., "We never intended EPA to do that!")

The modern treatment of administrative agencies as a repository for delegated power that can be more "efficiently" or "expertly" applied loses a core insight. As Judge Janice Rogers Brown of the U.S. Court of Appeals for the D.C. Circuit observed in *Association of American Railroads*, nondelegation is not some reactionary ban on a more efficient government, it is a limit that inheres in the natural scope of Congress's legitimate authority.[25] The erosion of the nondelegation doctrine has not only fueled the administrative state, it has resulted in a government that is largely disinterested in the distinctions and proper confines of executive, legislative, and judicial authority—despite the centrality those distinctions played in designing the Constitution and forming the framers' conceptions of liberty and tyranny.

II. THE ADMINISTRATIVE STATE'S PREMISES OF "EXPERTISE" AND "EFFICIENCY" RESULT IN UNFETTERED PREROGATIVE AND CONSOLIDATED POWER

As a former counsel to two Securities and Exchange Commissioners put it, "In an administrative law proceeding, the commission is akin to the prosecutor and then, in an appeal, the judge in the same case."[26] This observation evinces the generally inadequate separation of powers within administrative agencies. Professor Gary Lawson provided an illustrative example of how the consolidated authority within each administrative agency leads to it possessing almost total power over a given regulatory issue:

> Consider the typical enforcement activities of a typical federal agency—for example, of the Federal Trade Commission. The Commission promulgates substantive rules of conduct. The Commission then considers whether to authorize investigations into whether the Commission's rules have been violated. If the Commission authorizes an investigation, the investigation is conducted by the Commission, which reports its findings to the Commission. If the Commission thinks that the Commission's findings warrant an enforcement action, the Commission issues a complaint. The Commission's complaint that a Commission rule has been violated is then prosecuted by the Commission and adjudicated by the Commission. This Commission adjudication can either take place before the full Commission or before a semi-autonomous Commission administrative law judge. If the Commission chooses to adjudicate before an administrative law judge rather than before the Commission and the decision is adverse to the Commission, the Commission can appeal to the Commission. If the Commission ultimately finds a violation, then, and only then, the affected private party can appeal to an Article III court. But the agency decision, even before the bona fide Article III tribunal, possesses a very strong presumption of correctness on matters both of fact and of law.[27]

The procedures employed by administrative agencies in making, enforcing, and adjudicating their rules are equally unmoored from constitutional norms. The Notice of Proposed Rulemaking (NPRM), given to the public, is generally a part of the rulemaking process; crucially, it ensures public input. However, this important element has suffered in recent years.[28] When an administrative agency engages in rulemaking, the procedures by which the public may participate—such as receiving advanced NPRM and the opportunity to file comments on it—may be waived at the agency's discretion.[29] When an agency conducts adjudication before an ALJ, the Federal Rules of Evidence do not apply.[30] This allows parties to proffer unreliable and irrelevant evidence at the discretion of the ALJ. Further, probable cause is not required for an agency to conduct an administrative search, even when the same agency will then use the fruits of the search to bring the targeted individual or entity before an ALJ for prosecution.[31]

Agencies may also engage in functional rulemaking outside of the formal process itself. The judicial process allows parties to litigation to enter into consent decrees or settlements that end a lawsuit before costly litigation ensues and provides judicial supervision of the parties' respective commitments.[32] While these concepts can be laudable, administrative agencies have manipulated them to engage in rulemaking that can bind subsequent administrators, engage in settlement bargaining that exceeds the power delegated to the agency, and put the courts in the position of enforcing a settlement that could "require" agencies to take actions that exceed their delegated authority.[33] Even subsequent presidential elections that result in new agency administrators with different policy perspectives cannot undo the binding agreement made by a prior agency bureaucrat in litigation. Seventh Circuit Judge Frank Easterbrook explains the threat of "sue-and-settle" and its implications for the separation of powers:

> The separation of powers inside a government—and each official's concern that he may be replaced by someone with a different agenda—creates incentives to use the judicial process to obtain an advantage. The consent decree is an important element in the strategy. Officials of an environmental agency who believe that the regulations they

> inherited from their predecessors are too stringent may quickly settle a case brought by industry (as officials who think the regulations are not stringent enough may settle a case brought by a conservation group). A settlement under which the agency promulgated new regulations would last only for the duration of the incumbent official; a successor with a different view could promulgate a new regulation. Both parties to the litigation therefore may want a judicial decree that ties the hands of the successor. It is impossible for an agency to promulgate a regulation containing a clause such as "My successor cannot amend this regulation." But if the clause appears in a consent decree, perhaps the administrator gets his wish to dictate the policies of his successor. Similarly, officials of the Executive Branch may obtain leverage over the legislature [through a consent decree]. If prison officials believe their budget is too small, they may consent to a judgment that requires larger prisons, and then take the judgment to the legislature to obtain the funds.[34]

"Sue-and-settle" is yet another acute threat to the separation of powers. This process allows an administrative agency to expand executive power by arrogating undelegated legislative power with the imprimatur of a judicially enforceable settlement—often in lawsuits where the agency willingly settles with the plaintiffs precisely in order to enlarge its own powers. Because both parties consent to the settlement terms, courts rarely have the opportunity to review challenges to the agency's actual authority to promulgate the promised rules.[35]

The limited review courts exercise over agencies using consent decrees is a function of statutory law, but the judiciary's general reluctance to review an agency's statutory interpretation is a function of judicial choice. Since the Supreme Court's decision in *Chevron U.S.A. Inc. v. Natural Resources Defense Council, Inc.*, a court must defer to an agency's interpretation of its own authorizing statute if the interpretation is "permissible."[36] The Court's *Chevron* analysis morphed even beyond this, holding that agencies "may authoritatively resolve ambiguities in regulations," a position well beyond the discretion that the Administrative Procedure Act (APA) gave agencies regarding interpretive agency rules.[37]

Defenders of *Chevron* deference rightly note that Congress—not the Supreme Court—bears the initial blame for agency largesse by writing ambiguous statutes with vague delegations, inviting agency action.[38] Yet this response does not address the problem that *Chevron* deference poses to the separation of powers: How does the failure of Congress to write a clear law result in judicial failure to apply statutory-interpretation principles to agency interpretations? Why does a congressional decision to abrogate authority to an agency result in a judicial bias in favor of administrative agencies?[39] "Judicial restraint" cannot amount to judicial abdication and keep its legitimacy. The courts should not feel compelled to shirk their responsibility of judicial review, particularly when the majoritarian branches have decided to reallocate power among themselves in a manner that leaves unaccountable administrative agencies with so much unfettered discretion.[40]

It is not clear that *Chevron* deference has even fulfilled one of its core purposes: curbing the power of courts to issue arbitrary decisions. By retaining discretion over when *Chevron* deference applies and whether it applies a "hard look" at agency action or a very deferential review, courts retain significant discretion to manipulate what even Justice Scalia, long perceived as a strident defender of *Chevron* deference,[41] has characterized as a "judge-made doctrine[] of deference."[42] In *Massachusetts v. EPA*, for example, the Supreme Court held that "air pollutant" as defined within the Clean Air Act includes greenhouse gas emissions, despite EPA's decision to defer judgment on that very point, given the CAA's silence on the matter.[43] The Court did not explain why EPA's interpretation of its discretion could not receive *Chevron* deference; it simply decided that *Chevron* deference did not apply. Expansive delegation to make rules, combined with the deference that agencies experience on appeal, permits agencies—as Justice Scalia observed in the context of the SEC's criminal enforcement—to "in effect create (and uncreate) new crimes at will, so long as they do not roam beyond ambiguities that the laws contain."[44]

Even some defenders of *Chevron* deference take issue with the breadth to which it has been applied. In *Perez v. Mortgage Bankers Association*, for example, Justice Scalia explained how, "[h]eedless of the original design of the APA," which directed the "reviewing court . . . [to] interpret . . . statutory provisions," the Court adopted *Chevron* deference.[45] *Chevron* deference portended *Auer* deference,[46] allowing agencies to authoritatively resolve ambiguities in the rules they interpret.[47] This, too, runs afoul of the APA. The APA directs the "reviewing court . . . [to] determine the meaning or applicability of the terms of agency action."[48] As Justice Scalia concludes, "[b]y supplementing the APA with judge-made doctrines of deference," the Supreme Court has allowed agencies to bind the public not only to its statutory interpretations, but also to rules about how agencies make rules.[49]

Chevron deference, in tandem with *Auer* deference, creates a perverse incentive for an agency to circumvent all accountability to the constitutional branches. Suppose, for example, that an agency wants to impose a controversial regulation and therefore wishes to avoid opposition. The agency can manipulate the two deference doctrines to avoid having to answer for its regulation in either a public notice and comment period or before a court. The agency drafts a substantive regulation, but in a vague way so as to avoid exposing its controversial application(s). The agency's substantive regulation, as a "permissible" interpretation of the authorizing statute, receives *Chevron* deference—and the agency aims to ensure that a court applies *Chevron* by submitting that vague substantive regulation through all of the formal rulemaking procedures (such as notice and comment).[50] But the regulation's vagueness allows the agency to fill in the dirty details with its own interpretive rules, which need not be subject to notice and comment under *Auer* deference. Under this scheme, the controversial regulation never receives input from stakeholders through notice and comment or meaningful judicial review. Such manipulation, made possible by a passive judiciary, allows the administrative state to fully circumvent real checks and balances.

The discretion that *Chevron* deference affords courts—determining its breadth and depth, when it applies and when it does not—does little to prevent the courts from involving themselves in policy-making. The courts take center stage. Rather than prevent courts from interfering with the separation of powers, *Chevron* deference has ossified the courts' involvement in the contortion of those powers.

III. PROPOSING SOLUTIONS

Reviewing the predicament presented here for the separation of powers, our proposals to reinvigorate the separation of powers take two forms: (1) To the extent possible, realign the work of administrative agencies with the Constitution's separation-of-powers structure primarily by returning legislative power to Congress; and (2) impose a separation-of-powers construct on administrative agencies by reorganizing their structures and procedures.

A number of different efforts could return the power currently vested in administrative agencies to the Constitution's coordinate branches.

Congress has long considered adopting the REINS Act. This change to administrative procedures would reverse the delegation of authority for major regulations and would spell out a legislative procedure consistent with the Constitution to require that they be passed into law by both houses and signed by the President. By requiring that major rules be passed as legislation, the REINS Act reverses the burden of going forward currently in the Congressional Review Act (CRA).[51] It also restores powerful review over agency regulation to the President and Congress—making major regulations expressly accountable to the political branches.

Congressional action could also reform agency use of consent decrees. Currently, Federal Rule of Civil Procedure 24(a)(1) allows anyone to intervene in a lawsuit if given "an unconditional right to intervene by a federal statute." Congress can build on this by passing a statute that would subject all proposed consent decrees to notice and comment requirements.[52] The court could then consider such comments in evaluating the proposed consent decree, and parties with standing to challenge an action that would come from the consent decree could intervene in the suit and argue that the proposal is not in the public interest.[53] This would force courts to evaluate delegation questions in the context of settlements and mitigate sue-and-settle rulemaking.

The judiciary also possesses tools to realign administrative power with the Constitution. At least three sitting justices in *Perez*—Justices Scalia, Thomas, and Alito—have expressed a willingness to reevaluate *Auer* deference.[54] Moreover, Chief Justice Roberts in *City of Arlington* expressed a more general discomfort with the scope of modern regulatory power.[55] Parties challenging administrative rulemaking should take these cues and urge the Court to overrule *Auer* deference. Even if *Chevron* deference must remain in our jurisprudence, reversing *Auer* deference would eliminate the perverse incentive these two doctrines provide to an agency to circumvent accountability.

Additionally, while there does not yet appear to be a decisive appetite on the current Court to revisit *Chevron* deference, there is, as Justice Scalia noted in his opinion concurring in the judgment in *Perez*, some acknowledgment that *Chevron* is in tension with the APA requirement of courts to engage in statutory interpretation.[56] To the extent *Chevron* deference must remain, courts should insist that "permissible" agency interpretations of a statute must be—like permissible constitutional interpretation—governed by the original understanding of the words in the statute. Such an effort could better harmonize *Chevron* deference with the APA's directive.

If the Supreme Court were to reinvigorate the nondelegation doctrine, reining in *Chevron* directly becomes less critical. As Justice Scalia also notes in his *Perez* concurrence, "the rule of *Chevron*, if it did not comport with the APA, at least was in conformity with the long history of judicial review of executive action, where [s]tatutory ambiguities . . . were left to reasonable resolution by the Executive."[57] The nondelegation doctrine does not dispute that some executive action involves discretion, even as that discretion may resemble legislative policy-making. A reinvigorated nondelegation doctrine, one that asks the original question—as posed by Justice Thomas in *Association of American Railroads*—will better preserve the distinction between executive and legislative power.[58] The original structure of the Constitution dictates the proper judicial inquiry: "The question is whether the particular function requires the exercise of a certain type of power; if it does, then only the branch in which that power is vested can perform it."[59]

We also propose a number of procedural and structural reforms to administrative agencies. By enacting such reforms, Congress will better align the conduct of the administrative state with the principles of separated powers.

Every agency's executive, legislative, and judicial functions should be separated into different entities. Enforcement functions should be separated into one agency while rulemaking is placed into another, and adjudication preferably resides entirely with a court (either an Article I specialty court or an Article III court). This way, one agency is not making a rule, enforcing a rule, and adjudicating the enforcement of the very rule it made.

This separation of function could be accomplished by retaining the current rulemaking functions in the agencies. For example, EPA could continue to write the Clean Air Act and other environmental regulations assigned to it. However, the enforcement of those rules would be removed from EPA and assigned to law enforcement agencies depending on their function. In the case of many EPA programs that are designed to be enforced by the states, the states would serve as the inspectors, exercise police powers, and bring litigation to enforce the regulations. There need not be a federal enforcement role. For other agencies operating in an entirely federal context, the inspection function could be achieved by a consolidated federal inspection agency that has no police power. The police functions would be handled by federal law enforcement agencies, while the Department of Justice would bring any litigation.

This proposal would enhance the separation of powers by removing the inherent (or, at least, apparent) conflicts of interest within current agency administration. A recent report by the *Wall Street Journal*, concluding that the Securities and Exchange Commission prevailed against 90 percent of defendants in its administrative law courts—compared to 69 percent success in federal court during the same time period—from October 2010 to March 2015 identifies the potential conflicts.[60] Former administrative law judges have attested to being pressured by their respective agency to ensure that "the burden was on the people who were accused to show that they didn't do what the agency said they did."[61] By separating an agency's enforcement power from its review power, such conflicts may be better prevented.

To the extent possible, adjudicatory functions should be removed from administrative agencies—leaving them rulemaking power only. All of the federal ALJs could be consolidated into one court, ideally under Article III. If the matters that currently are heard before ALJs are somehow unfit for Article III courts, then Congress should create an Article I court to handle those administrative claims—or expand the jurisdiction of a preexisting Article I court (or courts) to handle such relevant claims. Not only would this further the separation of powers as a principle, it would also require procedural changes in administrative hearings, with the effect of restoring other constitutional safeguards that are effectively lost in unified administrative agencies. In all instances, the Federal Rules of Evidence should apply as they do in Article III courts and probable cause should be required for any administrative search pursuant to a regulation carrying a criminal penalty.

Reserving adjudicative functions to actual courts not only helps restore procedural protections to administrative adjudication; it also aids the separation of powers. Taking administrative adjudication out of agencies and putting it into courts acknowledges that administrative law courts practically exercise judicial power in adjudicating claims under agency rules. Rather than treat such adjudications as something else, this acknowledges them for what they are and provides the accordant procedural protections to litigants within them.

Such reforms would help reinvigorate the separation of powers within our modern government, which contends with them so rarely. Pursuing such reforms would remind the American people of the virtue of such an approach to government.

Rather than presuming that government is designed to fill in the "gaps" or "imperfections" or "inefficiencies" in society, the separation of powers presumes that individuals and civil society possess the tools and virtues necessary to regulate themselves. The coercive power of government should be a community's last resort and the product of consensus. Relearning this conception of government would go beyond simply preserving the separation of powers—it could facilitate the reinvigoration of public trust in non-government social institutions to address social questions. Moreover, it would help dispel the notion that a government that "does something"—meaning it passes more laws regulating conduct of some sort—is the government fit for a free people. As Alexander Hamilton noted in *Federalist* No. 73, "[i]t may perhaps be said that the power of preventing bad laws includes that of preventing good ones. . . . [But] [t]he injury which may possibly be done by defeating a few good laws will be amply compensated by the advantage of preventing a number of bad ones."[62] A government with separated powers that are appreciated by the people is a government that possesses the ability to preserve individual liberty.[63] Such is the form of government fit for a free people, and it is the government we hope to reclaim.

19.

SCANDAL AT THE IRS

Cleta Mitchell

Articles of Impeachment against Richard M. Nixon
Adopted July 27, 1974, House Judiciary Committee

Article 2: Using the powers of the office of President of the United States, Richard M. Nixon, in violation of his constitutional oath faithfully to execute the office . . . has repeatedly engaged in conduct violating the constitutional rights of citizens. . . . This conduct has included . . . the following:

He has, acting personally and through his subordinates and agents, endeavoured to obtain from the **Internal Revenue Service**, *in violation of the constitutional rights of citizens, confidential information contained in income tax returns for purposes not authorized by law, and to cause, in violation of the constitutional rights of citizens, income tax audits or other income tax investigations to be initiated or conducted in a discriminatory manner.*

Remember when President Nixon *tried* (unsuccessfully, it turns out) to use the Internal Revenue Service to punish his political enemies? That aborted effort was one of the grounds of the impeachment articles against Nixon passed by the House Judiciary Committee in July 1974. It was based on the demand by then White House Counsel John Dean that the IRS investigate, audit, and harass a list of 200 White House political enemies.

Nixon had, according to the Watergate tapes from May 13, 1971, demanded that the IRS commissioner appointee be "a ruthless son of a bitch, that he will do what he's told," and he insisted "that every income-tax return I want to see I see, [and] that he will go after our enemies and not go after our friends."[1] What Nixon had not counted on was that the individual appointed as IRS commissioner refused to comply with the White House demand that the IRS target the administration's political enemies.

Fast-forward almost four decades to February 2009. President Barack Obama has just taken office and has proposed a multibillion-dollar "Stimulus Package," which triggered the now-famous outburst from the floor of the Chicago Board of Trade by financial commentator Rick Santelli, who called for a new "tea party." Thus, the twenty-first-century Tea Party movement was born, with nationwide citizen opposition to the Obama administration's profligate spending and mushrooming deficits.

On April 15, 2009, citizens across the country held rallies to protest Obama administration policies. On September 12, 2009, the Taxpayer March on Washington attracted more than 500,000 participants by some estimates, with local rallies across the nation on the same day involving tens of thousands more. All were focused on opposition to the Obama administration's "tax and spend" policies. By the end of 2009, the Tea Party movement had grown to hundreds of groups nationwide, involving tens of thousands of patriotic Americans, many of whom had never before been actively involved in public policy issues or politics.

This spontaneous outpouring of civic engagement, deified by the Left when such movements involved issues they favor (gay rights, women's rights, anti-war protests, etc.), at once frightened and appalled the national media, liberal commentators, and, most importantly, the Obama administration and congressional Democrats. Then Speaker of the House Nancy Pelosi (D-CA) called the Tea Party movement "astroturf," alleging that it was being fueled by wealthy conservative donors and was not an "authentic" grassroots movement.[2]

Two events in early 2010 triggered a strong reaction by the Obama administration to the perceived threat from this rapidly growing citizen groundswell; it was that reaction that ultimately led the IRS to take action in an attempt to thwart the growing strength of the Tea Party.

On January 19, 2010, Republican Scott Brown won an upset victory in the Massachusetts special election to fill the Senate vacancy from Senator Edward Kennedy's death. Brown's victory was fueled in no small part by grassroots and Tea Party anger over Obamacare. President Obama's government-run health care legislation, the Affordable Care Act, had been introduced in Congress in November 2009 and immediately dubbed "Obamacare" by its many detractors and opponents. Tea Party Express (a federal PAC, not a 501(c)(4) social welfare organization) and dozens of other Tea Party and conservative groups played a major role in mobilizing support for Brown.

Two days later, on January 21, 2010, the Supreme Court struck down the prohibition on independent political speech by corporations and labor unions in *Citizens United v. Federal Election Commission*, 558 U.S. 310 (2010).

The Left erupted.

There is a history preceding *Citizens United*. The Left/Liberal/Progressive/Pro-Democratic forces had mobilized for the passage of the McCain-Feingold campaign finance law in 2002, which banned "soft money": contributions to the political parties in excess of the federal limits, as well as from both corporations and labor unions. After enactment of McCain-Feingold, during the 2004, 2006, and 2008 cycles, liberals and unions continued to spend hundreds of millions of soft money dollars during the elections, far outspending conservatives.[3] The Supreme Court's decision in *Citizens United* gave rise to the Left's collective fear that conservative voices might yet again be heard, something they believed they had vanquished with the enactment of McCain-Feingold in 2002.

For the three election cycles until *Citizens United* in January 2010, groups led by George Soros, Peter Lewis, Service Employees International Union (SEIU), and Emily's List controlled the electoral playing field, spending hundreds of millions of dollars to (unsuccessfully) defeat George W. Bush in 2004, then to (successfully) deliver control of Congress to the Democrats in 2006 and to elect Barack Obama in 2008.[4] Wealthy liberal donors and labor unions were quick to make the shift after 2002 from their previous large contributions to the Democratic

National Committee to new third-party efforts such as America Coming Together in 2004, followed in 2005 by the Soros-founded Democracy Alliance, which spawned and funded multiple leftist groups from its inception after the 2004 election.[5] After McCain-Feingold was enacted, pro-Democratic interest groups formed non-profit 527 political organizations that were actively engaged in the 2004, 2006, and 2008 election cycles, outspending conservative and pro-GOP 527s every cycle, with an almost 2–1 advantage by 2008.[6]

The 2008 presidential election was the first since the presidential taxpayer-financed system was established in which one candidate, Barack Obama, rejected government/taxpayer funds for both the primary and general elections, freeing him to raise private money. As a result, Barack Obama's total expenditures in 2008 were upwards of $745 million, ending the campaign with a surplus, whereas the Republican nominee, John McCain, dutifully accepted taxpayer funding for the general election and therefore had only $84 million to spend for his general election campaign.[7]

There were some on the right, concerned about the massive funding by liberal 527s, who decided to become actively involved in 2008. Attempting to counter the left-leaning 527s in 2008 who spent over $200 million that cycle, the U.S. Chamber of Commerce (a 501(c)(6) trade association) and two other tax-exempt organizations, Freedom-Watch and the Employee Freedom Action Committee (both 501(c)(4) organizations), together spent $86 million, only slightly more than the SEIU alone spent supporting Barack Obama's 2008 candidacy.[8]

Organizations established under Section 501(c) of the Internal Revenue Code are non-profit corporations, described in that section of the statute as one of several types of such entities. Exempt organizations do not pay corporate taxes on the income received from contributions or membership dues and are subject to limits on the program expenditures they are allowed to make for such things as partisan campaign activities.

Exempt organizations are corporations, albeit not-for-profit. Political expenditures by corporations and labor unions advocating the election or defeat of candidates was illegal under federal law until January 2010, when the Supreme Court in its *Citizens United* decision invalidated on First Amendment grounds the prohibition on independent political expenditures by corporations and labor unions.

After the removal of the threat of prosecution for illegal political activity and having seen the hundreds of millions of dollars spent by liberal interest groups in the preceding three election cycles, conservative donors and leaders began to harness their resources to fend off the liberal money machine. The leaders of the effort to persuade conservative donors to get off the sidelines and start competing were Charles and David Koch.[9]

The rise of the Tea Party movement, the shocking victory of Scott Brown, and the *Citizens United* decision struck terror in the White House and throughout the liberal community. It was one thing to have hundreds of millions of dollars in *progressive* money flowing at election time; it was quite another for conservatives to have the same opportunity. Obama supporters realized that *Citizens United* had removed the legal barrier that had made conservative donors reluctant to write checks.

The firestorm from the White House over *Citizens United* was instantaneous. President Obama castigated the Supreme Court about the decision during his January 27, 2010, State of the Union address and in his national radio address a few days later. Over the course of the next several months, President Obama, congressional Democrats, the liberal media, and commentators incessantly (and falsely) attacked *Citizens United*, and the Obama administration "orchestrated a sustained public relations campaign seeking to delegitimize the lawful political activity of conservative tax-exempt organizations and to suppress these groups' right to assemble and speak."[10]

The message from the White House was not lost on the IRS. IRS employees reviewing applications for exempt status submitted by Tea Party groups seeking recognition as social welfare organizations read the news and heard the President's "concerns."[11] The Issa Committee documented in its investigation that in February 2010, barely three weeks after President Obama's vociferous attacks on *Citizens United*, an IRS agent in the agency's Cincinnati office, charged with processing applications for exempt status, flagged an application from a Tea Party organization based on "potential media attention" and sent it to his superior rather than process it in the normal manner.[12]

Contrary to the response of the IRS commissioner who *refused* White House entreaties to use the agency to target Nixon's political enemies, the IRS under President Obama took its cues from the President, his allies in Congress, and the media and began concerted actions to thwart citizens opposing Obama's policies through the Tea Party movement.

Thus began the IRS scandal. The IRS flagged applications from hundreds of Tea Party groups and quarantined them in special IRS units, halting the review process while awaiting instructions from the IRS Counsel's office in Washington about how to handle applications from organizations with the words "tea party," "patriots," or "9/11" in their names—or where the issues of interest to the organization included "government spending, government debt or taxes," or where the group proposed to educate the public by advocacy or lobbying to "make America a better place to live," or where statements in the case file "criticize how the country is being run."[13]

Prior to fall 2009, an application for recognition as a Section 501(c)(4) social welfare organization could be expected to be processed by the IRS within a matter of *weeks*. Applications for recognition as charitable and educational organizations (Section 501(c)(3) groups) were normally processed in roughly six to nine months.

By August 2010, the applications for *certain* groups, based on their names and missions, were referred to the "special unit" within the IRS for "further screening," where they stayed for years, held in limbo by the offices of Lois Lerner, then director of the IRS Exempt Organizations Unit, and William Wilkins, the IRS Chief Counsel and the *only* political appointee in the IRS.

As the 2010 mid-term elections approached, the White House, congressional Democrats, and left-wing activists clamored for the IRS "do something" to "stop" Tea Party and conservative issue groups from playing a role in the 2010 elections. Lerner publicly acknowledged the pressure being placed on—and *felt by*—the IRS to do just that. And what the IRS did is now well documented: the agency stopped processing applications from the groups whose names and mission denoted opposition to Obama administration policies.

As reported in Breitbart News (among other sources),

> Lerner spoke to a small group at Duke's Sanford School of Public Policy on October 19, 2010, just two weeks before the wave election that brought the Tea Party and Republicans significant gains in

> Congress. During her appearance Lerner was asked about the flow of money from corporations to 501(c)(4) groups. "Everyone is up in arms because they don't like it" Lerner replied, adding "Federal Election Commission can't do anything about it; they want the IRS to fix the problem." . . . Lerner again emphasizes the political pressure the IRS was under at the time saying, "So everybody is screaming at us right now 'Fix it now before the election. Can't you see how much these people are spending?'" Lerner concludes by saying she won't know if organizations have gone too far in campaigning until she looks at their "990s next year."[14]

Clearly the IRS was feeling the political pressure—and succumbing to it. The IRS stopped processing—or granting—requests for exempt status from conservative and Tea Party organizations from 2010 until after the Treasury Inspector General for Tax Administration (TIGTA) report was issued in May 2013 and, even then, some groups did not receive their letters of determination of exempt status from the IRS until 2014.[15]

The reason? President Obama made known his displeasure for what he called "front groups with misleading names," and the IRS did its best to try to stem the tide of such conservative grassroots organizations.[16] All of this was documented by the TIGTA Russell George in his May 14, 2013, report, "Inappropriate Criteria Were Used to Identify Tax-Exempt Applications for Review" (the TIGTA Report).[17]

As a practitioner in the field who has submitted scores of applications for exempt status for many organizations over decades, it became apparent to me in early 2010 that something had changed at the IRS. Two examples follow from my own law practice: An application for exempt status was submitted in October 2009 for a Section 501(c)(4) organization formed to, among other things, "ensure accountability among elected officials."

The IRS did not respond to the application for recognition of exempt status until June 2010—more than eight months after the group's application was submitted. The response, when it came, was *not* from the Cincinnati office but from the IRS's Washington, D.C., office. Rather than inquiring about the content of the application, as had been my experience, the letter asked the group to explain, among other things, "all sources of funding" and give "a detailed summary of all past, current, and planned activities," including copies of all radio and television ads the group had sponsored in its opposition to Obamacare. The requested information was supplied in July 2010, but no letter of determination was received. In fact, the group did not hear from the IRS again until February 2012, when it received one of the "development letters" sent by the IRS to several hundred Tea Party groups demanding mountains of information (including identity of donors) that the Treasury Inspector General for Tax Administration later called "inappropriate."[18] My client did not receive its tax-exempt status until July 2013, two months after the TIGTA Report was released documenting the IRS targeting scandal and almost four years after filing.

Another client, True the Vote, applied for recognition in July 2010 as a 501(c)(3) charitable and educational organization whose mission is to protect the integrity of America's electoral process. That organization did not receive tax-exempt status until September 2013 and only *after* suing the IRS to obtain it. During that three-plus-year period, the IRS sent three separate "development letters" demanding voluminous inappropriate information, such as lists of attendees at meetings, transcripts of speeches to the group by public officials, the list of groups to whom the president of True the Vote had spoken in the last two years, as well as the list of groups during the coming year to whom the president of the organization planned to speak, and other similarly intrusive, burdensome questions. An IRS letter to True the Vote in February 2012 contained more than one hundred questions with parts, sub-parts, and sub-sub-parts. It was True the Vote's assigned agent who confirmed in October 2011 that the agents in the IRS Cincinnati office were hamstrung in processing applications from Tea Party groups because they were awaiting direction from their superiors in the IRS's Washington office. Many commentators, including Kim Strassel from the *Wall Street Journal*, have chronicled the relationship between the IRS scandal and the aggressive attacks by Obama and his administration against their political foes, who demanded that various government agencies from the Federal Election Commission to the Department of Justice to the IRS take action to silence opponents.[19] There is no evidence that *any* pro-Obamacare organization was subjected to similar scrutiny.

One would have thought that the TIGTA Report condemning the IRS targeting of Tea Party groups, preceded days earlier by Lois Lerner's "apology" for the targeting (although she lied about her direct knowledge of and role in it), would have forced an immediate halt to efforts by the Obama administration to curtail protected political speech.

In fact, the opposite happened.

On May 15, 2013, President Obama fired Acting IRS Commissioner Steven Miller and deployed Danny Werfel, then Director of the Office of Management and Budget, to the IRS "to ensure the IRS implements new safeguards to restore public trust and administers the tax code with fairness and integrity."[20]

Werfel immediately set about to codify the egregious treatment of social welfare organizations initiated over the previous three years. The June 2013 initiative was described in Orwellian doublespeak terms: "IRS Offers New Streamlined Option to Certain 501(c)(4) Groups Caught in Application Backlog."[21] According to Werfel, "the new 'streamlined' option gives certain groups that have waited far too long a quick and clear path to get their status resolved."[22]

The "new, streamlined option" required, however, that groups pledge to permanently forfeit their right to engage in the percentage of political speech and activity historically allowed by the IRS and to calculate as part of their "political expenditures" such things as "volunteer" activities—which have no definition in the Internal Revenue Code nor are the terms found in any guidelines from the IRS. Worse still, the process confirmed that the IRS had no intention of removing itself from the speech-policing business.

Not only was Werfel publicly touting a Hobson's choice "remedy" for citizens groups already subjected to multi-year viewpoint discrimination by the IRS, but unbeknownst to anyone outside the agencies, a small group within the Department of Treasury and the IRS was secretly developing far-reaching regulations to permanently restrict the political speech and association of all Section 501(c)(4) groups.

Originally planned for release on the Friday before Labor Day in 2013—but ultimately published on the Tuesday before Thanksgiving 2013—the regulations largely mirrored and would have institutionalized the "inappropriate" process that the IRS had been using. The Obama Treasury Department and the IRS have clearly undertaken the role of regulating citizen political speech and association, none of which has anything to do with collecting revenues to fund the federal government

When the proposed IRS regulations were released, citizens across the nation responded with understandable outrage. By the close of the comment period on February 27, 2014, more than 160,000 comments had poured into the IRS, almost entirely in opposition to the proposed speech regulations. That number was twice the total of all comments on all other Treasury and IRS proposals in the preceding seven years.[23]

Ultimately, the IRS was forced by the withering public pressure to withdraw the proposed regulations but advised that it would issue "revised" regulations sometime in 2015.

And what was the Obama administration doing during the IRS targeting scandal? Simply put: lying to Congress.

The Issa Report details the numerous instances in which senior IRS officials, including former Commissioner Doug Shulman, Acting Commissioner Steven Miller, and Exempt Organizations Director Lois Lerner repeatedly lied to Congress, denying and covering up the targeting of Tea Party and conservative groups before TIGTA issued its May 2013 report controverting their prior false statements to Congress.[24]

Shulman testified to the House Ways and Means Committee in March 2012 that there was no targeting of conservative groups. Yet the congressional investigations into that very targeting revealed that at the time of Shulman's denial, he *knew* that there was "a backlog of applications, delays in processing, and the use of inappropriate development questions."[25] In the early months of 2012, Lerner made multiple false statements to Congress as it sought to learn what the IRS was doing to hundreds of grassroots groups across the county. In personal meetings, telephone interviews, and written communications with congressional investigators, Lerner denied there were any changes in the criteria for evaluating applications for exempt status and stated (falsely) that the intrusive demands for proprietary information from grassroots organizations were "ordinary"—something the TIGTA Report specifically rebutted. In fact, at the very time Lerner was telling Congress that "nothing had changed" in the manner in which her unit handled such applications, the IRS, including Lerner, had already identified seven types of information that it had inappropriately demanded from conservative groups.

Between May 2012 and May 2013, Miller testified before Congress on at least six occasions, first as Deputy Commissioner, then as Acting Commissioner, and withheld information from Congress each time about the targeting. Yet in his interview with congressional investigators in November 2013—well after the targeting had been documented in the TIGTA Report—Miller admitted that he became aware of possible IRS misconduct in February 2012.

Has the Obama administration *ever* taken action to hold these individuals accountable for lying to Congress? It is a criminal offense—perjury—to lie to Congress. What has the Obama Justice Department done about these serious offenses? Nothing.

The Obama administration—aided and abetted by congressional Democrats and the liberal media—has done everything in its power to thwart and minimize the congressional investigations into the IRS scandal, hoping that it would simply fade away.

There are many fronts that continue to be explored by congressional oversight committees and citizen watchdog groups to reveal the full extent of the IRS scandal, all of which continue to face Obama administration stonewalling:

- the IRS pattern and practice of targeting for audits those who have been donors to conservative groups and GOP candidates, the reported instances of which are too numerous to be ignored;[26]
- the Department of Justice's fake "investigation" of the IRS scandal where the DOJ has yet to interview any of the Tea Party groups victimized by the IRS, choosing instead to interview only those responsible for the targeting, not to mention the DOJ's refusal to respond to the referral of Lois Lerner for criminal prosecution and the refusal by the U.S. Attorney for the District of Columbia to enforce the contempt citation against Lois Lerner passed by the House of Representatives in May 2014;[27]
- the extent of the communications between the IRS and the Executive Office of the President, with particular regard to the

disclosure by the IRS of confidential taxpayer information to the White House;[28]

- obtaining, reviewing, and *disclosing* all of the "missing" Lois Lerner e-mails—which may have been located by TIGTA but must still be produced and examined by Congress and the public;[29]
- the source(s) and impetus for the efforts to restrict the political speech and activities of citizens organizations through the issuance of new regulations to codify the abuses first developed during the Tea Party targeting, and the White House role in initiating the regulations;[30]
- the disregard by the IRS of its obligations to fully and promptly respond to Freedom of Information Act requests without forcing citizens to sue the agency to obtain documents to which citizens are entitled under the law.[31]

The Obama administration has set a shocking standard for politicizing federal agencies and then obfuscating, stonewalling, and denying its actions. Clearly, the IRS has come to see itself as the enforcer for a liberal president and his partisans in Congress and the media.

The IRS scandal can be laid squarely at the feet of the Obama White House and its determination to use every means available to silence its political enemies, critics, and citizens who oppose Obama administration policies.

The fact is that the IRS has become far more than a tax-collecting agency. The agency has too much power over the lives of every American, which makes it the "go-to" source for identifying, frightening, and silencing government critics. There is an opportunity at this point in our nation's history for Congress to curb the IRS's role and reduce its susceptibility to interject itself into the nation's political discourse and activities.

There has been far too little congressional oversight of the IRS and its operations and too many courts have given too much deference to the agency. This is the opportunity to reset the powers and impact of the IRS and to rebalance the agency so that it functions less like an uber-dictatorial monster and more like an agency responsible for revenue collections, an issue on which tax-exempt organizations have insignificant bearing.

There are ten changes in the law that Congress should enact to rein in the IRS:

1. Eliminate the procedure for applying for "exempt status" for all but charitable organizations. Only organizations seeking exemption from taxation under Section 501(c)(3) should be required to receive letters of determination of exempt status from the IRS, and those only because donors are entitled to tax deductions for their contributions. All other exempt organizations should simply note on their annual Form 990s the Code Section under which they operate. Citizens should not have to ask the IRS "Mother, may I?" for permission to organize and associate for lawful purposes.

2. Review organizations' compliance through random audits of their Form 990s but ensure that audits of Form 990s and exempt organizations are solely and truly random. Random and periodic reviews of Form 990s should be conducted to ensure an exempt organization's compliance with applicable provisions of the Internal Revenue Code and that the organization is operating in accordance with its stated exempt purpose. However, such audits should be initiated solely on a statistically random basis without consideration of or regard for the mission, ideological, or philosophical purpose of the exempt organization.

3. Political expenditures should not be subject to taxation, regulation, or reporting to the IRS. The United States Supreme Court has recognized the First Amendment rights of citizens to join together for purposes of making independent political expenditures and to engage in protected political speech and activities. Constitutionally guaranteed speech and activities should not be subject to taxation. Nor should the IRS be in the business of defining, regulating, or restricting political speech and activities. Congress should prohibit by statute the agency's involvement in this arena.

4. Congress should enumerate protected citizenship activities and prohibit the IRS from interfering with, penalizing, or taxing such activities. Congress should define the following as appropriate exempt activities by any exempt organization, recognized as being for the social welfare and the common good of the American people and not allowed to be restricted by the IRS in any manner: nonpartisan voter registration, nonpartisan get-out-the-vote activities, candidate debates, candidate forums, voter guides, grassroots lobbying, and meetings and public gatherings in which candidates for office present their positions and views on issues.

5. Eliminate donor disclosures to the IRS. Congress should repeal requirements that exempt organizations disclose their donors of over $5,000 to the IRS. This supposedly confidential schedule, filed only with the IRS, is susceptible to abuse by the IRS and others. It should be eliminated.

6. Prohibit politically motivated taxpayer audits. Congress should prohibit the IRS from using or relying upon any filings, campaign finance reports, or public information regarding a taxpayer's contributions to candidates, political organizations, parties, committees, or exempt organizations as a source for targeting or initiating audits of any taxpayer.

7. Prohibit the IRS from transferring confidential taxpayer information to state or local governments without notice to the taxpayer. Repeal current law allowing transfers of federal taxpayer information by the IRS to any other federal agency, or state or local government agency, without taxpayer notice, subpoena, or other form of due process.

8. Establish the taxpayer's "right to know" the contents of the taxpayer's file with the IRS. Require the IRS to furnish to any taxpayer upon that taxpayer's written request any and all information contained in that taxpayer's internal files within the IRS, including the identity by name and job title of any IRS employee who has inspected the taxpayer's confidential information, the date of the inspection, and the tax administration purpose that authorized the IRS employee's access to the taxpayer's information. Taxpayers include exempt organizations.

9. Ensure the proper functioning of the taxpayer confidentiality protections within the IRS. Establish a system for randomly and periodically testing the security of the IRS internal systems to ensure the provisions of Section 6103, the federal statute that supposedly guarantees the confidentiality of taxpayer information, are met. Report to Congress annually the results of the testing program.

10. Treat the IRS as any other federal agency. Congress should tighten oversight of the IRS to ensure it complies with all federal laws, including but not limited to the Administrative Procedure Act, the Paperwork Reduction Act, the Regulatory Flexibility Act, and the Freedom of

Information Act, and that it conducts all rulemaking of IRS regulations in accordance with procedures mandated by Congress.

The frightening conclusion from this episode in our nation's history is this: unless Congress enacts legislation to remove the IRS from the political speech-policing business, and unless those who call themselves journalists take these reprehensible actions seriously, and unless those who engage in this misbehavior are actually punished, the potential for future abuses is real and they are likely to recur. When? The very next time there is a tyrannical actor in the White House whose sympathetic minions in the federal agencies, including the IRS, are only too willing to do his (or her) bidding when dispatched to do battle against the President's political enemies.

20.

FEDERAL OVERREACH IN ENVIRONMENTAL REGULATION

"A Severe Blow to the Constitution's Separation of Powers"

Patrick Morrisey and Elbert Lin[1]

"American Electric Power is preparing to close six coal-fired power plants in four states on May 31 to comply with stricter federal emissions standards. . . . More than 250 workers will be affected."[2] That is the opening to an Associated Press story posted on April 6, 2015, out of Charleston, West Virginia.[3] It could be the same lede on dozens of other stories from greater Appalachia, however, documenting the consequences of increasingly aggressive and unelected federal environmental regulators on consumers, industry, and numerous state economies.

Whatever might be said as a matter of policy, a troubling trend is that the regulations having these effects are not sanctioned by elected representatives in Congress, as noted most recently by the United States Supreme Court in early 2014. The U.S. Environmental Protection Agency (EPA) received severe criticism from the Supreme Court for seeking to "seiz[e] expansive power that it admits the statute is not designed to grant."[4] EPA's actions earned it a stern rebuke on how the agency was threatening the

American form of democracy. "Under our system of government," the Court explained, "Congress makes laws and the President, acting at times through agencies like EPA, 'faithfully execute[s]' them."[5] EPA's attempt to "rewrite clear statutory terms to suit its own sense of how the statute should operate," the Court continued, "would deal a severe blow to the Constitution's separation of powers."[6]

The case—*Utility Air Regulatory Group v. EPA*—involved EPA rules that sought to incorporate greenhouse gas emissions into the statutory permitting obligations for the construction, modification, and operation of certain stationary sources (e.g., factories). The statutes only required permits for "major" stationary sources, defined as those emitting any covered air pollutant above a certain threshold: 100 or 250 tons per year, depending on the source.[7] EPA wanted to include greenhouse gas emissions as a covered pollutant under that regime but realized that doing so would "touch every household in the land" because millions of small sources, including large homes and schools, have greenhouse gas emissions beyond the statutory thresholds.[8] Conceding that this result would be "inconsistent with congressional intent," EPA argued that it was not bound to a "literal" reading of the statutes and promulgated a rule that simply revised the permitting thresholds for the purpose of greenhouse gas emissions.[9]

It was this patent and unapologetic revision of an act of Congress that drew the Supreme Court's ire. In no uncertain terms, the Court struck down EPA's attempt to remake the law: "An agency has no power to 'tailor' legislation to bureaucratic policy goals by rewriting unambiguous statutory terms."[10] The Court was particularly alarmed that EPA was "laying claim to extravagant statutory power over the national economy while at the same time strenuously asserting that the authority claimed would render the statute 'unrecognizable to the Congress that designed' it."[11]

A PATTERN OF "TAILOR[ING] LEGISLATION TO BUREAUCRATIC POLICY GOALS"

What especially disturbed the Supreme Court in the *Utility Air Regulatory Group* case—that EPA apparently viewed the law merely as an inconvenient hurdle on the way to its preferred policy outcome—is unfortunately commonplace today. At least four of EPA's recent signature projects bear the same hallmark. All four, described next, are inconsistent with the law and yet are, or were, being vigorously advanced.

Regulation of Power Plants under Section 112 of the Clean Air Act

In a case just decided by the Supreme Court in June 2015 against EPA, the agency had imposed costly technology-based requirements on power plants under Section 112 of the Clean Air Act, which governs the emissions of hazardous air pollutants. Most sources of hazardous air pollutants are automatically subject to Section 112 regulation.[12] At issue in the litigation was the fact that power plants are treated differently; EPA is given the choice to decide whether power plants should be regulated under Section 112 at all. The statute creates two threshold requirements to the regulation of power plants: (1) EPA "shall perform a study of the hazards to public health reasonably anticipated to occur as a result of emissions by" power plants; and (2) "after considering the results of the study," EPA "shall regulate" power plants "if the Administrator finds such regulation is *appropriate and necessary*."[13] In promulgating the rule, EPA had asserted that it is "require[d] . . . to find it *appropriate* to regulate" power plants if the agency determines that hazardous air pollutant emissions from power plants "pose an identified or potential hazard to public health or the environment."[14] At the same time, those public health hazards made it "*necessary* to regulate [power plants] under . . . [S]ection 112."[15]

One of several problems with EPA's approach was that it gave the word "appropriate"—in the phrase "appropriate and necessary"—no meaning. According to EPA, the existence of public health hazards made it *both* "appropriate" and "necessary" to regulate power plants under Section 112. But it is a long-standing rule of courts—and of common sense—that distinct words in statutes must be given distinct meanings. That was particularly true here, where one word typically conveys broad discretion and the other does not.

What is more, EPA relied in part on this flawed interpretation to justify its complete disregard of the rule's skewed cost-benefit ratio. By EPA's own calculations, the costs of the rule were projected to be $9.6 billion a year, while the benefits directly attributable to the reduction of hazardous air pollutants appeared to be only $4 to $6 million a year.[16] At best, that's a ratio of 1,600 to 1. A weighing of this extraordinary fact would fit naturally within the meaning of the word "appropriate," especially given that "consideration of cost is commonly understood to be a central component of ordinary regulatory analysis, particularly in the context of health, safety, and environmental regulation."[17] Yet according to EPA, "[i]t is reasonable to conclude that costs may not be considered."[18] Most of EPA's arguments, which turned on how other sources are treated under Section 112, failed to give sufficient weight to the fact that power plants are singled out under the statute for special consideration.

In the last decision of the October 2014 term, the Supreme Court found that EPA had violated the law by refusing to take costs into consideration. "[T]he phrase 'appropriate and necessary,'" the Supreme Court explained, "requires at least some attention to cost."[19] In the Court's view, EPA had failed even to act rationally: "[I]t is unreasonable to read an instruction to an administrative agency to determine whether 'regulation is appropriate and necessary' as an invitation to ignore cost."[20] Indeed, the opinion is a caution to all agencies, as the Court emphasized that "[c]onsideration of cost reflects the understanding that reasonable regulation ordinarily requires paying attention to the advantages *and* the disadvantages of agency decisions."[21] "No regulation is 'appropriate,'" the Court stressed, "if it does significantly more harm than good."[22]

Regulation of Power Plants under Section 111 of the Clean Air Act

While in the midst of defending one rule regulating emissions from power plants, EPA proposed two more, under a different part of the Clean Air Act. In January 2014, EPA formally proposed under Section 111(b) of the act nationwide standards for carbon dioxide (CO_2) emissions from *new* fossil fuel–fired power plants.[23] Then in June 2014, EPA invoked its authority under Section 111(d) of the act and proposed guidelines for CO_2 emissions from *existing* fossil fuel–fired power plants.[24] Each of these rules, as proposed, is also plainly beyond EPA's authority. Both rules are expected to be finalized in the summer of 2015.

Section 111(b). The proposed rule for new power plants, under Section 111(b), sets emissions limitations based on the application of partial carbon capture and storage—a particular method of reducing emissions. Section 111(b) authorizes EPA to issue standards of emissions for air pollutants that "reflect[] the degree of emission limitation achievable through the application of the best system of emission reduction which (taking into account the cost of achieving such reduction and any nonair quality health and environmental impact and energy requirements) the Administrator determines has been adequately demonstrated."[25] More simply stated: EPA must "identify the emission levels that are 'achievable' with 'adequately demonstrated technology.'"[26] In the proposed rule, EPA claims that level of technology—also called the "best system of emission reduction"—is partial carbon capture and storage.[27]

But EPA's claim relies on introducing an entirely new test for assessing the "best system of emission reduction." Over the years, the U.S. Court of Appeals for the D.C. Circuit—the court with the most and sometimes exclusive expertise over environmental matters—has interpreted the "best system of emission reduction" standard on a number of occasions and has adopted certain guidelines. Among those is that an "adequately demonstrated system" is one "which has been shown to be reasonably reliable, reasonably efficient, and which can reasonably be expected to serve the interests of pollution control without becoming exorbitantly costly in an economic or environmental way."[28] In turn, an "achievable standard" is one "which is within the realm of the adequately demonstrated system's efficiency and which, while not at a level that is purely theoretical or experimental, need not necessarily be routinely achieved within the industry prior to its adoption."[29] Notwithstanding these established and quite nuanced guidelines, EPA has invented in its proposed rule an entirely new test—whether the technology is "technically feasible"[30]—which the courts have never mentioned or adopted.

The proposal also clearly violates the Energy Policy Act of 2005, among other failures. That law *expressly* prohibits EPA from considering—for purposes of determining whether a technology is adequately demonstrated under Section 111(d)—technology used at facilities that are awarded either Clean Coal Power Initiative (CCPI) funding or advanced coal project tax credits.[31] In direct contravention of that mandate, EPA has expressly relied on several facilities that were awarded CCPI funding, advanced coal project tax credits, or both, as evidence that carbon capture and storage is adequately demonstrated.[32]

Whether EPA's final rule for new power plants will adhere to these patently unlawful proposals remains to be seen.

Section 111(d). As for the existing power plant rule, EPA has proposed under Section 111(d) CO_2 emissions targets for each state to hit by 2030—which together average a reduction of 30 percent nationwide over the next fifteen years.[33] To develop these aggressive targets, EPA used a combination of four "building blocks," which it has described as the "best system of emission reduction" for each state as a whole.[34] The four building blocks are (1) increased efficiency from coal-fired power plants; (2) increased use of natural gas–fired power plants; (3) increased use of low- or zero-carbon power sources, such as nuclear, wind, or solar; and (4) reduced energy demand from consumers.[35] Again, there are numerous legal problems with this approach, of which we highlight two.

The first issue is that the proposed rule attempts to regulate far more than what happens at any existing power plant—that is, it reaches well "beyond the fence." Only the first of EPA's building blocks takes place at the site of the affected power plant, while the remaining three require wide-ranging energy policies throughout a state. This is quintessential overreach.

EPA's Section 111(d) authority extends only to performance standards for *individual sources*. Section 111(d) permits EPA to require each state to "submit to the Administrator a plan which . . . establishes standards of performance *for any existing source* . . . to which a standard of performance under this section would apply *if such existing source* were a new source."[36] Furthermore, any EPA rules under Section 111(d) must "permit the State in applying a standard of performance *to any particular source* under a plan submitted under this paragraph to take into consideration, among other factors, the remaining useful life of the *existing source* to which such standard applies."[37] The language could not be clearer. What EPA has done—setting emissions targets based on activities and policies beyond the control of any individual existing power plant—thus far exceeds the agency's authority.

EPA has argued that the word "system" in "best system of emission reduction" permits it to consider a state's entire electrical system.[38] But this is pure misdirection. Section 111(d) does not authorize performance standards for a "system"; it provides for the creation of performance standards based on "*the application* of the best system of emission reduction" to an existing source.[39] As in the *Utility Air Regulatory Group* case, this is yet another transparent attempt to "bring about an enormous and transformative expansion in EPA's regulatory authority without clear congressional authorization."[40]

The second issue with this proposed rule is that it is barred by the existence of the Section 112 power plant rule. Section 111(d) provides that EPA can require states to issue "standards of performance for any existing source for any air pollutant . . . *which is not . . . emitted from a source category which is regulated under section [112]*."[41] As EPA itself has long admitted, a "literal reading" of this text means that EPA cannot use Section 111(d) to reach emissions from a source category already regulated under Section 112.[42] In EPA's words, "if source category X is a 'source category' regulated under section 112, EPA c[an] not regulate [hazardous] or non-[hazardous air pollutants] from that source category under section 111(d)."[43] So, because EPA has regulated power plants under Section 112, it is prohibited—under the agency's own understanding of the statute's "literal" text—from regulating those same plants under Section 111(d).

As in the *Utility Air Regulatory Group* case, EPA now asserts that it should be permitted to rewrite the plain statutory text. In a lengthy legal memorandum accompanying the proposed rule, EPA claims there is a stray amendment in the law as it was passed, which has not been included in the formal U.S. Code books, that muddies the otherwise clear statutory text.[44] EPA contends that this alleged ambiguity in the Statutes at Large (the books that compile acts of Congress in the form in which they are passed, before they are incorporated into the U.S. Code) can and must be resolved by the agency—in a way that just happens to permit both the Section 112 and the Section 111(d) rule.[45]

There is good reason, however, that EPA's lost-and-found amendment is not included in the code: it is clearly a drafting error that should simply be ignored. Specifically, the amendment was supposed to make a clerical correction to a cross-reference, but as a result of other substantive amendments in the same bill, the cross-reference was eliminated and the correction turned out to be unnecessary.[46] Under long-standing and undisputed legislative practice, such an extraneous clerical amendment is considered a mistake and given no meaning.[47] Indeed, even EPA itself previously admitted that the language is "a drafting error and therefore should not be considered."[48] Properly construed, there is no ambiguity, and EPA has no license to rewrite the statute.

Regulation Defining "Waters of the United States" under the Clean Water Act

Outside the air pollution context, EPA's primary rulemaking effort is its latest attempt to define the term "waters of the United States" for the purpose of the Clean Water Act. Under the Clean Water Act, EPA and the U.S. Army Corps of Engineers have authority to regulate "waters of the United States." Any discharge into the "waters of the United States" is unlawful without a federal permit.[49] The term, which is undefined in the act, is thus critical to determining the reach of the act.

Over the years, EPA and the Corps have failed to adopt a definition of "waters of the United States" that the Supreme Court has seen fit to approve. The latest effort by the Corps was rejected in 2006 by a fractured majority of the Court in a case called *Rapanos v. United States*. Two opinions—one by Justice Antonin Scalia and a second by Justice Anthony Kennedy—made up the majority.

In an opinion for four justices, Justice Scalia took a fairly bright-line view of the Clean Water Act's jurisdiction. He first concluded that the "only plausible interpretation" of "waters of the United States" includes "only those relatively permanent, standing or continuously flowing bodies of water"—bodies ordinarily described as streams, oceans, rivers, and lakes.[50] Next, recognizing that Clean Water Act jurisdiction also extends to wetlands "adjacent to" "waters of the United States," Justice Scalia limited such additional jurisdiction to wetlands that have a "continuous surface connection" to relatively permanent waters.[51] In all events, Justice Scalia rejected as "beyond parody" the application of the Clean Water Act to "ephemeral streams, wet meadows, storm sewers and culverts, directional sheet flow during storm events, drain tiles, man-made drainage ditches, and dry arroyos in the middle of the desert."[52]

Writing for himself, Justice Kennedy took a different approach. He concluded that jurisdiction under the act extends to any water or wetland with a "significant nexus" to "waters that are or were navigable in fact or that could reasonably be so made."[53] A "significant nexus" exists only where the wetlands, "alone or in combination with similarly situated lands in the region, significantly affect the chemical, physical, *and* biological integrity of other covered waters more readily understood as 'navigable.'"[54] Justice Kennedy would not bring within the scope of the act "drains, ditches, and streams remote from any navigable-in-fact water and carrying only minor water volumes toward it."[55]

In June 2015, EPA and the Corps published their most recent effort to define the act's jurisdiction, and they are again seemingly seeking to expand their jurisdiction from the "*waters* of the United States" to the "*lands* of the United States." The proposed rule defines the term "waters of the United States" in a cascading series of per se categories: (1) all waters susceptible to use in interstate or foreign commerce; (2) all interstate waters and wetlands; (3) the territorial seas; (4) all "tributaries" of the preceding waters; (5) all impoundments of waters otherwise identified as "waters of the United States"; and (6) all waters, including wetlands, that are "adjacent" to any of the preceding waters.[56] It then also includes on a case-specific basis, certain waters or sometimes-wet lands with a significant nexus to any water in the first three per se categories.[57] A "significant nexus" means that the water or wetland, "either alone or in combination with other similarly situated waters in the region, significantly affects the chemical, physical, *or* biological integrity of a water."[58]

At times, the proposal is so inconsistent with *both* tests put forth by the *Rapanos* majority that EPA and the Corps appear to be willfully ignoring the decision. For example, the proposed rule defines "tributaries"—which are per se included within the definition of "waters of the United States"—as any water with a bed and banks and high water mark that "contributes flow" to a water within one of the first three per se categories, and that may have one or more man-made or natural breaks (such as bridges, culverts, dams, debris piles, or boulder fields).[59] This definition, which permits breaks in flow, clearly cannot be squared with Justice Scalia's requirement of a "*continuous* surface connection" to a relatively permanent body of water.[60] Nor does any part of the definition account for Justice Kennedy's requirement that a covered non-navigable water "*significantly* affect the chemical, physical, *and* biological integrity of other covered waters more readily understood as 'navigable.'"[61]

The proposed rule's inclusion of all "adjacent" waters is similarly problematic. "Adjacent" is defined indiscriminately as all "bordering, contiguous or neighboring" waters and includes waters separated by "constructed dikes or barriers, natural river berms, beach dunes and the like."[62] There are surely waters within that sweeping definition that do not have a "continuous surface connection" to or "significantly affect the chemical, physical, and biological integrity" of any other waters. In fact, the definition of "neighboring"—a term that defines "adjacent"—expressly includes waters located within a "100-year floodplain," which is exactly what it sounds like.[63] If an isolated pond resides in an area that has a 1 percent chance of being flooded in any given year, that pond may well be considered part of "waters of the United States." No member of the *Rapanos* majority would endorse that view.

Several lawsuits were immediately filed upon the publication of the rule.[64]

WHAT TO DO WITH A PROBLEM LIKE EPA

When faced with an agency like EPA—which is bent on "seizing expansive power that . . . the statute[s] [are] not designed to grant"[65]—states, private regulated entities, and individual citizens must be willing and prepared to sue. The courts are our last check on the tyranny of unelected bureaucrats. As the Supreme Court showed in the *Utility Air Regulatory Group* case, there is hope still that the courts will look upon agency claims of "extravagant statutory power over the national economy" with "a measure of skepticism."[66]

There will be losses, of course. For every *Utility Air Regulatory Group*, there is an *EPA v. EME Homer City Generation, L.P.*—issued by the Supreme Court during the same term.[67] At issue there was EPA's determination of the duty of upwind states to reduce the pollution they send to downwind states—the so-called "Good Neighbor" obligation.[68] Under the Clean Air Act, states are responsible for maintaining attainment with EPA's National Ambient Air Quality Standards, which prescribe the maximum permissible levels of certain pollutants in the air.[69] The "Good Neighbor" obligation recognizes that air pollutants will travel from one state to another and requires a state to "prohibit[] . . . any source or other type of emissions activity within the State from emitting any air pollutant in *amounts* which will . . . contribute significantly to nonattainment in . . . any other State."[70] In *EME Homer City*, EPA had decided that upwind states would not be required to cut pollution in "amounts," as specifically stated in the statute, but rather were to cut all the pollution they could eliminate at a given cost.[71] A majority of the Supreme Court affirmed EPA's rule, to the chagrin of the dissenting justices, who rightly noted that the agency's approach had "no . . . textual justification at all."[72]

But challenges must be brought—and brought aggressively—because the goal of agencies like EPA is not necessarily to ultimately succeed in promulgating a rule, but rather to force through their policy ends by simply moving forward until they are ordered by a court to stop. There is no better example of that than the Section 112 regulation of power plants that was rejected in *Michigan v. EPA*. States and regulated entities promptly challenged the rule and eventually defeated it several years later, but in large part EPA had already accomplished what it set out to do. At oral argument before the Supreme Court, it was asserted that 90 percent of the capital cost of compliance had been spent.[73] And when EPA lost the lawsuit, it sought to reassure its supporters by touting that "investments have been made and most plants are already well on their way to making emissions reductions."[74] EPA had in practical terms achieved what the law and this country's elected representatives never intended it to do.

The worst that can be done with respect to an overreaching federal agency is to simply accept it and allow it, through sheer inertia, to remake this country according to the preferences of a handful of unelected bureaucrats.

21.

CRIMINAL LAW AND THE ADMINISTRATIVE STATE

How the Proliferation of Regulatory Offenses Undermines the Moral Authority of Our Criminal Laws

Michael B. Mukasey and John G. Malcolm

AN EVER-EXPANDING WEB OF CRIMINALIZED CONDUCT

It is conventional wisdom that the states have primary responsibility for protecting the health, safety, and general welfare of the people through the exercise of their "police power."[1] The federal government, however, has taken an increasingly expansive view of its role in combating crimes, thereby supplementing—or supplanting—the traditional role exercised by state and local authorities while broadening the scope of what is considered criminal behavior in our society.

There are nearly 5,000 federal criminal statutes scattered throughout the 51 titles of the federal code.[2] Some of these laws are incredibly broad. For example, in addition to dozens of statutes that penalize false statements or fraud in connection with individual federal programs, there are federal mail fraud[3] and wire fraud[4] statutes that seem to cover, with only slight hyperbole, any fraudulent scheme other than those perpetrated solely through in-person meetings or by carrier pigeon. There is also a federal false statements[5] statute that criminalizes any false statement pertaining to "any matter within the jurisdiction of" an ever-expanding government. And, in the case of the Lacey Act, it can be a crime *in this country* to violate another country's laws and regulations.[6]

Some criminal provisions appear within massive laws passed by Congress, and it is highly debatable whether most members of Congress even read or understood the law that they were passing. The Dodd-Frank Wall Street Reform & Consumer Protection Act, for example, is more than 800 single-spaced pages and contains over two dozen criminal offenses.[7] A prominent New York law firm published a summary of the bill that was more than 100 pages long, which noted that the act calls for 11 regulatory agencies to conduct 243 rulemakings and 67 studies.[8]

While the existence of too many federal criminal statutes covering too much conduct is a problem, it has helped spawn an even bigger problem: ambiguities in many of these statutes and broad delegations of authority to regulatory agencies have led to the proliferation of regulatory crimes and the concomitant increase in the power of unelected and unaccountable regulators to define what constitutes criminal behavior and then to enforce those definitions.

Buried within the Code of Federal Regulations, which is composed of approximately 200 volumes with over 80,000 pages, today there are an estimated 300,000 criminal regulatory offenses[9] ("public welfare" offenses). Nobody really knows the total number of regulatory offenses, although the number is immense. These regulations pose several problems. First, some of the regulations are vague and overbroad.[10] Second, many of these regulations are so abstruse that they may require a technical or doctoral degree in the discipline covered by the regulations to understand them. Third, there are so many regulations located in so many places that laypeople and small companies subject to those regulations would be unable to locate them, much less understand them, even if they had the resources to do so.[11] Fourth, the regulations often criminalize behavior that is not obviously morally wrong, so even the most intelligent among the population cannot by reason or common sense determine what behaviors are criminalized. In addition to actual regulations, there are also agency "guidance" documents and "frequently asked questions" that agencies sometimes try to pass off as having the same legal effect as regulations. Of course, this describes crimes only on the federal level. Each state has its own morass of criminal laws and regulations that people are presumed to know and which they must follow.

The result of all this is a vast web of criminalized conduct, much of which is not inherently immoral or blameworthy, that creates risks for an unwary public. The infamous Roman Emperor Caligula favored "publicizing" laws by writing them in fine print and posting them on boards affixed to the top of tall pillars.[12] Although that may not be the intent of regulators in the United States today, it is the practical reality for many individuals and small entities, especially those who cannot afford to keep high-priced, specialized attorneys on retainer to advise them. For them, such regulations might as well have been publicized by Caligula; they are equally inaccessible and incomprehensible.

In *Rogers v. Tennessee* (2001),[13] the Supreme Court of the United States cited "core due process concepts of notice, foreseeability, and, in particular, the right to fair warning as those concepts bear on the constitutionality of attaching criminal penalties to what previously had been innocent conduct." These are foundational elements—first principles—underlying the moral authority of our criminal laws. Then there is the well-known legal maxim *ignorantia juris non excusat*: ignorance of the law does not excuse violating the law, especially criminal laws. Yet considering the rows of library shelves needed to store the federal code (the laws themselves) and the Code of Federal Regulations, that maxim has been reduced to a cruel joke. This maxim made sense when the criminal laws in our country mirrored a commonly accepted moral code; it could fairly be said that if someone committed an act that reasonable people in society considered morally blameworthy, the person should not be surprised to discover, and could not use as an excuse unawareness, that such an act also constituted a criminal violation.[14] But that time has long since passed. Today, nobody knows or could reasonably know all of the laws that create potential criminal liability. The system is so complicated that sometimes even judges and lawyers have trouble discerning what the law is.[15] What hope do average citizens have?

The threat of unknown and unreasonable laws troubled the founders as well. In *Federalist* No. 62, James Madison warned, "It will be of little avail to the people that laws are made by men of their own choice if the laws be so voluminous that they cannot be read, or so incoherent that they cannot be understood . . . [so] that no man who knows what the law is today, can guess what it will be like tomorrow."[16] There is a serious problem when reasonable, intelligent people are branded as criminals for violating laws or regulations that they had no intent to violate, never knew existed, and would not have understood applied to their actions even if they had known about them. Additionally, there is a serious problem when reasonable people cannot plan their conduct and carry out their day-to-day lives because they do not know, and cannot with reasonable effort find out, what conduct the law prohibits.

At the end of this chapter, we suggest five measures Congress and state legislatures could take to solve the problem of over-criminalization, most of which could be implemented quickly if the political will could be mustered to approve them.

DELEGATING THE CRIMINAL LAW TO REGULATORY AGENCIES

One of the underpinnings of the Declaration of Independence and the Constitution is that a government's legitimacy and moral authority to exercise power arise from the "consent of the governed." This theory of governance was highly influenced by English philosopher John Locke, who wrote in 1690, "The power of the Legislative being derived from the People by a positive voluntary Grant and Institution . . . the Legislative can have no Power to transfer their Authority of making Laws, and place it in other Hands."[17]

Chief Justice John Marshall, however, distinguished between promulgating rules on "important" subjects, which is strictly a legislative function, and delegating power to others "to fill up the details."[18] Thus, regulatory offenses purport to flesh out and refine the details of federal statutes that Congress has enacted. In fact, the Supreme Court has held that Congress can delegate to Executive Branch agencies the ability "to fill up the details" so long as Congress provides an "intelligible principle" in the underlying statute to guide those agencies.[19] This is called the nondelegation doctrine.

Congress often passes broad statutes that are the result of compromise or a desire to avoid making tough choices that may prove politically unpopular.[20] The Clean Water Act[21] provides an illustration of this problem. Under that act, a party who discharges a pollutant into the "waters of the United States" without a permit can be criminally prosecuted. As the Supreme Court said in *Rapanos v. United States*,[22] over the past three decades, there has been an "immense expansion of federal regulation of land use that has occurred under the Clean Water Act—without any change in the governing statute—during the past five Presidential administrations." The Environmental Protection Agency and the U.S. Army Corps of Engineers have jurisdiction over "the waters of the United States," and they have claimed that that authority extends to "virtually any parcel of land containing a channel or conduit—whether man-made or natural, broad or narrow, permanent or ephemeral—through which rainwater or drainage may occasionally or intermittently flow."[23] The Court continued:

> On this view, the federally regulated "waters of the United States" include storm drains, roadside ditches, ripples of sand in the desert that may contain water once a year, and lands that are covered by floodwaters once every 100 years. Because they include the land containing storm sewers and desert washes, the statutory "waters of the United States" engulf entire cities and immense arid wastelands. In fact, the entire land area of the United States lies in some drainage basin, and an endless network of visible channels furrows the entire surface, containing water ephemerally wherever the rain falls. Any plot of land containing such a channel may potentially be regulated as a "water of the United States."[24]

Congress could, of course, have restricted the jurisdictional reach of the Clean Water Act by providing a narrow definition to the term "waters of the United States" so that it extended only to the traditional definition of navigable waters, that is, those used or susceptible to use in interstate or foreign commerce. Instead, Congress delegated authority to two federal agencies to define that term in order to avoid the pushback from irate landowners that would naturally follow any such congressional action. Indeed, the EPA and the Corps of Engineers have tried on many occasions since the passage of the Clean Water Act to expand their reach over wetlands and other "waters of the United States," to include remote, non-navigable creeks, streams, wetlands, and floodplains.[25]

This process results in the delegation of immense power to regulators, including the power to promulgate regulations that carry criminal penalties.[26] With two notable exceptions in 1935,[27] the Supreme Court has upheld every delegation to a regulatory agency, even in cases where congressional guidance has been virtually nonexistent or at best nebulous.[28]

The problem is compounded when courts defer, as some have done,[29] to an agency's interpretation of ambiguous statutes that contemplate criminal penalties under the *Chevron* doctrine.[30] However, Justices Antonin Scalia and Clarence Thomas have indicated that they are skeptical about whether Chevron deference should apply when an agency interprets a vague criminal statute. In *Whitman v. United States*,[31] the Supreme Court denied a criminal defendant's petition for a writ of certiorari challenging his insider trading conviction. While agreeing with the denial, Justice Scalia, joined by Justice Thomas, issued a statement indicating that he would be "receptive to granting" a petition seeking review on the issue of how much deference is due to an agency's interpretation of an ambiguous criminal law. He stated,

> I doubt the Government's pretensions to deference. They collide with the norm that legislatures, not executive officers, define crimes. When King James I tried to create new crimes by royal command, the judges responded that "the King cannot create any offence by his prohibition or proclamation, which was not an offence before." James I, however, did not have the benefit of *Chevron* deference. With deference to agency interpretations of statutory provisions to which criminal prohibitions are attached, federal administrators can in effect create (and uncreate) new crimes at will, so long as they do not roam beyond ambiguities that the laws contain. Undoubtedly Congress may make it a crime to violate a regulation, but it is quite a different matter for Congress to give agencies—let alone for us to *presume* that Congress gave agencies—power to resolve ambiguities in criminal legislation. The Government's theory [that agencies are entitled to such deference] . . . would . . . upend ordinary principles of interpretation. The rule of lenity requires interpreters to resolve ambiguity in criminal laws in favor of defendants.

> Deferring to the prosecuting branch's expansive views of these statutes "would turn [their] normal construction . . . upside-down, replacing the doctrine of lenity with a doctrine of severity."[32]

The relationship between criminal and administrative law dates back to the turn of the nineteenth century, when Congress established federal administrative agencies to protect the public from potential dangers posed by an increasingly industrialized society, and a regulatory framework that included both civil and criminal penalties for failing to abide by the rules those agencies promulgated. These regulations cover such aspects of our lives as the environment around us, the food we eat, the drugs we take, health, transportation, and housing, among many others. As the administrative state has grown, so too has the number of criminal regulations. As is the case with Congress, regulators have seemingly succumbed to the temptation to criminalize any behavior that they deem undesirable or which occasionally leads to a bad outcome.[33]

There are, however, important differences between criminal laws and regulations that are often overlooked, the most important of which is that they largely serve different purposes.[34] Blurring the two comes at a cost. Criminal laws are meant to enforce a commonly accepted moral code, set forth in language readily understood by an average person[35] and that clearly identifies the prohibited conduct, backed by the full force and authority of the government. Regulations, on the other hand, are meant to establish rules of the road to curb excesses and address consequences in a complex, rapidly evolving, highly industrialized society, with penalties attached for violations of those rules. While criminal laws are, or at least should be, narrowly drafted to provide "fair warning" to would-be violators, regulations are often drafted using broad, aspirational (and sometimes highly technical[36]) language to provide agencies with the flexibility they need to address health hazards and other societal concerns and to respond to new problems and changing circumstances, including scientific and technological advances.

There are certain kinds of crimes, such as murder, rape, arson, robbery, and fraud, which are referred to as *malum in se* offenses. These used to be, and to a large extent still are, the bread and butter of criminal enforcement. Such offenses are clearly morally opprobrious and are always prohibited, absent rare circumstances such as justifiable self-defense in a murder case. Bringing the moral force of the state in the form of a criminal prosecution to bear on such conduct is completely appropriate, indeed necessary, to maintain order and respect for the rule of law.

Regulatory crimes, however, generally are not *malum in se* offenses. Most regulatory crimes are *malum prohibitum* offenses, prohibiting acts that are not inherently blameworthy. Such offenses are "wrongs" only because Congress or regulatory authorities have said they are. They would not raise "red flags" to average citizens (or even to most lawyers and judges) who are unfamiliar with the voluminous, highly technical, and obscure contents of the Code of Federal Regulations. Unlike *malum in se* offenses, regulations do not generally prohibit morally indefensible conduct, although there are, of course, exceptions.[37] Rather, regulations *allow* conduct, but they circumscribe when, where, how, how often, and by whom certain conduct can be done, often in ways that are hard for the non-expert to understand or predict. Such regulatory infractions are enforced and penalized through the same traditional process used to investigate, prosecute, and penalize rapists and murderers, even though many of the people who commit such infractions were unaware that they were exposing themselves to potential criminal liability by engaging in routine activities as part of their everyday lives.

Each new criminal regulation necessarily gives investigators and prosecutors more power. Today, federal agents working for obscure regulatory bodies such as the U.S. Fish and Wildlife Service and the Food and Drug Administration are given guns and badges and are empowered to enforce regulatory crimes, with little sense of perspective and an unduly broad view of their authority.[38] When an investigator at a regulatory agency with a limited mandate is given such a hammer, every problem starts to look like a nail, and matters that should be handled civilly or administratively end up being handled criminally. Moreover, there will be a temptation for regulatory agents to pursue criminal cases to justify the authority they have been given and to lobby for future budgetary increases based on the number of charges they file or convictions they obtain.

Lavrentiy P. Beria, the influential chief of the secret police under Stalin, once said, "Show me the man, and I'll find you the crime." The United States is certainly not the former Soviet Union, but our criminal laws are numerous, and many are so dangerously overbroad that they create opportunities for prosecutors and investigators to abuse their power by targeting political or personal enemies. While the overwhelming majority of prosecutors and investigators in this country are people of high integrity who exercise good judgment and target truly bad actors, the average citizen should not have to rely on the discretion of prosecutors to decide when and against whom to enforce vague and overbroad laws. It is the job of the legislature to write clear laws so that people know ahead of time what conduct might subject them to criminal liability. We say that we have a government of laws and not of men; prosecutors and investigators, however well intentioned, are not disinterested players in the criminal justice process.

Moreover, regardless of the good intentions of federal officials, there is a significant difference between regulations that carry civil or administrative penalties for violations and those that carry criminal penalties. People caught up in the latter may find themselves deprived of their liberty and stripped of their rights to vote, sit on a jury, and possess a firearm, among other penalties that simply do not apply when someone violates a regulation that carries only civil or administrative penalties.

There is a unique stigma that is associated with being branded a criminal. A person stands to lose not only his liberty and certain civil rights, but also his reputation—an intangible yet invaluable commodity, precious to entities and people alike, that once damaged can be nearly impossible to repair. In addition to standard penalties that are imposed on those who are convicted of crimes, a series of burdensome collateral consequences often imposed by state or federal laws can follow a person for life.[39] For businesses, even a charge of a regulatory crime, let alone a conviction, can result in the "death sentence" of debarment from participation in federal programs—a power that some regulators exercise while a matter is still under investigation.[40] Legislators should be especially careful before promulgating regulations that can cause a person or entity to be unfairly branded as a criminal, to preserve the moral authority of our legal system and engender respect for the rule of law.

Many of these criminal prohibitions lack an adequate—or even any—*mens rea* ("guilty mind") requirement.[41] That may be acceptable when the goal is to penalize through the civil or administrative justice systems conduct that causes or threatens harm. But it is quite another matter to punish people through the criminal justice system when they have acted unwittingly. Although some heavily regulated entities receive notice about what is illegal, that is not the case for many people and small entities that end up acting at their peril, unaware of invisible trip wires that lie underfoot.

Throughout most of Anglo-American legal history, *mens rea* was considered an essential element of virtually every crime because it ensured that the criminal law ensnared only morally culpable parties.[42] In short, *mens rea* requires that someone must have acted with the intent to violate the law (or with the knowledge that his conduct violated the law) to be found guilty of a criminal offense. A *mens rea* requirement protects someone who engaged in accidental or innocent behavior from criminal prosecution but not from civil liability or administrative penalties.

Absent extraordinary circumstances[43] it should not be enough that the government proves that the accused possessed "an evil-doing hand"; the government should also have to prove that the accused had an "evil-meaning mind."[44] Indeed, recently, in *Elonis v. United States*, the Supreme Court reversed a man's conviction for transmitting threatening communications under 18 U.S.C. § 875(c) after he posted some deeply disturbing comments about his estranged wife (and others, including former co-workers) on his Facebook page that she regarded as threatening.[45] The Court read into the statute a *mens rea* requirement and reiterated the "basic principle that 'wrongdoing must be conscious to be criminal.'"[46] The Court focused on the actor's intent rather than the recipient's perception: "Having the liability turn on whether a 'reasonable person' regards the communication as a threat—regardless of what the defendant thinks—'reduces the culpability on the all-important element of the crime to negligence.'"[47] While the Court declined to identify exactly what the appropriate *mens rea* standard is under the statute and whether recklessness would suffice, the Court certainly recognized that a defendant's mental state is critical when he faces criminal liability and that when a federal criminal statute is "silent on the required mental state," a court should read into the statute "that *mens rea* which is necessary to separate wrongful conduct from 'otherwise innocent conduct.'"[48]

It is unavoidable that bad outcomes will occur from time to time, whether through willfulness, negligence, or sheer accident; however, the intent of the actor should make a difference in whether that person is criminally prosecuted or dealt with, perhaps severely, through the civil or administrative justice systems. As Oliver Wendell Holmes, Jr. once observed, "Even a dog distinguishes between being stumbled over and being kicked."[49]

REAL-LIFE CONSEQUENCES OF REGULATORY OVERREACH

Sadly, there are many laws and regulatory offenses on the books that are obscure or lack a *mens rea* requirement.[50] Injustices occur when unwitting people are criminally prosecuted for violating such provisions. Consider the following examples.

David McNab, Abner Schoenwetter, Robert Blandford, and Diane Huang were prosecuted for violating the Lacey Act, a statute that prohibits the importation of fish, wildlife, or plants "taken, possessed, transported, or sold in violation of . . . any foreign law."[51] Federal agents with the National Marine and Wildlife Fishery Service received an anonymous tip that McNab and the others were transporting a shipment of lobsters packed in plastic bags, rather than boxes, allegedly in violation of Honduran law. The tip also stated that many of the lobsters were undersized and some were egg-bearing or had their eggs removed, which also purportedly violated Honduran law. After contacting Honduran authorities, the agents seized the cargo, and McNab and the others were charged with criminal violations of the Lacey Act. Both prior to trial and after conviction, the defendants moved to dismiss the charges, arguing that these Honduran laws had never been validly enacted; thus they were unenforceable. The defendants offered the testimony of several Honduran law experts, a regional Honduran prosecutor, and the Attorney General of Honduras that these regulations were neither in effect nor legally binding at the time. Yet the trial judge accepted the testimony of a lower-ranking Honduran official from the Ministry of Agriculture and Livestock who testified on behalf of the U.S. government. The judge sentenced McNab, Schoenwetter, and Blandford to 97 months' imprisonment each and Huang to 24 months' imprisonment. A divided panel of the Eleventh Circuit Court of Appeals upheld their convictions[52] even though, while the appeal was pending, Honduran courts definitively ruled that these regulations had never been properly issued and were invalid, and the Constitution of Honduras appeared to require that the Honduran courts' orders be applied retroactively.[53] In other words, Honduran courts ruled that McNab and his co-defendants were correct in claiming that their actions did not violate Honduran law at the time, yet their convictions in this country under the Lacey Act for alleged violations of Honduran law were allowed to stand. This is a perverse result and a manifest injustice.

Wade Martin, a native Alaskan fisherman, sold ten sea otters to a buyer he thought was a native Alaskan; the authorities informed him that was not the case and that his actions violated the Marine Mammal Protection Act of 1972,[54] which criminalizes the sale of certain species, including sea otters, to non–native Alaskans. Because prosecutors would not have to prove that he knew the buyer was not from Alaska, Martin pleaded guilty and was sentenced to two years' probation and ordered to pay a $1,000 fine.[55] He lives with the stigma of a felony conviction.

Lawrence Lewis[56] was raised in the projects of Washington, D.C. Lewis worked as a janitor for the public school system, took night classes, and eventually worked his way up to chief engineer at Knollwood, a military retirement home. On occasion, some of the elderly patients at Knollwood would stuff their adult diapers in the toilets, causing a blockage and sewage overflow. To prevent harm to the patients, Lewis and his staff did what they were trained to do on such occasions and diverted the backed-up sewage into a storm drain that they believed was connected to the city's sewage-treatment system. It turned out, however, that the storm drain emptied into a remote part of Rock Creek, which ultimately connects with the Potomac River. This was unbeknownst to Lewis, as acknowledged by the Department of Justice in a court filing.

Nonetheless, federal authorities charged Lewis with felony violations of the Clean Water Act. To avoid a felony conviction and potential long-term jail sentence, Lewis was persuaded to plead guilty to a misdemeanor and was sentenced to one year of probation. And for what? Lewis's actions hardly compare with a large company dumping toxic chemicals into navigable waterways—which is what the Clean Water Act was intended to curb—but now he lives with the stigma of a criminal conviction.

Nancy Black,[57] a nationally renowned marine biologist, operates a whale-watching company and had a permit to research killer whales in Monterey Bay, California. On two different occasions, Black and her crew encountered a pod of orcas feasting on a dead gray whale. To catch this activity on film, Black had her crew remove a piece of blubber from the water, attach it to the boat with a rope, and then lower it back into the water. In an unrelated incident, the captain of one of her vessels whistled at a humpback whale to try to keep it in the vicinity. A crew member on her other boat encouraged whale-watcher passengers to do likewise. Black reprimanded both of them.[58]

When the wife of the chastened captain contacted the authorities to find out whether her husband had done anything wrong, an investigator with the National Oceanic and Atmospheric Administration began an investigation into potential harassment of a whale, a federal offense. The investigator contacted Black and asked her about the captain. She told the investigator that she had a videotape of the incident, produced to sell to that day's passengers as a memento of their experience, which she voluntarily provided to the agent. She did not, however, tell the investigator that the tape had been edited to cut out what she thought was extraneous footage. The footage that she provided included the captain whistling, but it did not include the crew member on the other boat egging on the passengers.[59]

Nothing happened to the captain or the crew member, but Nancy Black was charged with two felony counts for providing an edited video to the officer without disclosing that it was edited, as well as two misdemeanor violations of the Marine Mammal Protection Act for "feeding" killer whales. The government also sought forfeiture of her boats.[60] Facing the prospect of a felony conviction, a prison sentence, and loss of her property, and having already spent $100,000 in attorney's fees,[61] Black pled guilty to a misdemeanor. In doing so, she admitted that she had removed the blubber and then returned the same piece of blubber to the water, an activity which was not explicitly authorized by her permit, and that she had edited the video she had turned over to the inspector, which "could have" impeded the investigation.[62] That was it. Thus, a statute designed to protect mammals, not to impede harmless and potentially valuable research, was used to dragoon Nancy Black.[63]

Dr. Peter Gleason, a Maryland psychiatrist, dedicated much of his professional life to caring for the poor and underserved. Dr. Gleason got into trouble when he gave a series of paid lectures about Xyrem, a drug that had been approved by the FDA to treat narcolepsy but is also used to treat a variety of other medical conditions.[64] The conferences where Dr. Gleason spoke were sponsored by the manufacturer of Xyrem. While drug manufacturers are prohibited by law from promoting off-label usages of FDA-approved drugs, physicians face no such restrictions and they may prescribe a drug for off-label purposes and communicate with other physicians about the efficacy of the drug in treating those conditions.[65] Indeed, many new and efficacious uses of drugs have been discovered in this way. Nonetheless, Dr. Gleason found himself under indictment for allegedly conspiring with some of the drug manufacturer's representatives to promote off-label uses of Xyrem.[66] The federal government seized Dr. Gleason's assets, claiming that they were ill-gotten gains traceable to a so-called criminal conspiracy. Although he believed he had done nothing wrong, Dr. Gleason pleaded guilty to a misdemeanor to avoid the possibility of being branded a felon and losing his life's savings. He was sentenced to one year's probation and a $25 fine.[67]

A co-defendant, however, opted to fight. He persuaded the Second Circuit Court of Appeals that the First Amendment protects the right of physicians and manufacturers to convey truthful, factual information about the beneficial uses of drugs, including off-label uses.[68] Sadly, this vindication came too late for Dr. Gleason. Following his guilty plea, state medical authorities suspended Dr. Gleason's license, making it extremely difficult for him to practice psychiatry in any state. Dr. Gleason became increasingly despondent and hanged himself.[69]

FIVE STEPS TO HELP FIX THE PROBLEMS POSED BY CRIMINAL REGULATIONS

There are five steps Congress can take to rein in the proliferation of regulatory offenses and restore moral authority to our criminal law system. First, Congress should pass a law that requires the Attorney General and all regulatory agencies to identify all statutes and regulations that bear on the definition of criminal conduct or carry criminal penalties, and list them in a place that is easily accessible for free to the general public. This would have to be updated on an ongoing basis. Merely identifying and listing all such laws and regulations will not make them any less vague or hyper-technical, but it will provide members of the general public who want to stay on the right side of the law with a place to find out what is and is not a crime. This might prompt a prudent person to do additional research if he or she has continuing doubts about the legality of an action he or she wants to undertake. The government might argue that cataloging all criminal laws and regulations would be an unwieldy task but, if true, that only proves the need to do so.

Second, Congress should draft laws with precision and only when necessary. Legislators must resist pressure caused by the sensationalistic "headline of the day" from members of the public who demand that legislators "do something" to respond to a horrible event. Not infrequently, the complained-of conduct that led to the horrible event is already a federal crime. Even if it is not a federal crime, it might already be a state crime, and if so, there is no reason to make that same conduct a federal crime absent a unique federal interest. Further, legislators must resist pressure from lobbyists representing special interests who seek to gain a competitive, commercial advantage by criminalizing through regulations the business practices of their competitors.[70] When Congress responds to the latest high-profile problem or regulates at the behest of special interests, it risks developing criminal laws that do not reflect our social norms, a problem that imposes significant costs to society. Namely, a reasonable person will not be able to plan his conduct because the criminal laws are too unpredictable.

Third, Congress should pay more attention to *mens rea* standards. Absent extraordinary circumstances,[71] any new criminal laws should require proof beyond a reasonable doubt that the person acted with the intent to violate the law. Along these same lines, Congress should also pass a default *mens rea* provision for non-jurisdictional elements of existing criminal laws in which no *mens rea* has been provided. In other words, if there is an element of a criminal statute or regulation that is missing a *mens rea* requirement, a default standard should be inserted with respect to that element, unless Congress expressly states that it intends to enact a strict liability offense with no intent requirement.

Fourth, bureaucrats should not be making new crimes. Thus, Congress should not delegate its power to criminalize conduct to unelected officials in federal departments and agencies. If a matter is serious enough to send someone to prison, it is serious enough to be considered and voted upon by those who have been elected by (and are accountable to) the people. Furthermore, the Supreme Court should take more seriously the nondelegation doctrine and no longer permit the lower courts to allow agencies to create federal crimes through regulation.

Finally, Congress should consider adopting a mistake of law defense[72] to *malum prohibitum* offenses, which would place the burden of proof on the accused[73] and would sensibly balance society's interest in enforcing criminal laws with its perhaps greater interest in not saddling morally blameless people with criminal records.[74] While a mistake of fact defense has generally been recognized in this country for some crimes, such as when somebody charged with larceny defends himself by claiming that he honestly believed that the property he is accused of taking belonged to him, a mistake of law defense has not been recognized,[75] even though it has an ancient lineage.[76]

With a mistake of law defense, a person charged with violating an obscure criminal regulation could defend himself by proving that he reasonably and honestly (although mistakenly) believed that his conduct did not violate the law. Such a defense would require proof by the defendant that he did not know that his conduct was illegal and that a reasonable person in his position would not have known that such conduct was illegal. Therefore, if a person did not know that his conduct was illegal, but a reasonable person in his position would have known it, he loses; and if he knew that his conduct was illegal, he loses regardless of what a reasonable person in his position would have believed.

The existence of too many federal criminal statutes covering too much conduct is a serious problem. So is the proliferation of regulatory crimes and the immense power vested in unelected and unaccountable regulators to define what constitutes criminal behavior and to enforce those definitions. These reforms would go a long way toward ameliorating the serious and growing problem of unknowing and unwitting individuals and entities violating obscure or unknowable regulations and being branded criminals. The high risk of being ensnared in the vast web of criminalized conduct—much of which is not inherently immoral or blameworthy—diminishes the public's respect for the fairness and integrity of our criminal justice system, and *that* is something that should concern everyone.

22.

FTC OVERREACH ON ADVERTISING ENFORCEMENT THREATENS THE FREE FLOW OF VALUABLE INFORMATION

Maureen K. Ohlhausen[1]

INTRODUCTION

As the drafters of our Constitution recognized, a free society depends upon the free flow of information, including commercial information. Truthful advertising benefits consumers by informing them of products to serve their needs and desires. Conversely, fraudulent and deceptive advertising harms consumers by depriving them of the benefit of their bargain. Therefore, as a complement to its role in protecting the free flow of information and the vitality of the competitive marketplace, government has a legitimate role in preventing fraudulent and deceptive commercial information.

Unfortunately, the FTC has occasionally overreached when regulating advertising. The FTC's greatest overreach occurred during its "KidVid" effort in the late 1970s, when it sought to regulate television advertising to children. Specifically, the FTC concluded that much advertising to children was likely deceptive and unfair because of children's limited understanding of commercial messages. It therefore proposed major prohibitions, including a ban on all television advertising of any product directed to, or seen by, audiences with a significant proportion of young children who do not understand the commercial purpose of advertising.[2]

This sweeping regulatory agenda triggered a fierce backlash. Even the *Washington Post* criticized the commission for being a "National Nanny."[3] Congress demonstrated its particular disapproval of the FTC's overreach by refusing to fund the agency, closing the commission's doors for several days. Congress also passed new laws limiting the FTC's jurisdiction and prohibiting the FTC from regulating commercial advertising as unfair.[4]

Chastened by this backlash, the commission adopted restrained, case-by-case enforcement against deceptive advertisements. However, several recent advertising enforcement cases suggest that the FTC has resumed its overreach, albeit through more subtle methods. For example, as will be discussed in detail, the FTC recently demanded that two mobile app developers demonstrate through expensive drug-trial-like studies that their skin-mole tracking apps perform certain functions as well as a dermatologist, even though the companies never advertised such accuracy.[5] Such overreach threatens once again to undermine the FTC's mission of maximizing consumer welfare.

THE CONSTITUTION PROTECTS THE FREE FLOW OF COMMERCIAL INFORMATION

The Constitution protects free speech, including commercial speech. Over 200 years ago, the drafters of our Constitution recognized that a free society requires the free flow of information. The founders explicitly limited the government's ability to impede that free flow by adopting the First Amendment. Most people know that the First Amendment protects citizens' right to speak out on political issues, to express their views artistically, and to report on the events and issues of the day. But the First Amendment also prevents the government from unduly interfering with truthful commercial speech, including most advertising and marketing. Indeed, the government faces a high bar if it wishes to restrict such speech. If the commercial speech is not misleading and does not concern illegal activity, the government must demonstrate that it restricts no more speech than necessary to directly advance a substantial government interest.[6] Over the last twenty years, courts have applied this standard with increasing vigor to protect commercial speech.[7]

TRUTHFUL ADVERTISING BENEFITS CONSUMERS

Information is crucial to a well-functioning marketplace of ideas; but it is also crucial to a well-functioning marketplace. Indeed, as the Supreme Court recognized over thirty years ago, a "consumer's interest in the free flow of commercial information . . . may be as keen, if not keener by far, than his interest in the day's most urgent political debate."[8] The Court also noted that "intelligent and well informed" consumer decisions benefit that consumer, but they also benefit the market system more generally; therefore, the free flow of commercial speech is "indispensable."[9]

Both common sense and research show that consumers benefit greatly from accurate commercial information. Intuition and personal experience suggest that consumers make better decisions when they can easily compare their marketplace options, such as by using the many online and app-based tools available today. And empirical research has demonstrated that when consumers can compare their market options, prices tend to be lower and less varied.[10] Likewise, other studies have shown that when government restricts truthful advertising, prices rise and quality suffers.[11]

Consumers benefit from bountiful marketplace information not just through lower prices. FTC staff studied the dissemination of health information in the ready-to-eat cereal market and demonstrated how consumers and competition can benefit from advertising.[12] In 1984, the Kellogg Company began claiming on labels and in advertising that All-Bran cereal was high in fiber and that diets high in fiber could reduce cancer risk. The study notes that competitors soon responded with similar claims for their own high-fiber cereals and introduced more high-fiber products. Even more importantly, consumers began to make significant changes in their cereal choices, substantially increasing their consumption of high-fiber products. Thus, these advertising claims benefited consumers by delivering novel and valuable health information. Similarly, competition benefited because competitors greatly expanded the range of high-fiber cereal choices available in the market.

Just as truthful commercial speech benefits the marketplace, fraudulent and deceptive speech harms commerce and consumers. Thus, the government has a legitimate role in preventing fraudulent and deceptive speech. However, as government seeks to eliminate false and deceptive advertising, it must also avoid restricting consumers' access to truthful marketplace information. Actions that reduce consumers' access to truthful product information also reduce market efficiency, which harms consumers. As the FTC staff observed in a comment to the FDA on the First Amendment,

A flexible approach to commercial speech—one that encourages the dissemination of accurate speech and tailors restrictions to prevent speech that is false or misleading—will result in greater dissemination of valuable information with benefits for both consumers and competition. In contrast, the evidence indicates that broad restrictions on the dissemination of truthful commercial speech, while effectively stopping false or misleading information, can deprive consumers of useful information as well.[13]

FTC ADVERTISING ENFORCEMENT

After the KidVid debacle, the FTC built an advertising enforcement program that seeks to eliminate deceptive ads while maximizing the incentives to disseminate accurate information. This program relies upon a simple core principle: an advertiser must possess a reasonable basis for its advertising claims.[14] What constitutes a reasonable basis depends on how an advertiser presents and qualifies a claim. The FTC evaluates an advertisement's legality using a two-step process.

First, the FTC determines the claims of an ad, which may be express ("lose 5 pounds a week") or implied ("get a great beach body"). Implied claims exist on a continuum, from nearly express to vaguely implied. When determining what claims an ad makes, the FTC seeks to understand the net impression a reasonable consumer would take from the ad. The commission may undertake a net impression analysis and find implied claims when it can "conclude with confidence after examining the interaction of all the different elements in [an advertisement] that they contain a particular implied claim."[15] When the commission lacks such confidence (e.g., due to well-qualified claims or contradicting statements), however, it "will not find the ad to make the implied claim unless extrinsic evidence allows [it] to conclude that such a reading of the ad is reasonable."[16]

Once the FTC identifies an ad's claims, it determines the proper level of substantiation needed. The standard for substantiation differs depending on the type of claim. Many ads make an "establishment claim" describing the amount of support the advertiser has for the claim. For example, an ad might claim that a product is "scientifically proven" to be effective. When an advertiser makes such a claim, the commission expects that advertiser to have at least the level of support claimed in the ad. Qualified claims reflecting limited support therefore require less substantiation than an unqualified claim.

Not all ads make establishment claims, but many ads make at least one "efficacy claim," which is an express or implied claim about the product's effectiveness. The commission evaluates efficacy claims using six factors drawn from the 1972 *Pfizer* case.[17] These factors determine how much substantiation an advertiser must provide to support such a claim. The *Pfizer* factors are "the type of claim, the product, the consequences of a false claim, the benefits of a truthful claim, the cost of developing substantiation for the claim, and the amount of substantiation experts in the field believe is reasonable."[18]

Properly applied, the *Pfizer* analysis enables the FTC to balance the benefit from more evidence about a product's claimed attributes against the product's riskiness and the cost of suppressing potentially useful information about it. Claims about safe products that offer substantial possible benefits with few downsides need less substantiation. On the other hand, claims about risky products require more substantiation. Thus, under such an analysis, health- or disease-related claims about a safe product, such as a food,[19] require less substantiation than would health- or disease-related claims about a drug, because consumers risk less when consuming the safe product.

RECENT OVERREACHES IN FTC AD ENFORCEMENT

The FTC's approach to advertising enforcement has successfully removed many fraudulent claims from the marketplace while promoting the dissemination of useful information. However, in some recent cases the

FTC has overreached in its advertising enforcement, unconstitutionally limiting free speech and harming consumers in the process.

The FTC's advertising substantiation approach, described before, has historically entertained the possibility that advertising could make reasonable claims even absent fully conclusive science. Indeed, the FTC's past approach contemplated that claims on both sides of a scientific debate could have reasonable support. However, recent cases increasingly reflect an apparent belief by some at the commission that a claim can be reasonable only if supported by "settled" science and that only one side of a debate can be reasonable. This inefficiently high standard harms consumers because it restricts the flow of useful information to consumers about emerging areas of science and ultimately discourages scientific research in disputed areas.

The commission has imposed this inefficiently high standard in two ways. First, the FTC has directly imposed unduly strict standards in its settlements with companies, thereby chilling their free speech as well as the speech of similarly situated companies who would otherwise provide useful information to consumers. Second, the FTC has indirectly imposed too high a substantiation standard by interpreting ads to make much stronger claims than a reasonable consumer would take from the ad. I further describe both methods of overreach here.

FTC OVERREACH BY IMPOSING INAPPROPRIATELY STRICT SUBSTANTIATION STANDARDS IN CONSENTS

Most FTC advertising substantiation cases end in settlements. These settlements require defendants to possess specific levels of substantiation for future advertising claims. Although they only bind the party to the case, industry looks to these settlements to determine where the FTC draws the line between a substantiated and unsubstantiated claim. Thus, settlement orders can have a real effect on broader marketplace behavior.

Some recent FTC consent agreements have departed from the *Pfizer* balancing approach and, as a result, have imposed too high a level of substantiation on certain claims. Specifically, some recent cases have required advertisers to support future health- and disease-related claims, even for relatively safe products such as foods, with two randomized, controlled studies (also known as RCTs).[20]

RCTs are often referred to as the "gold standard" of scientific research. An RCT tests a treatment by establishing two randomly selected groups: a control group and an effect group. In an ideal study, the groups' sole difference is that the effect group receives the treatment while the control group receives a placebo. Such trials use blinding to avoid bias, and the strongest trials are double-blind: neither the subjects nor the researchers know which subjects are taking a placebo instead of the treatment.

For certain types of research, RCTs are the only methodology accepted by experts as adequate. However, RCTs are certainly not the only type of persuasive scientific evidence.[21] Furthermore, conducting RCTs can be difficult and can cost significant time and money relative to other types of testing, particularly for diseases that develop over a long period of time (such as osteoporosis) or for complex health conditions. In other cases, conducting an RCT could be unethical or immoral; for example, we do not conduct RCTs to determine the potential harm of chemicals suspected to be hazardous.

Under the *Pfizer* factors, requiring RCTs may be appropriate in some circumstances, such as where a product's use carries some significant risk, or where conducting RCTs may be low cost, as for conditions whose development or amelioration can be observed over a short time period. Thus, for example, I have been willing to support requiring two RCTs for short-term weight-loss claims because researchers can conduct such studies in a relatively brief amount of time and at a lower cost than for many other health claims.

In some cases, staff has sought to justify a two-RCT requirement as appropriate fencing-in relief. "Fencing in" denotes the commission's practice of extending a final consent order's scope beyond the specific product, parties, or type of conduct involved in the actual violation.[22] Fencing-in remedies seek to deter future unlawful conduct in related products or services through "provisions in a final Commission order that are broader in scope than the conduct that is declared unlawful."[23] For example, the FTC might prohibit a company that made unsubstantiated weight-loss claims about caffeine-imbued leggings from making similar unsubstantiated weight-loss claims about any drug or cosmetic.[24] Such fencing in protects consumers by subjecting past violators to potential fines if they extend their poor substantiation practices to other products or services.

Fencing in incentivizes known bad actors to behave properly toward consumers in spheres beyond the specific violation at issue. However, requiring unjustifiably high substantiation does not incentivize proper behavior. Instead, requiring past violators to obtain stricter-than-necessary substantiation for a claim imposes unnecessary costs on the distribution of useful information. This prevents consumers from accessing useful information without making them any safer. If the *Pfizer* factors indicate that reasonable scientific evidence such as a longitudinal study or a single RCT substantiates a particular advertising claim, requiring two RCTs offers no better protection to consumers. Instead, such a requirement simply increases the difficulty of making truthful claims that could be useful to consumers.[25]

As noted, when the FTC imposes an overly strict substantiation standard in a settlement, it affects more than just the party to the settlement and that party's customers. Including a two-RCT standard in such settlements implies that the FTC will require two RCTs to substantiate any health- or disease-related claims, even for relatively safe products. Manufacturers without two RCTs, but who possess otherwise adequate scientific evidence, may forgo making useful claims about these kinds of products out of fear that the FTC will determine such claims to be unsubstantiated. Requiring more numerous and rigorous studies for all health- or disease-related claims may increase confidence in such claims, but rather than spend the time and money to conduct such studies, companies may simply avoid providing information that would benefit consumers and focus instead on less scientific product attributes, like taste. If the FTC demands too high a level of substantiation in pursuit of certainty, it risks reducing consumers' access to information about emerging areas of science and weakening the pressure on firms to compete on the health features of their products.

Fortunately, the D.C. Circuit in a recent case agreed that imposing a two-RCT standard as a one-size-fits-all substantiation standard violates advertisers' First Amendment free speech rights. Specifically, in *POM Wonderful v. FTC*,[26] the court held that in imposing an "across-the-board, two-RCT substantiation requirement for any future disease-related claims by petitioners," the FTC had "fail[ed] to demonstrate how such a rigid remedial rule bears the requisite 'reasonable fit' with the interest in preventing deceptive speech."[27] The court noted that if a blanket two-RCT standard were imposed, "consumers may be denied useful, truthful information about products with a demonstrated capacity to treat or prevent serious disease."[28] The court's decision echoes my dissent from the FTC's two-RCT remedy in *POM*, where I stated that "[r]equiring a second RCT is not reasonably related to the violations at issue in this case because a second study would not cure any particular statistical or methodological problems," and while "requiring two RCTs" might "provide the Commission with some subjective comfort," it "does so at the expense of limiting consumer access to potentially useful information."[29]

I hope that the D.C. Circuit's conclusion in *POM* will encourage the FTC to rein in excessive substantiation requirements. The commission should apply the *Pfizer* balancing test in a more finely calibrated manner than it has in some recent consent orders to avoid imposing "unduly burdensome restrictions that might chill information useful to consumers in making purchasing decisions."[30]

FTC OVERREACH BY EXPANSIVELY INTERPRETING AN ADVERTISEMENT'S CLAIMS

The FTC has also imposed an inappropriately high level of substantiation by interpreting an advertisement too broadly. As I noted in the POM case, "We must keep in mind . . . that if we are too quick to find stronger claims than the ones reasonable consumers actually perceive, then we will inadvertently, but categorically, require an undue level of substantiation for those claims."[31]

Two recent FTC cases provide good examples of how the FTC requires too much substantiation by interpreting advertising too expansively.[32] These cases involve two mobile applications, MelApp and Mole Detective, designed to help users evaluate their risk of melanoma. To use the apps, a consumer photographs a skin lesion with their smartphone, and the apps then guide the user through self-evaluation and measurement[33] of the photo, based on the five "ABCDE" risk factors of melanoma.[34] Once the user completes the self-evaluation steps, the apps algorithmically generate and display a risk assessment, such as "Medium

Risk—This mole shows several symptoms of melanoma. Contact your dermatologist to get it checked immediately," or "Low Risk—This moles [*sic*] shows no symptoms of melanoma. Continue to track it and schedule your annual dermatology appointment."[35]

The advertisements for these apps described the apps as tools to improve self-assessments in conjunction with visits to dermatologists, emphasizing the importance of regular dermatologist visits. The ads also implied that using the apps would improve the users' chances of detecting melanoma but did not make specific accuracy claims, nor explain how much the users' chance of detecting melanoma would improve. The record contained no evidence that consumers interpreted the ads to promise melanoma detection as accurate and efficacious as a dermatologist.

The defendants' ads did not claim dermatologist-level accuracy, nor did the apps claim to substitute for medical care. Yet the commission majority position in these cases—from which I dissented[36]—effectively demanded that defendants demonstrate that their apps assess cancer risk as well as dermatologists. The settlement orders require a drug-trial-like level of substantiation: rigorous, well-accepted, blinded, human clinical tests to substantiate any claim that the app increases consumers' chances of detecting skin cancer in the early stages.[37] Both orders also impose the same high substantiation standard on any claim that an app "detects or diagnoses melanoma or risk factors of melanoma."[38]

Thus, the orders in these cases impose a high level of substantiation despite lacking evidence that the advertising claims require such substantiation. Regardless of the assurances in the majority's statement about what the orders require, the complaints imply—and the majority appears to agree[39]—that reasonable consumers expected the apps to substitute for professional medical care. This disconnect raises the possibility that the commission may use vague allegations to impose very high substantiation standards even for modest advertising claims.

CONCLUSION

Our Constitution and the FTC's historical approach under *Pfizer* recognize the important balance between preventing fraud and promoting the free flow of truthful commercial information. Recent, overly aggressive FTC advertising substantiation enforcement actions have disturbed this balance, "overprotecting" consumers by depriving them of useful information. Although the FTC no doubt has the best of intentions in requiring high levels of substantiation for advertising, this overreach ultimately harms consumers. Instead, the FTC should require appropriate levels of substantiation and more carefully interpret advertising claims. By doing so, the commission can protect consumers from false and deceptive advertising yet still ensure that consumers get the information they need to make decisions about the products they may purchase. Such an approach will maximize the free flow of truthful information that is vital to the functioning of a free society and a free market.

23.

PREEMPTION WITHOUT REPRESENTATION

E. Scott Pruitt[1]

In 2014, President Barack Obama announced a series of executive actions that (1) shielded many unlawfully present individuals from deportation, and (2) granted them federal benefits. This chapter will discuss how these executive actions were uniquely harmful to the vertical separation of powers found in our Constitution.

I. THE TAKE CARE CLAUSE

Article II, Section 3, of the United States Constitution contains a constitutional oddity. Requiring that "[the President] shall take Care that the Laws be *faithfully* executed,"[2] the section is one of only two provisions in the Constitution requiring an action to be taken with good intent.[3]

This requirement of faithfulness in execution is no small thing. William Maclaine proclaimed at the North Carolina ratifying convention that the Take Care Clause was "one of the [Constitution's] best provisions," while the nation's first president, George Washington, recognized that "to permit [the laws] to be trampled upon with impunity would be repugnant to" the duty imposed on him by the clause.[4]

The horizontal separation-of-powers rationale undergirding the Take Care Clause is readily apparent and oft-discussed. The United States Constitution creates a system of government by dividing powers horizontally among several equal and distinct parts—the well-known legislative, executive, and judicial branches.[5] The creation of three divided branches of government stands as structural protection against "abuse of power" and has thus far proven "critical to preserving liberty."[6] Within that constitutional scheme of horizontally divided power, Congress has been invested with "All legislative Powers,"[7] because "[t]he Founders of this Nation entrusted the law making power to the Congress alone."[8] By requiring the President—and hence the Executive Branch headed by the President—to "take Care that the Laws" made by Congress "be faithfully executed,"[9] the founders built into the constitutional structure a protection against executive detours into lawmaking—a structural protection ultimately aimed at protecting not just Congress but individual liberty as well.

In short, the founders recognized that when a branch of government pursues its own prerogatives, it has every incentive to do so vigorously. But when a branch is tasked with obeying the decisions of another branch,[10] there may well be times when it has every reason to pull its punches, at the expense of its co-equal branch. Thus, the faithfulness-in-execution requirement was made an integral part of Article II.

But the faithfulness-in-execution requirement serves a second, less-often-discussed purpose: to protect the *vertical* separation of powers between the states and the federal government, a relationship that in this context is defined largely by Article I, which gives exclusive lawmaking authority to Congress,[11] and the Supremacy Clause, which mandates that Congress's laws supersede state laws on the same subject.[12]

Much as they did with the horizontal separation of powers, "[t]he Framers concluded that allocation of powers between the National Government and the States enhances freedom, first by protecting the integrity of the governments themselves, and second by protecting the people, from whom all governmental powers are derived."[13] Federalism is "more than an exercise in setting the boundary between different institutions of government for their own integrity. . . . 'Rather, federalism secures to citizens the liberties that derive from the diffusion of sovereign power.'"[14] And like the horizontal separation of powers, the ultimate aim is the protection of individuals, whose freedom "rests on what might at first seem a counterintuitive insight, that 'freedom is enhanced by the creation of two governments, not one.'"[15]

When a state enters the Union, it agrees that validly enacted federal laws will supersede any conflicting state laws. But the basic constitutional bargain struck by the states assumes that preemption of state law occurs only through Congress, where the states have a voice and role in the process of creating the supreme federal laws. When the executive fails to faithfully execute Congress's laws, the states are, by operation of the Supremacy Clause, left unable to utilize their sovereign powers, while also left without a meaningful role in the creation of the federal law as executed. When that happens, the executive forecloses political advocacy as a remedy—it preempts state law through a process that involves no input from the states.

II. THE TAKE CARE CLAUSE'S BIGGEST TEST

In late 2014, the Executive Branch put the Take Care Clause to a first-of-its-kind test—one that implicated both rationales for the faithfulness-in-execution requirement.

To understand the situation fully, however, one must begin in 2008, when during his campaign for the presidency, Barack Obama urged Congress to comprehensively reform the Immigration and Nationality Act (INA). Candidate Obama stated that it was his "commitment" to the American people to champion "immigration reform that will secure our borders, . . . punish employers who exploit immigrant labor[,] . . . [and] bring[] the 12 million people who are here illegally out of the shadows. . . . That is a priority I will pursue from my very first day."[16]

This was hardly a novel idea. A piece of legislation known as the Development Relief and Education for Alien Minors Act (DREAM Act) had been before Congress in one form or another since 2001.[17] The DREAM Act would have given a select group of unlawfully present aliens the chance to earn legal status if they arrived in the United States when they were fifteen or younger, had lived in the United States for at least five years, had good moral character, were not inadmissible or removable under a number of specified grounds, had graduated from high school or obtained a GED, and had attended college or served in the military for two years.[18]

The DREAM Act had at times received bipartisan support, and the President called for its enactment in his 2011 State of the Union address, but it had repeatedly failed to receive Congress's approval.[19] Congress took up the proposal in 2006, 2007, 2009, 2010, and 2011 without passing it.[20] Congress rejected the legislation in a recorded vote most recently in December 2010, when forty-one Senators (including six members of the President's party) voted against cloture in the debate over the bill.[21]

Here things get constitutionally interesting: having failed to convince Congress to pass the DREAM Act, and in need of a boost to his hard-fought bid for re-election, President Obama in mid-2012 announced executive action titled Deferred Action for Childhood Arrivals (DACA), which would allow as many as 1.7 million eligible individuals to avoid deportation proceedings and apply for work authorization.[22] DACA was essentially the DREAM Act by different means—an amendment to the INA made in the complete absence of congressional action.

Specifically, the President and his Department of Homeland Security ordered federal immigration officials to extend "deferred action" to undocumented aliens who (1) had entered the United States before their sixteenth birthday, and (2) had been in the United States continuously for five years.[23] This was the DREAM Act, as the President acknowledged on June 15, 2012, when announcing the action: "This morning, Secretary Napolitano announced new actions my administration will take to mend our nation's immigration policy, to make it more fair, more efficient, and more just—specifically for certain young people sometimes called 'Dreamers.'"[24]

This candid admission by the President that he had effectively amended the INA was made even more remarkable by the fact that less than two years earlier he had declared, "I am president, I am not king. I can't do these things just by myself. We have a system of government that requires the Congress to work with the Executive Branch to make it happen. . . . That's what the Executive Branch means. I can't just make the laws up by myself."[25]

On this point, the President was correct; an American president is distinct from early English kings in many respects. Most relevant here, under English law, the king had until 1689 possessed the power to dispense of the laws enacted by Parliament.[26] In the hands of James II, the dispensing power had proved a dangerous thing, and it was rightly abolished,[27] never to be a part of the American constitutional tradition, as the United States Supreme Court recognized in *Kendall v. United States ex rel. Stokes*:

> It was urged at the bar, that the postmaster general was alone subject to the direction and control of the President, with respect to the execution of the duty imposed upon him by this law, and this right of the President is claimed, as growing out of the obligation imposed upon him by the constitution, to take care that the laws be faithfully executed. This is a doctrine that cannot receive the sanction of this court. It would be vesting in the President a dispensing power, which has no countenance for its support in any part of the constitution; and is asserting a principle, which, if carried out in its results, to all cases falling within it, would be clothing the President with a power entirely to control the legislation of congress, and paralyze the administration of justice.
>
> To contend that the obligation imposed on the President to see the laws faithfully executed, implies a power to forbid their execution is a novel construction of the constitution, and entirely inadmissible.[28]

In other words, by the early nineteenth century, the Supreme Court had thoroughly and unambiguously disposed of the notion that the United States Constitution conveyed on the American president a king's power to dispense of laws.

But a century and half later, an American president simultaneously disavowed and deployed just such a power. After taking this extraordinary action—an action he had previously, repeatedly, and emphatically denied he had the authority to take[29]—President Obama immediately began to insist that while he possessed the authority to implement DACA through executive action, DACA represented the outer limits of his executive authority:

> I am the Champion-in-Chief of comprehensive immigration reform. But what I've said in the past remains true, which is until Congress passes a new law, then I am constrained in terms of what I am able to

> do. What I've done is to use my prosecutorial discretion, because you can't enforce the laws across the board for 11 or 12 million people, there aren't the resources there. What we've said is focus on folks who are engaged in criminal activity, focus on people who are engaged in gang activity. Do not focus on young people, who we're calling DREAMers. . . . That already stretched my administrative capacity very far. But I was confident that that was the right thing to do. But at a certain point the reason that these deportations are taking place is, Congress said, "you have to enforce these laws." They fund the hiring of officials at the department that's charged with enforcing. And I cannot ignore those laws any more than I could ignore, you know, any of the other laws that are on the books. That's why it's so important for us to get comprehensive immigration reform done this year.[30]

Comprehensive immigration reform did *not* get done that year, at least not through Congress. But the self-described constraints on his ability to take further executive action proved no deterrent to President Obama, and on November 20, 2014, he took matters into his own hands, announcing executive action to simultaneously (1) put into force new "enforcement priorities" whereby most of the 11.3 million persons unlawfully present in the United States would not be considered "priorities" for deportation action,[31] and (2) create a program whereby nearly 5 million of such non-priority persons would be affirmatively shielded from deportation.[32]

Once again, the President was unabashed about what he had done, announcing in a November 25, 2014, speech, "I just took an action to change the law."[33]

This was unprecedented. Not only was the President announcing that he was dispensing with enforcement of large swaths of the INA; he was going one large step further, affirmatively granting federal benefits that were contrary to the INA's text and purpose.

To be fair, the Take Care Clause does not leave the Executive Branch without *any* discretion to determine when to take enforcement actions against individuals. But one thing is clear: the Executive Branch cannot, under the guise of exercising enforcement discretion, attempt to effectively rewrite the laws to match its policy preferences.[34] Put another way, enforcement decisions must further, rather than undermine, the congressional policy underlying the statutes the agency is charged with administering.[35] Likewise, the Executive Branch ordinarily cannot, as the Court put it in *Chaney*, "'consciously and expressly adopt[] a general policy' that is so extreme as to amount to an abdication of its statutory responsibilities."[36]

And even in instances where Congress has indicated that it intends the Executive Branch to retain enforcement discretion, and the enforcement decision furthers the congressional policy underlying the statute, the non-enforcement decisions can be characterized as exercises of enforcement discretion only when they are made on an individualized, case-by-case basis.[37]

The President's executive action appeared to fail these Take Care Clause prerequisites at every turn. It (1) was plainly an instance of the executive substituting its policy preferences for those of Congress; (2) undermined the purposes of the INA, by both failing to deport millions required by the INA to be deported and by encouraging further illegal immigration through the grant of benefits to those in violation of the INA; (3) amounted to an abdication of the executive's statutory responsibility to enforce the INA as written; and (4) was in practice anything but the "individualized" decision-making that is the hallmark of prosecutorial discretion.

III. THE STATES SUE TO PROTECT THEIR SOVEREIGN INTERESTS

This proved to be too much for the states, which reacted swiftly and strongly. Twenty-six states filed suit in a Texas federal court seeking to enjoin the President's dispensing of the INA[38] and promptly won an injunction preventing the President's executive action from taking effect.[39]

And rightly so. While the mainstream media focused on the affront to Congress's powers, the states were equally aggrieved. President Obama's extraordinary unilateral action in dispensing of the INA short-circuited the ordinary structures of accountability and undercut the constitutional structure for sounding complaints in the halls of Congress.

This preemption without representation nullified the states' interests in the advancement of territorial integrity and in the health and welfare of the states' people. "When a State enters the Union, it surrenders certain sovereign prerogatives"—the ones granted to the federal government in the Constitution.[40] Most significantly, by operation of the Supremacy Clause, a state surrenders the right to make state laws on certain subjects that are preempted by federal law.[41]

Despite the Supremacy Clause, states "are not relegated to the role of mere provinces or political corporations, but retain the dignity, though not the full authority, of sovereignty."[42] Indeed, the states' surrender of authority neither nullifies the state's interests in the advancement of territorial integrity nor its interest in the health and welfare of the state's people.[43] And in the context of immigration, the Supreme Court has recognized that the states "bear[] many of the consequences of unlawful immigration" such that the "pervasiveness of federal regulation does not diminish the importance of immigration policy to the States."[44]

When President Obama chose to rewrite the INA through executive action, he was taking an action that directly impaired the states' retained interests in the advancement of territorial integrity and health and welfare of the state's people, but in an area of law where the states are preempted entirely from engaging in the norm of sovereign self-help. Worse yet, he did all this without the states having had the opportunity to do what the Constitution contemplates with regard to the Supremacy Clause: participating through their congressional delegations in the crafting of the federal laws that preempt the states' ability to regulate.[45]

But even if the President's executive action were a proper exercise of discretion, the larger point is that the states—and not just Congress—have a significant stake in ensuring that the President faithfully executes the laws. And not only *can* the states seek to vindicate their interests, they *must*, because if they don't, the ultimate loser is our constitutional structure of horizontal and vertical separation of powers, a structure critical to the preservation of individual liberty.

24.

UNILATERAL ACTIONS OF PRESIDENT OBAMA IN VOTING AND ELECTIONS

Hans A. von Spakovsky

A hallmark of the Obama Justice Department has been its unilateral, constitutionally troublesome decisions to suspend enforcement of federal laws, including part of the National Voter Registration Act of 1993,[1] and to enforce other parts of the Voting Rights Act[2] in a racially discriminatory manner, contrary to the plain text and intent of the law.

The president has a clear constitutional duty to "take Care that the Laws be faithfully executed."[3] While no one questions that the administration and particularly the Justice Department have finite resources and therefore the ability to make enforcement choices and establish priorities, the president must make those enforcement choices "faithfully," which is defined by objectivity and nonpartisanship. As Professor Nicholas Quinn Rosenkranz says, "[I]t is important to remember the historical context of the clause: English kings had claimed the power to suspend laws unilaterally, but the Framers expressly rejected that practice."[4]

As a general principle, the decision whether to prosecute an individual is left to the discretion of the Executive Branch.[5] But the recognized concept of "prosecutorial discretion" does not give the president the authority to wholesale suspend the enforcement of a federal law or a particular section of a federal law. As Andrew McCarthy has written,

> Prosecutorial discretion is a common sense resource-allocation principle related to criminal law enforcement. It is not a generalized license to ignore congressional statutes, let alone effectively amend them.
>
> . . .
>
> . . . What Obama is doing is a perversion of prosecutorial discretion. It is an effort to delegitimize and effectively reverse laws he opposes on philosophical grounds. He is not saying the Executive Branch *lacks the resources* to enforce the immigration statutes and other federal law he finds uncongenial. He is proclaiming that *they should not be laws and he chooses not to execute them as such.*[6]

Finding a particular law "uncongenial" is exactly what happened in the administration's unilateral decision not to enforce Section 8 of the National Voter Registration Act (NVRA), one of the most important provisions of federal voting rights law. Intended to help maintain the integrity of the election process, Section 8 requires states to "conduct a general program that makes a reasonable effort to remove the names of ineligible voters from the official lists of eligible voters."[7]

Voter registration lists across the nation are in such poor condition that a 2012 study by the Pew Center on the States found that "approximately 24 million—one of every eight—voter registrations in the United States" are inaccurate, out of date, or duplicates.[8] As many as 1.8 million dead voters remained registered and nearly 2.8 million individuals were registered in multiple states.[9] Inaccurate voter registration rolls are the ore mined by those interested in stealing elections through voter fraud.

Ironically, as the U.S. Supreme Court pointed out when it upheld Indiana's voter ID law, other provisions in the NVRA "restricting States' ability to remove names from the lists of registered voters . . . have been partly responsible for inflated lists of registered voters."[10] In Indiana, a district court judge found that "as of 2004 Indiana's voter rolls were inflated by as much as 41.4%, and data collected by the Election Assistance Committee in 2004 indicated that 19 of 92

Indiana counties had registration totals exceeding 100% of the 2004 voting-age population."[11]

The Justice Department sued the State of Indiana in 2006 to enforce Section 8 because the state was not complying with the law by removing ineligible individuals from the voter registration list and had failed to "engage in oversight actions sufficient to ensure that local election jurisdictions identify and remove such ineligible voters."[12] Indiana agreed to settle the case, and a consent decree and order was entered "requiring Indiana to fulfill its list-maintenance obligation under § 8."[13]

The Justice Department's Civil Rights Division filed a similar lawsuit against Missouri in 2005 during the Bush administration because of its failure to comply with Section 8. The state's list maintenance was so inadequate or nonexistent in many counties that "at least 34 (nearly one-third) of the election jurisdictions in Missouri had more registered voters in November 2004 than there were persons of voting age," according to Census estimates.[14] In fact, one county had 153 percent of its Census voting-age population registered to vote.[15] Despite a favorable opinion from the Eighth Circuit Court of Appeals in 2008 reinstating the lawsuit after a district court dismissed it because of the lower court's misinterpretation of the requirements Section 8 imposes on states,[16] the Obama administration suddenly dismissed the lawsuit without explanation shortly after it came into office in 2009 without the state having taken any steps to clean up its voter rolls.[17]

The reason for this was clear: the administration refused to enforce a provision of federal law it did not like. An administration political appointee, Julie Fernandes, told lawyers in the Voting Section of the Civil Rights Division that the "Obama administration was not interested in enforcing" Section 8.[18] Witnesses who were interviewed by the Justice Department's inspector general "uniformly remembered" that Fernandes said that pursuing cases under Section 8 was not a priority because it did "not expand voter access."[19]

Before he was forced out by senior administration officials in the Justice Department (including Attorney General Eric Holder) because of his view that the Voting Rights Act (VRA) should be enforced in a race-neutral manner,[20] the former chief of the Justice Department's Voting Section, Christopher Coates, testified before the U.S. Commission on

Civil Rights that he recommended opening investigations of eight states that appeared to be violating Section 8 of the NVRA by not maintaining accurate voter registration lists.[21] Coates said his recommendations were ignored,[22] and the administration has not filed a single lawsuit to enforce the list-maintenance requirements of the NVRA during the entirety of its two terms.[23]

As Coates testified, prosecutorial discretion does not allow prosecutors "to decide not to do any enforcement of a law enacted by Congress because political appointees determined that they are not interested in enforcing the law. That is an abuse of prosecutorial discretion."[24] This policy-driven decision not to enforce a law duly passed by Congress, signed into law by a prior president, and enforced by an earlier administration, is a prime example of the administration circumventing the Legislative Branch. Such non-enforcement policies, according to liberal professor Jonathan Turley, "reduce the legislative process to a series of options for presidential selection ranging from negation to full enforcement. The Framers warned us of such a system and we accept it—either by acclaim or acquiescence—at our peril."[25] These actions by the Obama administration "challenge core principles of the separation of powers."[26]

Under another insidious, unilateral election policy, the Justice Department has engaged in racially discriminatory enforcement of the VRA, which fundamentally violates equal protection principles. In testimony before the U.S. Commission on Civil Rights, Christopher Coates, as well as former Voting Section lawyer J. Christian Adams, both described a culture of animus within the Civil Rights Division toward race-neutral enforcement of federal voting rights laws.[27] According to Coates, Julie Fernandes, the Deputy Assistant Attorney General, told Voting Section staff in a meeting that the Obama administration was only interested in filing "traditional" voting rights cases that would "provide political equality for racial- and language-minority voters."[28]

Both Coates and Adams said that this race-based approach to law enforcement was shared by the other political appointees in the Civil Rights Division: the belief that cases should not be brought against African Americans or other racial minorities if the victims happen to be white.[29] Fernandes's directions to the staff were no surprise: before she joined the Obama administration she claimed that the VRA was not written to protect all voters.[30] As former Commissioner Todd Gaziano of the U.S. Commission on Civil Rights pointed out, she was extremely critical of the Justice Department during the Bush administration for filing a successful lawsuit under the VRA against black officials in Noxubee County, Mississippi, for engaging in blatant racial discrimination against white voters.[31] According to Fernandes, "the law was written to protect black people."[32] Coates testified that everyone understood the policy Fernandes was implementing: it meant no more cases like the one in Mississippi or the New Black Panther Party voter intimidation case, in which party members threatened and intimidated white poll watchers and voters.[33]

While it is true that the Voting Rights Act was passed in 1965 because of widespread discrimination against blacks in the South that prevented them from registering and voting, Congress was very careful to craft a race-neutral law. The VRA was intended to ban *all* racial discrimination in voting, regardless of the race of the victims or the perpetrators. This is clear from the straightforward language of Section 2, the nationwide, permanent ban on voting discrimination in the VRA:

> No voting qualification or prerequisite to voting or standard, practice, or procedure shall be imposed or applied by any State or political subdivision in a manner which results in a denial or abridgement of the right of any citizen of the United States to vote on account of race or color, or in contravention of the guarantees set forth in section 10303(f)(2) [language minorities] of this title.[34]

The voting discrimination cases brought by the Justice Department under the VRA since 1965 have almost all been on behalf of racial minorities.[35] But as the protections of the VRA allowed racial and ethnic minorities to participate in the election process and to take over control of local jurisdictions where they are actually a majority of the population, it was inevitable that the Justice Department would eventually encounter a case such as *United States v. Brown*, the case in Noxubee County, Mississippi.[36]

In 2005, the Justice Department filed suit over voting discrimination by local black officials in Noxubee against white voters and candidates. The federal court found that the defendants had "engaged in racially motivated manipulation of the electoral process."[37] The court did not have to "look far to find ample direct and circumstantial evidence of an intent to discriminate against white voters which has manifested itself through practices designed to deny and/or dilute the voting rights of white voters in Noxubee County."[38]

Most importantly, the court concluded that the VRA protects all voters from racial discrimination. In fact, the defendants argued that it was a "perversion of the Act's historical and salutary purpose to 'eradicate inequalities in political opportunities that exist due to the vestigial effects of past purposeful discrimination' against blacks" for the Justice Department to bring the case.[39] The defendants said it was "preposterous" for the Justice Department to claim discriminatory behavior by blacks in Noxubee County was actionable.[40]

This argument was dismissed by the district court, which found that "where the proof establishes a specific racial intent by black election officials to disenfranchise white voters, Section 2 applies with ease. No one could reasonably argue that an election official's racially motivated decision to count the votes of black voters while rejecting those of white voters is discrimination that can be countenanced under any view of Section 2."[41] This decision was affirmed by the Fifth Circuit Court of Appeals.[42]

However, the position taken by the defendants is the same mistaken view of the VRA that Julie Fernandes and other Obama administration appointees brought to the Justice Department. It manifested itself internally in the reprimand of Voting Section chief Christopher Coates for asking new applicants for staff attorney positions whether they believed in the race-neutral enforcement of the VRA.[43] He was ordered to cease immediately and not ask that question[44] and was eventually driven out as the chief of the section, all with the explicit approval of Eric Holder.[45]

This unilateral, racially discriminatory enforcement policy first arose publicly in the unjustified dismissal of almost all of the voter intimidation case that had been filed against the New Black Panther Party (NBPP) for its misbehavior in 2008 in Philadelphia. Two members of the NBPP stood in front of a polling place located in a retirement community dressed in black Fascist-style paramilitary uniforms (one carrying a billy club), voicing threatening comments and hurling racial epithets at poll watchers and scaring off voters.[46]

Shortly before the Obama administration took over on January 20, 2009, the Justice Department filed a lawsuit under Section 11(b) of the VRA, which prohibits intimidation of voters and anyone else who is "urging or aiding any person to vote," which would include poll watchers.[47] As J. Christian Adams said, it was a "slam dunk" case of voter intimidation.[48] Christopher Coates said in an internal Justice e-mail that if the Black Panthers' actions did not violate Section 11(b), then he didn't "know what does."[49]

The NBPP didn't even bother to file an answer to the lawsuit, putting them in default.[50] However, just before the Voting Section was to obtain a final judgment, Coates was ordered to dismiss the entire lawsuit except for a reduced claim against one of the Panthers.[51] Instead of Coates asking for a nationwide injunction as originally proposed, the injunction was sharply limited to one defendant in Philadelphia.[52] According to both Coates and Adams, this decision had nothing to do with the actual merits of the case.[53]

The Justice Department claimed that political appointees within DOJ had nothing to do with the dismissal, even while it obstructed efforts by Congress[54] and the U.S. Commission on Civil Rights to investigate.[55] In a Freedom of Information Act lawsuit filed by Judicial Watch, federal district court Judge Reggie Walton concluded that Justice Department "documents reveal[ed] that political appointees within DOJ were conferring about the status and resolution of the *New Black Panther Party* case in the days preceding the DOJ's dismissal," which directly contradicted the sworn testimony of former Assistant Attorney General of Civil Rights Thomas Perez that "political leadership was not involved in that decision."[56] This included former Attorney General Eric Holder, who told the DOJ inspector general that he approved of the dismissal despite the fact that it overruled "the case team's recommendation."[57] Perez was never sanctioned for lying under oath; instead, he was promoted by President Obama to Secretary of the Department of Labor.

The Black Panther case demonstrates that even in the light of serious threats and intimidation by black defendants toward voters and poll watchers, the administration was unwilling to enforce the prohibitions of the VRA for racial reasons that would have shocked the members of Congress who voted in 1965 to protect *all* voters from this type of behavior.

Political appointees within the Justice Department violated their own oath to faithfully execute the law by selectively enforcing the VRA based on the race of the victims and the perpetrators. As Christopher Coates told the Commission on Civil Rights, in an "increasingly multiethnic society, that is a clear recipe to undermine the public's confidence in the legitimacy of our electoral process."[58] Moreover, it represented a basic violation of equal protection for a government law enforcement agency to enforce the law differently based on racial considerations.

This racially discriminatory attitude in the enforcement of Section 2 emerged again in the refusal of the Justice Department to help a retired Air Force officer, Arnold Davis, living in Guam. Because he is white, the territorial government refused to allow Davis, who has lived on the island since 1977, to register for a plebiscite on Guam's future relationship with the United States.[59] Only individuals considered "Native Inhabitants" were allowed to register with the "decolonization registry"[60]—a policy that excludes the majority of Guam citizens, including Davis, since only Chamorros (the racial designation given to the natives who originally inhabited Guam) are considered "Native Inhabitants."[61]

Davis was refused help by the Justice Department,[62] despite the fact that not allowing him to register based on his race is an obvious violation of the VRA, the Fifteenth Amendment, and the Equal Protection Clause of the Fourteenth Amendment. In 2000, in a similar case, the U.S. Supreme Court held that Hawaii's election system for the trustees of the Office of Hawaiian Affairs that only allowed "Native Hawaiians" to vote violated the Fifteenth Amendment.[63]

Guam's election restrictions are more extreme than anything that was in place in the South during the height of Jim Crow. Southern states such as Mississippi tried to make it as difficult as possible for blacks to vote through literacy tests, poll taxes, and other obstacles, but some small percentage of blacks were still able to get through this thicket of discrimination to actually register and vote. Guam, on the other hand, bars anyone who is white from voting in this plebiscite and even makes it a crime for a white person to try to register.[64] Yet not only did the Justice Department refuse to try to rectify this blatant discriminatory conduct by Guam, but in the midst of the private lawsuit that Davis was forced to file without the government's help, Eric Holder went on a "goodwill" visit to Guam in July 2012 to meet with the governor and members of the legislature who were responsible for the territorial government's discriminatory conduct.[65]

The Obama administration also applied this same discriminatory attitude to Section 5 of the VRA, which was effectively abolished by the U.S. Supreme Court in 2013 when it struck down the trigger formula for a jurisdiction to be covered under Section 5 in *Shelby County v. Holder*.[66] Passed in 1965, Section 5 was an emergency five-year provision that required a covered jurisdiction (nine states and parts of seven others)[67] to pre-clear any voting changes either with the Justice Department or a federal court in Washington, D.C.[68]

Section 5 specified that a jurisdiction could only obtain pre-clearance by proving that the voting change had neither "the purpose nor . . . the effect of denying or abridging the right to vote on account of race or color."[69] As with Section 2, Section 5 was designed to protect all voters who are a minority in their particular jurisdiction, regardless of their race. In fact, the triggering formula contained in Section 4 was based on the low registration or turnout of *all* voters in particular past elections, not just of black voters.[70]

Yet, as the DOJ inspector general (IG) reported, the "Civil Rights Division's current leadership" told the IG that it interpreted Section 5 as not being "applicable to White voters who are in the numerical minority in a particular jurisdiction."[71] So even in a jurisdiction like Noxubee County, Mississippi, where local black officials control the county government and have a proven history of discriminatory behavior, the Obama Justice Department would not review any Section 5 submissions of a voting change to ensure that it did not have a discriminatory purpose or effect on white voters—who are a racial minority in Noxubee County.

When queried about this racialist attitude by the IG, former Assistant Attorney General Thomas Perez claimed that this interpretation was the same as that of the prior administration.[72] However, the IG stated, "[A]t least three AAGs from the previous administration told the OIG that Division leadership at that time did not have a policy to interpret Section 5's retrogressive-effect prong such that it would not cover White citizens."[73]

This refusal to apply Section 5 in a race-neutral manner led to some very odd results. In 2009, the Justice Department objected under

Section 5 to a voting change in Kinston, North Carolina.[74] In a small town in which blacks were almost 65 percent of the registered voters, a referendum to change city council elections from partisan to nonpartisan was overwhelmingly approved in the November 2008 election.[75] However, DOJ claimed this would have a discriminatory effect on black voters because "[i]t is the partisan makeup of the general electorate" that allows the winner of the Democratic primary to win in the general election.[76] In other words, black voters would apparently not know whom to vote for without a party label next to a candidate's name. Not only was this patronizing attitude apparently intended to ensure the success of one particular political party, but the Justice Department ignored the effect, if any, this change would have on the actual racial minority in Kinston—white voters.

The political nature of this objection was further evidenced by what happened in litigation filed against the Justice Department by several Kinston residents and a candidate who claimed the objection to the referendum was wrong. When the lawsuit was at the appeals court stage and looked like it might be headed for the U.S. Supreme Court, the Justice Department suddenly changed its mind and notified Kinston in January 2012 that it was "reconsider[ing]" its objection to the referendum.[77] The Justice Department then withdrew its objection claiming there had been a "substantial change in operative fact," although the only "change" Justice cited was an increase of 0.8 percentage points in the black voter registration rate.[78] A logical inference was that the Justice Department wanted to moot the case so it would not reach the Supreme Court because the facts reflected so badly on the government's position.

All of this mal-enforcement and non-enforcement has been combined with the administration's all-out war on election integrity measures, in particular state voter ID laws. The Justice Department during the Bush administration pre-cleared the voter ID laws of Georgia and Arizona under Section 5 because there was no evidence that they were discriminatory.[79] Both laws were also subsequently upheld against challenges in the courts,[80] and the U.S. Supreme Court upheld Indiana's voter ID statute as constitutional in 2008 in *Crawford v. Marion County Election Board*.[81]

All of the data from states with photo ID requirements for voters show that claims that such laws are discriminatory or that they suppress the turnout of minority voters are wrong. States such as Georgia and Indiana saw increases in the turnout of voters in elections held after their voter ID laws became effective.[82] Yet that has not stopped the administration from invoking the VRA to challenge voter ID laws in other states,[83] or prevented administration officials like Eric Holder from making unproven and false claims that such laws are intended to "depress the vote of particular groups of people who are not supportive of the party that is advancing these photo ID measures."[84]

The political nature of these prosecutions is further evidenced by the fact that the "expert" data analysis firm hired by DOJ in its lawsuits against North Carolina and Texas is Catalist,[85] a self-proclaimed "progressive" campaign firm.[86] Catalist's website says that its mission is "to nurture a vibrant, growing, progressive community, and to work[] with that community towards a more just, equitable and tolerant America."[87]

Besides having as its clients many liberal advocacy organizations that have opposed voter ID laws in litigation, such as the Lawyers Committee for Civil Rights Under Law, the NAACP, and the American Civil Liberties Union (ACLU), Catalist is the campaign data consultant for numerous Democratic Party candidates, the Democratic Congressional Campaign Committee, the Democratic Governors Association, the Democratic Legislative Campaign Committee, and the Democratic Senatorial Campaign Committee.[88] A complaint filed with the Federal Election Commission claims that Catalist is actually a political action committee "financed, maintained and/or controlled, by the Democratic National Committee."[89]

What appears clear is that the administration has misused its authority under various federal voting rights laws to advance its own ideological agenda and to help ensure the election of candidates of the president's political party. This is an abuse of the executive power delegated to the president by the Constitution to "take Care that the Laws be faithfully executed." The highest duty of the Justice Department and the Executive Branch when it comes to federal law is to ensure that justice is administered in an objective, nonpartisan, racially neutral manner that meets both the letter and the spirit of the laws passed by the Legislative Branch and that satisfies the constitutional requirement of equal treatment under the law. This administration has failed that obligation.

25.

THE DESIGNATION OF SYSTEMICALLY IMPORTANT FINANCIAL INSTITUTIONS BY THE FINANCIAL STABILITY OVERSIGHT COUNCIL AND THE FINANCIAL STABILITY BOARD

Peter J. Wallison

Financial services is one of the most important and successful industries in the United States. In addition to banks, it includes insurers, asset managers, securities broker-dealers, finance companies, hedge funds, and others. The services of these companies enable main-street Americans to buy and sell assets, save for the future, purchase a home, send children to college, and retire comfortably. As important, financial services channel savings into financing for business, which in turn creates jobs and—through growth in productivity—improves the standard of living for all of us.

Financial regulation indisputably has a significant effect on the performance of financial institutions, and thus on economic growth. For this reason, Congress should have a major role in formulating the regulatory policies that affect the U.S. financial industry. However, Congress has generally not intervened in the development of bank capital regulation.

Basel I, II, and III were developed by bank regulators, approved by an international agreement among bank regulators, and subsequently applied (or will be applied) to the U.S. banking industry by U.S. regulators.

THE DODD-FRANK ACT, THE FSOC, AND GROWTH IN THE SCOPE OF REGULATION

In 2010, in the wake of the financial crisis, Congress adopted the Dodd-Frank Act, creating a special body known as the Financial Stability Oversight Council (FSOC). The FSOC is composed of the heads of all the federal financial regulators—the Federal Reserve, FDIC, SEC, the Consumer Financial Protection Bureau (CFPB), etc.—and a person appointed by the president and confirmed by the Senate as an expert in insurance, an industry that is not regulated by the federal government. The Secretary of the Treasury is the chair of the FSOC and has an effective veto over the FSOC's most important decisions since his affirmative vote is necessary for approval of any FSOC action. Because the act specifies that the members are the *heads* of the regulatory agencies—not the agencies themselves—virtually all the members are appointees of the administration in power. They are not required to represent their agencies' views and they do not; they seem generally to follow the directions of the Treasury Secretary.[1]

This in itself is highly unusual for a regulatory agency. In creating other regulatory agencies, particularly those that engage in financial regulation, Congress has generally set up bipartisan commissions to ensure that different views are brought to bear on contentious regulatory matters where significant parts of the economy could be harmed. The FSOC is unique in the sense that it is headed by the Secretary of the Treasury, usually a close political and economic advisor of the president. This, in addition to the fact that it is composed of the president's appointees, means that important and controversial decisions of the FSOC can be made on the basis of political or ideological factors rather than fully debated as technical regulatory or supervisory matters. There is strong evidence[2] that most of the members of the FSOC know little about the decisions they are asked to make and simply follow the directions of the Treasury Secretary.

Dodd-Frank enjoins the FSOC to "identify risks to the financial stability of the United States that could arise from the material financial distress or failure, or ongoing activities, of large interconnected bank holding companies or nonbank financial companies" (Section 112). The act designates all banks or bank holding companies with more than $50 billion in assets as systemically important financial institutions (SIFIs) and subjects them to special stringent regulation by the Federal Reserve Board, but it leaves to the FSOC the task of designating nonbank financial institutions as SIFIs. Section 113 authorizes the FSOC to designate a nonbank financial firm as a SIFI if "the Council determines that material financial distress at the U.S. nonbank financial company . . . could pose a threat to the financial stability of the United States." Firms so designated are then turned over to the Fed for prudential regulation, which Section 115 requires to be more "stringent" than the regulation to which firms of the same type are ordinarily subject. Section 115 and other provisions of the act suggest that this regulation be bank-like—that is, it should involve regulation of their capital and supervision of their risk-taking activities.

THE CONVENTIONAL NARRATIVE ABOUT THE FINANCIAL CRISIS AND MAJOR NEW OPPORTUNITIES FOR REGULATORS

Bank-like regulation of nonbank firms is a significant change in substantive U.S. regulatory policies. The 2008 financial crisis was a disaster for the American people, but it was a huge gift for financial regulators. After all major financial downturns, those who support government involvement in the economy claim that it would not have occurred if financial regulators had more power. Congress usually gives in to this argument, despite evidence that regulation is often ineffective or counterproductive. The collapse of the S&Ls in the late 1980s brought forth the Financial Institutions Reform, Recovery and Enforcement Act of 1989 (FIRREA) and the FDIC Improvement Act of 1991 (FDICIA). The Enron scandal in 2001 produced the Sarbanes-Oxley Act. All these new laws promised to prevent the recurrence of the prior events such as banking or financial crises, but the 2008 financial crisis demonstrates that the regulators they empowered have not performed as advertised.

By now, Congress should have recognized that increasing federal regulatory authority reduces economic growth without achieving the stability that regulators promise. Indeed, the opposite is usually the result. Although there has been no significant deregulation of the banking system in the last thirty years, many other areas of the economy—securities trading, communications, trucking, and air travel—have been deregulated, with huge benefits for the American people. The plain fact about banking regulation is that it creates repeating crises, which in turn bring forth additional regulation, culminating in more financial crises.[3]

The 2008 financial crisis had many elements of earlier crises, except in two respects: it was much larger than any previous crisis,[4] and it involved the whole financial system and not just depository institutions. Once again, the 2008 crisis produced a narrative to the effect that it could have been prevented if the regulators had had more power.[5] But in this case there was a difference in the regulation sought. Before the crisis, the only theory for applying federal prudential regulation to financial institutions justified merely the regulation of banks. Because banks were backed by the government, prudential regulation—requiring capital and controlling risk-taking—was necessary to prevent moral hazard and to protect the taxpayers who ultimately backed the FDIC. But after the 2008 crisis, which involved many large financial institutions other than banks, the conventional Washington narrative became something far more expansive: the failure of any large financial institution could be a danger to the entire financial system. This spawned a wholly new theory for regulation—that the risk-taking and capital position of *any* financial institution should be subject to prudential bank-like regulation if there is even a minimal case that its failure could cause a financial crisis. That's why the Dodd-Frank Act adopted the idea—implemented in Section 113 of the act—that any firm should be subject to this regime if its "financial distress" could cause "instability in the US financial system."

Because it is impossible to know in advance whether a particular institution's "distress" would cause "instability in the U.S. financial system" (whatever *that* is), the FSOC's authority is in effect a license to consign any financial institution of whatever size to stringent prudential regulation by the Fed.

However, the narrative that underlies this policy change was false. As described more fully in my book,[6] the financial crisis was not caused by insufficient regulation of the financial system; it was caused by government housing policies that built an enormous bubble between 1997 and 2007, suffusing the financial system with subprime and other low-quality mortgages. By 2008, more than half of all mortgages in the U.S.—that is, 31 million mortgages—were subprime or otherwise risky. Of these 31 million loans, 76 percent were on the books of government agencies, showing without question that the government created the demand for these low-quality loans.

When the housing price bubble deflated in 2007 and 2008, these mortgages defaulted in unprecedented numbers, severely weakening banks and other large financial institutions that held these mortgages in the form of mortgage-backed securities (MBSs). Banks were particularly hard hit, because government-mandated capital requirements had encouraged them to hold the very MBSs that lost substantial value when the mortgage defaults began. In March 2008, the government rescued Bear Stearns, a large investment bank, temporarily calming the market and creating the market expectation that the government would rescue all large financial firms. But this expectation was upended in September of the same year, when Lehman Brothers—a firm almost 50 percent larger than Bear Stearns—was allowed to fail; the result was the massive investor panic that we now know as the financial crisis.

The false idea that the crisis was caused by insufficient regulation of the private sector produced a major shift in regulatory policy, vastly increasing the potential reach of bank-like prudential regulation. Now, *all* large financial institutions in the U.S.—not just banks—could be subjected to bank-like prudential regulation unlike anything they had faced before. Given the unprecedented character of this power, Congress should look far more carefully than it has in the past at how this change in the scope of regulation is implemented.

THE SCOPE OF THE FSOC'S AUTHORITY

As noted earlier, the FSOC's authority flows from the language of Section 113 of the Dodd-Frank Act, which empowers the agency to designate as a SIFI any financial institution in the U.S. that it believes could cause "instability" in the U.S. financial system if it were to become "financially distressed" or fail. Aside from the vagueness of terms such as "financial distress" or "instability," no one can possibly predict what conditions in the future might contribute to or detract from the possibility that a firm's "financial distress" might cause financial instability. The result is an enormous—perhaps unprecedented—grant of discretionary power to the FSOC.

Moreover, the FSOC has not developed any standards to cabin or restrict its power. Quite the opposite. Since 2010, when the Dodd-Frank Act was signed into law, the FSOC has designated four firms as SIFIs: GE Capital (a subsidiary of the large manufacturer GE), AIG, Prudential Insurance, and MetLife. In every case, the bases for these designations were described in a very general public statement that provided no useful information about the standards applied. Although the companies involved were given detailed information, this information was not made public so that other firms could adjust their activities accordingly in order to avoid designation. Nor is there any way for Congress or anyone else to determine whether the FSOC is acting objectively and carefully with its extraordinary statutory mandate. For example, in summarizing its Prudential decision, the FSOC stated,

> Prudential is a *significant* participant in financial markets and the U.S. economy and is *significantly* interconnected to insurance companies and other financial firms through its products and capital markets activities. Because of Prudential's interconnectedness, size, certain characteristics of its liabilities and products, . . . material financial distress at Prudential could lead to an impairment of financial intermediation or of market functioning that would be sufficiently severe to inflict *significant* damage on the broader economy.[7]

Although this was a summary paragraph, it was never followed by any numerical or otherwise intelligible analysis of Prudential's effect on the market if it should encounter financial distress. In its twelve-page statement, the FSOC used the term "significant" forty-seven times. The most useful numerical data in the whole statement were the page numbers. Thus, the first concern that Congress should have about the FSOC is that it is failing to circumscribe or even define its discretionary authority in any way that will give financial institutions a way to change their activities in order to avoid a SIFI designation, or a way for Congress to determine whether the FSOC is carrying out its extraordinary mandate as Congress had intended. Or, indeed, whether the agency is acting arbitrarily in designating firms without a rational basis for doing so. If the agency is unable to meet these basic tests, its authority should be taken away.

Dodd-Frank suggests many factors that the FSOC should consider in addition to size—such factors as interconnectedness, leverage, and maturity mismatch—but the FSOC has refused to provide any indication of how these criteria will be weighted. For example, all financial firms are interconnected with others in some way, but what degree of interconnection will be considered a reason to designate a firm as a SIFI?[8] The failure to specify how it will define and weigh these issues preserves maximum discretion for the FSOC but provides no useful information to the regulated community. The FSOC's designations of AIG and GE Capital, which preceded the designation of Prudential, were similarly opaque.

Fortunately, this situation may change. In January 2015, MetLife filed suit against the FSOC to challenge its designation;[9] when and if the case is actually tried, we may finally have an opportunity to assess the quality of the FSOC's analysis and the criteria it used in reaching its designation decision. Moreover, in April 2015, GE announced that it would sell off many of the assets of GE Capital and seek a "de-designation" of the firm as a SIFI.[10] Whether and how the FSOC acts on this request will provide yet more information about what criteria the agency uses in making its designation decisions.

But there is another point that makes the FSOC's power particularly troubling. As noted earlier, the pattern established in bank regulation—and implicitly accepted by Congress—is that agreements among international regulators can become the rule in the U.S. without the express approval of Congress. This pattern was established with the capital accords of the Basel Committee on Bank Supervision in the 1980s. Bank regulators from the developed countries got together and decreed that while 8 percent risk-based capital was the suitable capital charge for the risk of a corporate loan, only 4 percent was necessary for a mortgage and 1.6 percent for high-quality mortgage-backed securities. These internationally agreed rules were made applicable to all U.S. banks by U.S. bank regulators. Congress never voted on any of this, but neither did Congress object. There was simply no debate on whether these rules were good policy.

It turned out that the Basel capital rules were terrible policy. They encouraged banks worldwide to buy mortgage-backed securities that were rated triple-A because the capital charge was so small. And when the MBS market collapsed in 2007 and 2008, the resulting bank losses led directly to a financial crisis because most banks had followed the incentives created by the Basel capital rules.[11] In other words, international regulatory accords, which can be very popular with *regulators* because they eliminate regulatory competition (usually called "opportunities for regulatory arbitrage" by the regulators), can be very bad policy, and can become law in the U.S. without any kind of serious debate in Congress. This experience should give Congress pause before it acquiesces in a similar process again.

This is especially true in SIFI designations, where the FSOC has wide discretionary authority from Congress to identify specific institutions for special and stringent treatment. It would be unprecedented and not within the likely contemplation of Congress if this judgment were to be made through an international agreement among regulators, without the thorough case-by-case decision-making that Congress almost certainly expected the FSOC to provide when it makes SIFI designations. Yet that seems to be exactly what is happening through the work of an international body of central banks, financial regulators, and government officials called the Financial Stability Board (FSB).

THE AUTHORITY OF THE FINANCIAL STABILITY BOARD

In September 2009, shortly after the financial crisis, the leaders of the G20 countries met in Pittsburgh. There, they authorized the FSB to effect "a fundamental reform of the financial system, to correct the fault lines that led to the global financial crisis and to rebuild the financial system as a safer, more resilient source of finance that better serves the real economy."[12] Both the Treasury and the Fed are members of the FSB, along with representatives of all the major developed countries and many other international government organizations.

It is important that the FSB was directed by the G20 leaders to bring about a fundamental reform of the international financial system. To the regulators and finance ministers that are part of the FSB process, the G20 leaders are their political masters. From their point of view, the FSB is carrying out the policies of their leaders. President Obama was of course part of the G20 leader group that directed the FSB to take steps that would make the financial system safer, so the Treasury is simply implementing this direction, as it would any other decision of the President. The political direction from the top undoubtedly makes it easier for the FSB to achieve consensus on specific steps. It also means that the FSB is not going to stop of its own accord until it gets a counter direction or meets an obstacle of some kind.

Thus far, the FSB has designated thirty-nine banks and nine insurance firms (including the U.S. insurers AIG, Prudential, and MetLife) as "global" SIFIs. In making these designations in July 2013, the FSB did not announce publicly either the standards that it used, if any, or the way the standards were applied to the banks or insurance firms designated as SIFIs. This is a pattern that, as outlined, has been repeated at the FSOC. It is typically adopted by regulators when they do not want to limit their discretion in the future. It is also the hallmark of a "we-know-it-when-we-see-it" approach to designation that cannot be what Congress had in mind for the FSOC.

One important question about how the FSB made its designations is the role of the Treasury and the Fed in the FSB's decision process. AIG and GE Capital were both designated as global SIFIs at about the time that the FSOC designated them as SIFIs in the United States. Prudential and MetLife, however, were designated as SIFIs in the U.S. *after* the FSB had acted—Prudential in September 2013 and MetLife in December 2014. This raises a serious question of objectivity and fairness in both cases. The Treasury and the Fed—the most important members of the FSOC—had, at the very least, acquiesced in the FSB's Prudential and MetLife decisions before the FSOC's decisions on both firms; it is highly unlikely that the FSB would have designated three U.S. insurers as global SIFIs if the Treasury and the Fed had objected. In testimony before Congress, Treasury Secretary Jack Lew has said that the FSB works by "consensus," which means a general agreement. In other words, the Treasury and Fed have gone beyond mere acquiescence; they have agreed with the designations of Prudential and MetLife as global SIFIs.

Instead of agreeing, the Treasury and Fed could have objected or abstained from the consensus because the process of designation in the U.S. was not complete, but there is no indication that they interposed any objection or abstained. In that case, it is inescapable that the Treasury and Fed had prejudged the designation of Prudential and MetLife before the decision was made by the FSOC. This should be unacceptable to Congress or to any fair-minded person. In a hearing on May 8, 2014, Congressman Scott Garrett tried but was unsuccessful in getting an answer from Treasury Secretary Lew on whether the Treasury had concurred in the FSB's Prudential designation. That is something that Congress must determine in order to decide whether the FSOC is carrying out a fair and honest inquiry when it designates financial firms as SIFIs or whether it is merely following the FSB.

RELATIONSHIP BETWEEN THE FSB AND THE FSOC

It is likely that the FSB, which has no enforcement mechanism of its own, expects to follow the pattern of the Basel Committee on Banking Supervision when it makes its designations. In that case, an agreement among all the central banks and financial regulators that are participating in the decision will designate certain financial institutions to be SIFIs, and any special regulation associated with designation will be carried out by their home country regulators. If this process is followed, the FSOC will simply implement the FSB's decisions in the United States. Congress will hold hearings, but there will be no legislation, no debate, and no vote. As noted already, it was a mistake for Congress not to raise questions about the Basel capital accords, and it would be another and more serious mistake for Congress to acquiesce in SIFI designations because they were made pursuant to an international "consensus" of regulators.

Congress must keep in mind that regulators are interested in broadening their authority, and when they can reach an international agreement on regulations, they enhance their authority because the regulated industries have fewer opportunities to avoid regulation by moving operations elsewhere. Regulators call this freedom of regulated firms to move elsewhere "regulatory arbitrage," but one advantage of regulatory competition (i.e., different rules in different places) is that it keeps regulation from stifling innovation and change. This is a key lesson to take away from the Basel capital accords.

Thus far, it appears that the FSOC is faithfully implementing the FSB policy and designation decisions. For example, in September 2013, the FSB recommended that if money market mutual funds do not adopt a floating net asset value, they should be subject to capital requirements in the same manner as are banks.[13] The FSOC then pressured the Securities and Exchange Commission to adopt similar rules for money market funds. In January 2014, the FSB indicated that all asset managers with assets of more than $100 billion may be subject to prudential regulation,[14] and the Office of Financial Research, another Treasury agency created by Dodd-Frank, produced two reports at the request of the FSOC to support the idea that large asset managers should be designated as SIFIs.[15] The FSB designated three U.S. insurance firms as SIFIs—AIG, Prudential, and MetLife—and the FSOC has followed suit by designating the same three firms. These parallel decisions again suggest that, unless Congress asserts its interests, the SIFI designation process will devolve into the implementation of the policies and decisions of the FSB. The result is that the unconstrained power delegated by Congress to the FSOC is effectively being exercised by the FSB, an international body unaccountable to the American people.

This also raises questions about the quality of the investigative and analytical work that the FSOC is supposed to do before declaring U.S. firms SIFIs under the Dodd-Frank Act—a concern that is fully validated by the kind of weak analysis the FSOC did in the Prudential case. There, the FSOC produced what can only be called a perfunctory decision. All the bank regulators, who know nothing about insurance regulation, voted for designating Prudential as a SIFI, but Roy Woodall, the sole voting member of the FSOC who has insurance expertise and is the Independent Person appointed to the FSOC because of his insurance knowledge, had this to say in his dissent:

> In making its Final Determination, the Council has adopted the analysis contained in the Basis [the FSOC's statement of its reasoning and analysis]. Key aspects of said analysis are not supported by the record or actual experience; and, therefore, are not persuasive. The underlying analysis utilizes scenarios that are antithetical to a fundamental and seasoned understanding of the business of insurance, the insurance regulatory environment, and the state insurance company resolution and guaranty fund systems. As presented, therefore, the analysis makes it impossible for me to concur because the grounds for the Final Determination are simply not reasonable or defensible, and provide no basis for me to concur.[16]

Woodall played it straight, but the decisions on Prudential and MetLife seem to have been baked in the cake before they were made by the FSOC. The fact that the FSB, the preceding July, had already determined that Prudential was a SIFI—with the concurrence of the Treasury and the Fed—made it all but inevitable that the FSOC would come to the same conclusion. Clearly, if the Basel Committee's procedures are followed in the FSB and acquiesced in by Congress, many large nonbank financial institutions in the U.S. may become subject to prudential bank-like regulation for reasons other than the objective analysis that Dodd-Frank expected the FSOC to apply.

Woodall has since broadened his concerns to include changes in federal law that might be brought about by the adoption of the FSB's rules in the U.S. In testimony to the Senate Banking Committee in April 2015, he noted,

> If U.S. Federal government officials at the FSB are to commit, on behalf of the U.S. to implement international insurance standards in the U.S., then, given the regulatory structure endorsed by Congress, I believe that the outcome of any such commitment should be consistent with proven effective State-based regulation and that any resulting agreement should contain express reservations preserving the discretion as to whether, or how, those standards will be implemented in the U.S.[17]

Woodall's remarks point to yet another issue that arises in the context of the FSOC's relationship with the FSB: whether the decisions of the FSB are expected to be adopted by all the members of the FSB, including the U.S. If so, this could have a substantial adverse impact on the functioning of U.S. capital markets in the future.

THE FSB, THE FSOC, AND SHADOW BANKING

The most problematic element of the FSB/FSOC relationship is the transparent effort of bank regulators in both organizations to get control of what they call "shadow banking." Since the financial crisis in 2008, central bankers and bank regulators worldwide have repeatedly called for controls on "shadow banking." Federal Reserve officials, including former Chair Ben Bernanke, have been among the most outspoken on this matter.[18] At the 2011 Cannes summit, and again at its Los Cabos summit in 2012, the G20 leaders called on the FSB to strengthen the oversight and regulation of "shadow banking."[19] It would be interesting to know what the G20 leaders thought they were approving when they endorsed a regulatory program for something as technical as shadow banking, especially since in 2011 it had not been defined by anyone, including the FSB.

The FSB finally defined shadow banking in 2012. Shadow banking, it said, is "credit intermediation involving entities and activities (fully or partially) outside the regular banking system."[20] Taken literally, this language is absurdly broad, since it covers all financial intermediation that is not subject to bank-like regulation, but in subsequent statements the FSB has not stepped back from the breadth of this definition.

It would be easy to define shadow banking narrowly and get at least some buy-in from the financial community. The defining characteristic of banks is that they perform something called maturity transformation—that is, they turn their short-term deposits into long-term assets by making loans. It's a risky business, and in the modern world it is somewhat protected by deposit insurance, which reduces the tendency of depositors to withdraw their funds (often called a "run") when they believe the bank's financial condition is weak.

During the financial crisis there were a number of institutions—Lehman Brothers and Bear Stearns being two—that failed or came close to failing because they attempted to use short-term repo financing to carry long-term assets like mortgages.[21] If we ignore the pejorative connotation associated with the term "shadow," the nonbanks that did what banks traditionally do could logically be called "shadow banks."

But although this might be a reasonable inference of what happened in the financial crisis, it is not the inference that the FSB chose to draw when it came to defining shadow banking. Thus, in 2012, it noted,

> [E]xperience from the crisis demonstrates the capacity for some non-bank entities and transactions to operate on a large scale in ways that create bank-like risks to financial stability (longer-term credit extension based on short-term funding and leverage). Such risk creation may take place at an entity level but it can also form part of *a complex chain of transactions, in which leverage* and maturity transformation occur in stages, and in ways that create multiple forms of feedback into the regulated banking system.[22]

As the FSB sees it, then, many entities in the shadow banking world work together to produce the maturity transformation that is the risky element of traditional banking. Former Fed Chair Ben Bernanke—a strong and persistent backer of regulating shadow banks—said in a 2012 speech,

> As an illustration of shadow banking at work, consider how an automobile loan can be made and funded outside of the banking system. The loan could be originated by a finance company that pools it with other loans in a securitization vehicle. An investment bank might sell tranches of the securitization to investors. The lower-risk tranches could be purchased by an asset-backed commercial paper (ABCP) conduit that, in turn, funds itself by issuing commercial paper that is purchased by money market funds.[23]

The problem with this, Bernanke went on, is that "although the shadow banking system taken as a whole performs traditional banking functions, including credit intermediation and maturity transformation, unlike banks, it cannot rely on the protections afforded by deposit insurance and access to the Federal Reserve's discount window to help insure its stability."[24]

Thus, to the extent that Bernanke reflects the underlying ideas circulating in the FSB—a good bet given the importance of the Fed in the world's financial system—the effort to control shadow banking is based on the idea that, while it can create risky maturity transformation, it does not have the necessary access to either the deposit insurance or the Fed's discount window that protect shadow banks against runs. Notably, despite heavy regulation by the Fed and other bank regulators, as well as deposit insurance and discount window access, three large insured banks—Wachovia, Washington Mutual, and IndyMac—had to be rescued during the financial crisis, while many other insured banks failed.

Nevertheless, based apparently on Bernanke's rationale, the FSB and the Fed are considering how to subject financial firms to prudential regulation. Thus, in September 2013, the FSB announced that it is "reviewing how to extend the SIFI Framework to global systemically important nonbank noninsurance (NBNI) financial institutions."[25] This category of firms, said the FSB, "includes securities broker dealers, finance companies, asset managers and investment funds, including hedge funds."[26]

This is troubling for two reasons. First, the persistent calls by bank regulators to get control of "shadow banking"—even before it had been defined—calls into question whether bank regulators are doing this because they honestly believe that shadow banking is a danger to the financial system or because shadow banking is a serious competitive threat to the traditional regulated banking system. Second, if they are successful in controlling what the FSB has now defined as shadow banking—that is, asset managers, securities firms, investment funds, finance companies, and hedge funds, among others—they may succeed in stifling the continued growth of the securities and capital markets in the United States, which have been far and away the main sources of financing for U.S. business. The following chart shows the growth of the capital markets as the sources of corporate financing compared to the banking sector.

The FSB is serious enough about this idea to suggest in January 2014 that asset managers with more than $100 billion under management could be designated as SIFIs.[27] Since pension funds, bond funds, and mutual

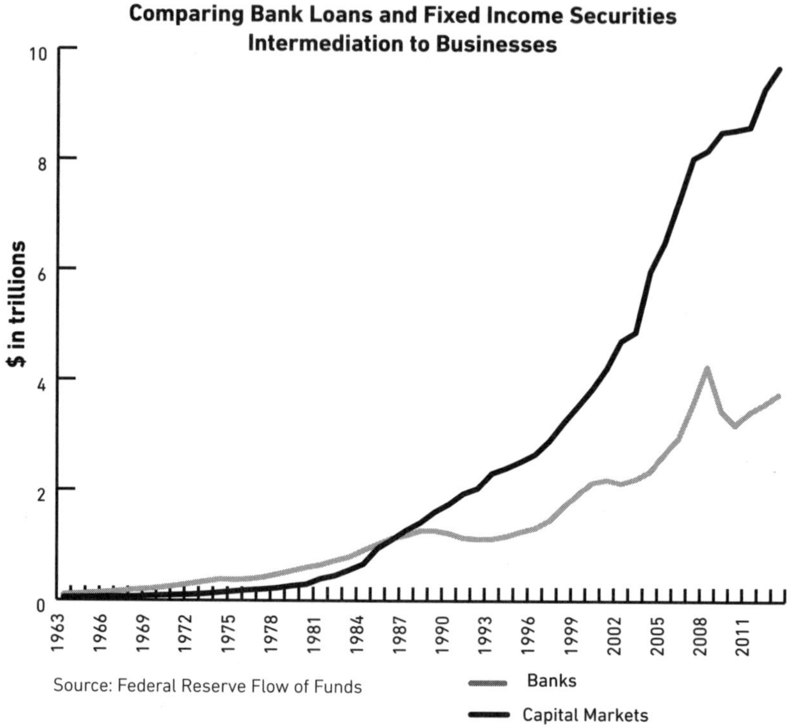

funds do not engage in maturity transformation on their own, this latest sally must come under the category of "*a complex chain of transactions,* in which leverage and maturity transformation occur in stages."[28]

It is important to understand, in this connection, that these investment funds and their managers are completely different from the banks or investment banks that suffered losses in the financial crisis. When a bank or investment bank suffers a decline in the value of its assets—as occurred when mortgages and mortgage-backed securities were losing value in 2007 and 2008—it still has to repay the full amount of the debt obligations it incurred to acquire those assets. Its inability to do so can lead to bankruptcy. But if a collective investment fund suffers the same losses, these pass through immediately to the fund's investors. The fund does not fail and thus cannot adversely affect other firms. In other words, investment funds cannot create systemic risks,[29] yet the FSB seems intent on including the largest firms in this industry among the

SIFIs it will designate. And, as outlined before, the FSOC seems to be following this lead.

The possibility that the FSB may adopt rules covering "complex chains of transactions," and thus attempt to place much of the U.S. capital markets under prudential regulation, has spawned considerable interest in Congress about whether the U.S. members of the FSB believe the FSB's rules are binding. Treasury Secretary Jack Lew has been less than candid about this issue. In a hearing on March 18, 2015, House Financial Services Committee Chair Jeb Hensarling noted that in the past the Secretary had said that the FSB "does not make rules for any of the national governments; every country has its own ability to make its own decisions for itself." If so, Hensarling asked, "why is it that the FSB found it necessary to grant exemptions [from compliance], specifically to the Chinese?" The Secretary reiterated his previous response: "we work in the FSB to try to get the kinds of standards that we think are appropriate in the United States to be adopted around the world so that the whole world will have high standards."[30] The Secretary apparently does not see the contradiction between saying that these standards are only voluntary and the idea that they will not be binding in the U.S. If indeed the U.S. hopes to get other countries to adopt the standards, it has to adopt the standards itself. So in effect the Secretary must expect that the standards will eventually become binding in the U.S.

This is not quite the same thing that occurs when bank regulators get together to agree on bank capital requirements. In that case, the U.S. regulators at least already have the authority from Congress to set bank capital requirements, even if Congress itself chooses not to review what the regulators have agreed to. However, in the case of "complex chains of transactions" in the capital markets—the current target of FSB proposals—there does not appear to be any direct statutory support for prudential regulation of these activities in the U.S. In that case, if prudential regulation is in fact imposed on the U.S. capital markets, it will bypass Congress and be based solely on an agreement among regulators.

THE EFFECTS OF REGULATION

The dollar effect of regulatory restrictions cannot be calculated. That is one of the reasons that economists do not try to estimate the effect of

Dodd-Frank on economic growth. But the effect can be seen in the results of individual financial firms. In March 2014, for example, JPMorgan Chase, the largest U.S. banking organization, cut back its projections for the coming year, announcing that its trading profits and return on equity would be down.[31] It noted that it would also add 3,000 new compliance employees, on top of the 7,000 it added the year before. But the total employees of the bank are expected to fall by 5,000 in the coming year.[32] Thus, compliance employees and their costs are being substituted for the personnel that are normally the sources of revenue and profit.

Often, these negative reports are blamed on slow business growth or lack of consumer spending, but this may be confusing cause and effect. If JPMorgan Chase were not substituting compliance officers for calling officers, the calling officers would be out in the market talking to businesses and offering them credit for expansion.

If what the FSB called the "SIFI Framework" is in fact extended to the rest of the financial system through decisions of the FSOC, the regulatory sclerosis that is affecting banks in the U.S. and elsewhere will be extended to the entire financial system and then to the economy as a whole. We can anticipate that credit will become more costly, simply because securities and capital markets entities will be doing a variation of what JPMorgan Chase is doing—hiring more compliance officials and substituting them for employees that are profitable for the firm. If credit is more expensive, some firms will be priced out of the market; the cost of borrowing will exceed the profit that could be earned from the additional productive resources put in place. If there is less borrowing, there will be less firm expansion and less equipment installed that will increase productivity. All of this will mean less economic growth.

There will also be less-tangible losses. If large capital markets firms are placed under bank-like supervision, they will take fewer risks. This is because it is the inclination of regulators and supervisors to reduce risk-taking for fear that it will cause losses for which they will be blamed. Less risk-taking will mean less innovation, fewer new efficiencies tried, and, again, slower growth. Yes, there will be fewer failures of financial firms, but at the same time there will be fewer new start-ups because there will be less credit for start-ups, which are riskier than established firms. It is important to note that the first new bank to be formed in the U.S since the adoption of Dodd-Frank was chartered in 2013, even as hundreds of banks have failed. Before Dodd-Frank, an average of one hundred new banks were chartered every year.[33]

CONCLUSION

Congress and the American people should be wary of the FSOC's extraordinary discretionary authority and its obscure relationship to the FSB. This authority is the result of a false narrative that the financial crisis was caused by insufficient regulation of the financial community. The restrictive Dodd-Frank Act was the natural consequence of this narrative. The actual cause of the crisis was the U.S. government's housing policies. Nevertheless, if Dodd-Frank cannot be repealed, Congress must consider both the FSOC's decision-making process on SIFI designations and the possibility that the FSB's effort to gain regulatory control of shadow banking will be imported into the U.S. as part of an international agreement among regulators. The potential adverse effects of these designations are too important to be left for consideration by regulators, who are eager to extend their control over the financial system.

Subjecting the U.S. financial system to prudential regulation by bank regulators will impair or eliminate the innovation and aggressiveness that has made the U.S. the world's financial leader and will consign all Americans to the slow-growth economy that excessive regulation inevitably produces.

26.

THE FTC, UNFAIR METHODS OF COMPETITION, AND ABUSE OF PROSECUTORIAL DISCRETION

Joshua D. Wright[1]

The Federal Trade Commission (FTC) has reached a critical point in its existence. Throughout its history, the agency has faced numerous criticisms for its overly expansive approach to antitrust and consumer protection enforcement as well as abuse of its prosecutorial discretion. Once again, the FTC is attracting significant criticism for an exceedingly broad view of its authority. Practitioners, academics, and even Congress have taken notice. A number of commissioners have raised concerns and are now considering reforms that would narrow the agency's interpretation of its enforcement authority. The FTC is, and always has been, fully capable of ending the controversy, eliminating the risk of legislative or judicial action that would curtail its authority, by issuing guidelines that delineate the scope of its authority and limit its prosecutorial discretion.

The FTC's law enforcement authority is rooted in Section 5 of the Federal Trade Commission Act.[2] Section 5's prohibition of "[u]nfair methods of competition" (UMC) and "unfair or deceptive acts or practices" (UDAP) evinces the agency's dual missions of pursuing competition and consumer protection, respectively. This chapter focuses upon the competition prong of Section 5, the FTC's UMC authority, which encompasses violations of the traditional antitrust laws as well as at least some conduct in an as-yet-undefined territory beyond the boundaries of those laws.[3]

The FTC's consumer protection activity in the 1960s and 1970s drew the attention of numerous critics from across the political and ideological spectrum, including Ralph Nader and "Nader's Raiders," as well as then professor Richard Posner, all of whom raised serious concerns about the ineffectiveness of the FTC and questioned the wisdom of the agency's continued existence.[4] The FTC's questionable activities culminated infamously in an attempt to ban advertising to children, prompting the *Washington Post* to declare the FTC a "national nanny."[5] The agency's overreach also garnered the attention of Congress, which allowed the FTC's funding to lapse, allowed the agency to shut down for a brief period, and then passed a law specifically limiting the FTC's "unfairness" rulemaking authority with respect to children's advertising.[6] In response, the FTC adopted a series of policy statements describing how it would evaluate conduct under its UDAP authority.[7] Doing so alleviated the public and Congress's concerns, and it legitimized and revitalized the FTC's consumer protection program. Its "unfairness" guidelines have even been codified into law.[8] The FTC has also had considerable success with its Horizontal Merger Guidelines, which have been widely adopted by federal courts and had broad influence upon antitrust thinking and doctrine.

But the FTC has refused to follow its useful experience with its UDAP authority to similarly define and constrain its competition authority. A full century into its existence, the FTC has failed to produce a useful UMC definition or even general guidelines as to when the agency will enforce its authority.[9] This failure has earned the FTC criticism both for failing to supply the public and the firms it regulates with some notion of what conduct will violate the law and for its apparent unwillingness to accept that its authority does and should have limits.

THE FTC'S UMC AUTHORITY

Congress intended Section 5 to reach business conduct outside the scope of the traditional antitrust laws, including the Sherman Act and the Clayton Act. The rationale for vesting an administrative agency with this broad authority was the commonly held expectation that an expert administrative body would exercise its authority in a manner that was responsive to changes in the marketplace and capable of expanding beyond current judicial interpretations of the antitrust laws. But its authority would be tempered by restrictions upon available remedies, which would be lighter than those available under the Sherman Act. Furthermore, FTC interpretations of Section 5 were intended to exclude the negative collateral effects of private litigation. Congress also designed the FTC to make full use of its expertise, giving it the complementary authority to conduct studies of business practices in order to understand their competitive implications.[10]

As Bill Kovacic (a former FTC chair) and Marc Winerman have explained, the institutional design features of the FTC's Section 5 authority were intended to "help make the Commission the preeminent vehicle for setting competition policy in the United States."[11] That is, the FTC's unique policy authority was intended to allow competition policy research and development that would guide the commission in identifying the appropriate standards of liability in its law enforcement efforts, while providing reliable guidance to the business community. Courts would "look to the Commission for guidance about how to frame and apply antitrust rules."[12] As we shall see, the FTC has simply not lived up to the goals Congress had in mind when designing its authority.

The FTC has now had over a century to demonstrate success in furthering U.S. competition policy under Section 5. Yet it has failed to do so. The FTC's last appellate court victory under Section 5 came in 1968.[13] Kovacic, a renowned FTC scholar and antitrust professor, sums up the FTC's record under Section 5: "One would be hard-pressed to come up with a list of ten adjudicated decisions that involved the FTC's application of Section 5 in which the FTC prevailed and the case can be said to have had a notable impact, either in terms of doctrine or economic effects."[14]

It has also failed to provide coherent guidance on when and under what circumstances it will seek to enforce its standalone UMC authority. There is no shortage of potential interpretations by scholars or individual commissioners of the FTC's UMC authority, but the FTC has failed to adopt any of them or offer one of its own.[15] Instead, the FTC has engaged in applications of its UMC authority that vary significantly over time. The FTC's UMC authority is, unfortunately, no more and no less than whatever a majority of commissioners believes it to be for any particular matter at any given time. For example, former FTC Chair Jon Leibowitz expressed his view that Section 5 broadly covers conduct that is "'collusive, coercive, predatory, restrictive, or deceitful,' or otherwise oppressive," but Chair Edith Ramirez views the FTC's UMC authority as more clearly tied to antitrust law's traditional measure of competitive effects.[16] Recently, some at the FTC have taken seriously even more provocative interpretations of Section 5. Former Chair Michael Pertschuk stated, in a highly publicized speech, that "no responsive competition policy can neglect the social and environmental harms produced as unwelcome by-products of the marketplace: resource depletion, energy waste, environmental contamination, worker alienation, the psychological and social consequences of producer-stimulated demands."[17]

The uncertainty caused by the commission's lack of commitment to providing coherent UMC guidance is exacerbated by both the perception that the commission enjoys significant legal and administrative advantages and the FTC's failure to garner the confidence of the antitrust bar that it can and will use its distinctive tools to influence competition law in a positive or even predictable direction.

THE FTC'S PERFORMANCE TO DATE

The FTC's recent forays into the development of its Section 5 UMC authority comprise nothing more than consent agreements, which set no legal precedent. Indeed, the last time a court opined on the scope of the FTC's UMC authority was over two decades ago, and the last time the Supreme Court opined on its scope was over four decades ago.[18] We can hardly expect any judicial guidance in the foreseeable future.

Some commentators defend the FTC's approach of piling up Section 5 UMC consent agreements by arguing that it mimics the virtues of the case-by-case, common law approach.[19] This view is understandable but misguided. Although the desire to strike the correct balance between flexibility and certainty is well intended, the so-called common law approach to defining the FTC's UMC authority is a recipe for unprincipled and inconsistent enforcement.[20] In the absence of an existing UMC standard or a judicial decision articulating such a standard, the regulated community must read any available tea leaves hidden within the growing collection of FTC consent orders.

Reliance upon this approach assumes that the common law virtues that have contributed to the traditional antitrust laws apply equally in the context of Section 5. Fundamental differences, however, distinguish the inputs and outputs of traditional litigation from the inputs and outputs of Section 5 enforcement. Consent decrees lack the benefit of the adversarial process associated with litigation. Furthermore, any opinion describing the commission's UMC analysis, often in the form of a statement issued in conjunction with the public release of the consent package, is highly unlikely to reflect the opinion of a neutral decision-maker, because the FTC is acting as both prosecutor and judge. Additionally, in order to minimize the costs associated with litigation, parties frequently enter into consent agreements with the FTC before it can develop a full evidentiary record upon which to conduct its analysis.[21]

Furthermore, the FTC has incentives to institute enforcement actions and extract consents even where it is unlikely to prevail in litigation. In the standalone Section 5 context alone, the past decade has produced at least four well-known examples of such consents: *Negotiated Data Solutions, LLC* (*N-Data*), *Motorola Mobility LLC and Google Inc.* (*Google/MMI*), *Bosch*, and *Intel*.[22] In *N-Data*, the commission challenged a patent holder's attempt to increase royalty rates above the small, one-time fee it committed many years prior to a standard-setting organization (SSO) to charge.[23] Following its ex ante contractual commitment regarding the royalty fee, the patent holder lawfully acquired monopoly power via the SSO's adoption of its technology in the relevant standard. The later attempt to increase royalty rates, the commission argued, violated Section 5 as both a UADP and a UMC.[24] Commissioner Kovacic's dissent criticized the FTC's legal analysis, which did not distinguish between the UADP and UMC violations and, indeed, appeared to extend the scope of UADP to encompass UMC.[25] Kovacic also pointed out that "[t]he prospect of a settlement can lead one to relax the analytical standards that ordinarily would discipline the decision to prosecute if the litigation of asserted claims was certain or likely. This is particularly the case when, as in this matter, the respondent has indicated during negotiations that, for various reasons, it will not litigate and will accept a settlement."[26]

Also in the standard-setting context, the FTC has challenged injunction-seeking efforts by Bosch and Google as UMC violations. In both cases, the patent holders had committed to licensing standard-essential patents (SEPs) on fair, reasonable, and non-discriminatory (FRAND) terms. In *Bosch*, Bosch had acquired a company that issued a letter of assurance to an SSO to offer licenses to potential SEPs on FRAND terms, but it did not discontinue previously initiated injunction actions against competitors implementing the SSO's standards.[27] In *Google/MMI*, MMI, and later Google, sought injunctions and exclusion orders against licensees after committing to license their SEPs on FRAND terms.[28] The commission found that seeking injunctions in this context violates commitments to license SEPs on FRAND terms and therefore constitutes a UMC violation.[29]

Finally, in *Intel*, the commission challenged loyalty discounts offered by Intel, which it concluded constituted de facto exclusive dealing arrangements in violation of Section 2 of the Sherman Act and Section 5. The discounts at issue in the matter had been in existence in the marketplace for nearly a decade, and there was substantial evidence to suggest there was intense competition in the market.[30] The commission thus was unlikely to prevail on a Section 2 theory because it would have been unable to prove actual anticompetitive effects. In the absence of a strong Section 2 case, the commission alleged UMC violations.

As these cases illustrate, the FTC has focused much attention upon high-tech markets where innovation often outpaces legal evolution. In *N-Data*, *Google/MMI*, and *Bosch*, the investigations focused on the perceived breach of commitments in the standard-setting context. There is no reason to think recourse to the antitrust laws is necessary in these cases, where state contract law and federal patent law are likely to be sufficient. Rather, bringing these actions within the purview of antitrust enforcement is likely to chill innovation and other pro-competitive conduct. This problem is particularly acute in cases like *Intel*, where the commission attempted to use Section 5 as a substitute for the Sherman Act due to deficiencies in its Section 2 case. Competition policy weighs heavily against using the antitrust laws where their application risks chilling pro-competitive behavior. Courts have rejected the commission's attempts to expand Section 5 in this way and likely would have done so in the cases described here.[31] Nevertheless, the commission pursued and obtained consent agreements in those cases rather than closing its investigations.

The pressure upon administrative agencies to engage in a large volume of activity, rather than to focus their efforts upon quality, leads them to open numerous investigations ending in consent agreements. As former Chair Kovacic has critically observed, "[t]he central and most heavily weighted criterion [for rating competition agencies] is the initiation of new cases. . . . This criterion generally equates activity with accomplishment. By this calculus, total case counts and trends in case counts become the measure of an agency's worth."[32]

The FTC enjoys legal and procedural advantages that deter the parties it investigates from litigating the merits of Section 5 UMC cases. The fact that the scope of UMC is subject to the whim of the commission's majority is one such advantage. It also leads to wide variation over time in how the commission prosecutes unfair methods of competition, making it difficult for firms to plan long-term strategies that involve conduct one commission might consider permissible and a subsequent commission might find offensive.

The uncertainty is exacerbated by the administrative procedures available to the commission for litigating UMC claims. Consider the following empirical observation. The FTC has voted out a number of complaints in administrative adjudication that have been tried by administrative law judges (ALJs) in the past two decades. In each of those cases, after the administrative decision has been appealed to the commission, the commission has ruled in favor of FTC staff and found liability. In 100 percent of cases where the ALJ ruled in favor of the FTC staff, the commission affirmed liability; and in 100 percent of the cases in which the ALJ found no liability, the commission reversed. This is a strong sign of an unhealthy and biased institutional process. By way of contrast, when the antitrust decisions of federal district court judges are appealed to the federal courts of appeal, the plaintiffs' win rate is much closer to 50 percent. One interpretation of these data is that the process at the FTC stacks the deck against the parties. Another is that the FTC has an uncanny knack for picking cases; a knack unseen heretofore within any legal institution.

The "omniscient agency" theory requires one to overcome the fact that commission decisions are appealed significantly more often than the judicial opinions of generalist judges in antitrust cases.[33] Furthermore, when appealed, commission decisions are reversed at a rate four times greater than antitrust opinions by generalist federal judges.[34] These observations are bolstered by criticisms of the FTC's performance in administrative adjudication every decade dating back to the 1960s.[35] In 1969, Posner published a well-known critique of the FTC's performance, in which he found the FTC enjoyed no comparative advantage over Article III courts, that the combination of an executive and adjudicative function was both a distinguishing characteristic of the FTC and a significant source of weakness, and that the agency had made no distinctive contribution to antitrust law through the administrative process.[36] In fact, Posner believed any contribution the FTC made to competition law was likely negative.[37] More recently, in comments to the FTC concerning its Section 5 workshop, former Assistant Attorney General for the Department of Justice's Antitrust Division Doug Melamed described administrative adjudication of antitrust cases as "a deeply flawed process," concluding "it is not suitable for the task of generating competition-law decisions that are sufficiently reliable and well-founded that they can be counted upon to send appropriate signals to economic actors about the conduct that the law requires of them."[38] At best, there exists a perception that the FTC enjoys procedural advantages that permit it to win cases it should not; at worst, the FTC enjoys actual procedural advantages.

The apparent procedural advantages, coupled with the vague and unbounded potential scope of the FTC's UMC authority, give businesses the incentive to settle Section 5 claims rather than going through lengthy and costly administrative litigation in which they are both deprived of any predictability of statutory interpretation and must confront a tribunal whose history predicts it will rule against them. The commission thus takes advantage of the uncertainty surrounding Section 5 by eliciting a settlement even though the challenged conduct very likely would not violate the traditional antitrust laws.

Congress established the FTC in large part because it expected the agency's work to contribute meaningfully to competition law and policy. The FTC's performance in administrative litigation gives little confidence that even if consent orders contribute to competition law and policy, they do so in a way that benefits competition and consumers. The FTC's performance over the past hundred years calls into question the desirability of vesting broad, potentially unbounded authority in the agency. Permitting the FTC to seek enforcement actions in unpredictable situations, providing it with the incentive to seek them even where it is unlikely to prevail in court, and discouraging businesses from defending themselves in litigation inevitably chills legitimate conduct that would have enhanced consumer welfare.

RECALIBRATING THE FTC'S UMC AUTHORITY

There is a growing consensus among those interested in competition law and policy that guidance would be helpful, if not required, when the commission uses Section 5 to reach beyond the scope of the traditional antitrust laws. Members of Congress have weighed in on the Section 5 debate, even reaching out to Chair Ramirez on multiple occasions to inquire about the commission's lack of guidance. Members of both the House and Senate have asked about Section 5 in oversight hearings. Members have sent a joint letter to the chair explaining their concerns about the lack of guidelines. Their concern is that the commission's use of its UMC authority is too expansive and potentially unauthorized by law.

Most recently, Representative Bob Goodlatte, Chair of the House Judiciary Committee, suggested Congress may recalibrate the FTC's UMC authority. He stated, "It is my hope that the Judiciary Committee will not need to take actions beyond writing letters and holding hearings."[39] Dispelling any ambiguity, counsel to the House Judiciary Committee has explained that Congress has three options for addressing the commission's use of Section 5: (1) writing letters, (2) holding hearings, and (3) proposing legislation.[40] There is only one option not yet tried: for Congress to severely limit or even strip the FTC of its standalone UMC authority altogether.

An alternative, and in my view preferable, option is for the commission to issue a policy statement providing guidance as to its interpretation of Section 5's UMC. Doing so would permit the agency to address the impediments to its enforcement efforts so that Section 5 can contribute meaningfully to the FTC's competition enforcement agenda. It would also provide certainty to the business community and encourage pro-competitive behavior otherwise forgone out of fear of crossing the currently undefined line between lawful and unlawful competitive conduct under Section 5.

It is appropriate now more than ever for the FTC to consider issuing guidelines explaining its interpretation of the scope of Section 5. The commission, as currently constituted, is closer to a consensus on a UMC interpretation than before. There is broad, albeit incomplete, agreement that Section 5 extends beyond the traditional federal antitrust laws. There is also broad agreement that one of the requirements for finding a UMC violation should be showing "harm (or likely harm) to competition," as the phrase has been developed under the traditional antitrust laws. This phrase has a specific meaning that is known to the antitrust bar and that is tethered to modern economics. Section 5's limited jurisprudence developed in the "pre-economic" era of antitrust analysis. The commission should be a leader in updating its methods—as it has done with the Horizontal Merger Guidelines—to be more reflective of modern economic thinking.

What remains is to define a UMC claim that will maximize the rate of return that the commission's enforcement efforts earn for customers. There is no shortage of potential definitions that would bring Section 5 jurisprudence and agency practice within the confines of "harm to competition" as understood in modern antitrust practice and improve the incorporation of economic analysis in UMC cases. I have urged the commission to adopt any of three different proposed UMC definitions, each of which incorporates a harm-to-competition element but would give different weight to efficiency justifications.[41] Although my view is that competition policy favors adoption of a UMC definition giving significant weight to efficiency, any of the proposed definitions would be a vast improvement over the status quo, which is no definition at all.

Continued exploitation of its vague UMC authority and administrative advantages harms competition law and policy and, importantly, consumers. The commission should take a lesson from its own history, in which the agency's overreach led Congress to nearly abolish its consumer protection authority. In the absence of proactive measures recognizing limiting principles, the FTC risks a legislative or judicial reaction that will require it to relinquish its standalone UMC authority altogether.

CONCLUSION

John Yoo

As we close the book on the Obama administration, the scandals keep coming. They seemed to buffet the White House from all directions: immigration, the IRS, Obamacare, and national security. Yet they all come from a common source: not Hillary Clinton's vast right-wing conspiracy but the inexorable growth of the administrative state. If conservatives are ever to reverse unaccountable government, they must fundamentally change their approach to constitutional law and the Executive Branch.

At first glance, the Obama administration's scandals seem unconnected. First came the failure to honestly account for the al Qaeda attack on the U.S. consulate in Benghazi, Libya. Despite warnings that terrorists sought to mark the eleventh anniversary of the September 11, 2001, attacks with assaults on American embassies, Hillary Clinton's State Department took no serious precautions.[1] Even as reports arrived that the attack on the U.S. consulate in Benghazi went beyond any mere protest, Secretary of State Hillary Clinton and President Obama were either paralyzed by indecision or rendered passive by indifference.[2] After the attacks killed the U.S. ambassador to Libya and U.S. security personnel, the White House concocted an unbelievable story blaming Arab unrest on an unknown maker of an unwatched anti-Muslim movie.[3]

The tax scandal followed. A Treasury Department inspector general reported that the Internal Revenue Service had targeted Tea Party and conservative groups for extra scrutiny and unfavorable treatment.[4] IRS official Lois Lerner's amateurish effort to get out in front of the damaging news by planting a question in a friendly forum failed.[5] She ended up pleading the Fifth before an investigating congressional committee, which has followed the trail from a Cincinnati IRS field office to IRS headquarters in Washington, D.C.[6] IRS officials are currently trying to run out the clock by resisting congressional demands for information before the end of 2016.

In yet another Beltway scandal, President Obama suspended central provisions of the very health care act on which he staked his presidency.[7] American businesses did not offer health care plans to all employees because the Department of Health and Human Services failed to issue standards for the plans.[8] States refused to cooperate with the administration in setting up exchanges to replace the market for health insurance policies, which threw regulators even further off the schedule demanded by the act. The administration gave out tax subsidies to all, even though the statute authorized them only in states that had set up health care exchanges.[9] Only *King v. Burwell*'s fanciful reading of the statutory language saved Obamacare's misuse of taxpayer funds.[10]

President Obama's refusal to enforce the law violates his constitutional duty to "take Care that the Laws be faithfully executed." While the President may refuse to enforce laws that themselves violate the Constitution, he cannot ignore a law simply because he doesn't care for its policies. Obama's failure to uphold his core constitutional responsibility shouldn't come as a surprise. In 2012, Obama ordered the Department of Homeland Security not to deport illegal aliens brought to the United States as children, even though it was required to by immigration laws.[11] In 2014, he unilaterally expanded his deferred prosecution program to allow millions more illegal aliens to remain in the country.[12] His Justice Department refuses to prosecute federal drug laws in states that have approved medical marijuana,[13] and his Solicitor General refused to defend the federal Defense of Marriage Act before the Supreme Court in *United States v. Windsor*.[14]

With its reputation for governing competence and political dexterity in shambles, the Obama administration suffered its worst blow in national security. A lowly network administrator for the National Security Administration—Edward Snowden, a stereotypical "IT guy"—stole some of the

U.S.'s dearest secrets and hightailed it to Hong Kong and Moscow, leaking U.S. eavesdropping programs as he fled. Obama's weakness plumbed its deepest depths when he could persuade neither Chinese President Xi Jinping nor Russian President Vladimir Putin to return Snowden.[15] Snowden's leaks have revealed far broader anti-terrorism surveillance of phone calls and e-mails than previously thought, throwing the branches of the U.S. government into a paroxysm of self-doubt, blame avoidance, and mutual recrimination. Obama has responded by agreeing to more judicial oversight of the NSA activities, becoming the first wartime American president to voluntarily reduce his Commander-in-Chief power in favor of the courts.[16]

These scandals may have traveled different vectors before they landed on the White House, but they all flow from the same source—the overgrowth of the administrative state. Introduced by one liberal president, Woodrow Wilson, expanded by a second, Franklin D. Roosevelt, and perfected by a third, Lyndon B. Johnson, the welfare state has metastasized under Barack Obama. It has a common formula. First, expand federal congressional powers beyond their enumerated constitutional limits. Second, delegate those powers to agencies and away from directly elected politicians in Congress. Third, insulate the civil servants so they can wield their discretion without accountability. Finally, force the courts to defer to Congress's delegation and to the agencies' regulations with little question.

The administrative state has reached its apotheosis in Obamacare. Congress claimed authority to take over one-sixth of the American economy rather than allowing the states and the markets to control supply and demand. Instead of passing the rules for this massive new government program themselves, the large Democratic majorities in Congress vested the power to regulate health care in the Department of Health and Human Services. An independent board of "experts" will decide critical questions such as the prices for medical procedures. Even the Supreme Court, with a majority of Republican-appointed Justices, would not stand in the way. In *NFIB v. Sibelius,* Chief Justice John Roberts, once the darling of conservatives, upheld the act's individual mandate as a constitutional tax even while holding it to violate the Commerce Clause.[17]

President Obama, however, can blame his travails at the end of his time in office on the very governing framework that produced his great health care victory in Congress, the Supreme Court, and the 2012 elections. Woodrow Wilson thought that the administrative state would allow experts to decide social problems scientifically without the dirty push-and-pull of partisan politics.[18] Rational management required the establishment of an administrative state that would overcome the inefficiencies of the separation of powers. Modern industrial capitalism demanded constant regulation and made fanciful the framers' ideal that divided government would allow liberty to flourish. But unaccountable bureaucracy lacks deliberation with accountability (the virtue of the Congress) and decision with vigor (the virtues of the President).

Instead, the welfare state has fulfilled the very fears that propelled the framers away from a multiple-headed executive selected by the legislature. Alexander Hamilton's defense of a sole President elected by the American people bears repeating. "A feeble execution is but another phrase for a bad execution," Hamilton argued in *Federalist* No. 70, "and a government ill executed, whatever may be in theory, must be, in practice, a bad government."[19] By contrast, "good government" required "energy in the executive" by a vigorous President who is "essential to the protection of the community from foreign attacks" and "the steady administration of the laws."[20]

Centralizing all executive authority in one head, rather than in multiple leaders, was critical to good government. A single executive would bring "[d]ecision, activity, secrecy, and dispatch," Hamilton wrote.[21] A plural executive would "conceal faults and destroy responsibility," allowing blame for failure to be shifted and avoiding accountability of punishment by public opinion.[22] A "cabal" within a council would "enervate the whole system of administration" and produce "habitual feebleness and dilatoriness."[23] To diffuse executive power among multiple parties would weaken authority and confusion would reign, frustrating the government's ability to respond to "the most critical emergencies of the state."[24]

Direct political accountability also fostered a successful executive. Hamilton and the Federalists established a four-year term of office with the possibility of re-election. In *Federalist* No. 71, Hamilton explained that this period would promote stability as well as "the personal firmness of the executive magistrate, in the employment of his constitutional powers."[25] A longer term with the opportunity for re-election gave a President the time to "plan and undertake the most extensive and arduous enterprises for the public benefit."[26] If his term were too short, popular opinion would sit foremost in the President's mind, and short-term political gain and hopes for re-election would come before the public interest. Longer terms created less rotation in offices and shifts in policy as new presidents took office. A "change in men" would create "a mutability of measures."[27]

Eligibility for re-election would allow the nation to gain from the experience and qualities of successful executives. For the Federalists, the prospect of re-election would encourage the chief executive to pursue policies in the broader public interest. Influenced by David Hume, the authors of the *Federalist* designed a system of government that would harness private interest to the national benefit. This was nowhere more so than in the design of the presidency. Hamilton described "the love of fame" as "the ruling passion of the noblest minds."[28] Pursuit of fame would encourage presidents to confront difficult challenges, but only if they could win re-election and their labors be rewarded.

President Obama's allegiance to the liberal administrative state guaranteed that his presidency would run aground on the very shoals marked out by the framers. Its operations are so vast and its reach so sprawling that it lies beyond the control or comprehension of any one man or group of men. Its dispersal of authority and dilution of responsibility produced the debacle in Benghazi, where no one felt responsible for the fates of American diplomats trapped in the consulate. The administrative state's broad sweep and ramshackle, complicated processes makes rational management impossible. Even President Obama does not know the full scope of his own health care act, nor can he and his aides figure out how to make its many moving parts work on time. His Justice Department instead resorted to the passive non-enforcement of the laws—the very reverse-image of a vigorous executive—to try to bring coherence to its health care schemes and to advance its policies.

This disease even infects Obama's handling of national security affairs, where the President's virtues of "decision, activity, secrecy, and dispatch"—as Hamilton described them in *Federalist* No. 70—should be at their height. Defending the nation's security is the President's paramount duty, as Abraham Lincoln's example reminds us during this 150th anniversary of the Civil War. But where earlier presidents stoutly defended their Commander-in-Chief power to protect the nation, Obama's response to the demands of the war on terror is to seek more judicial control over everything from surveillance to drones. At times Obama seems unaware of the surveillance and killing handed out by his intelligence agencies and shows little interest in directing them. It is difficult to imagine George Washington, Lincoln, or FDR responding to their national challenges with the embarrassment that afflicts Obama.

However much they may enjoy watching Obama flounder, conservatives can use these scandals as an opportunity to reform the administrative state. They should take caution from their previous effort, which unintentionally exacerbated the problems. When Ronald Reagan took office, conservatives did not radically downsize and transform the administrative state. Instead, they tried to tame it by rationalizing its decisions. Led by Chris DeMuth (later head of the American Enterprise Institute) and Douglas Ginsburg (later a judge of the powerful U.S. Court of Appeals for the D.C. Circuit), conservatives created a powerful nerve center within the White House's Office of Management and Budget (OMB) to oversee the sprawling welfare state. President Reagan issued an executive order requiring agencies to submit any major new regulations to OMB for cost-benefit review. Led by Antonin Scalia (later D.C. Circuit judge and Supreme Court Justice) and Robert Bork (also later D.C. Circuit judge and almost Supreme Court Justice), conservatives on the courts sought to spark economic growth by turning the agencies toward deregulation.

Three legal doctrines sat at the core of their campaign. First, the President must have the authority to fire the heads of any and all administrative agencies. Without the power of removal, presidents could not force the agencies to follow his deregulatory policies or to submit to the rigors of cost-benefit analysis. The removal theory of the executive crested in *Morrison v. Olson*, which upheld the independent counsel.[29] Second, as ultimately codified in the Supreme Court's 1984 decision *NRDC v. Chevron*, courts were to defer to agency interpretations of ambiguous laws, which had the effect of relocating even more lawmaking power to the Executive.[30] Third, courts were to defer to agency regulations unless they were "arbitrary and capricious," rather than giving them a "hard look."[31] Courts ought rarely overturn an agency decision on the merits.

For a time, this approach worked because the Reagan/Bush White House controlled the agencies, focused its domestic policy on cutting back regulations, and freed the animal passions of the economy. But what conservatives did not foresee is that a President committed to very different regulatory principles could free the administrative state from all control. The Progressive-created end run around the Constitution's checks not only made lawmaking easier through decree. It also eased the way for special interests by requiring them to capture the leaders of the Federal Reserve or the EPA alone, rather than persuading a majority of members of both the House and the Senate to adopt a favorable policy. In trying to remove policy from politics, Progressives made it significantly more vulnerable to special interests. And the Reagan Revolution, in trying to protect liberty from the excessive lawmaking of Congress, accepted the centralization of power in agencies that need never worry about voters, judges, or Congress. It is unclear whether the current state of our Republic should be the subject of an Elizabethan tragedy or comedy.

If the White House does not care to force the administrative state to act in a unitary, rational manner, then agencies will be free to pursue their own ideological agendas. If the President believes government can make economic decisions better than the market, then officials can act without any effective restraint. Conservative principles have only allowed the welfare state to become more effective in expanding its reach, ousting the private decisions of the markets, and undercutting the institutions of civil society.

Conservatives can begin reform by moving beyond the policies of the Reagan Revolution. Rather than make the administrative state more efficient and effective, perhaps the better answer is to disable and hobble it. First, conservatives should jettison some of the favorite legal doctrines of the current era. Rather than defer to agency interpretations of their laws, the courts should decide on their own whether regulations satisfy statutory requirements. Rather than give agencies wide room to run in formulating regulations, courts can give them a hard look or demand that they be based on scientific models and empirical evidence. Judges could resuscitate the pre–New Deal nondelegation doctrine, which once placed limits on Congress's freedom to give away its legislative power to the agencies. In the Supreme Court term that ended in June 2015, Justice Clarence Thomas called upon the Court to make exactly these changes.[32]

A more aggressive re-thinking of constitutional law could re-examine some separation-of-powers classics. Cases such as *INS v. Chadha*,[33] which struck down the legislative veto, or *Bowsher v. Synar*,[34] which limited the powers of congressional agencies, reduced Congress's ability to oversee the administrative state. If conservatives are going to impose new constraints, they must re-think some of their constitutional hostility toward Congress.

Another conservative revolution could come in the area of individual rights. Many conservative lawyers and judges, especially those who came to the fore during the Reagan years, believed that *Lochner v. New York*[35] was the great example of the evils of judicial activism.[36] In *Lochner*, the Supreme Court had struck down a limit on the working hours of bakers as a violation of their due process right to make contracts, a view that held sway from the end of the Civil War to the New Deal.[37] The framers of the Constitution and of the Reconstruction amendments shared a belief in natural rights. Nevertheless, conservatives agreed with the New Deal court's rejection of *Lochner* because it underlay their critique of the Warren Court's activism of the 1950s and 1960s.

Rejecting the restoration of natural rights has become a form of unilateral conservative disarmament. Often joined by a stray conservative, such as the ever-wandering Justice Anthony Kennedy, liberals do not hesitate to conjure new rights out of the Due Process Clause, from *Roe v. Wade*'s right to abortion to *Obergefell*'s right to gay marriage. By ignoring the natural rights that actually informed the framing, conservatives are pursuing an impoverished, defensive vision of constitutional law. As part of a strategy to reverse the growth of the administrative state, conservative thinkers must create a system of legal principles based on natural rights that judges can meaningfully enforce.

Conservatives need to recalibrate their revolution. While they are correct to follow the founders' fear of excessive lawmaking, the focus has been on the wrong source: Congress. Now constitutional doctrine must aim at liberty's nemesis—administrative agencies. Otherwise, our constitutional Republic might devolve into something akin to the statist governments of Europe. Obama's scandals, ironically, may give conservatives the opportunity to begin again.

AUTHOR BIOGRAPHIES

Jonathan H. Adler is the Johan Verheij Memorial Professor and Director of the Center for Business Law & Regulation at the Case Western Reserve University School of Law, where he teaches courses in administrative, constitutional, and environmental law. Professor Adler is the author or editor of five books and over a dozen book chapters. His articles have appeared in publications ranging from the *Harvard Environmental Law Review* and *Supreme Court Economic Review* to the *Wall Street Journal* and *USA Today*. He has testified before Congress a dozen times, and his work has been cited in the U.S. Supreme Court. Professor Adler is a contributing editor to *National Review Online* and a regular contributor to the popular legal blog *The Volokh Conspiracy*, hosted by Washingtonpost.com.

Bob Barr represented the 7th District of Georgia in the U.S. House of Representatives from 1995 to 2003. For the entire eight years he served in the House, Bob sat on the Judiciary Committee and was an active voice on legislation involving firearms issues and the Second Amendment. He was the primary sponsor of the legislation that passed the House in 1995 and would have repealed the "Clinton Gun Ban." Bob has served since 1997 as a member of the Board of Directors of the National Rifle Association, and he has attended several firearms-related international conferences in New York City at the United Nations and in Europe. Bob has authored many articles on the Second Amendment and frequently lectures on topics related thereto. In addition to practicing law in Atlanta, Georgia, he is an Adjunct Professor of Constitutional Policy at Kennesaw State University, a unit of the University of Georgia system.

In 1986 he was appointed by President Ronald Reagan to serve as the United States Attorney for the Northern District of Georgia, a position he held until 1990. He also served with the Central Intelligence Agency and has received degrees from the University of Southern California (BA), George Washington University (MA), and Georgetown University Law Center (JD).

Gerard V. Bradley is a Professor of Law at the University of Notre Dame, where he teaches Legal Ethics and Constitutional Law. At Notre Dame he directs (with John Finnis) the Natural Law Institute and co-edits *The American Journal of Jurisprudence*, an international forum for legal philosophy. Bradley has been a Visiting Fellow at the Hoover Institution of Stanford University and is a Senior Fellow of the Witherspoon Institute in Princeton, New Jersey. He served for many years as President of the Fellowship of Catholic Scholars.

Ronald A. Cass is Dean Emeritus of Boston University School of Law, President of Cass & Associates, PC, and Chair of the Center for the Rule of Law. He has received appointments from five U.S. Presidents, including as Commissioner and Vice Chair of the U.S. International Trade Commission; Member, Council of the Administrative Conference of the United States; and Member, Panel of Conciliators, International Centre for Settlement of Investment Disputes. He also has served as advisor or consultant to numerous government agencies in the U.S. and abroad and to entities fighting against government agencies as well. Dean Cass has been Chair, American Bar Association Section on Administrative Law and Regulatory Practice; Chair, Federalist Society Practice Group on Administrative Law and Regulation; President, American Law Deans Association; Life Member, American Law Institute; and Senior Fellow, International Centre for Economic Research. He has been a full-time faculty member at the University of Virginia and Boston University (where he was Melville Madison Bigelow Professor of Law) and has taught and lectured at leading universities around the world. His more than 125 published scholarly books, chapters, and articles include a leading textbook on administrative law (with Colin Diver, Jack Beermann, and Jody Freeman, now in its seventh edition, from Wolters Kluwer); a monograph on intellectual property law, *Laws of Creation: Property Rights in the World of Ideas* (with Keith Hylton, from Harvard University Press); and the internationally known book on discretion and legal process, *The Rule of Law in America* (Johns Hopkins University Press).

Linda Chavez is the president of Becoming American Institute in Boulder, CO, and chair of the Center for Equal Opportunity in Falls Church, VA, which she founded in 1995. She was the director of public liaison in the Reagan White House and staff director of the U.S. Commission on Civil Rights from 1983 to 1985. She served on the Subcommission on Human Rights of the U.N. Human Rights Commission from 1992 to 1996. She is the author of three books, including *Out of the Barrio: Toward a New Politics of Hispanic Assimilation* (Basic Books, 1991), and numerous articles on immigration, racial preferences, and language, which have appeared in the *New York Times*, *Washington Post*, and *Wall Street Journal*, among others. Chavez writes a weekly syndicated column on politics and public policy that appears in the *New York Post* and other newspapers. She earned a BA from the University of Colorado in 1970 and an MFA from George Mason University in 2012.

Charles J. Cooper is a founding member of the Washington, D.C., law firm of Cooper & Kirk, PLLC. Named by the *National Law Journal* as one of the ten best civil litigators in Washington, he has over thirty years of legal experience in government and private practice, with several appearances before the United States Supreme Court and scores of other successful cases on both the trial and appellate levels. Shortly after serving as law clerk to Judge Paul Roney of the Fifth Circuit Court of Appeals and to Justice William H. Rehnquist, Mr. Cooper joined the Civil Rights Division of the U.S. Department of Justice in 1981. In 1985 President Reagan appointed Mr. Cooper to serve as the Assistant Attorney General for the Office of Legal Counsel. Mr. Cooper reentered private practice in 1988; his litigation practice is national in scope and is concentrated in the areas of constitutional, commercial, civil rights, intellectual property, and health care litigation. Mr. Cooper was appointed by Chief Justice William H. Rehnquist as a member of the Standing Committee on Rules of Practice and Procedure of the Judicial Conference of the United States, and he served on the Committee from 1998 through 2005. Mr. Cooper is a member of the American Law Institute and the American Academy of Appellate Lawyers, and he has spoken and published extensively on a wide variety of constitutional and legal policy topics.

Dr. John C. Eastman is the Henry Salvatori Professor of Law and Community Service and former Dean at Chapman University's Dale E. Fowler School of Law. He is the founding Director of the Claremont Institute's Center for Constitutional Jurisprudence, which he represented as *amicus curiae* in several of the cases discussed in his essay, and is grateful for the fine research of several Chapman law school students and Blackstone fellows in the preparation of those briefs, some of which is included in his chapter. He also serves as Chair of the Board of the National Organization for Marriage.

Richard A. Epstein is the Laurence A. Tisch Professor of Law, New York University School of Law; the Peter and Kirsten Senior Fellow, the Hoover Institution; and the James Parker Hall Distinguished Service Professor of Law Emeritus and Senior Lecturer, the University of Chicago.

Dr. Harold Furchtgott-Roth, former commissioner of the Federal Communications Commission, is a senior fellow at the Hudson Institute, where he founded the Center on the Economics of the Internet. He is an adjunct professor of law at Brooklyn Law School and president of Furchtgott-Roth Economic Enterprises, an economics consulting firm. He is the author or coauthor of four books and over fifty professional papers and journal articles. His scores of op-eds and columns have been widely published. He is a member of the Legal Policy Advisory Board for the Washington Legal Foundation. Dr. Furchtgott-Roth received a PhD in economics from Stanford University and an SB in economics from the Massachusetts Institute of Technology.

Daniel M. Gallagher was a Commissioner of the U.S. Securities and Exchange Commission from 2011 to 2015. During that time, he focused on initiatives aimed at strengthening our capital markets and encouraging small business capital formation, including staunchly supporting the changes introduced by the JOBS Act. He was an early and outspoken advocate for conducting a holistic review of equity market structure; increasing focus on the fixed income markets; addressing the outsized power of proxy advisory firms; and eliminating special privileges for credit rating agencies. He also addressed the creeping federalization of corporate governance as well as the concerted efforts of special interest groups to manipulate the SEC's disclosure regime. He was a sharp critic of the Dodd-Frank Act and the encroachment of bank regulatory measures and prudential regulators into the capital markets and a vocal opponent of the disturbing trend toward empowering supranational groups to enact "one world" regulation outside established constitutional processes. Before 2011, he was alternately in the private sector and at the SEC, including serving as a partner at WilmerHale, as Deputy Director and Co-Acting Director of the SEC's Division of Trading and Markets, and as the General Counsel of Fiserv Securities, Inc.

Robert P. George is McCormick Professor of Jurisprudence and Director of the James Madison Program in American Ideals and Institutions at Princeton University. He has also taught at Harvard Law School. He is Chair of the U.S. Commission on International Religious Freedom and has served as a presidential appointee to the U.S. Commission on Civil Rights. He has also served on the President's Council on Bioethics and UNESCO's World Commission on the Ethics of Science and Technology. He was a Judicial Fellow at the Supreme Court of the United States, where he received the Justice Tom C. Clark Award. A Phi Beta Kappa graduate of Swarthmore College, he holds degrees in law and theology from Harvard and a doctorate in philosophy of law from Oxford University, in addition to many honorary degrees. He is a recipient of the U.S. Presidential Citizens Medal and the Honorific Medal for the Defense of Human Rights of the Republic of Poland and is a member of the Council on Foreign Relations. His most recent book is *Conscience and Its Enemies* (ISI Books).

The Honorable C. Boyden Gray is an attorney in Washington, D.C. He served as Counsel to Vice President and then President George H.W. Bush from 1981 to 1993 and as U.S. Ambassador to the European Union and U.S. Special Envoy to Europe for Eurasian Energy under President George W. Bush, among many other prestigious positions.

Samantha Harris, a native of Philadelphia, Pennsylvania, is the Director of Policy Research at the Foundation for Individual Rights in Education (FIRE). Samantha speaks and writes extensively on issues of free speech and due process on college and university campuses. She is a frequent commentator on radio and television, and her writing has appeared in numerous publications including the *New York Times*, the *Chronicle of Higher Education*, the *New York Post*, and the *Des Moines Register*. She received her JD in 2002 from the University of Pennsylvania Law School, where she served on the editorial board of the *Journal of Constitutional Law*, and received her AB, magna cum laude, from Princeton University in 1999. She lives outside of Philadelphia with her husband and three daughters.

Senator Orrin Hatch has been a stalwart voice for freedom and limited government throughout his nearly four decades of public service. As the most senior Republican, he currently presides over the Senate as President Pro Tempore and serves as Chair of the Senate Finance Committee. From these leadership positions, he is advancing a policy agenda to create jobs and increase prosperity by reforming the tax code and opening up foreign markets to American exports. As a longtime member and former Chair of the Senate Judiciary Committee, Senator Hatch has also been instrumental in fighting judicial activism and reshaping the federal courts. He has long been on the front lines of legislative battles to protect the free-market economy, preserve individual liberties, and respect the separation of powers under our Constitution. Senator Hatch and his wife, Elaine, have been married for more than fifty years. Together, they are the proud parents of six children, twenty-three grandchildren, and sixteen great-grandchildren.

William J. Haun is an associate in the Washington, D.C., office of Hunton & Williams LLP, practicing complex litigation in federal court. He will serve as a law clerk to Judge Janice Rogers Brown of the U.S. Court of Appeals for the D.C. Circuit during the 2016–2017 court term. He previously clerked for Judge Claude M. Hilton of the U.S. District Court for the Eastern District of Virginia. While in law school, he was a published member of the *Catholic University Law Review*, an executive editor of the *Harvard Journal of Law and Public Policy*'s symposium issue, and a research and teaching assistant to Professor Mark Rienzi. His publications have appeared in a variety of outlets, including *National Affairs*, *Engage*, *National Review Online*, and *Public Discourse*. Mr. Haun's article on EPA regulation of greenhouse gas emissions is often cited, including in a report on Cooperative Federalism from the U.S. Senate Committee on the Environment and Public Works and by the State of West Virginia in challenging EPA's proposed rule. He also was the principal draftsman of an *amici curiae* brief representing current and former governors, Congressman, and other elected officials in support of former Virginia Governor Bob McDonnell's appeal to the U.S. Court of Appeals for the Fourth Circuit. While serving as a legal intern at the Heritage Foundation, Mr. Haun worked under former U.S. Attorney General Edwin Meese. Mr. Haun is also a former John Marshall Fellow of the Claremont Institute. He received his Juris Doctor from the Catholic University of America and his Bachelor of Arts from American University—both with honors.

Thomas M. Johnson, Jr. is Of Counsel in the Washington, D.C., office of Gibson, Dunn & Crutcher. He practices in the firm's Litigation Department and is a member of the Labor and Employment Law and the Appellate and Constitutional Law Practice Groups. Before joining the firm, he clerked for one year for the Honorable Jerry E. Smith on the Fifth Circuit Court of Appeals in Houston, Texas. He received his law degree in 2005 from Harvard Law School, where he was Deputy Editor-in-Chief of the Harvard Journal for Law and Public Policy. He received his BA in Government from Georgetown University in 2002.

The Honorable F. Scott Kieff became a Commissioner of the U.S. International Trade Commission on October 18, 2013, after having been nominated by President Obama and confirmed by the Senate. Before swearing in, Commissioner Kieff took a leave of absence from serving as Fred C. Stevenson Research Professor at the George Washington University Law School in Washington, D.C., and resigned from Stanford University's Hoover Institution, where he was the Ray & Louise Knowles Senior Fellow. He previously taught at Washington University in St. Louis, as a Professor in the School of Law with a secondary appointment in the School of Medicine's Department of Neurological Surgery. Commissioner Kieff practiced law as a trial lawyer and patent lawyer at law firms in New York and Chicago and served as law clerk to U.S. Circuit Judge Giles S. Rich. While an academic, he regularly served as a testifying and consulting expert, mediator, and arbitrator. He studied law at Penn and biology and economics at MIT. He was recognized as one of the nation's "Top 50 under 45" by the magazine *IP Law & Business* in 2008 and was inducted as a Member of the European Academy of Sciences and Arts in 2012.

William J. Kilberg is a Partner with Gibson, Dunn & Crutcher, where he is the most senior partner in the Labor and Employment Law

Practice Group. A White House Fellow and Special Assistant to Secretary of Labor George P. Shultz in 1969–1970, Mr. Kilberg was appointed by President Nixon and unanimously confirmed by the Senate as Solicitor for the U.S. Department of Labor, a position he held from 1973 until 1977. Mr. Kilberg has served as president of the College of Labor and Employment Lawyers and was a founder of the Palmer National Bank, now United Bank. He currently serves on the boards of the Potomac School in McLean, Virginia; Oreck Materials Corp.; and the Virginia Israel Advisory Board. He is a Fellow of the American Bar Foundation.

Peter N. Kirsanow is a partner in the labor and employment practice group of Benesch, Friedlander, Coplan & Aronoff and a member of the U.S. Commission on Civil Rights. He was a member of the National Labor Relations Board between 2006 and 2008. Mr. Kirsanow has testified several times before various subcommittees of Congress regarding disparate impact.

Adam P. Laxalt is the 33rd Attorney General of the State of Nevada and lives in Reno with his wife, Jamie, and their daughter. When he took office on January 5, 2015, he was the youngest Attorney General in the nation. A fourth-generation Nevadan, Adam served his country as a Judge Advocate General in the Navy, where he was trained as a prosecutor and legal advisor. For his service, Adam was awarded the Joint Service Commendation Medal and Iraq Campaign Medal. He has also served as a Special Assistant U.S. Attorney, as an Assistant Professor of Law in the Leadership, Ethics and Law Department of the Naval Academy, and as a Special Advisor to the Undersecretary of State for Arms Control and International Security, John R. Bolton. Prior to being elected Attorney General, Adam was in private practice in Las Vegas. He graduated *magna cum laude* from Georgetown University and received his law degree from the Georgetown University Law Center.

Elbert Lin is the Solicitor General of West Virginia. The state's chief appellate lawyer, he also oversees the issuance of Attorney General Opinions and manages all legal issues and litigation involving the federal government for the West Virginia Attorney General. He is counsel of record for West Virginia in several cases challenging actions by the U.S. Environmental Protection Agency. Before joining the Attorney General's Office, Lin was a partner at Wiley Rein LLP in Washington, D.C., focused on appellate matters. A graduate of Yale University and Yale Law School, Lin has also been a trial attorney with the U.S. Department of Justice, primarily defending challenges to federal agency action. He served as a law clerk to U.S. Supreme Court Justice Clarence Thomas, U.S. Court of Appeals Judge William H. Pryor, Jr., and Senior U.S. District Judge Robert E. Keeton. Lin has been recognized by the *State Journal* as one of West Virginia's 40 under 40, by MavPAC as part of their nationally selected "Future 40," and by the Asian Pacific American Bar Association of the Greater Washington, D.C., area as a "Rising Star." Having grown up outside Chicago, Lin now lives in Charleston, West Virginia, with his wife and two young sons.

Greg Lukianoff is an attorney and the president and CEO of the Foundation for Individual Rights in Education (FIRE). He is the author of *Unlearning Liberty: Campus Censorship and the End of American Debate* and *Freedom From Speech*. He has published articles in the *Wall Street Journal*, the *Washington Post*, the *New York Times*, the *Los Angeles Times*, *TIME*, the *Boston Globe*, *Forbes*, *Reason*, and numerous other publications. He is a regular columnist for the *Huffington Post* and frequently appears on TV shows and radio programs, including *CBS Evening News*, *The Today Show*, and NPR's *Radio Times*. He has also authored a chapter in Templeton Press's anthology *New Threats to Freedom*, edited by Adam Bellow, as well as a chapter in *The State of the American Mind*, edited by Mark Bauerlein and Adam Bellow. Greg has testified before both the U.S. Senate and the House of Representatives about free speech issues on America's campuses. He is a graduate of American University and of Stanford Law School, where he focused on First Amendment and constitutional law.

John G. Malcolm is the Director and Ed Gilbertson and Sherry Lindberg Gilbertson Senior Legal Fellow of the Heritage Foundation's Edwin Meese III Center for Legal and Judicial Studies. An honors graduate from Columbia College and Harvard Law School, Malcolm clerked for federal judges in the Northern District of Georgia and on the Eleventh Circuit Court of Appeals. From 1990 to 1997, Malcolm served as an Assistant United States Attorney in Atlanta, Georgia, and an Associate Independent Counsel in Washington, D.C., where he investigated fraud and abuse at the Department of Housing and Urban Development. From

2001 to 2004, Malcolm served as a Deputy Assistant Attorney General in the Criminal Division at DOJ. While at the Justice Department, Malcolm received numerous awards including the Director's Award for Superior Performance by an Assistant United States Attorney. Between 1997 and 2001, Malcolm was a partner at his own firm, and from 2004 through 2009, Malcolm served as an Executive Vice President and Director of Worldwide Anti-Piracy Operations for the Motion Picture Association of America. In 2010, Malcolm served as a Distinguished Practitioner in Residence at Pepperdine Law School. From 2010 to 2012, Malcolm was the General Counsel at the U.S. Commission on International Religious Freedom.

David McIntosh is a leader for the principles of limited constitutional government and individual freedom. He is the President of the Club for Growth, the leading advocate for economic liberty. Former Congressman David McIntosh represented Indiana's Second Congressional District in the United States Congress from 1995 to 2000. As a freshman, David chaired the Subcommittee on Regulatory Relief. He passed the Congressional Review Act and held extensive oversight and field hearings to build a record of public support for regulatory relief initiatives in energy, biotechnology, pharmaceutical, health care, transportation, and technology sectors. Another issue that he championed was the elimination of the marriage penalty in the Federal Tax Code. David served during the Reagan administration as special assistant to Attorney General Edwin Meese III and as special assistant to President Reagan for Domestic Affairs. During the first Bush administration, he served as executive director of the President's Council on Competitiveness and assistant to the Vice President. The Competitiveness Counsel coordinated the cost-benefit review of major regulations and promoted legal reform measures. David is a co-founder of the Federalist Society for Law and Public Policy and serves on the Board of Directors. He remains active with several free-market and conservative think tanks and grassroots organizations. David has also had stints at the Hudson Institute and as a Professor of Economics at Ball State School of Business. Prior to the Club for Growth, David was a partner at Mayer Brown, LLP, in Washington, D.C. David graduated from the University of Chicago Law School in 1983 and with his BA, cum laude, from Yale University in

1980. He and his wife, Ruthie, are the proud parents of Ellie (age 17) and Davey (age 13).

Cleta Mitchell is a partner practicing political law in the Washington, D.C., office of Foley & Lardner LLP. Ms. Mitchell represents individuals, corporations, grassroots organizations, candidates, political party committees, elected officials, and others involved in political, policy, and advocacy activities. Through her representation of numerous conservative and Tea Party groups whose applications for exempt status were ensnared in the IRS targeting scandal, Ms. Mitchell learned firsthand how the IRS punishes and otherwise targets taxpayers for exercising their First Amendment rights. Ms. Mitchell graduated with High Honors from the University of Oklahoma and the University of Oklahoma College of Law. She is a former Oklahoma state legislator who served as a Fellow at the Institute of Politics at Harvard in 1981 and as the Shapiro Fellow at the School of Media and Public Affairs at George Washington University in 2001. Ms. Mitchell is Peer Review Rated as AV Preeminent by Martindale-Hubbell, is recognized in *The Best Lawyers in America* and the *Washington, D.C. Super Lawyers*, and was named a "Top Lawyer" in Washington, D.C., by the *Washingtonian* for political and campaign law. She is recognized nationally in *Chambers USA: America's Leading Business Lawyers* (2010–2015). In 2012, *National Journal* named her one of Washington's 25 Most Influential Women. She serves on the Board of Directors of the Lynde & Harry Bradley Foundation and is a former board member of the National Rifle Association and the American Conservative Union.

Patrick Morrisey was elected the Attorney General for the State of West Virginia in November 2012 and is the first Republican to serve as Attorney General in West Virginia since 1933. Since becoming Attorney General, Morrisey has made fighting fraud, waste, abuse, and corruption a top priority of the office. In addition, the Office of the Attorney General has worked to fight federal overreach, filing several lawsuits against the Environmental Protection Agency and other federal agencies, as well as *amicus* briefs before the U.S. Supreme Court on a number of issues, ranging from protecting the Second Amendment to defending state jobs and West Virginia's valuable energy resources. In practice since 1992, Morrisey worked on many high-profile health care matters prior to serving as Attorney General. Between 1999 and 2004, Morrisey served as the Deputy Staff Director and Chief Health Care Counsel to the U.S. House of Representatives Energy and Commerce Committee, helping draft and negotiate major legislation, including the Medicare Modernization Act of 2003 and the Bioterrorism and Public Health Preparedness Act of 2002. Morrisey graduated with honors from Rutgers College in 1989 and received a Juris Doctor from Rutgers Law School–Newark in 1992. A product of a working-class family, Morrisey is married and has a 16-year-old stepdaughter.

Michael B. Mukasey served as the 81st Attorney General of the United States, the nation's chief law enforcement officer, from November 2007 to January 2009. During that time, he oversaw the U.S. Department of Justice and advised on critical issues of domestic and international law. From 1988 to 2006, he served as a district judge in the United States District Court for the Southern District of New York, becoming chief judge in 2000. Judge Mukasey joined Debevoise & Plimpton LLP as a partner in the litigation practice in New York in February 2009, focusing his practice primarily on internal investigations, independent board reviews, and corporate governance.

Maureen K. Ohlhausen was sworn in as a Commissioner of the Federal Trade Commission on April 4, 2012. Prior to joining the Commission, Ohlhausen was a partner at Wilkinson Barker Knauer, LLP, where she focused on FTC issues, including competition law, privacy, and technology policy. Ohlhausen previously served at the Commission for over a decade, most recently as Director of the Office of Policy Planning, where she led the FTC's Internet Access Task Force. She was also an attorney advisor for former FTC Commissioner Orson Swindle, advising him on competition and consumer protection matters, and worked in the FTC General Counsel's Office. Before coming to the FTC, Ohlhausen spent five years at the U.S. Court of Appeals for the D.C. Circuit, serving as a law clerk for Judge David B. Sentelle and as a staff attorney. Ohlhausen graduated with distinction from George Mason University School of Law and with honors from the University of Virginia. Ohlhausen was on the adjunct faculty at George Mason University School of Law, where she taught privacy law and unfair trade practices. She served as a Senior Editor of the *Antitrust Law Journal* and a member of the American Bar Association Task Force on Competition and Public Policy. She has authored a variety of articles on competition law, privacy, and technology matters.

Troy A. Paredes was a Commissioner of the U.S. Securities and Exchange Commission from 2008 until 2013, having been appointed by President George W. Bush. At the SEC, Paredes was a strong advocate for small business, sensible disclosures that avoid the problem of information overload, data-based regulatory decision-making, and rigorous cost-benefit analysis. He also consistently expressed concerns about the overregulation and overreach of the Dodd-Frank Act. Since leaving government, Paredes has had an active consulting practice, advising companies on financial regulation, corporate governance, compliance, and public policy. Before becoming an SEC Commissioner, Paredes was a professor of law at Washington University in St. Louis and a professor of business (by courtesy) at Washington University's Olin Business School. Currently, he is the Distinguished Policy Fellow and Lecturer at the University of Pennsylvania Law School and a Lecturer on Law at Harvard Law School. Paredes is the author of numerous academic articles on financial regulation, corporate governance, innovation, and behavioral economics. He also is a coauthor (beginning with the fourth edition) of a multi-volume securities regulation treatise with Louis Loss and Joel Seligman entitled *Securities Regulation*. Paredes holds a bachelor's degree in economics from UC Berkeley and earned his JD from Yale Law School.

E. Scott Pruitt was elected Attorney General of Oklahoma in November 2010 and was reelected without opposition in 2014. He is recognized as a national leader in the effort to challenge federal overreach and unlawful executive action by the Obama administration. General Pruitt created Oklahoma's first "Federalism Unit" to help in the fight to restore the balance of power between the states and federal government. Before being elected Attorney General, Pruitt served eight years in the Oklahoma State Senate, where he was a leading voice for fiscal responsibility, religious freedom, and workers' compensation reforms. Pruitt and his wife, Marlyn, have been married for twenty-five years and have two children, McKenna and Cade.

Dean Reuter is Vice President and Director of Practice Groups at the Federalist Society for Law and Public Policy, where he has been employed since 2001. He also serves as a member of the board of directors of the federal Corporation for National and Community Services (CNCS). He served as Deputy Inspector General and Counsel to the Inspector General at CNCS from 1998 to 2000, immediately prior to which he was the Student Division Director of the Federalist Society. He is the co-editor of *Confronting Terror: 9/11 and the Future of American National Security* (Encounter Books). He served in the Legal Services Corporation from 1984 to 1991, conducting compliance oversight of federal grants. Mr. Reuter is graduated from Hood College and the University of Maryland School of Law, after completing his studies at Northwestern University School of Law. The views expressed in his contribution to the book are his own and do not necessarily reflect the views of the Federalist Society.

John Shu is an attorney in Newport Beach, California. He served both President George H.W. Bush and President George W. Bush and clerked for Judge Paul Roney, U.S. Court of Appeals for the 11th Circuit and Presiding Judge, U.S. Foreign Intelligence Surveillance Court of Review.

Lawrence VanDyke is the Solicitor General in the Office of the Nevada Attorney General. Prior to serving in that capacity, he was the Montana Solicitor General. Before that, Lawrence practiced law in the Appellate and Constitutional Law Practice Group of Gibson, Dunn & Crutcher LLP in its Washington, D.C., and Dallas, Texas, offices. He also clerked for Judge Janice Rogers Brown of the United States Court of Appeals for the District of Columbia Circuit. Lawrence graduated magna cum laude from Harvard Law School, where he also served as an editor of the *Harvard Law Review*. Before law school, he graduated with degrees in civil engineering and engineering management from Montana State University and worked for years in a family heavy civil construction business. Lawrence has been married to Cheryl VanDyke for over twenty years, and they have three children.

Hans A. von Spakovsky is a Senior Legal Fellow and Manager of the Election Law Reform Initiative in the Edwin Meese III Center for Legal and Judicial Studies at the Heritage Foundation. From 2006 to 2007, von Spakovsky was a member of the Federal Election Commission. He served as Counsel to the Assistant Attorney General for Civil Rights at the U.S. Department of Justice from 2002 to 2005. Prior to entering public service, von Spakovsky worked for seventeen years as a government affairs consultant, in a corporate legal department, and in private practice. He is a 1984 graduate of the Vanderbilt University School of Law and received a BS from the Massachusetts Institute of Technology in 1981. He is a member of the Policy Board of the American Civil Rights Union and the Public Interest Legal Foundation. Von Spakovsky is the coauthor of *Who's Counting? How Fraudsters and Bureaucrats Put Your Vote at Risk* (Encounter Books, 2012) and *Obama's Enforcer: Eric Holder's Justice Department* (HarperCollins/Broadside, 2014).

Peter J. Wallison holds the Arthur F. Burns chair in Financial Market Studies at the American Enterprise Institute (AEI) and is co-director of AEI's program on financial policy studies. Before joining AEI in 1999, he was a partner of Gibson, Dunn & Crutcher LLP, where he practiced banking, corporate, and financial law in the firm's Washington, D.C., and New York offices. He was general counsel of the Treasury Department from 1981 to 1985 and White House counsel for President Reagan from 1986 to 1987. From 1972 to 1976, he was counsel to Vice President Nelson Rockefeller. He is the author or coauthor of several books, including *Ronald Reagan: The Power of Conviction and the Success of His Presidency* and *Bad History, Worse Policy: How a False Narrative about the Financial Crisis Led to the Dodd-Frank Act*. His most recent book is *Hidden in Plain Sight: What Caused the World's Worst Financial Crisis and Why It Could Happen Again* (Encounter Books, 2015). He holds an honorary doctorate from the University of Colorado.

Joshua D. Wright was sworn in as a Commissioner of the Federal Trade Commission on January 11, 2013, to a term that expires in September 2019. Prior to joining the Commission, Wright was a professor at George Mason University School of Law and held a courtesy appointment in the Department of Economics. Wright is a leading scholar in antitrust law, economics, and consumer protection and has published more than sixty articles and book chapters, coauthored a leading casebook, and edited several book volumes focusing on these issues. Wright also served as co-editor of the *Supreme Court Economic Review* and a senior editor of the *Antitrust Law Journal*. Wright previously served the Commission in the Bureau of Competition as its inaugural Scholar-in-Residence from 2007 to 2008, where he focused on enforcement matters and competition policy. Wright's return to the Commission marks his fourth stint at the agency, after having served as an intern in both the Bureau of Economics and the Bureau of Competition in 1997 and 1998, respectively. Wright received his JD from UCLA in 2002 and his PhD in economics from UCLA in 2003, and graduated with honors from the University of California, San Diego, in 1998. He is a member of the California Bar.

John Yoo is the Emanuel Heller Professor of Law at the University of California at Berkeley and a Visiting Scholar at the American Enterprise Institute. His latest book, *Point of Attack: Preventive War, International Law, and Global Welfare* (Oxford University Press, 2014), presents a new understanding of the grounds of war to address today's security challenges. His other books address presidential power, national security, and international affairs: *Taming Globalization* (2012), *Confronting Terror* (2011), *Crisis and Command* (2010), *War by Other Means* (2006), and *The Powers of War and Peace* (2005). Professor Yoo has published numerous articles in the United States' leading law journals. He also regularly contributes to the editorial pages of the *Wall Street Journal*, *New York Times*, *Washington Post*, *Los Angeles Times*, *National Review*, and the *Weekly Standard*, among others. He has also been a columnist for his hometown newspaper, the *Philadelphia Inquirer*. Professor Yoo has served in all three branches of government. He was an official in the Office of Legal Counsel of the U.S. Department of Justice, where he worked on national security and terrorism issues after the September 11 attacks. He served as general counsel of the Senate Judiciary Committee under Chair Orrin Hatch of Utah. He has been a law clerk for Justice Clarence Thomas of the U.S. Supreme Court and Judge Laurence Silberman of the U.S. Court of Appeals in Washington, D.C. He has been a visiting professor at Seoul National University, the University of Trento, University of Chicago, and the Free University of Amsterdam. Professor Yoo graduated from Yale Law School, where he was an articles editor of the *Yale Law Journal*, and summa cum laude from Harvard College with a degree in American history.

ACKNOWLEDGMENTS

The editors wish to acknowledge, with much gratitude, the many contributors to this volume. We are both humbled by their enthusiastic participation in our venture. Their time and work helped transform the project from an idea into a book that we hope will make a lasting contribution to the study of the expanding powers of the federal government.

Our thanks also go to our scrupulous and diligent research assistants: Laurence Browning VanMeter, Anthony Rodregous, Josh Hammer, Nathan Curtisi, Nick Medling, and James Kilcup. We most especially thank Jordan Moliver, Daniel Chen, Gabriela Gonzalez-Araiza, and R. Sohan Dasgupta, who were diligent and thorough and worked with an alacrity that allowed us to move ever forward.

Roger Kimball and Katherine Wong of Encounter Books were tremendous in guiding our work and editing our manuscript. Our agent, Lynn Chu, as always, proved to be an editor and agent extraordinaire.

John Yoo would like to thank his wife, Elsa Arnett. Her love promotes his work, feeds his creativity, and sustains his life. He also thanks Dean Sujit Choudry of the Law School of the University of California, Berkeley, and Arthur Brooks of the American Enterprise Institute for providing congenial institutional homes.

Dean Reuter thanks his wife, Lou Anne, and his children, Taylor and Hannah, for their unwavering support, and his father, Roy Reuter, for his support and comments on early drafts.

NOTES

INTRODUCTION

1. See John W. Dawson & John Seater, "Federal Regulation and Aggregate Economic Growth," *J. Econ. Growth* 18 (2013): 137.

2. See ibid.

3. Ronald Bailey, "Federal Regulations Have Made You 75 Percent Poorer," *Reason* (June 21, 2013), http://reason.com/archives/2013/06/21/federal-regulations-have-made-you-75-per (on file with the editors).

4. See, e.g., Mark Tushnet, "Epstein's Best of All Possible Worlds: The Rule of Law," *U. Chi. L. Rev.* 80 (2013): 487; Thomas O. Sargentich, "Justice Stephen Breyer's Contribution to Administrative Law: Introduction," *Admin. L.J. Am. U.* 8 (1995): 713; Susan Rose-Ackerman, "Progressive Law and Economics—And the New Administrative Law," *Yale L.J.* 98 (1988): 341.

5. This is to paraphrase the title of a law review article. See Henry P. Monaghan, "Our Perfect Constitution," *N.Y.U. L. Rev.* 56 (1981): 353.

6. Ronald Reagan, U.S. President, "Farewell Speech After Two Terms of Office" (1988), http://www.pbs.org/wgbh/americanexperience/features/primary-resources/reagan-farewell/ (last visited Aug. 12, 2015) ("There's a clear cause and effect here that is as neat and predictable as a law of physics: As government expands, liberty contracts").

7. See Joseph Postell, Robert E. Moffit & Todd F. Gaziano, "How to Limit Government in the Age of Obama," Heritage Foundation, Lecture no. 1231 on Political Thought, June 25, 2013, http://www.heritage.org/research/reports/2013/06/how-to-limit-government-in-the-age-of-obama.

8. See generally George W. Carey, "The Separation of Powers in United States of America: Past and Present," *Historia Constitucional* 10 (2009): 263–295, http://www.historiaconstitucional.com/index.php/historiaconstitucional/article/viewFile/233/206.

9. Ibid., 272.

10. Letter from Thomas Jefferson to William C. Nicholas, Monticello, Sept. 7, 1803.

11. "Popular Names of Sections and Clauses," U.S. Constitution Online, http://www.usconstitution.net/constpop.html (last visited Aug. 12, 2015).

12. "U.S. Constitution – Article 1 Section 1," U.S. Constitution Online, http://www.usconstitution.net/xconst_A1Sec1.html (last visited Aug. 12, 2015) ("All legislative Powers herein granted shall be vested in a Congress of the United States").

13. "U.S. Constitution – Article 2 Section 1," U.S. Constitution Online, http://www.usconstitution.net/xconst_A2Sec1.html (last visited Aug. 12, 2015) ("The executive Power shall be vested in a President of the United States of America").

14. "U.S. Constitution – Article 3 Section 1," U.S. Constitution Online, http://www.usconstitution.net/xconst_A3Sec1.html (last visited Aug. 12, 2015) ("The judicial Power of the United States, shall be vested in one supreme Court, and in such inferior Courts").

15. Richard Primus, "The Limits of Enumeration," *Yale L.J.* 124 (2014): 576 (discussing the limiting dimension of enumerated powers).

16. James R. Rogers, "An Informational Rationale for Congruent Bicameralism," *J. Theor. Polit.* 13 (2001): 123 (elucidating the benefits of a bicameral legislature).

17. David W. Rohde & Dennis M. Simon, "Presidential Vetoes and Congressional Response: A Study of Institutional Conflict," *Am. J. Political Sci.* 29 (1985): 397 (outlining the veto and override process).

18. "How the Federal Courts Are Organized," Federal Judicial Center, http://www.fjc.gov/federal/courts.nsf/autoframe!openform&nav=menu1&page=/federal/courts.nsf/page/183 (last visited Aug. 12, 2015) (outlining the process of appointment and confirmation).

19. "How Cases Move Through Federal Courts," Federal Judicial Center, http://www.fjc.gov/federal/courts.nsf/autoframe!openform&nav=menu1&page=/federal/courts.nsf/page/287 (last visited Aug. 12, 2015) (outlining the process of judicial review; outlining life tenure, "good behavior" requirements, and congressional impeachment procedures).

20. Kate Stith, "Congress' Power of the Purse," *Yale L.J.* 97 (1987): 1343 (outlining the congressional "power of the purse" and its limiting effect on executive power).

21. Edwin Brown Firmage, R. Collin Mangrum & William Penn, "Removal of the President: Resignation and the Procedural Law of Impeachment," *Duke L.J.* 1974 (1975): 1023 (outlining impeachment procedures).

22. U.S. Const. amend. X; see generally Laird v. Tatum, 408 U.S. 1, 17 (1972); Kate Stith, "Congress' Power of the Purse," *Yale L.J.* 97 (1988): 1343.

23. Akhil Reed Amar, "Of Sovereignty and Federalism," *Yale L.J.* 96 (1987): 1425 (describing the federalism model).

24. Douglas G. Smith, "An Analysis of Two Federal Structures: The Articles of Confederation and the Constitution," *San Diego L. Rev.* 34 (1997): 249 (discussing how the constitutional grant of federal power created weaker authorizations then originally intended by the Articles of Confederation).

25. U.S. Const. art. I, § 8; U.S. Const. amend. XVI.

26. U.S. Const. amend. XVII.

27. Adrian Vermeule, "The Administrative State: Law, Democracy, and Knowledge," Harvard Public Law Working Paper No. 13-28, in *Oxford Handbook of the United States Constitution* (Oxford: Oxford UP, 2013).

28. See Edward Cline, "The Annotated Woodrow Wilson," *Capitalism Magazine* (Nov. 10, 2014), http://capitalismmagazine.com/2014/11/annotated-woodrow-wilson/; see also Ronald J. Pestritto, "Summary from Lecture on Woodrow Wilson and the Rejection of the Founders' Constitution" (2012), https://online.hillsdale.edu/document.doc?id=318.

29. Woodrow Wilson, *The State* (1889), 651.

30. D. Roderick Kiewiet & Mathew D. McCubbins, *The Logic of Delegation* (Chicago: University of Chicago Press, 1991).

31. Hon. Douglas Ginsburg, "Legislative Powers: Not Yours to Give Away, Report No. 2," Heritage Foundation (Jan. 6, 2011), http://www.heritage.org/research/reports/2011/01/legislative-powers-not-yours-to-give-away.

32. David Schoenbrod, *Power Without Responsibility: How Congress Abuses the People through Delegation* (New Haven, CT: Yale UP, 2008).

33. Walter J. Oleszek, "Congressional Oversight: An Overview," CRS (Feb. 22, 2010), http://fas.org/sgp/crs/misc/R41079.pdf.

34. Administrative Procedure Act, 5 U.S.C. §§ 551–559 [hereinafter APA].

35. See, e.g., Connor Raso, "Agency Avoidance of Rulemaking Procedures," *Admin. L. Rev.* 67, no. 1 (2015) (discussing agencies' systematic attempt to circumvent APA protocols such as notice and comment processes). Also, for example, under a phenomenon known as "sue-and-settle," agencies avoid formal rulemaking requirements and actually enlarge their powers by settling cases brought by regulation-friendly plaintiffs. Agencies also avoid formal rulemaking when they adopt "non-binding" guidance, letters, or policy statements less formal than regulations. However, the regulated community contravenes this non-binding guidance at its peril.

36. See, e.g., David Zaring, "The Dubious Campaigns to Fight Overregulation," *N.Y. Times* (June 3, 2014, 12:20 pm), http://dealbook.nytimes.com/2014/06/03/the-dubious-campaigns-to-fight-overregulation/?_r=0 (on file with the editors).

37. J.W. Hampton, Jr., & Co. v. United States, 276 U.S. 394, 404 (1928).

38. Chevron U.S.A. Inc. v. Natural Resources Defense Council, Inc., 467 U.S. 837 (1984) (stating that unless the agency's rule is unambiguously inconsistent with the statute, it will be upheld).

39. Auer v. Robbins, 519 U.S. 452 (1997) (stating that the agency must be deferred to when it is interpreting the scope of its own rules).

40. City of Arlington, Tex. v. FCC, 133 S. Ct. 1863 (2013) (stating that courts must defer to an agency's interpretation of a statutory ambiguity that relates to the scope of the agency's own regulatory powers unless the agency's construction is unambiguously wrong). The practical problem with *City of Arlington* is that it will pit the bureaucracy against itself, encouraging even more toxic inter-agency fights.

41. See U.S. Const. amend. V; Federal Rules of Evidence (FRE) (setting forth eleven articles governing the different evidentiary rules).

42. Thomas W. Merrill, "Article III, Agency Adjudication, and the Origins of the Appellate Review Model of Administrative Law," *Columbia L. Rev.* 111 (2011): 939.

43. For one such particularly personal narration of a regulated citizen's tribulations while being chased by a federal agency, see Michael J. Daugherty, *The Devil Inside the Beltway: The Shocking Exposé of the US Government's Surveillance and Overreach into Cybersecurity, Medicine and Small Business* (Broadland Press, 2013) (describing a small-business owner's "five-year journey of government power grabs and intimidation tactics").

44. Joan Solanes Mullor, "Why Independent Agencies Deserve Chevron Deference," InDret (Oct. 2010).

45. Edward Lazarus, "Life Tenure for Federal Judges: Should It Be Abolished?" CNN (Dec. 10, 2004, 4:08 pm), http://www.cnn.com/2004/LAW/12/10/lazarus.federal.judges/.

46. Richard B. Stewart, "Administrative Law in the Twenty-First Century," *N.Y.U. L. Rev.* 78 (2003): 437.

47. Lily Kahng, "The IRS Tea Party Controversy and Administrative Discretion," *Cornell L. Rev.* 99 (2013): 41.

48. See, e.g., Anne Flaherty, "GOP: Obama Aides Influenced 'Net Neutrality,'" *Salt Lake Trib.* (Mar. 17, 2015, 5:12 pm), http://www.sltrib.com/home/2303804-155/gop-obama-aides-influenced-net-neutrality (on file with the author); Brian Fung, "Read the E-mails that Republicans Say Show Obama Meddled in Net Neutrality," *Wash. Post* (Mar. 17, 2015), https://www.washingtonpost.com/blogs/the-switch/wp/2015/03/17/read-the-e-mails-that-republicans-say-show-obama-meddled-in-net-neutrality/ (on file with the author).

49. See, e.g., Gautham Nagesh & Brody Mullins, "Blindsided: How White House Thwarted FCC Chief on Net Rules," *Wall St. J.* (Feb. 5, 2015), http://www.wsj.com/articles/how-white-house-thwarted-fcc-chief-on-internet-rules-1423097522 (on file with the author).

CHAPTER 1

1. See 26 U.S.C. § 4980H(a)–(c).

2. Ibid.

3. See, e.g., Jed Graham, "ObamaCare Employer Mandate: A List of Cuts to Work Hours, Jobs," *Investor's Business Daily* (Sept. 5, 2014), http://news.investors.com/politics-obamacare/090514-669013-obamacare-employer-mandate-a-list-of-cuts-to-work-hours-jobs.htm; Ben Casselman, "Yes, Some Companies Are Cutting Hours in Response to 'Obamacare,'" *Five-Thirty-Eight* (Jan. 13, 2015), http://fivethirtyeight.com/features/yes-some-companies-are-cutting-hours-in-response-to-obamacare/.

4. See Patient Protection and Affordable Care Act, Pub. L. No. 111-148, § 1513(d), 124 Stat. 119 (2010) ("The amendments made by this section shall apply to months beginning after December 31, 2013.").

5. See Mark Mazur, "Continuing to Implement the ACA in a Careful, Thoughtful Manner," *Treasury Notes*, U.S. Department of the Treasury (July 2,

2013), http://www.treasury.gov/connect/blog/Pages/Continuing-to-Implement-the-ACA-in-a-Careful-Thoughtful-Manner-.aspx.

6. Ibid.

7. See Internal Revenue Service, Transition Relief for 2014 Under §§ 6055 (§ 6055 Information Reporting), 6056 (§ 6056 Information Reporting) and 4980H (Employer Shared Responsibility Provisions), NOT-129718-13 (July 9, 2013), http://www.irs.gov/pub/irs-drop/n-13-45.pdf.

8. See Shared Responsibility for Employers Regarding Health Coverage, 79 Fed. Reg. 8544, 8574 (Feb. 12, 2014).

9. Juliet Eilperin & Amy Goldstein, "White House Delays Health Insurance Mandate for Medium-Size Employers until 2016," *Wash. Post* (Feb. 10, 2014), http://www.washingtonpost.com/national/health-science/white-house-delays-health-insurance-mandate-for-medium-sized-employers-until-2016/2014/02/10/ade6b344-9279-11e3-84e1-27626c5ef5fb_story.html.

10. Ron Fournier, "Why I'm Sick of Defending Obamacare," *Nat'l J.* (Feb. 11, 2014), http://www.nationaljournal.com/white-house/why-i-m-getting-sick-of-defending-obamacare-20140211.

11. See 26 U.S.C. § 4980H(c)(5).

12. See Patient Protection and Affordable Care Act, Pub. L. No. 111-148, § 1401(e), 124 Stat. 119 (2010) ("The amendments made by this section shall apply to taxable years ending after December 31, 2013.").

13. See Sarah Kliff & Sandhya Somashekhar, "Health Insurance Marketplaces Will Not Be Required to Verify Consumer Claims," *Wash. Post* (July 5, 2013), http://www.washingtonpost.com/national/health-science/health-insurance-marketplaces-will-not-be-required-to-verify-consumer-claims/2013/07/05/d2a171f4-e5ab-11e2-aef3-339619eab080_story.html.

14. See Ezra Klein, "CBO Gives Us the Key to Health-Care Reform: The Employer Mandate," *Wash. Post* (July 2, 2009), http://voices.washingtonpost.com/ezra-klein/2009/07/cbo_gives_us_the_key_to_health.html.

15. See Letter from Mark Mazur, Assistant Secretary of the Treasury for Tax Policy, to Rep. Fred Upton, Chairman of the Committee on Energy and Commerce, U.S. House of Representatives (July 9, 2013), http://democrats.energycommerce.house.gov/sites/default/files/documents/Upton-Treasury-ACA-2013-7-9.pdf.

16. See Nicholas Bagley, "The Legality of Delaying Key Elements of the ACA," *New Engl. J. Med.* 370 (2014): 1967.

17. Ibid., 1968; Heckler v. Chaney, 470 U.S. 821 (1985).

18. Bagley, "Legality of Delaying," 1969.

19. Ibid.

20. See Joel Gehrke, "Treasury Didn't Check for Legal Authority Before Delaying Obamacare Mandate," *Wash. Exam.* (Mar. 20, 2014), http://washingtonexaminer.com /treasury-didnt-check-for-legal-authority-before-delaying-obamacare-mandate /article/2545995.

21. According to Politifact, the President made this statement over three dozen times. See "Obama: If You Like Your Health Care Plan, You'll Be Able to Keep Your Health Care Plan," Politifact.com, http://www.politifact.com /obama-like-health-care-keep/.

22. See 45 C.F.R. § 147.140(g).

23. The Department of Health and Human Services, for instance, predicted in June 2010, that between 40 and 67 percent of individual market policies would lose grandfather status in any given year. See 75 Fed. Reg. 34538, 34553 (June 17, 2010).

24. See Colleen McCain Nelson, Peter Nicholas & Carol E. Lee, "Aides Debated Obama Health-Care Coverage Promise," *Wall St. J.* (Nov. 2, 2013).

25. See "Statement by the President on the Affordable Care Act" (Nov. 14, 2013), http://www.whitehouse.gov/the-press-office/2013/11/14/statement -president-affordable-care-act.

26. See Letter from Gary Cohen, Director, Ctr. for Consumer Info. & Ins. Oversight, Dept. of Health & Human Servs. (Nov. 14, 2013), http://www .cms.gov/CCIIO/Resources/Letters/Downloads/commissioner-letter-11-14-2013 .pdf.

27. See 42 U.S.C. § 300gg–6.

28. See 26 U.S.C. § 5000A.

29. See Bagley, "Legality of Delaying," 1967.

30. Ibid.

31. See 42 U.S.C. 18011(a).

32. See 45 C.F.R. § 147.140(g).

33. For an extensive treatment of this issue, see Jonathan H. Adler & Michael F. Cannon, "Taxation without Representation: The Illegal IRS Rule to Expand Tax Credits under the PPACA," *Health Matrix* 23 (2013): 119.

34. See 42 U.S.C. § 18031(b)(I).

35. See 42 U.S.C. § 18041(c)(I).

36. See 26 U.S.C. § 36B(c)(2)(A)(i).

37. See 42 U.S.C. § 18041(c)(I).

38. See Robert Pear, "U.S. Officials Brace for Huge Task of Operating Health Exchanges," *N.Y. Times* (Aug. 5, 2012) ("When Congress passed legislation to expand coverage two years ago, Mr. Obama and lawmakers assumed that every state would set up its own exchange.").

39. Barack Obama, U.S. President, Remarks on Health Insurance Reform in Portland, Maine (Apr. 1, 2010), http://www.whitehouse.gov/the-press-office/remarks-president-health-insurance-reform-portland-maine.

40. Department of the Treasury, Internal Revenue Service, Health Insurance Premium Tax Credit, 77 Fed. Reg. 30377 (May 23, 2012), http://www.gpo.gov/fdsys/pkg/FR-2012-05-23/pdf/2012-12421.pdf.

41. Ibid., 30378.

42. See Lisa Rein, "Six Words Might Decide the Fate of Obamacare at the Supreme Court," *Wash. Post* (Mar. 1, 2015), http://www.washingtonpost.com/politics/why-six-words-might-hold-the-fate-of-obamacare-before-the-supreme-court/2015/03/01/437c2836-bd39-11e4-b274-e5209a3bc9a9_story.html.

43. See Letter from Mark J. Mazur, Assistant Secretary for Tax Policy, U.S. Treasury Department, to the Honorable Darrell Issa, Chairman, Committee on Oversight and Government Reform, U.S. House of Representatives (Oct. 12, 2012) (on file with author).

44. Ibid. (citing 42 U.S.C. § 18041(c)(1)) (emphasis added).

45. See 42 U.S.C. § 18024(d).

46. See Adler & Cannon, "Taxation without Representation."

47. See King v. Burwell, 576 U.S. ___ (No. 14-114, June 25, 2015).

48. Ibid. Slip op. at 21.

49. Ibid. Slip op. at 10, 12.

50. Ibid. Slip op. at 3, 21.

51. See, e.g., Andy S. Grewal, "Lurking Challenges to the ACA Tax Credit Regulations," *Bloomberg BNA Tax Insights* 98 DTR J-1 (May 2015), http://tinyurl.com/grewalACA.

52. See Ashley Parker, "House G.O.P. Files Lawsuit in Battling Health Law," *N.Y. Times* (Nov. 21, 2014), http://www.nytimes.com/2014/11/22/us/politics/obamacare-lawsuit-filed-by-republicans.html; Ron Johnson, "I'm Suing Over ObamaCare Exemptions for Congress," *Wall St. J.* (Jan. 5, 2014), http://

online.wsj.com/news/articles/SB10001424052702304325004579296140856419808.

53. For a list of administrative and legislative revisions to the PPACA, see Tyler Hartsfield and Grace-Marie Turner, "47 Changes to ObamaCare . . . So Far," Galen Institute (Jan. 7, 2015), http://www.galen.org/newsletters/changes-to-obamacare-so-far/.

54. "Pelosi: People Won't Appreciate Reform Until It Passes," *Politico* (Mar. 9, 2010), http://www.politico.com/livepulse/0310/Pelosi_People_wont_appreciate_reform_until_it_passes.html.

CHAPTER 2

1. Brady Handgun Violence Prevention Act, Pub. L. No. 103-159, 107 Stat. 1536 (1993).

2. The Public Safety and Recreational Firearms Use Protection Act, commonly referred to also as the "Clinton Assault Weapons Ban," was part of the Violent Crime Control and Law Enforcement Act of 1994. See Violent Crime Control and Law Enforcement Act of 1994, Pub. L. No. 103-322, § 110101, 108 Stat. 1796, 1996 (1994). It expired Sept. 13, 2004; § 110105, 108 Stat. at 2000.

3. White House, Office of Press Secretary, "Clinton Administration Reaches Historic Agreement with Smith and Wesson," Press Release (Mar. 17, 2000), http://clinton4.nara.gov/WH/New/html/20000317_2.html.

4. Allen Rostron, "Lawyers, Guns, & Money: The Rise and Fall of Tort Litigation Against the Firearms Industry," *Santa Clara L. Rev.* 46 (2006): 481, 497 (reviewing *Suing the Gun Industry: A Battle at the Crossroads of Gun Control and Mass Torts*, Timothy D. Lytton, ed. (University of Michigan Press, 2005)).

5. James Bennet, "True to Form, Clinton Shifts Energies Back to U.S. Focus," *N.Y. Times* (July 5, 1998), http://www.nytimes.com/1998/07/05/us/true-to-form-clinton-shifts-energies-back-to-us-focus.html.

6. U.S. Const. amend. II ("A well regulated Militia, being necessary to the security of a free State, the right of the people to keep and bear Arms, shall not be infringed.").

7. See McDonald v. Chicago, 561 U.S. 742, 791 (2010); District of Columbia v. Heller, 554 U.S. 570, 595 (2008).

8. Notwithstanding this agenda, President Obama, like his predecessors, regularly pays lip service to support for the Second Amendment, just as

every president states unequivocally that they would never, ever do anything while in office that would be "unconstitutional." For example, during a debate with Mitt Romney in 2012, Obama, when asked about steps his administration had taken or would take towards strengthening gun control, emphasized the strength of his "belief in the Second Amendment," just before launching into a discussion of why we need more gun control in America. "Transcript of Second Presidential Debate," *Fox News* (Oct. 16, 2012), http://www.foxnews.com/politics/2012/10/16/transcript-second-presidential-debate/.

9. See, e.g., James Barron, "Nation Reels After Gunman Massacres 20 Children at School in Connecticut," *N.Y. Times* (Dec. 14, 2012), http://www.nytimes.com/2012/12/15/nyregion/shooting-reported-at-connecticut-elementary-school.html?.

10. On January 16, 2013, Barack Obama announced the following list of twenty-three executive gun control measures, many of which his administration contended could be taken without congressional approval:

(1) Issue a Presidential Memorandum to require federal agencies to make relevant data available to the federal background check system.

(2) Address unnecessary legal barriers, particularly relating to the Health Insurance Portability and Accountability Act that may prevent states from making information available to the background check system.

(3) Improve incentives for states to share information with the background check system.

(4) Direct the Attorney General to review categories of individuals prohibited from having a gun to make sure dangerous people are not slipping through the cracks.

(5) Propose rulemaking to give law enforcement the ability to run a full background check on an individual before returning a seized gun.

(6) Publish a letter from ATF to federally licensed gun dealers providing guidance on how to run background checks for private sellers.

(7) Launch a national safe and responsible gun ownership campaign.

(8) Review safety standards for gun locks and gun safes (Consumer Product Safety Commission).

(9) Issue a Presidential Memorandum to require federal law enforcement to trace guns recovered in criminal investigations.

(10) Release a DOJ report analyzing information on lost and stolen guns and make it widely available to law enforcement.

(11) Nominate an ATF director.

(12) Provide law enforcement, first responders, and school officials with proper training for active shooter situations.

(13) Maximize enforcement efforts to prevent gun violence and prosecute gun crime.

(14) Issue a Presidential Memorandum directing the Centers for Disease Control to research the causes and prevention of gun violence.

(15) Direct the Attorney General to issue a report on the availability and most effective use of new gun safety technologies and challenge the private sector to develop innovative technologies.

(16) Clarify that the Affordable Care Act does not prohibit doctors asking their patients about guns in their homes.

(17) Release a letter to health care providers clarifying that no federal law prohibits them from reporting threats of violence to law enforcement authorities.

(18) Provide incentives for schools to hire school resource officers.

(19) Develop model emergency response plans for schools, houses of worship, and institutions of higher education.

(20) Release a letter to state health officials clarifying the scope of mental health services that Medicaid plans must cover.

(21) Finalize regulations clarifying essential health benefits and parity requirements within ACA exchanges.

(22) Commit to finalizing mental health parity regulations.

(23) Launch a national dialogue led by Secretaries Sebelius and Duncan on mental health.

"List: Obama's 23 Executive Actions on Gun Violence," *Wall St. J.* (Jan. 16, 2013, 12:23 pm), http://blogs.wsj.com/washwire/2013/01/16/list-obamas-23-executive-actions-on-gun-violence/.

11. Ibid.

12. G.A. Res. 67/234 B, Arms Trade Treaty (Apr. 2, 2013).

13. See John Kerry, U.S. Sec'y of State, "Remarks at the Arms Trade Treaty Signing Ceremony" (Sept. 25, 2013), http://www.state.gov/secretary/remarks/2013/09/214717.htm.

14. The Arms Trade Treaty, United Nations Off. for Disarmament Aff., http://www.un.org/disarmament/ATT/.

15. Ibid.

16. See Geneva Academy, *The Arms Trade Treaty 17* (2013), http://www.geneva-academy.ch/docs/publications/Arms%20Trade%20Treaty%203%20WEB%282%29.pdf.

17. Many of the dozens of provisions contained in the documents on which the ATT is based, or that reflect its "object and purpose," and which arguably would provide a justification for the Obama administration (or a subsequent, similarly disposed president) are provisions that would severely restrict civilian possession of any firearms (whether military or civilian) and would place control of determining, implementing, and enforcing such measures in the hands of the national government of a signatory nation. See Bob Barr, "The U.N. Comes After America's Guns," *Wash. Times* (Aug. 19, 2013), http://www.washingtontimes.com/news/2013/aug/19/barr-the-un-comes-after-americas-guns/.

18. As was done by President George W. Bush in 2002 after President Clinton signed the implementing instrument for the International Criminal Court (ICC) in December 2000. Luke A. McLaurin, "Can the President 'Unsign' a Treaty? A Constitutional Inquiry," *Wash. U. L. Rev.* 84 (2006): 1941.

19. Ibid., 1942.

20. This was the legal position of the Bush administration following its "unsigning" of the ICC implementing instrument. Ibid., 1944–1945.

21. See, e.g., Edwin Meese III, Baker Spring & Brett D. Schaefer, "The United Nations Convention on the Law of the Sea: The Risks Outweigh the Benefits," Heritage Foundation (May 16, 2007), http://www.heritage.org/research/reports/2007/05/the-united-nations-convention-on-the-law-of-the-sea-the-risks-outweigh-the-benefits.

22. "House Report: 'Choke Point' Targets Legal Businesses for Asphyxiation," Nat'l Rifle Ass'n Inst. for Legis. Action (May 30, 2014), https://www.nraila.org/articles/20140530/house-report-choke-point-targets-legal-businesses-for-asphyxiation.

23. See, e.g., "'Choke Point' Hearings Yield Predictable Responses from FDIC Chairman," Nat'l Rifle Ass'n Inst. for Legis. Action (Mar. 27, 2015), https://www.nraila.org/articles/20150327/choke-point-hearings-yield-predictable-responses-from-fdic-chairman.

24. Comm. on Oversight and Gov't Reform, U.S. House of Representatives, "The Department of Justice's Operation Choke Point: Illegally Choking Off Legitimate Businesses?" (2014), 1, http://oversight.house.gov/wp-content/uploads/2014/05/Staff-Report-Operation-Choke-Point1.pdf.

25. Ibid., 7–8.

26. Ibid., 1.

27. Rep. Blaine Luetkemeyer, U.S. House of Representatives, "FDIC and DOJ Commit to Luetkemeyer and Members an Investigation into Operation Choke Point," Press Release (Nov. 14, 2014), http://luetkemeyer.house.gov/news/documentsingle.aspx?DocumentID=398492.

28. Fed. Deposit Ins. Corp., Financial Institution Letter 5-2015, Statement on Providing Banking Services (2015), https://www.fdic.gov/news/news/financial/2015/fil15005.pdf.

29. Alan Zibel, "FDIC: Examiners Must Give Banks Written Notice on Risky Accounts," *Wall St. J.* (Jan. 28, 2015, 3:22 pm), http://www.wsj.com/articles/fdic-examiners-must-give-banks-written-notice-on-risky-accounts-1422476562.

30. Sari Horwitz, "Operation Fast and Furious: A Gunrunning Sting Gone Wrong," *Wash. Post* (July 26, 2011), http://www.washingtonpost.com/investigations/us-anti-gunrunning-effort-turns-fatally-wrong/2011/07/14/gIQAH5d6YI_story.html.

31. Katie Pavlich, "Documents Confirm Fast and Furious AK-47 Used in Phoenix Gang Assault," Townhall (Oct. 16, 2014), http://townhall.com/tipsheet/katiepavlich/2014/10/16/breaking-judicial-watch-confirms-fast-and-furious-rifle-used-in-phoenix-gang-assault-n1906153.

32. Horwitz, "Operation Fast and Furious."

33. Josh Gerstein, "Report Faults U.S. Attorney Dennis Burke for Fast and Furious Leak," *Politico* (May 20, 2013, 1:28 pm), http://www.politico.com/blogs/under-the-radar/2013/05/report-faults-former-us-attorney-dennis-burke-for-164374.html.

34. "House Votes to Hold Attorney General Holder in Contempt of Congress," *Fox News* (June 29, 2012), http://www.foxnews.com/politics/2012/06/28/house-holds-holder-contempt/.

35. Ibid.

36. "Our History—Our Story," Centers for Disease Control and Prevention (Apr. 26, 2013), http://www.cdc.gov/about/history/ourstory.htm.

37. Ibid.

38. See, e.g., Centers for Disease Control and Prevention, "Fiscal Year 2015 Justification of Estimates for Appropriation Committees" (2015), http://www.cdc.gov/fmo/topic/Budget%20Information/appropriations_budget_form_pdf/FY2015_CJ_CDC_FINAL.pdf.

39. See, e.g., U.S. Dep't of Health, Educ., and Welfare, "Healthy People: The Surgeon General's Report on Health Promotion and Disease Prevention 9-21 to -22" (1979), http://profiles.nlm.nih.gov/ps/access/NNBBGK.pdf. And, for an overview of the CDC's continuing effort to portray and treat violence in general as a public health issue, see Linda L. Dahlberg & James A. Mercy, "The History of Violence as a Public Health Issue," Centers for Disease Control and Prevention (2009), http://www.cdc.gov/violenceprevention/pdf/history_violence-a.pdf.

40. Larry Bell, "Why the Centers for Disease Control Should Not Receive Gun Research Funding," *Forbes* (Feb. 12, 2013, 8:00 am), http://www.forbes.com/sites/larrybell/2013/02/12/why-the-centers-for-disease-control-should-not-receive-gun-research-funding/.

41. Memorandum from Pres. Barack Obama to Kathleen Sebelius, Sec'y of Health and Human Services, "Engaging in Public Health Research on the Causes and Prevention of Gun Violence" (Jan. 16, 2013), https://www.whitehouse.gov/the-press-office/2013/01/16/presidential-memorandum-engaging-public-health-research-causes-and-preve.

42. Ibid.

43. Ibid.

44. Todd C. Frankel, "Why the CDC Still Isn't Researching Gun Violence, Despite the Ban Being Lifted Two Years Ago," *Wash. Post* (Jan. 14, 2015), http://www.washingtonpost.com/news/storyline/wp/2015/01/14/why-the-cdc-still-isnt-researching-gun-violence-despite-the-ban-being-lifted-two-years-ago/.

45. Inst. of Med. & Nat'l Research Council of the Nat'l Acads., "Priorities for Research to Reduce the Threat of Firearms-Related Violence" (2015), 2n2.

46. Ibid.

47. Bell, "Why the Centers for Disease Control."

48. In 2006, the Congress passed legislation, subsequently signed into law by President George W. Bush, requiring that the head of ATF be confirmed by the Senate. USA PATRIOT Improvement and Authorization Act of 2005, Pub. L. No. 109-177, § 504, 120 Stat. 192, 247 (2006). However, it was not until 2013 that the first such confirmation was accomplished. See, e.g., Sari Horwitz, "Senate Confirms ATF Director," *Wash. Post* (July 31, 2013), https://www.washingtonpost.com/world/national-security/senate-confirms-atf-director/2013/07/31/dc9b0644-fa09-11e2-8752-b41d7ed1f685_story.html.

It was during the period in which there was no confirmed ATF director that many problematic policies and regulatory steps were taken.

49. E.g., Brief of Appellants at 5, Ron Peterson Firearms, LLC v. Jones, 760 F.3d 1147 (10th Cir. 2014) (Nos. 13-2054, 13-2055).

50. Ron Peterson Firearms, LLC v. Jones, 760 F.3d 1147, 1153–1154 (10th Cir. 2014).

51. "NRA Supports Lawsuit Challenging the Obama Administration's Multiple Sales Reporting Requirement," Nat'l Rifle Ass'n Inst. for Legis. Action (Aug. 5, 2011), https://www.nraila.org/articles/20110805/nra-supports-lawsuit-challenging-the-ob.

52. Existing federal law required reporting to ATF of certain multiple sales of handguns but not rifles. See 18 U.S.C. § 923(g)(3)(A) (2012).

53. See Ron Peterson Firearms v. Jones, 760 F.3d 1151; 10 Ring Precision, Inc. v. Jones, 722 F.3d 711, 714 (5th Cir. 2013); Nat'l Shooting Sports Found. v. Jones, 716 F.3d 200, 203 (D.C. Cir. 2013).

54. Lawrence D. Pratt, "ATF Backs Down on Gun Sale Reports," *Am. Thinker* (June 28, 2014), http://www.americanthinker.com/articles/2014/06/atf_backs_down_on_gun_sale_reports.html.

55. Generally, federal law, pursuant to the federal Gun Control Act of 1968, prohibits the sale of firearms to or the possession by any person who:

- Has been convicted of, or is under indictment for, a crime punishable by imprisonment for more than one year;
- Is a fugitive from justice;
- Is an unlawful user of or addicted to a controlled substance;
- Is underage;
- Has been adjudicated as a mental defective or committed to a mental institution;
- Is unlawfully in the United States or has been admitted to the U.S. under a nonimmigrant visa;
- Has been dishonorably discharged from the military;
- Has renounced his or her U.S. citizenship;
- Is subject to a court order restraining him or her from harassing, stalking, or threatening an intimate partner, his or her child, or a child of a partner or engaging in other conduct that would place an intimate partner in reasonable fear of bodily injury to the partner or child; or

• Has been convicted of a misdemeanor crime of domestic violence. 18 U.S.C. § 922(d) (2012).

56. See Amended Definition of "Adjudicated as a Mental Defective" and "Committed to a Mental Institution," 79 Fed. Reg. 774, 775–776 (proposed Jan. 7, 2014) (to be codified at 27 C.F.R. pt. 478).

57. E.g., Firearms Industry Consulting Group, Comments in Opposition to Proposed Rule ATF 51P, 20–21 (Apr. 5, 2014), https://princelaw.files.wordpress.com/2014/04/ficg-atf-51p-comment.pdf.

58. See "List: Obama's 23 Executive Actions" ("4. Direct the Attorney General to review categories of individuals prohibited from having a gun to make sure dangerous people are not slipping through the cracks.").

59. "BATFE to Ban Common AR-15 Ammo," Nat'l Rifle Ass'n Inst. for Legis. Action (Feb. 13, 2015), https://www.nraila.org/articles/20150213/batfe-to-ban-common-ar-15-ammo.

60. Ibid.

61. See, e.g., Jeremy Diamond, "Obama Administration Scraps Bullet Ban After Push Back," *CNN* (Mar. 10, 2015), http://www.cnn.com/2015/03/09/politics/gun-rights-group-ad-campaign-armor-piercing-bullet-ban/.

62. Ibid.

63. See, e.g., Bureau of Alcohol, Tobacco, Firearms and Explosives, "Test, Examination and Classification of 7N6 5.45x39 Ammunition," Press Release (Apr. 7, 2014), https://www.atf.gov/news/pr/test-examination-and-classification-7n6-545x39-ammunition.

64. See "Another Week, Another Executive Gun Control Action: BATFE Reverses Prior Position on Pistol 'Stabilizing Braces,'" Nat'l Rifle Ass'n Inst. for Legis. Action (Jan. 16, 2015), https://www.nraila.org/articles/20150116/another-week-another-executive-gun-control-action-batfe-reverses-prior-position-on-pistol-stabilizing-braces.

65. See, e.g., Joe Palazzolo, "Silencers Loophole Targeted for Closure," *Wall St. J.* (Oct. 3, 2013, 7:36 pm), http://www.wsj.com/articles/SB10001424052702303492504579111243276511128.

66. See, e.g., "NRA Supports Lawsuit."

67. The Department of State is responsible for the export and temporary import of defense articles and services governed by 22 U.S.C. § 2778 of the Arms Export Control Act (AECA; see http://www.pmddtc.state.gov/regulations_laws/aeca.html) and Executive Order 13637. The International Traffic

in Arms Regulations (ITAR, 22 C.F.R. §§ 120–130) implements the AECA. International Traffic in Arms Regulations (ITAR), U.S. Dep't of State (July 7, 2015), https://www.pmddtc.state.gov/regulations_laws/itar.html.

68. "Exports of Firearms and Related Items FAQs," Bureau of Indus. and Sec., U.S. Dep't of Com., https://www.bis.doc.gov/index.php/policy-guidance/product-guidance/firearms (last visited July 8, 2015).

69. "Rule Change May Devastate International Travel for Hunters and Shooters," Nat'l Rifle Ass'n Inst. for Legis. Action (Mar. 20, 2015), https://www.nraila.org/articles/20150320/rule-change-may-devastate-international-travel-for-hunters-and-shooters.

70. Scott Olmsted, "Rule Change Snags Traveling American Hunters," *Am. Hunter* (Mar. 25, 2015), http://www.americanhunter.org/articles/2015/3/25/rule-change-snags-traveling-american-hunters/.

71. Juliet Eilperin, "Obama Administration Closes Two Gun Sale Loopholes," *Wash. Post* (Aug. 29, 2013), http://www.washingtonpost.com/blogs/post-politics/wp/2013/08/29/obama-administration-closes-two-gun-sale-loopholes/.

72. "Obama Administration Reverses Course, Forbids Sale of 850,000 Antique Rifles," *Fox News* (Sept. 1, 2010), http://www.foxnews.com/politics/2010/09/01/obama-administration-reverses-course-forbids-sale-antique-m-rifles/.

73. Ibid.

74. See previous notes and accompanying text.

75. Caring for Our Children Basics, 79 Fed. Reg. 75557, 75562 (Dec. 18, 2014).

76. See District of Columbia v. Heller, 554 U.S. 570, 630–35 (2008); Caring for Our Children Basics, 79 Fed. Reg. 75562.

77. Caring for Our Children Basics, 79 Fed. Reg. 75564.

CHAPTER 3

1. See Planned Parenthood of Southeastern Pennsylvania v. Casey, 505 U.S. 833, 850 (1992).

2. Hosanna-Tabor Evangelical Lutheran Church & Sch. v. EEOC, 132 S. Ct. 694, 706 (2012).

3. Burwell v. Hobby Lobby Stores, Inc., 134 S. Ct. 2751 (2014).

4. See Brief for United States as Amicus Curiae Supporting Petitioner, Town of Greece v. Galloway, 134 S. Ct. 1811 (2014) (No. 12-696); Brief for United States as Amicus Curiae Supporting Petitioner, Holt v. Hobbs, 135 S.

Ct. 853 (2015) (No. 13-6827); Brief for the Petitioner, EEOC v. Abercrombie & Fitch Stores, Inc., 135 S. Ct. 2028 (2015) (No. 14-86).

5. Patient Protection and Affordable Care Act § 2713, 42 U.S.C. § 300gg-13 (2012).

6. See Certain Preventive Services Under the Affordable Care Act, 77 Fed. Reg. 16501, 16502 (Mar. 21, 2012); see also "Birth Control: Medicines to Help You," U.S. Food and Drug Admin. (Jan. 8, 2015) (listing FDA-approved birth control products), http://www.fda.gov/ForConsumers/ByAudience/ForWomen/FreePublications/ucm313215.htm.

7. See Patient Protection and Affordable Care Act § 4980H, 26 U.S.C. § 4980H (2012).

8. Group Health Plans and Health Insurance Issuers Relating to Coverage of Preventive Services Under the PPACA, 76 Fed. Reg. 46621, 46623, 46626 (Aug. 3, 2011) (to be codified at 45 C.F.R. pt. 147).

9. Ibid.

10. E.g., Timothy M. Dolan, "ObamaCare and Religious Freedom," *Wall St. J.* (Jan. 25, 2012), http://www.wsj.com/articles/SB10001424052970203718504577178833194483196.

11. Coverage of Certain Preventive Services Under the Affordable Care Act, 79 Fed. Reg. 51092, 51093–51094 (Aug. 27, 2014) (to be codified at 26 C.F.R. pt. 54) (describing regulatory history of the "accommodation").

12. Ibid.

13. Ibid., 51094–51095, 51098.

14. Wheaton College v. Burwell, 134 S. Ct. 2806 (2014).

15. Little Sisters of the Poor Home for the Aged v. Sebelius, 134 S. Ct. 1022 (2014).

16. See Religious Freedom Restoration Act of 1993, 42 U.S.C. § 2000bb-1 (2012).

17. E.g., Priests for Life v. U.S. Dep't of Health and Human Servs., 772 F.3d 229, 257 (D.C. Cir. 2014).

18. Burwell v. Hobby Lobby Stores, Inc., 134 S. Ct. 2751, 2767 (2014).

19. Ibid.

20. Ibid., 2769.

21. Ibid., 2771.

22. See ibid., 2769–2770.

23. See ibid., 2782.

24. See, e.g., Jens Manuel Krogstad, Ana Gonzalez-Barrera & Mark Hugo Lopez, "Children 12 and Under Are Fastest Growing Group of Unaccompanied Minors at U.S. Border," Pew Research Ctr. (July 22, 2014), http://www.pewresearch.org/fact-tank/2014/07/22/children-12-and-under-are-fastest-growing-group-of-unaccompanied-minors-at-u-s-border/.

25. "About Unaccompanied Refugee Minors," Off. of Refugee Resettlement, U.S. Dep't of Health and Human Servs., http://www.acf.hhs.gov/programs/orr/programs/urm/about (last visited July 8, 2015).

26. Standards to Prevent, Detect, and Respond to Sexual Abuse and Sexual Harassment Involving Unaccompanied Children, 79 Fed. Reg. 77768, 77798 (Dec. 24, 2014) (to be codified at 45 C.F.R. pt. 411).

27. Ibid.

28. Ibid., 77784.

29. Executive Order 13672, 79 Fed. Reg. 42971 (July 21, 2014).

30. Implementation of Executive Order 13672, 79 Fed. Reg. 72985 (Dec. 9, 2014) (to be codified at 41 C.F.R. pt. 60).

31. See Employment Non-Discrimination Act of 2013, S. 815, 113th Cong. (2013).

32. See, e.g., Austin Ruse, "White House to Order Faith-Based Grant Recipients to Accept LGBT Applicants," Ctr. for Fam. & Hum. Rts. (May 28, 2015), https://c-fam.org/friday_fax/white-house-to-order-faith-based-grant-recipients-to-accept-lgbt-applicants/.

33. See Implementation of Executive Order 13672, 79 Fed. Reg. at 72986–72987 & n6.

34. U.S. Dep't of Justice, "Statement of the Attorney General on Litigation Involving the Defense of Marriage Act," Press Release (Feb. 23, 2011), http://www.justice.gov/opa/pr/statement-attorney-general-litigation-involving-defense-marriage-act; see also Defense of Marriage Act, Pub. L. No. 104-199, 110 Stat. 2419 (1996).

35. 133 S. Ct. 2675, 2683 (2013).

36. See U.S. Dep't of Justice, "Statement of the Attorney General."

37. See 133 S. Ct. 2695–2696.

38. Family and Medical Leave Act of 1993, 29 U.S.C. § 2611(13) (2012).

39. Family and Medical Leave Act of 1993, 60 Fed. Reg. 2180, 2191 (Jan. 6, 1995) (to be codified at 29 C.F.R. pt. 825).

40. See Family and Medical Leave Act, 79 Fed. Reg. 36445, 36454 (proposed June 27, 2014) (to be codified at 29 C.F.R. pt. 825).

41. Definition of Spouse Under the Family and Medical Leave Act, 80 Fed. Reg. 9989, 10000 (Feb. 25, 2015) (to be codified at 29 C.F.R. pt. 825).

42. Ibid., 9991. On Mar. 26, 2015, a federal district judge in Texas enjoined enforcement of the Final Rule against states within the Fifth Circuit acting as employers, concluding *inter alia* that the Final Rule exceeded the authority delegated to the Department by Congress under the FMLA. Texas v. United States, No. 7:15-cv-00056-O, 2015 WL 1378752, at *9 (N.D. Tex. Mar. 26, 2015).

43. See 42 U.S.C. § 2000bb-1 (2012).

44. Ibid.

45. See ibid.

46. To not "substantially burden" it, that is. Ibid.

47. See U.S. Const. art. II, § 3.

48. Elane Photography, LLC v. Willock, 309 P.3d 53 (N.M. 2013).

49. See ibid., 58–60.

50. See ibid., 78 (Bosson, J., concurring).

51. Ibid., 79–80.

52. Ibid., 80.

53. Ibid.

54. Ibid.

55. Ibid.

56. E.g., Randy Sly, "Obama Moves Away from 'Freedom of Religion' Toward 'Freedom of Worship,'" *Fox News* (July 23, 2010), http://www.foxnews.com/opinion/2010/07/23/randy-sly-obama-clinton-freedom-religion-freedom-worship-fort-hood.html.

57. Bronx Household of Faith v. Cmty. Sch. Dist. No. 10, 127 F.3d 207, 221 (2d Cir. 1997) (Cabranes, J., concurring in part and dissenting in part).

58. See ibid., 214–215.

59. See ibid.

60. See, e.g., McCreary Cty. v. Am. Civil Liberties Union of Kentucky, 545 U.S. 844, 860 (2005) (quoting Epperson v. Arkansas, 393 U.S. 97, 104 (1968)).

61. Transcript of Oral Argument, 26–27, Hosanna-Tabor Evangelical Lutheran Church & Sch. v. EEOC, 132 S. Ct. 694 (2012) (No. 10-553).

62. Transcript of Oral Argument, 27.

63. Ibid., 27–28.

64. Ibid., 28.

65. Hosanna-Tabor, 132 S. Ct. at 706.

66. Ibid.

67. Ibid.

68. Ibid.

69. Ibid.

70. Ibid.

71. Transcript of Oral Argument, 38, Obergefell v. Hodges, No. 14-556 (U.S. June 26, 2015); see also Bob Jones Univ. v. Simon, 416 U.S. 725 (1974).

72. See Valerie Jarrett, "Response to Your Petition on Conversion Therapy," WhiteHouse.gov (Apr. 8, 2015), https://petitions.whitehouse.gov/response/response-your-petition-conversion-therapy.

73. Jeremy Diamond, "Oregon Outlaws Gay Conversion Therapy, Joining Two Other States," *CNN* (May 20, 2015), http://www.cnn.com/2015/05/20/politics/oregon-outlaws-gay-conversion-therapy/.

74. Jarrett, "Petition on Conversion Therapy."

75. See ibid.

76. Paul McHugh & Gerard V. Bradley, "Sexual Orientation, Gender Identity, and Employment Law," *Pub. Discourse* (July 25, 2013), http://www.thepublicdiscourse.com/2013/07/10636/.

77. Paul McHugh, "Transgenderism: A Pathogenic Meme," *Pub. Discourse* (June 10, 2015), http://www.thepublicdiscourse.com/2015/06/15145/.

78. See Welsh v. United States, 398 U.S. 333, 340 (1970); United States v. Seeger, 380 U.S. 163, 176 (1965).

79. See Brief for the United States, 6–7, Welsh v. United States, 398 U.S. 333 (1970) (No. 76); Brief for the United States, 9–10, Seeger v. United States, 380 U.S. 163 (1965) (No. 50).

80. See Welsh, 398 U.S. 343–344; Seeger, 380 U.S. 165–166.

81. See note 4.

CHAPTER 4

1. See, e.g., *The Federalist* No. 47 (Madison).

2. See, e.g., *The Federalist* No. 78 (Hamilton).

3. See, e.g., *The Federalist* No. 48 (Madison) ("The legislative department is everywhere extending the sphere of its activity, and drawing all power into its impetuous vortex.").

4. 476 U.S. 837 (1984) [hereinafter Chevron].

5. See 5 U.S.C. § 706 (2012).

6. See, e.g., National Labor Relations Bd. v. Hearst Publ'ns, Inc., 322 U.S. 111 (1943); Gray v. Powell, 314 U.S. 402 (1941); Norwegian Nitrogen Prods. Co. v. United States, 288 U.S. 294 (1933). See also Ronald A. Cass, Colin S. Diver, Jack M. Beermann & Jody Freeman, *Administrative Law: Cases & Materials*, 6th ed. (Wolters Kluwer, 2011), 155–158, 167–168; Thomas W. Merrill, "Judicial Deference to Executive Precedent," *Yale L.J.* 101 (1992): 969.

7. 47 U.S.C. § 307 (2012).

8. See National Broadcasting Co. v. United States, 319 U.S. 190 (1943).

9. Smiley v. Citibank (South Dakota), N. A., 517 U.S. 735, 740–741 (1996).

10. See, e.g., Motor Vehicle Manufacturers Ass'n v. State Farm Mutual Automobile Ins. Co., 463 U.S. 29 (1903) (pre-Chevron); FCC v. Fox Television Stations, Inc., 556 U.S. 502 (2009) (post-Chevron).

11. See, e.g., Ronald A. Cass, "Vive la Deference? Rethinking the Balance Between Administrative and Judicial Discretion," *Geo. Wash. L. Rev.* 83 (2015) (forthcoming); Antonin Scalia, "Judicial Deference to Administrative Interpretations of Law," *Duke L.J.* 1989 (1989): 511, 516. See also Peter L. Strauss, "'Deference' Is Too Confusing Let's Call Them 'Chevron Space' and 'Skidmore Weight,'" *Colum. L. Rev.* 112 (2012): 1143.

12. The thought on judicial responsibility to pronounce the law when a case or controversy properly puts the legal question before the court traces back to Hamilton's essay in *Federalist* No. 78, though the common citation is to John Marshall's opinion in Marbury v. Madison, 5 U.S. (1 Cranch) 137, 177 (1803). The notion that administrators may be granted broad scope for decision and that other branches might cede authority to them occurs in various guises, not all as problematic as extreme judicial deference to administrative interpretations. See, e.g., Jerry Mashaw, "Prodelegation: Why Administrators Should Make Political Decisions," *J.L. Econ. & Org.* 1 (1985): 81.

13. 515 U.S. 687 (1995).

14. See ibid., at 714–736 (Scalia, J., dissenting).

15. 549 U.S. 497 (2007).

16. 42 U.S.C. § 7521(a)(1) (emphasis added).

17. See generally Massachusetts v. EPA, 549 U.S. 497.

18. See, e.g., Ronald A. Cass, "Massachusetts v. EPA: The Inconvenient Truth About Precedent," *Va. L. Rev.* 93 (2007), in Brief 75.

19. 529 U.S. 120 (2000) [hereinafter Brown & Williamson Tobacco].

20. No. 14-114 (June 25, 2015) [hereinafter Burwell].

21. See, e.g., Brown & Williamson Tobacco. The "traditional tools" approach was part of *Chevron* from the outset, as Justice Stevens's opinion declared:

> The judiciary is the final authority on issues of statutory construction and must reject administrative constructions which are contrary to clear congressional intent. If a court, employing traditional tools of statutory construction, ascertains that Congress had an intention on the precise question at issue, that intention is the law and must be given effect.

Chevron, n9.

22. Brown & Williamson Tobacco.

23. Ibid.

24. Pub. L. No. 111-148, 124 Stat. 119.

25. See 26 U.S.C. § 36B (2012).

26. See, e.g., Burwell.

27. 759 F.3d 358, 372 (4th Cir. 2014).

28. Indeed, it is difficult to credit the Court's statutory construction as an appropriate, much less an unambiguously compelling, reading of the law. See, e.g., Burwell (Scalia, J., dissenting).

29. Ibid.

30. 531 U.S. 457, 468 (2001) [hereinafter Whitman].

31. Ibid., 465–469, 481–486.

32. See Burwell.

33. Ibid.

34. Ibid.

35. 533 U.S. 218 (2001) [hereinafter Mead].

36. See, e.g., World Customs Organization (WCO), Harmonized Tariff Schedule for the United States (2015) [hereinafter HTSUS].

37. See Mead.

38. Ibid.

39. The characterization of decisions having "the effect of law" engages another aspect of determining what administrative actions are eligible for *Chevron* deference. While some Supreme Court decisions exclude from *Chevron* eligibility only agency actions that are not taken to constitute authoritative decisions of the agency, a few decisions place a broader set of determinations outside that realm. That distinction, however, was important to the majority opinion in Mead, which analogized the Customs Service's decisions on tariff classifications to "interpretations contained in policy statements, agency manuals, and enforcement guidelines." Ibid. (citing Christensen v. Harris County, 529 U.S. 576, 587 (2000)).

40. Ibid.

41. 323 U.S. 134 (1944) [hereinafter Skidmore].

42. Ibid.

43. "Agency Pre-emption: Speak Softly But Carry a Big Stick?" *Chapman L. Rev.* 11 (2008): 363, 381–382 (panel presentation at 2006 Federalist Society National Lawyers' Convention).

44. See, e.g., Jack M. Beermann, "End the Failed Chevron Experiment Now: How Chevron Has Failed and Why It Can and Should Be Overruled," *Conn. L. Rev.* 42 (2010): 779; Colin S. Diver, "Statutory Interpretation in the Administrative State," *U. Pa. L. Rev.* 133 (1985): 549; Cynthia R. Farina, "Statutory Interpretation and the Balance of Power in the Administrative State," *Colum. L. Rev.* 89 (1989): 452; Ronald M. Levin, "The Anatomy of Chevron: Step Two Reconsidered," *Chi.-Kent L. Rev.* 72 (1997): 1253; Thomas W. Merrill & Kristin E. Hickman, "Chevron's Domain," *Geo. L.J.* 89 (2001): 833; Richard J. Pierce, Jr., "Chevron and Its Aftermath: Judicial Review of Agency Interpretations of Statutory Provisions," *Vand. L. Rev.* 41 (1988): 301; Peter L. Strauss, "One Hundred Fifty Cases per Year: Some Implications of the Supreme Court's Limited Resources for Judicial Review of Agency Action," *Colum. L. Rev.* 87 (1987): 1093.

45. See, e.g., Cass, "Rethinking"; Scalia, "Judicial Deference." See also Ronald A. Cass, *The Rule of Law in America* (Baltimore: Johns Hopkins University Press, 2001), 4–19, 28–29; Michael Dorf, "Prediction and the Rule of Law," *UCLA L. Rev.* 42 (1995): 651, 680–689; Michael Oakeshott, "The Rule of Law," in *On History and Other Essays* (Barnes & Noble, 1983), 119, 130–132, 136–140; Antonin Scalia, "The Rule of Law as a Law of Rules," *U. Chi. L. Rev.* 56 (1989): 1175.

46. City of Arlington v. FCC, 133 S. Ct. 1863, 1874 (2013).

47. See, e.g., Beermann, "End the Failed Chevron Experiment Now"; John F. Duffy, "Administrative Common Law in Judicial Review," *Tex. L. Rev.* 77 (1998): 113; William N. Eskridge, Jr. & Lauren E. Baer, "The Continuum of Deference: Supreme Court Treatment of Agency Statutory Interpretation from Chevron to Hamdan," *Geo. L.J.* 96 (2008): 1083; Orin S. Kerr, "Shedding Light on Chevron: An Empirical Study of the Chevron Doctrine in the U.S. Courts of Appeal," *Yale J. on Reg.* 15 (1998): 1.

48. See, e.g., Kenneth Bamberger & Peter L. Strauss, "Chevron's Two Steps," *Va. L. Rev.* 95 (2009): 611; Merrill & Hickman, "Chevron's Domain," 834; Matthew Stephenson & Adrian Vermeule, "Chevron Has Only One Step," *Va. L. Rev.* 95 (2009): 597; Cass Sunstein, "Chevron Step Zero," *Va. L. Rev.* 92 (2006): 187.

49. The authors are not in agreement on this point. Compare Cass, "Rethinking," at part IV, with Mistretta v. United States, 488 U.S. 361, 415–416 (1989) (Scalia, J., dissenting). We do agree, however, that if a judicially administrable test could be identified, it would be desirable (and consistent with the Constitution's design) to adopt and enforce it. After all, congressional adventurism and expansionism were central concerns of the framing generation. See, e.g., *The Federalist* No. 48 (Madison). See also Gary Lawson, "Delegation and Original Meaning," *Va. L. Rev.* 88 (2002): 327; David Schoenbrod, "Separation of Powers and the Powers that Be: The Constitutional Purposes of the Delegation Doctrine," *Am. U. L. Rev.* 36 (1987): 355. That said, it remains that the "if" in the initial sentence is a serious caveat.

50. See, e.g., Cass, "Rethinking"; Kenneth A. Shepsle, "The Strategy of Ambiguity: Uncertainty and Electoral Competition," *Am. Pol. Sci. Rev.* 66 (1972): 555.

CHAPTER 5

1. Jens Manuel Krogstad & Jeffrey Passel, "5 Facts About Illegal Immigration in the U.S.," Pew Research Ctr. (Nov. 18, 2014), http://www.pewresearch.org/fact-tank/2014/11/18/5-facts-about-illegal-immigration-in-the-u-s/.

2. Barack Obama, Remarks by the President in Address to the Nation on Immigration (Nov. 20, 2014) (transcript available at https://www.whitehouse.gov/the-press-office/2014/11/20/remarks-president-address-nation-immigration).

3. Barack Obama, Remarks by the President at Univision Townhall (Mar. 28, 2011) (transcript available at https://www.whitehouse.gov/the-press-office/2011/03/28/remarks-president-univision-town-hall).

4. See Matt Wolking, Office of Speaker of the House John Boehner, "22 Times President Obama Said He Couldn't Ignore or Create His Own Immigration Law" (Nov. 19, 2014), http://www.speaker.gov/general/22-times-president-obama-said-he-couldn-t-ignore-or-create-his-own-immigration-law.

5. Drew Desilver, "Executive Actions on Immigration Have a Long History," Pew Research Ctr. (Nov. 21, 2014), http://www.pewresearch.org/fact-tank/2014/11/21/executive-actions-on-immigration-have-long-history/.

6. DACA was initiated by President Obama on August 15, 2012. See Alejandro Maorkas, "Deferred Action for Childhood Arrivals," White House Blog (Aug. 15, 2012, 11:55 am), https://www.whitehouse.gov/blog/2012/08/15/deferred-action-childhood-arrivals-who-can-be-considered.

7. Memorandum from Jeh Charles Johnson, Sec'y, U.S. Dept. of Homeland Sec., to Thomas S. Winkowski, Acting Director, U.S. Immigration & Customs Enforcement, et al., 1 (Nov. 20, 2014) (on file with author), http://www.dhs.gov/sites/default/files/publications/14_1120_memo_prosecutorial_discretion.pdf.

8. Ben Gitis & Laura Collins, "The Budgetary and Economic Costs of Addressing Unauthorized Immigration: Alternative Strategies," Am. Action Forum (Mar. 6, 2015), http://americanactionforum.org/research/the-budgetary-and-economic-costs-of-addressing-unauthorized-immigration-alt.

9. John T. Bennett, "Conservatives Lose as House Funds DHS," DefenseNews (Mar. 3, 2015), http://www.defensenews.com/story/defense/policy-budget/congress/2015/03/03/dhs-homeland-security-shutdown-freedom/24326143/.

10. Memorandum from Jeh Charles Johnson to Thomas S. Winkowski et al.

11. U.S. Dep't of Homeland Sec., "Secretary Napolitano Announces Deferred Action Process for Young People Who Are Low Enforcement Priorities," Press Release (June 15, 2012), http://www.dhs.gov/news/2012/06/15/secretary-napolitano-announces-deferred-action-process-young-people-who-are-low; see also Memorandum from Janet Napolitano, Sec'y, U.S. Dep't of Homeland Sec., to David V. Aguilar, Acting Comm'r, U.S. Customs & Border Protection, et al., 1 (June 15, 2012), http://www.dhs.gov/xlibrary/assets/s1-exercising-prosecutorial-discretion-individuals-who-came-to-us-as-children.pdf.

12. See Development, Relief, and Education for Alien Minors Act of 2001, S. 1291 107th Cong. (2001).

13. See, e.g., Shankar Vedantam, "DREAM Act Defeat Reveals Failed Strategy," (Dec. 19, 2010), http://www.washingtonpost.com/wp-dyn/content/article/2010/12/18/AR2010121803271.html.

14. See Memorandum from Lake Research Partners to America's Voice, 1 (Nov. 13, 2012), http://amvoice.3cdn.net/f7a2462c34a8aaa78d_27m6iv0js.pdf.

15. Memorandum from Janet Napolitano to David V. Aguilar et al.

16. Crane v. Napolitano, 2013 WL 8211660, at *1 (N.D. Tex. July 31, 2013), aff'd sub nom. Crane v. Johnson, 783 F.3d 244 (5th Cir. 2015).

17. Ibid., 783 F.3d at 255.

18. Obama, Address to the Nation on Immigration.

19. Michael D. Shear, "Obama, Daring Congress, Acts to Overhaul Immigration," (Nov. 20, 2014), http://www.nytimes.com/2014/11/21/us/obama-immigration-speech.html?_r=0.

20. Ibid.

21. Ibid.

22. Ashley Parker & Robert Pear, "Ending Days of Chaos at the Capitol, Senate Passes $1.1 Trillion Spending Bill," (Dec. 14, 2014), A28, http://www.nytimes.com/2014/12/14/us/senate-spending-package.html?_r=0.

23. Sean Sullivan, "House Passes Bill Fully Funding the Department of Homeland Security," (Mar. 3, 2015), http://www.washingtonpost.com/politics/house-passes-bill-fully-funding-the-department-of-homeland-security/2015/03/03/9d62484a-c1c5-11e4-9ec2-b418f57a4a99_story.html.

24. Complaint at 26, Texas v. United States, 2015 WL 648579 (S.D. Tex. Feb. 16, 2015) (No. 14-cv-00254), aff'd, 787 F.3d 733 (5th Cir. 2015).

25. Ibid., *35.

26. Ibid., *36.

27. Ibid., *50.

28. Texas, 787 F.3d at 743.

29. Keith E. Whittington, *Constitutional Interpretation: Textual Meaning, Original Intent, & Judicial Review* (Lawrence: UP of Kansas, 1999), 211.

30. Jake Sherman & Anna Palmer, "GOP Mulls Its Own Immigration Plan," *Politico* (Nov. 18, 2014, 1:08 pm), http://www.politico.com/story/2014/11/gop-immigration-plan-112991.html.

31. Jens Manuel Krogstad, "Top Issue for Hispanics? Hint: It's Not Immigration," Pew Research Ctr. (June 2, 2014), http://www.pewresearch.org/fact-tank/2014/06/02/top-issue-for-hispanics-hint-its-not-immigration/.

32. Mark Hugo Lopez et al., "Latino Support for Democrats Falls, but Democratic Advantage Remains: Hispanics and Their Views of Immigration Reform," Pew Research Ctr. (Oct. 29, 2014), http://www.pewhispanic.org/2014/10/29/chapter-5-hispanics-and-their-views-of-immigration-reform/.

33. "How Groups Voted in 2012," Roper Center, http://www.ropercenter.uconn.edu/polls/us-elections/how-groups-voted/how-groups-voted-2012/ (last visited July 13, 2015).

34. Katie Packer Gage, "Don't Repeat Mitt Romney's Mistake on Immigration," *Politico* (June 16, 2015), http://www.politico.com/magazine/story/2015/06/dont-repeat-mitt-romneys-mistake-on-immigration-119087.html#.VaPwpvlVijR.

35. Ibid.

36. Jens Manuel Krogstad et al., "Children 12 and Under Are Fastest Growing Group of Unaccompanied Minors at U.S. Border," Pew Research Ctr. (July 22, 2014), http://www.pewresearch.org/fact-tank/2014/07/22/children-12-and-under-are-fastest-growing-group-of-unaccompanied-minors-at-u-s-border/.

37. Ana Gonzalez-Barrera & Jens Manuel Krogstad, "With Help from Mexico, Number of Child Migrants Crossing U.S. Border Falls," Pew Research Ctr. (Apr. 28, 2015), http://www.pewresearch.org/fact-tank/2015/04/28/child-migrants-border/.

38. "Unauthorized Immigrant Population Trends for States, Birth Countries and Regions," Pew Research Ctr. (Dec. 11, 2014), http://www.pewhispanic.org/2014/12/11/unauthorized-trends/.

39. Border apprehensions have traditionally been used as a proxy for the flow of illegal immigrants into the United States. The number of border apprehensions peaked in 1986 and 2000, when nearly 1.7 million persons were apprehended trying to cross the border illegally. Leslie Sapp, U.S. Dep't of Homeland Sec., Apprehensions by the U.S. Border Patrol 2005–2010 (2011), 1, http://www.dhs.gov/xlibrary/assets/statistics/publications/ois-apprehensions-fs-2005-2010.pdf.

40. Pub L. No. 99-603, 101 Stat. 3359 (codified as amended in scattered sections of 8 U.S.C.).

41. See U.S. Citizenship & Immigration Servs., "Do I Need to Use Form I-9," http://www.uscis.gov/i-9-central/complete-correct-form-i-9/who-needs-use-form-i-9/do-i-need-use-form-i-9 (last updated Mar. 8, 2013).

CHAPTER 6

1. The author gratefully acknowledges the assistance of Harold Reeves in the research and preparation of this chapter. The author also notes that he and his law firm represent the Community Financial Services Association and Advance America, Inc., in a suit asserting claims under the Administrative Procedure Act and the Constitution against the banking regulatory agencies for their enforcement of Operation Choke Point against the payday lending industry. The case is Community Financial Services Association v. FDIC, 14-cv-00953, U.S. District Court, District of Columbia (Washington).

2. Frank Keating, "Justice Puts Banks in a Choke Hold," *Wall St. J.* (Apr. 24, 2014, 7:21 pm), http://on.wsj.com/1eiMUtj.

3. See, e.g., Dennis A. Ross, "Don't Buy the Spin: Operation Choke Point Targets Legal Businesses," Am. Banker (May 4, 2015, 10:00 am), www.americanbanker.com/bankthink/dont-buy-the-spin-operation-choke-point-targets-legal-businesses-1074104-1.html.

4. E-mail from a Counsel, Legal Division, FDIC, to Marguerite Sagatelian, Senior Counsel, Consumer Enforcement Unit, FDIC (Aug. 28, 2013, 9:32 am), FDICHOGR00007424; E-mail from a Counsel, Legal Division, FDIC, to Marguerite Sagatelian, Senior Counsel, Consumer Enforcement Unit, FDIC (Mar. 9, 2013, 2:53 pm), FDICHOGR00005178.

5. E-mail from Thomas J. Dujenski, Regional Director, Atlanta Region, Federal Deposit Insurance Corporation, to Mark Pearce, Director, Division of Consumer Protection, Federal Deposit Insurance Corporation (Nov. 27, 2012, 20:40:05), FDICHOGR00006585.

6. See 12 U.S.C. § 1831p-1(f) (outlining the range of standards for safety and soundness to be prescribed by the prudential regulators pursuant to Section 39 of the Federal Deposit Insurance Act); see also 12 U.S.C. § 1831p-1(e)(1)(A) (even when a bank fails to meet these prescribed standards for safety and soundness, the regulators have no power to decide how the bank will be made safe and sound; they may only require that the bank submit a satisfactory compliance plan to show how the bank plans to bring itself into compliance).

7. The OCC handbook reflected the traditional understanding of reputation risk as a risk to a bank's business reputation arising from the provision of products and services by the bank itself. See OCC, "Bank Super-vision Process," *Comptroller's Handbook* 121 (2007), http://www.occ.gov/publications/publications-by-type/comptrollers-handbook/bsp-2.pdf ("The assessment of reputation risk recognizes the potential impact of the public's opinion on a bank's franchise value. This risk is inherent in all bank activities. Banks that actively associate their name with products and services, such as with fiduciary services, are more likely to have higher reputation risk exposure. As the bank's vulnerability to public reaction increases, its ability to offer competitive products and services may be affected."). In 2003, the bank regulators first acknowledged that bank services provided by third parties in the name of the bank could affect the reputation of the bank itself because of the increased risk of confusion on the part of the customer as to who is providing the service. See also FDIC et al., "Weblinking: Identifying Risks and Risk Management Techniques," Press Release, 3–4, https://www.fdic.gov/news/news/press/2003/pr3403a.html (last updated Apr. 23, 2003).

8. Financial Institution Letter, FIL-44-2008, Guidance for Managing Third-Party Risk (June 6, 2008).

9. Letter from Rep. Jeb Hensarling, Chairman, H. Comm. on Fin. Servs., to Janet Yellen, Chair, the Federal Reserve System (May 22, 2014).

10. Ibid., 10, quoting email from a Counsel, Legal Division, FDIC, to Marguerite Sagatelian, Senior Counsel, Consumer Enforcement Unit, FDIC (Aug. 28, 2013, 9:32), FDICHOGR00007424.

11. Ibid., 11, quoting email from a Counsel to Marguerite Sagatelian.

12. FDIC, "Managing Risks in Third-Party Payment Processor Relationships," Supervisory Insights No. 1 (2011), 3, https://www.fdic.gov/regulations/examinations/supervisory/insights/sisum11/managing.html (last modified July 2014).

13. *Guilty until Proven Innocent? A Study of the Propriety & Legal Authority for the Justice Department's Operation Choke Point: Hearing Before the H. Comm. on the Judiciary*, 113th Cong. § 5, 5 (2014), http://judiciary.house.gov/_cache/files/30804b28-f604-4e22-80c5-201db94c0cdc/113-114-88724.pdf (statement of Chair Bob Goodlatte).

14. See Letter from M. Anthony Lowe, Regional Director, FDIC Chicago Regional Office to a depository institution subject to FDIC's super-

visory authority (Feb. 15, 2013), http://oversight.house.gov/wp-content/uploads/2014/10/Regional-Director-Letter.pdf. (The House Committee on Oversight and Government Reform has released only a redacted copy of the letter.)

15. Financial Crimes Enforcement Network, FIN-2014-G001, BSA Expectations Regarding Marijuana-Related Businesses, 1 (Feb. 14, 2014), www.fincen.gov/statutes_regs/guidance/pdf/FIN-2014-G001.pdf.

16. See 5 U.S.C. §§ 551–559, 701–708.

17. See 5 U.S.C. §§ 553(b); Center for Auto Safety v. Nat'l Highway Traffic Safety Administration, 452 F.3d 798, 806 (D.C. Cir. 2006) (as the terminations experienced by payday lenders, gun dealers, pawn shops, and other disfavored merchants amply attest, the revised standard of reputation risk is a "*de facto* rule or binding norm that could not properly be promulgated absent the notice and comment rulemaking required by § 553 of the APA"); see also 5 U.S.C. § 706(2)(D) (providing that a reviewing court must set aside agency action that is "without observance of procedure required by law").

18. See United States v. Johnson, 632 F.3d 912, 931 (5th Cir. 2011) ("The purpose of notice-and-comment rulemaking is to assure fairness and mature consideration of rules having a substantial impact on those regulated.") (quotations omitted).

19. See 5 U.S.C. § 706(2)(A) (providing that a reviewing court must set aside agency action that is "arbitrary, capricious, an abuse of discretion, or otherwise not in accordance with law").

20. See 5 U.S.C. § 706(2)(C) (The APA requires a reviewing court to set aside agency action "in excess of statutory jurisdiction, authority, or limitations, or short of statutory right.").

21. See 12 U.S.C. § 1831p-1.

22. See Wisconsin v. Constantineau, 400 U.S. 433 (1971) (Due Process Clause requires that "an individual must be given notice and an opportunity to be heard before being branded with such "a badge of infamy" as being publicly identified as an alcohol abuser.); Tozzi v. HHS, 271 F.3d 308, 309 (D.C. Cir. 2001) ("When the government attached an inherently pejorative and damaging term . . . to a product, the probability of economic harm" to the purveyor of that product "increases exponentially."); National Council of Resistance of Iran v. United States Department of State, 251 F.3d 192, 204 (D.C. Cir. 2001)

(organization could state a claim under *Constantineau* on the ground that the label "deprived [them] of the previously held right to . . . hold bank accounts").

23. Philip Hamburger, *Is Administrative Law Unlawful?* (Chicago: University of Chicago Press, 2014), 1–2.

24. Maureen Harrison, *The Speeches of Ronald Reagan*, Steve Gilbert, ed. (Excellent Books, 2004), 12.

25. Ibid., 64.

CHAPTER 7

1. The views expressed here are Professor Eastman's, of course, and do not necessarily reflect the views of the organizations with which he is affiliated. This chapter was drawn from a larger article on the same subject, delivered at a symposium on "The Future of Families and of Family Law in America," sponsored by the Marriage and Family Law Research Project at the J. Reuben Clark Law School at Brigham Young University, and to be published in the *Ave Maria Law Review*.

2. United States v. Windsor, 133 S. Ct. 2675, 2711 (2013) (Scalia, J., dissenting).

3. See John C. Eastman, "Philosopher King Courts: Is the Exercise of Higher Law Authority Without a Higher Law Foundation Legitimate?" *Drake L. Rev.* 54 (2006): 831 (elaborating on the theoretical foundations and attendant problems inherent in this dispute); see also John C. Eastman, "Judicial Review of Unenumerated Rights: Does Marbury's Holding Apply in a Post-Warren Court World?" *Harv. J.L. & Pub. Pol'y* 28 (2005): 713.

4. Hawaii Revised Statutes § 572-1 (1985); Baehr v. Lewin, 74 Haw. 530, 852 P.2d 44 (1993).

5. The case's history after remand is a bit tortured. Following the Hawaii Supreme Court's "strict scrutiny" ruling, the Hawaii legislature passed legislation reasserting the traditional definition of marriage and chastising its Supreme Court for breaching fundamental separation of powers requirements. It also created a commission to study the issue, however, and the trial court put the case on hold pending the study. The trial court reopened the case in September 1996 and ruled a few months later that the Hawaii marriage law was unconstitutional under the 1993 strict scrutiny ruling of the Hawaii Supreme Court. Baehr v. Miike, 65 USLW 2399 (Hawaii Cir. Ct., Dec. 3, 1996). But the trial court then immediately stayed its own ruling pending appeal, and while the appeal was

pending, the voters of Hawaii amended their state Constitution in November 1998 to codify the traditional definition of marriage, effectively overruling the Hawaii Supreme Court's 1993 decision and rendering the legal challenge based on the state Constitution's Equal Protection Clause moot. Baehr v. Miike, 92 Haw. 634, 994 P.2d 566, No. 20371, 1999 Haw. LEXIS 391 (Haw. Dec. 9, 1999).

6. U.S. Const. art. IV, § 1.

7. See, e.g., Nevada v. Hall, 440 U.S. 410, 424 (1979) ("the Full Faith and Credit Clause does not require a State to apply another State's law in violation of its own legitimate public policy"); see also Alaska Packers Ass'n v. Industrial Accident Comm'n, 294 U.S. 532, 547 (1935) ("A rigid and literal enforcement of the full faith and credit clause, without regard to the statute of the forum [State], would lead to the absurd result that, whenever conflict arises, the statute of each state must be enforced in the courts of the other, but cannot be in its own.").

8. Defense of Marriage Act, Pub. L. No. 104-199, 110 Stat. 2419 (1996) (codified as amended at 1 U.S.C. § 7 and 28 U.S.C. § 1738C); H.R. Rep. No. 104-664, at 2 (1996).

9. 28 U.S.C. § 1738C.

10. 1 U.S.C. § 7.

11. 156 *Cong. Rec.* S6597 (2010) (Kagan Confirmation Hearing, response to Senator Specter, Question #14).

12. Ibid. (response to Senator Specter, Question #17).

13. Gill v. Office of Personnel Management, No. 09-10309 (D. Mass., filed Sept. 18, 2009); Smelt v. United States, No. 09-00286 (C.D. Cal., filed Mar. 9, 2009).

14. See, e.g., *Testimony of Elena Kagan, Hearing on Confirmation of Elena Kagan as Associate Justice of the Supreme Court* (acknowledging that, while Solicitor General, she had substantial enough involvement in both *Smelt* and *Gill* to require that she recuse herself if either case came before the Supreme Court).

15. See Memorandum in Support of Defendant United States of America's Motion to Dismiss, 10–15, Smelt v. United States, No. 09-00286, Dkt. #25 (C.D. Cal., filed June 11, 2009).

16. See ibid., 18 (citing Catalano v. Catalano, 170 A.2d 726, 728–729 (Conn. 1961) (marriage of uncle to niece, "though valid in Italy under its laws,

was not valid in Connecticut because it contravened the public policy of th[at] state")); see also Jo Becker, *Forcing the Spring: Inside the Fight for Marriage Equality* (New York: Penguin Press, 2014), 249–250 (describing how the President "hit the roof" when he saw the news headlines about the brief, including one that read, "Obama DOJ Compares Gay Marriage to Incest").

17. Reply Memorandum in Support of Defendant United States of America's Motion to Dismiss, 2, Smelt v. United States, No. 09-00286, Dkt. #44 (C.D. Cal., filed Aug. 17, 2009).

18. Ibid.

19. Becker, *Forcing the Spring*, 251 (quoting Tony West).

20. See notes 15–17, citing Intervenor's Brief (Doc. 42 at 8–9), and studies by the American Academy of Pediatrics, http://aappolicy.aappublications.org/cgi/content/full/pediatrics;109/2/339 (Feb. 2002 policy statement); American Psychological Association, http://www.apa.org/pi/lgbc/policy/parents.html (July 2004 policy statement); American Academy of Child and Adolescent Psychiatry, http://www.aacap.org/cs/root/policy_statements/gay_lesbian_transgender_and_bisexual_parents_policy_statement (June 1999 policy statement); American Medical Association, http://www.ama-assn.org/ama/pub/about-ama/our-people/member-groups-sections/glbt-advisory committee/ama-policy-regarding-sexual-orientation.shtml (AMA Policy Regarding Sexual Orientation); Child Welfare League of America, http://www.cwla.org/programs/culture/glbtqposition.htm (Position Statement on Parenting of Children by Lesbian, Gay, and Bisexual Adults); Memorandum of Law in Support of Defendants' Motion to Dismiss, 3, Gill v. Office of Personnel Management, No. 09-10309 (D. Mass., filed Sept. 18, 2009) (emphasis added).

21. See Gill v. Office of Pers. Mgmt., 699 F. Supp. 2d 374, 397 (D. Mass. 2010); see also Mass. v. U.S. Dep't of Health & Human Servs., 698 F. Supp. 2d 234, 249, 253 (D. Mass. 2010) (a companion case brought by the Commonwealth of Massachusetts where the district court also ruled that Section 3 of DOMA exceeded Congress's powers under the Spending Clause and violated the Tenth Amendment). On appeal, the Department of Justice filed a brief defending DOMA but then filed a revised brief "altering its position," "arguing that the equal protection claim should be assessed under a 'heightened scrutiny' standard and that DOMA failed under that standard." This revised brief was filed after the Attorney General announced in a parallel case out of New York

that the Obama administration would no longer defend DOMA. See Smelt v. United States, Act III.

22. Order Granting Defendant's Motion to Dismiss, Smelt v. United States, No. 09-00286 (C.D. Cal. Aug. 24, 2009).

23. Peter Baker, "Kagan Is Sworn in as the Fourth Woman, and 112th Justice, on the Supreme Court," *N.Y. Times* (Aug. 8, 2010), A13, http://www.nytimes.com/2010/08/08/us/08kagan.html?_r=0 (available on Aug. 7, 2010).

24. United States v. Windsor, No. 10-cv-08435, Dkt. #1 (S.D. N.Y., filed Nov. 9, 2010).

25. Ibid., Dkt. #6 (Dec. 3, 2010); Dkt. #8 (Jan. 28, 2011).

26. Becker, *Forcing the Spring*, 257 (recounting Kaplan's initial refusal to agree to an extension until West called her directly and begged for the extension, adding, "The attorney general of the United States is asking you for time").

27. Office of Public Affairs at the U.S. Department of Justice, "Statement of the Attorney General on Litigation Involving the Defense of Marriage Act," Press Release (Feb. 23, 2011), http://www.justice.gov/opa/pr/statement-attorney-general-litigation-involving-defense-marriage-act (hereinafter "AG Statement").

28. Pederson v. Office of Personnel Management, No. 10-1750 (D. Conn., filed Nov. 9, 2010) (a cased filed in the federal district court for the District of Connecticut on the same day that the Windsor case had been filed in Manhattan; it was filed on behalf of six same-sex couples and one same-sex widower who alleged that because of DOMA, they were denied a variety of federal benefits that were available to heterosexual couples); "AG Statement."

29. Ibid.; Becker, *Forcing the Spring*, 248 (recounting that the President and Attorney General independently decided that a "heightened scrutiny" standard should be adopted in the government's responses in the pending cases and shared their views with each other when they bumped into each other in the hallway outside the State Dining Room in the White House on Super Bowl Sunday, February 6, 2011, where the Obamas had set up big-screen televisions for a small, informal Super Bowl party).

30. AG Statement.

31. See AG Statement; see also, e.g., Mass. v. U.S. Dep't of Health & Human Servs., 682 F.3d 1, 7 (1st Cir. 2012) ("The Justice Department filed a brief in this court defending DOMA against all constitutional claims. Thereafter, altering its position, the Justice Department filed a revised brief arguing that the

equal protection claim should be assessed under a 'heightened scrutiny' standard and that DOMA failed under that standard.").

32. See Attorney General William French Smith, Press Release, 5 (May 6, 1982) ("[T]he Department of Justice has the responsibility to defend acts of Congress unless they intrude on executive powers or are clearly unconstitutional.") (cited in Note, "Executive Discretion and the Congressional Defense of Statutes," *Yale L.J.* 92 (1983): 970, 975n19).

33. League of Women Voters of California v. F.C.C., 489 F. Supp. 517, 518 (C.D. Cal. 1980).

34. See Notification to Joint Leadership Group from Senate Legal Counsel in Respect to League of Women Voters v. F.C.C., reprinted in 125 *Cong. Rec.* 35416 (1979) (cited in Note, "Executive Discretion and the Congressional Defense of Statutes": 970, 1000 ("Congressional Defense of Statutes").

35. League of Women Voters of California v. F.C.C., 547 F. Supp. 379, 381 (C.D. Cal 1982), aff'd sub nom. F.C.C. v. League of Women Voters of California, 468 U.S. 364 (1984) (The statute was then ultimately held by the courts to be unconstitutional.).

36. Clinton v. City of New York, 524 U.S. 417 (1998).

37. See, e.g., Robert J. Delahunty & John Yoo, "Dream On: The Obama Administration's Non-Enforcement of the Immigration Laws, the DREAM Act, and the Take Care Clause," *Tex. L. Rev.* 91 (2013): 781.

38. The Declaration of Independence para. 4 (U.S. 1776).

39. See Sydney George Fisher, *The Struggle for American Independence* (Ulan Press, 2011), 131 ("the colonists, as good Whigs and lovers of liberty, would surely not uphold the wicked dispensing power of the Stuart Kings against whom their . . . ancestors had fought").

40. See Virginia Declaration of Rights § 7 (1776) ("That all power of suspending laws, or the execution of laws, by any authority without consent of the representatives of the people, is injurious to their rights, and ought not be exercised."); Delaware Declaration of Rights § 7 (1776) ("That no power of suspending Law . . . ought be exercised unless by the legislature"); Vermont Constitution of 1786, ch. I, § XVII ("The power of suspending laws, or the execution of laws, ought never be exercised, but by the Legislature, or by any authority derived from it, to be exercised in such particular cases only as the Legislature shall expressly provide for.").

41. See Americanus I, *Virginia Independent Chronicle*, reprinted in *The Documentary History of the Ratification of the Constitution* 8, Virginia No. 1, John P. Kaminski et al., eds. (Charlottesville: University of Virginia Press, 2009), 203–204 (arguing that under the Constitution, the President had no power to affect laws without participation of Congress); Virginia Ratification Debates, reprinted in *The Documentary History of the Ratification of the Constitution* 10, Virginia No. 3, 1552 (proposing an explicit amendment to prohibit a "power of suspending laws"); Gary Lawson & Christopher D. Moore, "The Executive Power of Constitutional Interpretation," *Iowa L. Rev.* 81 (1995–1996): 1267, 1304–1305 (reviewing scholarship demonstrating that Take Care Clause was a "textual rejection by the framers of the various royal devices for avoiding executive implementation of the laws"); see also Kendall v. U.S. ex rel. Stokes, 37 U.S. 524, 613 (1838) (holding that there is no "dispensing power" in the President); United States v. Smith, 27 F. Cas. 1192, 1230 (C.C.D.N.Y. 1806) ("The president of the United States cannot control the statute, nor dispense with its execution."). Cf. "American Bar Association Task Force on Presidential Signing Statements and the Separation of Powers Doctrine" (2006), 18, http://www.greenmountainpac.com/ABA_SigningStatementsTF.pdf ("because the 'take care' obligation of the President requires him to faithfully execute all laws, his obligation is to veto bills he believes are unconstitutional. He may not sign into law and then emulate King James II by refusing to enforce them.").

42. H.R. Rep. No. 104-664, at 13, reprinted in 1996 U.S.C.C.A.N. 2905.

43. See, e.g., Smelt v. County of Orange, 374 F. Supp. 2d 861, 880 (C.D. Cal. 2005), aff'd in part, vacated in part, remanded, 447 F.3d 673 (9th Cir. 2006); In re Kandu, 315 B.R. 123, 145 (Bankr. W.D. Wash. 2004); Wilson v. Ake, 2004 WL 3334722 (M.D. Fla.).

44. See Consolidated Mem. of Points and Authorities in Support of Defendants' Motion to Dismiss and in Opposition to Plaintiff's Motion for Summary Judgment, Gill v. Office of Personnel Management, 2010 WL 1935803 (Apr. 30, 2010); see also Dragovich v. U.S. Dep't of the Treasury, 764 F. Supp. 2d 1178, 1189 (N.D. Cal. 2011) ("Federal Defendants disavow the governmental interests identified by Congress in passing the DOMA, and instead assert a post-hoc argument that the DOMA advances a legitimate governmental interest in preserving the status quo.").

45. U.S. Brief in Support of Plaintiff's Mot. for Summary Judgment (Dkt. #71) (hereinafter "U.S. Brief Supporting SJ"), 22.

46. See, e.g., New York Lawyers Code of Professional Responsibility, Canon 7, Ethical Consideration 7-1 ("The duty of a lawyer, both to the client and to the legal system, is to represent the client zealously within the bounds of the law."); see also 28 U.S.C. § 530B(a) ("An attorney for the Government shall be subject to State laws and rules, and local Federal court rules, governing attorneys in each State where such attorney engages in that attorney's duties, to the same extent and in the same manner as other attorneys in that State.").

47. See, e.g., U.S. Brief Supporting SJ, 4.

48. Ibid., 22, 24–25.

49. Ibid., 5n1.

50. Ibid., 22.

51. See the Attorney General's Duty to Defend the Constitutionality of Statutes, 5 U.S. Op. Off. Legal Counsel 25 (O.L.C.), 1981 WL 30934, *25 (emphasis added); see also 4A Op. O.L.C. 55, 55 (1980) (noting that even when the Attorney General believes a statute to be unconstitutional, "he can best discharge the responsibilities of his office by defending and enforcing" it).

52. Memorandum and Order Granting Intervention, Dkt. #26 (June 2, 2011).

53. See ibid., Dkt. #20, 49, 71, 72.

54. United States v. Windsor, No. 12-63 (hereinafter "Windsor Cert.") (cert. petition filed July 16, 2012); Brief of the United States on Petition for Writ of Certiorari Before Judgment, Windsor v. United States, No. 12-63, *13 (2012) (hereinafter "Windsor Cert. U.S. Brief") (citing Sup. Ct. R. 11 and Golinski Pet. 13–16, a separate DOMA challenge in the Ninth Circuit Court of Appeals).

55. Windsor Cert. U.S. Brief, *9 (emphasis of language of intermediate scrutiny added).

56. Windsor Cert.

57. See, e.g., Lyle Denniston, "Kagan, DOMA, and Recusal," SCOTUSBlog (Nov. 2, 2012), http://www.scotusblog.com/2012/11/kagan-doma-and-recusal/.

58. Windsor Cert. U.S. Brief, *11–36.

59. See ibid.

60. Ibid., *37 (citing United States v. Virginia, 518 U.S. 515, 535–536 (1996)).

61. Ibid., *9, *11, *39, and *41.

62. E.J. Graff, "Retying the Knot," in *Same-Sex Marriage: Pro and Con*, ed. Andrew Sullivan (New York: Vintage, 2004), 135–138.

63. http://www.abrahamlincolnonline.org/lincoln/speeches/lyceum.htm.

CHAPTER 8

1. For the past several years I have advised several hedge funds on the various issues arising out of the ongoing dispute over Fannie and Freddie. My thanks to Rachel Bukberg, University of Chicago Law School, class of 2016, for her usual excellent research assistance on this essay.

2. 12 U.S.C. § 4501(7) (2013).

3. U.S. Const. art. II, § 3.

4. See generally Richard A. Epstein, "The Government Takeover of Fannie Mae and Freddie Mac: Upending Capital Markets with Lax Business and Constitutional Standards," *N.Y.U. J.L. & Bus.* 10 (2014): 379.

5. For information about the FHFA, see http://www.fhfa.gov.

6. Housing and Economic Recovery Act of 2008, Pub. L. 110-289, 122 Stat. 2654 (2008).

7. Richard A. Epstein, "The Public Trust Doctrine," *Cato J.* 7 (1987): 411, 417 (proposing the following test for state givings: "Nor shall public property be transferred to private use, without just compensation").

8. See generally Richard A. Epstein, "The History of Public Utility Regulation in the United States Supreme Court: Of Reasonable and Nondiscriminatory Rates," *J. Sup. Ct. Hist.* 38 (2013): 345.

9. See Federal National Mortgage Association Charter Act, 12 U.S.C. § 1719(g) (2012) (Fannie Mae); cf. Federal Home Loan Mortgage Corporation Act, 12 U.S.C. § 1455(l) (2012) (Freddie Mac); ibid.

10. 12 U.S.C. § 1719(g)(1)(C)(i–iv) (2012).

11. 12 U.S.C. § 4617 (2012).

12. 12 C.F.R. § 1237.3(b) (2012).

13. 12 U.S.C. § 4617(b)(2)(D) (2012).

14. Conservatorship and Receivership, 76 Fed. Reg. 35724, 35730 (June 20, 2011).

15. U.S. Dep't of Treas., "Statement by Secretary Henry M. Paulson, Jr. on Treasury and FHFA Action to Protect Financial Markets and Taxpayers," Press Release (Sept. 7, 2008), http://www.treasury.gov/press-center/press-releases/Pages/hp1129.aspx; ibid.

16. See FHFA, Senior Preferred Stock Purchase Agreements, Conservatorship, http://www.fhfa.gov/Conservatorship/Pages/Senior-Preferred-Stock-Purchase-Agreements.aspx (last visited July 13, 2015).

17. Starr Int'l Co. v. Fed. Res. Bank of N.Y., 906 F. Supp. 2d 202 (S.D.N.Y. 2012), aff'd, 742 F.3d 37 (2d Cir. 2014) (dealing only with the preemption issue).

18. See Richard A. Epstein, "A Tale of Two Bailouts: AIG, Fannie and Freddie and Beyond," *Forbes* (Nov. 26, 2014), http://www.forbes.com/sites/richardepstein/2014/11/26/a-tale-of-two-bailouts-aig-fannie-and-freddie-and-beyond/; cf. Ryan v. Tad's Enters, Inc., 709 A.2d 682, 690 (Del. Ch. 1996).

19. See Saxton v. FHFA, No. 1:15-cv-00047 (N.D. Iowa May 28, 2015).

20. See, e.g., Pumpelly v. Green Bay Co., 80 U.S. 166, 177–178 (1871).

21. Perry Capital LLC v. Lew, 2014 WL 4829559, nos. 13-1053 (RCL), 13-1439 (RCL), 13-1025 (RCL) (D.D.C. Sept. 30, 2014), https://scholar.google.com/scholar_case?case=5303049630589577280&q=Perry+Capital+v.+Lew&hl=en&as_sdt=400006.

22. 12 U.S.C. § 4617(b)(2)(A) (2012).

23. Ibid.

24. Penn. Cent. Transp. Co. et al. v. N.Y.C., 438 U.S. 104 (1978).

CHAPTER 9

1. See generally the *Federalist Papers*, http://thomas.loc.gov/home/histdox/fedpapers.html (on file with the author). See also Gregory E. Maggs, "A Concise Guide to the Federalist Papers as a Source of the Original Meaning of the United States Constitution," *B.U. L. Rev.* 87 (2007): 801, 802n2 ("Hamilton, Madison, and Jay originally published most of the essays in newspapers. Hamilton also collected these essays in a two-volume book called *The Federalist: A Collection of Essays Written in Favour of the New Constitution, As Agreed Upon by the Federal Convention September 17, 1787* (1788). In compiling this work, Madison edited the essays and added new ones that had not appeared in newspapers.") (internal citations omitted).

2. *The Federalist* No. 47 (Madison), p. 324 (J. Cooke, ed., 1961). See also INS v. Chadha, 462 U.S. 919, 960–961 (1983) (Powell, J., concurring in judgment) (citing Levi, "Some Aspects of Separation of Powers," *Colum. L. Rev.* 76 (1976): 369, 374).

3. See generally Maeva Marcus, "Separation of Powers in the Early National Period," *Wm. & Mary L. Rev.* 30 (1989): 269; ibid., 270 (quoting John Jay's "Charge to the Grand Jury of the Circuit Court for the District of New York" (Apr. 12, 1790) (John Jay Papers, Columbia University) (the Framers "have at Length very unanimously agreed vizt. that its Powers should be divided into three, distinct, independent Departments—the Executive, legislative and judicial. But how to constitute and ballance them in such a Manner as best to guard against Abuse and Fluctuation, & preserve the constitution from Encroachments, are Points on which there continues to be a great Diversity of opinions, and on which we have all as yet much to learn.")); ibid., 271 (characterizing some inter-branch impositions as "not entirely consistent with a strict separation of powers").

4. See ibid.

5. See Act of Feb. 4, 1887, ch. 104, §§ 18, 21, 24 Stat. 379, 386–387 (establishing the Interstate Commerce Commission within the control of the Secretary of the Interior); Act of Mar. 2, 1889, ch. 382, §§ 7–8, 25 Stat. 855, 861–862 (eliminating the requirement that the Secretary of the Interior approve salaries and expenses and authorizing the Commission to report directly to Congress).

6. *The Federalist* No. 47 (Madison), p. 324 (J. Cooke, ed., 1961).

7. See, e.g., Harold Furchtgott-Roth, "A Tough Act to Follow," Am. Enterprise Inst. (2006), https://www.aei.org/wp-content/uploads/2014/06/-a-tough-act-to-follow-the-telecommunications-act-of-1996-and-the-separation-of-powers_152737976914.pdf (on file with the author).

8. "FCC: What We Do," https://www.fcc.gov/what-we-do (on file with the author) ("An independent U.S. government agency overseen by Congress, the [FCC] is the United States' primary authority for communications law, regulation and technological innovation.").

9. Kirti Datla & Richard L. Revesz, "Deconstructing Independent Agencies (and Executive Agencies)," *Cornell L. Rev.* 98 (2013): 769, 818–820. Even if it is true that "'consultation and coordination on general policy issues of national interest naturally occurs' between the President and the [commission's] chair," that is not reason enough to excuse the erosion of the separation of powers. Ibid., 820 (quoting Peter L. Strauss, "The Place of Agencies in Government: Separation of Powers and the Fourth Branch," *Colum. L. Rev.* 84 (1984): 573, 591).

10. See, e.g., Marshall J. Breger & Gary J. Edles, *Independent Agencies in the United States: Law, Structure, and Politics* (New York: Oxford UP, 2015), 410–411.

11. See Kenneth Culp Davis & Richard J. Pierce, Jr., *Administrative Law Treatise*, 3rd ed. (New York: Aspen, 1994), § 2.5, 46 ("The characteristic that most sharply distinguishes independent agencies is the existence of a statutory limit on the President's power to remove the head (or members) of an agency."); Peter L. Strauss, *An Introduction to Administrative Justice in the United States* (Durham, NC: Carolina Academic Press, 1989), 15 ("Because [independent commission] members are appointed for fixed terms from which they cannot be dismissed without formal cause, they are more remote from presidential influence and control than the more usual 'executive' agency.").

12. Humphrey's Ex'r v. United States, 295 U.S. 602, 624, 625–626 (1935) (internal quotation marks and citation omitted).

13. City of Arlington v. FCC, 668 F.3d 229, 240 (5th Cir. 2012).

14. See Humphrey's Ex'r v. United States, 295 U.S. 623–628; see also Morrison v. Olson, 487 U.S. 654, 690–691 (1998); Wiener v. United States, 357 U.S. 349, 355–356 (1958).

15. Free Enterprise Fund and Bestead and Watts, LLP v. Public Company Accounting Oversight Board et al., 561 U.S. 477, 530 (2009) (Breyer, J., dissenting) (quoting James Madison, *Annals of Cong.* 1 (1789): 611–612).

16. Humphrey's Ex'r, 295 U.S. 624 (quoting S. Rep. No. 597, at 10–11 (1914)).

17. See ibid.; see also Datla & Revesz, "Deconstructing Independent Agencies," 771 ("the purpose of these agencies' structural features was recharacterized from promoting expertise to fostering independence from the President"). The understanding in some circles is that focused expertness "springs only from that continuity of interest, that ability and desire to devote fifty-two weeks a year, year after year, to a particular problem." James M. Landis, *The Administrative Process* (New Haven, CT: Yale UP, 1938), 23.

18. See generally Jody Freeman & Jim Rossi, "Agency Coordination in Shared Regulatory Space," *Harv. L. Rev.* 125 (2012): 1131, 1173–1181 (explaining the role of presidential oversight); Note, "Independence, Congressional Weakness, and the Importance of Appointment: The Impact of Combining Budgetary Autonomy with Removal Protection," *Harv. L. Rev.* 125 (2012): 1822, 1831–1838 (analyzing the effect of an independent funding source on executive

and legislative impositions on agencies); Marshall J. Breger & Gary J. Edles, "Established by Practice: The Theory and Operation of Independent Federal Agencies," *Admin. L. Rev.* 52 (2000): 1111, 1131–1133 (articulating that the need for administrators with "technical competence," "apolitical experience," and deftness in "scientific management" enabled the creation of independent agencies).

19. 47 U.S.C. § 151 et seq.

20. "FCC: FCC Adopts Strong, Sustainable Rules to Protect the Open Internet" (Feb. 26, 2015), https://www.fcc.gov/document/fcc-adopts-strong-sustainable-rules-protect-open-internet; "Protecting and Promoting the Open Internet," Report and Order on Remand, Declaratory Ruling and Order, GN Docket No. 14-28, FCC 15-24 (rel. Mar. 12, 2015), https://apps.fcc.gov/edocs_public/attachmatch/FCC-15-24A1.pdf (hereinafter "2015 Order").

21. Anne Flaherty, "GOP: Obama Aides Influenced 'Net Neutrality,'" *Salt Lake Trib.* (Mar. 17, 2015, 5:12 pm), http://www.sltrib.com/home/2303804-155/gop-obama-aides-influenced-net-neutrality (on file with the author); Brian Fung, "Read the E-mails that Republicans Say Show Obama Meddled in Net Neutrality," *Wash. Post* (Mar. 17, 2015), https://www.washingtonpost.com/blogs/the-switch/wp/2015/03/17/read-the-e-mails-that-republicans-say-show-obama-meddled-in-net-neutrality/ (on file with the author).

22. 47 U.S.C. § 251 et seq.

23. "The term 'telecommunications service' means the offering of telecommunications [the transmission, between or among points specified by the user, of information of the user's choosing, without change in the form or content of the information as sent and received] for a fee directly to the public, or to such classes of users as to be effectively available directly to the public, regardless of the facilities used." 47 U.S.C. §§ 153(53), (50).

24. "The term 'information service' means the offering of a capability for generating, acquiring, storing, transforming, processing, retrieving, utilizing, or making available information via telecommunications, and includes electronic publishing, but does not include any use of any such capability for the management, control, or operation of a telecommunications system or the management of a telecommunications service." 47 U.S.C. § 153(24).

25. Federal-State Joint Board on Universal Service, Report to Congress, 13 F.C.C.R. 11501, 11540, para. 81 (1998).

26. Inquiry Concerning High-Speed Access to the Internet Over Cable and Other Facilities et al., Declaratory Ruling and Notice of Proposed Rulemaking, 17 F.C.C.R. 4798, 4821, para. 36 (2002) ("Cable Modem Order"), aff'd sub nom. Nat'l Cable & Telecomms. Ass'n v. Brand X Internet Servs., 545 U.S. 967 (2005).

27. Nat'l Cable & Telecomms. Ass'n v. Brand X Internet Servs. 545 U.S. 967, 987–989 (2005).

28. Appropriate Framework for Broadband Access to the Internet over Wireline Facilities et al., Report and Order and Notice of Proposed Rulemaking, 20 F.C.C.R. 14853 (2005); United Power Line Council's Petition for Declaratory Ruling Regarding the Classification of Broadband over Power Line Internet Access Service as an Information Service, Memorandum Opinion and Order, 21 F.C.C.R. 13281 (2006); Appropriate Regulatory Treatment for Broadband Access to the Internet over Wireless Networks, Declaratory Ruling, 22 F.C.C.R. 5901 (2007).

29. See Framework for Broadband Internet Service, Notice of Inquiry, 25 F.C.C.R. 7866, 7894, paras. 63–64 (2010).

30. Michael K. Powell, Chairman, FCC, "Preserving Internet Freedom: Guiding Principles for the Industry," Remarks at the Silicon Flatirons Symposium on "The Digital Broadband Migration: Toward a Regulatory Regime for the Internet Age," 3 (Feb. 8, 2004), https://apps.fcc.gov/edocs_public/attachmatch/DOC-243556A1.pdf.

31. See Appropriate Framework for Broadband Access to the Internet over Wireline Facilities; Review of Regulatory Requirements for Incumbent LEC Broadband Telecommunications Services; Computer III Further Remand Proceedings: Bell Operating Company Provision of Enhanced Services; 1998 Biennial Regulatory Review—Review of Computer III and ONA Safeguards and Requirements; Inquiry Concerning High-Speed Access to the Internet over Cable and Other Facilities Internet over Cable Declaratory Ruling; Appropriate Regulatory Treatment for Broadband Access to the Internet over Cable Facilities, Policy Statement, 20 F.C.C.R. 14986 (2005).

32. See Comcast Corp. v. FCC, 600 F.3d 642 (D.C. Cir. 2010).

33. Preserving the Open Internet, Report and Order, 25 F.C.C.R. 17905 (2010), vacated in part, Verizon v. FCC, 740 F.3d 623 (D.C. Cir. 2014).

34. 47 U.S.C. § 1302.

35. See Verizon, 740 F.3d 635–649.

36. See ibid., 650–659.

37. See ibid., 657.

38. See Cellco P'ship v. FCC, 700 F.3d 534 (D.C. Cir. 2012).

39. See Verizon, 740 F.3d 656–659.

40. Ibid., 659.

41. See Protecting and Promoting the Open Internet, Notice of Proposed Rulemaking, 29 F.C.C.R. 5561, 5647 (2014) (hereinafter "2014 NPRM").

42. See ibid., 5563, para. 4.

43. See ibid., 5583, para. 62.

44. Nagesh & Mullins, "Blindsided."

45. Ibid.

46. The White House, "Net Neutrality: President Obama's Plan for a Free and Open Internet" (Nov. 10, 2014), http://www.whitehouse.gov/net-neutrality (hereinafter "Obama Net Neutrality Statement").

47. 47 U.S.C. § 160 et seq. Under section 10(c), any telecommunications carrier or a class thereof is entitled to file a petition with the commission asking that the commission apply the forbearance prerogative. Should the commission fail to act on a forbearance petition within one year (extended by three months, if necessary), the petition is "deemed granted." 47 U.S.C. § 160 (c). See also AT&T Inc. v. FCC, 452 F.3d 830, 834–837 (D.C. Cir. 2006) (analyzing Forbearance Order, 20 F.C.C.R. 9361).

48. There is no evidence that any ISP has ever engaged in paid prioritization, and many had expressly denied any interest in the practice during the FCC's proceeding.

49. See "Obama Net Neutrality Statement."

50. Ibid.

51. See Nagesh & Mullins, "Blindsided."

52. FCC, "FCC Chairman Tom Wheeler's Statement on President Barack Obama's Statement Regarding Open Internet," Press Release (Nov. 10, 2014), https://apps.fcc.gov/edocs_public/attachmatch/DOC-330414A1.pdf.

53. Ibid.

54. "2015 Order."

55. For a skeptical view on the commission's application of forbearance in the network neutrality order, see Harold Furchtgott-Roth, "The FCC Forbears from the Rule of Law," *Forbes* (Apr. 14, 2015), http://www.forbes.com/sites/haroldfurchtgottroth/2015/04/14/the-fcc-forbears-from-the-rule-of-law.

56. "2015 Order," 3.

57. The 2015 Order also imposed a going-forward "conduct standard," under which an ISP may not unreasonably interfere with or unreasonably disadvantage end users' ability to select, access, and use broadband Internet access service or the lawful Internet content, applications, services, or devices of their choice, or edge providers' ability to make lawful content, applications, services, or devices available to end users. See "2015 Order," paras. 20–21.

58. Susan Crawford, "A Tale of Two Commissioners," BackChannel (May 26, 2015), https://medium.com/backchannel how-the-fcc-found-its-backbone-960331bfac95.

59. Ibid.

60. See, e.g., Breger & Edles, "Established by Practice," 1138 and n131 ("The critical element of independence is the protection—conferred explicitly by statute or reasonably implied—against removal except 'for cause.'"). In addition, then Professor Elena Kagan opined that the "core legal difference" between independent and executive agencies is that the President lacks the power to unilaterally remove personnel from the former whereas he or she retains it with respect to the latter. Elena Kagan, "Presidential Administration," *Harv. L. Rev.* 114 (2001): 2245, 2376.

61. 47 U.S.C. § 154 (a).

62. See Kenneth C. Cole, "Presidential Influence on Independent Agencies," *Annals Am. Acad. Pol. & Soc. Sci.* 221 (May 1942): 74 ("Only individuals who have no ambition to succeed themselves in their present jobs can be uninfluenced by th[e] fact" that their re-nomination or other patronage possibilities depend on their being compliant with presidential wishes). This personnel-selection angle always "casts a shadow" on the substantive legitimacy of the policies these personnel render. Ibid.

63. See, e.g., Christopher S. Yoo, "U.S. vs. European Broadband Deployment: What Do the Data Say?" U. of Penn., Inst. for Law & Econ. Research Paper No. 14-35 (June 3, 2014), http://papers.ssrn.com/sol3/papers.cfm?abstract_id=2510854. See also Harold Furchtgott-Roth, "In Search of a Captive Audience: Susan Crawford's Captive Audience," *Fed. Comm. L.J.* 65 (2013): 312, 314–332.

64. Jason Koebler, "The Path to Community Broadband Runs Through an Army of Telecom Lawyers," Motherboard (July 25, 2014), http://motherboard

.vice.com/read/the-path-to-community-broadband-runs-through-an-army-of-telecom-lawyers (on file with the author).

65. Lawrence J. Spiwak, "The FCC's New Municipal Broadband Preemption Order Is Too Clever by Half," *Bloomberg News* (Apr. 13, 2015), http://www.bna.com/fccs-new-municipal-n17179925222/ (on file with the author); see also Federal Communications Commission, "Connecting America: The National Broadband Plan," (Mar. 16, 2010), p. 153, http://hraunfoss.fcc.gov/edocs_public/attachmatch/DOC-296935A1.pdf (on file with the author).

66. 740 F.3d 641.

67. Ibid., 660n2 (Silberman, J., concurring in part and dissenting in part).

68. 501 U.S. 452, 461.

69. Arizona v. Inter Tribal Council of Arizona, Inc., 133 S. Ct. 2247, 2256 (2013).

70. 541 U.S. 125 (2004).

71. Ibid., 138 ("§ 253 would not work like a normal preemptive statute if it applied to a governmental unit. It would often accomplish nothing, it would treat States differently depending on the formal structures of their laws authorizing municipalities to function, and it would hold out no promise of a national consistency.").

72. Ibid., 133–134.

73. See Allan Holmes, "Chattanooga Wants Feds to Pre-empt Broadband Ban," The Center for Public Integrity (July 10, 2014), http://www.publicintegrity.org/2014/07/10/15057/chattanooga-wants-feds-pre-empt-broadband-ban (on file with the author) ("Wheeler asked to meet with Chattanooga Mayor Andy Berke in June to discuss the city's plans for expanding its network. Wheeler told the mayor that any preemption of state laws would have to come out of the public utilities that ban or place barriers on cities that want to build or expand broadband networks.").

74. Tenn. Code Ann. § 7-52-601(a).

75. Tom Wheeler, "Removing Barriers to Competitive Community Broadband," FCC Blog (June 10, 2014), http://www.fcc.gov/blog/removing-barriers-competitive-community-broadband (on file with the author).

76. Petition of the Electric Power Board of Chattanooga, Tennessee, Pursuant to Section 706 of the Telecommunications Act of 1996, for Removal of Barriers to Broadband Investment and Competition, WC Docket No. 14-116 (filed July 24, 2014).

77. Petition of the City of Wilson, North Carolina, Pursuant to Section 706 of the Telecommunications Act of 1996, for Removal of Barriers to Broadband Investment and Competition, WC Docket No. 14-115 (filed July 24, 2014).

78. "Community-Based Broadband Solutions: The Benefits of Competition and Choice for Community Development and High-Speed Internet Access," The Exec. Office of the President, The White House (Jan. 2015), https://www.whitehouse.gov/sites/default/files/docs/community-based_broadband_report_by_executive_office_of_the_president.pdf (on file with the author).

79. "Fact Sheet: Broadband that Works: Promoting Competition & Local Choice in Next-Generation Connectivity," Office of the Press Sec'y, The White House (Jan. 13, 2015), https://www.whitehouse.gov/the-press-office/2015/01/13/fact-sheet-broadband-works-promoting-competition-local-choice-next-gener (on file with the author).

80. "Community-Based Broadband Solutions," 3.

81. Ibid., 18–19.

82. Letter from Lawrence E. Strickling, Assistant Sec'y, U.S. Dep't of Commerce, to Tom Wheeler, Chairman, FCC (Jan. 14, 2015), http://apps.fcc.gov/ecfs/document/view?id=60001013458_(on file with the author). In May 2009, President Obama had issued a memorandum announcing the Administration's general policy on preemption. See Memorandum from the White House, Office of the Press Sec'y, to the Heads of Exec. Dep'ts & Agencies (May 20, 2009). The President's memorandum declared "that preemption of State law by executive departments and agencies should be undertaken only with full consideration of the legitimate prerogatives of the States and with a sufficient legal basis for preemption." Ibid. Needless to say, the President's statements regarding government-operated broadband networks could not have diverged more sharply from this guidance.

83. "2015 Order," paras. 153–167.

84. City of Wilson, North Carolina Petition for Preemption of North Carolina General Statute Sections 160A-340 et seq., The Electric Power Board of Chattanooga, Tennessee Petition for Preemption of a Portion of Tennessee Code Annotated Section 7-52-601, Memorandum Opinion and Order, 30 F.C.C.R. 2408, 2506 (2015) (dissenting statement of Comm'r Ajit Pai).

85. See Pet. for Review, Tennessee v. FCC & United States, Case No. 15-3291 (6th Cir, filed Mar. 20, 2015), http://www.fedregsadvisor.com/files/2015/03/State-of-Tenessee-v-FCC.pdf (on file with the author); see Mot.

for Leave to Intervene, Tennessee v. FCC & United States, Case No. 15-3291 (6th Cir, filed Mar. 20, 2015), http://www.tellusventure.com/downloads/fcc/naruc_motion_to_intervene_muni_broadband_13apr2015.pdf (on file with the author).

86. See John Eggerton, "Divided FCC Votes to Expand E-Rate" (Dec. 11, 2014), http://www.multichannel.com/news/fcc/divided-fcc-votes-expand-e-rate/386230 (on file with the author).

87. See, e.g., Jerry Hausman & Howard Shelanski, "Economic Welfare and Telecommunications Regulation: The E-Rate Policy for Universal Service Subsidies," *Yale J. on Reg.* 16 (1999): 19, https://www.heartland.org/policy-documents/economic-welfare-and-telecommunications-regulation-e-rate-policy-universal-service; Jerry Hausman, "Taxation by Telecommunications Regulation," *Tax Policy and the Economy*, vol. 12, ed. James M. Poterba (Cambridge, MA: MIT Press, 1998), 29; Christopher DeMuth, "The Strange Case of the E-Rate," Am. Enterprise Inst. On the Issues (July 1998).

88. See 47 U.S.C. §§ 254(h)(1)(B), 254(h)(2).

89. See Schools and Libraries Universal Service Support Mechanism and a National Broadband Plan for Our Future, Sixth Report and Order, 25 F.C.C.R. 18762, 18780–18783, paras. 35–40 (2010).

90. See "FCC: Taking the Next Step in E-Rate Modernization" (Nov. 17, 2014), https://www.fcc.gov/blog/taking-next-step-e-rate-modernization (on file with the author).

91. See "President Obama Unveils ConnectED Initiative to Bring America's Students into Digital Age," The White House, Press Release (June 6, 2013), https://www.whitehouse.gov/the-press-office/2013/06/06/president-obama-unveils-connected-initiative-bring-america-s-students-di (on file with the author) (hereinafter "White House ConnectED Release").

92. See "FCC: High-Speed Services for Internet Access: Status as of June 30, 2008," tbl. 16 (2009), http://www.fcc.gov/Daily_Releases/Daily_Business/2009/db0723/DOC-292191A1.pdf.

93. See "White House ConnectED Release."

94. "Fact Sheet: ConnectED: President Obama's Plan for Connecting All Schools to the Digital Age," The White House (June 6, 2013), https://www.whitehouse.gov/sites/default/files/docs/connected_fact_sheet.pdf (on file with the author).

95. Susan Jones, "Reporters Laugh When Obama's Spokesman Denies Another 'End Run' Around Congress," *CNS News* (Aug. 15, 2013), http://www.cnsnews.com/news/article/reporters-laugh-when-obamas-spokesman-denies-another-end-run-around-congress (on file with the author).

96. Ibid.

97. Modernizing the E-Rate Program for Schools and Libraries, Notice of Proposed Rulemaking, 28 F.C.C.R. 11304, 11469 (2013) (statement of Acting Chairwoman Mignon Clyburn).

98. Mary Jo Madda, "FCC Approves E-Rate Reform to Boost Funding for Broadband," edSurge (July 10, 2014), https://www.edsurge.com/n/2014-07-11-fcc-approves-e-rate-reform-to-boost-funding-for-broadband (on file with the author).

99. Tom Wheeler, "Helping American Students Compete in a Digital World," FCC Blog (Jan. 24, 2014, 3:30 pm), http://www.fcc.gov/blog/helping-american-students-compete-digital-world (on file with the author).

100. Barack Obama, President of the U.S., State of the Union address (Jan. 28, 2014), http://www.washingtonpost.com/politics/full-text-of-obamas-2014-state-of-the-union-address/2014/01/28/e0c93358-887f-11e3-a5bd-844629433ba3_story.html (on file with the author).

101. FCC, "Statement from FCC Chairman Tom Wheeler on the State of the Union Address and the FCC's E-Rate Program," Press Release (Jan. 28, 2014), https://apps.fcc.gov/edocs_public/attachmatch/DOC-325328A1.pdf (on file with the author).

102. FCC, "FCC to Invest Additional $2 Billion in High-Speed Internet in Schools and Libraries," Press Release (Feb. 3, 2014), https://apps.fcc.gov/edocs_public/attachmatch/DOC-325403A1.pdf (on file with the author).

103. U.S. Dep't of Educ., Inst. of Educ. Scis., Nat'l Ctr. for Educ. Statistics, "Fast Facts," http://nces.ed.gov/fastfacts/display.asp?id=372 (on file with the author).

104. Ibid.

105. Edward Wyatt, "FCC Says It Will Double Spending on High-Speed Internet in Schools and Libraries," *N.Y. Times* (Feb. 1, 2014), http://www.nytimes.com/2014/02/02/us/fcc-says-it-will-double-spending-on-high-speed-internet-in-schools-and-libraries.html_(on file with the author).

106. Tom Wheeler, Chairman, FCC, Prepared Remarks at National Digital Learning Day, 1, 3 (Feb. 5, 2014), http://transition.fcc.gov/Daily_Releases/Daily_Business/2014/db0205/DOC-325447A1.pdf (on file with the author).

107. Modernizing the E-Rate Program for Schools and Libraries, Notice of Proposed Rulemaking, 29 F.C.C.R. 8870 (2014).

108. Modernizing the E-Rate Program for Schools and Libraries, Second Report and Order and Order on Reconsideration, 29 F.C.C.R. 15538 (2014).

109. Ibid., 15635 (dissenting statement of Comm'r Ajit Pai).

110. Datla & Revesz, "Deconstructing Independent Agencies," 771; Landis, *The Administrative Process*, 38.

111. Humphrey's Ex'r, 295 U.S. 624.

CHAPTER 10

1. A special thank you to John Cook for his valuable contributions to this essay.

2. See, e.g., Bureau of Labor Statistics, Business Employment Dynamics, http://www.bls.gov/bdm/home.htm. Although not without dispute, the right answer to sluggish economic growth may be to foster demand by promoting small businesses as engines of job creation. See generally J.D. Harrison, "Who Actually Creates Jobs: Start-ups, Small Businesses or Big Corporations?" *Wash. Post* (Apr. 25, 2015), http://www.washingtonpost.com/business/on-small-business/who-actually-creates-jobs-start-ups-small-businesses-or-big-corporations/2013/04/24/d373ef08-ac2b-11e2-a8b9-2a63d75b5459_story.html.

3. See generally Joseph Schumpeter, *Capitalism, Socialism and Democracy* (New York: Harper and Bros., 1942).

4. See, e.g., Troy A. Paredes, Commissioner, U.S. Securities & Exchange Commission, "Remarks at The SEC Speaks in 2011" (Feb. 4, 2011), https://www.sec.gov/news/speech/2011/spch020411tap.htm.

5. See generally *Hearing on Venture Exchanges and Small-Cap Companies (Mar. 10, 2015) Before the Subcommittee on Securities, Insurance, and Investment of the U.S. Senate Committee on Banking, Housing, and Urban Affairs*; *Hearing on Legislative Proposals to Enhance Capital Formation and Reduce Regulatory Burdens, Part II (May 13, 2015) Before the Subcommittee on Capital Markets and Government Sponsored Enterprises of the U.S. House of Representatives Committee on Financial Services.*

6. See Rule 12b-2 (17 C.F.R. § 240.12b-2); Regulation S-K, Item 10(f)(1) (17 C.F.R. § 229.10(f)(1)). "Float" refers to the value of common equity held by persons not affiliated with the issuer; it is calculated by multiplying the number of shares held by non-affiliates by the current price per share in the principal market for the common equity. Ibid.

7. See Regulation S-X, Article 8 (17 C.F.R. § 210.8-01 et seq.).

8. See Regulation S-K, Item 10(f) (table listing scaling provided across Regulation S-K). The "smaller reporting company" concept was created in 2007 when the commission terminated the separate reporting regime for "small business issuers" under Regulation S-B and replaced it with eased reporting requirements under Regulation S-K for smaller reporting companies. See Rel. No. 33-8876, Smaller Reporting Company Regulatory Relief and Simplification (Dec. 19, 2007).

9. See, e.g., General Instruction A(2) to Form 10K.

10. See Jumpstart Our Business Startups (JOBS) Act of 2012 § 103, amending Sarbanes-Oxley § 404.

11. Section 5 of the '33 Act establishes the basic system for SEC oversight of interstate offers and sales of securities in the U.S. (i.e., public offerings), including the requirement for registration of such offerings with the SEC and the burdens and restrictions incident thereto.

12. Rules 504 and 505 are promulgated pursuant to Section 3(b) of the '33 Act. Section 3(b) permits the SEC to exempt certain small issuances from Section 5's registration requirements.

13. "Accredited investor" is defined to include a number of large institutions as well as natural persons whose net worth exceeds $1 million or whose income exceeds $200,000 (or $300,000 when combined with a spouse's income). See Rule 501(a) of Regulation D (17 C.F.R. § 230.501(a)). Rule 506 is a safe harbor for offerings under Section 4(a)(2) (formerly Section 4(2)) of the '33 Act, the private offering exemption. See generally SEC v. Ralston Purina Co., 346 U.S. 119 (1953) (concluding that an offering where the investors are able to "fend for themselves" is not a public offering subject to Section 5).

14. Rule 506 preempts state "blue sky" laws that otherwise generally require registration of those offerings with each state in which offers or sales of securities are made. Rules 504 and 505 do not preempt state blue sky laws. Thus, a small business may choose to use the Rule 506 exemption so as to avoid the expense, burdens, and uncertainty of state registration.

15. Regulation A was adopted by the commission in 1936 under Section 3(b) of the '33 Act. See, e.g., Rel. No. 33-9741, Amendments for Small and Additional Issues Exemptions under the Securities Act (Regulation A) (Mar. 25, 2015).

16. As noted, Rule 506 of Regulation D is a safe harbor based on the private offering exemption of Section 4(a)(2). One of the tenets of the private offering exemption had been that advertising an offering and general solicitation are inconsistent with what it means for an offering to be "private." Therefore, Rule 506 did not allow such activity. The JOBS Act changed this. The legislation mandated that the SEC eliminate the ban on advertising and general solicitation for Rule 506 offerings. The SEC created a new class of offerings under Rule 506(c) to which the ban on advertising and general solicitation does not apply so long as the issuer takes reasonable steps to verify the accredited status of the ultimate purchasers of securities. See Rel. No. 33-9415, Eliminating the Prohibition Against General Solicitation and General Advertising in Rule 506 and Rule 144A Offerings (July 10, 2013).

Regulation A had become widely criticized as not being useful because there was no state blue sky preemption afforded to Regulation A offerings and because of the small size ($5 million) of offerings permitted under the regulation. See U.S. Government Accountability Office, "Securities Regulation: Factors That May Affect Trends in Regulation A Offerings, GAO-12-839 (July 3, 2012). The JOBS Act permitted the SEC to preempt blue sky registration and qualification requirements for Regulation A offerings to qualified purchasers and also raised the offering limit to $50 million. The SEC implemented these provisions in 2015 in what many refer to as "Regulation A+." Regulation A+ has two "tiers." Tier 1, for offerings between $0 and $20 million, requires concurrent registration with the SEC and the states but does not require ongoing reporting with the SEC. Tier 2, for offerings between $0 and $50 million, preempts states' role in approving the offering but requires continuing compliance with a particularized periodic reporting regime.

17. An EGC is a company that has annual gross revenues of less than $1 billion. An EGC maintains that status until (i) its revenues are $1 billion or more, (ii) the fifth anniversary of its IPO, (iii) it issues over $1 billion in non-convertible debt over the prior three years, or (iv) it becomes a "large accelerated filer" (i.e., it has over $700 million in non-affiliate float). See Securities Act § 2(a)(19).

18. The JOBS Act smooths the path to an IPO for these companies—the "on ramp"—by, for example, permitting confidential filing of draft registration statements with the commission, allowing an EGC to present fewer years of audited financial statements and other selected financial data than is the case for other issuers, and exempting EGCs from the costly independent internal controls audit required by Section 404(b) of the Sarbanes-Oxley Act.

19. Forms of crowdfunding already exist. The most common—which sprung up before the JOBS Act—is donation-based crowdfunding, where a group of people donates money to a cause or a business in exchange for a product, such as a T-shirt, or some other tangible benefit. Equity-based crowdfunding, on the other hand, is simply another form of securities offering, which, if done on an interstate basis, would trigger SEC registration and disclosure obligations.

The JOBS Act directed the SEC to create an alternative regulatory framework to facilitate crowdfunding as a new way for very small businesses to raise capital. In addition to the "wisdom of the crowd," a notable investor protection that was included is a cap on how much an investor can invest; this, in turn, caps how much an investor can lose. The SEC has proposed a regime to implement this provision of the JOBS Act but has yet to adopt final rules. See Rel. No. 33-9470, Crowdfunding (Oct. 23, 2013). In the meantime, crowdfunding on the basis of other exemptions from the registration and mandatory disclosure provisions of the '33 Act (e.g., the intrastate exemption of Section 3(a)(11) of the '33 Act and the new Rule 506(c) exemption for unlimited offerings to investors using general solicitation) has been advancing apace.

20. Daniel M. Gallagher, Commissioner, U.S. Securities & Exchange Commission, "Whatever Happened to Promoting Small Business Capital Formation?" (Sept. 17, 2014), http://www.sec.gov/News/Speech/Detail/Speech/1370542976550. That is, rather than an incremental approach to regulation based on tweaking the "crazy quilt" of existing rules, regulations, exemptions, no-action letters, interpretive guidance, and the like when problems arise, or when Congress tells the SEC to do so, the SEC should proactively evaluate small business funding needs and determine how to align the commission's rules and regulations with those needs, so that the SEC is promoting, rather than impeding, capital formation. See Daniel M. Gallagher, Commissioner, U.S. Securities & Exchange Commission, "Crazy Quilt Chart of Regulation" (June 3, 2015), http://www.sec.gov/news/statement/crazy-quilt-chart-of-regulation.html.

21. Moreover, liquidity can be important for employees of a private company, who will want to turn at least some of their securities into cash in a "liquidity event." Accordingly, liquidity can help start-up companies hire, reward, and retain the talent they need to grow and prosper over time.

22. Section 12(g) of the '34 Act requires a company with a certain number of shareholders to provide periodic disclosures to the public, even if the company has not engaged in a public offering. Title V of the JOBS Act increased the number of shareholders of record triggering mandatory '34 Act reporting for companies other than banks to 2,000 persons or 500 persons who are not accredited investors. The threshold had been 500 shareholders. Banks received their own special thresholds in Title VI of the JOBS Act.

23. The inability of employees to find a ready market for their shares could force an employer to go public before the company is ready in order to give employees (and other shareholders) liquidity. If an employer is determined to stay private, employees (and other shareholders) might not be able to sell for an extended period of time. Secondary liquidity for the private securities could help a start-up or other small business attract and keep the employees it needs to succeed. Here, one solution may be to formalize the so-called "Section 4(a)(1½)" exemption, which would facilitate the "private" resale of securities initially sold in a private offering. See Gallagher, "Crazy Quilt Chart of Regulation." The SEC's Small Business Advisory Committee on June 3, 2015, endorsed this idea.

24. Regulation A shares can be listed on an exchange, and the SEC's final Reg. A+ rule even included some accommodations to help Regulation A issuers achieve exchange listing—particularly, permitting certain issuers in a Tier 2 offering to concurrently register that class of securities under the '34 Act using short-form Form 8-A rather than the more burdensome Form 10. However, if such issuers were to list on any of the current exchanges, they would immediately become subject to full Section 13 (i.e., unscaled) reporting obligations, thereby eliminating the benefit of the scaled periodic regime that would otherwise result from a Regulation A Tier 2 offering.

25. NYSE's small cap market, NYSE MKT, is a separate exchange (formerly the American Stock Exchange). By contrast, the NASDAQ Capital Market is a tier within NASDAQ's exchange.

26. Listing standards are standards that a company must satisfy to be listed (i.e., trade) on an exchange. They include rules for the size of the company

(e.g., the company generally must have a minimum share price, a minimum capitalization or revenues, and a minimum number of publicly traded shares), the conduct of the company, and corporate governance (e.g., audit committee requirements), as well as reporting and other disclosure obligations. Listing on an exchange also triggers '34 Act reporting obligations under Section 12(b) of the '34 Act, meaning an issuer must comply with the disclosure requirements under Section 13 of the '34 Act, including SEC Forms 10-K, 10-Q, 8-K, and so forth.

27. While we focus on venture exchanges in this essay, we'd also welcome ideas for greater secondary liquidity of privately placed securities and improvements to the OTC market.

28. See Rel. No. 33-8876, Smaller Reporting Company Regulatory Relief and Simplification (Dec. 19, 2007).

29. Ibid.

30. An issuer might be expected to migrate out of a venture exchange once it reaches a certain size because the benefits of a main-tier listing could exceed those of remaining on the venture exchange. If many issuers remain on the venture exchange even when they are able to meet the requirements of trading on a main exchange, it would highlight the need to evaluate whether we have overburdened companies listing on our main tier stock exchanges.

31. For example, Rule 611 of Reg. NMS, alternatively known as the "trade-through rule" or the "order protection rule," generally seeks to avoid "trade-throughs"—execution at other than the best price available, which could mean a price on other exchanges or venues. See generally SEC Equity Market Structure Advisory Committee, Memorandum, Rule 611 of Regulation NMS (Apr. 30, 2015), https://www.sec.gov/spotlight/emsac/memo-rule-611-regulation-nms.pdf.

32. See, e.g., James Angel et al., "Equity Trading in the 21st Century," Marshall School of Business Working Paper No. FBE 09-10 (Feb. 23, 2010); James Angel et al., "Equity Trading in the 21st Century: An Update" (June 21, 2013), http://www.q-group.org/wp-content/uploads/2014/01/Equity-Trading-in-the-21st-Century-An-Update-FINAL1.pdf.

33. See, e.g., IPO Task Force, "Rebuilding the IPO On-Ramp: Putting Emerging Companies and the Job Market Back on the Road to Growth" (Oct. 20, 2011), http://www.sec.gov/info/smallbus/acsec/rebuilding_the_ipo_on-ramp.pdf, 13–14.

34. See, e.g., Charles Collver, Financial Economist, Division of Trading and Markets, "A Characterization of Market Quality for Small Capitalization US Equities," U.S. Securities & Exchange Commission (Sept. 2014), http://www.sec.gov/marketstructure/research/small_cap_liquidity.pdf ("The smallest stocks with market capitalization less than $100 Million are exceptionally illiquid relative to larger stocks with capitalizations between $1 Billion and $5 Billion. They have wider quoted and effective spreads and trade lower dollar volumes. These measures tend to improve monotonically with market cap. The smallest stocks exhibit much less depth on average than stocks in larger capitalization ranges."). See also Stephen Luparello, Director, Division of Trading and Markets, U.S. Securities & Exchange Commission, *Testimony on Venture Exchanges and Small-Cap Companies before the U.S. Senate Subcommittee on Securities, Insurance, and Investment, Committee on Banking, Housing, and Urban Affairs* (Mar. 10, 2015), http://www.sec.gov/news/testimony/testimony-venture-exchanges.html.

35. While the following discussion contemplates choices that the venture exchange itself would make in determining how to set itself up, an alternative to consider would be to permit each venture exchange to leave some or all of these decisions (depending, for example, upon operational and technological complexity and the degree of investor confusion) to each company listing there—in effect, allowing each venture-exchange-listed company to decide for itself how its shares will trade.

36. To be sure, we believe that this has its benefits by promoting competition. Even if there were less competition for where the stock of a particular small cap company trades, there could still be competition among venture exchanges to gain listings in the first place.

37. See '34 Act § 12(f).

38. The market structure changes do not need to be as categorical as we have described them. There could be shades of gray. For example, rather than banning off-exchange trading, it could be permitted so long as there is a sufficiently meaningful benefit (e.g., size or price improvement) if the trade were to occur elsewhere.

39. This is not unprecedented; other jurisdictions are experimenting with this approach already. While we should not blindly follow their lead, looking to their experience may be instructive. For example, on Europe's Euronext, the most liquid securities are traded continuously while less liquid securities are

traded at call auctions at 11:30 AM and 4:30 PM. See Euronext, "Trading Rules & Methods," https://www.euronext.com/trading/trading-methods (last accessed June 12, 2015). In 2013, India instituted a similar requirement, although by December of that year it had to "rationalize" the criteria due to decreased volumes in some of the shares under the call-auction mechanism. See, e.g., Securities and Exchange Board of India, Circular No. CIR/MRD/DP/6/2013 (Feb. 14, 2013) (directing stock exchanges to, at the beginning of every quarter, identify listings meeting certain illiquidity criteria and shift them to trade on a periodic call-auction basis).

NYSE and NASDAQ both have call auctions at open and at close but continuous trading for the rest of the day. Continuous trading has the advantage of enabling buyers and sellers to execute nearly instantaneously, but the liquidity is diffuse throughout the day; periodic call auctions require all willing buyers and sellers to concentrate their liquidity at the preordained times.

40. Perhaps a venture exchange could permit listed companies to determine their own tick size—a possibility to explore. It is not clear that a larger tick size would necessarily result in better market quality for small cap companies. The SEC has a pilot program under way to determine if it might. See Rel. No. 34-74892, Order Approving a National Market System Plan to Implement a Tick Size Pilot Program (May 6, 2015). The same spirit that animated the drive for that pilot program—for example, that increased tick sizes might incentive market-makers to provide liquidity and might lead to more research—could also apply to venture exchanges. We don't know if these results will materialize from larger tick sizes or, even if they do, if the costs of wider spreads will outweigh the benefits. Whatever is learned from the tick size pilot would have a bearing on the proper market structure for venture exchanges.

41. See, e.g., Troy A. Paredes, "Blinded by the Light: Information Overload and Its Consequences for Securities Regulation," *Wash. U. L.Q.* 81 (2003): 417; Daniel M. Gallagher, Commissioner, U.S. Securities & Exchange Commission, "Remarks to the Forum for Corporate Directors, Orange County, California" (Jan. 24, 2014), http://www.sec.gov/News/Speech/Detail/Speech/1370540680363.

42. In 1996, Congress upended the parallel securities regulatory regime that had existed since 1933—state securities regulation sitting alongside federal securities regulation—by determining that certain securities are of such a national character that preempting state securities regulation with respect to those securi-

ties was warranted. In so doing, Congress greatly streamlined regulatory compliance burdens with respect to the sale of those securities. But this statute—the National Securities Markets Improvement Act of 1996 (NSMIA)—limited preemption to so-called "covered securities." Included within the definition of "covered securities" are securities that are (a) listed on the NYSE, AMEX, or NASDAQ's national market system; (b) listed on a national securities exchange that has "listing standards that the Commission determines by rule . . . are substantially similar to the listing standards applicable" under (a); or (c) is a security at least as senior as a security under (a) or (b). See '33 Act § 18(b).

43. Following NSMIA's passage, NASDAQ sought to have the SEC designate its SmallCap Market as falling within the scope of Section 18 to get the benefit of blue sky preemption; this request was rejected. One of the grounds for rejection was that the minimum share price for preferred shares on the SmallCap Market would have been $4, while on the AMEX at the time it was $10. See Rel. No. 33-7494, Covered Securities Pursuant to Section 18 of the Securities Act of 1933 (Jan. 2, 1998) (also citing minimum distribution requirements for preferred stock and warrants, as well as a less-stringent maintenance standard). NASDAQ reapplied in 2006 on behalf of its Capital Market (formerly known as SmallCap Market) in conjunction with its transition to a registered exchange and after having beefed up its listing standards to make them substantially similar to one of the named markets. The SEC approved the designation. See Rel. No. 33-8791, Covered Securities Pursuant to Section 18 of the Securities Act of 1933 (Apr. 18, 2007).

44. Cf. Rel. No. 33-9741, Amendments for Small and Additional Issues Exemptions under the Securities Act (Regulation A) (Mar. 25, 2015) (federal protections, even properly scaled ones, sufficient to justify preemption of state blue sky laws). In the long run, Congress should consider finding a different basis for blue sky preemption than substantial similarity with incumbent industry participants, with its attendant effects of stifling innovation and competition.

45. These are the Section 13 reporting obligations. See General Instruction A(2) to Form 10K for the exceptions.

46. Scaling for smaller companies has a rich history at the SEC, from Regulations A and D—which are themselves a form of scaling of otherwise-applicable regulatory obligations—to a scaled '34 Act reporting regime solely for small businesses. See Rel. No. 33-8876, Smaller Reporting Company Regulatory Relief and Simplification (Dec. 19, 2007).

47. Consider the disclosure requirements for smaller reporting companies. The current cut-off for scaled disclosure applies to companies with $75 million in float, which does not align well with commonly accepted market definitions of "nanocap" (up to $50 million in float) and "microcap" (up to $300 million). Tailoring the definition of a "smaller reporting company" to the microcap level and then seeking even greater reductions in disclosures for a new category of, say, "smallest reporting company" could yield improvements. This more refined breakdown would represent a realization that enterprises in these various size bands present different types of concerns and that concerns that may warrant more costly regulation for some companies are not appropriate for others. A finer gradient by company size could, in turn, promote a more calibrated cost-benefit analysis than is the case today, with respect to weighing whether the benefits of disclosure truly justify the costs for smaller companies, including the smallest. Moreover, cost-benefit analysis could be improved by taking into consideration the total burden of the reporting regime on small business. Currently, when the commission adopts new rules, it analyzes only the incremental costs and benefits imposed by the specific rule under consideration. It does not consider the broader picture of whether the overall regulatory burden is appropriate. Even if no single rule can be seen as the "straw that breaks the camel's back," it is still possible for the cumulative regulatory burden to discourage companies from going public.

48. See generally Troy A. Paredes, Commissioner, U.S. Securities & Exchange Commission, "Statement at Open Meeting to Adopt a Final Rule Regarding Shareholder Approval of Executive Compensation and Golden Parachute Compensation" (Jan. 25, 2011), http://www.sec.gov/news/speech/2011/spch012511tap-3.htm (refusing to support the "say-on-pay" final rule because the commission did not exempt smaller reporting companies or provide a phase-in period for newly public companies from the say-on-pay shareholder vote); Daniel M. Gallagher, Commissioner, U.S. Securities & Exchange Commission, "Dissenting Statement at an Open Meeting Proposing Mandated Pay versus Performance Disclosures" (Apr. 29, 2015) (citing absence of an exemption for smaller reporting companies and emerging growth companies as a reason for opposing the proposed rule requiring pay versus performance disclosures), http://www.sec.gov/news/statement/dissent-proposing-mandated-pay-versus-performance-disclosures.html; Daniel M. Gallagher, Commissioner, U.S. Securities & Exchange Commission, "Dissenting Statement at an Open

Meeting to Propose Compensation Clawback Listing Standards" (July 1, 2015) (dissenting, in part, because the proposed rule does not exclude smaller reporting companies or EGCs), http://www.sec.gov/news/statement/dissenting-statement-compensation-clawback-listing-standards.html.

49. By way of contrast, the BX Venture Market that the SEC approved has scaled quantitative standards but governance standards that are "generally comparable to those of other exchanges." See Rel. No. 34-64437, Self-Regulatory Organizations; NASDAQ OMX BX, Inc.; Order Granting Approval of Proposed Rule Change and Amendment No. 1 Thereto and Notice of Filing and Order Granting Accelerated Approval to Amendment No. 2 Thereto to Create a Listing Market on the Exchange (May 6, 2011).

50. For current SEC investor education efforts, see generally the website for the SEC's Office of Investor Education and Advocacy at http://investor.gov.

51. In this regard, the NYSE used to have three-letter symbols and NASDAQ four-letter symbols. Prefacing venture listings with some consistent label (e.g., VX) might help encourage investors to evaluate the risks and rewards of investing in a venture-exchange-listed company.

52. See, e.g., Arthur Levitt, "Op-Ed, A Small-Cap Idea with Little to Recommend It: The SEC's Plan to Create Special Exchanges Sounds Like a Solution in Search of a Problem," *Wall St. J.* (Mar. 2, 2015); Luis A. Aguilar, Commissioner, "The Need for Greater Secondary Market Liquidity for Small Businesses," U.S. Securities & Exchange Commission (Mar. 4, 2015), http://www.sec.gov/news/statement/need-for-greater-secondary-market-liquidity-for-small-businesses.html.

53. For example, this is a prime metric by which the Toronto stock market venture exchange measures success. See TMX Group, "TSX Venture Exchange Celebrates 600 Graduates," Press Release (Oct. 30, 2014) (noting that the total number of companies to graduate from TSX Venture Exchange to the "main" Toronto Stock Exchange platform from January 1, 2000, to October 30, 2014, had reached 600).

CHAPTER 11

1. The authors wish to recognize and thank Mr. Adam White, Esq. for his invaluable assistance. Mr. White is an attorney in Washington, D.C. He clerked for Judge David Sentelle, U.S. Court of Appeals for the D.C. Circuit.

2. Dodd-Frank characterizes the Consumer Financial Protection Bureau in a variety of inconsistent ways. The act calls it an "independent bureau" established "in the Federal Reserve System," Dodd-Frank § 1011(a), or an "independent agency," § 1100D(a). But the act also calls it an "Executive agency," § 1011(a). For present purposes we discuss it as an "executive agency," despite its independence from the presidency, because the CFPB's current leadership certainly acts in a manner consistent with the policy goals of this particular President.

3. "Congressional Profiles," http://history.house.gov/Congressional-Overview/Profiles/111th. See also "Alphabetical List: Senators," http://www.gpo.gov/fdsys/pkg/CDIR-2009-12-01/pdf/CDIR-2009-12-01-STATISTICALINFORMATION-2.pdf.

4. See, e.g., Ronald D. Orol, "Obama Signs Sweeping Bank-Reform Bill into Law," *MarketWatch* (July 21, 2010), http://www.marketwatch.com/story/story/print?guid=2B007AF9-98C4-46BD-B7B6-09545EF8ADEF. The law is named after Senator Chris Dodd (D-CT) and Congressman Barney Frank (D-MA).

5. See, e.g., Cody Vitello, "The Wall Street Reform Act of 2010 and What It Means for Joe & Jane Consumer," *Loy. Consumer L. Rev.* 23 (2010–2011): 99. See also Securities Exchange Act of 1934, 15 U.S.C. § 78(a) et seq.

6. Dodd-Frank Wall Street Reform and Consumer Protection Act, Pub. L. 111-203 (July 21, 2010), http://www.gpo.gov/fdsys/pkg/PLAW-111publ203/pdf/PLAW-111publ203.pdf.

7. One of this chapter's authors is co-lead counsel in a constitutional challenge to the CFPB's structure. Shortly before this work went to press, the D.C. Circuit held unanimously that the lead plaintiff, a West Texas community bank, has standing to litigate those constitutional claims. State Nat'l Bank of Big Spring et al. v. Lew et al., No. 13-5247, 2015 WL 4489885 (D.C. Cir. July 24, 2015).

8. C. Boyden Gray & John Shu, "The Dodd-Frank Wall Street Reform & Consumer Protection Act of 2010: Is It Constitutional?" *Engage* 11, no. 3 (Dec. 2010), http://www.fed-soc.org/publications/detail/the-dodd-frank-wall-street-reform-consumer-protection-act-of-2010-is-it-constitutional-2.

9. See generally U.S. Const. arts. I, II, and III. See also U.S. Const. art. III, § 3, cl. 4, stating that the president must "take Care that the Laws be faithfully executed."

10. Today, the Bureau is more commonly known as the Consumer Financial Protection Bureau, or CFPB.

11. NLRB v. Noel Canning, 573 U.S. ___ (2014).

12. Josh Gerstein, "Supreme Court Strikes Down Obama Recess Appointments," *Politico* (June 26, 2014), http://www.politico.com/story/2014/06/supreme-court-recess-appointments-108347.html.

13. U.S. Senate, Roll Call Votes, 113th Cong., 1st Session (July 16, 2013), http://www.senate.gov/legislative/LIS/roll_call_lists/roll_call_vote_cfm.cfm?congress=113&session=1&vote=00174. The vote was 66–34.

14. "Sec. 11. That a Commission is hereby created and established to be known as the Inter-State Commerce Commission, which shall be composed of five Commissioners, who shall be appointed by the President, by and with the advice and consent of the Senate . . . Any Commissioner may be removed by the President for inefficiency, neglect of duty, or malfeasance in office. Not more than three of the Commissioners shall be appointed from the same political party." The ICC Termination Act of 1995, P.L. 104-88 (1995), abolished the Interstate Commerce Commission.

15. See, e.g., Panama Refining Co. v. Ryan, 293 U.S. 388 (1935) (striking § 9(c) of the National Industrial Recovery Act of 1933 because Congress improperly delegated power to the President); R.R. Ret. Bd. v. Alton R.R. Co., 295 U.S. 330 (1935) (striking the Railroad Retirement Act of 1934); A.L.A Schechter Poultry Corp. v. United States, 295 U.S. 495 (1935) (striking § 3 of the National Industrial Recovery Act of 1933 and the National Recovery Administration's "codes of fair competition"); Louisville Joint Stock Land Bank v. Radford, 295 U.S. 555 (1935) (striking the Frazier–Lemke Emergency Farm Bankruptcy Act of 1934); Humphrey's Ex'r v. United States, 295 U.S. 602 (1935) (invalidating President Roosevelt's removal of President Calvin Coolidge's and President Herbert Hoover's appointees to the Federal Trade Commission, an independent regulatory agency); United States v. Butler, 297 U.S. 1 (1936) (striking the Agricultural Adjustment Act of 1933 and the Agricultural Adjustment Administration); Carter v. Carter Coal Co., 298 U.S. 238 (1936) (striking the Bituminous Coal Conservation Act of 1935); Ashton v. Cameron Cnty. Water Improvement Dist. No. 1, 298 U.S. 513 (1936) (striking the Municipal Bankruptcy Act of 1934, also known as Sumners-Wilcox); Morehead v. New York ex rel. Tipaldo, 298 U.S. 587 (1936) (striking New York's state labor commission's minimum wage).

16. See, e.g., W. Coast Hotel Co. v. Parrish, 300 U.S. 379 (1937); Steward Mach. Co. v. Davis, 301 U.S. 548 (1937); Nat'l Labor Rel. Bd. v. Jones & Laughlin Steel Corp., 301 U.S. 1 (1937). Justice Owen Roberts's controversial joining of the Parrish majority is commonly known as "The Switch in Time to Save Nine," referring to President Roosevelt's "court-packing plan," the Judicial Procedures Reform Bill of 1937. The Judiciary Act of 1869, 16 Stat. 44, established the U.S. Supreme Court's makeup of the Chief Justice and eight associate justices, any six of whom constitute a quorum.

17. Dodd-Frank, § 1011(a).

18. Despite certain statutory exceptions, such as § 1029 (auto dealers, which was one of the compromises needed for the law's passage) and § 1075 (interchange fees, also known as the Durbin Amendment), the CFPB is taking aggressive steps to get around them. See notes 80–84.

19. Dodd-Frank, §§ 1022(a), (b)(1), (b)(2), (b)(4).

20. Dodd-Frank, § 1022(b)(3)(A) (emphasis added).

21. Dodd-Frank, § 1022(b)(4). But cf. Reg'l Rail Reorg. Act Cases, 419 U.S. 102 (1974) (due process takings claims, in some circumstances, satisfied collaterally in the Court of Claims). Courts generally review an administrative agency's decision on an arbitrary and capricious standard, i.e., whether the agency's action is reasonable and based on a proper consideration of the circumstances; the courts generally give that agency what is known as *Chevron* deference. Chevron U.S.A., Inc. v. Natural Res. Def. Council, Inc., 467 U.S. 837 (1984). The classic *Chevron* two-step test is where a reviewing court determines (1) whether Congress spoke directly to the precise question at issue (Congress's unambiguously expressed intent controls); and (2) if the statute is silent *or ambiguous* (emphasis added) with respect to the specific question, the court must review whether the agency's answer is based on a permissible construction of the statute. See also Natural Res. Def. Council, Inc. v. U.S. Envtl. Prot. Agency, 966 F.2d 1292, 1297 (9th Cir. 1992). The act's deferential requirements essentially means that the CFPB's interpretations will trump those of other agencies. Dodd-Frank, § 1022(b)(4)(B).

22. Dodd-Frank, § 1023.

23. Dodd-Frank, § 1011(a).

24. See, e.g., Rachel E. Barkow, "Insulating Agencies: Avoiding Capture Through Institutional Design," *Tex. L. Rev* 89 (2010): 15, 73–74.

25. See, e.g., Dodd-Frank § 1017(a)(4)(E).

26. Dodd-Frank, § 1017(a)(1).

27. Dodd-Frank, § 1017(a)(2)(C).

28. Dodd-Frank, §§ 1017(c)(2), (c)(3).

29. Dodd-Frank, § 1017(c)(1).

30. Dodd-Frank, § 1017(a)(2). The percentage was 10 percent for FY2011, 11 percent for FY2012, and 12 percent for FY2013 and beyond. The CFPB's budget is also entitled to the percent increase in the employment cost index. See also Board of Governors of the Federal Reserve System, 96th Annual Report 2009 (May 2010), http://www.federalreserve.gov/boarddocs/rptcongress/annual09/pdf/ar09.pdf.

31. Dodd-Frank, §§ 1017(e)(1), (e)(2).

32. Oddly, the act requires that the CFPB director prepare reports and appear before Congress regarding, *inter alia*, "a justification of the budget request of the previous year." See, e.g., Dodd-Frank, § 1016(c)(2).

33. CFPB, "The CFPB Strategic Plan, Budget, and Performance Plan and Report" (Feb. 2015), http://files.consumerfinance.gov/f/201502_cfpb_report_strategic-plan-budget-and-performance-plan_FY2014-2016.pdf. The CFPB had 1,379 full-time employees or equivalents (FTEs) in FY2014, an estimated 1,537 FTEs for FY2015, and 1,690 FTEs for FY2016. Ibid., 15.

34. Ibid., 21.

35. See, e.g., CFPB organizational chart, available at http://www.consumerfinance.gov/the-bureau/.

36. CFPB, "The CFPB Strategic Plan, Budget, and Performance Plan and Report" (Apr. 2013), 81, http://files.consumerfinance.gov/f/strategic-plan-budget-and-performance-plan-and-report-FY2012-14.pdf.

37. The FTC's FY2014 actual total budget was $334 million with 1,145 FTEs agency-wide. The FTC Bureau of Competition (antitrust) received $146 million. Fiscal Year 2016 Congressional Budget Justification, Federal Trade Commission (Feb. 2, 2015), https://www.ftc.gov/system/files/documents/reports/fy-2016-congressional-budget-justification/2016-cbj.pdf. The CFPB's duties overlap somewhat with the FTC's (e.g., payday lending, deceptive mortgage practices), which was founded on September 16, 1914. See, e.g., ibid. at 7, 97. The Securities & Exchange Commission's FY2014 enacted total budget was $1.46 billion, with 1,294 FTE's. FY2015 Congressional Budget Justification, FY2015 Annual Performance Plan, FY2013 Annual Performance Report,

U.S. Securities & Exchange Commission, http://www.sec.gov/about/reports/secfy15congbudgjust.pdf.

38. Dodd-Frank, § 1012(c)(2).

39. Ibid.

40. Dodd-Frank, § 1012(c)(3).

41. Dodd-Frank, § 1012(c)(1).

42. Mark Bialek, CFPB Inspector General, "Letter Evaluating CFPB Headquarters Renovation," CFPB Office of the Inspector General (June 30, 2014), http://financialservices.house.gov/uploadedfiles/ig_report_regarding_cfpb_headquarters.pdf.

43. Ibid.

44. Ibid.

45. Ibid.

46. Ibid.

47. Testimony of Richard Cordray, CFPB Director (Mar. 3, 2014), U.S. House of Representatives Committee on Financial Services, http://tinyurl.com/pbgyo9b.

48. Dodd-Frank, § 1021(b)(2).

49. Dodd-Frank, § 1031.

50. Dodd-Frank, § 1036(a)(1)(B).

51. Dodd-Frank, § 1036(a)(3).

52. Dodd-Frank, § 1031(d).

53. See, e.g., Dodd-Frank, §§ 1022(a), (b)(1), (b)(2), (b)(4).

54. Dodd-Frank, § 1031(e).

55. Dodd-Frank, §§ 1022(b)(2).

56. Administrative Procedure Act, 5 U.S.C. §§ 500–504, §§ 551–559, §§ 561–570(a).

57. Kate Davidson, "Trying to Stay Above the Politics: A Conversation with Richard Cordray," *American Banker* (Mar. 23, 2012), http://www.americanbanker.com/issues/177_58/cordray-cfpb-supervision-enforcement-consumers-UDAAP-UDAP-1047798-1.html.

58. Dodd-Frank, § 1022(b).

59. Senator Ted Kaufman (D-DE), who voted for Dodd-Frank, said that "the bill delegates too much authority to the regulators. . . . Congress largely has decided instead to punt decisions to the regulators, saddling them with a mountain of rule-makings and studies." The Congressional Record, 111th Cong.,

2nd Session, 156, no. 105, Daily Edition (July 15, 2010), S5885, http://www.gpo.gov/fdsys/pkg/CREC-2010-07-15/pdf/CREC-2010-07-15-pt1-PgS5870-2.pdf.

60. Dodd-Frank, § 1054(a).

61. Dodd-Frank, §§ 1055(b), (c). The civil penalties go up to $1,000,000 per day for a knowing violation. Ibid.

62. Dodd-Frank, §§ 1054(f), 1055(a).

63. Although Dodd-Frank, § 1029 is titled "Exclusion for Auto Dealers," § 1029(a) is titled "Sale, Servicing, And Leasing of Motor Vehicles Excluded," not just automobiles. § 1029(f) defines "motor vehicle" to include, for example, recreational boats and motorcycles and also defines "motor vehicle dealer."

64. Dodd-Frank, §§ 1029(c), (d).

65. Congress felt comfortable exempting automobile dealers from CFPB regulation because the Fed, the FTC, and the full range of state consumer protection statutes still strictly regulated them. See, e.g., "Consumer Financial Protection Bureau (CFPB) 101," Nat'l Auto. Dealers Ass'n (Sept. 2014), https://www.nada.org/WorkArea/DownloadAsset.aspx?id=21474838551. State statutes governing fraud and automobile dealers have long demanded disclosure and strictly prohibited dealers from forcing F&I products upon their customers, or even suggesting that an F&I product is required or will help obtain financing approval. See, e.g., "Finance & Insurance Best Practices for Minnesota Dealers," Minn. Auto. Dealers Ass'n, http://tinyurl.com/q66m6ry.

66. See, e.g., Kimberly Long, "Serving the Right Mix of F&I Products," *Auto Dealer Today* (Nov. 2011), http://tinyurl.com/ok42vzr.

67. Dodd-Frank, § 1029(b).

68. Dodd-Frank, § 1029(b)(2).

69. CFPB, "Indirect Auto Lending and Compliance with the Equal Credit Opportunity Act," Bulletin 2013-02 (Mar. 21, 2013), http://files.consumerfinance.gov/f/201303_cfpb_march_-Auto-Finance-Bulletin.pdf.

70. Ibid.

71. See, e.g., Dodd-Frank, §§ 1022(b)(2), 1031(e). See also Administrative Procedure Act, 5 U.S.C. §§ 500–504, §§ 551–559, §§ 561–570(a).

72. Ibid.

73. Ibid.

74. Ibid. See also Regulation B, 12 C.F.R. § 1002.2(l). On June 25, 2015, the U.S. Supreme Court decided Texas Dep't of Hous. & Community Affairs v. The Inclusive Communities Project, Inc., holding that the Fair Housing Act

authorizes disparate impact claims. This case strengthens the CFPB's disparate impact approach. While the CFPB will almost certainly apply this FHA case to ECOA and other consumer protection claims, Justice Kennedy's opinion imposed important limitations on disparate impact liability in order "to protect potential defendants against abusive disparate-impact claims."

75. See CFPB, "Fair Lending, Lending Discrimination," Bulletin 2012-04 (Apr. 18, 2012), http://files.consumerfinance.gov/f/201404_cfpb_bulletin_lending_discrimination.pdf.

76. See, e.g., Ricci v. DeStefano, 557 U.S. 557, 57–78 (2009). See also Wards Cove Packing Co. v. Atonio, 490 U.S. 642 (1989).

77. Ibid.

78. Ibid.

79. CFPB Bulletin 2013-02 (Mar. 21, 2013).

80. See *The Godfather* (Paramount Pictures, 1972).

81. CFPB, "Consumer Financial Protection Bureau to Hold Auto Lenders Accountable for Illegal, Discriminatory Markup," CFPB Fact Sheet (Mar. 21, 2013), http://files.consumerfinance.gov/f/201303_cfpb_march_-Auto-Finance-Factsheet.pdf.

82. Cf. Tupac Shakur, Big Syke (feat. Prince Ital Joe), *Thug Life: Vol. 1* (Out Da Gutta Records, Interscope Records, Sept. 26, 1994).

83. The CFPB, like any other administrative agency, should not be permitted to exceed its statutory authority and flaunt other federal statutes because its in-house attorneys were unusually and aggressively creative in achieving its director's personal policy preferences, especially when Congress clearly expressed its intent with a statutory exception. It also should not be permitted to issue non-rules, which are essentially rules, and use them as such.

84. Senator Elizabeth Warren (D-MA), "The Unfinished Business of Financial Reform," Remarks at the Levy Institute's 24th Annual Hyman P. Minsky Conference (Apr. 15, 2015), http://www.warren.senate.gov/files/documents/Unfinished_Business_20150415.pdf.

85. Letter from Richard Cordray to U.S. Representative Terri Sewell (D-AL) (June 20, 2013), http://www.cfpbmonitor.com/files/2013/06/06-21-13_CFPB-Letter-on-Auto-Lending1.pdf.

86. See Jim Henry, "CFPB Faces Legal Hurdle in Regulating F&I Products," *Automotive News* (Oct. 15, 2014), http://tinyurl.com/nh5fxr7.

87. CFPB, "Defining Larger Participants of the Automobile Financing Market and Defining Certain Automobile Leasing Activity as a Financial Product or Service," Final Rule, RIN: 3170-AA46 (June 2015), http://files.consumerfinance.gov/f/201506_cfpb_defining-larger-participants-of-the-automobile-financing-market-and-defining-certain-automobile-leasing-activity-as-a-financial-product-or-service.pdf. See also CFPB, "Automobile Finance Examination Procedures" (June 2015), http://files.consumerfinance.gov/f/201506_cfpb_automobile-finance-examination-procedures.pdf.

88. CFPB, "CFPB to Oversee Nonbank Auto Finance Companies; Bureau Publishes Exam Procedures for Supervised Companies in $900 Billion Market," Press Release (June 10, 2015), http://www.consumerfinance.gov/newsroom/cfpb-to-oversee-nonbank-auto-finance-companies.

89. Ibid.

90. Bernie Woodall and Ben Klayman, "U.S. Auto Sales End 2014 Strong but Slower Growth Looms," *Reuters* (Jan. 5, 2015), http://tinyurl.com/q47ms73. These numbers do not include sales of manufacturers' certified pre-owned vehicles, for which manufacturers' finance arms often extend purchase loans on terms very favorable to the consumer. There appear to be no confirmable hard data available on how many (1) supplementary finance and insurance product transactions the automobile dealers and manufacturers' finance arms made in 2014, (2) how many loans or leases the manufacturers' finance arms acquired from other entities in 2014, and (3) how many loans or leases the automobile dealers and manufacturers' finance arms refinanced. As of this writing, it is unknown whether the CFPB considers supplementary finance and insurance products separate transactions from the primary lease or purchase loan, especially if several different products are bundled into a single vehicle lease or purchase.

91. CFPB, Final Rule, RIN: 3170-AA46. See also Dodd-Frank § 1002(15)(A)(xi)(II).

92. Dodd-Frank, § 1054(a).

93. Dodd-Frank, §§ 1055(b), (c). The civil penalties go up to $1,000,000 per day for a knowing violation. Ibid.

94. Dodd-Frank, §§ 1054(f), 1055(a). For example, the Securities and Exchange Commission prevailed in 90 percent of the cases before its own administrative law judges in the time period from October 2010 to March 2015. The SEC prevailed in 69 percent of the cases in federal court over the same time period. The SEC prevailed in 95 percent of administrative appeals from January

2010 to Mar. 2015. At the SEC, like the CFPB, the agency is the prosecutor, the judge, and the court of appeals in these cases. Moreover, the agencies pay the administrative law judges' salaries. The agencies also are able to better control the evolution of legal doctrine when before its own administrative law judges. Jean Eaglesham, "SEC Wins with In-House Judges," *Wall St. J.* (May 6, 2015), http://www.wsj.com/articles/sec-wins-with-in-house-judges-1430965803.

95. 12 C.F.R. §§ 1081.201, 1081.206.

96. CFPB, "Rules of Practice for Adjudication Proceedings," Final Rule, RIN: 3170-AA05 (June 2012), http://files.consumerfinance.gov/f/201206_cfpb_final-rule_rules-of-practice-for-adjudication-proceedings.pdf.

97. 12 C.F.R. § 1081.208.

98. See, e.g., Amanda West Abshire and Herrmann Lawson, "CFPB Enforcement Action Appeals: Quick Resolution with Unchecked Discretion," *JD Supra Business Advisor* (May 22, 2015), http://tinyurl.com/pemcw3z. See also 12 C.F.R. §§ 1081.400–1081.407.

99. Ibid. See also, CFPB, Final Rule, RIN: 3170-AA05 (June 2012).

100. Ibid.

101. Trey Garrison, "CFPB Director: PHH Corp. Took Kickbacks for Mortgage Insurance Referrals," HousingWire.com (June 4, 2015), http://www.housingwire.com/articles/print/34100-cfpb-director-phh-corp-took-kickbacks-for-mortgage-insurance-referrals. The kickbacks were mortgage reinsurance premiums that mortgage insurers paid to a PHH subsidiary. In re PHH Corp., No. 2014-CFPB-0002 (Consumer. Fin. Prot. Bureau) (case documents from January 29, 2014–June 24, 2015), http://www.consumerfinance.gov/administrativeadjudication/2014-cfpb-0002.

102. Trey Garrison, "What to Expect When You're Expecting a CFPB Administrative Action," HousingWire.com (July 6, 2015), http://www.housingwire.com/articles/print/34389-what-to-expect-when-youre-expecting-a-cfpb-administrative-action.

103. In re PHH Corp., No. 2014-CFPB-0002 (Consumer Fin. Prot. Bureau, June 4, 2015) (Decision of the Director (Public Version)), http://files.consumerfinance.gov/f/201506_cfpb_decision-by-director-cordray-redacted-226.pdf. See also In re PHH Corp., No. 2014-CFPB-0002 (Consumer Fin. Prot. Bureau, June 4., 2015) (Final Order), http://files.consumerfinance.gov/f/201506_cfpb_final_order_227.pdf.

104. Ibid.

105. Ibid. For example, Director Cordray determined that PHH accrued a new RESPA violation each time the mortgage insurers paid PHH a reinsurance premium, not when the underlying mortgage loan closed, as the ALJ found. Director Cordray also determined that any premium monies that PHH paid out to insurance claimants was irrelevant to disgorgement calculations, i.e., that PHH must disgorge its ill-gotten *revenue*, not its ill-gotten *profit*. Ibid.

106. Ibid.

107. Ibid.

108. Ibid. The U.S. Courts of Appeal will give the trial court great deference to its fact-finding and may only review questions of law de novo.

109. PHH Corp. v. CFPB, No. 15-1177 (D.C. Cir. filed June 19, 2015).

110. See, e.g., Lydia DePillis, "A Watchdog Grows Up: The Inside Story of the Consumer Financial Protection Bureau," *Wash. Post* (Jan. 11, 2014).

111. See, e.g., U.S. House of Representatives Committee on Financial Services, June 25, 2015, *Oversight and Investigations Subcommittee, Hearing Entitled "Examining Continuing Allegations of Discrimination and Retaliation at the Consumer Financial Protection Bureau," Memorandum*, 114th Cong. (June 22, 2015), http://financialservices.house.gov/uploadedfiles/062515_oi_memo.pdf.

112. Angela Martin, Esq., Senior Enforcement Attorney, CFPB Office of Enforcement, *Testimony of Angela Martin Before the House Committee on Financial Services Subcommittee on Oversight and Investigations, U.S. House of Representatives*, 113th Cong. (Apr. 2, 2014), http://financialservices.house.gov/uploadedfiles/hhrg-113-ba09-wstate-amartin-20140402.pdf.

113. Ibid.

114. See, e.g., Congressman Sean Duffy (R-WI), Chairman, Opening Statement, *Hearing Entitled "Examining Continuing Allegations of Discrimination and Retaliation at the Consumer Financial Protection Bureau," U.S. House of Representatives Committee on Financial Services, Subcommittee on Oversight and Investigations*, 114th Cong. (June 25, 2015), http://tinyurl.com/pqrtdqf.

115. See, e.g., U.S. House of Representatives Committee on Financial Services, Subcommittee on Oversight and Investigations, *Hearing Entitled "Examining Continuing Allegations of Discrimination and Retaliation at the Consumer Financial Protection Bureau," U.S. House of Representatives*, 114th Cong. (June 25, 2015), http://financialservices.house.gov/calendar/eventsingle.aspx?EventID=399269.

116. Ibid., Congressman Sean Duffy (R-WI), Opening Statement (June 25, 2015).

117. Rachel Witkowski, "CFPB Grapples with Spike in Employee Bias Complaints," *American Banker* (June 15, 2015), http://www.americanbanker.com/news/law-regulation/cfpb-grapples-with-spike-in-employee-bias-complaints-1074889-1.html?zkPrintable=1&nopagination=1.

118. Rachel Witkowski, "CFPB Staff Evaluations Show Sharp Racial Disparities," *American Banker* (Mar. 6, 2014), http://www.americanbanker.com/issues/179_44/cfpb-staff-evaluations-show-sharp-racial-disparities-1066045-1.html?zkPrintable=1&nopagination=1.

119. Ibid.

120. Ibid.

121. Trey Garrison, "The Claim: Discrimination, Intimidation Culture Runs Through CFPB," HousingWire.com (June 18, 2014), http://www.housingwire.com/articles/30367-discrimination-intimidation-culture-runs-through-cfpb.

122. Misty Raucci, *Testimony Before the U.S. House of Representatives Committee on Financial Services, Subcommittee on Oversight and Investigations Subcommittee, Hearing Entitled "Examining Continuing Allegations of Discrimination and Retaliation at the Consumer Financial Protection Bureau," U.S. House of Representatives*, 113th Cong. (Mar. 28, 2014), http://financialservices.house.gov/uploadedfiles/hhrg-113-ba09-wstate-mraucci-20140402.pdf.

123. Ibid.

124. Ibid.

125. Rachel Witkowski, "Democrats, Republicans Vow to Continue Probe into CFPB Employment Practices," *American Banker* (Apr. 2, 2014), http://www.americanbanker.com/issues/179_64/democrats-republicans-vow-to-continue-probe-into-cfpb-employment-practices-1066664-1.html?zkPrintable=true.

126. Kevin A. Williams, CFPB Office of Consumer Response, *Testimony Before the U.S. House of Representatives Committee on Financial Services, Subcommittee on Oversight and Investigations, Hearing Entitled "Examining Continuing Allegations of Discrimination and Retaliation at the Consumer Financial Protection Bureau," U.S. House of Representatives*, 113th Cong. (June 18, 2014), http://www.gpo.gov/fdsys/pkg/CHRG-113hhrg91149/html/CHRG-113hhrg91149.htm. See also Nicholas Ballasy, "Witness Details Alleged CFPB Gender, Racial Discrimination," *Credit Union Times* (Apr. 2, 2014), http://www.cutimes.com/2014/04/02/witness-details-alleged-cfpb-gender-racial-discrim.

127. Florine Williams, CFPB Office of Civil Rights, *Testimony Before the U.S. House of Representatives Committee on Financial Services, Subcommittee on Oversight and Investigations, Hearing Entitled "Examining Continuing Allegations of Discrimination and Retaliation at the Consumer Financial Protection Bureau," U.S. House of Representatives*, 114th Cong. (June 25, 2015), http://financialservices.house.gov/uploadedfiles/hhrg-114-ba09-wstate-fwilliams-20150625.pdf.

128. Kelly Riddell, "Bureaucrats Gone Wild: Feds Describe Racial Hostility, Discrimination inside New Obama Agency," *Wash. Times* (Aug. 27, 2014), http://www.washingtontimes.com/news/2014/aug/27/us-consumer-financial-protection-bureau-employees-/print/. Naraghi earned top performance marks and promotions at the Federal Reserve. His CFPB managers, however, graded him at the lowest performance review level, allegedly in retaliation for Naraghi's pointing out to CFPB management that the bureau was not using a consistent, objective risk model when evaluating bank performance, resulting in CFPB bank examinations that were skewed in favor of whatever predetermined result the CFPB management and/or the CFPB examiner wanted. Ibid. See also Angela Martin, Esq., *Testimony Before Congressman Patrick McHenry (R-NC), "Allegations of Discrimination and Retaliation and the CFPB Management Culture," U.S. House of Representatives Financial Services Committee, Subcommittee on Oversight and Investigations Subcommittee*, 113th Cong. (Apr. 2, 2014), http://tinyurl.com/orqx587.

129. Witkowski, "CFPB Staff Evaluations Show Sharp Racial Disparities."

130. Ibid. It is perhaps also no surprise that the CFPB demonstrated an "abysmal record of non-compliance" with Congress's requests for information. Alan Zibel, "Hensarling Wants Quicker Responses from 'Stonewalling' Agencies," *Wall St. J.* (Mar 3, 2015), http://tinyurl.com/qc2mg7c.

131. Ibid.

132. Ibid.

133. Rob Blackwell, "CFPB Employee Rating Disparities Go Beyond Just Race, Agency Says," *American Banker* (May 19, 2014), http://www.americanbanker.com/issues/179_96/cfpb-employee-rating-disparities-go-beyond-just-race-agency-says-1067575-1.html.

134. Ibid.

135. Ibid. These statistical disparities, along with causality evidence, would likely support a disparate impact claim against the CFPB, especially because

the CFPB admitted that its employee evaluations contained "broad-based" and "statistically significant disparities." Ibid.

136. Trey Garrison, "Sound and Fury at CFPB Racial Discrimination Hearing," HousingWire.com (Apr. 2, 2014), http://www.housingwire.com/articles/29531-sound-and-fury-at-cfpb-racial-discrimination-hearing. See also *Testimony of Angela Martin, Esq. Before Congressman Patrick McHenry (R-NC)* (Apr. 2, 2014).

137. Ryan Smith, "CFPB Discriminates Against Women, Minorities—Union Rep," *Mortgage Professional America* (May 22, 2014), http://www.mpamag.com/news/cfpb-discriminates-against-women-minorities--union-rep-18311.aspx ("women and minority employees were being underpaid when compared to similarly situated white male colleagues").

138. See, e.g., Joe Sims, "How Racism Sparked Capitalism's Financial Crisis," *People's World* (Jan. 30, 2009), http://www.peoplesworld.org/how-racism-sparked-capitalism-s-financial-crisis. Congressman Frank strongly believed that racism played a role in the collapse. See, e.g., Sam Dealey, "Barney Frank's Fannie and Freddie Racism Regarding the Financial Crisis," *U.S. News & World Report* (Oct. 8, 2008), http://www.usnews.com/opinion/blogs/sam-dealey/2008/10/08/barney-franks-fannie-and-freddie-racism-regarding-the-financial-crisis.

139. Robert Cauldwell, President, NTEU Chapter 335, *Testimony Before the U.S. House of Representatives Committee on Financial Services, Subcommittee on Oversight and Investigations, Hearing Entitled "Examining Continuing Allegations of Discrimination and Retaliation at the Consumer Financial Protection Bureau," U.S. House of Representatives*, 114th Cong. (June 25, 2015), http://financialservices.house.gov/uploadedfiles/hhrg-114-ba09-wstate-rcauldwell-20150625.pdf.

140. Witkowski, "CFPB Grapples with Spike in Employee Bias Complaints."

141. Ibid.

142. See, e.g., Arthur Postal, "Administration: 'No Sequels Here' Where Financial Oversight Is Concerned," InsuranceNewsNet (May 27, 2015), http://tinyurl.com/nvynrsp.

143. See, e.g., Brian Honea, "Wisconsin Representative Continues CFPB Reform Efforts with Series of Proposals," *DSNews* (Mar. 6, 2015), http://tinyurl.com/oua2kcv. Congresswoman Maxine Waters (D-CA) has been one of the CFPB's strongest defenders. Ibid.

144. Todd Zywicki & Chad Reese, "Redundant Today, Essential Tomorrow," *U.S. News & World Report* (June 30, 2015), http://tinyurl.com/q96meaa.

145. Financial Regulatory Improvement Act of 2015, S. 1484, U.S. Senate, 114th Cong. (June 2, 2015), https://www.congress.gov/bill/114th-congress/senate-bill/1484/text.

146. Consumer Financial Protection Bureau Accountability Act of 2015, S. 1383, U.S. Senate, 114th Cong. (May 19, 2015), http://tinyurl.com/psefwye.

147. Reforming CFPB Indirect Auto Financing Guidance Act of 2015, H.R. 1737, U.S. House of Representatives, 114th Cong. (Apr. 13, 2015), http://tinyurl.com/o8a53kr.

148. Ibid.

149. Bureau Advisory Commission Transparency Act of 2015, H.R. 1265, U.S. House of Representatives, 114th Cong. (Apr. 14, 2015), http://tinyurl.com/nhoqxrc.

150. Ibid.

151. Ibid.

152. Bureau of Consumer Financial Protection Advisory Boards Act of 2015, H.R. 1195, U.S. House of Representatives, 114th Cong. (Apr. 22, 2015), http://tinyurl.com/oglxdqt.

153. Ibid.

154. Newt Gingrich, "A Government Snoop That Puts the NSA to Shame," *Wall St. J.* (July 7, 2015), http://tinyurl.com/p8bxe7w.

155. Ibid.

156. Shahien Nasiripour, "CFPB Begins Probe of Student Loan Servicers, Signaling Stronger Rules," *Huffington Post* (May 14, 2015), http://tinyurl.com/nnpbqz3.

157. Ibid.

158. Lydia Wheeler, "CFPB Rules Would Decrease Payday Loan Volume by 70 Percent, Report Says," *The Hill* (May 28, 2015), http://tinyurl.com/oas3qzh. See also CFPB, "CFPB Considers Proposal to End Payday Debt Traps," Press Release (Mar. 26, 2015), http://www.consumerfinance.gov/newsroom/cfpb-considers-proposal-to-end-payday-debt-traps/.

159. Arthur Baines, Marsha Courchane & Steli Stoianovici, "Economic Impact on Small Lenders of the Payday Lending Rules under Consideration by the CFPB," Comty. Fin. Svcs. Ass'n of Am. (May 12, 2015), http://www.crai.com/sites/default/files/publications/Economic-Impact-on-Small-Lenders-of-the-Payday-Lending-Rules-under-Consideration-by-the-CFPB.pdf; CFPB, Outline of Proposals under Consideration and Alternatives Considered, CFPB

Small Business Advisory Review Panel for Potential Rulemakings for Payday, Vehicle Title, and Similar Loans (Mar. 26, 2016), http://files.consumerfinance.gov/f/201503_cfpb_outline-of-the-proposals-from-small-business-review-panel.pdf.

160. Bowles v. Willingham, 321 U.S. 503, 537 (1944) (Roberts, J., dissenting).

CHAPTER 12

1. Special thanks to Will Creeley, Susan Kruth, and Azhar Majeed for their invaluable assistance with this chapter.

2. Laura Kipnis, "Sexual Paranoia Strikes Academe," *Chron. of Higher Educ.* (Feb. 27, 2015), http://chronicle.com/article/Sexual-Paranoia-Strikes/190351.

3. Petition for Administrative Response to Prof. Kipnis, https://docs.google.com/forms/d/12sbmVqpNGQPY-QEYG5N7-VIUsXigVg3l9itcX4yTDcA/viewform.

4. Olivia Exstrom, "Students Carry Mattresses, Pillows to Protest Professor's Controversial Article," *Daily Northwestern* (Mar. 10, 2015), http://dailynorthwestern.com/2015/03/10/campus/students-carry-mattresses-pillows-to-protest-professors-controversial-article.

5. Laura Kipnis, "My Title IX Inquisition," *Chron. of Higher Educ.* (May 29, 2015), http://chronicle.com/article/My-Title-IX-Inquisition/230489.

6. Ibid.

7. Ibid.

8. Brock Read, "Laura Kipnis Is Cleared of Wrongdoing in Title IX Complaints," *Chron. of Higher Educ.* (May 31, 2015), http://chronicle.com/blogs/ticker/laura-kipnis-is-cleared-of-wrongdoing-in-title-ix-complaints/99951.

9. Natasha Vargas-Cooper, "Feminist Students Protest Feminist Prof for Writing About Feminism," *Jezebel* (May 29, 2015, 5:30 pm), http://jezebel.com/feminist-students-protest-feminist-prof-for-writing-abo-1707714321.

10. Greg Lukianoff, "P.C. Never Died," *Reason* (Feb. 2010), http://reason.com/archives/2010/01/11/pc-never-died.

11. See Walter Olson, "Rule by 'Dear Colleague' Letter: The Department of Education's Stealth Regulation," CATO Institute: Cato at Liberty (Apr. 10, 2015, 9:30 am), http://www.cato.org/blog/rule-dear-colleague-letter-time-end-stealth-regulation-department-education.

12. 20 U.S.C. § 1681.

13. Alexander v. Yale, 459 F. Supp. 1, 5 (D. Conn. 1977) ("[I]t is perfectly reasonable to maintain that academic advancement conditioned upon submission to sexual demands constitutes sex discrimination in education."); see also Alexander v. Yale, 631 F.2d 178 (2d Cir. 1980) (affirming decision of District Court).

14. North Haven Bd. of Educ. v. Bell, 456 U.S. 512 (1982).

15. Grove City Coll. v. Bell, 465 U.S. 555 (1984).

16. For early examples of such policies, see UWM Post, Inc. v. Board of Regents of the Univ. of Wis. Sys., 774 F. Supp. 1163 (E.D. Wis. 1991); Doe v. Univ. of Mich., 721 F. Supp. 852 (D. Mich. 1989).

17. Eugene Volokh, "Freedom of Speech, Cyberspace, Harassment Law, and the Clinton Administration," *Law & Contemp. Probs.* 63 (2000): 299.

18. Ibid., 315.

19. Anthony Lewis, "Abroad at Home; Living in a Cocoon," *N.Y. Times* (Nov. 27, 1995), http://www.nytimes.com/1995/11/27/opinion/abroad-at-home-living-in-a-cocoon.html.

20. See, e.g., Doe v. Petaluma City Sch. Dist., 949 F. Supp. 1415 (N.D. Cal. 1996); Bosley v. Kearney R-1 Sch. Dist., 904 F. Supp. 1006 (W.D. Mo. 1995).

21. U.S. Dep't of Educ., Off. for Civil Rights, "Sexual Harassment Guidance: Harassment of Students by School Employees, Other Students, or Third Parties" (Mar. 13, 1997), http://www2.ed.gov/about/offices/list/ocr/docs/sexhar01.html.

22. Davis v. Monroe County Bd. of Educ., 526 U.S. 629, 650 (1999).

23. U.S. Dep't of Educ., Off. for Civil Rights, "Revised Sexual Harassment Guidance: Harassment of Students by School Employees, Other Students, or Third Parties" (Jan. 19, 2001), http://www2.ed.gov/about/offices/list/ocr/docs/shguide.pdf.

24. U.S. Dep't of Educ., Off. for Civil Rights, "Dear Colleague Letter on First Amendment" (July 28, 2003), http://www2.ed.gov/about/offices/list/ocr/firstamend.html.

25. U.S. Dep't of Educ., Office for Civil Rights, "Sexual Harassment: It's Not Academic" (Sept. 2008), http://www2.ed.gov/about/offices/list/ocr/docs/ocrshpam.html.

26. U.S. Dep't of Educ., Off. for Civil Rights, "Dear Colleague Letter on Harassment and Bullying" (Oct. 26, 2010), http://www2.ed.gov/about/offices/list/ocr/letters/colleague-201010.pdf.

27 See Memorandum from Samantha Harris, Found. for Individual Rights in Educ., to U.S. Commission on Civil Rights (May 26, 2011), https://www.thefire.org/pdfs/6aefda8e736cc0f8d633980f9549eeae.pdf.

28. U.S. Dep't of Educ., Off. for Civil Rights, "Dear Colleague Letter on Sexual Violence" (Apr. 4, 2011), http://www2.ed.gov/about/offices/list/ocr/letters/colleague-201104.pdf.

29. KC Johnson, "The Strange Justice of Campus Rape Trials," *Minding the Campus* (Dec. 15, 2013), http://www.mindingthecampus.org/2013/12/the_strange_justice_of_rape_tr.

30. Samantha Harris, "The Feds' Mad Assault on Campus Sex," *N.Y. Post* (July 20, 2011), http://nypost.com/2011/07/20/the-feds-mad-assault-on-campus-sex.

31. Anonymous, "An Open Letter to OCR," *Inside Higher Ed* (Oct. 28, 2011), https://www.insidehighered.com/views/2011/10/28/essay-ocr-guidelines-sexual-assault-hurt-colleges-and-students.

32. Administrative Procedure Act, 5 U.S.C. § 553.

33. According to the U.S. Court of Appeals for the D.C. Circuit, a court must examine the language used by the agency to determine whether the agency has created a "binding norm." As an example, the court noted that it has "found decisive the choice between the words 'will' and 'may.'" Community Nutrition Inst. v. Young, 818 F.2d 943, 946 (D.C. Cir. 1987). Guidance from the Executive Branch itself confirms this: The Office of Management and Budget's "Final Bulletin for Agency Good Guidance Practices" warns against using words like "must" and "shall" in documents not subject to notice and comment.

34. Letter from Anurima Bhargava, Chief, Civil Rights Div., U.S. Dep't of Justice, and Gary Jackson, Reg'l Dir., Off. for Civil Rights, U.S. Dep't of Educ., to Royce Engstrom, President, Univ. of Montana, and Lucy France, Univ. Counsel, Univ. of Montana (May 9, 2013), http://www.justice. gov/opa/documents/um-ltr-findings.pdf. See also Resolution Agreement Among the Univ. of Montana-Missoula, the U.S. Dep't of Justice, Civil Rights Div., Educ. Opportunities Section and the U.S. Dep't of Educ., Off. for Civil Rights, https://d28htnjz2elwuj.cloudfront.net/pdfs/e020f15363aa692736fbdc55f94840f6.pdf.

35. Resolution Agreement.

36. Ibid.

37. See, e.g., DeJohn v. Temple Univ., 537 F.3d 301, 317–318 (3rd Cir. 2008); Booher v. Bd. of Regents, N. Ky. Univ., 1998 U.S. Dist. LEXIS 11404 (E.D. Ky. July 21, 1998); UWM Post, Inc. v. Bd. of Regents of the Univ. of Wis., 774 F. Supp. 1163 (E.D. Wisc. 1991); Doe v. Univ. of Mich., 721 F. Supp. 852 (E.D. Mich. 1989).

38. Letter from Found. for Individual Rights in Educ. et al., to Anurima Bhargava, Chief, Civil Rights Div., U.S. Dep't of Justice, and Seth Galanter, Acting Assistant Sec'y for Civil Rights, Off. for Civil Rights, U.S. Dep't of Educ. (July 16, 2013), https://www.thefire.org/fire-coalition-letter-to-departments-of-education-and-justice.

39. Senator John McCain, "Senator John McCain Sends Letters to DOJ and EPA on Obama Administration Settlement Abuse," Press Release (June 26, 2013), http://www.mccain.senate.gov/public/index.cfm/2013/6/post-818fd6f0-b009-240c-b963-7b7bb47f03fb.

40. Doug Lederman, "Into the Lawyers' Den," *Inside Higher Ed* (June 21, 2013), https://www.insidehighered.com/news/2013/06/21/ocr-official-explains-harassment-policies-skeptical-college-lawyers.

41. Samantha Harris, "A Massive Burden," *Inside Higher Ed* (June 13, 2013), https://www.insidehighered.com/views/2013/06/13/essay-criticizes-education-dept-approach-sexual-harassment.

42. Resolution Agreement Among the Univ. of Montana-Missoula, the U.S. Dep't of Justice, Civil Rights Div., Educ. Opportunities Section and the U.S. Dep't of Educ., Off. for Civil Rights (May 9, 2013), 10.

43. Ibid., 13. See also Martin Kidston, "UM Faculty Balk at DOJ Demand for Sexual-Assault Training Rosters," *Missoulian* (Sept. 26, 2013), http://missoulian.com/news/local/um-faculty-balk-at-doj-demand-for-sexual-assault-training/article_9f7e5056-265d-11e3-b14e-0019bb2963f4.html.

44. Martin Kidston, "UM Meets Initial Goals of DOJ Sex Assault, Harassment Agreement," *Missoulian* (Nov. 6, 2013), http://missoulian.com/news/local/um-meets-initial-goals-of-doj-sex-assault-harassment-agreement/article_464c4148-4681-11e3-8ee7-0019bb2963f4.html.

45. University of Montana Policy on Discrimination, Harassment, Sexual Misconduct, Stalking, and Retaliation (adopted Aug. 2013), http://www.umt.edu/policies/human-resources/DiscriminationHarassmentSexualMisconductStalkingRetaliation.php).

46. Letter from Catherine Lhamon, Assistant Sec'y for Civil Rights, U.S. Dep't of Educ., to Greg Lukianoff, President, Found. for Individual Rights in Educ. (Nov. 14, 2013), https://www.thefire.org/letter-from-department-of-education-office-for-civil-rights-assistant-secretary-catherine-e-lhamon-to-fire.

47. U.S. Dep't of Educ., Off. for Civil Rights, "Dear Colleague Letter on First Amendment" (July 28, 2003), http://www2.ed.gov/about/offices/list/ocr/firstamend.html.

48. See http://www.thefire.org/spotlight.

49. Jake New, "Justice Delayed," *Inside Higher Ed* (May 6, 2015), https://www.insidehighered.com/news/2015/05/06/ocr-letter-says-completed-title-ix-investigations-2014-lasted-more-4-years.

50. Allie Grasgreen, "Holding Colleges Responsible," *Inside Higher Ed* (June 11, 2013), https://www.insidehighered.com/news/2013/06/11/student-activists-spur-sexual-assault-complaints-some-say-education-department.

51. Michael Stratford, "Obama Seeks Funding Boost," *Inside Higher Ed* (Feb. 3, 2015), https://www.insidehighered.com/news/2015/02/03/obama-seeks-boost-higher-education-spending-and-proposes-some-loan-reforms-have.

52. Task Force on Fed. Regulation of Higher Educ., "Report: Recalibrating Regulation of Colleges and Universities," (Feb. 12, 2015), 36, http://www.help.senate.gov/imo/media/Regulations_Task_Force_Report_2015_FINAL.pdf.

53. White House Task Force to Protect Students from Sexual Assault, "Report: Not Alone" (Apr. 2014), https://www.notalone.gov/assets/report.pdf.

54. Ibid.

55. Ibid.

56. Not Alone: Together Against Sexual Assault, http://www.notalone.gov.

57. Joe Cohn, "Legislative Rush on Campus Sexual Assault Threatens Student Rights," *The Hill* (Sept. 29, 2014), http://thehill.com/blogs/congress-blog/education/219026-legislative-rush-on-campus-sexual-assault-threatens-student.

58. Campus Safety and Accountability Act, S. 590, 114th Cong. (2015).

59. Task Force on Fed. Regulation of Higher Educ., "Report: Recalibrating Regulation of Colleges and Universities," 1.

60. Kipnis, "My Title IX Inquisition."

61. Jeannie Suk, "The Trouble with Teaching Rape Law," *New Yorker* (Dec. 15, 2014), http://www.newyorker.com/news/news-desk/trouble-teaching-rape-law.

CHAPTER 13

1. William Blackstone, *Commentaries on the Laws of England*, vol. 1 (Oxford: Clarendon Press, 1765), *146.

2. President Obama has said this a number of times, perhaps most famously when the Senate did not pass the American Jobs Act (S. 1549, 112th Cong. (2011)), a $447 billion proposal. Barack Obama, "More Jobs for Americans: Stand with President Obama to Continue the Fight for Jobs," YouTube (Oct. 12, 2011), https://www.youtube.com/watch?v=Ziy1SYTvLgI.

3. "President Obama Speaks on Getting our Veterans Back to Work," The White House (Nov. 7, 2011), transcript available at https://www.whitehouse.gov/photos-and-video/video/2011/11/07/president-obama-speaks-getting-our-veterans-back-work#transcript.

4. For a more thorough summary of Obamacare deadline delays, see David Nather & Susan Levine, "A Brief History of Obamacare Delays," *Politico* (Mar. 24, 2014, 11:43 pm), http://www.politico.com/story/2014/03/obamacare-affordable-care-act-105036.html

5. 26 U.S.C.A. § 5000A(3)(1)(A)

6. This is described as a hardship exemption on the HealthCare.gov website, but it is not listed in the actual C.F.R. that governs eligibility standards for exemptions. See 45 C.F.R. § 155.605 (2015); 2015 tax year exemptions from the fee for not having health coverage, HealthCare.gov, https://www.healthcare.gov/fees-exemptions/exemptions-from-the-fee/#hardshipexemptions (last visited July 25, 2015).

7. 42 C.F.R. § 431.400 (2012); Julie Appleby, "Administration Unexpectedly Expands Payments for Medicare Advantage Plans," *Kaiser Health News* (Nov. 16, 2010), http://khn.org/news/medicare-advantage-bonuses/.

8. King v. Burwell, 125 S. Ct. 2480 (2015).

9. Utility Air Regulatory Group v. E.P.A. 134 S. Ct. 2427 (2014).

10. Dan Lamothe, "Taliban Official Swapped for Bowe Bergdahl Could Return to Battlefield, General Says," *Wash. Post* (Feb. 3, 2015), https://www.washingtonpost.com/news/checkpoint/wp/2015/02/03/taliban-official-swapped-for-bowe-bergdahl-could-return-to-battlefield-general-says/; John Bresnahan and Seung Min Kim, "Attorney General Eric Holder Held in Contempt of Congress," *Politico* (June 28, 2012, 4:43 pm), http://www.politico.com/news/stories/0612/77988.html.

11. 41 U.S.C.A. § 6502 (2011); Melanie Trottman, "Labor Department Moves to Raise Minimum Wage for Federal Contractors," *Wall St. J.* (June 12, 2014, 5:08 pm), http://www.wsj.com/articles/labor-department-moves-to-raise-minimum-wage-for-federal-workers-1402607272.

12. Motoko Rich, "'No Child' Law Whittled Down by White House," *N.Y. Times* (July 6, 2012), http://www.nytimes.com/2012/07/06/education/no-child-left-behind-whittled-down-under-obama.html.

13. Reno v. Flores, 113 S. Ct. 1439, 1453 (1993) ("We have stated that, at least in certain contexts, the Attorney General's exercise of discretion under § 1251(a)(1) requires 'some level of individualized determination.'").

14. Burgess Everett and Seung Min Kim, "Senate Goes for 'Nuclear Option,'" *Politico* (Nov. 22, 2013, 5:09 pm), http://www.politico.com/story/2013/11/harry-reid-nuclear-option-100199.html.

15. U.S. Const. art. II, § 2, cl. 2.

16. See NLRB v. Noel Canning, 134 S. Ct. 2550 (2014).

17. See Chevron U.S.A. v. Natural Resources Defense Council, Inc., 467 U.S. 837 (1984).

18. For a more thorough discussion of the injury-in-fact requirement of Article III standing, see Lujan v. Defenders of Wildlife, 504 U.S. 555, (1992) ("[O]ur cases have established that the irreducible constitutional minimum of standing contains three elements: first, the plaintiff must have suffered an 'injury in fact'—an invasion of a legally-protected interest which is (a) concrete and particularized . . . and (b) 'actual or imminent.'") (citations omitted).

19. 12 U.S.C.A. § 5491 (2010); Michael D. Shear & Jessica Silver-Greenberg, "Payday Loan Rules Proposed by Consumer Protection Agency," *N.Y. Times* (Mar. 26, 2015), http://www.nytimes.com/2015/03/27/business/dealbook/consumer-protection-agency-proposes-rules-on-payday-loans.html.

20. "Tennessee Among 7 States Getting Extended NCLB Waiver," *Wash. Post* (July 23, 2015), http://www.washingtonpost.com/national/tennessee-among-7-states-getting-extended-nclb-waiver/2015/07/23/e9e77d5c-315f-11e5-a879-213078d03dd3_story.html.

CHAPTER 14

1. The views expressed herein are not properly attributable to the International Trade Commission (ITC) or any of its other members or staff and take no position on pending or proposed legislative or other governmental actions.

This chapter is adapted from James E. Daily & F. Scott Kieff, "Benefits of Patent Jury Trials for Commercializing Innovation," *Geo. Mason L. Rev.* 21 (2014): 865. The author gratefully acknowledges the many helpful contributions from Steve Dove, Mitch Ginsburg, Rebecca Gordon, Mary Beth Jones, Troy Paredes, Dean Pinkert, and Dean Reuter.

2. The term "institution" is used here to refer to the set of human-imposed restraints, including laws, rules, and norms, while the term "organization" is used to refer to groups of individuals. See Douglass C. North, "Economic Performance Through Time," in *Nobel Lectures in Economic Sciences 1991–1995*, ed. Torsten Persson (Singapore: World Scientific, 1997), 112–123.

3. Sometimes, agency responsiveness to politics and fashion is seen as a feature rather than a flaw. See, e.g., Richard B. Stewart & Cass R. Sunstein, "Public Programs and Private Rights," *Harv. L. Rev.* 95 (1982): 1193 (describing the public values theory of agencies).

4. See, e.g., David A. Hyman & William E. Kovacic, "Why Who Does What Matters: Governmental Design and Agency Performance," *Geo. Wash. L. Rev.* 82 (2014): 1446; see generally, Richard J. Pierce, Jr., *Administrative Law Treatise*, 5th ed. (New York: Aspen, 2010).

5. See generally John M. Dobson, *Two Centuries of Tariffs, the Background and Emergence of the United States International Trade Commission* (Washington, D.C.: International Trade Commission, 1976).

6. See generally Stephen Breyer, *Breaking the Vicious Circle: Toward Effective Risk Regulation* (Cambridge, MA: Harvard UP, 1993); Landis, *The Administrative Process.*

7. Dobson, *Two Centuries of Tariffs*, 87–89. To be sure, the Federal Election Commission was eventually created much later in the twentieth century to follow the model of the ITC's structure for independence, but because its docket is so inherently political (elections!), it is widely recognized as more vulnerable to partisan politics.

8. Rather than the more typical five members of the other commissions.

9. Rather than the more typical five-year terms for members of the other commissions.

10. Rather than the more typical chairmanships of the other commissions, which can last through a presidential term and be terminated by the President.

11. Rather than the practical ability on most other commissions for the chair and the two other members who are of the President's political party to all together control the majority on most votes.

12. Rather than the greater administrative role typically played by the chair at other commissions.

13. Rather than the proximity the other commissions typically have to one of the major political parties, political branches, or one of the houses of Congress, depending on the overall power dynamics in government at the time.

14. In part, this is related to the basic internal structure and organization of the commission, including the chair's primary role in hiring senior leadership and setting the agenda.

15. The CADC is marked with an asterisk because it reviews only the FTC among the other lower tribunals listed in the figure. The CAFC reviews the PTO, ITC, and District Court patent decisions.

16. While the DOJ and FTC of course do consider ordinary patent issues of validity, infringement, and patent remedy (as distinct from antitrust remedy) on their way to adjudicating their core antitrust docket, they do not enter final judgments of patent invalidity, infringement, or patent remedy (such as damages or injunction against infringement or exclusion from importation).

17. See, e.g., Robin Jacob, "One Size Fits All?" in *Perspectives on Properties of the Human Genome Project*, ed. F. Scott Kieff (Amsterdam: Elsevier, 2003), 455 ("No one outside America, for instance, regards the use of jury trial as remotely sensible."); Robin Jacob, "Abolish Patents?" Ideas Lab (Nov. 1, 2012), http://archive.ideaslaboratory.com/2012/11/01/robin-jacob-abolish-patents/ ("Could the patent system be improved, for instance in the US by abolishing jury trial . . . ?"); Mark Lemley, "Why Do Juries Decide If Patents Are Valid?" Stanford Public Law Working Paper No. 2306152 (2013), 66 ("Jury trials in patent cases are extraordinarily expensive; reducing their number would presumably result in both quicker and cheaper resolution of patent disputes."). See also Kimberly A. Moore, "Judges, Juries, and Patent Cases—An Empirical Peek Inside the Black Box," *Fed. Circuit B.J.* 11 (2001): 209 (arguing that the technical nature of patent cases makes juries unsuitable fact finders, or worse, that juries are biased in favor of patentees); Am. Intell. Prop. L. Ass'n, Law Practice Mgmt. Comm., Report of the Economic Survey 2007 1-91 (2007) (reporting a private party's litigation costs for patent cases between approximately $2 and $5 million, depending on amount of likely damages at stake).

18. See, e.g., S. Leslie Misrock & F. Scott Kieff, "Latent Cures for Patent Pathology: Do Our Civil Juries Promote Science and the Useful Arts?" in *Symposium on Science in Crisis at the Millennium at Geo. Wash. U. Ctr. for Hist. of Recent Sci.*, ed. Horace Freeland Judson (Sept. 19, 1996), printed in Chisum et al., *Principles of Patent Law* (1st ed., 1998), 1368 (exploring various mechanisms available under the Federal Rules of Civil Procedure and Federal Rules of Evidence to improve the patent jury trial and showing how the jury trial can be largely avoided for many patent cases by using techniques gleaned from the historical context of that right at the time of the framing of the U.S. Constitution); Charles Miller et al., "The Use of Alternative Dispute Resolution Methods for Civil Actions Against the Patent Office: A Letter to the Editor," *J. Pat. & Trademark Off. Soc'y* 79 (1997): 29 (exploring alternative dispute resolution techniques in patent cases involving the Patent Office); Charles Miller et al., "Executive Order Allows PTO Action Arbitration—ADR Can Resolve Civil Claims by Private Parties Against the PTO," *Nat'l L. J.* 19 (Jan. 27, 1997): C18 (col. 4); F. Scott Kieff, "How Ordinary Judges and Juries Decide the Seemingly Complex Technological Questions of Patentability over the Prior Art," in Kieff, *Perspectives on Properties of the Human Genome Project* (exploring the role of lay judges and juries in deciding historical and technological fact questions in patent cases); F. Scott Kieff, "The Case for Registering Patents and the Law and Economics of Present Patent-Obtaining Rules," *B.C. L. Rev.* 45 (2003): 55 (exploring why it makes sense for lay judges and juries in deciding historical and technological fact questions in patent cases); F. Scott Kieff, "The Case for Preferring Patent Validity Litigation over Second Window Review and Gold Plated Patents: When One Size Doesn't Fit All, How Could Two Do the Trick?" *U. Penn. L. Rev.* 157 (2009): 1937 (exploring comparative case for relying on litigation of validity issues before lay juries and judges rather than deciding these issues using enhanced administrative procedures before the Patent Office); James E. Daily & F. Scott Kieff, "Anything Under the Sun Made by Humans: Patent Law Doctrines as Endogenous Institutions for Commercializing Innovation," *Emory L.J.* 62 (2013): 967 (exploring the effects that a broader or narrower view of patentable subject matter can have on the commercialization of innovation and the diversity of the marketplace for new technologies).

19. See, e.g., Stephen J. Adler, *The Jury: Trial and Error in the American Courtroom* (New York: Times Books, 1995), reviewed in Richard A. Posner, "Juries on Trial," *Commentary* (Mar. 1, 1995), 49 (the 1985 award to Pennzoil

of $10.5 billion in a contract interference in Texas case against Texaco, then largely based in New York, over the acquisition of Getty Oil, after which the jurors explained "that they added $1 billion to the award for each of the Texaco lawyers from New York they had most despised").

20. See, e.g., 28 U.S.C. § 1861 (1994) (the Jury Selection and Service Act of 1968 does require that juries be selected from a "fair cross section of the community").

21. See Fla. Dep't of Revenue v. Piccadilly Cafeterias, Inc., 128 S. Ct. 2326, 2339 (2008) ("[I]t is not for us to substitute our view of . . . policy for the legislation which has been passed by Congress." (quoting In re Hechinger Inv. Co. of Del., 335 F.3d 243, 256 (3d Cir. 2003))).

22. See, e.g., Richard B. Stewart & Cass R. Sunstein, "Public Programs and Private Rights," *Harv. L. Rev.* 95 (1982): 1193 (describing the public values theory of agencies).

23. B. Zorina Khan & Kenneth L. Sokoloff, "History Lessons: The Early Development of Intellectual Property Institutions in the United States," *J. Econ. Persp.* 15 (2001): 233, 235.

24. F. Scott Kieff, "On Coordinating Transactions in Intellectual Property: A Response to Smith's Delineating Entitlements in Information," *Yale L.J.* 117 (2007): Pocket Part 101, 102; see also Henry E. Smith, "Intellectual Property as Property: Delineating Entitlements in Information," *Yale L.J.* 116 (2007): 1742, 1751–1752.

25. See Kieff, "On Coordinating Transactions," 102.

26. See Smith, "Intellectual Property as Property," 1745. The ability of commercialization approaches toward the patent system to avoid the need for careful governmental tracing highlights an additional difficulty associated with the various theories of the patent system that focus on specific, targeted inducements, which is getting the amount of the inducement just right. Cf. Michael Abramowicz & John F. Duffy, "The Inducement Standard of Patentability," *Yale L.J.* 120 (2011): 1590, 1605 (arguing patent validity determinations should turn on whether the particular invention would have been made or disclosed but for the inducement of the patent); Edmund W. Kitch, "Graham v. John Deere: New Standards for Patents," *Sup. Ct. Rev.* 1966: 293, 301 ("a patent should not be granted for an innovation unless the innovation would have been unlikely to have been developed absent the prospect of a patent").

27. See Smith, "Intellectual Property as Property," 1763–1765.

28. See, e.g., Naomi R. Lamoreaux & Kenneth L. Sokoloff, "Intermediaries in the U.S. Market for Technology, 1870–1920," in *Finance, Intermediaries, and Economic Development*, ed. Stanley L. Engerman et al. (Cambridge: Cambridge UP, 2003), 209, 210–211; Khan & Sokoloff, "History Lessons," 235.

29. See Giles S. Rich, "The Relation Between Patent Practices and the Anti-Monopoly Laws," *J. Pat. & Trademark Off. Soc'y* 24 (1942): 159, reprinted in *Fed. Cir. B.J.* 14 (2004–2005), 5, 21, 37, 67, 87 (five-part series of articles). The other principal drafter, who also wrote a great deal about the statute, was Pat Federico.

30. See, e.g., Jon Thurber, "Obituaries—Judge Giles Rich; Patent Law Authority," *L.A. Times* (June 14, 1999), A22, http://articles.latimes.com/1999/jun/14/news/mn-46460; Richard A. Oppel, Jr., "Obituary—Giles S. Rich, Oldest Active Federal Judge, Dies at 95," *N.Y. Times* (June 12, 1999), Section A, http://www.nytimes.com/1999/06/12/business/giles-s-rich-oldest-active-federal-judge-dies-at-95.html.

31. Abraham Lincoln, "Second Lecture on Discoveries and Inventions" (1859), reprinted in *The Collected Works of Abraham Lincoln*, vol. 3, ed. Roy P. Basler (New Brunswick, NJ: Rutgers UP, 1953), 356, 363 (emphasis added and emphasis omitted).

32. See Reiner v. I. Leon Co., 285 F.2d 501, 503 (2d Cir. 1960) (Hand, J.) ("There can be no doubt that the Act of 1952 meant to change the slow but steady drift of judicial decision that had been hostile to patents."); Picard v. United Aircraft Corp., 128 F.2d 632, 643 (2d Cir. 1942) (Frank, J., concurring) (discussing the role of predictable rules for patent enforcement in helping a smaller "David" compete with a larger "Goliath").

33. Pauline Newman, "The Federal Circuit in Perspective," *Am. U. L. Rev.* 54 (2005): 821, 822–823 (reviewing history of the 1982 statute designed to strengthen the U.S. patent system and included as a major domestic policy initiative of the Carter administration before being signed into law by the Reagan administration).

34. For the relevant conclusions of the study, see the Indus. Advisory Subcomm. on Patent & Info. Policy, Report on Patent Policy, in Advisory Committee on Industrial Innovation: Final Report 147, 155 (1979). The statute that resulted is the Federal Courts Improvement Act of 1982, P.L. 97-164, 96 Stat. 25 (Apr. 2, 1982).

35. See, e.g., Michael Kremer, "Patent Buyouts: A Mechanism for Encouraging Innovation," *Q.J. Econ.* 113 (1998): 1137 (suggesting the government buy out patents after conducting an auction to determine an appropriate buyout price to better address these same fields and others); Steven Shavell & Tanguy van Ypersele, "Rewards Versus Intellectual Property Rights," *J.L. & Econ.* 44 (2001): 525 (suggesting government-sponsored cash rewards as partial or full replacements for patents and to better address fields where the disparity between average cost and marginal cost is typically large, citing as examples biotechnology and computer software, which are both focal points in today's debates about patentable subject matter).

36. See generally F. Scott Kieff, "Property Rights and Property Rules for Commercializing Inventions," *Minn. L. Rev.* 85 (2001): 697, 705–717 (critiquing rewards-focused approaches to patents); see also Daniel F. Spulber, "Should Business Method Inventions Be Patentable?" *J. Legal Analysis* 3 (2011): 265, 298–304.

37. Kieff, "Property Rights," 712. As suggested by Abramowicz and Duffy, important cost savings also can accrue if other patent examination bodies are allowed to bring to bear their own expertise in evaluating the validity of given patents. Michael Abramowicz & John F. Duffy, "Ending the Patenting Monopoly," *U. Pa. L. Rev.* 157 (2009): 1541.

38. This basically means one party's significant investment that is specific to only one use followed by the other party's use of guile to take undo advantage of that investment. See, e.g., Oliver Williamson, *The Economic Institutions of Capitalism: Firms, Markets, Relational Contracting* (Cheltenham, UK: Edward Elgar, 1985), 61–63.

39. See Kieff, "The Case for Registering Patents," 76–99.

40. See ibid., 99–105.

41. F. Scott Kieff & Anne Layne-Farrar, "Incentive Effects from Different Approaches to Holdup Mitigation Surrounding Patent Remedies and Standard-Setting Organizations," *J. Competition L. & Econ.* 9 (2013): 19 (showing how hold-up can be better addressed by reliance on such a fact-based approach instead of allowing open textured policy debates about the possibility of hold-up in general to drive outcomes in particular cases without any factual underpinnings adjudicated in those cases).

42. See generally Kieff, "The Case for Registering Patents"; see also Kieff, "The Case for Preferring Patent Validity Litigation."

43. Although so-called bench trials, which occur without a jury, also rely on detailed factual records developed through the rules of evidence and procedure, a benefit of the jury trial is that it allows for a separation between the judge as decider of questions of law and jury as decider of questions of fact, as well as a dynamic interaction between these two decision-makers. Although a full comparison of jury and bench trials is beyond the scope of this essay, juries have a long tradition of being viewed favorably as tools for making factual determinations. Dimick v. Schiedt, 293 U.S. 474, 486 (1935) ("Maintenance of the jury as a fact-finding body is of such importance and occupies so firm a place in our history and jurisprudence that any seeming curtailment of the right to a jury trial should be scrutinized with the utmost care."); Kevin Casey, Jade Camara & Nancy Wright, "Standards of Appellate Review in the Federal Circuit: Substance and Semantics, *Fed. Cir. B.J.* 11 (2001): 279, 307–309 (the "substantial evidence" standard applied to jury fact-finding is more stringent than the "clearly erroneous" standard applied to judicial fact-finding). Likewise there are several features of a jury trial, such as *voir dire* and the diversity of views that can emerge during deliberation among a large panel, that can reduce the influence of the fashion or political beliefs held by any one person, such as a judge. James J. Gobert, "In Search of the Impartial Jury," *J. Crim. L. & Criminology* 79 (1988): 269, 279–280, 317, 325. The adversarial process of the trial can mitigate risks associated with so-called "groupthink" and other potential shortcomings of group decision-making.

44. See Kieff, "The Case for Preferring Patent Validity Litigation," 1950.

45. John F. Duffy, "The Federal Circuit in the Shadow of the Solicitor General," *Geo. Wash. L. Rev.* 78 (2010): 518 (showing how lobbying efforts before the Solicitor General's Office can influence outcomes in Supreme Court patent cases).

46. Ibid.

47. Cf., Lemley, "Why Do Juries Decide" (arguing that limiting juries to patent damages would "encourage (or perhaps even require) that damages be separated from infringement and validity and tried separately").

48. See, e.g., Kieff, "The Case for Preferring Patent Validity Litigation," 1957–1958. For a recent example of the use sanctions to deter bad faith arguments, see Raylon, LLC v. Complus Data Innovations, Inc., 700 F.3d 1361 (Fed. Cir. 2012).

49. This issue is the subject of a pending U.S. Supreme Court case. Octane Fitness, LLC v. Icon Health and Fitness, Inc., 134 S. Ct. 49 (Oct. 1, 2013) (mem.) (granting cert).

50. 35 U.S.C. § 285.

51. David A. Root, Note, "Attorney Fee-Shifting in America: Comparing, Contrasting, and Combining the 'American Rule' and 'English Rule,'" *Ind. Int'l & Comp. L. Rev.* 15 (2005): 583, 585–591 (discussing American uses of fee-shifting and the history of the English rule).

52. See, e.g., Dennis Crouch, "Judicial Network of the Patent Trial and Appeals Board (PTAB)," Patently-O (Dec. 12, 2013), http://patentlyo.com (citing and linking to Patent Public Advisory Committee Meeting Patent Trial and Appeal Board Update of Dec. 12, 2013). Some have expressed concern that the PTO's newly enhanced procedures for reexamining patents, combined with its dramatically expanded board of administrative patent judges, will favor large, politically effective businesses in their efforts to delay or prevent small business from having enforceable patents. See, e.g., Steven J. Moore, "The AIA: A Boon for David or Goliath?" IPWatchdog (Aug. 15, 2013, 7:45 am), http://www.ipwatchdog.com.

53. See Notice of Public Hearings Competition and Intellectual Property Law and Policy in the Knowledge-Based Economy, 66 Fed. Reg. 58146, 58147 (Nov. 20, 2001) (announcing joint hearings and explaining the reasons for them); see also Federal Trade Commission, "Muris Announces Plans for Intellectual Property Hearings," Press Release (Nov. 15, 2001) (collecting sources, including links to Federal Register Notice and to speech by Chair Timothy Muris, and questioning these and other aspects of the patent system), http://www.ftc.gov/opa/2001/11/iprelease.htm (last visited Nov. 13, 2003); and Federal Trade Commission Report, "The Evolving IP Marketplace: Aligning Patent Notice and Remedies with Competition" (Mar. 2011), http://www.ftc.gov/news-events/events-calendar/2010/05/evolving-ip-marketplace (summarizing decade of hearings and prior reports and their lineage up to the 2011 report). For some recent critiques of these approaches, see Richard A. Epstein, F. Scott Kieff & Daniel F. Spulber, "The FTC, IP, and SSOs: Government Hold-Up Replacing Private Coordination," *J. Competition L. & Econ.* 8 (2012): 19; F. Scott Kieff & Anne Layne-Farrar, "Incentive Effects from Different Approaches to Holdup Mitigation Surrounding Patent Remedies and Standard-Setting Organizations," *J. Competition L. & Econ.* 9 (2013): 19. For information on the budgets of the

FTC and DOJ, see U.S. Dep't of Justice Antitrust Division, Congressional Submission for FY 2013 Performance Budget (2012); U.S. Fed. Trade Comm'n, Fiscal Year 2013 Congressional Budget Justification (2012).

54. U.S. Dep't of Justice Antitrust Division, Congressional Submission for FY 2013 Performance Budget 2 (2012) (noting that "intellectual property issues involving patents, copyrights, trademarks, or trade secrets are instrumental in the Division's work," while listing this IP focus as one of the only three topics selected for special callout in a box of text at the beginning of this budget justification); U.S. Fed. Trade Comm'n, Fiscal Year 2013 Congressional Budget Justification 32 (2012) (noting that "issues in antitrust matters increasingly intersect with intellectual property concerns. . . . In FY 2012 and beyond, the FTC expects to expend significant and specialized resources to enhance its ability to investigate and litigate complex matters involving high-tech segments of the economy.").

55. See Kieff, "The Case for Registering Patents," 1949.

56. Of the five main areas of the ITC's operations, IP-based work (so-called Ops 2) is only one of them, with the other areas being the commission's largest operational area, Ops 1, import injury investigations, which focuses on antidumping and countervailing duty cases; Ops 3, industry and economic analysis, which prepares reports under Section 332 of the Tariff Act of 1930 and other similar statutes; Ops 4, trade information services, which maintains and publishes an extensive repository of trade- and tariff-related data regularly used by governments, academics, and business, including the entire Harmonized Tariff Schedule of the U.S. (HTSUS), contributions to the International Trade Data System (ITDS), the set of U.S Commitments under Schedule XX of the GATT/WTO and under GATS, and support for U.S. contributions to the WTO Integrated Database; and Ops 5, trade policy support, through which the ITC helps trade policy makers in the U.S. executive and legislative branches by providing objective consultation involving research and data compilation and analysis, often including formal details of ITC staff to these other parts of the U.S. government. U.S. Int'l Trade Comm'n, Agency Financial Report 8 (2013).

57. Am. Intellectual Prop. L. Ass'n, Law Practice Mgmt. Comm., Report of the Economic Survey 34–35 (2013) (finding that Section 337 litigation is about 10–20 percent less expensive for the parties than patent litigation in general, depending on the amount at risk).

58. Colleen Chien, "Patently Protectionist? An Empirical Analysis of Patent Cases at the International Trade Commission," *Wm. & Mary L. Rev.* 50 (2008): 63, 102.

59. U.S. Int'l Trade Comm'n, "Budget Justification Fiscal Year 2013" (2012), http://www.usitc.gov/press_room/documents/budget_2013.pdf. According to the ITC's budget justification, there were 20 more active actions in 2013 over 2012 with a marginal cost of $50,900. Ibid., 29–30. The ITC sets a goal of 13.5 months per action, giving a marginal cost of an action from start to finish of $57,262. Ibid., 25.

60. Neither Kieff nor Daily were involved in the case.

61. Compare, e.g., Philip Elmer-DeWitt, "How the ITC Forced a Veto in the Samsung-Apple Patent Case," *CNNMoney* (Aug. 5, 2013, 6:13 am), http://tech.fortune.cnn.com (claiming that the majority in the case only ordered a ban in order to allow the administration to veto it and quoting with approval a statement by patent commentator Florian Mueller that "the ITC ruling is a serious threat to innovation and competition"), with Philip Elmer-DeWitt, "Apple v. Samsung: Justice Delayed Is Justice Denied," *CNNMoney* (Feb. 17, 2013, 2:45 pm), http://tech.fortune.cnn.com (decrying the slow pace of patent litigation and quoting with approval a statement by Florian Mueller that "[t]he unwillingness of many U.S. courts to adjudicate patent infringement cases within reasonable periods of time is slowly but surely becoming a serious issue for the competitiveness of the innovative part of the U.S. economy").

62. See 337-TA-794 Commission Opinion (Public Version), July 18, 2013 (including pp. 41–66 focusing on affirmative defenses relating to the SSO and pp. 105–119 focusing on the remedy, the public's interest in the remedy, and how the remedy was tailored to address the public's interest).

63. See, e.g., In the Matter of Certain Baseband Processor Chips, Inv. No. 337-TA-543, USITC Pub. 4258 (Oct. 1., 2011) (Final) (a less strict exclusion order that balanced the public interest with the protection of intellectual property); In the Matter of Certain Personal Data and Mobile Communications Devices, Inv. No. 337-TA-710, USITC Order 124 (Sep. 19, 2012) (a limited exclusion order to account for consumer effects, including the ability to get replacements phones under warranty or insurance; the order was also delayed for four months to allow service providers time to adapt).

64. Memorandum from U.S. Trade Rep. Michael B.G. Froman to Int'l Trade Comm'n Chairman Irving A. Williamson (Aug. 3, 2013), http://www.ustr.gov/sites/default/files/08032013%20Letter_1.pdf.

65. Of course, this is not always the case, as the interests of small business and entrepreneurs can gain significant political momentum from time to time.

66. See, e.g., Susan Decker & Brian Wingfield, "Samsung Loses Bid for Obama Veto of Apple-Won Import Ban," *Bloomberg* (Oct. 8, 2013) (highlighting significant public speculation about the role of political pressure and domestic bias in the Executive Branch's decision to intervene against the ITC in the decision to enforce Samsung's patents against Apple, but not soon thereafter in the ITC's decision in the related proceedings to enforce Apple's patents against Samsung); and Deanna Tanner Okun, "Commentary: Listen to the Factual Record on the ITC, Not the Broken One," *Roll Call* (Nov. 25, 2013) (discussing politics behind efforts to amend statute to eliminate ITC role in broad categories of patent cases).

67. At the same time, broad understandings of organizational psychology suggest that whatever a group is doing usually does reflect, to at least some extent, intentions that actually are present within the group and in that sense would not fairly be characterized as unintended. Furthermore, broad understandings of political science suggest that often what a group does (such as the laws passed or enforced within a larger society) is the product of a complex interaction among the relative power and intensity of preferences of particular individuals and subgroups within the larger whole and therefore typically will reflect the intentions of some members while being unintended, if not even disliked, by others. See, e.g., Daniel A. Farber & Philip P. Frickey, "Legislative Intent and Public Choice," *Va. L. Rev.* 74 (1988): 423; Duncan Black, *The Theory of Committees and Elections* (Cambridge: Cambridge UP, 1958).

CHAPTER 15

1. The authors are very grateful to Eugene Scalia and Laura Mumm for reviewing a draft of this chapter and providing their excellent comments and suggestions.

2. See the National Labor Relations Act of 1935, Pub. L. No. 74-198, 49 Stat. 449 (codified as amended at 29 U.S.C. § 151 et seq. (2012)).

3. See the Labor Management Relations Act of 1947, Pub. L. No. 80-101, 61 Stat. 136 (codified in various sections of 29 U.S.C. § 151 et seq. (2012)).

4. See Edward Rohrbach, "Shultz, Meany Keep Golf Date," *Chicago Trib.* (Aug. 22, 1971), 1–5.

5. Gerald Mayer, Cong. Research Serv., RL32553, Union Membership Trends in the United States 12 (2004); Bureau of Labor Statistics, Economic News Release: Union Members Summary (Jan. 23, 2015), http://www.bls.gov/news.release/union2.nr0.htm (last visited June 10, 2015).

6. "The Shrinking American Labor Union," *N.Y. Times* (Feb. 7, 2015), BU6.

7. See generally NLRB v. Noel Canning, 503 U.S. ___, 134 S. Ct. 2550 (2014).

8. Steven Greenhouse, "After Push for Obama, Unions Seek New Rules," *N.Y. Times* (Nov. 8, 2008), A33.

9. See Representation—Case Procedures, 79 Fed. Reg. 74308 (Dec. 15, 2014) (to be codified at 29 C.F.R. pts. 101, 102, and 103).

10. Exec. Order No. 13496, 29 C.F.R. § 471 (2010); Exec. Order No. 13494, 3 C.F.R. § 13494 (2009).

11. See, e.g., Heidi Shierholz & Lawrence Mishel, "A Decade of Flat Wages," *Economic Policy Institute* (Aug. 21, 2013), http://www.epi.org/publication/a-decade-of-flat-wages-the-key-barrier-to-shared-prosperity-and-a-rising-middle-class/ (last visited June 10, 2015).

12. See Mark J. Perry, "US Middle Class Has Disappeared into Higher-Income Groups; Recent Stagnation Explained by Changing Household Demographics?" AEIdeas (Feb. 4, 2015, 7:14 pm), https://www.aei.org/publication/middle-class-disappeared-higher-income-groups-recent-stagnation-explained-changing-household-demographics/ (last visited June 10, 2015); see also Dionne Searcey & Robert Gebelhoff, "Middle Class Shrinks Further as More Fall Out Instead of Climbing Up," *N.Y. Times* (Jan. 26, 2015), B1.

13. See generally Emin Dinlersoz & Jeremy Greenwood, "The Rise and Fall of Unions in the U.S.," Population Studies Ctr., Univ. of Penn., PSC Working Paper Series, PSC 12-02 (2013); see also Jeffrey M. Hirsch & Barry T. Hirsch, "The Rise and Fall of Private Sector Unionism: What Next for the NLRA?" *Fla. St. U. L. Rev.* 34 (2007): 1133, 1137–1139.

14. See generally Kim B. Clark, "Unionization and Firm Performance: The Impact on Profits, Growth and Productivity," Nat'l Bureau of Econ. Research, Working Paper No. 990 (1982).

15. See generally Stephen Bronars et al., "The Effects of Unions on Firm Behavior: An Empirical Analysis Using Firm-Level Data," *Indus. Relations* 33 (1994): 426.

16. See ibid.

17. See, e.g., Harry Katz et al., "Crisis and Recovery in the U.S. Auto Industry: Tumultuous Times for a Collective Bargaining Pacesetter," in *Collective Bargaining Under Duress*, ed. Howard R. Stanger et al. (Champaign, IL: Labor and Employment Relations Assn., 2013), 48–54.

18. See Claus Schnabel, "Trade Unions in Europe: Dinosaurs on the Verge of Extinction?" *Vox* (Nov. 18, 2013), http://www.voxeu.org/article/trade-unions-europe (last visited June 10, 2015).

19. See Tom McGinty & Brody Mullins, "Political Spending by Unions Far Exceeds Direct Donations," *Wall St. J.* (July 10, 2012), http://www.wsj.com/articles/SB10001424052702304782404577488584031850026 (last visited June 10, 2015).

20. Hirsch & Hirsch, "The Rise and Fall of Private Sector Unionism," 1137; Bureau of Labor Statistics, Union Members Summary.

21. Steven Greenhouse, "Most U.S. Union Members Are Working for the Government, New Data Shows," *N.Y. Times* (Jan. 23, 2010), B1.

22. See generally Chris Edwards, "Public Sector Unions and the Rising Costs of Employee Compensation," *Cato J.* 30 (2010): 87.

23. See generally Lincoln Fed. Labor Union No. 19129 v. Northwestern Iron & Metal Co., 335 U.S. 525 (1949) (holding state "right to work" laws are constitutional).

24. See Complaint and Notice of Hearing, The Boeing Company & Int'l Ass'n of Machinists & Aerospace Workers District Lodge 751, Case 19-CA-32431, NLRB Region 19 (Apr. 20, 2011).

25. See George F. Will, "The NLRB vs. Boeing: Obama Administration Puts Politics before the Economy," *Seattle Times* (May 14, 2011), http://www.seattletimes.com/opinion/the-nlrb-vs-boeing-obama-administration-puts-politics-before-the-economy/ (last visited June 10, 2015).

26. See Aaron Vehling, "NLRB Invites Briefs on Union Fees for Non-members," *Law360* (Apr. 17, 2015, 7:00 PM ET), http://www.law360.com/articles/644547/nlrb-invites-briefs-on-union-fees-for-nonmembers (last visited June 10, 2015).

27. Int'l Ass'n of Machinists & Aerospace Workers, Local Union No. 697 & Ronnie G. Carroll, 223 NLRB 832, 834 (1976).

28. See ibid., 835.

29. See Representation—Case Procedures, 76 Fed. Reg. 80138 (Dec. 22, 2011) (codified in various sections of 29 C.F.R. pts. 101, 102, and 103).

30. Office of the General Counsel, NLRB, Memorandum GC 12-03, i, 4 (Mar. 8, 2011).

31. Gregory Korte, "Obama's Fourth Veto Protects Unionization Rules," *USA Today* (Mar. 31, 2014), http://www.usatoday.com/story/news/politics/2015/03/31/obama-nlrb-unionization-ambush-election/70718822/ (last visited June 10, 2015).

32. Ben James, "Election Petitions Surge After NLRB Union Rule Takes Effect," *Law360* (May 28, 2015, 8:24 PM ET), http://www.law360.com/articles/661024/election-petitions-surge-after-nlrb-union-rule-takes-effect (last visited June 10, 2015).

33. Specialty Healthcare & Rehabilitation Center of Mobile & United Steel Workers, District 9, 357 NLRB No. 83, 2011 WL 3916077, *17 (Aug. 26, 2011).

34. See, e.g., Macy's, Inc. & Local 1445, United Food & Commercial Workers Union, 361 NLRB No. 4, 2014 WL 3613065, *10 (July 22, 2014).

35. See, e.g., Nestlé Dreyer's Ice Cream Co. v. NLRB, 361 NLRB No. 95, 2014 WL 5781271 (Nov. 5, 2014), appeal docketed Nos. 14-2222, 1402339 (4th Cir. 2015).

36. See Exec. Order No. 13496.

37. Ibid.

38. Notification of Employee Rights Under the National Labor Relations Act, 76 Fed. Reg. 54006 (Aug. 30, 2011).

39. Ibid., 54031.

40. National Ass'n of Manufacturers v. NLRB, 717 F.3d 947, 955–959 (D.C. Cir. 2013).

41. Ibid.

42. 29 U.S.C. § 157.

43. See generally Office of the General Counsel, NLRB, Memorandum OM 11-74 (Aug. 18, 2011); Office of the General Counsel, NLRB, Memorandum OM 12-31 (Jan. 24, 2012); Office of the General Counsel, NLRB, Memorandum OM 12-59 (May 30, 2012).

44. Karl Knauz Motors, Inc. & Robert Becker, 358 NLRB No. 164, 2012 WL 4482841, *1 (Sept. 28, 2012).

45. Ibid.

46. Costco Wholesale Corp. & United Food and Commercial Workers Union, Local 371, 358 NLRB No. 106, 2012 WL 3903806, *1–2 (Sept. 7, 2012).

47. Ibid.

48. Banner Health System & James A. Navarro, 358 NLRB No. 93, 2012 WL 3095606, *2 (July 30, 2012).

49. See Memorandum from Barry J. Kearney, Associate General Counsel, Division of Advice, NLRB to Cornele A. Overstreet, Regional Director, Region 28, NLRB, SWH Corporation d/b/a Mimi's Café Case 28-CA-084365, 3 (Oct. 31, 2012).

50. D.R. Horton, Inc. & Michael Cuda, 357 NLRB No. 184, 2012 WL 36274, *1 (Jan. 3, 2012).

51. D.R. Horton, Inc. v. NLRB, 737 F.3d 344, 361–362 (5th Cir. 2013).

52. Murphy Oil USA, Inc. & Sheila M. Hobson, 361 NLRB No. 72, 2014 WL 5465454, *1 (Oct. 28, 2014).

53. S. 2814, 113th Cong. (2014).

54. See Teamwork for Employees and Managers Act of 1995, H.R. 743, 104th Cong. (1995).

CHAPTER 16

1. Alexis de Tocqueville, *Democracy in America*, vol. 2 (Knopf Vintage Ed., 1990), 109.

2. Richard Henry Sander and Stuart Taylor, *Mismatch: How Affirmative Action Hurts Students It's Intended to Help, and Why Universities Won't Admit It* (New York: Basic, 2012).

3. "Assessing the Impact of Criminal Background Checks and the Equal Employment Opportunity Commission's Conviction Records Policy," U.S. Commission on Civil Rights (Dec. 2013).

4. Griggs v. Duke Power, 401 U.S. 424 (1971).

5. Ricci v. DeStefano, 557 U.S. 557, 563 (2009).

6. Ibid., 594.

7. Docket No. FR-5508-F-02 Implementation of the Fair Housing Act's Discriminatory Effects Standard (Feb. 15, 2013).

8. Ibid., § 5.152.

9. But see Texas Department of Housing and Community Affairs v. The Inclusive Communities Project, 576 U.S. ___ (2015) (holding that the act does make cognizable disparate impact claims).

10. Docket No. FR-5508-F-02 (Feb. 15, 2013), 1.

11. Chevron U.S.A., Inc. v. Natural Resources Defense Council, Inc., 467 U.S. 837 (1984).

12. See, e.g., Ricci v. DeStefano.

13. Parents Involved in Community Schools v. Seattle School District No. 1, 551 U.S. 701 (2007); see Section 903.2(a)(3); Docket No. FR-5173-P-01 § 5.152.

14. Docket No. FR-5173-P-01 § 5.152.

15. Equal Employ. Opp'ty Comm., Enforcement Guidance on the Consideration of Arrest and Conviction Records in Employment Decisions under Title VII of the Civil Rights Act of 1964 [hereinafter "Guidance"].

16. "Guidance," 13 ("Although there may be social science studies that assess whether convictions are linked to future behaviors, traits, or conduct with workplace ramifications, and thereby provide a framework for validating some employment exclusions, such studies are rare at the time of this drafting.").

17. See "Guidance," n14. The "Guidance" relies upon a study of New Zealand youths that found that adolescent criminal convictions did not predict counterproductive work behaviors in adulthood; see Brent W. Roberts et al., "Predicting the Counterproductive Employee in a Child-to-Adult Prospective Study," *J. App. Psychol.* 92 (2007): 1427, 1430. This study is not terribly useful because criminal behavior in adolescence is quite common, but most people desist during or shortly after adolescence; see John H. Laub and Robert H. Sampson, "Understanding Desistance from Crime," *Crime & Justice* 28 (2001): 1, 6 ("[B]ased on the available data, desistance occurs most often during and after adolescence. Based on the evidence, desistance is normative for most offenders."). If indeed "it is statistically aberrant to refrain from crime during adolescence" (ibid., citation omitted), it is unsurprising that adolescent criminal convictions in and of themselves do not predict the presence of counterproductive work behaviors in adulthood. See also Alfred Blumstein & Jacqueline Cohen, "Characterizing Criminal Careers," *Science* 237 (1987): 985, 989 (there is a "rapid buildup of participation [in crime] in the early teen years, followed by steady termination of criminal careers in the later teen years and early 20s").

18. See Alfred Blumstein et al., "Delinquency Careers: Innocents, Desisters, and Persisters," *Crime and Justice* 6 (1985): 1987 (stating that at least a third of cohort members from multiple delinquency studies are arrested, but most have only one or a few contacts with the justice system; however, if a cohort member has six or more contacts with the criminal justice system the probability of recidivism is 80 percent); see also Blumstein and Cohen, "Characterizing Criminal Careers" ("common belief suggests that offenders are about to terminate their criminal careers by age 30. . . . however, it becomes clear that among those offenders who do remain active, mean residual careers length actually rises until about age 30, is fairly flat through the 30s, and then begins to decline rapidly in the early 40s").

19. Charlie Savage, "Countrywide Will Settle a Bias Suit," *N.Y. Times* (Dec. 21, 2011), http://www.nytimes.com/2011/12/22/business/us-settlement-reported-on-countrywide-lending.html?_r=0.

20. United States v. Countrywide (C.D.C. 2011) (No. 2:11-cv-10540-PSG-AJW), complaint, 13–14, http://www.justice.gov/crt/about/hce/documents/countrywidecomp.pdf.

21. Ibid., 17.

22. United States v. Fort Davis State Bank (W.D. Tex. 2013) (No. 4:13-cv-00077-RAJ), complaint.

23. United States v. Countrywide (C.D.C. 2011) (No. 2:11-cv-10540-OSG-AJW), consent order, 5, http://www.justice.gov/crt/about/hce/documents/countrywidesettle.pdf.

24. CFPB v. National City Bank (W.D. Pa. 2013) (No. 2:13-cv-01817-CB), consent order, 3.

25. United States v. Fort Davis State Bank, consent order, 9.

26. See, e.g., United States v. Countrywide (C.D.C. 2011) (No. 2:11-cv-10540-OSG-AJW), consent order, 5, http://www.justice.gov/crt/about/hce/documents/countrywidesettle.pdf.

27. Ibid., 10; see also CFPB v. National City Bank (W.D. Pa. 2013) (No. 2:13-cv-01817-CB); United States v. Fort Davis State Bank (W.D. Tex. 2013) (No. 4:13-cv-00077-RAJ), consent order, 12.

28. Paul Sperry, "BofA Must Pay Excess Settlement Funds to ACORN Clones," *Investor's Business Daily* (Jan. 4, 2012), http://news.investors.com/010412-596657-doj-orders-boa-to-fund-community-groups.htm?src=HPLNews.

29. See generally Letter from National Civil Rights, Fair Housing, and Consumer Organizations to Senate Banking Committee (Feb. 24, 2014), http://www.nclc.org/images/pdf/credit_discriminatio/ltr-housing-finance-feb2014.pdf.

CHAPTER 17

1. The authors would like to thank Ethan Foster and Luke Holladay for their assistance with this chapter from its inception to its final draft. We are particularly grateful for their research, substantive contributions, and edits throughout the chapter's development.

2. Cf. United States v. Riverside Bayview Homes, Inc., 474 U.S. 121, 123 (1985) (describing the Corps of Engineers' 1975 regulation that expanded jurisdiction to tributaries of navigable waters for the first time).

3. Rapanos v. United States, 547 U.S. 715, 723 (2006) (plurality opinion) (quoting The Daniel Ball, 10 Wall. 557, 563 (1871)).

4. Riverside Bayview Homes, 474 U.S. at 139.

5. See Rapanos, 547 U.S. 748 (plurality opinion); Solid Waste Agency of N. Cook Cnty. v. U.S. Army Corps of Engineers, 531 U.S. 159, 172 (2001) (SWANCC).

6. SWANCC, 531 U.S. 174.

7. Ibid.

8. Ibid., 167, 171–172.

9. Rapanos, 547 U.S. 748 (plurality opinion).

10. Ibid., 739–742.

11. Ibid., 767.

12. Ibid., 780 (Kennedy, J., concurring).

13. Clean Water Rule: Definition of "Waters of the United States," 80 Fed. Reg. 37054, 37104 (June 29, 2015) (to be codified at 33 C.F.R. pt. 328.3(a)) [hereinafter "Final Rule"].

14. Ibid., 37126 (to be codified at 40 C.F.R. pt. 401.11(3)(iii)); see Patrick Morrisey et al., "Re: Comments of the Attorneys General of West Virginia, et al. on the Proposed Definition of 'Waters of the United States'" (Oct. 8, 2014), 5–6, http://www.regulations.gov tracking number 1jy-8etb-nher [hereinafter "Multistate Comment"].

15. See Multistate Comment, 7.

16. Rapanos, 547 U.S. 778 (where Justice Kennedy worried about deference to an agency interpretation if it "would permit federal regulation whenever

wetlands lie alongside a ditch or drain, however remote and insubstantial, that eventually may flow into traditional navigable waters") (Kennedy, J., concurring).

17. See Final Rule, 37126 (to be codified at 40 C.F.R. pt. 401.11(3)(iv)).

18. Ibid.

19. Ibid.

20. See Rapanos, 547 U.S. 746 (plurality opinion) (recognizing that the Corps of Engineers' definition of adjacent "extended beyond reason to include . . . the 100-year floodplain of covered waters").

21. See Multistate Comment, 9.

22. See Final Rule, 37058 (emphasis added).

23. Rapanos, 547 U.S. 780 (Kennedy, J., concurring) (emphasis added).

24. See Final Rule, 37126.

25. See Rapanos, 547 U.S. 753 (arguing that neither Riverside Bayview nor SWANCC supported the case-by-case approach) (plurality opinion). Ibid., 798 (characterizing the holding of Riverside Bayview to preclude case-by-case jurisdictional determinations) (Stevens, J., dissenting).

26. See ibid., 809 (worrying that the case-by-case determination will "increase the time and resources spent processing permit applications") (Stevens, J., dissenting).

27. Multistate Comment, 10.

28. Rapanos, 547 U.S. 721, 738 (plurality opinion).

29. Ibid., 738.

30. Ibid., 758 (Roberts, C.J., concurring).

31. Edward J. DeBartolo Corp. v. Florida Gulf Coast Bldg. & Constr. Trades Council, 485 U.S. 568, 575 (1988).

32. SWANCC 531 U.S. 172–173; see also Rapanos, 547 U.S. 737–738 (plurality opinion).

33. Final Rule, 37084.

34. See ibid., 37126.

35. See Gregory v. Ashcroft, 501 U.S. 452, 468 (1991).

36. See Rapanos, 547 U.S. 738 (plurality opinion) (calling water rights a "quintessential state and local power"); SWANCC 531 U.S. 173 (refusing to "permit[] federal encroachment upon a traditional state power").

37. See Waters of the United States Regulatory Overreach Protection Act of 2015, H.R. 594, 114th Cong. (2015) (boasting a bipartisan group of 185 cosponsors at this writing).

38. Navigation and Navigable Waters, 33 U.S.C. § 1251(b) (Agencies must "recognize, preserve, and protect *the primary responsibilities and rights of States* . . . to plan the development and use . . . of land and water resources.") (emphasis added).

39. See Final Rule, 37059–37060.

40. See Multistate Comment, 6.

41. Rapanos, 547 U.S. 734.

42. 33 U.S.C. § 1251(a) (emphasis added).

43. David Sunding, "Review of 2014 EPA Economic Analysis of Proposed Revised Definition of Waters of the United States," Waters Advocacy Coalition (May 15, 2014), 2. Though Dr. Sunding's article critiqued the economic analysis of the proposed rule, the portions of his critique included here apply equally to the economic analysis of the final rule.

44. Ibid.

45. See ibid., 5–7.

46. Memorandum from the Nevada Association of Counties to Donna Downing, Jurisdictional Team Leader, Wetland Division, U.S. Environmental Protection Agency, and Stacey Jensen, Regulatory Community of Practice, U.S. Army Corps of Engineers (Nov. 6, 2014), 2, http://www.regulations.gov tracking number 1jy-8ffv-xw0t [hereinafter "NACO"].

47. See Final Rule, 37073 ("The rule excludes for the first time certain waters and features over which the agencies have generally not asserted CWA jurisdiction.").

48. See ibid.

49. Ibid., 37099.

50. Ibid., 37057.

51. Ibid., 37083.

52. Ibid., 37058.

53. See ibid., passim.

54. Ibid., 37063 (internal citation omitted).

55. 33 U.S.C. §§ 1311, 1319, 1365; Civil Monetary Penalty Inflation Adjustment Rule, 74 Fed. Reg. 626, 627 (2009).

56. The Section 404 Permit Program authorizes the Corps of Engineers to issue permits for the discharges of fill or dredged material into waters of the United States. Any States wishing to implement the program must submit a proposal to, and receive approval from, the administrator of the EPA. See, e.g.,

New Jersey Dept. of Environmental Protection and Energy Section 404 Permit Program Approval, 59 Fed. Reg. 9933 (Mar. 2, 1994) (to be codified at 40 C.F.R. pt. 233).

57. NACO, 4.

58. See Final Rule, 37099.

59. Rapanos, 547 U.S. 721 (citing David Sunding & David Zilberman, "The Economics of Environmental Regulation by Licensing: An Assessment of Recent Changes to the Wetland Permitting Process," *Natural Resources J.* 42 (2002): 59, 74–76).

60. Ibid. (explaining that "for backfilling his own wet fields, Mr. Rapanos faced 63 months in prison").

61. Clean Water Act of 1977 (CWA), 33 U.S.C. §§ 1313(a)–(b) (1977).

62. Ibid., § 1313(d)(1)(C).

63. Ibid., § 1342.

64. Final Rule, 37060.

65. Memorandum of Agreement with the Sec'y, 40 C.F.R. § 233.14 (June 25, 2015).

66. See, e.g., Brian Sandoval, "Nevada Exec. Budget: 2013–2015" (2013), 1, http://budget.nv.gov/uploadedFiles/budgetnvgov/content/StateBudget/FY_2014-2015/Nevada_Executive_Budget_2013-2015.pdf.

67. In fact, the agencies have not produced evidence showing that federal regulation is superior to state and local regulation. Dr. Sunding believes the opposite is likely true. See Sunding, "Review of 2014 EPA Economic Analysis," 26.

68. See, e.g., Nevada Attorney General, "Attorney General Laxalt Files Suit Challenging Federal Overreach in New 'Waters of the United States' Rule," Press Release (June 29, 2015), http://ag.nv.gov/News/Press_Releases/.

CHAPTER 18

1. *The Federalist* No. 47 (Madison) (J. Cooke, ed., 1961).

2. Debra Cassens Weiss, "Scalia Bests Breyer for Senate Zingers, Asserts 'Every Banana Republic' Has a Bill of Rights," *ABA Journal* (Oct. 6, 2011, 12:30 pm), http://www.abajournal.com/news/article/scalia_bests_breyer_for_senate_zingers_asserts_every_banana_republic_has_a_/ (on file with the authors).

3. *The Federalist* No. 47 (Madison), p. 324 (J. Cooke, ed., 1961).

4. See, e.g., City of Arlington, Tex. v. FCC, 133 S. Ct. 1863, 1877–1878 (2013) (Roberts, C.J., dissenting) ("Although modern administrative agencies fit most comfortably within the Executive Branch, as a practical matter they exercise legislative power, by promulgating regulations with the force of law; executive power, by policing compliance with those regulations; and judicial power, by adjudicating enforcement actions and imposing sanctions on those found to have violated their rules. The accumulation of these powers in the same hands is not an occasional or isolated exception to the constitutional plan; it is a central feature of modern American government."). Even the majority opinion, written by Justice Scalia, concedes that this "discomfort with the growth of agency power . . . is perhaps understandable" (see 1873n4), even as it disagrees—as a matter of form—that agencies exercise "legislative" and "judicial" power as understood by the Constitution.

5. Morrison v. Olson, 487 U.S. 654, 698 (1988) (quoting *The Federalist* No. 73 (Hamilton), p. 442 (Clinton Rossiter, ed., 1961)).

6. U.S. Const. art. II, § 3.

7. See Morrison, 487 U.S. 697–734 (Scalia, J., dissenting).

8. Woodrow Wilson, "The Art of Governing," in *The Papers of Woodrow Wilson*, vol. 5 (69 vols.), ed. Arthur S. Link (Princeton: Princeton UP, 1966–1994), 52 [hereinafter *PWW*] (emphasis in original).

9. Wilson, "Government By Debate," in *PWW* 2:224 (1882).

10. Wilson, "Notes for Lectures at the Johns Hopkins," in *PWW* 7:122 (1891).

11. Wilson, "Notes for Lectures," in *PWW* 7:134–138 (1891).

12. See Mistretta v. U.S., 488 U.S. 361, 426 (1989) (Scalia, J., dissenting). Indeed, as Justice Scalia also notes in discussing John Locke's "Second Treatise of Government," "[s]trictly speaking, there is no acceptable delegation of legislative power." See ibid., 419–420.

13. See, e.g., Mich. v. U.S. Envtl. Prot. Agency, 192 L. Ed. 2d 674, 688 (2015) (Thomas, J., concurring) (stating that even if the Supreme Court, in approving agency deference when deference should not exist, "escape[s] the jaws of Article III's Vesting Clause, it runs headlong into the teeth of Article I's, which vests '*[a]ll* legislative Powers herein granted' in Congress") (citing U.S. Const. art I., § 1) (emphasis added).

14. See, e.g., Mass. Const. of 1780, pt. 1, art. 30; see also Va. Const. of 1776, pt. II ("The legislative, executive, and judiciary departments shall be

separate and distinct, so that neither exercise the powers properly belonging to the other.").

15. See Gary Lawson, "Symposium, Changing Images of the State: the Rise and Rise of the Administrative State," *Harv. L. Rev.* 107 (1994): 1231, 1240.

16. See Mistretta, 488 U.S. 417 (Scalia, J., dissenting).

17. 135 S. Ct. 1225, 1251 (2015) (Thomas, J., concurring in judgment).

18. See City of Arlington, Tex., 133 S. Ct. 1863 (2013) (Roberts, J., dissenting) ("[T]he citizen confronting thousands of pages of regulations—promulgated by an agency directed by Congress to regulate, say, 'in the public interest'—can perhaps be excused for thinking that it is the agency that is really doing the legislating."); see also Ass'n of Amer. R.R., 135 S. Ct. 1237 (2015) (Alito, J., concurring) (explaining that the result of such "broad general directives" of delegation has been that "the other branches of Government have vested powers of their own that can be used in ways that resemble lawmaking").

19. See Mistretta, 488 U.S. 372.

20. See Christina Farr, "The Specter of D.C. Overregulation Haunts Health Entrepreneurs," *Venture Beat* (Mar. 20, 2013), http://venturebeat.com/2013/03/20/the-specter-of-d-c-overregulation-haunts-health-entrepreneurs/.

21. Mich., 192 L. Ed. 2d 688 ("Statutory ambiguity . . . becomes an implicit delegation of rulemaking authority, and that authority is used not to find the best meaning of the text, but to formulate legally binding rules to fill in gaps based on policy judgments made by the agency rather than Congress.").

22. See Randolph J. May, "Why Stovepipe Regulation No Longer Works: An Essay on the Need for a New Market-Oriented Communications Policy," *Fed. Comm. L.J.* 58 (2006): 103, 104; see ibid., 106–107 ("However serviceable these definitional constructs may have been at an earlier time . . . they are no longer serviceable in a world in which digital technology is rapidly displacing analog.").

23. See, e.g., William J. Haun, "The Clean Air Act as an Obstacle to the Environmental Protection Agency's Anticipated Attempt to Regulate Greenhouse Gas Emissions from Existing Power Plants," Federalist Society White Paper (Mar. 2013), 6–7n27, http://www.fed-soc.org/publications/detail/the-clean-air-act-as-an-obstacle-to-the-environmental-protection-agencys-anticipated-attempt-to-regulate-greenhouse-gas-emissions-from-existing-power-plants (on file with the authors).

24. See *The Federalist* No. 51 (Madison) (J. Cooke, ed., 1961).

25. See Ass'n of Am. Railroads v. U.S. Dep't of Transp., 721 F.3d 666, 677 (D.C. Cir. 2013).

26. Jean Eaglesham, "SEC Wins with In-House Judges," *Wall St. J.* (May 6, 2015), http://www.wsj.com/articles/sec-wins-with-in-house-judges-1430965803 (quoting Bradley Bondi); see also Tumey v. Ohio, 273 U.S. 510, 523 (1927) (conflict of interest exists when a party, someone who by definition benefits from tilting the requisite "burden of proof" in their own favor, is judge in the same cause).

27. See Lawson, "Symposium, Changing Images of the State," 1248–1249.

28. "Federal Rulemaking: Agencies Could Take Additional Steps to Respond to Public Comments," U.S. GAO Report (Dec. 2012), http://www.gao.gov/assets/660/651052.pdf (on file with the authors) (For the 568 major rules and approximately 30,000 non-major rules issued by agencies between 2003 and 2010, "[a]gencies did not publish a notice of proposed rulemaking (NPRM), enabling the public to comment on a proposed rule, for about 35 percent of major rules and about 44 percent of non-major rules published during [this period]."); ibid. ("[A]gencies, though not required, often requested comments on major final rules issued without an NPRM, but they did not always respond to the comments received.").

29. Agencies may invoke a "good cause" exception if notice of a proposed rule seems to the agency to be "impracticable, unnecessary, or contrary to the public interest." 5 U.S.C. § 553(b)(B). See Pierce, *Administrative Law Treatise*, § 6.8; Ellen R. Jordan, "The Administrative Procedure Act's 'Good Cause' Exemption," *Admin. L. Rev.* 36 (1984): 113, 116–117 ("Agencies which listen and respond to public comment enhance their legitimacy and accountability, both of critical importance when decisionmaking is delegated to a nonrepresentative, politically insulated body."). For judicial reasoning on this issue, see also United States v. Utesch, 596 F.3d 302, 308–309 (6th Cir. 2010). To be fair, however, "agencies sometimes solicit public comments on . . . rules" even when it is "not required to do so." "Federal Rulemaking," 2. But agency administrators are fallible human beings and there is no evidence that the gratuitous NPRMs on non-major rules are not in some way intended to deflect public and media scrutiny, not to mention congressional oversight, when NPRM is withheld on major rules.

30. 42 C.F.R. § 93.519(b).

31. The Supreme Court has recognized that an administrative search without probable cause cannot be a pretext for law enforcement activity. See New York v. Burger, 482 U.S. 691, 716–717, n27 (1987). This recognition has little practical effect, however, because many regulatory violations come with criminal penalties. Additionally, *Burger*'s holding—that there is no "pretext" when a police officer conducted the administrative inspection at issue and the discovered evidence is used in a criminal prosecution—precludes a court from finding "pretext" in many agency searches without probable cause. See, e.g., United States v. Aukai, 497 F.3d 955 (9th Cir. 2007) (*en banc*) (holding that TSA airport searches for weapons are permissible administrative searches).

32. See, e.g., Rufo v. Inmates of Suffolk County Jail, 502 U.S. 367, 378–379 (1992).

33. If it is true that "private enforcers" can inflict this directly on agencies, then it follows that it is even more effective for agency administrators to do so themselves. But see David Freeman Engstrom, "Agencies as Litigation Gatekeepers," *Yale L.J.* 123 (2013): 616, 630–631. Private enforcers, as plaintiffs, are masters of their suits, but the agencies, when entering into settlement agreements, are defendants to the suit but masters of their houses. Agency administrators can game the settlement, particularly when a willing enabler is suing them—and foist on future administrators those (sometimes draconian) settlement terms.

34. Frank Easterbrook, "Justice and Contract in Consent Judgments," *U. Chi. L. Forum* 1987 (1987): 19, 33–34.

35. Sue-and-settle may also be used as a tool to divest legitimate discretion from agencies so that they may be unable to take actions that the suing parties find objectionable. This form of sue-and-settle raises questions as to the ability of a court to deprive the executive branch of authority lawfully delegated to it by Congress—an equally troubling outcome for the separation of powers. See generally Jeremy Rabkin & Neal Devins, "Averting Government by Consent Decree: Constitutional Limits on the Enforcement of Settlements with the Federal Government," *Stan. L. Rev.* 40 (1987): 203 (discussing the various separation of powers concerns implicated by sue-and-settle with case studies).

36. See Chevron U.S.A. Inc. v. Natural Resources Defense Council, Inc., 467 U.S. 837, 842 (1984).

37. See Perez v. Mortg. Bankers Ass'n, 135 S. Ct. 1199, 1211 (2015) (Scalia, J., concurring in judgment).

38. See, e.g., City of Arlington, Tex., 133 S. Ct. 1874 ("The fox-in-the-henhouse syndrome is to be avoided not by establishing an arbitrary and undefinable category of agency decisionmaking that is accorded no deference, but by taking seriously, and applying rigorously, in all cases, *statutory* limits on agencies' authority.") (emphasis added).

39. Professor Phillip Hamburger explores these issues extensively in his article "Chevron Bias," Columbia Public Law Research Paper No. 14-417 (2014), http://ssrn.com/abstract=2477641 (on file with the authors).

40. Cf. Hettinga v. United States, 677 F.3d 471, 481 (D.C. Cir. 2012) (Brown, J., concurring) ("The judiciary has worried incessantly about the 'countermajoritarian difficulty' when interpreting the Constitution. But the better view may be that the Constitution created the countermajoritarian difficulty in order to thwart more potent threats to the Republic.").

41. See Michael Herz, "Textualism and Taboo: Interpretation and Deference for Justice Scalia," *Cardozo L. Rev.* 12 (1991): 1663 ("Justice Scalia is a fierce, sometimes strident defender of Chevron.").

42. See Perez, 135 S. Ct. 1211 (Scalia, J., concurring in judgment).

43. See Mass., 549 U.S. 497, 532–534 (2007).

44. See Whitman v. United States, *cert. denied*, 135 S. Ct. 352, 353 (2014) (statement of Scalia, J., joined by Thomas, J.) ("Undoubtedly, Congress may make it a crime to violate a regulation . . . but it is quite a different matter for Congress to give agencies—let alone for us to *presume* that Congress gave agencies—power to resolve ambiguities in criminal legislation.") (emphasis in original).

45. See Perez, 135 S. Ct. 1211 (Scalia, J., concurring in judgment) (quoting 5 U.S.C. § 706).

46. Auer v. Robbins, 519 U.S. 452 (1997).

47. See Perez, 135 S. Ct. 1211 (Scalia, J., concurring in judgment).

48. See 5 U.S.C. § 706.

49. See ibid.

50. *Chevron* deference, though within the discretion of courts, tends to operate under what administrative law scholars refer to as a "pay me now or pay me later" scheme. See, e.g., E. Donald Elliott, "Re-Inventing Rulemaking," *Duke L.J.* 41 (1992): 1490, 1491. In other words, an agency that submits a rule through the formal rulemaking procedures is likely to see that rule receive deference on judicial review, while a rule made through less formal procedures

is more apt to receive less or no deference. See, e.g., Note, "Tentative Interpretations: The Abracadabra of Administrative Rulemaking and the End of Alaska Hunters," *Vand L. Rev.* 67 (2014): 875, 882–887 (discussing "[p]ay [m]e [n]ow or [p]ay [m]e [l]ater: [t]he [c]hoice [b]etween [p]rocedural [e]ase and [j]udicial [d]eference").

51. The CRA was designed for Congress to expeditiously pass joint resolutions overturning regulations of which it disapproved. See generally 5 U.S.C. § 801. Yet "[the act] has not been particularly effective, largely because it is difficult to enact congressional resolutions of disapproval that are still subject to presidential veto, nor have there even been many attempts to use it." Jonathan Adler, "Placing 'REINS' on Regulations: Assessing the Proposed REINS Act," *N.Y.U. J. Legis. & Pub. Pol'y* 16 (2013): 1, 19. The proposed REINS Act, on the other hand, would subject major agency regulations (defined by the White House Office of Management and Budget as imposing more than $100 million of costs on the economy or other such anticompetitive costs) to congressional approval and presidential signature. For a detailed analysis of the proposed REINS Act, see generally Adler, "REINS," 1.

52. It is unlikely that Congress will disapprove most consent decrees. Nonetheless, the possibility of close congressional scrutiny might help produce qualitatively superior decrees in the first place.

53. For more possible solutions related to the abuse of consent decrees, see *The Use and Abuse of Consent Decrees in Federal Rulemaking: Hearing Before the Subcommittee on the Courts, Commercial and Administrative Law, Committee on the Judiciary, United States House of Representatives,* 112th Cong. (Feb. 3, 2012), http://judiciary.house.gov/_files/hearings/Hearings%202012/Grossman%20 02032012.pdf (written testimony of Andrew M. Grossman, Visiting Legal Fellow, the Heritage Foundation).

54. 135 S. Ct. 1210 (Alito, J., concurring in part and concurring in judgment); see ibid., 1211 (Scalia, J., concurring in judgment); see ibid., 1213 (Thomas, J., concurring in judgment).

55. City of Arlington, Tex., 133 S. Ct. 1886 (Roberts, C.J., dissenting) (stating that today, federal agencies draw from a "potent brew of executive, legislative, and judicial power" in light of the "dramatic shift in power" that has happened "over the last 50 years from Congress to the Executive—a shift effected through the administrative agencies").

56. See Perez, 135 S. Ct. 1211–1212 (Scalia, J., concurring in judgment) ("Heedless of the original design of the APA, we have developed an elaborate law of deference to agencies' interpretations of statutes and regulations.").

57. See ibid., 1212 (Scalia, J., concurring in judgment) (internal citation and quotation marks eliminated).

58. See Ass'n of Am. R.R., 135 S. Ct. 1242 (Thomas, J., concurring in judgment); ibid., 1241–1250 (discussing the Constitution's original structure and some post-founding judicial history, including the Marshall Court's treatment of the separation of powers).

59. See ibid., 1242.

60. Eaglesham, "SEC Wins."

61. See ibid. (quoting former SEC administrative law judge Lillian McEwen). There are a number of instances where ALJs allege interference with their decisional independence by agency officials, though these instances do not necessarily result in review of an Article III court. See, e.g., Mahoney v. Donovan, 721 F.3d 633 (D.C. Cir. 2013), *cert. denied*, 134 S. Ct. 2724 (2014); see also Tunik v. Merit Sys. Prot. Bd., 407 F.3d 1326, 1329 (Fed. Cir. 2005).

62. *The Federalist* No. 73 (Hamilton), pp. 443–444 (Clinton Rossiter, ed., 1961). The courts do not get to decide that because, in a given instance, a good law is worth keeping, the constitutional separation of powers might be suspended (if only for a moment).

63. Candace H. Beckett, "Separation of Powers and Federalism: Their Impact on Individual Liberty and the Functioning of Our Government," *Wm. & Mary L. Rev.* 29 (1988): 635, 639 (The framers "designed a system to block the overreach—a system of government that would *safeguard liberty* by avoiding the entrapments of tyranny. The framers dispersed constitutional authority among the three branches of government and between the national and state governments. To further control power, they made the different national and state officials answerable to different constituencies.") (emphasis added).

CHAPTER 19

1. Douglas Martin, "Johnnie M. Walters, Ex-I.R.S. Chief, Dies at 94," *N.Y. Times* (June 26, 2014), B19, http://www.nytimes.com/2014/06/26/us/politics/johnnie-m-walters-ex-irs-chief-dies-at-94.html.

2. Ryan Powers, "Pelosi: Tea Parties Are Part of an 'Astroturf' Campaign by 'Some of the Wealthiest People in America,'" ThinkProgress (Apr. 15, 2009, 4:37 pm), http://thinkprogress.org/politics/2009/04/15/37578/pelosi-astroturf/.

3. "Total Outside Spending by Election Cycle, Excluding Party Committees," OpenSecrets, https://www.opensecrets.org/outsidespending/cycle_tots.php (last visited July 2, 2015).

4. "Partnership for America's Families, 2004 Election Cycle," The Center for Responsive Politics, https://www.opensecrets.org/527s/527events.php?id=1 (last visited July 2, 2015); Ivan Osorio, "Organization Man: How Andrew Stern Plans to Transform the Union Movement," Labor Watch (Dec. 2009), http://capitalresearch.org/wp-content/uploads/2013/07/LW1209.pdf.

5. See generally, "COMMUNITY. STRATEGY. INVESTMENT. IMPACT.," Democracy Alliance, http://www.democracyalliance.org/home (last visited July 2, 2015); see also Kenneth P. Vogel, "Inside the Vast Left Wing Conspiracy," *Politico* (June 23, 2014, 5:01 am), http://www.politico.com/story/2014/06/inside-the-vast-liberal-conspiracy-108171.html; Democracy Alliance Investment Recommendations, "2012–2014 DA Portfolio" (Spring 2014), http://s3.documentcloud.org/documents/1202744/da-portfolio2012-2014-042714.pdf.

6. 26 U.S.C. § 527 (Westlaw) (defining "political organizations" as entities established for primarily political purposes and referred to by their Internal Revenue Code section number); Steve Weissman & Suraj Sazawal, "Soft Money Political Spending by 501(c) Nonprofits Tripled in 2008 Election," Campaign Finance Institute (Feb. 25, 2009), http://www.cfinst.org/press/preleases/09-02-25/Soft_Money_Political_Spending_by_Nonprofits_Tripled_in_2008.aspx.

7. Federal Election Commission, "2008 Presidential Campaign Financial Activity Summarized: Receipts Nearly Double 2004 Total," Press Release (June 8, 2009), http://www.fec.gov/press/press2009/20090608PresStat.shtml.

8. John D. McKinnon & Dionne Searcey, "Donors to GOP Group Drew IRS Scrutiny," *Wall St. J.* (May 31, 2013), http://www.wsj.com/articles/SB10001424127887324682204578517563566848922.

9. See generally "About Us," Freedom Partners, https://freedompartners.org/us/ (last visited July 2, 2015) (describing how the Freedom Partners Chamber of Commerce was established as the Association for American Innovation in 2011).

10. Letter from Rep. Darrell Issa et al., Majority Staff, Committee on Oversight and Government Reform, to Members, Committee on Oversight and Government Reform (Sept. 17, 2013), http://oversight.house.gov/wp-content/uploads/2013/09/2013-09-17-Interim-update-on-IRS-Investigation-of-tax-exempt-applicants1.pdf.

11. Non-profit corporations apply to the IRS to be recognized as operating within one of the Internal Revenue Code's categories of "exempt organizations," confirming in the application that the organization will conduct its activities in a manner consistent with IRS rules for that type of entity.

12. H.R. Rep., Committee on Oversight and Government Reform, The Internal Revenue Service's Targeting of Conservative Tax-Exempt Applicants: Report on Findings for the 113th Congress, at 144 (2014), http://oversight.house.gov/wp-content/uploads/2014/12/December-2014-IRS-Report.pdf (hereinafter "Issa Report").

13. Jonathan Weisman & Matthew L. Wald, "I.R.S. Focus on Conservatives Give G.O.P. an Issue to Seize On," *N.Y. Times* (May 13, 2013), A1.

14. John Sexton, "Lois Lerner Discusses Political Pressure on the IRS in 2010," *Breitbart News* (Aug. 6, 2013), http://www.breitbart.com/blog/2013/08/06/lois-lerner-discusses-political-pressure-on-the-irs-in-2010/.

15. Letter from J. Russell George, TIGTA, to Rep. Sander Levin (June 26, 2013), http://online.wsj.com/public/resources/documents/TIGTAFinalResponseToRepLevin06262013.pdf (reporting to Congress 292 conservative/Tea Party groups whose applications had been sequestered and subjected to inappropriate targeting, compared to 6 liberal or progressive groups).

16. The White House, "Weekly Address: President Obama Castigates GOP Leadership for Blocking Fixes for the Citizens United Decision," Press Release (Sept. 18, 2010), https://www.whitehouse.gov/the-press-office/2010/09/18/weekly-address-president-obama-castigates-gop-leadership-blocking-fixes-.

17. Memorandum from Michael E. McKenney, Acting Deputy Inspector General for Audit, to Acting Commissioner, Tax Exempt and Government Entities Division (May 14, 2013), https://www.treasury.gov/tigta/auditreports/2013reports/201310053fr.pdf.

18. See generally ibid.

19. See Kimberley A. Strassel, "Conservatives Became Targets in 2008," *Wall St. J.* (May 23, 2014), http://www.wsj.com/articles/SB10001424127887324659404578501411510635312.

20. The White House, "President Obama Appoints Daniel Werfel as Acting Commissioner of Internal Revenue," Press Release (May 16, 2013), https://www.whitehouse.gov/the-press-office/2013/05/16/president-obama-appoints-daniel-werfel-acting-commissioner-internal-reve.

21. IRS, "FS-2013-8, IRS Offers New Streamlined Option to Certain 501(c)(4) Groups Caught in Application Backlog" (2013), http://www.irs.gov/uac/Newsroom/IRS-Offers-New-Streamlined-Option-to-Certain-501c4-Groups-Caught-in-Application-Backlog.

22. Ibid.; see also Commissioner Daniel Werfel, "Charting a Path Forward at the IRS: Initial Assessment and Plan of Action," IRS (June 24, 2013), http://www.irs.gov/pub/newsroom/Initial%20Assessment%20and%20Plan%20of%20Action.pdf.

23. See IRS, "IR-2014-42, Prepared Remarks of Commissioner of Internal Revenue Service John Koskinen before the National Press Club" (2014), http://www.irs.gov/uac/Newsroom/Prepared-Remarks-of-Commissioner-of-Internal-Revenue-Service-John-Koskinen-before-the-National-Press-Club-2014.

24. Issa Report, 54–87.

25. Ibid.

26. Kimberley A. Strassel, "Obama's Enemies List—Part II," *Wall St. J.* (July 19, 2012), http://www.wsj.com/articles/SB10000872396390444464304577537233908744496; Daniel Strauss, "Coburn: Romney Donors Fear They Were Targeted by IRS," The Hill (May 23, 2013, 3:30 pm), http://thehill.com/video/senate/301565-coburn-indications-out-of-oklahoma-that-irs-audited-romney-donors-.

27. See Tom Fitton, "IRS Cover-Up Expands to Justice Department," *Breitbart News* (Feb. 3, 2015), http://www.breitbart.com/big-government/2015/02/03/irs-cover-up-expands-to-justice-department/; "New Documents Offer Glimpse into Criminal Investigation of Obama IRS Scandal," Judicial Watch (Feb. 5, 2015), http://www.judicialwatch.org/press-room/press-releases/new-documents-offer-glimpse-criminal-investigation-obama-irs-scandal/; see also Committee on Ways and Means, "Ways and Means Committee Refers Lois Lerner to Department of Justice for Criminal Prosecution," Press Release (Apr. 9, 2014), http://waysandmeans.house.gov/ways-and-means-committee-refers-lois-lerner-to-department-of-justice-for-criminal-prosecution/; Committee on Ways and Means, "IRS Abuse: Committee Seeks DOJ Update on Lerner Criminal Referral," Press Release (May 28, 2015), http://waysandmeans.house

.gov/irs-abuse-committee-seeks-doj-update-on-lerner-criminal-referral/; see also John Bresnahan & Rachael Bade, "DOJ: No Contempt Charges for Former IRS Official Lois Lerner," *Politico* (Apr. 1, 2015, 2:16 pm), http://www.politico.com/story/2015/04/lois-lerner-no-contempt-charges-justice-department-116577.html (last updated Apr. 1, 2015, 5:09 pm).

28. Robert W. Wood, "In 'Lost' Trove of IRS Emails, 2,500 May Link White House to Confidential Taxpayer Data," *Forbes* (Nov. 27, 2014, 8:09 pm), http://www.forbes.com/sites/robertwood/2014/11/27/in-lost-trove-of-irs-emails-2500-may-link-white-house-to-confidential-taxpayer-data/; Sarah Westwood, "Cause of Action Presses IRS on Taxpayer Data Shared with White House," *Wash. Exam.* (Feb. 25, 2015, 8:02 am), http://www.washingtonexaminer.com/cause-of-action-presses-irs-on-taxpayer-data-shared-with-white-house/article/2560679.

29. "Federal Court Issues Ruling Compelling IRS to Provide Answers on Lerner IRS Emails," Judicial Watch (June 8, 2015), http://www.judicialwatch.org/press-room/press-releases/judicial-watch-federal-court-issues-ruling-compelling-irs-to-provide-answers-on-lerner-irs-emails/; Kelly Phillips Erb, "TIGTA on Lerner Emails: Potential Criminal Activity," *Forbes* (Mar. 2, 2015), http://www.forbes.com/sites/kellyphillipserb/2015/03/02/tigta-on-lerner-emails-potential-criminal-activity/.

30. Committee on Ways and Means, "Hatch, Ryan Demand Complete Documents from Treasury on Efforts to Change Rules for Tax-Exempt Groups," Press Release (June 10, 2015), http://waysandmeans.house.gov/hatch-ryan-demand-complete-documents-from-treasury-on-efforts-to-change-rules-for-tax-exempt-groups/.

31. See generally *Ensuring Transparency Through the Freedom of Information Act (FOIA): Hearing Before H.R. Comm. on Oversight and Government Reform* (2015), http://oversight.house.gov/hearing/ensuring-transparency-through-the-freedom-of-information-act-foia/.

CHAPTER 20

1. The authors have participated or are currently participating in administrative proceedings or litigation involving each of the rules discussed in this essay. They also would like to acknowledge the efforts of General Counsel Misha Tseytlin and Assistant Attorney General J. Zak Ritchie.

2. "AEP Closing Coal-fired Plants," *Bluefield Daily Telegraph* (Apr. 6, 2015, 5:00 am), http://www.bdtonline.com/news/aep-closing-coal-fired-plants/article_d5f4cc3a-dc02-11e4-9000-6f1313dc83a9.html.

3. Ibid.

4. Util. Air Regulatory Grp. v. EPA, 134 S. Ct. 2427, 2444 (2014).

5. Ibid., 2446 (alteration in original) (quoting U.S. Const. art. II, § 3).

6. Ibid.

7. See ibid., 2435–2436.

8. Regulating Greenhouse Gas Emissions Under the Clean Air Act, 73 Fed. Reg. 44354, 44355 (July 30, 2008); Prevention of Significant Deterioration and Title V Greenhouse Gas Tailoring Rule, 75 Fed. Reg. 31514, 31533 (June 3, 2010) (to be codified at 40 C.F.R. pts. 51, 52, 70, and 71).

9. Prevention of Significant Deterioration and Title V Greenhouse Gas Tailoring Rule, 75 Fed. Reg. 31541–31542.

10. Util. Air Regulatory Grp., 134 S. Ct. 2445.

11. Ibid., 2444.

12. See Clean Air Act § 112(c), 42 U.S.C. § 7412(c) (2012).

13. Clean Air Act § 112(n)(1)(A), 42 U.S.C. § 7412(n)(1)(A) (2012) (emphasis added).

14. National Emission Standards for Hazardous Air Pollutants, 76 Fed. Reg. 24976, 24987 (proposed May 3, 2011) (to be codified at 40 C.F.R. pts. 60 and 63) (emphasis added).

15. National Emission Standards for Hazardous Air Pollutants, 77 Fed. Reg. 9304, 9363 (Feb. 16, 2012) (to be codified at 40 C.F.R. pts. 60 and 63) (emphasis added).

16. See White Stallion Energy Ctr., LLC v. EPA, 748 F.3d 1222, 1263 (D.C. Cir. 2014) (Kavanaugh, J., dissenting); see also National Emission Standards for Hazardous Air Pollutants, 77 Fed. Reg. 9305–9306, 9428.

17. White Stallion Energy Ctr., 748 F.3d 1261 (Kavanaugh, J., dissenting).

18. National Emission Standards for Hazardous Air Pollutants, 76 Fed. Reg. 24989.

19. Michigan v. EPA, No. 14-46, slip op., 6–7 (U.S. June 29, 2015), http://www.supremecourt.gov/opinions/14pdf/14-46_10n2.pdf.

20. Ibid., 7–8.

21. Ibid., 7 (emphasis in original).

22. Ibid.

23. Standards of Performance for Greenhouse Gas Emissions from New Stationary Sources: Electric Utility Generating Units, 79 Fed. Reg. 1430 (proposed Jan. 8, 2014) (to be codified at 40 C.F.R. pts. 60, 70, 71, and 98).

24. Carbon Pollution Emission Guidelines for Existing Stationary Sources: Electric Utility Generating Units, 79 Fed. Reg. 34830 (proposed June 18, 2014) (to be codified at 40 C.F.R. pt. 60).

25. Clean Air Act §§ 111(a)(1), (b), 42 U.S.C. §§ 7411(a)(1), (b) (2012).

26. Sierra Club v. Costle, 657 F.2d 298, 330 (D.C. Cir. 1981).

27. Standards of Performance for Greenhouse Gas Emissions from New Stationary Sources: Electric Utility Generating Units, 79 Fed. Reg. 1433.

28. Essex Chemical Corp. v. Ruckelshaus, 486 F.2d 427, 433 (D.C. Cir. 1973).

29. Ibid., 433–434.

30. Standards of Performance for Greenhouse Gas Emissions from New Stationary Sources: Electric Utility Generating Units, 79 Fed. Reg. 1463.

31. See 42 U.S.C. § 15962(i) (2012) ("No technology, or level of emission reduction, solely by reason of the use of technology, or the achievement of the emission reduction, by 1 or more facilities receiving assistance under this Act, shall be considered to be . . . adequately demonstrated for purposes of [Section 111]."); 26 U.S.C. § 48A(g) (2012) ("No use of technology (or level of emission reduction solely by reason of the use of the technology), and no achievement of any emission reduction by the demonstration of any technology or performance level, by or at one or more facilities with respect to which a credit is allowed under this section, shall be considered to indicate that the technology or performance level is . . . adequately demonstrated for purposes of section 111 of the Clean Air Act.").

32. See Letter from Rep. Fred Upton et al., U.S. House of Representatives, to Gina McCarthy, Adm'r, EPA (Nov. 15, 2013), http://energycommerce.house.gov/sites/republicans.energycommerce.house.gov/files/letters/20131115EPA.pdf.

33. Carbon Pollution Emission Guidelines for Existing Stationary Sources: Electric Utility Generating Units, 79 Fed. Reg. 34830, 34832 (proposed June 18, 2014) (to be codified at 40 C.F.R. pt. 60).

34. Ibid., 34834–34835.

35. Ibid., 34836.

36. Clean Air Act § 111(d), 42 U.S.C. § 7411(d) (2012) (emphases added).

37. Ibid. (emphases added).

38. EPA, Legal Memorandum for Proposed Carbon Pollution Emission Guidelines for Existing Electric Utility Generating Units 54 (June 2, 2014), http://www2.epa.gov/sites/production/files/2014-06/documents/20140602-legal-memorandum.pdf.

39. 42 U.S.C. § 7411(a)(1) (emphasis added).

40. Util. Air Regulatory Grp. v. EPA, 134 S. Ct. 2427, 2444 (2014).

41. 42 U.S.C. § 7411(d) (emphasis added).

42. Proposed National Emission Standards for Hazardous Air Pollutants, 69 Fed. Reg. 4652, 4685 (proposed Jan. 30, 2004) (to be codified at 40 C.F.R. pts. 60 and 63).

43. Revision of December 2000 Regulatory Finding on the Emissions of Hazardous Air Pollutants, 70 Fed. Reg. 15994, 16031 (Mar. 29, 2005) (to be codified at 40 C.F.R. pt. 63).

44. EPA, Legal Memorandum for Proposed Carbon Pollution Emission Guidelines, 21.

45. Ibid., 23.

46. See West Virginia v. EPA, No. 14-1146 (D.C. Cir. June 9, 2015), Final Brief of Petitioners, 40–46, http://www.ago.wv.gov/publicresources/epa/Documents/Final%20WV%20opening%20brief%20-%20reduced%20.pdf.

47. Ibid.

48. Revision of December 2000 Regulatory Finding on the Emissions of Hazardous Air Pollutants, 70 Fed. Reg. 16031.

49. Rapanos v. United States, 547 U.S. 715, 723 (2006).

50. Ibid., 739.

51. Ibid., 742.

52. Ibid., 734 (internal quotation marks omitted).

53. Ibid., 759 (Kennedy, J., concurring).

54. Ibid., 780 (emphasis added).

55. Ibid., 781.

56. Clean Water Rule: Definition of "Waters of the United States," 80 Fed. Reg. 37054, 37117–37118 (June 29, 2015) (to be codified at 33 C.F.R. pt. 328, 40 C.F.R. pts. 110, 112, 117, 122, 230, 300, 302, and 401).

57. Ibid., 37118.

58. Ibid., 37119 (emphasis added).

59. Ibid.

60. Rapanos, 547 U.S. 742 (emphasis added).

61. Ibid., 780 (Kennedy, J., concurring) (emphasis added).

62. Clean Water Rule: Definition of "Waters of the United States," 80 Fed. Reg. 37118.

63. Ibid., 37118–37119.

64. John Siciliano, "22 States Sue EPA over Water Rule," *Wash Exam.* (June 30, 2015, 5:41 pm), http://www.washingtonexaminer.com/22-states-sue-epa-over-water-rule/article/2567358?custom_click=rss.

65. Util. Air Regulatory Grp. v. EPA, 134 S. Ct. 2427, 2444 (2014).

66. Ibid.

67. 134 S. Ct. 1584 (2014).

68. Ibid., 1593.

69. See 42 U.S.C. §§ 7409, 7410(a)(1) (2012).

70. 42 U.S.C. § 7410(a)(2)(D)(i) (emphasis added).

71. See EME Homer City Generation, 134 S. Ct. 1606.

72. Ibid., 1610 (Scalia, J., dissenting).

73. Michigan v. EPA, No. 14-46 (U.S. 2015), Transcript of Oral Argument, 82.

74. Ben Wolfgang, "Supreme Court Strikes Down Obama Power-Plant Regulations," *Wash. Times* (June 29, 2015), http://www.washingtontimes.com/news/2015/jun/29/court-rules-against-epa-power-plant-mercury-limits/.

CHAPTER 21

1. See Jacobson v. Massachusetts, 197 U.S. 11, 38 (1905) ("The safety and health of the people of Massachusetts are, in the first instance, for that commonwealth to guard and protect. They are matters that do not ordinarily concern the national government.").

2. See *The Crimes on the Books and Committee Jurisdiction: Hearing Before the H. Comm. on the Judiciary*, 113th Cong. (2014) (Testimony of John Baker), http://judiciary.house.gov/_cache/files/44135b93-fe36-43dc-a91b-3412fe15e1f4/baker-testimony.pdf.

3. 18 U.S.C. § 1341.

4. 18 U.S.C. § 1343.

5. 18 U.S.C. § 1001.

6. See United States v. McNab, 331 F.3d 1228, 1239 (11th Cir. 2003) (rejecting argument that the Lacey Act term "any foreign law" applies only to foreign statutes, not regulations).

7. See Tiffany M. Joslyn, "Criminal Provisions in the Dodd-Frank Wall Street Reform & Consumer Protection Act," http://www.fed-soc.org/publications/detail/criminal-provisions-in-the-dodd-frank-wall-street-reform-consumer-protection-act.

8. Summary of the Dodd-Frank Wall Street Reform and Consumer Protection Act, Enacted into Law on July 21, 2010 (Davis Polk & Wardwell, LLP, Washington, D.C.), July 21, 2010 (on file with the author).

9. *Over-Criminalization of Conduct/Over-Federalization of Criminal Law: Hearing Before the Subcomm. on Crime, Terrorism & Homeland Sec. of the H. Comm. on the Judiciary*, 111th Cong. (2009), 7 (testimony of former Attorney General Dick Thornburgh, transcript), http://judiciary.house.gov/_files/hearings/pdf/Thornburgh090722.pdf.

10. Although courts are reluctant to invoke it, under the void-for-vagueness doctrine, a criminal statute that "fails to give a person of ordinary intelligence fair notice that his contemplated conduct is forbidden by the statute" (United States v. Harriss, 347 U.S. 612, 617 (1954)) or is so indefinite that "it encourages arbitrary and erratic arrests and convictions" (Papachristou v. Jacksonville, 405 U.S. 156, 162 (1972)) is void for vagueness. See also Chicago v. Morales, 527 U.S. 41, 55 (1999); Kolender v. Lawson, 461 U.S. 352, 357 (1983); Grayned v. City of Rockford, 408 U.S. 104, 108–109 (1972); Bouie v. City of Columbia, 378 U.S. 347, 350–351 (1964); United States v. Reese, 92 U.S. 214, 221 (1876) ("It would certainly be dangerous if the legislature could set a net large enough to catch all possible offenders, and leave it to the courts to step inside and say who could be rightfully detained, and who should be set at large."). See generally Anthony G. Amsterdam, Note, "The Void-for-Vagueness Doctrine in the Supreme Court," *U. Pa. L. Rev.* 109 (1960): 67 (discussing the historical development of the void-for-vagueness doctrine). Similarly, the common law rule of lenity requires courts to resolve any ambiguity in a criminal statute in the defendant's favor because of the unfairness that would come with punishing somebody for not correctly understanding an ambiguous criminal law. See United States v. Santos, 553 U.S. 507, 514 (2008).

11. Although rare, on at least one occasion, the Supreme Court has addressed the issue of whether it constitutes a due process violation to convict

somebody for violating an obscure criminal provision that nobody could be expected to know unless explicitly informed of its existence. In Lambert v. California, 355 U.S. 225 (1957), the Court, by a 5–4 margin, overturned the defendant's conviction for violating a local ordinance contained in the Los Angeles municipal code that required any ex-felon to report to the sheriff after being present in Los Angeles for five days.

12. See Blackstone, *Commentaries*, vol. 1, *46 (noting that Caligula "wrote his laws in a very small character, and hung them up upon high pillars, the more effectually to ensnare the people"); Screws v. United States, 325 U.S. 91, 96 (1945) (plurality opinion).

13. 532 U.S. 451, 459 (2001).

14. See Cheek v. United States, 498 U.S. 192, 199 (1991) (the rule that ignorance of the law is no defense is "[b]ased on the notion that the law is definite and knowable").

15. For example, federal campaign finance laws contain many criminal provisions. As the U.S. Supreme Court noted in Citizens United v. Federal Election Commission, at that time, "[t]he FEC had adopted 568 pages of regulations, 1,278 pages of explanations and justifications for those regulations, and 1,771 advisory opinions since 1975." 103 U.S. 876, 895 (2010). During oral argument in McCutcheon v. Federal Election Commission, a case involving a challenge to the constitutionality of aggregate limits on individual contributions to national parties and federal candidates, Justice Antonin Scalia said, "this campaign finance law is so intricate that I can't figure it out." McCutcheon v. FEC, 134 S. Ct. 1434 (2014) (No. 12-536), transcript of Oral Argument, 17, http://www.supremecourt.gov/oral_arguments/argument_transcripts/12-536_21o2.pdf. See also William J. Stuntz, "Self-Defeating Crimes," *Va. L. Rev.* 86 (2000): 1871 ("Ordinary people do not have the time or training to learn the contents of criminal codes; indeed, even criminal law professors rarely know much about what conduct is and isn't criminal in their jurisdictions.")

16. *The Federalist* No. 62 (Madison), pp. 323–324 (George W. Carey & James McClellan, eds., 2001).

17. John Locke, *The Second Treatise of Civil Government* (1690), 141.

18. Wayman v. Southard, 23 U.S. (10 Wheat.) 1, 41 (1825).

19. See, e.g., J.W. Hampton, Jr., & Co. v. United States, 276 U.S. 394, 406 (1928) ("In determining what [Congress] may do in seeking assistance from another branch, the extent and character of that assistance must be fixed according

to common sense and the inherent necessities of the government co-ordination." So long as "Congress shall lay down by legislative act an intelligible principle to which the person or body authorized to [exercise the delegated authority] is directed to conform, such legislative action is not a forbidden delegation of legislative power.").

20. See, e.g., Margaret H. Lemos, "The Consequences of Congress's Choice of Delegate: Judicial and Agency Interpretations of Title VII," *Vand. L. Rev.* 63 (2010): 363, 369–370 ("Indeed, as public choice theorists have argued, delegations can be particularly useful to Congress with respect to divisive issues. Congress often legislates to please certain constituencies. But different groups tend to want different solutions to problems; legislation that responds to the wishes of one group may draw the ire of another. The problem is particularly acute when interest group differences cut across party lines. Legislation in such circumstances threatens high political costs and minimal gains, as any conclusive solution will divide supporters of both parties. One option is to do nothing, but inaction is a risky strategy when constituents are clamoring for a legislative response to some pressing problem. Instead, Congress often opts for legislation that addresses the problem generally but leaves the most contentious details unresolved. By delegating the ultimate decision to an agency, Congress can take credit for doing something while dodging the blame from disappointed constituents."); Neal Devins & Michael Herz, "The Battle That Never Was: Congress, the White House, and Agency Litigation Authority," *Law & Contemp. Probs.* 61 (1998): 205, 215–216 ("As public choice theory suggests, lawmakers often devise legislation at the behest of powerful interest groups. . . . [S]ince interest groups often compete with each other (including industry and environmentalists, unions and business), legislation is often ambiguous."); Joseph A. Grundfest & A.C. Pritchard, "Statutes with Multiple Personality Disorders: The Value of Ambiguity in Statutory Design and Administration," *Stan. L. Rev.* 54 (2002): 627, 628 ("Ambiguity serves a legislative purpose. When legislators perceive a need to compromise, they can, among other strategies, 'obscur[e] the particular meaning of a statute, allowing different legislators to read the obscured provisions the way they wish.'" (quoting Abner J. Mikva & Eric Lane, *Legislative Process* (New York: Aspen, 1997), 779–780)); Lisa Schultz Bressman, "*Chevron*'s Mistake," *Duke L.J.* 58 (2009): 549, 568 ("Congress might aim to write just enough policy to receive a positive response for its action, while deflecting any negative attention for the burdensome details to the agency."); Jonathan

R. Macey & Geoffrey P. Miller, "The Canons of Statutory Construction and Judicial Preferences," *Vand. L. Rev.* 45 (1992): 647, 666 ("As interest groups have become more specialized and as more interest groups have succeeded in gaining voice in the policymaking process, consensus has become more difficult to achieve. Congress has adopted, therefore, the strategy of passing increasingly broad and amorphous enabling legislation that delegates controversial matters to administrative agencies.").

21. 33 U.S.C. §§ 1251–1387 (2012).

22. 547 U.S. 715, 722 (2006).

23. Ibid.

24. Ibid.

25. See, e.g., Waters of the United States, 79 Fed. Reg. 76, 22188 (Apr. 21, 2014), http://www.gpo.gov/fdsys/pkg/FR-2014-04-21/pdf/2014-07142.pdf; Tony Francois, "The Waters of the United States Rule: Not About Water," Liberty Blog (Feb. 9, 2015), http://blog.pacificlegal.org/2015/waters-united-states-rule-not-water/.

26. There are many instances where Congress grants a broad delegation to regulatory agencies to promulgate regulations, violations of which can result in criminal prosecution. For example, pursuant to 42 U.S.C. §§ 6921(a) & (b), the EPA is granted broad authority to characterize and list "hazardous materials," which it has done on several occasions: 40 C.F.R. § 261.3 (2010) (generally defining "hazardous waste"); §§ 261.20–261.24(a) (defining as hazardous waste solid waste that has the characteristics of ignitability, corrosivity, reactivity, or toxicity); §§ 261.4, 261.38–261.40 (defining "exclusions" from "hazardous waste"); § 261.5 (defining special requirements for hazardous waste generated by "conditionally exempt small quantity generators"); § 261.6 (defining requirements for "recyclable materials" as an exemption from "hazardous waste"); § 261.10 (specifying criteria for identifying "the characteristics of hazardous waste"); § 261.11 (defining requirements for listing "hazardous waste"); § 261.24(b) (listing "toxic wastes"); § 261.31 (listing hazardous wastes from "nonspecific sources"); § 261.32 (listing hazardous wastes from "specific sources"). Violations of provisions pertaining to hazardous waste can subject individuals or entities to criminal prosecution under 42 U.S.C. § 6928. Pursuant to 29 U.S.C. § 655(b), the Department of Labor is empowered to establish national occupational health and safety standards. Once established, DOL may require the use of signs warning employees about particular hazards, the use of particular types of protective gear,

and the type and number of medical examinations for particular employees. Violations of such rules can result in criminal prosecution pursuant to 29 U.S.C. § 666. And Congress has empowered the President to list articles and services that are subject to strict export restrictions because of their potential military uses. The State Department has done so under far-reaching International Traffic in Arms Regulations (ITAR), 22 C.F.R. §§ 120–130, violations of which may result in criminal prosecution.

27. See Panama Refining Co. v. Ryan, 293 U.S. 388 (1935); A.L.A. Schechter Poultry Corp. v. United States, 295 U.S. 495 (1935).

28. The Supreme Court of the United States has given the "green light" to Congress to delineate the "general policy" and broad boundaries of delegated authority. See, e.g., Mistretta v. United States, 488 U.S. 361, 372 (1989): "Applying this 'intelligible principle' test to congressional delegations, our jurisprudence has been driven by a practical understanding that in our increasingly complex society, replete with ever changing and more technical problems, Congress simply cannot do its job absent an ability to delegate power under broad general directives. Accordingly, this Court has deemed it 'constitutionally sufficient' if Congress clearly delineates the general policy, the public agency which is to apply it, and the boundaries of this delegated authority." Congress has certainly taken advantage of this broad latitude, as have regulatory agencies.

29. See, e.g., Nat'l Rifle Ass'n v. Brady, 914 F.2d 475, 479, n3 (4th Cir. 1990) (deferring to ATF's interpretation of a regulation requiring that licensees maintain records concerning receipt and disposition of their personal firearms); United States v. Flores, 404 F.3d 320, 326–327 (5th Cir. 2005) (deferring to ATF's interpretation as set forth in 27 C.F.R. § 478.11 of the phrase "illegally or unlawfully in the United States" in 18 U.S.C. § 922(g)(5)(A)); United States v. Atandi, 376 F.3d 1186, 1189 (10th Cir. 2004) (deferring to ATF's interpretation as set forth in 27 C.F.R. § 478.11 of the phrase "illegally or unlawfully in the United States" in 18 U.S.C. § 922(g)(5)(A)); NLRB v. Oklahoma Fixture Co., 332 F.3d 1284, 1286–1287 (10th Cir. 2003) (*en banc*) (deferring to NLRB's interpretation of the term "membership dues" in the Labor Management Relations Act exception to a criminal prohibition on employer payments to labor organizations); United States v. Kanchanalak, 192 F.3d 1037, 1047, and n17 (D.C. Cir. 1999) (deferring to FEC's interpretation of soft money regulation requiring political committees to report the "true" sources of their soft money donations).

30. In Chevron U.S.A., Inc. v. Natural Resources Defense Council, 467 U.S. 837, 842–843 (1984), the Court held that unless Congress has clearly expressed its intent, reviewing courts should defer to an agency's interpretation of an ambiguous statute so long as that interpretation is reasonable.

31. 574 U.S. ___ (2014), *cert. denied* (Nov. 10, 2014) (No. 14-29) (Scalia, J., dissenting).

32. Ibid. (citations omitted).

33. See Lawrence M. Friedman, *Crime and Punishment in American History* (New York: Basic, 1993), 282–283: "There have always been regulatory crimes, from the colonial period onward. . . . But the vast expansion of the regulatory state in the twentieth century meant a vast expansion of regulatory crimes as well. Each statute on health and safety, on conservation, on finance, on environmental protection, carried with it some form of criminal sanction for violation. . . . Wholesale extinction may be going on in the animal kingdom, but it does not seem to be much of a problem among regulatory laws. These now exist in staggering numbers, at all levels. They are as grains of sand on the beach." Indeed, the mere existence of criminal regulations dramatically alters the relationship between the regulatory agency and the regulated power. All an agency has to do is suggest that a regulated person or entity *might* face criminal prosecution and penalties for failure to follow an agency directive, and the regulated person or entity will likely fall quickly into line without questioning the agency's authority. For an excellent article discussing the pressures that companies face when confronted with the possibility of, and the lengths to which they will go to avoid, criminal prosecution, see Richard A. Epstein, "The Dangerous Incentive Structures of Nonprosecution and Deferred Prosecution Agreements," Heritage Foundation, Legal Memorandum No. 129 (June 26, 2014), http://www.heritage.org/research/reports/2014/06/the-dangerous-incentive-structures-of-nonprosecution-and-deferred-prosecution-agreements. See also James R. Copeland, "The Shadow Regulatory State: The Rise of Deferred Prosecution Agreements," Manhattan Institute for Policy Research (May 2012), http://www.manhattan-institute.org/html/cjr_14.htm.

34. See Paul J. Larkin, Jr., "Regulation, Prohibition, and Overcriminalization: The Proper and Improper Uses of the Criminal Law," *Hofstra L. Rev.* 42 (2014): 745.

35. See, e.g., United States v. Harriss, 347 U.S. 612, 617 (1954) (government cannot enforce a criminal law that cannot be understood by a person

of "ordinary intelligence"); Connally v. Gen. Constr. Co., 269 U.S. 385, 391 (1926) (discussing persons of "common intelligence").

36. See, e.g., Vidrine v. United States, 846 F. Supp. 2d 550, 561–569 (W.D. La. 2011) (containing discussion of whether the substance the defendant was charged with storing was "hazardous waste," which would constitute a crime, or "used oil," which would not constitute a crime, and noting that the case agent ignored the fact that there was an internal debate among EPA employees and state authorities on that question).

37. For example, the Securities and Exchange Commission promulgated Rule 14a-9, which prohibits the making of false or misleading statements in connection with the solicitation of proxies, 17 C.F.R. § 240.14a-9, and Rule 10b-5, which prohibits material omissions or misleading statements or employing any device, scheme, or artifice to defraud in connection with the purchase or sale of any security, 17 C.F.R. § 240.10b-5, language which closely mirrors language in the enabling statute, the Securities Exchange Act of 1934.

38. For examples of the consequences to citizens of regulatory overcriminalization, see the following Heritage Foundation publications: "USA vs. You," www.heritage.org/usavsyou (July 10, 2014); *One Nation Under Arrest: How Crazy Laws, Rogue Prosecutors, and Activist Judges Threaten Your Liberty*, ed. Paul Rosenzweig, 2nd ed. (2013).

39. An inventory of collateral consequences is maintained by the American Bar Association, accessible at American Bar Association, National Inventory of the Collateral Consequences of Conviction, http://www.abacollateralconsequences.org/. In short, individuals convicted of crimes face consequences extending beyond the end of their actual sentences, potentially lasting their entire lives. Examples include being barred from entering a variety of licensed professional fields and receiving federal student aid. The Internet has spawned numerous websites designed specifically to catalog, permanently retain, and publicize individuals' criminal histories—all but guaranteeing perpetual branding as a criminal. These websites can demand payment from individuals in exchange for removing their mug shots and related personal information. For additional discussion about the detrimental nature of collateral consequences, see "Collateral Damage: America's Failure to Forgive or Forget in the War on Crime," National Association of Criminal Defense Lawyers (2014), http://thf_media.s3.amazonaws.com/2014/pdf/Collateral%20Damage%20FINAL%20Report.pdf.

40. See, e.g., Peggy Little, "The Debarment Power—No Do Business with No Due Process" (Apr. 25, 2013), http://executivebranchproject.com/the-debarment-power-no-do-business-with-no-due-process/#sthash.ord4YN0x.dpuf; Steven Gordon & Richard Duvall, "It's Time to Rethink the Suspension and Debarment Process" (July 3, 2013), http://www.mondaq.com/unitedstates/x/248174/Government+Contracts+Procurement+PPP/Its+Time+To+Rethink+The+Suspension+And+Debarment+Process.

41. See, e.g., Graham Hughes, "Criminal Omissions," *Yale L.J.* 67 (1958): 590, 595: "For it was in the latter half of the nineteenth century that the great chain of regulatory statutes was initiated in England, which inaugurated a new era in the administration of the criminal law. Among them are the Food and Drugs Acts, the Licensing Acts, the Merchandise Marks Acts, the Weights and Measures Acts, the Public Health Acts and the Road Traffic Acts. With these statutes came a judicial readiness to abandon traditional concepts of *mens rea* and to base criminal liability on the doing of an act, or even upon the vicarious responsibility for another's act, in the absence of intent, recklessness or even negligence." (footnotes omitted); Edwin Meese III & Paul J. Larkin, Jr., "Reconsidering the Mistake of Law Defense," *J. Crim. L. & Criminology* 102 (2012): 725, 744–745: "[T]he environmental laws often do not require proof of the same type of mental state and actions that ordinary crimes demand. Some criminal environmental laws require proof of the same 'evil meaning' mind demanded by common law crimes. But most can lead to a conviction if a person knew what he was doing, even if he did not know that what he was doing was illegal or wrongful, and sometimes even if he merely acted negligently. Moreover, the 'knowledge' necessary to establish a violation can be imputed to a person from the knowledge of others in his company. As far as the necessary criminal acts go, a person can be held liable not only for his own actions, but also for the conduct of others under his supervision because of his position in the company. In some instances, a person can be held criminally liable for *not* reporting a crime. Finally, '[i]gnorance or mistake-of-law are generally not valid defenses, except perhaps for a specific intent crime that requires a knowing violation.'" (citations omitted).

42. See, e.g., Oliver Wendell Holmes, Jr., *The Common Law* (1881), *50 ("It is not intended to deny that criminal liability . . . is founded on blameworthiness. Such a denial would shock the moral sense of any civilized community; or, to put it another way, a law which punished conduct which would not be

blameworthy in the average member of the community would be too severe for that community to bear."); Blackstone, *Commentaries*, vol. 4 (1769), *20–21 (distilling the act of criminality to "this single consideration, the want or defect of *will*") (emphasis in original); United States v. Morissette, 342 U.S. 246, 250 (1952): "The contention that an injury can amount to a crime only when inflicted by intention is no provincial or transient notion. It is as universal and persistent in mature systems of law as belief in freedom of the human will and a consequent ability and duty of the normal individual to choose between good and evil."

43. The Supreme Court has upheld the constitutionality of strict liability crimes on a number of occasions. See Shevlin-Carpenter Co. v. Minnesota, 218 U.S. 57 (1910) (holding that a corporation can be convicted for trespass without proof of criminal intent); United States v. Balint, 258 U.S. 250 (1922) (holding that a real person can be convicted of the sale of narcotics without a tax stamp without proof that he knew that the substance was a narcotic); United States v. Behrman, 258 U.S. 280 (1922) (Balint companion case) (holding that a physician can be convicted of distributing a controlled substance not "in the course of his professional practice" without proof that he knew this his actions exceeded that limit); United States v. Dotterweich, 320 U.S. 277 (1943) (holding that the president of a company can be convicted of distributing adulterated or misbranded drugs in interstate commerce without proof that he even was aware of the transaction). However, a number of commentators have criticized the existence and proliferation of such laws. See, e.g., Lon L. Fuller, *The Morality of Law*, rev. ed. (New Haven, CT: Yale UP, 1969), 77 ("Strict criminal liability has never achieved respectability in our law."); H.L.A. Hart, "Negligence, Mens Rea, and Criminal Responsibility," in *Punishment and Responsibility: Essays in the Philosophy of Law* (New York: Oxford UP, 1968), 136, 152 ("strict liability is odious"); Francis B. Sayre, "Public Welfare Offenses," *Colum. L. Rev.* 33 (1933): 55, 72 ("To subject defendants entirely free from moral blameworthiness to the possibility of prison sentences is revolting to the community sense of justice; and no law which violates this fundamental instinct can long endure."); A.P. Simester, "Is Strict Liability Always Wrong?" in *Appraising Strict Liability*, ed. A.P. Simester (Oxford: Oxford UP, 2005), 21 (strict liability is wrong because it "leads to conviction of persons who are, morally speaking, innocent"); Herbert Wechsler, "The Challenge of a Model Penal Code," *Harv. L. Rev.* 65 (1952): 1109: "The most that can be said for such provisions [prescribing liability

without regard to any mental factor] is that where the penalty is light, where knowledge normally obtains and where a major burden of litigation is envisioned, there may be some practical basis for a stark limitation of the issues; and large injustice can seldom be done. If these considerations are persuasive, it seems clear, however, that they ought not to persuade where any major sanction is involved."; Richard G. Singer, "The Resurgence of Mens Rea: The Rise and Fall of Strict Criminal Liability," *B.C. L. Rev.* 30 (1989): 337, 403–404; Rollin M. Perkins, "Criminal Liability without Fault: A Disquieting Trend," *Iowa L. Rev.* 68 (1983): 1067–1070.

44. See Morissette, 342 U.S. 251–252 ("Crime, as a compound concept, generally constituted only from concurrence of an evil-meaning mind with an evil-doing hand, was congenial to an intense individualism and took deep and early root in American soil.").

45. Elonis v. United States, 575 U.S. ___ (2015).

46. Ibid., 9 (quoting Morissette v. United States, 342 U.S. 246, 252 (1952).).

47. Ibid., 13.

48. Ibid., 12 (quoting Carter v. United States, 530 U.S. 255, 269 (2000).).

49. Wendell Holmes, Jr., *The Common Law*, *3.

50. See, e.g., 18 U.S.C. § 707 (providing a criminal penalty of up to six months' imprisonment for the unauthorized use of a 4-H club's logo); 36 C.F.R. § 261.22(a) (unauthorized use or reproduction of "Smokey Bear" logo); 36 C.F.R. § 261.22(b) (unauthorized use or reproduction of "Woodsy Owl" logo); 36 C.F.R. § 2.15(a)(2) (failure to keep a pet on a leash that does not exceed six feet in length in a public building, public transportation vehicle, or location designated as a swimming beach); 36 C.F.R. § 2.10(b)(1) (digging or leveling the ground at a campsite); 36 C.F.R. § 2.11 (picnicking in a non-designated area); 36 C.F.R. § 2.12(a)(1) (operating a "motorized toy, or an audio device, such as a radio, television set, tape deck or musical instrument, in a manner . . . [t]hat exceeds a noise level of 60 decibels measured on the A-weighted scale at 50 feet"); 36 C.F.R. § 2.14(a)(5) ("[b]athing, or washing food, clothing, dishes, or other property at public water outlets, fixtures or pools" not designated for that purpose); 36 C.F.R. § 2.16(e) ("Allowing horses or pack animals to proceed in excess of a slow walk when passing in the immediate vicinity of persons on foot or bicycle"); 36 C.F.R. § 2.18(d)(1) (operating a snowmobile that makes "excessive noise"; "Excessive noise for snowmobiles manufactured after July 1,

1975 is a level of total snowmobile noise that exceeds 78 decibels measured on the A-weighted scale measured at 50 feet. Snowmobiles manufactured between July 1, 1973 and July 1, 1975 shall not register more than 82 decibels on the A-weighted scale at 50 feet. Snowmobiles manufactured prior to July 1, 1973 shall not register more than 86 decibels on the A-weighted scale at 50 feet. All decibel measurements shall be based on snowmobile operation at or near full throttle."); 36 C.F.R. § 2.20 (using roller skates, skateboards, roller skis, coasting vehicles, or similar devices in non-designated areas); 36 C.F.R. § 2.22(a)(3) (failing to turn in found property to the park superintendent "as soon as practicable"); and 36 C.F.R. § 3.17(b) (using a surfboard on a beach designated for swimming).

51. 16 U.S.C. § 3372(a)(2)(A). This is the same law that was used to investigate the Gibson Guitar Company for importing wood for guitar frets that allegedly violated export laws in India and Madagascar—which, in the case of Madagascar, were not even written in English. In order to avoid indictment, Gibson Guitar agreed to pay a $300,000 fine and a $50,000 community service payment to the National Fish and Wildlife Foundation and to withdraw claims for the $260,000 worth of wood that had been seized by federal agents. See "Justice Hits Gibson Guitars with $300G Fine Over Fingerboards," *Fox News* (Aug. 6, 2012), http://www.foxnews.com/politics/2012/08/06/justice-hits-gibson-guitars-with-300g-fine-over-fingerboards/; Daniel Dew & Gavriel Swerling, "DOJ Bullies Gibson Guitar into Submission: Will Congress Allow This to Happen Again?" *Daily Signal* (Aug. 7, 2012), http://dailysignal.com/2012/08/07/doj-bullies-gibson-into-submission-will-congress-allow-this-to-happen-again/. For an excellent article arguing that the criminal provisions of the Lacey Act are unconstitutional, see Paul J. Larkin, Jr., "The Dynamic Incorporation of Foreign Law, and the Constitutional Regulation of Federal Lawmaking," *Harv. J.L. & Pub. Pol'y* 38 (forthcoming 2015) (arguing that the criminal provisions of the Lacey Act are unconstitutional).

52. McNab v. United States, 331 F.3d 1228, 1232 (11th Cir. 2003).

53. As Judge Peter Fay noted in his dissenting opinion, "Article 96 of the Honduran Constitution specifically provides, '[t]he Law does not have retroactive effect, except in penal matters when the new law favors the delinquent [i.e., criminally convicted] or the person that is prosecuted.'" Ibid., 1249. Judge Fay added, quite correctly, "I think we would be shocked should the tables be reversed and a foreign nation simply ignored one of our court rulings because it caused some frustration or inconvenience." Ibid., 1251.

54. 16 U.S.C. §§ 1371–1423.

55. See Gary Fields & John R. Emshwiller, "As Federal Crime List Grows, Threshold of Guilt Declines," *Wall St. J.* (Sept. 27, 2011), http://online.wsj.com/articles/SB10001424053111904060604576570801651620000.

56. See Gary Fields & John R. Emshwiller, "A Sewage Blunder Earns Engineer a Criminal Record," *Wall St. J.* (Dec. 12, 2011), http://online.wsj.com/articles/SB10001424052970204903804577082770135339442; *Regulatory Crime: Identifying the Scope of the Problem: Hearing Before the H. Comm. on the Judiciary*, 113th Cong. (2013) (Testimony of Lawrence Lewis), http://judiciary.house.gov/_files/hearings/113th/10302013/Lawrence%20Lewis%20Testimony.pdf. For a videotaped interview with Lawrence Lewis, go to http://dailysignal.com/2013/07/05/diverted-from-the-straight-and-narrow-path-for-diverting-sewage/.

57. Daniel Dew, "Save the Whales NOAA," *Daily Signal* (Sept. 2, 2012), http://dailysignal.com/2012/09/05/save-the-whales-noaa/.

58. Evan Bernick, "Much Ado About Blubber: Marine Biologist Faces Fines, Probation for Research," *Daily Signal* (Dec. 20, 2013), http://dailysignal.com/2013/12/20/much-ado-blubber-marine-biologist-faces-fines-probation-research/.

59. Ibid.

60. Ibid.

61. George Will, "Blowing the Whistle on Leviathan," *Wash. Post* (July 27, 2012), http://www.washingtonpost.com/opinions/george-will-blowing-the-whistle-on-leviathan/2012/07/27/gJQAAsRnEX_story.html.

62. Bernick, "Much Ado About Blubber."

63. This saga is reminiscent of a case involving Robert Eldridge, Jr., who was also charged with violating the Marine Mammal Protection for freeing a whale that was caught in his fishing net rather than reporting the ensnarement to federal authorities so that they could free the whale. Facing the prospect of a felony conviction, Eldridge pleaded guilty to a misdemeanor. See Fields & Emshwiller, "As Federal Crime List Grows."

64. Harvey Silverglate, "A Doctor's Posthumous Vindication," *Wall St. J.* (Dec. 25, 2012), http://online.wsj.com/news/articles/SB10001424127887323981504578174973015235686?mg=reno64-wsj.

65. Ibid.

66. Alex Berenson, "Indictment of Doctor Tests Drug Marketing Rules," *N.Y. Times* (July 22, 2006), http://www.nytimes.com/2006/07/22/business/22drugdoc.html?pagewanted=all&_r=3&.

67. Silverglate, "A Doctor's Posthumous Vindication."

68. United States v. Caronia 703 F.3d 149, 169 (2nd Cir. 2012).

69. Silverglate, "A Doctor's Posthumous Vindication."

70. See Paul J. Larkin, Jr., "Co-opting the Criminal Justice System for Anti-Competitive Purposes," Heritage Foundation (Sept. 3, 2014), http://www.heritage.org/research/commentary/2014/9/coopting-the-criminal-justice-system-for-anticompetitive-purposes. This is most evident in the area of licensing restrictions, where several states have passed laws making it a crime to practice certain professions without a license, even when public safety does not appear to be an issue, at least not a legitimate one. See, e.g., Fla. Stat. Ann. § 476.194 (unlicensed practice of barbering is a misdemeanor) (West 2014); Ky. Rev. Stat. §§ 317A.020(2), 317A.990 (West 2014) (unlicensed practice of cosmetology is punishable by a fine or incarceration); Penn. Stat. Ann. §§ 63:551, 63:565 (West 2014) (unlicensed practice of barbering is punishable by a $600 fine or 90 days' incarceration); Tenn. Code Ann. §§ 62-4-108, 62-4-129 (West 2014) (unlicensed practice of "cosmetology, manicuring or aesthetics" is a misdemeanor); Title 59 O.S. Section 199.6(c) (unlicensed practice of cosmetology in Oklahoma is a misdemeanor). Such anti-competitive regulations, enforceable by criminal penalties, are also promulgated on occasion by federal regulators. For example, the Environmental Protection Agency has, on occasion, promulgated new regulations (many of which can be found in 40 C.F.R. pt. 60), violations of which can result in criminal prosecution, that contain "grandfather" provisions exempting existing producers, which obviously creates a barrier to entry for new, would-be competitors. See Thomas J. Dean and Robert L. Brown, "Pollution Regulation as a Barrier to New Firm Entry: Initial Evidence and Implications for Future Research," *Acad. Management J.* 38 (1995): 288–303; OECD Policy Roundtable Report, Environmental Regulation and Competition (2006). The Raisin Marketing Order, established under Agriculture Marketing Agreement Act, 7 U.S.C. § 608c(1), is another example of federal regulatory power used to benefit an entrenched interest. The order, which is promulgated by the Secretary of Agriculture, creates a cartel-like Raisin Administrative Committee, composed mainly of well-established raisin growers, which requires that a certain percentage of raisins be surrendered to a raisin reserve. The effect is to reduce supply, thus

raising prices for raisins, which prevents small raisin producers from competing with well-entrenched producers by offering their raisins at lower prices. Raisin handlers who refuse to turn over the requisite raisins or otherwise violate the order face potential criminal penalties. See 7 U.S.C. § 608c(14) (setting forth penalties upon "conviction" for violating the order); Horne v. Dept. of Agriculture, 569 U.S. ___, 133 S. Ct. 2053, 2057 (2013) ("Handlers who violate the Secretary's marketing orders may be subject to civil and criminal penalties.").

71. Such circumstances might include conduct that is universally recognized as being wrongful or inherently dangerous. See, e.g., United States v. Park, 421 U.S. 658 (1975) (maintenance of rat-infested food warehouses); United States v. Int'l Minerals & Chem. Corp., 402 U.S. 558 (1971) (transportation of hazardous waste); United States v. Freed, 401 U.S. 601 (1971) (possession of hand grenades); United States v. Dotterweich, 320 U.S. 277 (1943) (sale of mislabeled drugs).

72. See Meese & Larkin, "Reconsidering the Mistake of Law Defense."

73. See, e.g., Smith v. United States, 133 S. Ct. 714, 718–720 (2013) (defendant can be required to prove that he withdrew from a conspiracy); Dixon v. United States, 548 U.S. 1, 17 (2006) (defendant can be required to prove duress or necessity); Martin v. Ohio, 480 U.S. 228, 233, 235 (1987) (defendant can be required to prove that he acted in self-defense); Patterson v. New York, 432 U.S. 197, 208–210 (1977) (defendant can be required to prove that he acted due to extreme emotional disturbance).

74. Congress has, on occasion, enacted laws setting forth the elements of a defense, such as the insanity defense. See Insanity Defense Reform Act of 1984, 18 U.S.C. § 20 (2012). It should be noted, however, that if Congress fails to create such a statutory defense, the Supreme Court has stated that while federal courts do not have the authority to create common law crimes, they do have the authority, in limited circumstances, to develop common law defenses. See, e.g., Jacobson v. United States, 503 U.S. 540, 548–549 (1992) (entrapment defense); United States v. Bailey, 444 U.S. 394, 409–415 (1980) (duress or necessity defense); United States v. Penn. Indus. Chem. Corp., 411 U.S. 655, 673–675 (1973) (defense of reliance on opinions of government officials interpreting a federal law within their jurisdiction); Sinclair v. United States, 279 U.S. 263, 299 (1929) (reliance on advice of private counsel); Brown v. United States, 256 U.S. 335, 343–344 (1921) (self-defense); Rowe v. United States, 164 U.S. 546, 555–558 (1896) (self-defense); Beard v. United States, 158 U.S. 550, 555–556

(1895) (self-defense); Davis v. United States, 160 U.S. 469, 476–477 (1895) (insanity defense).

75. There is an exception to this, albeit an indirect one. In criminal cases in which the government must prove willfulness, such as criminal tax prosecutions, a defendant can defend himself by claiming that he did not know that his conduct was illegal and requiring the government to prove otherwise. In such cases, however, the defendant is not so much presenting an affirmative mistake of law defense, which might exonerate him even if the government proved its case-in-chief, as he is seeking to demonstrate that the government has not met its burden of proving beyond a reasonable doubt that the defendant acted willfully, an essential element of the crime.

76. See Ronald A. Cass, "Ignorance of the Law: A Maxim Reexamined," *Wm. & Mary L. Rev.* 17 (1976): 671, 685. Although a mistake of law defense traces its roots back to Roman law, Roman law distinguished between "ignorance as a defense to actions under the *jus gentium*, the law derived from the common customs of the Italian tribes and thought to embody the basic rules of conduct any civilized person would deduce from proper reasoning," to which a mistake of law defense could not be raised, and "the more compendious and less common-sense *jus civile*," as to which "women, males less than 25 years old, soldiers, peasants, and persons of small intelligence" could raise a mistake defense if he or she "had not had the opportunity to consult counsel familiar with the laws." Ibid. (footnotes omitted).

CHAPTER 22

1. The views expressed in these remarks are my own and do not necessarily reflect the views of the Federal Trade Commission or any other commissioner.

2. See FTC Staff Report on Television Advertising to Children (Feb. 1978); Notice of Proposed Rulemaking on Children's Advertising, 43 Fed. Reg. 17967 (1978).

3. See, e.g., Editorial, "The FTC as National Nanny," *Wash. Post* (Mar. 1, 1978), A22.

4. See Federal Trade Commission Improvements Act of 1980, Pub. L. No. 96-252, 94 Stat. 374 (1980).

5. See Health Discovery Corporation, No. C-4516 2015 WL 802712 (F.T.C. Feb. 23, 2015) [hereinafter "MelApp Order"]; Stipulated Final Judgment and Order for Permanent Injunction and Other Equitable Relief Against

Defendants Kristi Zuhkle Kimball and New Consumer Solutions LLC [hereinafter "Mole Detective Order"], https://www.ftc.gov/system/files/documents/cases/150223avromorder.pdf.

6. Central Hudson Gas & Electric Corp. v. Public Service Commission of New York, 447 U.S. 557, 566 (1980).

7. See, e.g., Sorrell v. IMS Health, Inc., 131 S. Ct. 2653 (2011); Thompson v. Western States Medical Center, 535 U.S. 357 (2002); United States v. United Foods, 533 U.S. 405 (2001); Lorillard Tobacco Co. v. Reilly, 533 U.S. 525 (2001); Greater New Orleans Broad. Ass'n v. United States, 527 U.S. 173 (1999); R.J. Reynolds Tobacco Co. v. FDA, 696 F.3d 1205 (D.C. Cir. 2012).

8. VA State Bd. of Pharmacy v. VA Citizens Consumer Council, 425 U.S. 748, 763 (1976).

9. Ibid., 764.

10. See, e.g., James C. Cooper, "Price Levels and Dispersion in Online and Offline Markets for Contact Lenses," FTC Bureau of Economics Working Paper No. 283 (2006), http://www.ftc.gov/reports/prices-price-dispersion-online-offline-markets-contact-lenses; Jeffrey R. Brown & Austan Goolsbee, "Does the Internet Make Markets More Competitive? Evidence from the Life Insurance Industry," *J. Pol. Econ.* 110 (2002): 481; Alan T. Sorensen, "Equilibrium Price Dispersion in Retail Markets for Prescription Drugs," *J. Pol. Econ.* 108 (2000): 833; Erik Brynjolfsson & Michael D. Smith, "Frictionless Commerce? A Comparison of Internet and Conventional Retailers," *Mgm't Sci.* 49 (2000): 563.

11. See, e.g., James H. Love & Jack H. Stephen, "Advertising, Price and Quality in Self-regulating Professions: A Survey," *Int'l J. Econ. Bus.* 3 (1996): 227; Frank H. Stephen, "Advertising, Consumer Search Costs, and Prices in a Professional Service Market," *Applied Econ.* 26 (1994): 1177; J. Howard Beales & Timothy J. Muris, *State and Federal Regulation of National Advertising*, ed. Christopher C. DeMuth & Jonathan R. Macey (Washington, D.C.: AEI Press, 1993), 8–9; James H. Love et al., "Spatial Aspects of Competition in the Market for Legal Services," *Regional Stud.* 26 (1992): 137; Deborah Haas-Wilson, "The Effect of Commercial Practice Restrictions: The Case of Optometry," *J.L. & Econ.* 29 (1986): 165; John Kwoka, "Advertising and the Price and Quality of Optometric Services," *Am. Econ. Rev.* 74 (1984): 211; Timothy J. Muris & Fred S. McChesney, "Advertising and the Price and Quality of Legal Services: The Case for Legal Clinics," *Am. B. Found. Res. J.* 1 (1979): 179; Roger Feldman &

James Begun, "The Effects of Advertising: Lessons from Optometry," *J. Hum. Resources* 13 (1978): 247; J.F. Cady, "An Estimate of the Price Effects on Restrictions on Drug Price Advertising," *Econ. Inquiry* 14 (1976): 490; Lee Benham, "The Effect of Advertising on the Price of Eyeglasses," *J.L. & Econ.* 15 (1972): 337.

12. P. Ippolito & A. Mathios, "Health Claims in Advertising and Labeling: A Study of the Cereal Market," FTC Staff Report (1989).

13. FTC Staff Comment Before the Department of Health and Human Services Food and Drug Administration, Docket No. 02N-0209 (Sept. 2002), http://www.ftc.gov/sites/default/files/documents/advocacy_documents/ftc-staff-comment-food-and-drug-administration-concerning-first-amendment-issues/fdatextversion.pdf.

14. FTC Policy Statement Regarding Advertising Substantiation (appended to Thompson Med. Co., Inc., 104 F.T.C. 648, 839 (1984)).

15. In re Thompson Med. Co., 104 F.T.C. 648, 788–789 (1984); In re Telebrands Corp., 140 F.T.C. 278, 290 (2005) (citing Thompson Medical).

16. Thompson Med. Co., 104 F.T.C 789; Telebrands, 140 F.T.C. 291 (citing Thompson Med. Co.)

17. In re Pfizer, Inc., 81 F.T.C. 23 (1972).

18. See also FTC Policy Statement Regarding Advertising Substantiation (appended to Thompson Med. Co., Inc., 104 F.T.C. 648, 839 (1984)).

19. The FDA designates most food ingredients as GRAS (generally recognized as safe). 21 C.F.R. § 170.30 (2015). Vitamins and minerals are treated as foods by the FDA and are also GRAS. See "Guidance for Industry: Frequently Asked Questions about GRAS," FDA (Dec. 2004), http://www.fda.gov/Food/GuidanceRegulation/GuidanceDocumentsRegulatoryInformation/IngredientsAdditivesGRASPackaging/ucm061846.htm#Q1.

20. See, e.g., Dannon Co., Inc., No. C-4313, 151 F.T.C. 62 (Jan. 31, 2011); Nestle Healthcare Nutrition, Inc., No. C-4312, 151 F.T.C. 1 (Jan. 12, 2011).

21. See, e.g., Trisha Greenhalgh, "How to Read a Paper: Getting Your Bearings (Deciding What the Paper Is About)," *British Med. J.* 315 (July 26, 1997): 243 (describing randomized controlled trials, cohort studies, case-control studies, cross sectional surveys, and case reports as examples of scientific evidence in the medical field).

22. See, e.g., FTC v. Colgate-Palmolive, Co., 380 U.S. 374, 391 (1965) ("We think it reasonable for the Commission to frame its order broadly enough to prevent respondents from engaging in similarly illegal practices in future advertisements."); FTC v. Ruberoid Co., 343 U.S. 470, 474–475 (1952) (holding that the commission's order encompassing "wholesalers, retailers, and roofing contractors or applicators" was "reasonably related to the facts," even though only retailers and applicators were affected by Ruberoid's violation); Telebrands Corp., 457 F.3d 354, 357, 362 (4th Cir. 2006) (holding that a reasonable relationship existed between Telebrand's violation involving advertisements for an abdominal belt and the commission's remedy that encompassed future "manufacturing, labeling, advertising, promotion, offering for sale, or distribution of" the actual product as well as that of "any food, drug, dietary supplement, device, or any other product, service or program") (emphasis omitted); Kraft, Inc. v. FTC, 970 F.2d 311, 326 (7th Cir. 1992) ("The FTC has discretion to issue multi-product orders, so-called 'fencing-in' orders, that extend beyond violations of the Act to prevent violators from engaging in similar deceptive practices in the future."); Am. Home Prods. Corp. v. FTC, 695 F.2d 681, 705 (3rd Cir. 1982) ("'Fencing in' often takes the form, as in this case, of a multi-product order.").

23. Telebrands Corp. v. FTC, 457 F.3d 354, 357n5; see also, e.g., Colgate-Palmolive, Co., 380 U.S. 394–395; FTC v. Ruberoid Co., 343 U.S. 473; Kraft, Inc. v. FTC, 970 F.2d 326.

24. Compare, e.g., Wacoal America, Inc., No. C-4496, Decision and Order § I (prohibiting representations that the covered product, caffeine-imbued leggings, cause substantial weight or fat loss or reduce unclad body size) with § II (prohibiting misrepresentations regarding weight-loss effect of the covered product or of any drug or cosmetic).

25. A more specific requirement would not "fence in" proven violators; rather, it would "wall off" truthful claims that would be quite valuable to consumers. See J. Howard Beales III, Timothy J. Muris & Robert Pitofsky, "In Defense of the Pfizer Factors," George Mason University Law & Economics Research Paper Series, No. 12-49 (May 2012), 35, http://www.law.gmu.edu/assets/files/publications/working_papers/1249InDefenseofPfizer.pdf.

26. POM Wonderful, LLC v. FTC, 777 F.3d 478 (D.C. Cir. 2015).

27. Ibid., 499, 503 (2015) (quoting Board of Trustees v. Fox, 492 U.S. 469, 480 (1989)).

28. Ibid., 502.

29. POM Wonderful LLC, No. 9344, 2013 FTC LEXIS 6, Opinion of the Commission, n36 (F.T.C. Jan. 10, 2013).

30. FTC Staff Comment Before the Food and Drug Administration In the Matter of Assessing Consumer Perceptions of Health Claims, Docket No. 2005N-0413 (2006), 5–6, http://www.ftc.gov/be/V060005.pdf.

31. Concurring Statement of Commissioner Maureen K. Ohlhausen, POM Wonderful, Docket No. 9344 (Jan. 10, 2013), 3, https://www.ftc.gov/public-statements/2013/01/concurring-statement-commissioner-maureen-k-ohlhausen-matter-pom-wonderful.

32. MelApp Order; Mole Detective Order.

33. For example, MelApp requires the user to measure the diameter of the lesion, and Mole Detective has the user trace the lesion's border on the photo.

34. The visible risk factors for melanoma are *A*symmetry, uneven *B*order, multiple *C*olors, *D*iameter greater than 6 mm, and *E*volution. Lesions with one or more of these characteristics are more likely to be melanoma. The ABCDE methodology assesses risk; the only way to diagnose a melanoma is through a biopsy. See generally John D. Whited et al., "Does This Patient Have a Mole or a Melanoma?" *JAMA* 279 (Mar. 4, 1998): 696. Dermatologists highly recommend that consumers regularly perform self-examinations using these risk factors to increase their chances of detecting melanoma in the early stages.

35. See Fed. Trade Comm'n, New Consumer Solutions LLC, Mole Detective Complaint, Exhibits A–E at Ex. D, https://www.ftc.gov/system/files/documents/cases/150223avromcmptexha-e.pdf.

36. I agreed with the majority that the companies claimed, without substantiation, that the apps' automated risk assessments were more accurate than a user's unaided self-assessment using the ABCDE factors, and I therefore would have supported complaints narrowly challenging this claim. Further, I would have supported orders prohibiting claims that an app "detects melanoma or risk factors of melanoma, thereby increasing, as compared to unaided self-assessment, users' chances of detecting melanoma in early stages," unless substantiated by competent and reliable scientific evidence. These narrower claim interpretations and corresponding substantiation requirements are more consistent with FTC precedent.

37. Mole Detective Order, 5. The MelApp Order includes a similar prohibition. See MelApp Order, 3.

38. Mole Detective Order, 5; MelApp Order, 3.

39. "Commissioner Ohlhausen . . . believes . . . that it is not reasonable to read the ads as claiming that the automated assessment is as accurate as a dermatologist. We disagree." Statement of Chairwoman Ramirez, Commissioner Brill, and Commissioner McSweeny, Health Discovery Corporation & FTC v. Avrom Boris Lasarow (Feb. 23, 2015), 1, https://www.ftc.gov/system/files /documents/public_statements/626041/150223moledetectiveerjbtmstmt.pdf.

CHAPTER 23

1. The author would be remiss in failing to note that many of the ideas contained in this chapter were formulated together with his friend David B. Rivkin, a staunch defender of the horizontal and vertical separation of powers required by the United States Constitution.

2. U.S. Const. art. II, § 3.

3. The other is Article IV, Section 1, which requires that "Full *Faith* and Credit shall be given in each State to the public Acts, Records, and judicial Proceedings of every other State." U.S. Const. art. IV, § 1 (emphasis added).

4. Saikrishna Prakash, "The Essential Meaning of Executive Power," *U. Ill. L. Rev.* 2003 (2003): 701, 725.

5. Free Enter. Fund v. Pub. Co. Accounting Oversight Bd., 561 U.S. 477, 483 (2010).

6. See Bowsher v. Synar, 478 U.S. 714, 721–722, 730 (1986).

7. U.S. Const. art. I, § 1.

8. Youngstown Sheet & Tube Co. v. Sawyer, 343 U.S. 579, 589 (1952).

9. U.S. Const. art. II, § 3.

10. Or, in the case of the Full Faith and Credit Clause, when one sovereign state is required to recognize the judgments of a sister state. See U.S. Const. art. IV, § 1.

11. See U.S. Const. art. I, § 1.

12. See U.S. Const. art. VI, cl. 2.

13. Bond v. United States, 131 S. Ct. 2355, 2364 (2011).

14. Ibid. (quoting New York v. United States, 505 U.S. 144, 181 (1992)).

15. Ibid. (quoting Alden v. Maine, 527 U.S. 706, 758 (1999)).

16. Senator Barack Obama, Speech Before the National Association of Latino Elected and Appointed Officials (June 28, 2008), http://www.cfr.org /immigration/obamas-speech-naleo-immigration/p16689.

17. See Elisha Barron, "Recent Development, The Development, Relief, and Education for Alien Minors (DREAM) Act," *Harv. J. on Legis.* 48 (2011): 623, 631–634.

18. See DREAM Act of 2011, S. 952, 112th Cong. §§ 3, 5 (2011).

19. Robert J. Delahunty & John C. Yoo, "Dream On: The Obama Administration's Nonenforcement of Immigration Laws," *Tex. L. Rev.* 91 (2013): 781, 789.

20. Ibid.

21. Ibid.

22. Jeffrey S. Passel & Mark H. Lopez, "Up to 1.7 Million Unauthorized Immigrant Youth May Benefit from New Deportation Rules," Pew Hispanic Ctr. (Aug. 14, 2012), 3, http://www.pewhispanic.org/files/2012/12/unauthroized_immigrant_youth_update.pdf.

23. Janet Napolitano, Sec'y, U.S. Dep't of Homeland Sec., "Secretary Napolitano Announces Deferred Action Process for Young People Who are Low Enforcement Priorities," Press Release (June 15, 2012), http://www.dhs.gov/news/2012/06/15/secretary-napolitano-announces-deferred-action-process-young-people-who-are-low.

24. President Barack Obama, Remarks by the President on Immigration (June 15, 2012), http://www.whitehouse.gov/the-press-office/2012/06/15/remarks-president-immigration.

25. Interview by Eddie Sotelo with President Barack Obama in Los Angeles, CA, *LA Times* (Oct. 25, 2010), http://latimesblogs.latimes.com/washington/2010/10/transcript-of-president-barack-obama-with-univision.html.

26. See Delahunty & Yoo, "Dream On," 803–804.

27. See ibid., 805–807.

28. 37 U.S. 524, 612–613 (1838).

29. See, e.g., Glenn Kessler, "Obama's Royal Flip-Flop on Using Executive Action on Illegal Immigration," *Wash. Post* (Nov. 18, 2014), http://www.washingtonpost.com/blogs/fact-checker/wp/2014/11/18/obamas-flip-flop-on-using-executive-action-on-illegal-immigration/.

30. "Univision News Transcript: Interview with President Barack Obama," *Univision* (Mar. 5, 2014) (emphasis added), http://communications-univisionnews.tumblr.com/post/79266471431/univision-news-transcript-interview-with-president.

31. See Memorandum from Jeh Johnson, Sec'y of Homeland Sec., to Thomas S. Winkowski, Acting Dir., U.S. Immigration and Customs Enforcement, et al., "Policies for the Apprehension, Detention and Removal of Undocumented Immigrants" (Nov. 20, 2014), 3–4, http://www.dhs.gov/sites/default/files/publications/14_1120_memo_prosecutorial_discretion.pdf.

32. Memorandum from Jeh Johnson, Sec'y of Homeland Sec., to León Rodriguez, Dir., U.S. Citizenship and Immigration Servs., et al., "Exercising Prosecutorial Discretion with Respect to Individuals Who Came to the United States as Children and with Respect to Certain Individuals Who Are the Parents of U.S. Citizens or Permanent Residents" (Nov. 20, 2014), 4, http://www.dhs.gov/sites/default/files/publications/14_1120_memo_deferred_action.pdf; Amanda Peterson Beadle, "President Obama Announces Immigration Executive Action," Am. Immigration Council (Nov. 20, 2014), http://immigrationimpact.com/2014/11/20/president-obama-announces-immigration-executive-action/.

33. Daniel Halper, "Obama Admits: 'I Just Took an Action to Change the Law,'" *Wkly. Standard* (Nov. 25, 2014, 7:42 pm), http://www.weeklystandard.com/blogs/obama-admits-i-just-took-action-change-law_820167.html.

34. See Heckler v. Chaney, 470 U.S. 821, 832–833 (1985).

35. Cf. Youngstown Sheet & Tube Co. v. Sawyer, 343 U.S. 579, 637 (1952) (Jackson, J., concurring) ("When the President takes measures incompatible with the expressed or implied will of Congress, his power is at its lowest ebb.").

36. 470 U.S. 833n4 (quoting Adams v. Richardson, 480 F.2d 1159, 1162 (D.C. Cir. 1973) (*en banc*)).

37. See, e.g., Kenney v. Glickman, 96 F.3d 1118, 1123 (8th Cir. 1996); Crowley Caribbean Transp., Inc. v. Peña, 37 F.3d 671, 676–677 (D.C. Cir. 1994).

38. The President's lawyers (predictably) argued that the States lacked standing to challenge the executive actions. See Texas v. United States, No. B-14-254, 2015 WL 648579, *9 (S.D. Tex. Feb. 16, 2015).

39. Ibid., *62.

40. Massachusetts v. EPA, 549 U.S. 497, 519 (2007).

41. See U.S. Const. art. VI, cl. 2; Lorillard Tobacco Co. v. Reilly, 533 U.S. 525, 540–541 (2001).

42. Alden v. Maine, 527 U.S. 706, 715 (1999).

43. See Massachusetts, 549 U.S. 518–520 (2007).

44. Arizona v. United States, 132 S. Ct. 2492, 2500 (2012). For example, the executive's dispensing of the INA allows individuals who have committed crimes to remain in the United States when the crimes aren't considered significant enough. See Byron York, "Drunk Drivers, Sex Abusers, Drug and Gun Offenders Not Top Deportation Priorities," *Wash. Exam.* (Nov. 22, 2014, 8:49 am), http://www.washingtonexaminer.com/after-obama-action-dhs-sets-new-immigration-rules-drunk-drivers-sex-abusers-drug-dealers-gun-offenders-not-top-deportation-priorities/article/2556517. State penitentiaries currently house such individuals at significant costs to the states. These individuals would normally be deportable under the INA, but the President's dispensing of the INA allows them to stay in the United States after their release from prison.

45. Nor could the President plausibly argue that he was exercising a power delegated to him by Congress. While executive branch agencies routinely preempt state laws through rulemaking, when they do so, they are exercising legislative power delegated to them by Congress, which they must exercise consistently with statutory directives. In those instances, the Executive Branch has been expressly delegated the power to preempt. Enforcement discretion, on the other hand, is a purely executive power, and one that cannot, consistent with the Constitution, effect preemption of state laws.

CHAPTER 24

1. National Voter Registration Act of 1993, 52 U.S.C. §§ 20501–20511 (2015).

2. Voting Rights Act of 1965, 52 U.S.C. §§ 10301–10702 (2015).

3. U.S. Const., Art. II, § 3.

4. *The President's Constitutional Duty to Faithfully Execute the Laws: Hearing Before the H. Comm. on the Judiciary*, 113th Cong. (2013), 2 (statement of Nicholas Quinn Rosenkranz, Professor, Georgetown University Law Center) (footnote omitted), http://judiciary.house.gov/_cache/files/c2b96776-4a12-4495-b902-899266641e2d/rosenkranz-testimony.pdf.

5. Heckler v. Chaney, 470 U.S. 821, 831 (1985).

6. Andrew C. McCarthy, *Faithless Execution: Building the Political Case for Obama's Impeachment* (Encounter Books, 2014), 79–81 (italics in original).

7. National Voter Registration Act of 1993 § 8, 52 U.S.C. § 20507 (2015).

8. Pew Center on the States, "Inaccurate, Costly, and Inefficient: Evidence that America's Voter Registration System Needs an Upgrade" (2012), 1, http://www.pewtrusts.org/~/media/legacy/uploadedfiles/pcs_assets/2012/PewUpgradingVoterRegistrationpdf.pdf.

9. Ibid., 1, 4.

10. Crawford v. Marion Cty. Election Bd., 553 U.S. 181, 192 (2008) (citation omitted).

11. Ibid. (citations omitted).

12. Ibid., 234 (Souter, J., dissenting).

13. Ibid.

14. United States v. Missouri, No. 05-4391-CV (W.D. Mo.), complaint, 6–7.

15. Ibid., 7.

16. United States v. Missouri, 535 F.3d 844, 850–851 (8th Cir. 2008).

17. Hans von Spakovsky, "Politics? What Politics?" *Nat'l Review* (May 14, 2009, 4:00 am), http://www.nationalreview.com/article/227501/politics-what-politics-hans-von-spakovsky.

18. John Fund & Hans von Spakovsky, *Who's Counting? How Fraudsters and Bureaucrats Put Your Vote at Risk* (Encounter Books, 2012), 146–147.

19. Office of Inspector Gen., U.S. Dep't of Justice, "A Review of the Operations of the Voting Section of the Civil Rights Division" (2013), 100.

20. John Fund & Hans von Spakovsky, *Obama's Enforcer: Eric Holder's Justice Department* (Broadside Books, 2014), 98–99.

21. Christopher Coates, *Prepared Testimony for Hearing Before the U.S. Comm'n on Civil Rights* (Sept. 24, 2010), 15, http://www.usccr.gov/NBPH/TestimonyChristopherCoates_09-24-10.pdf.

22. Ibid.

23. J. Christian Adams, "A Primer on 'Motor Voter': Corrupted Voter Rolls and the Justice Department's Selective Failure to Enforce Federal Mandates," Heritage Foundation, Legal Memorandum No. 139 (Sept. 25, 2014), 10, http://thf_media.s3.amazonaws.com/2014/pdf/LM139.pdf.

24. Coates, *Prepared Testimony*, 16.

25. *The President's Constitutional Duty to Faithfully Execute the Laws: Hearing Before the H. Comm. on the Judiciary*, 113th Cong. (2013) (statement of Jonathan Turley, Professor, George Washington University Law School), http://judiciary

.house.gov/_cache/files/2d1fda91-18a4-467f-818c-62025feaaa6f/120313-turley-testimony.pdf.

26. Ibid.

27. Fund & von Spakovsky, *Who's Counting?*, 146; *Hearing Before the U.S. Comm'n on Civil Rights* (July 6, 2010) (testimony of J. Christian Adams), 58, http://www.usccr.gov/NBPH/07-06-2010_NBPPhearing.pdf.

28. Fund & von Spakovsky, *Who's Counting?*, 146–147.

29. U.S. Comm'n on Civil Rights, "Race Neutral Enforcement of the Law? The U.S. Department of Justice and the New Black Panther Party Litigation" (2010) (statement of Comm'r Todd Gaziano, U.S. Comm'n on Civil Rights), 109, http://www.usccr.gov/NBPH/USCCR_NBPP_report.pdf.

30. See ibid., 109–110.

31. See ibid.

32. Ibid., 110.

33. Ibid., 109.

34. 52 U.S.C. § 10301 (2015).

35. See, e.g., Hans von Spakovsky, "This Is the First Lawsuit Filed Alleging White Voters' Voting Are Being Diluted," *Daily Signal* (Jan. 16, 2015), http://dailysignal.com/2015/01/16/first-lawsuit-filed-alleging-white-voters-voting-rights-diluted/.

36. 494 F. Supp. 2d 440 (S.D. Miss. 2007).

37. Ibid., 449.

38. Ibid.

39. Ibid., 480.

40. Ibid.

41. Ibid., 486.

42. United States v. Brown, 561 F.3d 420, 438 (5th Cir. 2009).

43. Office of Inspector Gen., U.S. Dep't of Justice, "A Review of the Operations," 160–161.

44. Ibid., 160.

45. Fund & von Spakovsky, *Obama's Enforcer*, 99.

46. Fund & von Spakovsky, *Who's Counting?*, 139–141.

47. Ibid., 142–143; see also Voting Rights Act of 1965 § 11(b), 52 U.S.C. § 10307(b) (2015).

48. Fund & von Spakovsky, *Who's Counting?*, 142.

49. Ibid., 143.

50. Ibid.

51. Ibid.

52. Ibid.

53. See J. Christian Adams, *Injustice: Exposing the Racial Agenda of the Obama Justice Department* (Regnery, 2011), 130–131; Fund & von Spakovsky, *Who's Counting?*, 146.

54. See, e.g., U.S. Comm'n on Civil Rights, "Race Neutral Enforcement of the Law?," 92n303.

55. See, e.g., ibid., ii.

56. Judicial Watch, Inc. v. United States Dep't of Justice, 878 F. Supp. 2d 225, 235–236 (D.D.C. 2012) (italics in original).

57. Office of Inspector Gen., U.S. Dep't of Justice, "A Review of the Operations," 71.

58. Coates, *Prepared Testimony*, 19.

59. Hans von Spakovsky, "DOJ Ignores Guam Voting Discrimination," *Nat'l Review* (Nov. 22, 2011, 4:00 am), http://www.nationalreview.com/article/283749/doj-ignores-guam-voting-discrimination-hans-von-spakovsky.

60. Davis v. Guam, 785 F.3d 1311, 1313–1314 (9th Cir. 2015).

61. See John Fund, "New Jim Crow in Guam: Where's Holder?" *Nat'l Review* (July 16, 2012, 4:00 am), http://www.nationalreview.com/article/309449/new-jim-crow-guam-wheres-holder-john-fund.

62. von Spakovsky, "DOJ Ignores Guam Voting Discrimination."

63. Rice v. Cayetano, 528 U.S. 495, 498–499 (2000).

64. See 3 Guam Code Ann. § 21009 (2014).

65. See "U.S. Attorney General Eric Holder Visits Guam," U.S. Dep't of Interior (July 16, 2012), http://www.doi.gov/oia/press/2012/07162012b.cfm.

66. 133 S. Ct. 2612, 2631 (2013).

67. For a list of the states formerly covered by Section 5, see "Section 5 Covered Jurisdictions," U.S. Dep't of Justice, http://www.justice.gov/crt/about/vot/sec_5/covered.php (last visited June 24, 2015).

68. See Voting Rights Act of 1965 § 5, 52 U.S.C. § 10304 (2015).

69. Ibid.

70. Voting Rights Act of 1965 § 4(b), 52 U.S.C. § 10303(b) (2015), invalidated by Shelby Cty., 133 S. Ct. 2631. Under Section 4, a jurisdiction was covered if it had a test or device that denied or abridged the right to vote on account of race or color and had registration or turnout below 50 percent in the 1964, 1968, or 1972 presidential elections. Ibid.

71. Office of Inspector Gen., U.S. Dep't of Justice, "A Review of the Operations," 89.

72. Ibid., 91n76.

73. Ibid.

74. Fund & von Spakovsky, *Who's Counting?*, 147–148.

75. Ibid., 148.

76. Letter from Loretta King, Acting Assistant Att'y Gen., U.S. Dep't of Justice, to James P. Cauley III (Aug. 17, 2009), http://www.justice.gov/crt/records/vot/obj_letters/letters/NC/l_0perez90817.php.

77. Letter from Thomas E. Perez, Assistant Att'y Gen., U.S. Dep't of Justice, to James P. Cauley III (Jan. 30, 2012), http://www.bjmurphy.org/wp-content/uploads/2012/02/USDOJ-Letter-Pre-Cleared-2012-02-10.pdf.

78. Letter from Thomas E. Perez, Assistant Att'y Gen., U.S. Dep't of Justice, to James P. Cauley III (Feb. 10, 2012), http://www.bjmurphy.org/wp-content/uploads/2012/02/USDOJ-Letter-Pre-Cleared-2012-02-10.pdf.

79. E.g., Hans von Spakovsky, "Lessons from the Voter ID Experience in Georgia," Heritage Foundation, Issue Brief No. 3541 (Mar. 19, 2012), 1, http://thf_media.s3.amazonaws.com/2012/pdf/ib3541.pdf; Hans von Spakovsky, "No, *New York Times*, Requiring Proof of Citizenship to Vote Isn't 'Voter Suppression,'" *Nat'l Review* (Mar. 24, 2014, 6:32 pm), http://www.nationalreview.com/corner/374100/no-new-york-times-requiring-proof-citizenship-vote-isnt-voter-suppression-hans-von.

80. See Gonzalez v. Arizona, 677 F.3d 383, 407, 408 (9th Cir. 2012) (*en banc*) (upholding Arizona law against challenges under Section 2 of the VRA and the Fourteenth Amendment's Equal Protection Clause), aff'd on other grounds, Arizona v. Inter Tribal Council of Arizona, Inc., 133 S. Ct. 2247 (2013); Common Cause/Georgia v. Billups, 554 F.3d 1340, 1346 (11th Cir. 2009) (upholding Georgia law against challenge under the Fourteenth Amendment's Equal Protection Clause).

81. 553 U.S. 181, 185–189 (2008).

82. See von Spakovsky, "Voter ID Experience in Georgia," 3; Hans von Spakovsky, "Voter Photo Identification: Protecting the Security of Elections," Heritage Foundation, Legal Memorandum No. 70 (July 13, 2011), 1, http://thf_media.s3.amazonaws.com/2011/pdf/lm0070.pdf; see also Hans von Spakovsky, "Revisiting the Lessons from the Voter ID Experience in Kansas: 2014," Heritage Foundation, Issue Brief No. 4380 (Apr. 10, 2015), 3, http://thf_media

.s3.amazonaws.com/2015/pdf/IB4380.pdf; Hans von Spakovsky, "Lessons from the Voter ID Experience in Tennessee," Heritage Foundation, Issue Brief No. 4180 (Mar. 25, 2014), 3, http://thf_media.s3.amazonaws.com/2014/pdf/IB4180.pdf.

83. See, e.g., U.S. Dep't of Justice, "Justice Department to File New Lawsuit Against State of Texas Over Voter I.D. Law," Press Release (Aug. 22, 2013), http://www.justice.gov/opa/pr/justice-department-file-new-lawsuit-against-state-texas-over-voter-id-law.

84. Noah Rothman, "Eric Holder: Voter ID Used to 'Depress the Vote' of People Who Don't Support GOP," *Mediaite* (Jan. 24, 2014, 3:40 pm), http://www.mediaite.com/tv/eric-holder-voter-id-used-to-depress-the-vote-of-people-who-dont-support-gop/.

85. Hans von Spakovsky, "The Justice Department's War on Texas' Voter ID Law," *Daily Signal* (Apr. 27, 2015), http://dailysignal.com/2015/04/27/the-justice-departments-war-on-texas-voter-id-law/.

86. "About Us," Catalist, http://catalist.us (last accessed June 25, 2015).

87. "Careers," Catalist, http://www.catalist.us/careers/careers.html (last accessed June 25, 2015).

88. "Clients," Catalist, http://catalist.us/clients/clients.html (last accessed June 25, 2015).

89. Mark Tapscott, "Watchdog Calls for Federal Probe of Powerful Democratic Campaign Data Firm," *Wash. Exam.* (Feb. 21, 2015, 12:20 pm), http://www.washingtonexaminer.com/watchdog-calls-for-federal-probe-of-powerful-democratic-campaign-data-firm/article/2560530.

CHAPTER 25

1. See, e.g., this GAO report recommending greater transparency for FSOC's designation process: http://www.gao.gov/assets/670/667096.pdf.

2. See, e.g., this Norton Rose Fulbright blog post, noting how FSOC designations of systemically important financial institutions (SIFIs) are usually unanimous: http://www.regulationtomorrow.com/us/not-surprisingly-yet-not-unanimously-fsoc-designates-metlife-as-a-sifi/.

3. See Stijn Claessens & Laura Kodres, "The Regulatory Responses to the Global Financial Crisis: Some Uncomfortable Questions," http://www.imf.org/external/pubs/ft/wp/2014/wp1446.pdf ("After crises, however, reforms remain often incomplete. One of the difficulties in making overall progress is that crises

tend to instill forward momentum on obvious failings, but often ignore the underlying, deeper causes.")

4. See the first substantive slide of this Treasury presentation for a comparison of the 2007–2009 recession to other recessions since 1974: http://www.treasury.gov/resource-center/data-chart-center/Documents/20120413_FinancialCrisisResponse.pdf.

5. See, e.g., the majority Report of the Financial Crisis Inquiry Commission, from which I dissented: http://www.aei.org/files/2011/01/26/Wallisondissent.pdf.

6. Peter J. Wallison, *Hidden In Plain Sight: What Really Caused the World's Worst Financial Crisis and Why It Could Happen Again* (Encounter Books, 2015).

7. Financial Stability Oversight Council, Basis for the Financial Stability Oversight Council's Final Determination Regarding Prudential Financial, Inc. (Sept. 19, 2013), p. 2 [emphasis added].

8. See, e.g., "Primer: FSOC's SIFI Designation Process for Nonbank Financial Companies," a blog post by American Action Forum ("While many determining factors are mentioned as being part of the evaluation process, no determinant is weighted as more heavily signaling of requiring designation, making the process appear highly subjective."), http://americanactionforum.org/research/primer-fsocs-sifi-designation-process-for-nonbank-financial-companies.

9. http://www.bloomberg.com/news/articles/2015-01-13/metlife-sues-over-too-big-to-fail-designation-by-u-s-regulators.

10. http://blogs.wsj.com/moneybeat/2015/04/10/ge-looks-to-check-out-of-hotel-california-of-added-federal-oversight/.

11. See, e.g., Jeffrey Friedman, "A Perfect Storm of Ignorance," http://www.cato.org/policy-report/januaryfebruary-2010/perfect-storm-ignorance.

12. Financial Stability Board, "Overview of Progress in Implementation of the G20 Recommendations for Strengthening Financial Stability," Report of the Financial Stability Board to G20 Leaders (Sept. 5, 2013), p. 3.

13. Ibid., p. 24.

14. Financial Stability Board, "Assessment Methodologies for Identifying Non-Bank Non-Insurer Global Systemically Important Financial Institutions: Proposed High-Level Framework and Specific Methodologies," consultative document (Jan. 8, 2014), www.financialstabilityboard.org/publications/r_140108.pdf.

15. See, e.g., http://financialresearch.gov/reports/files/ofr_asset_management_and_financial_stability.pdf.

16. Roy Woodall, Views of the Council's Independent Member having Insurance Expertise, p. 1, http://www.treasury.gov/initiatives/fsoc/council-meetings/Documents/September%2019%202013%20Notational%20Vote.pdf.

17. http://www.banking.senate.gov/public/index.cfm?FuseAction=Files.View&FileStore_id=9c4cb361-2d62-4d3c-9597-a1643068cfb8.

18. See, e.g., http://www.federalreserve.gov/newsevents/speech/bernanke20120409a.htm; http://www.federalreserve.gov/newsevents/speech/bernanke20130510a.htm.

19. https://g20.org/wp-content/uploads/2014/12/Declaration_eng_Cannes.pdf; http://www.financialstabilityboard.org/2012/11/r_121118/.

20. FSB, "Strengthening Oversight and Regulation of Shadow Banking," consultative document (Nov. 18, 2012), p. 1.

21. See, e.g., Understanding Repurchase Agreements, p. 6, https://www.blackrock.com/cash/literature/whitepaper/understanding-repurchase-agreements.pdf.

22. FSB, "Strengthening Oversight and Regulation of Shadow Banking," p. 1 [emphasis added].

23. Ben Bernanke, "Fostering Financial Stability," Speech at 2012 Federal Bank of Atlanta Financial Markets Conference, p. 2.

24. Ibid.

25. FSB, "Progress and Next Steps Towards Ending 'Too-Big-to-Fail,'" Report of the Financial Stability Board to the G-20 (Sept. 2, 2013), p. 17.

26. Ibid.

27. Assessment Methodologies for Identifying Non-Bank Non-Insurance Global Systemically Important Financial Institutions, https://www.iosco.org/library/pubdocs/pdf/IOSCOPD435.pdf.

28. FSB, Strengthening Oversight and Regulation of Shadow Banking, Consultative Document, November 18, 2012, p. 1.

29. See Peter J. Wallison, "Unrisky Business: Asset Management Cannot Create Systemic Risk," *Financial Services Outlook* (Jan. 2014).

30. http://www.c-span.org/video/?c4531621/hensarling-lew.

31. Dan Fitzpatrick, "J.P. Morgan Dims Its Light on 2014," *Wall St. J.* (Feb. 26, 2014).

32. Ibid.

33. Ryan Tracy, "A Local Bank in Amish Country Flourishes Amid Dearth of Small Lenders," *Wall St. J.* (Mar. 29, 2015), http://www.wsj.com/articles/a-local-bank-in-amish-country-flourishes-amid-dearth-of-small-lenders-1427677879.

CHAPTER 26

1. This article is based upon various speeches I have made and articles I have written regarding the Federal Trade Commission's use of its Section 5 "unfair methods of competition" authority. Joshua D. Wright, "Revisiting Antitrust Institutions: The Case for Guidelines to Recalibrate the FTC's Section 5 Unfair Methods of Competition Authority," No. 4-2013 Concurrences Review No. 58727 (2013); Joshua D. Wright, Comm'r, Fed. Trade Comm'n, "Judging Antitrust: Remarks at the Global Antitrust Institute Invitational Moot Court Competition" (Feb. 21, 2015); Joshua D. Wright, Comm'r, Fed. Trade Comm'n, "Section 5 Recast: Defining the Federal Trade Commission's Unfair Methods of Competition Authority" (June 19, 2013); Joshua D. Wright, Comm'r, Fed. Trade Comm'n, "Section 5 Revisited: Time for the FTC to Define the Scope of Its Unfair Methods of Competition Authority" (Feb. 26, 2015); Joshua D. Wright, Comm'r, Fed. Trade Comm'n, "What's Your Agenda?" (Apr. 11, 2013). The views expressed herein are my own and do not reflect those of the commission or any of its commissioners. I thank my advisor, Angela Diveley, for many discussions on this topic and her assistance in preparing this article.

2. 15 U.S.C. § 45(a) (2012).

3. 15 U.S.C. §§ 1–7 (Sherman Antitrust Act); 15 U.S.C. §§ 12–27 (Clayton Act).

4. See Edward F. Cox et al., *The Nader Report on the Federal Trade Commission* (New York: Baron, 1969); ABA Comm'n, Report of the ABA Commission to Study the Federal Trade Commission 92-118 (1969) (separate statement of Richard A. Posner).

5. "The Post's Sweet Talk, Circa 1978," *Wash. Post* (May 19, 2008), http://www.washingtonpost.com/wp-dyn/content/article/2008/05/18/AR2008051802379.html (providing a "lightly edited version" of the original Mar. 1, 1978, editorial).

6. See Public Statement, J. Howard Beales, "Advertising to Kids and the FTC: A Regulatory Retrospective That Advises the Present," 7–8, https://www.ftc.gov/sites/default/files/documents/public_statements/advertising-kids-and

-ftc-regulatory-retrospective-advises-present/040802adstokids.pdf (revised version of remarks before the George Mason Law Review 2004 Symposium on Antitrust and Consumer Protection Competition, Advertising, and Heath Claims: Legal and Practical Limits on Advertising Regulation).

7. Deception Policy Statement, appended to Cliffdale Associates, Inc., 103 F.T.C. 110, 174 (1984), cited with approval in Kraft, Inc. v. FTC, 970 F.2d 314 (7th Cir. 1992), *cert. denied*, 507 U.S. 909 (1993); Unfairness Policy Statement, appended to International Harvester Co., 104 F.T.C. 949, 1070 (1984).

8. See 15 U.S.C. § 45(n) (2012).

9. For ease of reference, the remainder of this chapter will refer to the FTC's standalone UMC authority simply as its Section 5 or UMC authority.

10. William E. Kovacic & Marc Winerman, "Competition Policy and the Application of Section 5 of the Federal Trade Commission Act," *Antitrust L.J.* 76 (2010) 929, 932.

11. Ibid.

12. Ibid., 932.

13. See ibid., 941 (citing FTC v. Texaco, Inc., 393 U.S. 223 (1968)).

14. Ibid., 933–934.

15. E.g., Rambus, Inc., 2006 WL 2330118, *9 (Leibowitz, Comm'r, concurring) (Section 5 prohibits conduct that is "collusive, coercive, predatory, restrictive, or deceitful, or otherwise oppressive" (internal quotation marks omitted); Neil W. Averitt, "The Meaning of 'Unfair Methods of Competition in Section 5 of the Federal Trade Commission Act,'" *B.C. L. Rev.* 21 (1980): 227, 299 ("In exercising these broad powers the Commission can act to prevent several different types of unfairness: violations of the letter of one of the other antitrust statutes; incipient violations; violations of their underlying spirit; violations of settled business norms; violations of competition policy as declared by the agency; and, on occasion, violations that could be characterized as unfair acts or practices."); Amanda Reeves & Maurice Stucke, "Behavioral Antitrust," *Indiana L.J.* 86 (2011): 1527, 1583–1585; Wright, "Section 5 Revisited" (providing three potential interpretations, all requiring competitive harm and prohibiting the use of Section 5 as a method of circumventing well-established judicial interpretations of the traditional antitrust laws, but each permitting a different application of the efficiencies defense); Michael Pertschuk, "Remarks Before the Annual Meeting of the Section on Antitrust and Economic Regula-

tion," Association of American Law Schools, Atlanta, GA (Dec. 27, 1977); Edith Ramirez, Chairwoman, Fed. Trade Comm'n, "Unfair Methods and the Competitive Process: Enforcement Principles for the Federal Trade Commission's Next Century" (Feb. 13, 2014) ("[T]he Commission will condemn [as a Section 5 violation] conduct only where . . . the likely competitive harm outweighs the cognizable efficiencies."); Maureen K. Ohlhausen, Comm'r, Fed. Trade Comm'n, "Section 5: Principles of Navigation: Remarks at the U.S. Chamber of Commerce" (July 25, 2013) (favoring a Section 5 standard in which the likely harm disproportionately outweighs the cognizable efficiencies); Joe Sims, "A Report on Section 5, Global Competition Policy" (Nov. 2008), http://www.jonesday.com/files/Publication/c597157d-198a-48b9-a842-af0f2ad22bdd/Presentation/PublicationAttachment/f9f6a38c-b154-4bbb-9378-b848acef7437/Sims-Nov08%20(1).pdf (cautioning against "reinvigoration" of Section 5 and broad application beyond the traditional antitrust laws).

16. Rambus, Inc., 2006 WL 2330118, *9 (internal quotation marks omitted); Ramirez, "Unfair Methods"; *Hearing: Oversight of the Antitrust Enforcement Agencies*, 114th Cong. (2015).

17. Pertschuk, "Remarks Before the Annual Meeting."

18. FTC v. Abbott Labs, 853 F. Supp. 526 (D.D.C. 1992); see James Campbell Cooper, "The Perils of Excessive Discretion: The Elusive Meaning of Unfairness in Section 5 of the FTC Act," *J. Antitrust Enforcement* 3 (2015): 87, 88n8; FTC v. Sperry & Hutchinson Co., 405 U.S. 233 (1972).

19. E.g., Sharis Pozen & Anne Six, "Section 5 Guidelines: Fixing a Problem that Doesn't Exist?" *Competition Pol'y Int'l* (Sept. 16, 2013); Ramirez, "Unfair Methods."

20. Jan M. Rybnicek & Joshua D. Wright, "Defining Section 5 of the FTC Act: The Failure of the Common Law Method and the Case for Formal Agency Guidelines," *Geo. Mason L. Rev.* 21 (2014): 1287.

21. See generally Douglas H. Ginsburg & Joshua D. Wright, "Antitrust Settlements: The Culture of Consent," in *William E. Kovacic: An Antitrust Tribute Liber Amicorum*, ed. N. Charbit, E. Ramundo, A. Chehtova & A. Slater (Institute of Competition Law, 2012), 177 (discussing the rise, and competitive implications, of consent decrees as a method of terminating antitrust enforcement actions).

22. Negotiated Data Solutions, LLC, File No. 051-0094 (Jan. 23, 2008); Motorola Mobility LLC, File No. 121-0120 (Jan. 3, 2013); Robert Bosch

GmbH, File No. 101-0081 (Apr. 24, 2013); Intel Corp., Docket No. 9341 (Aug. 4, 2010).

23. Negotiated Data Solutions, LLC, File No. 051-0094 (Jan. 23, 2008), Analysis of Proposed Consent Order to Aid Public Comment.

24. Ibid., Complaint ¶¶38–39.

25. Ibid., Dissenting Statement of Commissioner William E. Kovacic, 2.

26. Ibid., 3.

27. Robert Bosch GmbH, File No. 101-0081 (Apr. 24, 2013).

28. Motorola Mobility LLC, File No. 121-0120 (Jan. 3, 2013).

29. Statement of the Federal Trade Commission, Robert Bosch GmbH, File No. 101-0081 (Apr. 24, 2013); Statement of the Federal Trade Commission, Motorola Mobility LLC, File No. 121-0120 (Jan. 3, 2013).

30. See Joshua D. Wright, "An Antitrust Analysis of the Federal Trade Commission's Complaint Against Intel," George Mason University Law and Economics Research Paper Series 10-27, International Center for Law and Economics Antitrust and Competition Policy White Paper Series (June 8, 2010), 15, http://www.law.gmu.edu/assets/files/publications/working_papers/1027AntitrustAnalysisofFTCsComplaint.pdf.

31. See, e.g., Boise Cascade Corp. v. FTC, 637 F.2d 573, 582 (9th Cir. 1980) (rejecting a UMC claim where well-forged case law under the traditional antitrust laws was adequate to reach the conduct at issue).

32. William E. Kovacic, "Rating the Competition Agencies: What Constitutes Good Performance?" *Geo. Mason L. Rev.* 16 (2009): 903, 908 (citing a campaign speech by then Senator Barack Obama, implying that the number of cases filed is indicative of the U.S. antitrust agencies' performance); see also Eric Holder, Att'y Gen., Dep't of Justice, Remarks at 63rd Spring Meeting of the American Bar Association Section of Antitrust Law (Apr. 17, 2015) ("[T]hen-Senator Barack Obama vowed that, if he were elected President, he would step up enforcement activity in a comprehensive way. . . . That's exactly what we've done. . . . [T]he Antitrust Division's criminal program has prosecuted 385 individuals and 129 corporations over the course of the Obama Administration. We have obtained more than $5 billion in fines and penalties. . . . We have challenged numerous mergers. . . . Two mergers foundered at trial, while many others were abandoned or entirely restructured as a result of our enforcement measures.").

33. Joshua D. Wright & Angela M. Diveley, "Do Expert Agencies Outperform Generalist Judges? Some Preliminary Evidence from the Federal Trade

Commission," *J. Antitrust Enforcement* 1 (2012): 82, 96. Appeals are useful for evaluating the commission's performance in that they provide a "signal generated by actual costs incurred by the parties who, informed by their own economic experts, have determined the initial court committed a reversible error." Reversals signal that this was indeed the case.

34. Ibid., 97.

35. See Richard Posner, "The Federal Trade Commission," *U. Chi. L. Rev.* 37 (1969): 47; Malcolm B. Coate & Andrew N. Kleit, "*Does It Matter that the Prosecutor Is Also the Judge? The Administrative Complaint Process at the Federal Trade Commission*," *Managerial & Decision Econ.* 19 (1998): 1; Terry Calvani, "The Federal Trade Commission: *A* Proposal *for Radical* Change," *Antitrust L. Bull.* 34 (1989): 185; Terry Calvani & Angela M. Diveley, "The FTC at 100: A Modest Proposal for Change," *Geo. Mason L. Rev.* 21 (2014): 1169; Philip Elman, "*A* Modest Proposal *for Radical Reform*," *ABA J.* 56 (1970): 1045; A. Douglas Melamed, Comments to the Federal Trade Commission, Workshop Concerning Section 5 of the FTC Act 10 (Oct. 14, 2008), http://www.ftc.gov/sites/default/files/documents/public_comments/section-5-workshop-537633-00004/537633-00004.pdf.

36. Posner, "The Federal Trade Commission," 53–54.

37. Ibid., 54–60. Posner's findings focused largely upon documenting abuse of the administrative process. The vast majority of enforcement actions pursued in administrative adjudication involved conduct that was "overwhelmingly likely" to be efficient, and only a handful of the over 250 cases he reviewed were economically justified.

38. Melamed, Comments to the Federal Trade Commission, 10.

39. *Hearing: Oversight of the Antitrust Enforcement Agencies*, 114th Cong. (2015) (opening remarks of Rep. Bob Goodlatte, Chairman, H. Comm. on the Judiciary).

40. BakerHostetler, "The Past, Present, and Future of Section 5 of the FTC Act: Perspectives from the Commission, the Judiciary, and Congress" (Feb. 2015), 7.

41. Wright, "Section 5 Revisited" (The proposed definitions also prohibit the use of Section 5 to circumvent unfavorable case law under the traditional antitrust laws); ibid., 21.

CONCLUSION

1. S. Rep. No. 113-134, Review of the Terrorist Attacks on U.S. Facilities in Benghazi, Libya, Sept. 11–12, 2012, together with Additional Views, at 9-27 (2014), http://www.intelligence.senate.gov/sites/default/files/publications/113134.pdf (last accessed Aug. 14, 2015).

2. See ibid. Mark Mazzetti, Eric Schmitt & David D. Kirkpatrick, "Benghazi Attack Called Avoidable in Senate Report," *N.Y. Times* (Jan. 15, 2014), http://www.nytimes.com/2014/01/16/world/middleeast/senate-report-finds-benghazi-attack-was-preventable.html.

3. See S. Rep. No. 113-34, at 32–37.

4. Gregory Corte, "Planted Question Gambit Backfires on IRS officials," *USA Today* (May 18, 2013), http://www.usatoday.com/story/news/politics/2013/05/18/irs-scandal-planted-question/2216747/.

5. Abby D. Phillip, "IRS Planted Question about Tax Exempt Groups," *ABC News* (May 17, 2013), http://abcnews.go.com/blogs/politics/2013/05/irs-planted-question-about-tax-exempt-groups/.

6. Rebecca Kaplan, "Lois Lerner Pleads the Fifth Again, Doesn't Testify on IRS Targeting," *CBS News* (Mar. 5, 2014), http://www.cbsnews.com/news/lois-lerner-pleads-the-fifth-again-doesnt-testify-on-irs-targeting/.

7. David Nather and Susan Levine, "A Brief History of Obamacare Delays," *Politico* (Mar. 25, 2014), http://www.politico.com/story/2014/03/obamacare-affordable-care-act-105036.html.

8. See ibid.

9. King v. Burwell, 135 S. Ct. 2480, 2487 (2015).

10. Ibid., 2490 (arguing against construing "established by the State" in its "most natural sense").

11. U.S. Citizenship and Immigration Services, Consideration of Deferred Action for Childhood Arrivals (DACA) (Aug. 3, 2015), available at http://www.uscis.gov/humanitarian/consideration-deferred-action-childhood-arrivals-daca (last accessed Aug. 14, 2015); see Julia Preston & John H. Cushman, Jr., "Obama to Permit Young Migrants to Remain in U.S.," *N.Y. Times* (June 15, 2012), http://www.nytimes.com/2012/06/16/us/us-to-stop-deporting-some-illegal-immigrants.html.

12. U.S. Citizenship and Immigration Services, Executive Actions on Immigration (Apr. 15, 2015), available at http://www.uscis.gov/immigrationaction (last accessed Aug. 14, 2015).

13. David Stout and Solomon Moore, "U.S. Won't Prosecute in States That Allow Medical Marijuana," *N.Y. Times* (Oct. 19, 2009), http://www.nytimes.com/2009/10/20/us/20cannabis.html.

14. See Eric Holder, Letter from the Attorney General to Congress on Litigation Involving the Defense of Marriage Act, the United States Department of Justice (Feb. 23, 2011), http://www.justice.gov/opa/pr/letter-attorney-general-congress-litigation-involving-defense-marriage-act (last accessed Aug. 14, 2014).

15. Eleni Himaras, Yuliya Fedorinova & Ekaterina Shatalova, "Snowden Lands in Moscow as Hong Kong Rejects U.S. Warrant," *Bloomberg News* (June 23, 2013), http://www.bloomberg.com/news/articles/2013-06-23/snowden-leaves-hong-kong-as-u-s-seeks-his-extradition; Steven Lee Myers & Andrew E. Krameraug, "Defiant Russia Grants Snowden Year's Asylum," *N.Y. Times* (Aug. 1, 2013), http://www.nytimes.com/2013/08/02/world/europe/edward-snowden-russia.html.

16. President Barack Obama, "Fact Sheet: The Administration's Proposal for Ending the Section 215 Bulk Telephony Metadata Program," The White House (Mar. 27, 2014), https://www.whitehouse.gov/the-press-office/2014/03/27/fact-sheet-administration-s-proposal-ending-section-215-bulk-telephony-m (last accessed Aug. 14, 2015).

17. 132 S. Ct. 2566 (2012).

18. Woodrow Wilson, "The Study of Administration," *PSQ* 2 (1887): 197.

19. *The Federalist* No. 70 (Hamilton).

20. Ibid.

21. Ibid.

22. Ibid.

23. Ibid.

24. Ibid.

25. *The Federalist* No. 71 (Hamilton).

26. *The Federalist* No. 72 (Hamilton).

27. Ibid.

28. Ibid.

29. 487 U.S. 654 (1988).

30. 467 U.S. 837 (1984).

31. Motor Vehicle Mfrs. Ass'n of U.S., Inc. v. State Farm Mut. Auto. Ins. Co., 463 U.S. 29 (1983).

32. Michigan v. E.P.A., 135 S. Ct. 2699, 2712 (2015) (Thomas, J., concurring).

33. 462 U.S. 919 (1983).

34. 478 U.S. 714 (1986).

35. 198 U.S. 45 (1905).

36. For example, Robert Bork labeled Lochner "the symbol, indeed the quintessence, of judicial usurpation of power." Robert H. Bork, *The Tempting of America: The Political Seduction of the Law* (New York: Free Press, 1990), 44.

37. Lochner, 198 U.S. 64–65; West Coast Hotel Co. v. Parrish, 300 U.S. 379 (1937) (ending the Lochner era).

INDEX

Abbott, Greg, 76
abortion, 45
Adams, J. Christian, 322, 325
Administrative Procedure Act (APA)
  agency non-compliance, 246
  banking industry non-compliance, 87
  CFPB, requirements for, 157
  CFPB non-compliance, 158
  DOE non-compliance, 177
  federal regulators violation of, 87
  immigration policies violating, 76–77
  non-compliance, results of, 9, 188
  OCR non-compliance, 170–171, 174, 177
  public notice and comment requirement, 11, 87, 177
  reforms required, 188
  requirement of courts to engage in statutory interpretation, 250
  requirements of, 9
  SEC overreach and, 145
  Section 706 and *Chevron* doctrine, 58, 69, 250
  statutory rulemaking requirements, 158
administrative state, 240–248, 366, 368–370. *See also* agencies
advertising, FTC overreach on regulating, 299–309
Advice and Consent Clause, 210
Affirmatively Furthering Fair Housing (AFFH), 223–225
Affordable Care Act (ACA)
  health exchanges, 21–24, 61–62, 364
  health insurance plans, private/preexisting, 18–20
  preventive care and screenings for women requirement, 43
  Supreme Court ruling, 365
  Tea Party movement against, 257
Affordable Care Act (ACA), Obama's abuses of executive power
  ad hoc implementation and enforcement of, 13–25
  laws, defying and rewriting of existing, 182–184
  misuse of taxpayer funds (subsidies), 21–24, 182–183, 364, 365
  preexisting health insurance plan fix announced, 18–19
  statutory mandates, waiving or delaying, 14–17, 182–184
  tax credit regulation, 22–24

agencies
binding agreements, 245
function of, 243
funding, control over, 9
independent, 118–119, 135, 193
New Deal expansion of, 153, 241
off-roading, 88–89
regulations, eradicating outdated, 9–10
separation of powers and, 118, 239–240, 248, 249–253
use of consent decrees, 249
agency accountability
APA non-compliance, 246
to the branches, 248–249
circumventing, incentives for, 248, 250
Congressional oversight, 8–10
judical, 189
judicial review, 57–69, 246–248, 252
lack of, 11
Scalia's *Morrison* dissent on, 240
agency overreach. *See also* Consumer Financial Protection Bureau (CFPB)
Congressional solutions to, 165–167
lawmaking authority, 189
laws, interpretation of, 10, 58, 189
agency power/authority
accumulation of, 7
agency rules, interpreting, 246–248, 250
concentration of, 4–5, 244–248
Congressional delegation of legislative power to, 7–8, 10–11, 68–69, 189, 241–243, 247, 249, 286–287, 297–298
criminal regulation, 286–293
enforcement actions, adjudicating, 10, 245–246
executive power, expanding, 246
judicial deference to, 10–11, 58, 65–66, 189, 241, 246–248, 368–369
law, administrative discretion of application of the, 59–63
lawsuit settlements to enlarge, 246
limiting, 9, 240, 370
nondelegation doctrine impact on, 243
reforming, 9–10, 249–253
statutory limits on, 67–68
Wilson's vision of, 241
AIG, 110–111, 339, 341
air pollution regulation, 59–60
Alappat decision, 200
Alexander v. Yale, 171
Ali, Russlynn, 173
Alito, Samuel, 249
al Qaeda attack on U.S. consulate, 363, 367
America Coming Together, 257–258
America Invents Act, 202
American Electric Power, 271
American International Group, 107
American Trucking Associations Inc., Whitman.v., 63, 64
ammunition, controls on, 37, 38. *See also* gun control
Antitrust Division (DOJ), 192, 358
antitrust issues, 194, 202
antitrust law, 351–360
Apple, 204

apps, FTC overreach in regulating, 307–308
Arms Trade Treaty (ATT) (UN), 29, 30–31, 39
Articles of Confederation, 6, 117
Ashcroft, Gregory v., 128, 130
Association of American Railroads, Department of Transportation v., 242, 243, 250
ATF (Bureau of Alcohol, Tobacco, Firearms, and Explosives), 29, 33–34, 36–38
at-will employment policies, 218
Auer deference, 10, 247–248, 249–250
auto lenders, 158–162, 167

Babbit v. Sweet Home Chapters of Communities for a Great Oregon, 58–63
Bagley, Nicholas, 16–17, 20
bailouts (2008), 107–114
banking industry
  capital regulation, 331–332
  disparate impact accusations, 226–228
  home loans, 105–115, 162, 226–228, 335, 338, 344
  maturity transformation, 343–344
  Operation Choke Point, 29, 31–33, 81–90
  reputation risk standard applied to, 83–85, 87–89
banking industry regulation
  APA non-compliance, 87
  arbitrary and abusive agency action, 87
  Constitutional violations, 87
  depriving citizens of due process of law, 31–33, 81–90
  financial crises and, 334
  power assumed by, 87
  prudential, 334–335, 342, 345
  shadow banking, 343–347
  statutory authority exceeded, 87
Bank of America, 228
Basel Committee on Bank Supervision, 337–338, 340, 342
Bear Stearns, 335, 344
Begala, Paul, 28
Benson decision, 200
Beria, Lavrentiy P., 290
Bernanke, Ben, 343–345
Biden, Joe, 28
binding rules of conduct, 87
Bipartisan Legal Advisory Group of the U.S. House of Representatives (BLAG), 99, 103
Black, Nancy, 294–295
Blackstone, William, 181
Blandford, Robert, 293–294
Bloomberg, Michael, 36
Bob Jones University, 51
Boehner, John, 76, 78
Boeing Corporation, 214–215
Bork, Robert, 368
Bosch, 355, 356
Bosson, Richard C., 48–49
Boswell, James, 69
Bowsher v. Synar, 370
Brady Bill, 27
Brand X decision, 121
broadband networks, 120–130
Bronx Household of Faith, 49
Brown, Janice Rogers, 243
Brown, Scott, 257, 259

Brown, United States v., 323–324
Brown & Williamson Tobacco Co., Food & Drug Administration v., 60–63, 67
bullying, 173
Bureau Advisory Commission Transparency Act, 166
Bureau of Alcohol, Tobacco, Firearms, and Explosives (ATF), 29, 33–34, 36–38
Bureau of Consumer Financial Protection Advisory Boards Act, 166
Burwell, King v., 24, 60–65, 67, 364
Burwell v. Hobby Lobby Stores, 42, 45, 48
Bush, George H. W., and administration, 27, 200, 369
Bush, George W., and administration, 53, 321, 328–329

cable modem service, 121
Caligula, 285
Campus Accountability and Safety Act (CASA), 178–180
Carter, Jimmy, and administration, 97, 198
Casey, Planned Parenthood v., 41
Catholic schools, 54
Cauldwell, Robert, 164
CDC Foundation (CDC), 34–35
censorship, politically correct, 171
Centers for Disease Control and Prevention (CDC), 29, 34, 35, 36
Chadha, INS v., 370
Chaney, Heckler v., 17, 317
charitable organizations
  contraception mandate (HHS) exception, 43
  tax-exempt status, 87–88
Chevron deference, 10, 223, 247–248, 250, 288, 368
Chevron doctrine, 57–69, 189, 250
Chevron U.S.A. Inc. v. Natural Resources Defense Council, Inc., 57, 246–247, 368
children
  childcare for child-migrants, 45
  FTC regulating advertising to, 299–300, 352
  HHS firearms guidelines and childcare, 39
  immigrants, illegal, 45, 72–77, 79–80, 314–315, 364
churches, 42, 45
citizens, EPA penalties and litigation costs for water use, 235–236
citizenship, 49, 74
Citizens United v. Federal Election, 257, 258–259
City of Arlington, 10, 249
City of New York, Penn Central Transportation C. v., 114
Civil Rights Act, 173–174, 222
Civil Rights Division (DOJ), 321, 322
Clean Air Act, 59–60, 63, 184, 190, 247, 273–278
Clean Coal Power Initiative (CCPI), 275–276
Clean Water Act, 230, 234, 236, 278–280, 287, 294
Clinton, Bill, and administration, 27–28, 34, 36, 93, 121, 219
Clinton, Hillary, 39, 363

Clyburn, Mignon, 132
Coates, Christopher, 321–326
Code of Federal Regulations, 284–285, 290
Commerce Clause, 233
Commerce Department, 38
commercial advertising, 300
commercial speech, 300–302
Communications Act, 58, 119, 122–123, 124
competition law, 358
confirmation process, undermining the, 186–188, 210
Congress
  ability to oversee the administrative state, 370
  accountability, avoiding through delegation of powers, 243, 286–287, 297–298
  All legislative Powers, 312
  authority of, over financial regulations, 337–338
  DOMA and, 93, 99, 102
  executive overreach era and, 181–190
  nondelegation doctrine, 68, 241–242, 243, 250, 286, 298
  senators, system of direct election, 7
Congressional power
  agencies, delegation to, 7–8, 10–11, 189, 241–243, 247, 286–287, 297–298
  FSOC, delegation to, 341
  of impeachment, 5–6
  Obama's usurping of, 184–186, 211, 214, 314–318, 320–329
  shift of power away from, 17
Congressional Review Act (CRA), 249
ConnectED Initiative, 131–133
conscientious objector provisions, 53
consent decrees, 249
Constitutional Interpretation (Whittington), 78
Consumer Credit Protection Act, 159
Consumer Financial Civil Penalty Fund, 155
Consumer Financial Protection Bureau (CFPB)
  authority, 153–154, 156–158, 190
  budget, 9, 154–155
  data-mining, 166–167
  discriminatory and retaliatory practices, 162–165, 167
  disparate impact, 226–227
  Dodd-Frank and the, 153–154
  enforcement actions, 156–158, 160–161
  headquarters renovation, 155–156
  Investment Review Board, 155
  mandate, 153
  objectives, 156
  overreach, 155–156, 158–162, 165–168
  RESPA interpretation by, 162
  structure, 154–156, 168
Consumer Financial Protection Bureau Accountability Act, 166
Consumer Financial Protection Fund, 154
consumer information, CFPB data gathering, 167

consumers
  Internet Freedoms, 122
  truthful advertising, benefit to, 301–302, 306–307
contraception mandate, HHS, 43–46, 48
Cordray, Richard, 152, 156, 157, 161
Corker, Bob, 154
Costco, 214–217
Countrywide, 226–228
Cox, Archibald, 53
Crawford, Susan, 125
Crawford v. Marion County Election Board, 328–329
crime, regulatory, 290–291
criminal background checks, 222, 225–226
criminal laws
  moral authority of, 285, 289–290, 291–292
  purpose, 289
  regulations vs., 289
criminal regulation, 284, 286–293, 296–298
criminals, stigma associated, 291, 294
crowdfunding, 142
Cruz, Ted, 75–76

data-mining, CFPB, 166–167
data roaming rules, FCC, 123
Davis, Arnold, 326–327
Davis v. Monroe County Board of Education, 172–173, 180
Dean, John, 256
Defense of Marriage Act (DOMA), 46–47, 91–104, 364
deference, language of, 58–63. *See also* judicial deference
Deferred Action for Childhood Arrivals (DACA) program, 72–77, 80, 314–315
Deferred Action for Parents of Americans (DAPA), 73–78
DeMarco, Edward, 107, 111
Democracy Alliance, 258
DeMuth, Chris, 368
Department of Education (DOE), 167, 171, 178, 190. *See also* Office for Civil Rights (OCR) (DOE)
Department of Health and Human Services
  ACA, interpretations of the, 18, 20, 61–62, 364
  authority, 182
  contraception mandate, 43–46, 48
  "Engaging in Public Health Research on the Causes and Prevention of Gun Violence" (Presidential Memorandum) (Obama), 35
  gun control, 30, 39
  regulatory authority, 365
Department of Homeland Security (DHS), 72–77, 80, 314, 364
Department of Housing and Urban Development (HUD), 223–225
Department of Justice (DOJ)
  budget, 202–203
  duty of the, 97, 99
  enforcement actions, 226–228, 320
  IP-focused work, 202–203
  law, enforcing the, 364
  patents, antitrust scrutiny of, 202, 204

political influence driving outcomes, 200
racial discrimination, 226–228, 322, 323–328
sexual assault investigation, 174–176
sexual assault training programs, 178
smartphone wars patent case, 204
voting rights enforcement, 322–328
Department of Justice (DOJ), Obama and the
decisions to suspend enforcement of federal laws, 319
demands action to silence opponents, 262
DOMA case, 94–103
Operation Choke Point, 31–33, 81–90
Operation Fast and Furious, 33–34
political pressures on, 192
Department of Labor (DOL), 46, 47, 216–217
Department of Transportation v. Association of American Railroads, 242, 243, 250
DeStefano, Ricci v., 222, 226
DiPaolo, John, 175
discrimination. *See also* racial discrimination
anti-discrimination laws, OCR enforcement of, 173–174
auto lenders liability under CFPB, 158–159
on the basis of sex, 46, 170, 171
on the basis of sexual orientation, 46
CFPB discriminatory and retaliatory practices, 162–165, 167
disparate impact, 159, 221–228
Dodd-Frank Wall Street Reform and Consumer Protection Act, 152–167, 190, 284, 332–341, 348–349. *See also* Financial Stability Oversight Council (FSOC)
Donnelly, Joe, 75
DREAM Act (Development Relief and Education for Alien Minors Act), 74, 313–315
D. R. Horton, Inc. decision, 218
Droney, Christopher, 101
drug laws, 364
due process of law
on campus, threats to, 169–180
Fifth Amendment, 88, 95
Fourteenth Amendment, 370
Operation Choke Point depriving citizens of, 31–33, 81–90
protections, campus judicial systems, 180
Duffy, Sean, 163, 166
Duke Power, Griggs v., 222, 225
Durbin, Dick, 74

Earnest, Josh, 132
economy
federal regulation, effect on, 2, 334, 348
truthful advertising, benefit to, 301–302
unions and the, 211–213

education. *See also* Department of Education (DOE); schools
for investors, 148–149
legislative power, Obama's usurping of, 185
No Child Left Behind Act, 185
EEOC, Hosanna-Tabor Evangelical Lutheran Church and School v., 42, 50–51
efficacy claims in advertising, 303
Eilperin, Juliet, 15
Elane Photography, 48–49
elections, Obama's abuse of power over, 319–329
Elliott, Cameron, 161–162
EME Homer City Generation L.P., EPA v., 280–281
emergency contraception mandate, 45–46
emerging growth companies (EGCs), 142, 144
Emily's List, 257
Employee Free Choice Act, 210
Employee Freedom Action Committee, 258
employees
CFPB discriminatory and retaliatory practices against, 162–165, 167
notice of employees' rights, 216–217
protections of collective action, 218
speech rights in the workplace, 214–218
employers
employee discipline by, 217
PPACA mandate, 14–17, 24
religious non-profits, 43–45, 48
undocumented workers, penalty for hiring, 80
unions effect on, 211–212
employment
criminal background checks, EEOC and, 222, 225–226
disparate impact in, 222, 225–228
hostile work environments, 163
at-will employment policies, 218
Employment Non-Discrimination Act (ENDA), 46
endangered species, 59
Energy Policy Act, 275
"Engaging in Public Health Research on the Causes and Prevention of Gun Violence" (Presidential Memorandum) (Obama), 35
entrepreneurism, 137–139, 141, 142
Environmental Protection Agency (EPA)
Good Neighbor policy, 280–281
recommendations to reform, 280–281
Science Advisory Board, 235
Environmental Protection Agency (EPA) overreach
carbon dioxide regulation, 190
claim to statutory power, 271–272
greenhouse gas emissions, attempts to regulate, 60, 242–243, 247, 272
judicial criticism, 271–272
law, attempt to remake the, 271–278

power plant regulation, 273–278, 281
waters of the United States, regulating the, 230, 278–280, 287
Environmental Protection Agency, Massachusetts v., 59–60, 247
EPA, Michigan v., 281
EPA, Utility Air Regulatory Group v., 272, 277, 280
EPA v. EME Homer City Generation L.P., 280–281
Equal Credit Opportunity Act (ECOA), 158–159
equal dignity for equal love, 48–49, 51
Equal Employment Opportunity Commission (EEOC), 42, 50, 222, 225–226
equal protection, 95, 101
Equal Protection Clause, 92, 223–224, 326
E-Rate subsidy mechanism increase, FCC, 130–133
establishment claims in advertising, 303
evil, the greatest, 81
Executive Branch
actions, judicial review of, 250
agency resources, authority to prioritize, 16–17
Begala's characterization of, 28
enforcement discretion, 19
nondelegation doctrine, 241
re-election, 366–367
resources, authority to prioritize, 16–17
successful, accountability in, 366
Take Care Clause requirement, 48, 76, 97–98, 106, 240, 311–316, 319, 329, 364
Executive Branch, power of the
of the purse, 5–6
to suspend laws unilaterally (prosecutorial discretion), 314–320
veto power, 5, 98
Executive Branch overreach
administrative state as conspirator to, 11
agency model to mitigate, 194–195, 203–207
Congress in enabling, 190
congressional solutions to, 152, 165–168
enabling, 152–165
judicial pushback, 114
Exempt Organizations Unit (IRS), 260
"Exercising Prosecutorial Discretion with Respect to Individuals Who Came to the United State as Children.Who Are Parents of U.S. Citizens or Permanent Residents" (Johnson), 73
extraordinary cases exception, *Chevron* doctrine, 60–63, 67, 68

Fair Housing Act, 223
Family and Medical Leave Act (FMLA), 47
FCC, Verizon v., 122–123, 127
FDIC Improvement Act (FDICIA), 333
Federal Advisory Committee Act, 166

Federal Communications
Commission (FCC)
creation of, 119
E-Rate subsidy mechanism
increase, 130–133
Executive Branch relationship,
118–120, 134–135
independence, 118–120, 122–
126, 134–135
Notice of Proposed Rulemaking,
123, 126
Obama and the, 11, 120–121,
123–126, 130–133
Open Internet Order, 122, 125
rulemaking authority, 119
state sovereignty, preemption of,
126–130
Federal Communications
Commission (FCC) regulatory
authority
delegation of, 242–243
ISPs, 120–126
radio licenses, 58, 63
to remove barriers to
infrastructure investment, 121–
122, 127, 131, 134, 242–243
statutory right to, 243
Federal Deposit Insurance Act,
82–83
Federal Deposit Insurance
Corporation (FDIC), 31–33,
81–90
Federal Election, Citizens United v.,
257, 258–259
Federal Election Commission, 262,
329
federal firearms licenses (FFLs), 36,
38
Federal Home Loan Mortgage
Corporation (Freddie Mac),
105–115
Federal Housing Finance Agency
(FHFA), 107–114
federalism, 312–313
Federalist Papers, 117, 229, 239–240,
241, 252, 285–286, 366–367
Federal National Mortgage
Association (Fannie Mae), 105–
115
Federal Reserve, 81–90, 110–111,
339–340, 345. *See also* Consumer
Financial Protection Bureau
(CFPB)
*Federal Reserve Bank of New York,
Starr International Co. v.*, 111
Federal Reserve Bank of New York
bailout, 110–111
Federal Reserve Board, 333
Federal Rule of Civil Procedure, 249
Federal Rules of Evidence, 245
Federal Trade Commission (FTC)
budget, 202–203
consumer protection program,
352
establishment, reasons for, 358
funding, 352
guidance, lack of, 359
Horizontal Merger Guidelines,
352
independence, 118
IP-focused work, 202–203
ITC compared, 192
law enforcement authority, 351
litigation advantages, 357–358
mission, 300, 351–352
smartphone wars patent case, 204

structure, 193–194
UDAP authority, evaluating, 352
UMC authority, 351–361
Federal Trade Commission (FTC)
overreach
in advertising, 299–300, 302–304, 352
antitrust scrutiny of patents, 202
competition authority, 351–361
consents, extracting, 355–359
jurisdiction, laws limiting, 300
limiting, 352
patent royalty fees, 355
UMC enforcement actions, 355–359
Federal Trade Commission Act, 351
felons, financial services for, 86
Fernandes, Julie, 321, 322–323, 324
Fifth Amendment, 88, 95, 101
Financial Crimes Enforcement Network (Treasury Department), 86
financial crisis (2007), 106–107
financial crisis (2008-2009), 151, 334–344, 349
financial industry. *See also* systemically important financial institutions (SIFIs)
delegation of power to the, 334–335
Fannie/Freddie fiasco, 105–115
investor education, 148–149
investor protection, 140, 143
propriety of regulatory actions, pursuant to statutory powers, 107–114
financial industry oversight
Financial Stability Board (FSB), 338–347
Financial Stability Oversight Board (FSOB), 331–349
Financial Stability Oversight Council (FSOC), 332–347, 351–353
financial industry regulation. *See also* banking industry regulation; Consumer Financial Protection Bureau (CFPB)
bank-like prudential, 332, 334–335, 342, 345
of capital markets, 347
Congressional authority required for, 337–338
Dodd-Frank Act, 151–168, 190, 284, 332–341, 352–353
effects of, 347–348
financial crisis and, 338
growth in scope of, 332–333
innovation, effect on, 341, 348, 349
international, 337–339
objectivity and fairness, 337, 339
Financial Institutions Reform, Recovery and Enforcement Act (FIRREA), 333
Financial Regulatory Improvement Act, 166
Financial Stability Board (FSB), 338–347
Financial Stability Oversight Board (FSOB), 331–349
Financial Stability Oversight Council (FSOC), 336–349. *See also* Dodd-Frank Wall Street Reform and Consumer Protection Act

firearms retailers, 31–33, 36
firearms trafficking, 33–34, 38. *See also* gun control
First Amendment. *See also* freedom of speech
  campus harassment policies and the, 173, 175
  freedom of association, 50
  freedom of worship, 49–50
  free flow of information protections, 300, 302
  OCR restrictions on the, 175
  prohibition on independent political expenditures, 258, 267
Food & Drug Administration v. Brown & Williamson Tobacco Co., 60–63, 67
Food and Drug Administration (FDA), 35–36, 242, 295–296
Fort Davis State Bank, 228
Fourteenth Amendment, 326, 370
Francis, James, 96
Frank, Jerome, 154, 198
fraud, anti-fraud enforcement, 148–149
Freddie Mac (Federal Home Loan Mortgage Corporation), 105–115
freedom of association, 50
freedom of speech. *See also* speech
  commercial speech, 300–302
  Constitutional protections, 300–302, 306–307
  OCR restrictions on, 170–173, 175, 179
  rights to convey truthful information, 296
  university restrictions on, 171–172
  in the workplace, 214–218
freedom of worship, 49–52
Freedom-Watch, 258
FTC, POM Wonderful v., 306–307
Full Faith and Credit Clause, 93

G20 countries, 339–340, 343
Gage, Katie Packer, 79
Garrett, Scott, 340
Gaziano, Todd, 323
GE, 336–337
GE Capital, 339
Geithner, Timothy, 111
gender equality, 51, 55
gender identity, 46
George, Russell, 260
George III, 98
Gill, 95, 99, 102
Ginsburg, Douglas, 368
Gleason, Peter, 295–296
Goldstein, Amy, 15
Goodlatte, Bob, 359
Good Neighbor obligation, 280–281
Google/MMI, 355, 356
governance theory, 286
government contractors
  emergency contraception mandate, 45–46
  non-discrimination requirements, 46
grants, federal, 46
Greenberg, Hank, 111
greenhouse gas emissions, EPA regulation of, 60, 243, 247, 272
Gregory v. Ashcroft, 128, 130
Griggs v. Duke Power, 222, 225
Griswold, Erwin, 53
Guam, voter rights, 326–327

Guantanamo Bay, prisoner releases from, 184
Guinta, Frank, 166
gun control
ammunition, controls on, 37, 38
CDC and, 34, 35, 36
Clinton White House, 27–28, 34, 36
firearms exporting/re-importing, 38
firearms retailers, 31–33, 36
firearms trafficking, 33–34, 38
Obama's abuse of executive power in, 29–35, 82–90
Operation Choke Point, 29, 31–33, 82–90
Operation Fast and Furious, 29, 33–34

Hackett, Rick, 160
Hamburger, Philip, 88–89
Hamilton, Alexander, 117, 252–253, 366–367
Hand, Learned, 198
Hanen, Andrew S., 76–78
harassment, 171–175, 180
Harmonized Tariff System of the United States (HTSUS), 65
Hatch, Orrin, 74, 152
Hawaii, 92, 326
Health Care and Education Reconciliation Act (HCERA), 13
health care reform. *See* Affordable Care Act (ACA)
health information, benefit to consumers with dissemination of, 301
health insurance. *See also* Affordable Care Act (ACA)
private, pre-existing, 18–20
subsidies, 21–24, 182–183, 364, 365
health insurance exchanges, 21–24, 61–62, 364
Heckler v. Chaney, 17, 317
Heller, 39
Hensarling, Jeb, 347
Hobby Lobby Stores, Burwell v., 42, 45, 48
Holder, Eric, 28, 32, 33, 45–46, 96, 325–326, 329
Holder, Shelby County v., 327
Holmes, Oliver Wendell, Jr., 65, 292–293
Holtz-Eakin, Douglas, 73
home ownership, 105–115, 335. *See also* mortgage industry
homosexuality, 51–52, 99, 162–165
Honduran law, violation of, 293–294
Horizontal Merger Guidelines, 352, 360
Hosanna-Tabor Evangelical Lutheran Church and School v. EEOC, 42, 50–51
hospitals, religious, 43
House Oversight and Government Reform Committee, 32–33
housing, public, 223–225
Housing and Community Development Act, 106
Housing and Economic Recovery Act (HERA), 107–110, 112
housing boom, 106, 335

housing policy, financial crisis and U.S., 349
Huang, Diane, 293–294
Huguenins (*Elane Photography* case), 48–49
Hume, David, 367

IBM, 200
immigrants, illegal, 71–73, 80
Immigration and Customs Enforcement (ICE), 74–75
Immigration and Nationality Act (INA), 313–314, 316–317
immigration law, 73–76, 80
immigration reform, 71–80, 185–186, 313–318
Immigration Reform and Control Act (IRCA), 80
impeachment power, 5–6
independent commissions, described, 118–119
IndyMac, 345
ineligible cases, *Chevron* doctrine, 64
information, FTC restriction of free flow of, 299–309
information service, 121
innovation, 242–243, 341, 348, 349
INS v. Chadha, 370
integrated information service classification, 121
Intel, 356
Intel, 355
intellectual property (IP), 202–204
International Trade Commission (ITC), 191–194, 203–207
International Traffic in Arms Regulations (ITAR), 38
Internet Freedoms, 122
Internet service providers (ISPs), regulation of, 120–126
Interstate Commerce Commission (ICC), 118
inventions, patents for, 197–199
Investment Review Board (CFPB), 155
investors
  education for, 148–149
  protections, 140, 143
IPO market, 142
IRS
  501(c)(4) Groups streamlined option, 263
  legislative changes recommended, 267–269
  Nixon impeachment and the, 255–256, 259
  non-profit corporations and the, 258
  Obama's influence over, 11
IRS overreach
  employer mandates (ACA), authority to delay, 14–17
  exempt status applications, response to, 259–262
  health exchanges ruling, 61–62
  noncompliance penalties waved, 16
  Obama's influence in, 259–261, 262, 265–266
  restricting political speech and association, 263–264
  targeting scandal, 257, 259–263, 264–265
  tax credit regulation for health insurance, 22–23, 24, 182
  tax liabilities, deferred payments authorized by, 16

Issa, Darrell, 32
Issa Report, 264

Jacobs, Dennis, 101
James I, 288
James II, 314–315
Jarrett, Valerie, 51–52
Jay, John, 117
Jefferson, Thomas, 4–5
Johnson, Jeh, 73, 77
Johnson, Lyndon B., and administration, 200, 365
Johnson, Samuel, 69
JPMorgan Chase, 348
judicial activism, 370
judicial deference. *See also Chevron* deference
  administrative decisions and controlling authority, 66–69
  to agency authority, 10–11, 58, 65–66, 189, 241, 246–248, 368–369
  extraordinary cases exception, 67, 68
  FHFA breach of fiduciary duty, 112–114
  to Secretary of the Interior, 59
judicial systems, campus, 180
judiciary
  ACA, Supreme Court ruling, 365
  accountability, 11
  appropriate role of, 92, 189
  established canons of statutory construction rejected, 63–65
  power of the, 5–6
  review of agency decisions, uniform rule for, 57–69, 252
  Supreme Court nominees, confirmation process, 186
  unconstitutionality of DOMA ruling, 100
  vesting clause / nondelegation of power, 241
Jumpstart Our Business Startups (JOBS) Act, 141–142, 143, 144

Kagan, Elena, 93–94, 95, 101–102
Kaplan, Roberta, 96
Katzenbach, Nicholas, 200
Kellogg Company, 301
Kendall v. United States ex rel. Stokes, 315
Kennard, Bill, 121
Kennedy, Anthony, 103, 232, 278–280, 370
Kennedy, Edward, 257
Kennedy, John F. administration, 200
Kerry, John, 29, 39
King, Martin Luther, Jr., 226–228
King v. Burwell, 24, 60–65, 67, 364
Kipnis, Laura, 169–180
Klein, Ezra, 16
Koch, Charles, 259
Koch, David, 259
Kovacic, Bill, 355, 356, 361

Lacey Act, 284, 293–294
Lamberth, Royce, 113–114
Lanza, Adam, 29
lawlessness, 103–104
laws
  agency discretion in application of, 59–63

agency interpretations of, 10, 58, 189
Constitutional power of Congress to write, 182–184
defying and rewriting of existing, Obama's, 182–184, 314–329, 364
Executive Branch, power of the, 314–320
threat of unknown and unreasonable, 285–286
Lawson, Gary, 242, 244
League of Women Voters, 98
Lee, Mike, 75
Lehman Brothers, 107, 335, 344
Leibowitz, Jon, 353
lenity doctrine, 288
Lerner, Lois, 260–261, 263, 264–265, 364
Lew, Jack, 340, 347
Lew, Perry v., 113–114
Lewis, C. S., 81, 90
Lewis, Lawrence, 294
Lewis, Peter, 257
LGBTQ, 51–52, 162–165
liberty, safeguarding, 4, 181
libraries, 131–133
Lincoln, Abraham, 103–104, 198, 367, 368
Little Sisters of the Poor, 44
Lochner v. New York, 370
Locke, John, 286–293
Lockhart, James, 107
Lowe, M. Anthony, 86
Lynch, Loretta, 28, 32

Maclaine, William, 311
Madison, James, 117–118, 134, 229, 239, 285–286
major questions rule, *Chevron* doctrine, 63
Manchin, Joe, 75
marijuana, medical, 364
Marine Mammal Protection Act, 294, 295
Marion County Election Board, Crawford v., 328–329
marriage
Defense of Marriage Act (DOMA), 46–47, 91–104, 364
defined, 92, 93
same-sex unions, 51, 92–93, 101
Marshall, John, 286
Martin, Angela, 163
Martin, Wade, 294
Massachusetts v. Environmental Protection Agency, 59–60, 247
Mazur, Mark, 17
McCain, John, 175, 258
McCain-Feingold campaign finance law, 257–258
McCarthy, Andrew, 320
McHugh, Paul, 52
McNab, David, 293–294
Mead Corp., United States v., 65–68
Meany, George, 210
Medicare Advantage program, 182
Melamed, Doug, 358
MelApp, 307–308
mens rea standard, 291–292
MetLife, 336–337, 339, 341–342
Michigan v. EPA, 281
Miller, Steven, 263, 264–265
minimum wage, 184–185

minorities
CFPB discriminatory and retaliatory practices, 162–165, 167
voting power, 79
Mississippi, 74–75
Missouri Municipal League, Nixon v., 128, 130
mistake of fact defense, 298
mistake of law defense, 298
mobile ISPs, 122–123, 124
Mole Detective, 307–308
monopolies, regulation of, 108
Monroe County Board of Education, Davis v., 172–173, 180
Montesquieu, 117, 134
moral authority
of churches, 42
of our criminal laws, 285, 289–290, 291–292
Morrison v. Olson, 240, 368
Mortgage Bankers Association, Perez v., 247, 249–250
mortgage industry, 105–115, 162, 226–228, 335, 338, 344
Motorola Mobility LLC and Google Inc. (Google/MMI), 355, 356
motor vehicle dealer exemption, 158–162

Nader, Ralph, 352
Nader's Raiders, 352
Napolitano, Janet, 73, 314
Naraghi, Ali, 164
National Ambient Air Quality Standards (EPA), 280
National City Bank, 228
National Defense Authorization Act, 184
National Firearms Act, 38
National Firearms Act Trusts, 37–38
National Labor Relations Act (NLRA) (Wagner Act), 209, 213, 214, 217–218
National Labor Relations Board (NLRB), 209–219
National Labor Relations Board v. Noel Canning, 152
National Oceanic and Atmospheric Administration, 295
National Rifle Association (NRA), 28, 36
National Security Administration, 364–365
National Treasury Employees Union (NTEU), 164
National Urban League, 228
National Voter Registration Act (NVRA), 320, 322
Natural Resources Defense Council, Chevron U.S.A. Inc. v., 57, 246–247, 368
natural rights, 370
Negotiated Data Solutions, LLC (-DATA), 355
net neutrality, 120–126, 243
Nevada, 229–237
Nevada Association of Counties, 234–235
New Black Panther Party (NBPP) voter intimidation case, 323, 324–325
New Deal, 188, 241
New York, Lochner v., 370

NFIB v. Sibelius, 365
Nixon, Richard, and administration, 210, 255–256, 259
Nixon v. Missouri Municipal League, 128, 130
NLRB Reform Act, 219
No Child Left Behind Act, 185
Noel Canning, National Labor Relations Board v., 152
nonbank financial institutions. *See* systemically important financial institutions (SIFIs)
nonbank noninsurance (NBNI) financial institutions, 345
nondelegation doctrine, 68, 241–242, 243, 250, 286, 298
non-profit employers, religious, 43–44, 48
Notice of Proposed Rulemaking (NPRM), 87, 123, 126, 245

Obama, Barack
  agency regulations, request to eradicate outdated, 9
  on classifications of sexual orientation, 96–97
  governing competence, 364–365, 367–368
  on unconstitutionality of DOMA, 96–97
Obama, Barack, abuses of executive power. *See also* Affordable Care Act (ACA); *specific departments*
  absolute power claimed by, 88
  accountability for, 188–189
  Clean Air Act, 184
  confirmation process, undermining the, 186–188, 210
  Congressional response, 187–190
  disparate impact, 223–228
  Dodd-Frank Act, 151–168
  Guantanamo Bay prisoner release, 184
  gun control, 29–35, 82–90
  immigration policy, 71–72, 114, 185–186, 313–318
  laws, defying and rewriting of existing, 182–184, 314–329, 364
  legislative power, usurping, 184–186, 211, 214, 314–318, 320–329
  minimum wage executive order, 184–185
  pen and phone strategy, 184
  recess appointments, 152, 186–187, 210
  resource prioritization, 16–17
  Supreme Court rulings on, 184
  unilateralism threats, 182
  unions, 210–212, 214, 218–219
  voting and elections, 319–329
  won't take no for an answer position, 182
Obama, Barack, election of
  educational platform, 131–133
  financing, 258
Obamacare. *See* Affordable Care Act (ACA)
Obama White House
  administrative state, 88, 365–367
  on *Citizens United* ruling, 259
  DOMA position, 95–96

enforcement discretion, claim to, 17
governing competence, 364–365
gun control agenda, 28–29
health care reform, 13–25
overreaching granted authority, 12
religion, remapping, 48–52, 53–55
scandals, 363–364, 367
tax and spend policies, 256
Obergefell, 370
O'Connor, Sandra Day, 61
Office for Civil Rights (OCR) (DOE)
hostile environment theory, 170
Obama White House and the, 170–171, 173–174
Office for Civil Rights (OCR) (DOE) overreach
APA non-compliance, 170–171, 174, 177
authority, claims to, 180
campus oversight, 174–179
congressional solutions to, 180
Dear Colleague letter (April 2011), 174, 177
Dear Colleague letter (October 2010), 173–174
enforcement actions, 173–174, 178–179
freedom of speech restrictions, 170–173, 175–176
national effects of, 176
redefining sexual harassment, 173–176
reporting mandates, 174, 176
Title IX enforcement, 171–172, 176, 178–179
Office of Civil Rights (OCR) (CFPB), 163, 164, 177
Office of Consumer Response (CFPB), 164
Office of Equal Opportunity & Fairness (CFPB), 163
Office of Financial Research (Treasury), 341
Office of Investor Education and Advocacy (SEC), 149
Office of Management and Budget (OMB), 368
Office of Minority & Women Inclusion (CFPB), 163
Office of the Comptroller of the Currency, 81–90
Office of Unfair Import Investigations (ITC), 204
Olson, Morrison v., 240, 368
omniscient agency theory, 358
on-line gambling businesses, 84
Open Internet Order (FCC), 122, 125
Operation Choke Point, 29, 31–33, 82–90
Operation Fast and Furious, 29, 33–34
Operation Hope, 228
originalism movement, 92
Oversight and Investigations Subcommittee, 163

Pai, Ajit, 130, 133–134
Paperwork Reduction Act, 145
Parrish decision, 167
PATCO strike, 211, 213
Patent Act, 198

Patent and Trademark Office (PTO) (DOC), 192, 194–195, 200, 202, 204
patent jury trials, benefits of, 195–196, 199–202
patents, 194–199, 201–207
Patient Protection and Affordable Care Act (PPACA). *See* Affordable Care Act (ACA)
Paulson, Henry, 107, 110–111
payday lenders, 82–83, 85–86, 167
peer harassment, 174
Pelosi, Nancy, 256
Penn Central Transportation C. v. City of New York, 114
Perdue, David, 166
Perez, Thomas, 175, 325, 327
Perez v. Mortgage Bankers Association, 247, 249–250
Perlmutter, Ed, 166
Perry v. Lew, 113–114
Pertschuk, Michael, 353
Pfizer case, 303, 304, 305, 306, 307, 308
PHH Corporation, 161–162
Pittenger, Robert, 166
place of celebration rule, 47
Planned Parenthood v. Casey, 41
PNC, 228
POM Wonderful v. FTC, 306–307
pornography dealers, 84
Posner, Richard, 352, 358
Powell, Michael, 122
power
  governmental accumulation of, 7
  liberty and unaccountable, 90
  states role in federal, 6
power plants, EPA regulation of, 273–278, 281
PPACA (Patient Protection and Affordable Care Act). *See* Affordable Care Act (ACA)
preemption without representation, 311–318
Priorities for Research to Reduce the Threat of Firearms-Related Violence (National Academy of Science), 35
property rights, 114, 197, 199
prosecutorial discretion, abuses of, 182–184, 314–329, 351–361, 364. *See also* Take Care Clause
Prudential Insurance, 336–337, 339, 341–342
public housing, 223–225
Putin, Vladimir, 365

race, classification by, 223–224
racial discrimination. *See also* discrimination
  disparate impact and, 159, 221–228
  in law enforcement, 322
  OCR focus on, 170
  in voting rights, 319, 322–328
racism, CFPB, 164
radio licenses, 58, 63
Ramirez, Edith, 353, 359
Rapanos v. United States, 231, 232, 233, 234, 278–279, 287
Raucci, Misty, 163–164
Reagan, Ronald, and administration, 79, 90, 97, 198, 211, 213, 368, 369–370

Real Estate Settlement Procedures Act (RESPA), 162
recess appointments, 152, 186–187, 210
Recess Appointments Clause, 186–187
Reforming CFPB Indirect Auto Financing Guidance Act, 166
refusal-to-defend, 103
regulations, purpose, 289
regulatory authority and economic growth, 2, 334
regulatory competition, 340–341
Regulatory Flexibility Act, 145
Regulatory Improvement Act, 9
regulatory overreach
  innovation, effect on, 242–243
  real-life consequences of, 293–296
  recommended actions to repair problems posed by, 296–298
REINS Act, 249
religion, Obama White House remapping of, 48–52, 53–55
Religious Freedom Restoration Act (RFRA), 44–45, 47–48
religious identity, 42–43
religious institutions, HHA contraception mandate and, 43–45
religious liberty, 41–52
reparative therapies for minors, 52
reproductive freedom, 43–46, 48
reputation, 291
reputation risk standard, 83–85, 87–89
Revised Sexual Harassment Guidance (OCR), 172
Ricci v. DeStefano, 222, 226
Rich, Giles S., 197–198
right-to-work laws, 209, 214–215
Riverside Bayview Homes, United States v., 230–231
Roberts, John, 24, 233, 249, 365
Roberts, Owen, 167
Roe v. Wade, 370
Rogers v. Tennessee, 285
Romney, Mitt, 79
Roosevelt, Franklin D., 153, 209, 365, 368
Rosenberg, Mark, 36
Rosenkranz, Nicholas Quinn, 319
rule of an elite, 90
rule of law
  Operation Choke Point and the, 84, 87, 88–90
  refusal-to-defend threat to, 103
  reputation risk standard subverting the, 84, 87
  threats posed to the, 92

same-sex attraction, 52
same-sex marriage, 51, 92–93, 101
Samsung, 204
Sandy Hook Elementary School shooting, 29, 34–35
Santelli, Rick, 256
Sarbanes-Oxley Act, 142, 148, 333
Scalia, Antonin, 24, 91–92, 222, 231, 240, 247–248, 249–250, 278–279, 288, 368
Schoenwetter, Abner, 293–294
schools. *See also* education; universities

hostile educational environments, 172, 174
Obama's educational platform, 131–133
religious, 54
Title IX and the, 169–179
violence in, 29, 34–35
Science Advisory Board (EPA), 235
Scott, David K., 172
Searching for and Cutting Regulations that Are Unnecessary Burdensome (SCRUB) Act, 9
Secretary of the Interior, judicial deference to, 59
Securities Exchange Act, 141, 143, 151
Securities Exchange Commission (SEC)
conflicts of interests within, 251
FSOC pressure on, money market fund rules, 341
independence, 118
ITC compared, 192
Office of Investor Education and Advocacy, 149
small business and the, 137–138, 141–143
venture exchanges and the, 140, 143–150
Seeger, 53
segregation, HUD's interpretation of, 224–225
Selective Service, conscientious objector provisions, 53
senators, system of direct election, 7
Senior Preferred Stockholder Agreement (SPSA), 110–111
separation of powers
in an administrative state, 239–253
agencies threat to, 239–240
agencies without, 118
agency circumvention of, 248
agency reforms and, 249–253
Constitution ensuring, 5–6, 181
division of powers vs., 241
erosion of, 6, 240–244
historically, 117–118
horizontal, 5–6
liberty, safeguarding, 312
Obama's undermining of, 181–190
Obama White House challenging, 322
purpose, 181, 312
solutions proposed to reinvigorate the, 249–253
sue-and-settle threat implications for, 245–246
vertical, 6, 312–313
Service Employees International Union (SEIU), 257, 258
Seventeenth Amendment, 7
severity doctrine, 288
sex, discrimination on the basis of, 46, 170
sexual abuse, 52, 171–174, 175, 177, 180
sexual assault on campus, 175, 178, 180
sexual harassment, 171–173, 174, 175, 180
Sexual Harassment Guidance (OCR), 172
"Sexual Harassment: It's Not Academic" (OCR), 173

sexual orientation, 46, 48–49, 52, 55, 96–97, 101–103, 162–165
sexual-orientation classifications, 99
sexual orientation/gender identity (SOGI) non-discrimination rules, 46
sexual self-determination, 48, 51
sexual violence, 174
sexual violence complaints, 177
shadow banking, 343–347
Shelby, Richard, 166
Shelby County v. Holder, 327
Sherman Act, 352–354, 356
Shulman, Doug, 264
Shultz, George, 210
Sibelius, NFIB v., 365
Silberman, Laurence, 127–128
Skidmore v. Swift & Co., 65–68
small business
  capital formation, SEC and, 137–138, 141–143
  crowdfunding, 142
  economic importance of, 137–140
  Operation Choke Point and, 29, 82, 86
  venture exchanges, 143–150
smartphone wars, 204
Smelt case, 94, 102
Smith & Wesson, 28
Snowden, Edward, 364–365
social media, 217–218
Solicitor General, role of, 93–94
Solid Waste Agency of Northern Cook County (SWANCC) v. United States Army Corps of Engineers, 231, 233
Soros, George, 36, 257, 258
Soviet Union, 90
Specialty Healthcare decision, 215
speech. *See also* freedom of speech
  political, 257, 263–264
  politically correct, 171
  regulation of fraudulent and deceptive, 302
speech codes, 171–172
Spyer, Thea, 96
Starr International Co. v. Federal Reserve Bank of New York, 111
State Department, anti-firearms agenda, 29, 38–39
state law, preemption without representation, 313, 317–318
states
  broadband networks, 126–130
  compensation and pension costs, results to, 213
  FCC preemption of sovereignty, 126–130
  federal law, surrender of authority to, 313, 318–319
  federal Treasury, supporting the, 7
  health insurance exchanges, 21–24, 61–62, 182–183, 364
  health insurance plans, 20
  legal recognition of same-sex unions, 93
  power of, shift to the federal level, 6
  right-to-work laws, 214–215
  senators' accountability to, 7
  water regulation, undermining authority of, 235–238
Strassel, Kim, 262
Straub, Chester J., 101
student loan servicing industry / student debt market, 167

sue-and-settle threat, 245–246
Suk, Jeannie, 179–180
Sunding, David, 234
Sunshine Act, 193
Supremacy Clause, 313, 318
Supreme Court nominees, confirmation process, 186
Sutherland, George, 118–119, 134–135
Sweet Home Chapters of Communities for a Great Oregon, Babbit v., 58–63
Swift & Co., Skidmore v., 65–68
Synar, Bowsher v., 370
systemically important financial institutions (SIFIs), 333, 337, 340–346, 349, 352–353

Taft-Hartley Act, 209, 213–214, 217
Take Care Clause, 48, 76, 97–98, 106, 240, 311–316, 319, 329, 364
Takings Clause, 112
tariff classification for day planners, 65–66
Tariff Commission, 192
Task Force on Federal Regulation of Higher Education, 179
Tauro, Joseph L., 95
Taussig, Frank W., 192
Taxpayer March, 256
tax subsidies for health insurance, 21–24, 182–183, 364, 365
TEAM Act, 219
Tea Party Express, 257
Tea Party movement, 256–257, 259–261, 363–364
Telecommunications Act, 121–122, 124, 127, 131, 242–243
television advertising regulation, 300
Tennessee, Rogers v., 285
Tenth Amendment, 230, 233
terrorism
  domestic, 29, 34–35
  foreign, 363, 365
Terry, Brian, 33
Thatcher, Margaret, 213
Third Amendment, 111–113
Thomas, Clarence, 242, 249, 250, 288, 370
TIGTA Report, 260, 261, 263, 264–265
Title IX, 169–179
tobacco regulation, 35–36, 60–62
Tocqueville, Alexis de, 221
trademarks, 202
Treasury Department, 14–17, 22–24, 86, 107–114, 263–264, 339–340
Treasury Inspector General for Tax Administration (TIGTA), 260, 261
tributaries, defined, 231, 279
True the Vote, 262
Truman, Harry S, 209
Turley, Jonathan, 322
tyranny, 117–118, 221, 239

UADP, 355
U.N. Convention on the Law of the Sea, 31
undocumented workers, penalty for hiring, 80
unions, 164, 209–219, 257, 258

United States, Rapanos v., 231, 232, 233, 234, 278–279, 287
United States, Whitman v., 288
United States Army Corps of Engineers, 278–280, 287
United States Army Corps of Engineers, Solid Waste Agency of Northern Cook County (SWANCC) v., 231, 233
United States Chamber of Commerce, 258
United States consulate, al Qaeda attack on, 363, 367
United States Customs Service, 65–66
United States ex rel. Stokes, Kendall v., 315
United States v. Brown, 323–324
United States v. Mead Corp., 65–68
United States v. Riverside Bayview Homes, 230–231
United States v. Windsor, 47, 91–92, 97, 98, 99, 101, 103, 364
universities. *See also* education; schools
  contraception mandate exception, 43–44
  free speech and due process of law, threats to, 169–180
  judicial systems, 180
  OCR/DOJ involvement, 178
  OCR investigations of, 172, 177
  OCR Title IX requirements, 174–177
  sexual assault complaints against, 178
University of Montana, 175–176, 179
Utility Air Regulatory Group v. EPA, 272, 277, 280

vehicle title loan industry, 167
venture exchanges, 143–150
Verizon, 122
Verizon v. FCC, 122–123, 127
Verrilli, Donald, 51
veto
  Executive Branch, 5, 182–184
  legislative, 370
voter ID law, 320–321, 328–329
voter intimidation, 323, 324–325
votes, minority, 79
voting, Obama's abuses of executive power over, 319–329
Voting Rights Act (VRA), 319, 321–327, 329

Wachovia, 345
Wade, Roe v., 370
Wagner, Ann, 156
Wagner Act, 209, 213, 214, 217–218
Walton, Reggie, 325
war on women, 51
Warren, Elizabeth, 160
Washington, George, 311, 368
Washington Mutual, 345
waters
  ephemeral, 231–232, 234, 278, 287
  navigable, 230–231, 232, 279–280, 287
waters of the United States, 230–231, 234–237, 287
welfare state, 365–366
Welsh, 53

Werfel, Danny, 263
West, Tony, 95, 96
wetlands, 231, 232, 234, 278
Wheaton College, 44
Wheeler, Tom, 123, 124–125, 128–129, 132–133
White House Task Force to Protect Students From Sexual assault, 178
Whitman v. American Trucking Associations, Inc., 63, 64
Whitman v. United States, 288
Whittington, Keith E., 78
Wilkins, William, 260
Wilson, Woodrow, 7, 240–241, 365, 366
Windsor, Edith, 96
Windsor, United States v., 47, 91–92, 97, 98, 99, 101, 103, 364
women
  CFPB discriminatory and retaliatory practices, 162–165
  contraception mandate, HHS, 43–46, 48
  war on, 51
Woodall, Roy, 341–343
workplace. *See* employees; employment
worship, 49–50

Xi Jinping, 365

Yale, Alexander v., 171

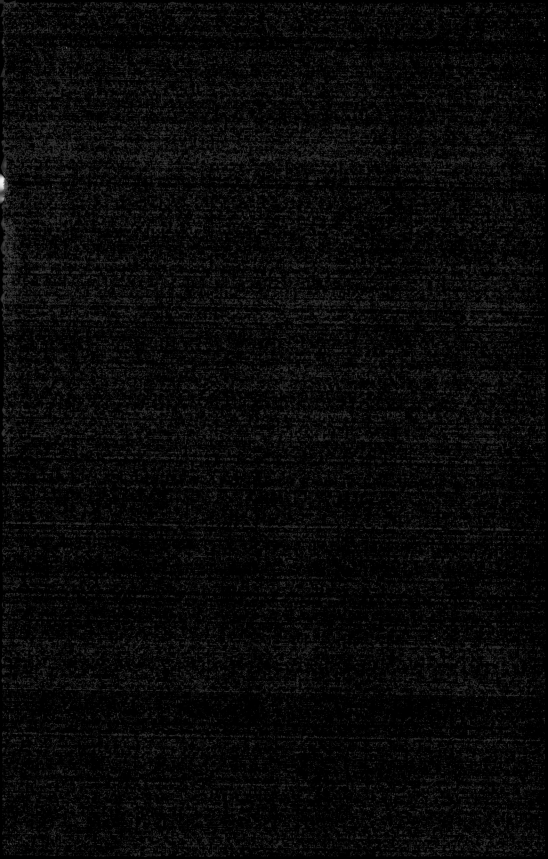